Obligations and Responsibilities: Ireland and the United Nations, 1955–2005

Essays marking fifty years of Ireland's United Nations membership

MICHAEL KENNEDY
AND
DEIRDRE McMAHON
(EDITORS)

IPA
INSTITUTE OF PUBLIC
ADMINISTRATION

First published in 2005 by
Institute of Public Administration
57–61 Lansdowne Road
Dublin 4, Ireland

in association with
Department of Foreign Affairs

A catalogue record for this book is available from the British Library.

ISBN 1 904541 36 4

Cover design by Slick Fish Design, Dublin
Typeset by Carole Lynch, Sligo
Printed in Ireland by Future Print, Dublin

Table of contents

Abbreviations

ANC	Armée National Congolaise
APC	Armoured Personnel Carrier
APSO	Agency for Personal Service Overseas
ATCP	aid to the civil power
CFSP	Common Foreign and Security Policy
CIVPOL	United Nations Civilian Police
CONCP	Conference of Nationalist Organisations of the Portuguese Colonies
COPS	Political and Security Committee
CTC	Counter-Terrorism Committee
DAC	Development Assistance Committee
DCI	Development Co-operation Ireland
DEA	Department of External Affairs (to 1971)
DFA	Department of Foreign Affairs (from 1971)
DRC	Democratic Republic of the Congo
DROPS	Demountable Rack Offloading and Pickup System
EAD	Euro-Arab Dialogue
EAPC	Euro-Atlantic Partnership Council
ECE	Economic Commission for Europe
ECO	European Coal Organisation
ECITO	European Central Inland Transport Organisation
ECOSOC	Economic and Social Council
EEC	European Economic Community
EECE	Emergency Economic Commission for Europe
EPC	European Political Co-operation
ERP	European Recovery Program (Marshall Plan)
ESDP	European Security and Defence Policy
EU	European Union
EUPM	European Union Police Mission
EUFOR	European Union Force in Bosnia and Herzegovina
EURRF	European Union Rapid Reaction Force
FAO	Food and Agriculture Organisation
FCÁ	An Fórsa Cosanta Áitúil

FYR	Federal Yugoslav Republic
GATT	General Agreement on Tariffs and Trade
GHQ	General Headquarters
IAAM	Irish Anti-Apartheid Movement
IAEA	International Atomic Energy Agency
IBRD	International Bank for Reconstruction and Development (World Bank)
ICC	International Criminal Court
ICRC	International Committee of the Red Cross
IIA	International Institute of Agriculture
ILO	International Labour Organisation
IMF	International Monetary Fund
IRA	Irish Republican Army
KFOR	Kosovo Force
MDGs	Millennium Development Goals
MINURSO	United Nations Mission for the Referendum in Western Sahara
MPLA	Movimento Popular da Libertação d'Angola
NAI	National Archives of Ireland, Dublin
NATO	North Atlantic Treaty Organisation
NPT	Nuclear Non-Proliferation Treaty
OAU	Organisation of African Unity
OECD	Organisation for Economic Co-operation and Development
OEEC	Organisation for European Economic Co-operation
ONUC	Opération de Nations Unies au Congo
ONUMOZ	United Nations Operation in Mozambique
ORGA	Official Records of the General Assembly
OSCE	Organisation for Security and Co-operation in Europe
PDF	Permanent Defence Force (Ireland)
PfP	Partnership for Peace
PICAO	Provisional International Civil Aviation Organisation
PLO	Palestine Liberation Organisation
PMUN	Irish Permanent Mission to the United Nations (New York)
POLISARIO	Frente Popular para la Liberación de Saguia El-Hamra y Rio de Oro Front
RENAMO	National Resistance of Mozambique
RF	Rhodesian Front
RUC	Royal Ulster Constabulary
SFOR	Stabilisation Force
SHIRBRIG	Stand-By Force High Readiness Brigade
SWAPO	South West African People's Organisation

TNA	The National Archives, Kew, London
UAR	United Arab Republic
UCDA	University College Dublin, Archives Department
UKUN	United Kingdom Mission to the United Nations
UN	United Nations
UNAIDS	Joint United Nations Programme on HIV/AIDS
UNAMET	United Nations Assistance Mission in East Timor
UNAVEM II	United Nations Angola Verification Mission
UNCP	United Nations Civilian Police
UNCTAD	United Nations Conference on Trade and Development
UNDP	United Nations Development Programme
UNECE	United Nations Economic Commission for Europe
UNEF I	United Nations Emergency Force I
UNEF II	United Nations Emergency Force II
UNFPA	United Nations Population Fund
UNIPTF	United Nations International Police Task Force
UNITA	União Nacional pela Independência de Angola
UNMIK	United Nations Interim Administration in Kosovo
UNFICYP	United Nations Force in Cyprus
UNHCHR	United Nations High Commissioner on Human Rights
UNHCR	United Nations High Commissioner for Refugees
UNICEF	United Nations International Children's Emergency Fund, from 1953 United Nations Children's Fund
UNIFIL	United Nations Interim Force in Lebanon
UNIPTF	United Nations International Police Task Force
UNMEE	United Nations Mission in Ethiopia and Eritrea
UNMIL	United Nations Mission in Liberia
UNMO	United Nations Military Observer
UNO	United Nations Organisation
UNOGIL	United Nations Observation Group in Lebanon
UNOSOM II	United Nations Operation in Somalia II
UNPROFOR	United Nations Protection Force
UNPSG	United Nations Police Support Group
UNRRA	United Nations Relief and Rehabilitation Administration
UNRWA	United Nations Relief and Works Agency
UNSAS	United Nations Stand-By Arrangement System
UNSETPSA	United Nations Special Educational Training Programme for Southern Africa
UNSCOP	United Nations Special Committee on Palestine
UNTAC	United Nations Transitional Authority in Cambodia
UNTAES	United Nations Transitional Administration for Eastern Slavonia

UNTAG	United Nations Transition Assistance Group
UNTSA	United Nations Trust Fund for South Africa
UNTSO	United Nations Truce Supervision Organisation
WEO	Western Europe and Others
WEU	Western European Union
WFP	World Food Programme
WHO	World Health Organisation

Acknowledgements

Firstly, our thanks are due to the Minister for Foreign Affairs, Dermot Ahern TD and the Secretary-General of the Department of Foreign Affairs, Dermot Gallagher. The Minister and his Department originated the idea for this volume in late 2004, hoping that it would be in print by the occasion of the fiftieth anniversary of Ireland's joining the United Nations. In achieving this goal the editors had the support of a great many people in what became a collaborative venture of considerable proportions and we thank them and acknowledge their support.

At the National Archives of Ireland, Director of the National Archives of Ireland, Dr David Craig and the Keeper of the National Archives of Ireland, Ken Hannigan. At Military Archives, Cathal Brugha Barracks, Dublin its Director, Commandant Victor Laing and his colleagues Commandant Pat Brennan and Commandant Dermot O'Connor. At the University College Dublin Archives Department, Seamus Helferty and Orna Somerville. We also thank Natalie Ceeney, the Chief Executive of the National Archives, Kew, London.

The Department of Foreign Affairs was ever supportive of this project and our thanks are due to Anne Barrington, Brian Cahalane, Julian Clare, David Cooney, John Deady, Eoin Duggan, Karl Gardner, Rory Murphy, James O'Shea and Miriam Tiernan. At the Department of Justice we thank John Lohan and Seán Murphy.

At the Royal Irish Academy, we would like to thank the President of the Academy, Professor James Slevin; the Executive Secretary, Patrick Buckley; the Secretary, Dr Howard Clarke and the Honorary Academic Research Officer, Professor Frank Imbusch.

At the Institute of Public Administration we thank Declan MacDonagh, Eileen Kelly, Jim Power, Hanna Ryan and Tom Turley. We would also like to thank Geraldine Begley for compiling the index.

We thank our colleagues at The Centre for Historical Research of Mary Immaculate College and the University of Limerick who have organised a series of seminars during 2005–06 to commemorate fifty years of Irish membership of the United Nations and to which a number of the authors in this volume are contributing.

Our special thanks to Professor Eunan O'Halpin of the Department of History and the Centre for Contemporary Irish History at Trinity College

Dublin who began the preparatory work for this volume following initial contacts from the Department of Foreign Affairs and who has provided constant support and encouragement to the editors and authors.

We would also like to thank Alan Kennedy, Sanchia O'Connor, Kate O'Malley, Simon Nolan and Dr Susannah Riordan who read and commented on a number of the chapters, Colonel James Fagan and Colonel Tom Furlong for allowing us to reproduce photographs in their possession, and Professor Ronan Fanning.

The editors would like particularly to put on record their gratitude to the contributors for keeping so promptly to deadlines and for doing anything and everything possible to ensure that this project met its final deadline and was published in time for the fiftieth anniversary of Ireland's admission to the United Nations.

MICHAEL KENNEDY
DEIRDRE McMAHON
September 2005

Preface

MINISTER FOR FOREIGN AFFAIRS,
DERMOT AHERN TD

This book marks an historic milestone – the fiftieth anniversary of Ireland's membership of the United Nations, which coincides with the sixtieth anniversary of the foundation of the UN itself.

Ireland's commitment to the UN remains central to our foreign policy. Earlier this year, I was honoured to have been asked by the Secretary-General to be one of his Envoys on UN Reform, which was a recognition of Ireland's contribution over many years. One of our main priorities over the coming period is to take forward implementation of the reform measures agreed at the World Summit in New York in September.

The essays in this book, which has been most ably edited by Michael Kennedy of the Royal Irish Academy and Deirdre McMahon of Mary Immaculate College, Limerick, illuminate various facets of our activity at the UN, not least but by no means only in the first years of membership. While many – but not all – of the specific issues involved may seem remote, there are important thematic continuities.

In our early days of membership, the UN was grappling with the problems caused by the Cold War. Ireland, viewed benignly by both sides, as well as by newly independent countries, played a more significant role than that of many other countries of similar size.

This was in no small measure due to the calibre of the people involved at the political and official levels. The holders of the office of Taoiseach at the time – Eamon de Valera, Seán Lemass and John A Costello – are revealed to have played an important role on key issues. The intense involvement of Frank Aiken – one of my predecessors not just as Minister for Foreign Affairs but as a TD for Louth – was remarkable but Liam Cosgrave was also very engaged. Outstanding diplomats such as Freddie Boland, Con Cremin, Conor Cruise O'Brien and Éamon Kennedy helped establish Ireland's credibility as a serious and innovative player.

In the decades since, successive governments and Ministers for Foreign Affairs, supported by generations of dedicated and able officials, have continued to ensure that Ireland makes a principled and intelligent contribution to the UN, above all in our periods as a member of the Security Council in 1962, 1981–1982 and 2001–2002. While membership of the European Union has significantly changed the context within which our foreign policy is developed, through active participation in EU co-ordination at the UN we have if anything been able to strengthen the practical impact of our approach.

In the history of the United Nations, peacekeeping stands out and we must never forget the eighty-five Irish soldiers who have given their lives in the cause of peace. One essay recalls the Irish contribution in the Congo, which the author rightly describes as a 'remarkable commitment'. Despite the killing of ten Irish soldiers in the Niemba ambush, Ireland continued contributing to the Congo Mission for another three years. Our lengthy deployment in UNIFIL is also covered in some detail as is the role of the Garda Síochána in service to the UN. The chapters on peacekeeping and military issues reinforce the need for troop deployment to be preceded by a full understanding of the political situation in recipient countries, an analysis of the potential threats facing our soldiers as well as the provision of appropriate equipment.

Ireland's contribution to the negotiation of the Nuclear Non-Proliferation Treaty is covered – Frank Aiken was asked to be the first signatory of the Treaty in recognition of Ireland's role. The Treaty's twin aims of non-proliferation and disarmament remain valid today and Ireland continues to be at the forefront of efforts to sustain the Treaty's effectiveness.

The contribution of the Irish delegation to discussions on decolonisation, which dominated the early years of our membership, is striking. Indeed it is noteworthy that UN membership has grown from seventy-six states in 1955 to 191 today, largely due to decolonisation. Many of these new members were of course in Africa, where we now have an increased presence thanks to our Development Cooperation Programme, which is a vital dimension of our foreign policy. Thanks to the ongoing expansion in our Official Development Assistance, we have been able to increase our support for the UN's own Funds and Programmes, which address humanitarian and development needs throughout the world.

The background to Ireland's sometimes overlooked membership of the Security Council in 1962 is dealt with comprehensively and illustrates the complex implications of the expansion of membership to include decolonised African and Asian states. The involvement of Seán Lemass as Taoiseach in the eventual decision to let Ireland's name go forward for election is further evidence of the role of successive Taoisigh in Irish foreign policy.

Taken together, the book provides an illuminating insight into the formulation and articulation of Irish foreign policy in a key arena. Drawing on a rich variety of archival material it should be of interest to public representatives, students, officials and the general public. It should also contribute to greater knowledge and discussion of our role in the UN. I am delighted that my Department has supported its publication.

DERMOT AHERN TD, MINISTER FOR FOREIGN AFFAIRS
December 2005

Introduction

MICHAEL KENNEDY
AND DEIRDRE McMAHON

When in January 2005 the Department of Foreign Affairs first discussed the issue of a commemorative volume of essays to mark fifty years of Ireland's membership of the United Nations with the editors it was thought that potential contributors might have unpublished pieces to hand that could easily become chapters for the book. Such was the interest in the project amongst contributors that the chapters below, researched and written between January and September 2005, represent new and original research into Ireland's relationship with the United Nations. In most cases the chapters were written specifically for this volume. Together they illustrate how, fifteen years after the initial release of the archives of the Department of Foreign Affairs in 1990, research into Irish diplomatic history is flourishing, though internationally diplomatic history has entered one of its periodic cyclical downturns and is currently out of fashion in many parts of the world. First and foremost, this volume commemorates fifty years of Irish United Nations membership. It is also a sign of the ongoing vitality in research into Irish foreign policy and shows the continuing awareness amongst those who follow the course of Ireland's foreign policy of the central position of the United Nations to the development of Ireland's external relations.

Examinations of Ireland's United Nations policy have in the past concentrated largely on the six years between Ireland's joining the United Nations in December 1955 and Ireland's first application to join the EEC in August 1961. The release of the Department of Foreign Affairs archives saw a rush of early publications of the variety 'Ireland and ...', with the blank being filled with the areas judged to be of key historical importance to Irish foreign policy. For the United Nations, it was Joseph Skelly's *Ireland and the United Nations* that became the first strongly primary-source based monograph to focus on Irish United Nations policy.[1] During the years immediately

---

[1] Jospeh M. Skelly, *Ireland and the United Nations 1945–1965: National interests and the international order* (Dublin, 1997).

following its publication, the broad sweep of Skelly's book, which centred on the 1955 to 1961 period, perhaps put researchers off examining in more detail the territory it covered. That was only a short-term effect. The chapters below show that though Skelly was able to sketch out a broad interpretative framework, the complexity of the field he was covering was such that, having digested his analysis and findings, historians and political scientists have returned to the area to reconsider the lie of the land initially sketched out by Skelly.

This study shows that Dublin had a much more nuanced and layered United Nations policy than the catch-all terms of Cosgrave's 'three principles' or Aiken's activist independent position indicate. The pivotal 1955 to 1961 period is returned to in many chapters in the volume. It is the focus of those by Edward Burke, Richard Heaslip and Michael Kennedy re-examining Ireland's earliest engagements with United Nations peacekeeping and Ireland's Security Council policy prior to its first period on the Council through 1962. Yet a quick browse through the table of contents will show that the book places those years in a wider context by situating them within fifty years of Ireland's United Nations membership.

The United Nations celebrates its sixtieth anniversary in 2005 and the volume takes the story of Irish interaction with the United Nations back to the final years of the Second World War. Contributions by Till Geiger and Deirdre McMahon show that Ireland, though failing to gain admission to the United Nations in 1946, was not immune to the work of the United Nations before December 1955. They also show that Ireland had a hitherto unacknowledged degree of interaction with United Nations technical organisations and that there was an ongoing debate on the need for Irish membership of the United Nations and the role of the United Nations system in government circles.

Aoife Bhreatnach, John Terence O'Neill, Kevin O'Sullivan and Greg Spelman open new territory completely in the history of Irish engagement with the United Nations. They take the story on beyond the previous terminal date of 1961, the end of what has often been called Ireland's 'Golden Age' at the United Nations, to explain how Ireland dealt with the changes in the nature of the General Assembly in the 1960s as it became dominated by the Afro-Asian group. It was not, as Spelman and Bhreatnach show, a case of simply dropping the United Nations in preference for the European Economic Community, but of adopting a more nuanced policy. That policy could be activist; but the parameters of Ireland's activism were now much more conservative because though they themselves were unchanged, the General Assembly had become more radical and Ireland's 'radicalism' looked much more restrained as a consequence. O'Sullivan and O'Neill show how the United Nations of the 1960s to the 1990s led to changes in the nature of Irish United Nations policy and Irish involvement in peacekeeping operations as Irish ministers and diplomats had to permanently deal with issues far beyond the traditional remit of Irish foreign policy.

Together the essays expand the picture of Irish interaction with the United Nations in the ten years 1945 to 1955 and the thirteen years from 1961 to 1974 (31 December 1974 being at time of writing the limit of the 30-year rule under which state papers are released in Ireland under the National Archives Act) by placing the six years following admission to the United Nations in the context of wider Irish foreign policy. Chapters on aspects of contemporary Irish United Nations policy by Eileen Connolly and John Doyle, Ben Tonra, Rory Miller and Ray Murphy show how in the subsequent thirty years the United Nations has remained a cornerstone of Irish foreign policy because of, rather than in spite of, Irish membership of the European Union (EU). Through the EU, Ireland now has a much greater economic and political reach globally to its foreign policy but that policy remains underpinned by the values enshrined in the United Nations Charter. Those authors also illustrate the enduring involvement of members of the Irish Defence Forces and members of an Garda Síochána in United Nations peacekeeping operations.

In broad terms the contributors have expanded the historiography of Ireland's United Nations policy by widening the understanding of that policy in the period prior to membership in 1955 and following the end of Ireland's 'Golden Age' at the United Nations in 1961. Whilst in no way aiming or pretending to be a complete survey of Ireland's United Nations policy to the present day, the contributors have overcome a significant historiographical hurdle in the analysis of Irish United Nations policy. Traditionally accounts of Ireland's United Nations policy began in 1955 and petered out some time in the early 1960s, the simple approach being to talk of the Europeanisation of Irish foreign policy in the years surrounding Ireland's first application to the EEC in 1961 with Lemass' pro-EEC agenda taking predominance over Aiken's preference for active non-alignment in New York. Quite what happened between the EEC application and the conclusion of the nuclear non-proliferation treaty in 1968 and Ireland's attempt to bring the outbreak of the Troubles in Northern Ireland before the Security Council in 1969 was unclear.

Partly 'what happened' was unclear because the picture was much more complex and Cosgrave's three principles and Aiken's non-alignment lacked the dimensions necessary to conduct United Nations policy in the 1960s. In addition, there was no similar handy summary of policy by which to judge policy or synopsise its rationale. Aiken and his officials had now to cope with a changed General Assembly in the 1960s as the Cold War divide was replaced by a divide between the developed and developing world, between the North and South, between the 'old' members of the United Nations and the 'new' Afro-Asian states who had joined following their independence from colonial rule in the 1960s.

Noel Dorr has addressed the position of the Security Council in the early months of the Troubles with a critical assessment of the role of the Security Council in attempting to reduce tension between Britain and Ireland. Prior to the outbreak of the Troubles in Northern Ireland in 1969, the key goals of Irish foreign policy aspired to EEC membership and to developing diplomatic relations with Africa and the Far East. Foreign policy became more complex as the 1960s continued and the relative ease with which United Nations policy was conducted during the 'Golden Age' no longer existed. The chapters on the 1960s show how Irish United Nations policy responded to this change, revealing a realisation that there were limits to the 'radicalism' it had adopted in the late 1950s and that the agendas of the new United Nations members were not similar to Irish agendas.

We can now see the 'Golden Age' in the wider context of post-war and contemporary Irish foreign policy. What is immediately clear is that Irish United Nations policy from 1955 to 1961 is not simply six years of activism at New York following ten years of international isolation or simply a period of activism preceding a reorientation of foreign policy in favour of Europe and membership of the EEC. Rather, Irish engagement with the United Nations was a continuum from 1945, despite the failure to obtain membership in August 1946, through the early years of activism and on to maturity as part of a wider foreign policy also encompassing EEC membership in the 1970s. Those who understand the centrality of United Nations membership to Irish foreign policy will know this, but the concentration on the years 1955 to 1961 has skewed the historical and interpretative perspective. This volume provides a counterpoint to that perspective.

The views expressed in the articles in this volume are the authors' own and do not necessarily reflect the views of the Minister for Foreign Affairs.

Chapter One

'Our Mendicant Vigil is Over.'
Ireland and the United Nations, 1946–55

DEIRDRE McMAHON

Over the last decade the release of Irish official and private papers has shed
considerable light on Irish relations with the United Nations, both before and
after December 1955.[1] This new material reveals the labyrinthine negotiations
and manoeuvrings which paved the long road to eventual admission but it
also questions previous assumptions about Irish foreign policy in the uncertain decade after 1945. How did wartime neutrality affect post-war relations
with Britain and America? Was Ireland really as isolated as subsequent commentators claimed? How far can we discern continuities and discontinuities
in the United Nations policy of the four administrations which were in
power from 1945–55?

The term 'United Nations' was first used in the 'Declaration by United
Nations' of January 1942 when, following the attack on Pearl Harbour and
the entry of America into the Second World War, representatives of twenty-
six nations affirmed their determination to pursue the war against the Axis
Powers. In October 1943 the foreign ministers of the USSR, the United
States of America, Great Britain and China signed the Moscow Declaration,
clause 4 of which stated that the ministers 'recognised the necessity of establishing at the earliest practicable date a general international organisation,
based on the principle of the sovereign equality of all peace-loving states, and
open to membership by all such states, large and small, for the maintenance
of international security'. A year later, at the Dumbarton Oaks conference in
Washington DC, the same four powers drafted the structure of the future

---

[1] These include the Department of Foreign Affairs records which are in the National Archives, as
well as the extensive private collections of Eamon de Valera, Frank Aiken and John A. Costello in
the UCD Archives Department. The latter were not available to Joseph Morrison Skelly when he
wrote about the period 1946–55 in his article 'Ireland, the Department of External Affairs, and the
United Nations, 1946–55: a New Look', in *Irish Studies in International Affairs*, 7 no. 4 (1996) pp.
63–80.

United Nations Organisation (UNO). It was to consist of four main bodies: (1) the General Assembly; (2) the Security Council; (3) the International Court of Justice and (4) the Economic and Social Council. Another important feature of the Dumbarton Oaks plan for UNO was that member states were to place their armed forces at the disposal of the Security Council. The absence of such a provision for the League of Nations after the First World War was widely recognised as one of the main reasons for the League's failure. No decision was reached at Dumbarton Oaks concerning the proposed voting procedure at the Security Council. This was subsequently worked out at the Yalta Conference five months later in February 1945. However, the plan to give the Big Five – the United States, Britain, the USSR, China and France – veto rights in the Security Council provoked strenuous opposition when the representatives of the forty-five states invited to the first conference met at San Francisco from April to June 1945 to draft the United Nations Charter.

The Irish government had watched these developments with great interest but also uncertainty as to what shape the new organisation would assume. In November 1943, just ten days after the Moscow Declaration, the Taoiseach and Minister for External Affairs, Eamon de Valera, told the Dáil that when the new organisation came into being 'there need be no doubt that this country will, as in the past, be prepared to take its full share in endeavouring to secure international peace and security'.[2] In June 1944 de Valera emphasised that any new organisation must acknowledge the sovereign character and free association of its member states; it must also 'provide a framework within which all nations, great and small, will play a due part in building a just and stable international order'.[3] These concerns were familiar from de Valera's involvement with the League of Nations in the 1930s and they were to be amplified over the next two years as de Valera and his officials watched uneasily as the new organisation evolved.

In October 1944, the Irish High Commissioner in Canada, John Hearne, reported to Dublin on a recent conversation with Edward J. Phelan, the Irishman who was Acting Director of the International Labour Organisation (ILO). This had been an affiliated agency of the League of Nations and Phelan, who had been on the receiving end of Soviet hostility to the ILO in the 1930s, considered the USSR to be

the great question mark of the future. No one can say how she is going to fit herself into any world organisation. She had been isolated for nearly twenty years in a very abyss of isolation. Russia is unused to the idea and to the methods of international cooperation. She is now reviving all her old claims in South Eastern Europe. She is playing a

---

[2] *Dáil Deb*, vol. 91, col. 1681, 9 Nov. 1943.
[3] *Dáil Deb*, vol. 94, col. 1358, 28 Jun. 1944.

lone hand on the Polish question … If these experiences are going to be repeated later on, say, in the Far East, she will be at loggerheads with the United States in a few years from now … The problem of security resolved itself into that of the Big Four holding together when the war was over. He [Phelan] seemed to doubt that they would hold together.[4]

There was much speculation about the potential membership of UNO and particularly whether it would include neutrals. The Irish Legation in Washington quoted a report in the *New York Times* on 25 February 1945, just after the Yalta conference, that Spain, Sweden, Switzerland, Portugal, Argentina 'and possibly Eire' had been banned from the San Francisco gathering. Only a change of government, it was reported in 'responsible quarters', might win some of these countries a place in the good graces of the major powers. However, the Irish position 'was considered a bit different … Although neutral, she has been making an important contribution to Britain's economy through man-power resources and volunteers for the fighting forces'.[5] Robert Brennan, the Irish Minister in Washington, noted that Irish-American groups were agitating for Irish representation at San Francisco but he was being non-committal: 'The line I am taking is that as Americans they are quite entitled to take any view they like in the matter. If the time comes when there is a world organisation we want to get into, their help will be useful'.[6]

A gloomy account of the proceedings in San Francisco was relayed back to Dublin by John Hearne who had just met Seán Lester, the last Secretary-General of the League of Nations. A League delegation was present in San Francisco but Lester had been told by a junior State Department official that as he was from a neutral state he could not attend. The Soviets also raised Lester's presence at the executive committee of the conference but here he received strong support from the British Foreign Secretary, Anthony Eden, and the Permanent Secretary of the British Foreign Office, Sir Alexander Cadogan. Lester stayed but he was not impressed by what he saw.[7] Speaking from the heart as a dedicated League official, he was troubled by the cynicism of its successor.

> The League had been sustained for years by a certain indefinable but unmistakeable moral authority deriving not only from the faith and idealism of its founders and from world wide popular support. The strongest force in the world was the moral conscience of mankind. At San Francisco you had a belated lip service to the ideas of international

---

[4] NAI DFA 417/1, Hearne to Walshe, 17 Oct. 1944.

[5] Ibid. Cable from Washington Legation to DEA, 26 Feb. 1945.

[6] Ibid. Brennan to Walshe, 5 Apr. 1945.

[7] As an added humiliation Lester was put on the ninth row of the gallery in the San Francisco Opera House (where the conference was being held) so he must have seen very little.

justice etc. shamefacedly dragged in as an afterthought in the discussions … The framers of the new world system did not even pretend to acknowledge any objective moral standard or law binding upon Nations as upon individuals.

As for the British, Lester thought they had now discounted continental Europe as a significant source of support for some time to come.[8]

Lester's pessimism appeared to be shared by de Valera. In July 1945, during the Dáil debate on the Department of External Affairs vote, he stressed the dilemma of small states like Ireland. From a preliminary glance at the new United Nations Charter, which had been signed in San Francisco at the end of June, he doubted whether the United Nations would be any more effective than the League and he was certain that small nations would have nothing like the influence they had in Geneva.[9] But it is worth recalling that de Valera had been equally despondent about the League in the 1930s yet played a prominent role in its proceedings. A similar pattern was to emerge in his views on the United Nations: while he had major reservations about the organisation, he was determined that Ireland should be a member.

A key factor in Irish policy was what the other neutrals would do. In August 1945 the Irish High Commissioner in London, J.W. Dulanty, informed External Affairs that Sweden was applying for observer status at the United Nations. This prompted an overly optimistic assessment by the legal adviser at External Affairs, Michael Rynne: 'We have no enemies in the Security Council at the moment (even Russia would scarcely oppose an Irish application just now)'.[10] Copies of the United Nations Charter were distributed to TDs shortly after this but de Valera told them that the government did not intend to apply just yet for United Nations membership.

However, the prospects for Irish membership dimmed over the next two months. As Rynne noted at the beginning of December, the Soviets and their satellites were against any applications for membership at the first UNO meeting the following year and were particularly hostile to the ex-neutrals. Given the existing international tension which Rynne thought could lead to a third world war, it was perhaps better to hold off from joining the United Nations. 'Over-caution … is preferable to the risk, however slight it may prove to be, of blindly leading this country into a Great Power conflict more terrible than that from which we were so recently happily spared'.[11]

---

[8] NAI DFA 417/1, Hearne to Walshe, 28 May 1945. De Valera was loyal to the League for as long as possible and even wanted its technical activities and functions to be maintained after the war. However, it was finally dissolved in April 1946. See Michael Kennedy, *Ireland and the League of Nations 1919–1946: International Relations, Diplomacy and Politics* (Dublin, 1996), pp. 244–49.

[9] *Dáil Deb*, vol. 97, cols 2780–1, 19 July 1945.

[10] NAI DFA 417/33 Pt 1, memorandum by Rynne, 23 Oct. 1945.

[11] Ibid. memorandum by Rynne, 5 Dec. 1945

As Cold War tension escalated, Irish membership of the United Nations was discussed by the United States and British governments. Sumner Welles, the former United States Under-Secretary of State, wrote in the *New York Herald Tribune* on 2 January 1946 that resentment at the 'stubborn neutrality' of the Irish should not justify their exclusion from the United Nations since their state was 'wholly democratic'. Three weeks later there was a meeting at the Foreign Office in London to discuss new UNO members. Of the neutrals there was agreement that Portugal and Iceland deserved special consideration since they had allowed their bases to be used by Allied forces but Irish membership would probably require a cabinet decision.[12] The Dominions Office, which had responsibility for Anglo-Irish relations, was not sure what Irish policy was: perhaps, like Switzerland, the Irish would prefer perpetual neutrality. There was also the question whether they wanted to be proposed for membership by the British government.[13] The Dominions Office explained loftily:

Our reasons are that it is desirable to bring Eire back into the Western European fold, and that cooperation with her in an international organisation is the best means of promoting cooperation in e.g. defence and economic matters, which is valuable for purely British reasons. At the same time we do not want to give the Eire Government the opportunity of rebuffing us ... There might be a better chance of success if the hint was given jointly by the United Kingdom and United States Governments or by a Dominion Government ... It would, however, be awkward if the Soviet Government objected to Eire, and if we were only able to get in some of our candidates and were not able to mobilise the requisite degree of United States support for Eire. We could, of course, always threaten to veto other candidates unless Eire were accepted by the other Great Powers, but it might not be practical to push this policy beyond a certain point.[14]

The Dominions Secretary, Lord Addison (a veteran of Asquith's pre-1914 governments), drafted a memorandum for the cabinet which reminded his colleagues that 'our general policy towards Eire as agreed by the Cabinet last year ... is to rebuild and restore friendly relations' and to that end he recommended support for Irish membership of the United Nations'. Given the

---

[12] TNA FO371/57253/U1217/1217/70, Foreign Office note, 26 Jan. 1946. In a letter to the Foreign Office on 11 March 1946, Godfrey Shannon of the DO emphasised that since the British government had consistently refused to recognise, on constitutional grounds, Irish neutrality, British representatives at the United Nations should 'avoid referring to Eire as "neutral"'. This advice fell on deaf ears at the FO since officials there continued to include Ireland among the other wartime neutrals. FO371/57254/U2960/1217/70.

[13] Ibid. note by F. Cumming-Bruce (Dominions Office), Jan. 1946.

[14] TNA FO371/57253/U1438/1217/70, note by Dominions Office, 31 Jan. 1946.

Irish record at the League, he expected them to be sympathetic to the Western European attitude on international problems. The only potential difficulty was partition but Addison doubted if there was much to be gained by raising partition at the United Nations: 'on the contrary, we should be presented with a convenient opportunity for stating our own position'.[15] The prospect that de Valera would raise partition at UNO was a recurrent British fear. When the Foreign Office got wind of Addison's draft memorandum, officials tried to head him off by saying that it was unnecessary but the Dominions Office replied that he was determined to refer the matter to the cabinet 'in view of the explosive quality of anything to do with Eire in this count'. In the event the extraordinary decision was taken to withdraw Addison's memorandum pending the Home Secretary's discussion of the matter with the Northern Ireland government. In a letter to the Home Secretary, Chuter Ede, Addison considered this a dangerous precedent: 'it is clear that that Government, in accordance with their usual policy, would at once object to our facilitating the admission of Eire to UNO, and the Cabinet would then be faced with the awkward necessity of over-ruling Northern Ireland in the matter'. Ede agreed but thought the Northern Ireland government should at least be informed.[16]

The Foreign Secretary, Ernest Bevin, landed something of a bombshell in mid-March when, in a minute for the Prime Minister (Clement Attlee), he expressed categorical opposition to any British support for Irish membership of UNO: 'my reason is because I fear that as soon as she became a member of the United Nations she would immediately raise the question of the "partition" of Ireland. In my opinion, we would do better to take no action and wait upon events'. Bevin's minute led to a ministerial meeting on 21 March between himself, Ede, Addison and their officials. The Soviets, Bevin argued, might exploit partition by demanding that Ireland be admitted as a thirty-two county unit. It might also be argued that partition was an arbitrary act imposed on Ireland by the British government purely for reasons of defence. Bevin was against pressing the claims of neutral states to UNO membership not only because of partition in the Irish case but also because of the nature of the Salazar and Franco regimes on the Iberian peninsula. Addison was not convinced by Bevin's arguments on partition and thought it unlikely that de Valera would apply on behalf of a thirty-two county Ireland. But Attlee agreed with Bevin and after this the Foreign Office blew cold on Irish admission to UNO. In a minute for the Permanent Under-Secretary, Sir Orme Sargent, J.G. Ward made no secret of where his sympathies lay.

---

[15] TNA FO371/57253/U1985/1217/70, draft memorandum, 14 Feb. 1946.
[16] Ibid. minute by J.G. Ward for Sir Alexander Cadogan, 6 Feb. 1946; FO371/57254/U3219/1217/70, Addison to Ede, 21 Feb. 1946; Ede to Addison, 4 Mar. 1946.

The Dominions Office, as usual, have been showing a remarkable zeal on behalf of Eire. (Being myself of Ulster descent, I will forbear to comment.) The Dominions Office actually asked that we should make it a condition of our going along with the United States in regard to Sweden, Portugal and Iceland, that they should undertake to make an approach to Eire ... I do not think we can possibly do this and, moreover, if Eire does file an application, the U.S. will probably have to vote for her ... The Dominions Office would also like us to omit the consultation with the Home Secretary about Eire. This I think we should firmly resist, since we can hardly admit the Dominions Office contention that the goodwill of Eire is more important to the United Kingdom than the goodwill of Northern Ireland.[17]

In Berne the Irish Minister, Frank Cremins, recorded a conversation with Professor Sir Charles Webster, the distinguished diplomatic historian who was currently special adviser to Philip Noel-Baker, Minister of State at the Foreign Office. Webster had served on the British delegations at Dumbarton Oaks and San Francisco and told Cremins that in his opinion it would be a long time before any neutral was admitted to UNO although he stressed that this was not British policy, '*we* want the neutrals in'. Webster thought that the renunciation by Britain of an attack on Ireland during the war 'was one of the greatest renunciations in history' but complained that it was little appreciated in Ireland. Cremins demurred and said de Valera fully appreciated it; Cremins privately thought that 'having aggressed us for at least twenty-five generations, we were entitled to a little rest' but refrained from saying so. On one subject Webster was firm: 'Ireland, through her failure to assist the Allies when America entered the war, lost for ever the sympathy of the USA'. Cremins replied that there had certainly been a lot of propaganda to that effect but that subsequently there had been a reaction.[18]

By July 1946 Argentina was the only ex-neutral to be admitted to the United Nations. With regard to the other new international organisations, Ireland was one of the founder members of the World Health Organisation (WHO), was intending to apply for membership of the Food and Agriculture Organisation (FAO), but had not been approached to join UNESCO nor the International Monetary Fund and the World Bank. De Valera continued to make pessimistic comparisons between UNO and the League, and F.H. Boland, the new DEA Secretary, told the British Representative in Ireland, Sir John Maffey, that United Nations membership had little to offer Ireland.

---

[17] TNA FO371/159728/UN331/31/78, minute by Ward, 18 Jun. 1946.
[18] NAI DFA 417/33 Pt.1, Cremins to External Affairs, 2 May 1946.
[19] TNA FO371/59729, Maffey to Dominions Office, 2 Jul. 1946; Archer (Dublin) to Shannon (DO), 3 Jul. 1946.

The American Minister, David Gray, also thought the signs discouraging.[19] The reason for these soundings was that the British and the Americans had now decided to support Irish membership and de Valera was informed of this on 5 July. He was pleased to have British support but told Maffey it was somewhat embarrassing to apply for admission without being sure of support beforehand, as had been the case with the League. He was anxious to know the views of the other members of the Security Council and, Maffey noted, attached particular importance to Sweden and Portugal. De Valera made no attempt to link partition to UNO and indeed was 'most friendly and reasonable throughout'.[20]

Maffey's reference to Sweden and Portugal indicated which way the wind was blowing at Iveagh House. On 12 July, the Portuguese Chargé d'Affaires, de Freitas, told Boland that his government had also been assured of British and American support for any Portuguese application to join UNO. However, the Portuguese government was lukewarm, believing that the Soviets would veto any application but apart from this the organisation was an unattractive proposition as its character and future were still so uncertain. For the Portuguese the major factor was Spain because as long as agitation against Spain persisted, joining UNO was impossible.[21] The Swedish Chargé was similarly unenthusiastic and told Boland that his government did not intend to apply for membership as it did not know what the Soviet attitude would be.[22]

But as the deadline for applications approached at the beginning of August, the Portuguese and Swedish governments changed their minds and thus Ireland, Portugal and Sweden decided to submit formal membership applications. De Valera received the necessary authorisation from the Dáil on 25 July. During the debate he reiterated his misgivings about the current structure of UNO and the Charter. Regarding partition, he doubted whether membership would bring about unity but neither would it hinder it. 'I do not think we could effectively help ourselves simply by remaining outside … Within the organisation we might be able to protect our immediate interests better inside the organisation than outside it'.[23] While most of the Fine Gael front bench agreed that it was better not to raise partition, it was, interestingly, the former party leader, W.T. Cosgrave, who judged that partition

> should never be absent from the minds or from the consideration of the representatives of this country, either in the United Nations or elsewhere … so long as Partition continues, harmonious, cordial and friendly relations between this country and Great Britain can never be

---

[20] Ibid. Maffey to DO, 8 Jul. 1946.
[21] NAI DFA 417/33 Pt.1, unsigned memorandum (by Boland ?), 12 Jul. 1946.
[22] Ibid. minute by Boland for de Valera, 16 Jul. 1946.
[23] *Dáil Deb*, vol. 102, cols. 1323–26, 24 Jul. 1946.

established on the basis on which they might rest if Partition ceased to exist ... I think that as soon as the opportunity presents itself this country will raise the matter of Partition. Whether it is considered by the United Nations as a whole, or by some committee of it, our contribution to world affairs and to a full participation ... would be far greater, far more effective and far more encouraging to the people of this country in making them participate in a fuller measure if the problem of Partition were solved.[24]

When Boland met the Swedish Chargé, Thorsing, the day after the Dáil vote, the latter reported that the Soviets were apparently 'positive' although they were dissatisfied with the attitude of the Security Council towards the applications of its satellites, particularly Albania and Outer Mongolia.[25] The Irish application was lodged on 2 August. Such was the Irish optimism that to mark Ireland's admission to UNO de Valera was already making enthusiastic plans for his first visit to the United States since 1930. Boland sent Robert Brennan details of the delegation and told him that de Valera wanted to visit New York, Boston, Philadelphia, Chicago and San Francisco. Brennan advised de Valera that if he was visiting all these cities, then he would have to address meetings as 'he cannot go to them and not meet thousands of people without disappointing them ... if meetings are to be organised, promoters will have to start immediately'.[26]

Initially, the omens seemed promising. The Norwegian Secretary-General of the United Nations, Trygve Lie, made hopeful comments to both Frank Cremins and Sean Lester. The applications of Afghanistan, Transjordan and Ireland came before the membership committee on 12 August. In a cable to the Foreign Office, the head of the United Kingdom delegation, Sir Alexander Cadogan, reported that while the Irish had the support of Britain, the United States, China, France, Holland and Brazil, the Soviets referred to the absence of diplomatic relations with Ireland and 'would not (repeat not) support [Irish] application'.[27] The Irish and Portuguese applications were essentially at the mercy of the barter politics which were emerging with such force as the Cold War took hold. These barter politics were to frustrate Irish admission for the next nine years. If the Western powers wouldn't accept Soviet satellites such as Albania and Outer Mongolia, then the Soviets would veto states like Ireland and Portugal sponsored by the Western powers.

The veto on Ireland and Portugal was confirmed on 30 August. Sweden, however, was accepted. The terseness of the statement which de Valera issued

---

[24] Ibid. cols. 1460–63, 25 Jul. 1946.
[25] NAI DFA 417/33 Pt.1, minute by Boland for de Valera, 26 Jul. 1946.
[26] Ibid. Boland to Brennan, 30 Jul. 1946; Brennan to Boland, 8 Aug. 1946.
[27] TNA FO371/59732/UN1284/31/78, cable from Cadogan to Foreign Office, 12 Aug. 1946.

indicated the depth of his disappointment. Comment was unnecessary, he said, the position was self-explanatory.[28] What de Valera found especially frustrating about the Soviet attitude was that they kept shifting their grounds for rejecting the Irish application, at one moment citing the lack of diplomatic relations and at another castigating Ireland's war record and alleged sympathy with the Axis. In a circular despatch to Irish overseas missions, Boland did his best to put a brave face on the rejection. De Valera 'is satisfied that we have lost nothing by the non-success of our application. The fact that our application was supported by all the members of the Security Council except Russia, and that even Poland dissociated herself from the Russian attitude was very satisfactory'. As to the future, there was no question of making a second application; if at a later date the Security Council wanted to review its decision, then it was up to the Council to do so.[29]

In one quarter at least there was satisfaction at the Irish failure. The Irish minister to the Holy See, Joseph Walshe, reported that Vatican officials 'have no belief in UNO' and indeed would have been happier if the Irish government had been less precipitate in its application.[30] On 12 September de Valera met Herbert Morrison, Lord President of the Council in Attlee's cabinet, who was on holiday in Ireland. Morrison wrote that de Valera 'took "a shrug of the shoulders" attitude' towards the Soviet veto but noted perceptively that the rejection 'may have offended his dignity'.[31] There is no doubt that for de Valera, despite his reservations about UNO, membership was a way of re-establishing his and Ireland's international position in the post-war world. For the moment he had failed but neither would he beg for admission, least of all to the Soviets, and on that he remained adamant for the next nine years. One of the most galling aspects was that in September 1934 he had supported the admission of the USSR to the League of Nations and had declared on that occasion: 'I represent a country which, if you consider its political and religious ideals, is as far apart as the poles from Soviet Russia; but I would be willing to take the responsibility of saying openly and frankly here that I would support and vote for the entry of Russia into the League'.[32] It was a stance that was opposed by, among others, the *Irish Independent*, which remained implacably hostile to the USSR. 'Russian opposition to Ireland is indeed a tribute and a compliment', the *Independent* observed sourly on 31 August 1946.

There was a brief revival of Irish hopes in November–December 1946 when a special sub-committee of UNO's Political and Security Committee recommended that the Security Council re-examine the rejected applications

---

[28] UCDA, De Valera Papers [DVP], P150/2823, statement, 30 Aug. 1946.
[29] NAI DFA 417/33 Pt. 1, circular despatch by Boland, 4 Sept. 1946.
[30] Ibid. Walshe to Boland, 4 Sept. 1946.
[31] TNA FO371/59734/31/78, extract from cabinet memorandum by Lord President, 16 Oct. 1946.
[32] Maurice Moynihan ed., *Speeches and Statements by Eamon de Valera 1917–1973* (Dublin, 1980) p. 259.

of Albania, Transjordan, Ireland, Portugal and Outer Mongolia. This was approved by seven votes to four, with the USSR, Ukraine, Czechoslovakia and Chile against. Gromyko, the Soviet representative, insisted that an applicant's war record must be taken into account. The Indian delegate, Vijaya Lakshmi Pandit, warmly supported Ireland.

> There is no doubt that Ireland is a peace-loving nation. Perhaps Ireland was a little too peace-loving during the War. Ireland could not be admitted as an original member of the United Nations because at that time, the definition of a peace-loving country was that it should have declared War. That definition is no longer applicable. We feel that Ireland fully satisfies the conditions laid down in Article 4 of the Charter. India has always had a certain fundamental sympathy with Ireland. Ireland, like India, has fought long and hard for her freedom. Indeed our earlier patriots used to follow Irish methods for obtaining freedom. Later, however, thanks to the gospel of non-violence elaborated by Mahatma Gandhi, we have been following a different and, I believe, nobler method for the achievement of freedom. This, however, does not detract from our admiration for the tenacity and vigour with which Ireland has conducted her own struggle.[33]

There were further expressions of support from the Canadian delegate Louis St Laurent (then Minister for External Affairs and future Prime Minister) who commented that while many disagreed with Ireland's wartime neutrality, at least that neutrality demonstrated that the Irish placed a high value on peace and could pursue an independent foreign policy. Paul Hasluck, an Australian delegate, argued that consideration of applicants' war records should be ruled out; UNO 'is not an association of belligerent nations, but an association of peace-loving States'.[34]

De Valera and Boland were clearly determined that this time the Irish must be more active in their own interests and not floundering in the wake of the other neutrals and Britain and America. On 9 November Boland cabled Hearne in Ottawa and asked him to go at once to New York and 'by personal contacts and discussions with individual delegates advise us (a) what are prospects of agreement on new admissions being reached at present Assembly and (b) whether there is any action to be taken here to improve prospects of our admission'. Seán Lester was also in New York and could help Hearne with contacts. The cable ended with the admonition that his presence in New York 'should appear to have some other object and your attendance at meetings etc. to be purely casual'.[35] It is not surprising that such a delicate task was given to

---

[33] NAI DFA 417/33 Pt. 2, statement, 8 Nov. 1946.
[34] Ibid. *Irish Times*, 7 Nov. 1946, *Irish Press* 8 Nov. 1946.
[35] Ibid. cable from Boland to Hearne, 9 Nov. 1946

Hearne rather than to Robert Brennan in Washington whose work always had more to do with propaganda than strict diplomacy. Hearne was close to de Valera who had entrusted to him the drafting of the 1937 constitution. He had been in External Affairs since the 1920s and had a network of contacts from the Commonwealth conferences and from the League of Nations which he had regularly attended. He was to play a vital behind-the-scenes role from now until 1955.

Once in New York Hearne lost no time speaking to UNO delegates from Canada, Australia, New Zealand, South Africa and India. Hasluck told him bluntly that as long as the British held out against Albania the Soviets would obstruct Irish admission. Hearne informed him that his government would much prefer an adjournment to a second rejection. Two of the South African delegates sought Hearne's advice on aspects of the 1936 External Relations Act (which he had drafted). One of them said to Hearne: 'I am a Dutch South African. I have been brought up on Mr de Valera. We all admire him in South Africa. I have a point to make to you. The British Commonwealth can be made whatever the French in Canada, the Dutch in South Africa, and the Irish all over but especially in Ireland, want it to be. That's a point, isn't it ?'[36]

Hearne consulted Seán Lester and E.J. Phelan who were in the city, both of whom were pessimistic about Irish chances in the current session. Lester, speaking with 'great emphasis', warned against any anti-partition campaign in the United States while Phelan consoled Hearne with the philosophical observation that 'events aren't logical, developments aren't predictable anymore. Nothing makes sense … I don't think that the *Russians* know what they will do next week or before the session ends'. Hearne also renewed acquaintance with Ben Cockram from the Commonwealth Relations Office (formerly Dominions Office), whom he had known at League meetings in the 1930s and with Cadogan whom he had also met at Geneva. Perhaps the most interesting of Hearne's encounters were those with the Polish delegation. Boland had asked Hearne to thank Oscar Lange for supporting Ireland when he was President of the Security Council in August-September; 'you might be able to get light from him as to strength of and reasons for Russian attitude. For your information Warsaw is sounding us indirectly about recognition but at the moment there is no change in our attitude'. Hearne wrote an evocative report of his meeting with Stanczyk, another of the Polish delegates, as they walked up and down Park Avenue.

> We talked about the similarity of the Irish and Polish struggles for freedom and unity; about the Polish treasures 'lost' in Canada; and, inevitably, of the United Nations. 'The United Nations', Mr Stanczyk said, 'why do we call it so ? There is no United Nations, no broad basic policy of the peace organisation agreed on by all. The Great Powers are

---

[36] Ibid. Hearne to Boland, 2 Dec. 1946

at war in the United Nations. Who can say what the result will be?' ... Of Ireland Mr Stanczyk said 'Ireland must join the United Nations, but who knows when, next year perhaps?' I said that our Government and people were grateful to Dr Lange for his speech on our candidature. 'But that was the voice of Poland', Mr Stanczyk remarked with a stab at propaganda ... I observed 'Russia is the trouble'. Stanczyk squeezed my arm, and at once relaxed the pressure as if he was going too far. He said nothing ... We spoke of other things, the glory and horror of New York in her wealth and luxury, the future of America in world affairs, her doubtful destiny as the custodian of the European heritage ... But we spoke no more of Ireland and the United Nations.[37]

Hearne's *envoi* was prescient as Ireland's application once again ran into the sands. On 10 December reconsideration of the applications was deferred by the Security Council with the Soviets bringing up Irish conduct during the war. 'Snubbed Again' ran the headline in the *Irish Independent* which from now on became a vocal critic of the United Nations. Bishop Michael Fogarty of Killaloe expressed his relief at the exclusion from UNO which was 'bad company' for Ireland.

Irish resentment of this politicking surfaced in the row which happened shortly after this. Ireland and Spain were both members of the Provisional International Civil Aviation Conference (PICAO). On 12 December 1946 the Political and Security Committee of the United Nations General Assembly passed a resolution banning Spain from membership of international agencies or organisations affiliated to UNO. De Valera was incensed by this and told the Spanish Minister, Count d'Artaza, that if Ireland had been a member of UNO he would have gone to the Assembly in person and voted against the resolution.

The action of the United Nations Organisation in attempting to dictate what regime a particular State should have was a thoroughly bad principle; if, however, such a principle were to be adopted, it could only be justified at all if it were applied impartially; and to single out Spain on the ground of alleged defects in the present regime in that country, while ignoring what was happening in countries further east in Europe, was just one-sided and hypocritical.[38]

Since the Canary Islands were an essential link in Atlantic air traffic control, Irish officials considered that expulsion could not be justified in the interests

[37] Ibid. The Polish treasures referred to were the Polish Royal Collections which were shipped to Canada for safety in 1939 and only returned in 1961.
[38] NAI DFA 417/22, minute by Boland for heads of mission, 4 Jan. 1947.

of civil aviation. In any event PICAO was not yet formally affiliated to UNO.[39] When this happened in May 1947 Spain was expelled not only from PICAO but from the ITU (International Telecommunications Union). However, Spain did participate in the Marshall Plan and in NATO, and in November 1950 United Nations sanctions were lifted although it was banned from UNESCO in 1952. Spain eventually joined UNO at the same time as Ireland.

The DEA still had not given up hope and in March 1947 Boland instructed the heads of mission in Washington, London, Paris, Ottawa and Canberra to glean 'any scrap of information [that] may be useful … and may give us a fairly reliable indication of our prospects'.[40] This yielded immediate results with a report from Dulanty in London of a meeting with the new Polish Ambassador there, Jerzy Michalowski. Michalowski had tried to persuade Gromyko to support the Irish application but to no avail. He told Dulanty that the Soviets felt their prestige was adversely affected by a small country like Ireland declining to have diplomatic relations and that 'our attitude was in the nature of an affront to their dignity'. When Gromyko complained of the Irish record in the war, Michaolowski pointed out that he had voted for Swedish admission.

> Mr Gromyko's rejoinder was that Sweden was in an extremely difficult situation because of the strategical importance of her geographical position. There had been considerable pressure put on her by Germany. There had been no such pressure on Ireland, and the Ambassador formed the impression that Mr Gromyko thought that we had really been against the Allies.

'A curious view for the representative of the country that had made a pact with Hitler', was Dulanty's barbed response.[41] Expressions of sympathy came from Lester Pearson of Canada, from Argentina, from Australia but at the end of July 1947 the Soviets, following a furious debate over Albania's application, once more rejected the Irish application. 'Humiliated Again', fulminated the *Irish Independent* on 31 July. But this time, obviously feeling that nothing more was to be gained from a low-key response, de Valera let fly in a forthright interview he gave to the *New York Times* on 1 August.

> The reasons given by the Russian representative are obviously a pretence. The statement that Ireland expressed sympathy with the Axis is simply untrue. The Irish people are genuinely a democratic people, who, whilst they do not desire to interfere with the manner in which

---

[39] NAI DFA 417/16, Spain and UNO 1946–55.
[40] NAI DFA 417/33 Pt. 2, Boland to Heads of Mission, 21 March 1947.
[41] Ibid. Dulanty to Boland, 21 March 1947.

other peoples organise their social life or govern themselves, dislike for their part and fundamentally, dictatorships of whatever variety ... As for Ireland's attitude during the war, Ireland remained neutral ... but she would have defended herself to the best of her ability if attacked. Russia did not enter the war until she was attacked and for almost two years preceding her entry, Russia assisted Germany in accordance with the terms of a trade agreement which she made with Germany before the war. Moreover the immediate preparatory step to Germany's attack on Poland on September 1st, 1939, was the conclusion of the famous Non-Aggression Pact between Russia and Germany ... That Agreement was interpreted by everyone at the time as giving Germany a free hand to go ahead.

The Russian view of the qualities required in a nation for entry into the United Nations Organisation is a strange one. If Russia, which attacked Finland, Poland, Esthonia [sic], Latvia, Lithuania, can be regarded as qualifying as a peace-loving nation it is difficult to see how a nation which kept the peace and scrupulously fulfilled its obligations as a member of the League of Nations can rightly be regarded as not qualifying ... Russia's action in this matter ... is clearly an abuse of power and it is obvious that no organisation in which such action is possible will command the people's respect or can long endure.[42]

The interview won de Valera much praise in the United States, Australia and Europe. During a rushed visit to Ottawa, Hearne's former League acquaintance, Ben Cockram, now in charge of UNO affairs at the British Embassy in Washington, took time out to visit him and ask what implications de Valera's interview had for the Irish application. Hearne assured him that it had not been withdrawn.[43] When the General Assembly approved Ireland for membership, a move which had no legal significance as the Security Council was responsible for deciding on new members, the Soviet permanent representative to the United Nations, Andrei Vyshinsky, declared that Ireland and Portugal were fascist states which supported Franco's Spain. Hector McNeil, the head of the British delegation, dismissed this with scorn. 'To say that Ireland is Fascist is to suggest that they don't have a representative government. They conduct elections in the full blaze of publicity; their citizens go freely and sometimes noisily to the polls. Nobody is in any doubt about the ability of the Irish to conduct elections and freely to elect a government.'[44] In Ottawa Hearne had a chance encounter with the Governor-General, Lord Alexander, at the reception to mark the marriage of Princess Elizabeth to Prince Philip. Alexander came up to Hearne and said

---

[42] UCDA DVP, P150/2823.
[43] NAI DFA 417/33 Pt. 3, Hearne to Boland, 6 Sept. 1947.
[44] *Irish Press*, 18 Nov. 1947.

'our exclusion [from UNO] is the highest compliment ever paid to our country'. Alexander, as Hearne noted, 'always refers to himself in public and in private as an Irishman',[45] an intriguing observation given the dramatic events which unfolded in Canada ten months later and in which Alexander played a leading role.

Irish citizens went 'noisily to the polls' in February 1948 and Fianna Fáil, after sixteen long years in power, was replaced by a five party coalition led by John A. Costello; the new Minister for External Affairs was Seán MacBride. There were straws in the wind that MacBride's UNO policy might depart from that of his predecessor. In a speech six months earlier he had proposed that instead of seeking admission to UNO he would like the government to offer prizes, on the lines of the Nobel Prizes, for books, plays and films which would impress on people that another world war would be the end of civilisation. Such a course, he thought, would be 'more effective, cheaper and dignified than another application for membership of UNO'.[46] On 20 July 1948, five months after he became minister, he told the Dáil that 'at some time in the near future, it may become necessary that the Government should consider whether our application for membership of the United Nations Organisation should be withdrawn'. He had delayed doing so because he was reluctant to take steps which might indicate 'a lack of faith in any attempt that was being made to discuss world problems at a conference table. No matter how abortive or how fruitless such conferences may prove, it is still the only way of avoiding conflict.'[47] This caused some alarm in Washington and prompted a letter to MacBride from the American Minister, George Garrett. The State Department would view 'with regret' the withdrawal of Ireland's application as it would be open to the interpretation that Ireland was 'now less anxious to play her part in the community of nations'. A withdrawal would also reflect badly on UNO at a time when every effort was needed to maintain its authority. The United States government, Garrett assured MacBride, would continue to support Irish admission as it fulfilled the qualifications for membership set out in the Charter. MacBride was mollified by Garrett's letter and said his government had no intention of withdrawing its application although there was much public scepticism about UNO.[48]

But MacBride was no nearer than de Valera to UNO membership. In December 1948 the General Assembly once again passed a resolution, thirty-eight votes to six, in favour of Irish membership. There were signs, however, that Soviets were tiring of this campaign of attrition and in June

[45] NAI DFA 417 Pt. 3, Hearne to Boland, 21 Nov. 1947.
[46] Irish Times, 16 Aug. 1947.
[47] Dáil Deb, 112, 903–4, 20 Jul. 1948.
[48] NAI DFA 417/33 Pt. 3, Garrett to MacBride, 26 Aug. 1948; MacBride to Chapin, 28 Sept. 1948.

1949 they proposed a bloc barter of admissions, seven Western states for five pro-Soviet states, but this was rejected and in September 1949 they again vetoed Ireland and Portugal, this time in company with Austria, Finland, Italy, Jordan and Ceylon. In an interview which de Valera gave to *America*, the Jesuit weekly, in December 1949 the most he would say in favour of UNO was that it was at least 'a forum for discussion – or for disagreement'. His hostility to the Soviets had not abated.

> We used to read of the tortures which the savages inflicted on their captives. That was in what we considered as savage times. But now we have governments regarded as civilised making a policy and practice of torture. Think of the 'confessions' in the Soviet courts ... Russia has conquered country after country outside her own borders, either by force or by the workings of little groups of Communists from within. How are all these subjected peoples to be freed ? How are the Russians to be compelled to withdraw to their own territory? I hate to think of force – but sometimes force suggests itself as the only answer.

When the interviewer suggested that force was a dubious solution, de Valera replied ruminatively that 'in the long run, in the very long run, perhaps force is not an answer anywhere'.[49]

The intense frustration which Irish isolation was causing was illustrated in a letter which James Dillon, the Minister for Agriculture, wrote to Costello in January 1951. Dillon had always taken a great interest in international affairs and his opposition to neutrality had led to his departure from Fine Gael in 1942 (he subsequently rejoined). Every free country in Europe, he commented in exasperation, except those on the Soviet frontiers, were now members of NATO. Ireland was isolated and now that Spain had escaped from that dilemma, 'Ireland's isolation is more marked and more incongru-ous in a world situation of Communism versus the rest'. In an obvious tilt at MacBride, Dillon declared that 'we are becoming the universal wooden spoon wherewith any mischief-maker feels himself free to stir up any convenient pot of broth which he wishes to see boiling over without any risk to himself, while at the same time securing the maximum irritation to Great Britain or/and the USA'. Dillon wanted a comprehensive Irish-American defence treaty which would, he predicted, 'inevitably expedite the disappear-ance of Partition' and establish Ireland as a kind of Atlantic Pearl Harbour.[50] Nothing came of Dillon's grandiose ideas as the Costello administration collapsed four months later.

Between 1946 and 1950 only nine states – Afghanistan, Iceland, Sweden,

---

[49] *America*, 24 Dec. 1949.
[50] UCDA, John A. Costello Papers [JACP], P190/562.

Thailand, Pakistan, Yemen, Burma, Israel, Indonesia – were admitted to UNO. A further sixteen states had submitted applications since 1946, thus creating a logjam which was becoming more untenable by the year. The Soviets increasingly favoured a bloc barter solution but the British, the Americans and the Chinese were lukewarm. Further difficulties were caused by American attempts to secure Japanese admission, a move opposed by the Soviets, and by American insistence that every application had to be examined on its merits. External Affairs was still sensitive to any suggestion that the government was begging for admission. On 16 March 1952, Basil Collins, second secretary at the Irish Embassy in Washington, made what he thought was an innocuous broadcast on United Nations Radio for St Patrick's Day. At the end of his talk Collins commented that Ireland was still debarred from the United Nations, 'that nobly conceived organisation through the operation of the veto ... many times by the Soviet Union'. He hoped that 'we may yet be enabled to have our voice heard'. The Secretary of the Department of External Affairs, Sean Nunan, marked this passage in the transcript of the broadcast and reminded Collins that 'public opinion here will not stand for anything in the nature of a "plea" ... for admission to UNO'. The Minister, Frank Aiken, had made this crystal clear. With the Soviets now in favour of a bloc barter, 'we are fast coming to the point where the responsibility for our non-admission will rest on the USA, rather than the USSR!'[51]

By 1953 the very name UNO induced exhaustion among External Affairs officials. When Joe Brennan, press officer in Washington, wrote to Conor Cruise O'Brien in the Political Section at External Affairs that the journal *Catholic World* was interested in publishing an article on Ireland and UNO, O'Brien replied that he saw 'no advantage in publicity for our attitude to UNO ... we are making no special efforts to promote acceptance, and, in the present state of things', he concluded dispiritedly, 'such efforts would in any case be of no avail'.[52] By the following year there were now nineteen states with pending applications, of which five were Communist states. The United States was still opposing bloc admission of these five but began to float the idea of associate membership among the Soviet-vetoed applicants. The Italian government, according to Denis Devlin at the Irish Embassy in Rome, was against the idea and no longer seemed interested in joining UNO.[53] Ceylon was also opposed and the idea seems to have been dropped. The tenth anniversary of UNO occurred in 1955 but, as one External Affairs official wrote, after nine years of waiting such was the general apathy and lack of

[51] NAI DFA 417/33 Pt. 4, Nunan to Hearne (Washington), 22 Apr. 1952.

[52] Ibid. DFA 417/33/1, correspondence between Brennan and O'Brien, Nov.–Dec. 1953.

[53] Ibid. DFA 417/33, Pt. 6, Devlin to Sean Murphy (DEA Secretary), 13 Oct. 1954.

[54] Ibid. minute by Eamon Kennedy, 22 Apr. 1955.

[55] Ibid. J.D. Brennan to Murphy, 11 Jul. 1955.

enthusiasm in the country it was unlikely the government would embark on any commemoration ceremonies.[54] A Spanish diplomat, Jose Sebastian de Erice, suggested that Ireland establish permanent observer status at UNO but External Affairs thought that nothing was to be gained from observer status and in any event the cost, as much as £10,000 p.a., was prohibitive.[55]

Of rather more concern to John Hearne, now Ambassador in Washington, was the United States voting record at UNO on colonial issues. The United States had supported France on Algeria and the British on Cyprus. The Norwegian Foreign Minister, Dr Halward Lange, had visited Washington the previous week and told the Secretary of State, John Foster Dulles, that 'Norway had a long history of colonial status and pointed out the danger to NATO of the principal members of UNO throwing their influence against the trend of freedom amongst present day colonial peoples'. Hearne agreed. 'The upsurge of nationalism in Asia and Africa since the end of World War II is as strong as the upsurge of nationalism in Europe after World War I', and the recent Bandung Conference and the UNO vote on Algeria showed that the world was dividing on racial lines. For Hearne, the recent arms deal between Czechoslovakia and Egypt was an even more ominous portent: 'for the balance of power is a balance of armaments. And the Middle East has, in that connection, become a witch's cauldron'.

Colonial issues were also of concern to Seán MacBride as was evident in a letter he wrote to the Taoiseach, Costello, in November 1955. Some continental papers were predicting that, if admitted to the United Nations, the Irish would take an anti-colonialism stand at UNO. But partition was MacBride's main priority as he tried to predict where the various UNO members, current and future, stood on the issue. Spain, Italy, Iceland, France, Greece, Luxembourg and Belgium would probably support Ireland on partition; Portugal and Turkey would be friendly but uncommitted unless the United States signalled its support. Within the British Commonwealth, India and South Africa were uncertain, Australian and New Zealand would probably be opposed, while Canada might abstain. Thus the attitude of the US was vitally important especially regarding states being pressured by Britain. Under British influence, the State Department had always avoided committing itself on partition. If the issue came before UNO MacBride believed it could no longer avoid the issue; 'I believe that through Congressional and/or Presidential intervention the State Department could be compelled to take our side'.[56] But Costello had heard enough siren voices on partition in his first administration and told the Dáil that there was nothing to be gained from raising partition 'at inopportune times or on inappropriate occasions or by giving the impression that we are blind to all issues of international policy

[56] UCDA, JACP, P190/849 (2), MacBride to Costello, 19 Nov. 1955.
[57] *Dáil Deb*, vol. 156, col. 409, 17 Apr. 1955.

save that of Partition alone'.[57]

On 16 December 1955 Ireland was finally admitted to UNO along with Albania, Austria, Bulgaria, Cambodia, Ceylon, Finland, Hungary, Italy, Jordan, Laos, Libya, Nepal, Portugal, Romania and Spain. The *Irish Independent* grumbled that 'nobody can say that the circumstances of our mendicant vigil for nine years awaiting the outcome of these intrigues and bargains has been quite in accord with our national dignity' but at least Ireland was finally in.[58]

---

[58] *Irish Independent*, 16 Dec. 1955.

Chapter Two

A belated discovery of internationalism? Ireland, the United Nations and the reconstruction of Western Europe, 1945–60

TILL GEIGER

In his wartime statements, the Taoiseach and Minister for External Affairs, Eamon de Valera, developed the arguments which informed three generally accepted narratives on Irish wartime neutrality: neutrality kept Ireland out of the war, preserved the integrity of the Irish state, and asserted strongly the rights of small nations to sovereignty and territorial integrity. As Geoffrey Roberts has pointed out, de Valera's single-minded determination to preserve the sovereignty and integrity of independent Ireland could be described as a policy of moral indifference.[1] De Valera stressed in Dáil Éireann in September 1939 that the interests of Ireland (as a partitioned nation, the northern portion of which was still subjugated by a great power) had to take precedence over all other considerations.[2] He portrayed war as evil and a direct result of great power politics.

This narrative of neutrality shaped de Valera's response to the Anglo-American Dumbarton Oaks proposals for a united nations organisation published in autumn 1944. In a speech to the College Historical Society at Trinity College, Dublin, in November 1944, de Valera argued that while only the creation of an international state would insure world peace, the formation of a world government remained unlikely in the foreseeable future. In the absence of an international super-state, he feared that merely replacing the League of Nations with another international organisation would not improve

---

[1] Geoffrey Roberts, 'Three narratives of neutrality: historians and Ireland's war', in Brian Girvin and Geoffrey Roberts, eds., *Ireland and the Second World War: Politics, Society and Remembrance* (Dublin, 2000), pp. 165–72.

[2] Maurice Moynihan (ed.), *Speeches and Statements by Eamon de Valera, 1917–1973* (Dublin, 1980), pp. 416–20.

the position of small nations in the world or provide the vital guarantees of sovereignty that they needed. Indeed, he voiced his concerns that the envisaged international organisation would be controlled by the great powers and would dominate smaller nations. As a result, de Valera remained reluctant to endorse the Anglo-American proposals wholeheartedly or commit Ireland to joining the new international organisation despite the country's support for the League of Nations. This view was fully supported by the editorial opinion of the leading Irish newspapers.[3]

De Valera's scepticism about the new world organisation never completely vanished in the following two years which led up to Ireland's application to join the United Nations in July 1946. In a debate on a financial vote relating to Ireland's contribution to the League of Nations in June 1946, de Valera told the Dáil that the final assembly of the League of Nations had decided to dissolve the organisation and transfer its assets to the United Nations. In asking the Dáil to approve Ireland's final annual payment to the League, de Valera used his speech to reflect on the failure of what he called 'possibly the greatest experiment in international co-operation'. From its inception until 1931, the League largely had lived up to the expectations of its founders. De Valera suggested that the League had then failed because member states proved unwilling to uphold the Covenant's security guarantees for all member states and to do so if necessary by force.[4]

While the debate focused primarily on the reasons for the failure of the League, some voices expressed their hope for the success of the United Nations and demanded that the Taoiseach set out the government's position on the United Nations rather than dwell on the past.[5] In his reply, de Valera reminded opposition TDs that Ireland would have to apply for United Nations membership and that its accession should not be regarded as a foregone conclusion given that any application had to be endorsed by the Security Council and by a two-thirds majority in the General Assembly. At the same time, he insisted that the Irish government would have to assess whether it would be in the country's interest to apply for United Nations membership. In this context, he repeated his concerns about the organisational structure of the United Nations which he first voiced in his speech to the College Historical Society in November 1944:

---

[3] National Archives of Ireland (hereafter NAI), Department of the Taoiseach (hereafter DT) S13590, press clippings on inaugural meeting of College Historical Society, 2 and 3 November 1944. On this speech, see also Till Geiger, 'Introduction. Ireland, Europe and the Marshall Plan: the legacy of American power', in Till Geiger and Michael Kennedy (eds.), *Ireland, Europe and the Marshall Plan* (Dublin, 2004), p. 27. On Ireland's involvement in the League of Nations, see Michael Kennedy, *Ireland and the League of Nations, 1919–46: International relations, diplomacy and politics* (Dublin, 1996).

[4] *Dáil Deb.*, vol. 101, cols. 2429–33, 26 June 1946.

[5] *Dáil Deb.*, vol. 101, cols. 2433–48, 26 June 1946.

My own view is that the present organisation does not appear as satisfactory from the point of view of the small nations as the old League of Nations was. However, we have not had the settling of that. Inasmuch as it is the large Powers which will have, in the main, to supply the force which is necessary to support the rule of law, it is not unnatural that the large nations should claim considerable power in what they regard as certain vital matters, but I think that could be secured by an arrangement somewhat better than the present one. However, I do not think there will be anything gained by my discussing changes and improvements in the existing organisation. I think I have made it clear that our general desire would be to form part of a security organisation and that the very serious question of whether we should or should not apply will come up for consideration probably when the peace treaties have been signed and a peace situation has been reached.[6]

Given this ambivalent statement, the government's announcement that it intended applying for United Nations membership in July 1946 seemed to be a sudden u-turn to outsiders.[7]

The opening of the Irish archives has enabled historians to shed more light on the reasons for de Valera's change of heart in summer 1946, which earlier authors such as Norman MacQueen had found so puzzling.[8] In an article published in 1986, Ronan Fanning has shown that Britain signalled to the Irish government that it and the United States would support an Irish application. This signal of support convinced Irish politicians that they should seek United Nations membership without delay.[9] In a more recent article, Joe Skelly has demonstrated that the possibility of Irish membership of the United Nations was discussed within the Department of External Affairs as early as 1945. These discussions revealed some concerns about whether membership and particularly Article 43 of the Charter would be compatible with Irish neutrality. By early 1946 it became obvious that growing rifts between the superpowers would make it unlikely that member states would be called upon to make troops and bases available to the United Nations in a future war. Therefore, de Valera seemed more sanguine about Ireland joining the United Nations in his speech to the Dáil in June 1946 than on previous occasions. While Skelly underlines the importance of Anglo-American signals that they would support Ireland's application, he interprets Dublin's quick decisive action as a sign of general support for the

---

[6] *Dáil Deb.*, vol. 101, cols. 2448–55, 26 June 1946.

[7] Norman MacQueen, 'Ireland's entry to the United Nations, 1946–56', in Tom Gallagher and James O'Connell (eds.), *Contemporary Irish Studies* (Manchester, 1983), pp. 65–7.

[8] MacQueen, 'Ireland's entry', pp. 65–9.

[9] Ronan Fanning, 'The Anglo-American alliance and the Irish application for membership of the United Nations', *Irish Studies in International Affairs*, vol. 2, no. 2 (1986), pp. 35–61.

United Nations.[10] However, de Valera repeated his reservations about the United Nations in his opening speech in the debate.[11] When closing the debate he stressed that the ultimate test of whether Ireland should apply for United Nations membership should be whether membership would improve the country's ability to protect its freedom from the potential threat of great power intervention, as had almost happened during the recent war from Britain and the United States.[12] His statements hardly amounted to a ringing endorsement of either the United Nations or the desirability of international co-operation.

Irish policymakers were not just sceptical about the United Nations, they were similarly reserved about the Anglo-American proposals for a new international economic order unveiled at the Bretton Woods conference in 1944. In a memorandum to de Valera, his unofficial economic adviser, Professor Timothy Smiddy, argued that small nations would fare better if they stayed outside the international trading system to protect their domestic economies from any future international economic crises.[13] However, even though the Irish government did not join the International Monetary Fund (IMF) or the International Bank for Reconstruction and Development (IBRD or World Bank), its economy became intrinsically linked with the Bretton Woods system through its membership of the sterling area and currency union with Britain. While Ireland accumulated substantial sterling balances during the Second World War, the Irish government depended in the immediate postwar period on the willingness of the British government to convert these balances into dollars in order to purchase vital supplies to assist economic recovery. In contrast to Ireland, Britain had sell most of its overseas assets in order to finance weapons and materials purchases from the United States before the inception of Lend-Lease. As a consequence of its accumulated wartime debts, Britain had to approach the United States for a massive loan in autumn 1945. In order to receive such a loan, Britain had to agree to make sterling convertible within a year of ratification of the agreement. Britain partly used the American loan to make dollars available to other members of the sterling area in 1946–47. However, the British sterling crisis in August 1947 forced the British government to suspend sterling convertibility and limit the drawing of sterling area countries including Ireland on the sterling area dollar pool. Other western European countries faced similar economic crisis due their diminished foreign currency reserves. As a consequence, most western European countries including Ireland could no longer purchase vital imports from the dollar area. The general economic crisis and the sterling crisis in particular forced Ireland to accept the ERP loan offered by the

---

[10] Joseph Morrison Skelly, 'Ireland, the Department of External Affairs, and the United Nations, 1946–55: A new look', *Irish Studies in International Affairs* 7 (1996), pp. 63–78.

[11] *Dáil Deb.* vol. 102 , cols. 1308–26, 24 July 1946.

[12] *Dáil Deb.* vol. 102 , cols. 1463–81, 25 July 1946.

[13] NAI DT S13590, 'Small nations', memorandum by Smiddy for de Valera, 31 Oct. 1946.

American government despite the government's concern about the long-term financial implications for the Irish economy.[14]

Some historians of Ireland's involvement in the European Recovery Program (ERP or Marshall Plan) have argued that through the Marshall Plan the country became drawn into the process of European economic co-operation, paving the way for its application to join the European Economic Community in August 1961.[15] Charged with coordinating Ireland's relationship with American Marshall aid administrators and the Organisation for European Economic Co-operation (OEEC), the Department of External Affairs expanded considerably to meet the considerable challenges of multilateral international cooperation.[16] Gary Murphy has argued that Ireland's participation in the ERP allowed the Department of External Affairs to take a leading role in shaping the country's policy towards European integration.[17] This view challenges the more traditional view of Brian Girvin among others that the insular outlook of many Irish policymakers led to isolationist policies and a dogged adherence to economic nationalism, which held back the country's economic development in the 1950s. Girvin argues that in contrast to the governments of other small European countries, Irish policymakers did not realise the growing interdependence of European states in a new emerging bipolar world. Therefore, the Irish government failed to adopt more forward-looking policies to develop its economy and integrate it into the emerging European market.[18]

On balance, the existing historiography on Irish foreign policy in the immediate postwar period suggests that Irish policymakers were reluctant to participate in the efforts to create a framework for increased international cooperation after the end of the war. For all their differences of interpretation, historians of Ireland's entry to the United Nations seem to agree that after the failure of Ireland's application to the United Nations in 1946 the country remained firmly outside the United Nations system until its entry in

---

[14] Till Geiger, 'Why Ireland needed the Marshall Plan but did not want it: Ireland, the Sterling Area and the European Recovery Program, 1947–1948', *Irish Studies in International Affairs* 11 (2000), 193–215.

[15] Bernadette Whelan, 'Integration or isolation?: Ireland and the invitation to join the Marshall Plan', in Michael Kennedy and Joseph Skelly (eds.), *Irish foreign policy, 1919–1966: From independence to internationalism* (Dublin, 2000), pp. 203–21; and Gary Murphy, ' "An exercise that had to be undertaken": the Marshall Plan and the genesis of Ireland's involvement in European integration', in Geiger and Kennedy (eds.), *Ireland, Europe and the Marshall Plan*, pp. 81–101. The seminal study on Ireland's involvement in the Marshall Plan remains: Bernadette Whelan, *Ireland and the Marshall Plan* (Dublin, 2000).

[16] Michael Kennedy, 'The challenge of multilateralism: the Marshall Plan and the expansion of the Irish diplomatic service', in Geiger and Kennedy (eds.), *Ireland, Europe and the Marshall Plan*, pp. 102–30.

[17] Murphy, 'Genesis', p. 101.

[18] For the most recent exposition of this argument, see Brian Girvin, 'Did Ireland benefit from the Marshall Plan?: Choice, strategy and the national interest in a comparative context', in Geiger and Kennedy (eds.), *Ireland, Europe and the Marshall Plan*, pp. 182–220.

1955. At the same time, most historians of Ireland's involvement in the Marshall Plan argue that the country's participation benefited from being involved in the process of European economic cooperation and integration in spite of clinging to protectionist policies. Both these consensus views seem flawed as they rest on rather narrow views of international cooperation in this period. The exclusive focus on Ireland's membership of the United Nations has meant that historians have ignored Ireland's membership in the newly formed specialised international organisations, which became part of the United Nations system during the late 1940s. Moreover, the emphasis on the ERP has led historians to ignore Ireland's involvement in the efforts to assist European recovery prior to the announcement of the Marshall Plan offer in June 1947. Out of these efforts emerged the United Nations Economic Commission for Europe (UNECE), which held its first session in July 1947 at the same time as western European governments met in Paris to discuss the American Marshall plan offer.[19] This chapter will broaden the debate about Ireland's involvement in international affairs in the immediate postwar period by examining Ireland's accession to the Food and Agriculture Organisation (FAO) and its involvement in the UNECE. The examination of Ireland's involvement in these two international organisations shows that despite some initial reluctance, Ireland participated much more widely, albeit selectively, in international cooperation in this period. Far from being isolated, this chapter underlines that the extent of Ireland's involvement in international cooperation depended on the willingness of Irish policymakers to engage positively with the emerging challenge of multilateralism.

Ireland and the question of membership in specialised international organisations, 1946

The existing historical literature has focused almost exclusively on Ireland's failed application to join the United Nations in the summer of 1946. This emphasis creates the slightly distorted picture that Ireland remained firmly outsides the emerging international order. However, even prior to the application to the United Nations, Irish policymakers faced the question whether or not the country should join some of the specialised agencies being set up under the umbrella of the United Nations.

Following the San Francisco conference of 26 June 1945 and the establishment of the United Nations, the members of international organisations that had been part of the League of Nations system considered their future in the light of the demise of its former umbrella organisation. In the case of the International Labour Organisation (ILO), the membership decided to

---

[19] On the developments leading to the creation of the UNECE, see Walt Rostow, 'The Economic Commission for Europe', *International Organization*, vol. 3, no. 2 (1949), pp. 254–68; and David Wightman, *Economic Co-Operation in Europe: A study of the United Nations Economic Commission for Europe* (London, 1956), pp. 3–24.

seek recognition as a United Nations specialised organisation in 1946. As an existing member, Ireland simply remained a part of the ILO, despite the fact that the organisation became a part of the United Nations system of specialised organisations.[20] At the same time, a number of new international organisations were being set up in this period. For example, Ireland became a member of the International Civil Aviation Organisation in 1944, because it was seen as a vital link in the future of transatlantic air travel. Moreover, the American government used its aviation agreement with Ireland to outmanoeuvre the British government over transatlantic air routes.[21] In the case of newly created international organisations such as the World Health Organisation (WHO) and the Food and Agriculture Organisation (FAO), Irish ministers adopted a more cautious approach. De Valera told the Dáil in June 1946 that the government had been invited to join the planned WHO.[22] Indeed, Ireland would become one of the organisation's founding members in 1948.[23]

Even more interesting is the case of the Food and Agriculture Organisation (FAO). The FAO had been founded at a conference in Hot Springs, Virginia, in 1943 even before the United Nations had been set up. Indeed, the FAO had held its first inaugural conference in Quebec City in 1945. In early 1946 the government came under considerable pressure from some TDs to join the FAO. In March 1946, the Minister for Agriculture, James Ryan, had to endure some searching questions whether or not the Irish government intended to apply for FAO membership. His replies demonstrated that the minister was ill-informed about the FAO and its membership. Opposition speakers had pointed out that United Nations membership was not a requirement for membership in the FAO. However, since the government had not been invited to join the organisation, ministers seemed reluctant to seek membership.[24]

A few days earlier, the Irish legation in Washington had informed the department on the impeding merger between the International Institute of Agriculture (IIA) and the FAO. The American government asked for Irish support to dissolve the IIA at the forthcoming meeting of the IIA at the end of March 1946. American officials stressed that the FAO would welcome former neutrals to join the organisation after the dissolution of the IIA. As the FAO was not a part of the United Nations, Ireland would not be debarred from membership provided its application gained the approval of two-thirds

[20] *Dáil Deb.*, vol. 101, col. 2452, 26 June 1946. At the time, the ILO was headed by the Irishman Edward Phelan who had risen to become ILO director-general in 1940. He continued in this post until his retirement in 1948.

[21] Joseph P. O'Grady, 'A troubled triangle: Great Britain, Ireland, the United States and civil aviation, 1944–45'. *Journal of Transport History* 15, no. 2 (1994) pp. 179–96.

[22] *Dáil Deb.*, vol.101, col. 2453, 26 June 1946.

[23] Miriam Hederman, *The Road to Europe: Irish attitudes to European integration, 1948–61* (Dublin, 1983) p. 48.

[24] *Dáil Deb.*, vol. 100, col. 187–8, 21 Mar. 1946.

of the current membership.[25] Faced with the imminent demise of the IIA, the Irish government began to consider applying for FAO membership. As part of this process, the Department of External Affairs contacted its legation in Washington to find out whether it might be possible for Ireland to join the FAO without having to apply for membership under some sort of 'golden bridge' arrangement. The department's secretary, Frederick Boland, also contacted the Irish legation in Berne and Lisbon in order to find out the positions of the Swiss and Portuguese governments.[26] Neither government had any reservations about joining the FAO. During a stopover at Shannon on 5 June 1946, the FAO director-general, Sir James Boyd-Orr, stressed that he would fully support an Irish application for FAO membership. Indeed, he thought that the Irish government would commit a grave error if it stayed outside the FAO.[27] Later the same month, de Valera confirmed that Ireland would probably apply for FAO membership, as membership in specialised international organisations entailed only obligations, which Ireland could fulfil.[28] After taking soundings in Washington, the Minister for Agriculture submitted a memorandum to the Cabinet in August 1946 recommending that Ireland should join the FAO and send a representative to the organisation's next conference in September. In contrast to his earlier statements, the minister stressed that joining the organisation was vital for Ireland because the FAO conference would discuss the allocation of world food supplies.[29] At their next Cabinet meeting on 13 August 1946, ministers agreed that Ireland should submit its application to join the FAO without delay and send a representative to attend the upcoming FAO conference in Copenhagen.[30] The following Monday, the Department of Agriculture submitted a further memorandum suggesting that two of its officials together with an official from the Department of Industry and Commerce should attend the conference.[31] Ministers approved this suggestion at their next meeting a day later. Indeed, the Cabinet decided that three other departments (External Affairs, Local Government and Public Health, and Agriculture) were to send an official if the country's application was accepted by the conference.[32] A week later, ministers decided that if the conference approved Ireland's application, Ryan himself should travel to Copenhagen to head the Irish delegation.[33]

---

[25] NAI DFA 332/229, Devlin to Boland, 19 Mar. 1946.

[26] Ibid., Boland to Cremins, 25 Apr. 1946; Boland to Brennan, 25 Apr. 1946; Boland to O'Donovan, 25 Apr. 1946.

[27] *Irish Times*, 11 Sept. 1946.

[28] *Dáil Deb.*, vol. 101, col. 2453, 26 June 1946.

[29] NAI DT S13875A, Memorandum for the Government submitted by the minister for Agriculture, 10 Aug. 1946.

[30] Ibid., Extract from Cabinet Minutes, G.C.4/186, item 6, 13 Aug. 1946.

[31] Ibid.: Memorandum for the Government submitted by the Minister for Agriculture, 19 Aug. 1946.

[32] Ibid., Extract from Cabinet Minutes, G.C.4/187, item 2, 20 Aug. 1946.

[33] Ibid., Extract from Cabinet Minutes, G.C.4/188, item 1, 28 Aug. 1946.

As planned, a small Irish delegation consisting of three officials from the Departments of External Affairs, Industry and Commerce and Agriculture travelled to Copenhagen in order to attend the opening session of the conference as observers. On their arrival, the officials discovered that the term 'Eire' instead of 'Ireland' was being used in all conference documentation and official notices. The outraged Irish officials led by the Minister to Sweden, John Belton, protested in the strongest terms to the FAO director-general, who agreed to instruct his secretariat to correct the documentation. The following day Belton confirmed that most documentation had indeed been changed. However, just before the conference was due to discuss the Irish application on the morning of 3 September 1946, the Secretary-General, M. Lavally, came to see Belton to tell him that the British government would make a formal protest if the Irish delegation insisted on using Ireland to describe the Irish state in its application to join the FAO. After consultation, the Irish delegation decided to hold firm despite the possibility that a formal British protest might undermine the prospects of the Irish application in the assembly. When the Irish officials tried to inform the chairman of the conference, the Danish minister to Washington, of their position, they found themselves embroiled in a confrontation with two members of the British delegation including the Northern Ireland Minister for Agriculture, Rev Robert Moore. Moore and a Ministry of Food official argued that the Irish government could not use the word 'Ireland' because the six northern countries were part of the United Kingdom. The Irish officials countered that Ireland was the English word for Éire and every country except Britain accepted Ireland to refer to the Irish state. Moore rejected this argument saying that he did 'not care what foreigners called us; in Northern Ireland they never called us anything except Eire'. However, the chairman did not respond too kindly to this remark and decided that 'Ireland' should be used and if the British delegation decided to make a protest the matter should be referred to the General Committee.[34]

As a consequence of this argument, the conference session opened 30 minutes late. In the following debate on the Irish application, the country was always referred to by 'Ireland'. The Irish application was approved with twenty-four votes with two countries opposing Irish membership. The Polish representative stated that his country voted against Irish membership, because Ireland did not have diplomatic relations with his country.[35] However, the row over the use of 'Ireland' rumbled on. The following day, the Irish delegation much to its dismay discovered that the FAO deputy secretary-general, a former British civil servant, had changed all references to

---

[34] NAI DFA 332/29, Belton to Boland, 8 Sept. 1946.
[35] *Irish Press*, 4 and 5 Sept. 1946; the second country voting against the Irish application was Czechoslovakia, see NAI DFA 332/29, 'Second session of F.A.O. conference held in Copenhagen, September 1946', memorandum by McCann, 23 Sept. 1946.

'Ireland' to 'Eire' except those in the speech of the Irish delegate '... in the interest of consistent reporting'. Belton again protested in the strongest terms, refusing to accept the apologies of the deputy secretary-general and his protestation that he was an impartial international civil servant. While the chairman reprimanded the deputy secretary-general, he told Belton that this matter should be resolved amicably as soon as possible by a meeting of the two delegations. While Belton agreed to a meeting, he objected to Britain being solely represented by Moore, because Northern Ireland was not an international entity. In the end, the British delegation tried to persuade the Irish representatives to accept an explanatory footnote to clarify that the word Ireland referred to the territory of the former Irish Free State. By this stage, the Irish delegation had been joined by Ryan and several additional Irish officials. After some deliberation, Ryan suggested that if the British footnote was inserted in the conference proceedings then the Irish delegation would insist on the insertion of an additional note containing articles 2 and 3 of the 1937 Irish constitution. However, the Irish addendum proved unacceptable to the British delegation, which approached Ryan in order to agree a footnote text. In the end the matter remained unresolved and the British delegation referred the matter for decision to London.[36]

Aside from the furore over the country's proper designation, Hugh McCann reported that the conference discussed two issues of particular interest from the perspective of the Department of External Affairs: the FAO director's proposal for a World Food Board and the short-term problem of the world food situation. McCann's report only briefly touched on the latter issue. The conference urged all member states to take urgent steps to alleviate the impending food crisis arising from the gap between available food supplies and growing demand. The discussion revealed particular concern about the likely impact of the dissolution of the United Nations Relief and Rehabilitation Administration (UNRRA) at the end of the year.[37]

McCann devoted slightly more space to the deliberations surrounding the proposals for a World Food Board. The proposals envisaged an expansion of world food production to meet the current severe worldwide food shortages by mechanising agricultural production. In order to prevent overproduction, as happened during the interwar period, the report stressed the need for the expansion of consumer demand. This expansion would require the development of third world countries in order to absorb surplus agricultural labour freed by increased mechanisation. The authors of the report expressed their hope that the World Bank would provide the finance for large-scale development projects. However, the report pointed out that these plans for the expansion of world food production crucially depended on the stabilisation

---

[36] NAI DFA 332/29, Belton to Boland, 8 Sept. 1946.
[37] Ibid., 'Second session of F.A.O. conference held in Copenhagen, September 1946', memorandum by McCann, 23 Sept. 1946.

of food prices. The report argued that food prices for key commodities might be stabilised through international commodities agreements, particularly for staple foods such as bread grain, rice and, exceptionally, citrus fruit concentrates, dried fruit, vegetables, some livestock products and fish. The intention of these proposals was to insure the supply of sufficient food to the world's population at reasonable prices.[38]

The conference charged a preparatory commission with the task of considering the proposals in detail. During the discussion of the proposals in a committee, the Irish delegate objected to the manner in which the membership of the commission had been agreed behind closed doors. However, he did not pursue the matter because Ireland did not have any fundamental reservations about the proposed composition of the commission particularly because it would have the right to be represented by an observer during the commission's deliberations. In his report, McCann noted that support for the proposals for a World Food Board grew during the conference. The speech of the director-general of UNRRA, Fiorello La Guardia, seemed to particularly persuade many delegates of the merits of the proposals by its realism.[39]

After the conference, Ryan toured Danish and Swedish farms before returning via London for talks with the British Minister for Food, John Strachey. While in London, Ryan told an *Irish Press* reporter that he welcomed the world food plan outlined by the FAO director at the conference, because it would prevent a slump in agricultural processes for the foreseeable future.[40] While Ireland might have benefited from these proposals as an importer of bread grain, it is hard to see whether Ireland would indeed benefit directly as a food producer as Ryan thought. As the British delegation noted at the conference, the proposed scheme might harm some farmers if cereal prices were stabilised prior to the stabilisation of other agricultural prices. In particular, livestock producers would suffer if meat prices collapsed due to a general economic downturn. Faced with high cereal prices, they would be forced out of business and thereby would contribute to the collapse of the agricultural sector and potentially a worldwide depression.[41] As a major importer of cereals, including animal feed, a sudden downturn in meat prices would have had a major impact on Irish agriculture.

As this analysis shows, the Irish government regarded FAO membership as highly desirable. However, Irish ministers were evasive about applying for membership until they received reassurances that Ireland's application was likely to succeed.[42] At the same time, the FAO conference offered Irish

[38] Ministry of Food, *Food and Agriculture Organisation of the United Nations: Summary of the Report of the Preparatory Commission on World Food Proposals*, Cmd. 7032 (London, 1946).

[39] NAI DFA 332/29, 'Second session of F.A.O. conference held in Copenhagen, September 1946', memorandum by McCann, 23 Sept. 1946.

[40] *Irish Press*, 20, and 29 Sept. 1946.

[41] NAI DFA 332/29, 'Second session of F.A.O. conference held in Copenhagen, September 1946', memorandum by McCann, 23 Sept. 1946.

[42] Ibid., Commins to Boland, 26 July 1946.

diplomats a welcome opportunity to re-establish contact with the international community. To improve its relationship with other countries, the Irish delegation hosted a dinner party for twenty guests including senior FAO officials, two Danish ministers, the heads of delegations from Commonwealth countries and the American under-secretary of state for agriculture. The Indian delegation greeted the admission of Ireland to the FAO particularly warmly. Indian delegates privately emphasised '… the common bond of sympathy which existed between India and Ireland'.[43] Far from feeling excluded from the international community, the Irish delegation encountered considerable goodwill among the other member states. However, in order to capitalise on this goodwill, the Irish government would have to cooperate with the other member states at an international level.

Ireland and the Emergency Economic Committee for Europe

In the immediate aftermath of the war, most European countries suffered from severe shortages of food and raw materials. While Ireland was one of the few countries with a food surplus, its economy was affected by shortages of coal and fertilisers in particular. In the final phase of the war, the allies had set up a number of small organisations including the European Coal Organisation (ECO), the European Central Inland Transport Organisation (ECITO) and the Emergency Economic Committee for Europe (EECE), to ease these shortages by allocating the available supplies between European countries. Ireland remained initially outside this system of international cooperation on postwar recovery.

In February 1946, M.E. Dockrell TD asked Eamon de Valera in his role as Minister for External Affairs whether or not the country had been invited to attend the Emergency Conference on European Cereal Supplies. In replying to repeated questions, de Valera proved rather evasive. Highlighting the fact that no invitation had been received, his reply reflected a degree of hurt pride that Ireland had not yet been invited: 'Our existence, I take it, is known. Those immediately responsible know of our existence, and, if they thought we would be of any value in the matter, we would be invited.' Not only did he rule out making representations to the EECE which was organising the conference, but also, if Ireland was invited, he stressed he would like to know more about the terms of the conference before sending a delegation.[44]

In the end, the Minister for Industry and Commerce, Seán Lemass, attended the Emergency Conference on European Cereal Supplies in London at the beginning of April 1946. The conference adopted a number of resolutions urging European governments to maximise the forthcoming harvest and decided to adopt an international system of allocation for bread and animal

---

[43] Ibid., 'Second session of F.A.O. conference held in Copenhagen, September 1946', memorandum by McCann, 23 Sept. 1946.
[44] Dáil Deb., vol. 99, cols. 1177–8, 20 Feb. 1946.

feed grain.[45] While Ireland itself experienced serious grain shortages, Boland argued in the aftermath of the conference that Ireland should reduce its food consumption to make more food available to the International Red Cross[46] for shipment to France and Italy. In June and July 1946, Ireland provided 285 tons of bacon and cattle to UNRRA for shipment to Germany, Austria and Hungary.[47] However, the continued shortages forced most European countries to tighten bread rationing and increase the extraction rate of flour from wheat. The continued difficulties of obtaining sufficient bread grain forced the Irish government to adopt bread rationing in autumn 1946.[48] In order to be considered for future allocation of cereals, the government decided in May 1947 that Ireland should join the International Wheat Council and the Cereals Committee of the International Emergency Food Council. The government appointed the commercial attaché in its Washington legation, Tom Commins, to represent Ireland on both institutions.[49]

In April 1947, Cremin informed the department that the Economic and Social Council had approved the formation of the United Nations Economic Commission for Europe. Once the UNECE had been established the EECE, ECO and ECITO would cease to exist and their functions would be taken over by the new commission.[50] At the time, Ireland only belonged to the EECE as an associate member. However, American officials prevailed on the Irish government to join the ECO, because their government was committed to ship American coal to Europe only on the basis of ECO allocations. Therefore, American coal shipments to Ireland were causing the Truman administration some embarrassment. However, the Department of Industry and Commerce initially opposed Ireland becoming a member of the ECO and the formation of the UNECE potentially complicated matters. Irish officials feared that the country might not receive any coal and fertiliser allocations because it was not a United Nations member. Therefore, the Irish government now decided to join the ECO as an associate member in order to ensure continued supply of American coal even though the ECO would only exist for a few more months. At the same time, some officials raised the question whether Ireland should become an associate member of UNECE rather than just ECO although they remained concerned that non-members would play only a minor role in the work of the UNECE. Therefore, the officials felt that if Ireland planned only to become involved in the work of UNECE in matters of coal allocation, then it would be better to join ECO now rather than having to be invited as a consultative member once UNECE was up and running.[51]

---

[45] 'Resolutions adopted by the Emergency Conference on European Cereals (3–6 April 1946)', MCE European Navigator (http://www.ena.lu/mce.cfm) 2004 [accessed: 9 August 2005].

[46] NAI DFA 408/22/4, minute by Boland for Cremin, 15 May 1946.

[47] Ibid., note by Cremin, 14 June 1946; note by Cremin, 30 July 1946.

[48] *Dáil Deb.*, vol. 104, cols. 590–608, 29 Jan. 1946.

[49] NAI DT S13875A, minute by Nolan for Leydon, 9 May 1947.

[50] NAI DFA 408/100, minute by Cremin for McCann, 15 Apr. 1947.

[51] Ibid., minute by McCann for Cremin, 8 May 1947.

While other countries became convinced through their involvement in the EECE, the ECO and the ECITO of the value of international cooperation, officials in the Department of External Affairs were rather dismissive about the value of these organisations for Ireland:

> Apart from being a source of information and providing a forum to ventilate our grievances in relation to the treatment we are receiving in the matter of the allocation of fertilisers, I think it can safely be said that we derived no very great other advantages from our association with the workings of the EECE.[52]

If indeed the international cooperation in the emergency organisations paved the way for the formation of the UNECE and created a willingness among European governments to cooperate, then Irish policymakers failed to absorb this lesson of the response of other European governments to the ongoing economic crisis caused by the devastation of the recent war.[53]

Ireland and the UNECE

Besides the continued need for international economic cooperation, there was a growing concern among American and European policymakers that the growing tensions between the west and east would lead to the division of Europe into two rival economic blocs disrupting traditional trading patterns. These policymakers hoped that through the formation of a European-wide organisation for economic cooperation, the UNECE, this schism could be prevented. However, the announcement of the Marshall Plan followed by the Soviet rejection of the American offer deepened the rift between eastern and western Europe.[54]

While Ireland reluctantly decided to participate in the Marshall Plan and joined the OEEC, it could not become a full member of the UNECE. Nevertheless, the UNECE decided to invite all non-member states in Europe with the exception of Spain to become associate members. Associate members were entitled to attend the meetings of its committees in a consultative capacity.[55] Because the main work of the UNECE was carried out by its various technical committees, the opportunity to participate in their deliberations provided Ireland with an opportunity to cooperate with other European countries outside the context of the Marshall Plan. The public sessions of the UNECE soon became a forum for cold war rhetoric rather than a forum for constructive economic cooperation. As a consequence, most work tended to be done in the technical committees, which collected valuable statistics and

---

[52] Ibid.
[53] Rostow, 'Economic Commission for Europe', pp. 254–6.
[54] Wightman, *Economic co-operation*, pp. 25–51.
[55] NAI DFA 408/100, minute by Cremin for McCauley, 2 Oct. 1947.

compiled useful reports. Nevertheless, active participation in the UNECE offered governments an opportunity to study how other countries were dealing with the massive problems of postwar economic recovery.[56]

After having been invited by the UNECE secretary-general, Gunnar Myrdal, to participate in the commission's work as an associate member, officials from the Department of Industry and Commerce discussed at some length in October 1947 the issue of whether Ireland should attend committee meetings. They decided that it would be more appropriate if officials from the Department of Local Government attended the panel on housing problems. At the same time, officials felt that Ireland had little to contribute to the discussions of the timber and fertiliser subcommittees because these subcommittees would be primarily concerned with expanding the production of these commodities. While Ireland produced neither timber nor nitrogen fertiliser in significant quantities, the domestic economy was severely affected by shortages of both commodities. Therefore, officials disagreed on the usefulness of attending these subcommittees. In the case of the timber subcommittee, officials in the department shared the view of the Land Commission that Ireland could neither gain from nor contribute to the deliberations of that subcommittee. While some officials felt nothing useful could be gained by attending the fertiliser subcommittee, others argued that 'it is possible that participation, even in a consultative capacity, in the work of any Sub-Committee with distribution problems would be beneficial to the country as a whole'. The department decided that a principal officer, E. Burke of the department's Fuel Section, would attend a meeting of the Coal Committee. Despite this exception, officials agreed that the question of whether an Irish representative should attend a committee meeting should be decided on a case-by-case basis. Therefore, the Department of Industry and Commerce suggested that the Department of External Affairs should circulate the agendas of future meetings and ask the relevant departments whether they intended to send a representative.[57] In his reply to the Department of External Affairs, one of the deputy secretaries in the Department of Industry and Commerce, J. Williams, stated that his minister, Seán Lemass, felt that Ireland should be represented at the meetings of the various committees and subcommittees. If a particular meeting did not justify sending a representative from Dublin to attend, the Irish minister to Switzerland should attend as an observer. Moreover, the Department of Industry and Commerce stressed in correspondence the importance of receiving the papers of the various committees in order to stay informed about the work of the UNECE.[58]

---

[56] On the work of the UNECE and its committees, see Wightman, *Economic co-operation*, pp. 55–192.

[57] NAI Department of Industry and Commerce (hereafter DIC) FT 5/47, minute by Connolly for Williams, 13 Nov. 1947.

[58] Ibid., Williams to Boland, 20 Nov. 1947.

This correspondence seems to suggest that Lemass attached considerable importance to Ireland being a part of international organisations, in marked contrast to the dismissive attitude of the officials in his department. His attendance at various European conferences in 1946 and 1947 had impressed on him the value of international cooperation. It is hard to discern whether Ireland would have played a more prominent role in the UNECE, if Fianna Fáil had been re-elected in February 1948. However, it is more than likely that even if Lemass had remained Minister for Industry and Commerce, Ireland's involvement in the Marshall Plan and Organisation for European Economic Co-operation would have taken precedence over a more active participation in the work of the UNECE.

From 1947 the Department of External Affairs regularly notified other departments of meetings of working parties by the UNECE, although most declined to attend them. Notable exceptions were the Department of Agriculture and the Central Statistics Office. The Department of Agriculture participated in the work of the Committee on Agricultural Problems since its establishment in 1949. Officials clearly found the committee's reports useful and remained committed to contribute to its work.[59] The Central Statistics Office regularly sent representatives to the Conference of Statistical Experts.[60] The Irish government regularly received the papers generated by the UNECE. In general, officials felt that UNECE documents sent to Dublin contained little of interest for the Irish government.[61] For example, the responsible official in the Department of Foreign Affairs, Jack Molloy, filed the papers relating to the eighth, ninth and tenth session of the UNECE without reading them.[62] Moreover, there is no indication in the files of Ireland's diplomatic mission to Switzerland that Irish diplomats there attended the meetings of UNECE committees as observers.[63]

Against the aspirations of the founders of the UNECE, the Cold War prevented the recovery of East-West trade in the late 1940s. Concerned that this trend might delay the economic recovery of Europe, a trade committee was set up to address this problem. The committee's deliberations soon reached stalemate, however, because eastern European governments used the meetings to criticise the western strategic trade controls. In 1951, the UNECE secretariat initiated talks on the future of East-West trade which made some limited progress by mid-1955. At the trade consultations in April 1954, experts from the United States and every European country except Ireland and Spain

---

[59] NAI DFA 408/137/32, O'Doherty to Murphy, 31 Mar. 1956.

[60] See correspondence contained in NAI DFA 408/137/26.

[61] NAI DIC FT 5/49: minutes to Duff, Hegarty, O'Riordan and Connolly, 2, 10 and 11 Feb. 1949.

[62] See NAI DFA 408/137/23; NAI DFA 408/137/29 I and II; and NAI DFA 408/137/30. I was unable to locate files relating to earlier sessions in the finding aids to the records of the DFA held at the NAI in Dublin.

[63] The only file in the Berne Embassy release relating to the UNECE (NAI DFA 2001/9/158) starts at the end of April 1956.

attended.[64] From the inception of these negotiations, the secretariat invited Ireland to send a representative to them. However, Irish policymakers refused these requests outright. In July 1952, one official commented that there was a general consensus among government departments '… that we have no economic interest in attending the proposed Conference; our political interest would be against it'.[65] Six month later, another official reaffirmed this view to the Minister for External Affairs, Frank Aiken, that Ireland was not interested in East-West trade because of the government's policy '… to have as little as possible to do with the Communist countries'.[66] Aiken agreed that in the light of this policy the government should not be represented at the planned meeting of the trade committee in early 1953. As Cold War tensions eased after Stalin's death, Aiken asked for a general review of the government's restrictive policy on trade with Eastern European countries in July 1954, citing the decision of other countries to expand their trade with countries behind the Iron Curtain.[67]

As this analysis shows, Ireland participated rather selectively in the work of the UNECE. In the case of the UNECE conferences on East-West trade, political rather than economic considerations influenced government decisions even if such decisions isolated Ireland from the attempts of other governments to develop international economic cooperation further. By standing aside, Irish policymakers had to learn about such developments indirectly from UNECE documents.

Ireland at the 11th session of the United Nations Economic Commission for Europe

With the easing of Cold War tensions after Stalin's death, Eastern European governments started participating actively in the workings of the UNECE rather than using the commission's sessions as a platform for propaganda statements.[68] At the same time, the membership of the UNECE increased considerably. After Ireland joined the United Nations officially on 14 December 1955, it automatically became a full member of the UNECE – at the same time as Albania, Austria, Bulgaria, the Federal Republic of Germany, Finland, Hungary, Italy, Portugal, Romania and Spain.[69]

---

[64] Wightman, *Economic co-operation*, pp. 213–27.

[65] NAI DFA 408/137/19, minute by Biggar for Fay, 22 July 1952.

[66] Ibid., minute by Fay for Aiken, 2 Feb. 1953.

[67] NAI DFA 305/57/132/4, 'Trade with communist-controlled countries', memorandum to the Government by the Minister for External Affairs and the Minister for Industry and Commerce, 18 September 1954. On Ireland's trade with Eastern Europe, see Till Geiger, 'Ireland and East-West Trade, 1945–1960', paper presented at the 'East-West Trade and The Cold War' conference organised by the Department of History, University of Jyväskylä, 20–23 November 2003. [paper available on conference web site: http://www.cc.jyu.fi/~pete/EWGeiger.pdf].

[68] NAI DT S16023A, Minutes of 219th meeting of the Inter-Departmental E.R.P. Committee, 7 June 1956.

[69] United Nations Economic Commission for Europe, *Annual Report (31 March 1955–21 April 1956)*, E/2868, E/ECE/237, New York: United Nations, 23 Apr. 1956, p. 22.

A month before the eleventh session of the UNECE was to meet in Geneva on 5 April 1956, the American ambassador to Dublin, William Taft III, urged the Irish government to attend the forthcoming meeting 'if at all possible'. Privately, American officials urged Irish policymakers to be represented by a sizeable delegation as the new Eastern European members were likely to be represented in strength. The United States government was anxious to insure sufficient representation of 'free nations' to counterbalance 'the increased voting strength of the Soviet Bloc'. In particular, American policymakers were eager to avoid the possibility of the Soviet bloc using its vote to influence the agenda or the election of officers.[70] The Minister for External Affairs, Liam Cosgrave, instructed his staff to contact the Department of the Taoiseach about whether an Irish delegation should attend. Initially, the Government Secretary, Maurice Moynihan, felt the enquiry required no decision until the interdepartmental Foreign Trade Committee had decided whether a delegation should be sent.[71] At its next meeting, the Foreign Trade Committee discussed the matter. In the meeting, the representative of the Department of Industry and Commerce chairing the meeting argued that his department saw no reason to send a delegation on purely trade grounds. Other matters were outside the committee's remit such as the discussion on coal supplies and the development of tourism, which might be of interest to other departments. He argued that only a small delegation should be sent with the Department of External Affairs taking the lead. In general, the Department of Industry and Commerce opposed 'sending staff to international organisations unless vital interests were involved'. The meeting asked the Department of External Affairs to contact other departments on whether or not they would like to send representatives to attend the UNECE session.[72] The Department of External Affairs duly contacted the other departments but none was interested in sending an official to Geneva.[73] Only the Department of Agriculture offered some observations on the items on the agenda, which the delegation did not receive until after the item in question had already been discussed. The reluctance of other departments meant that Ireland was represented by its Minister to Switzerland, Hugh McCann, and an official of the department's Economic Section from Dublin, Jack Molloy. Only Albania and Iceland sent a similarly small delegation to this session of the UNECE.[74]

In his opening remarks as chairman, the Polish diplomat, Juliusz

---

[70] NAI DT S16023A, Taft to Cosgrave, 1 Mar. 1956; NAI DFA 408/32, minute by Coffey, 29 Feb. 1955.

[71] Ibid., Coffey to Nolan, 8 Mar. 1956.

[72] Ibid., Minutes of a meeting of the Foreign Trade Committee, 16 Mar. 1956.

[73] Ibid., Coffey to Nolan, 20 Mar. 1956.

[74] United Nations Economic Commission for Europe, *Annual Report 1955/56*, 50–4.; see also NAI DT S16023A, Murphy to Nolan, 6 Apr. 1957.

Katz-Suchy,[75] welcomed the new member states and encouraged them to take full part in the deliberations of the various committees. He said that the recent compromise deal over United Nations membership had been a victory for international understanding and was bound to improve international relations. Even during the heady days of the cold war, the UNECE as the only existing all-European organisation had tried to solve shared economic problems in the spirit of co-operation. Indeed, he hoped that the current improvement of East-West relations would lead to an extension of economic cooperation in Europe. By extending European economic cooperation, the spirit of Geneva might be preserved and international peace strengthened.

In his report on the 11th session, Molloy noted that the Soviet Union introduced at the last minute three resolutions on the preparation of an All-European Agreement on Economic Co-operation, on extending economic contacts between western and eastern Europe, and on establishing a committee on the peaceful use of atomic energy. Most western countries favoured postponing the discussion of the Soviet proposal for an All-European Agreement on Economic Co-operation. The assembly decided to await further clarification of the Soviet proposal and then consult governments over the coming months. While the commission adopted the proposal for increased economic contacts, the Irish delegation abstained as instructed given Ireland's policy of not admitting diplomats, trade officials and business representatives from eastern European countries. In the case of the proposal for co-operation in the field of atomic energy, the commission decided to await the outcome of the current negotiations about the formation of an International Atomic Energy Agency at the United Nations before discussing this matter further. While other countries used the debate on the secretariat's *Economic Survey of Europe in 1955* to make long and in some cases propagandistic statements on their country's economic development, the Irish delegation found it lacked the necessary information to make a similar statement. Therefore, Molloy recommended that future Irish delegations to UNECE meetings would need to be briefed properly on Ireland's economic and financial situation. Indeed, he noted

> The absence of our participation in the debate on this and other items of the Agenda during this Session was somewhat conspicuous and would be more so next year, particularly as we would not then have the excuse that we were new members who had not been able fully to participate in the working of the Commission during the year.

[75] The head of the Polish Foreign Trade Institute, Katz-Suchy, had been elected vice-chairman at the previous year's session in March 1955, but became chairman automatically when the Belgian diplomat, Max Suetens, died suddenly in the intervening period; NAI DT S16023A: Opening statement of Dr. Juliusz Katz-Suchy, 5 Apr. 1956 [E/ECE/244, 5 April 1956]. Prior to the 11th session, the French ambassador approached Sean Murphy to insure that Ireland would support the move of other western countries to replace him with the Belgian ambassador to Switzerland, Mr Forthomme at the meeting; NAI DFA 408/137/32, minute by Murphy, 19 Mar. 1956.

The Irish delegation had planned to make a statement during the discussion of the UNECE's working programme for the coming year. The intention was to explain that Ireland had hitherto not become involved in the commission's work because it had not been a full member. Nevertheless, the delegation would have confirmed Ireland's interest in participating fully in the work of the commission particularly in the areas of agriculture, coal and housing in the future. However, the opportunity did not arise, because the item was not discussed.[76]

In contrast to Molloy, McCann analysed the political dealings at the 11th session in his separate report. He described at length the caucuses of western and eastern European countries at the conference, expressing his surprise that the Yugoslavian delegation attended the western caucus. When discussing the reaction of other countries to the Soviet initiative on deepening economic relations between eastern and western Europe, McCann noted with surprise that the Portuguese delegation supported all three resolutions. The Portuguese representative told McCann that Portugal recently abandoned its opposition to trading with eastern European countries because it realised that the country could benefit from an expansion of East-West trade. The Spanish delegation similarly supported improved economic relations with Eastern Europe, but absented itself during the vote on the Soviet proposals because of the likely political fallout in Spain from anything but a no vote.[77]

As this analysis shows, most Irish policymakers saw no virtue in attending UNECE meetings, feeling that the deliberations did not affect any vital Irish interests. Having been approached by the American and other western governments to send a sizeable delegation, the Department of External Affairs realised the political importance of being represented at the 11th session. Due to financial constraints, the department decided to send only two representatives. While Molloy was clearly sceptical about the value of attending the UNECE meeting without proper briefing, McCann's report revealed on the one hand the deeply political nature of the UNECE meetings and on the other hand the importance of participating at a time of easing Cold War tensions and real prospects of improved economic relations between the two blocs. Improvements in East-West trade relations might also lead to a strengthening of the UNECE and therefore, as Dublin's representative to the OEEC, William Fay noted, it would be vital for Ireland to be represented and participate in the work of the commission.[78]

Gunnar Myrdal's visit to Dublin, June 1956

After the 11th session, Myrdal embarked on a tour of the capitals of the new member states. At the end of April 1956, he wrote to the Department of

---

[76] NAI DFA 408/137/32, minute by Molloy to Warnock, 26 May 1956.
[77] Ibid., 'Political aspects of the 11th session of the Economic Commission for Europe', report McCann for Murphy, 23 Apr. 1956.
[78] Ibid., Fay to Warnock, 18 Apr. 1956.

External Affairs to arrange a visit to Dublin.[79] In a phone conversation with McCann, Myrdal explained that he had already made arrangements to visit Madrid and Lisbon. He planned a stopover in Ireland on his return from the United States on 6 June for two days.[80] Minister Cosgrave responded to Myrdal's letter three weeks later after UNECE officials pressed for a reply.[81] Molloy wrote to McCann indicating that the department was trying to arrange meetings with the minister and officials from the economic departments.[82]

Representatives from other departments were invited to the meeting of the interdepartmental ERP committee in early June a few days before the actual visit. The response of the responsible official in the Department of Industry and Commerce is rather illuminating:

> This visit seems to be in competition with the recent visit of M. Sergent of OEEC. As I attended on the behalf of this Dept., the ERP Ctte. Meeting with M. Sergent I suppose I should attend this also. We have no concrete 'axe to grind' with the ECE as far as this Dept. is concerned.[83]

During his visit to Dublin, Myrdal attended a meeting of the interdepartmental ERP Committee to discuss the commission's work relating to Ireland.[84] In the meeting, he explained the current working practices of the commission. He stressed that the work in the committees and sub-committees had been primarily of a technical nature and was often confined to the exchange of statistical data. However, he hoped that work could now turn to more practical matters. In the discussion, Myrdal clarified the relationship between the UNECE and other international organisations such as the FAO and the OEEC as well as with the United Nations Economic and Social Council (ECOSOC). Discussing the various level of participation in the work of UNECE, he noted Ireland was the only member country besides Albania which did not have a permanent representative in Geneva. While Irish officials showed great interest in the work of the commission, it became obvious that they primarily saw the UNECE reports as a valuable source of information rather than thinking about participating actively in the deliberations of the various committees. Among the assembled Irish officials, only the deputy director of the Central Statistics Office, M. D. McCarthy, regularly attended the biannual meetings of the Conference of Statistical Experts. He highlighted the current work of the conference in standardising international statistics

---

79 NAI 2001/9/158, Myrdal to Cosgrave, 27 Apr. 1956.
80 Ibid., McCann to Secretary, 27 April 1956.
81 Ibid., minute to McCann, 18 May 1956; letter Cosgrave to Myrdal, 19 May 1956.
82 Ibid., Molloy to McCann, 19 May 1956.
83 NAI DIC FT5/70, minute by Cahill to Kennan, 4 June 1956.
84 NAI DT S16023A, Coffey to Murray, 2 June 1956.

and its value. He argued therefore that the conference should meet on an annual basis.[85]

Two weeks after the visit, Myrdal invited Tadhg O'Sullivan in the absence of McCann in Austria to attend the informal lunch club organised by the UNECE secretariat to inform the permanent representatives of the work of the secretariat. At the lunch, O'Sullivan was seated on Myrdal's left. Myrdal used the occasion to impress on O'Sullivan that Ireland should appoint a permanent delegate to the UNECE in Geneva. Given this pressure, O'Sullivan spoke to the German consul general and permanent UNECE representative, Herr Thierfeller, about the arrangements for the West German representation in Geneva. As a new member, West Germany had a delegation of five members of staff based in Geneva. Indeed, in introducing O'Sullivan, Myrdal highlighted the fact that Ireland had not yet appointed a permanent representative and therefore he had been given a place of honour at the table. Among the other new faces introduced on the occasion, O'Sullivan noted, were six new members to the Soviet delegation. He thought this a sign that the Soviet government was enlarging its UNECE delegation 'perhaps as a means of pursuing its new policy of "competitive co-existence".'[86] After speaking about his visits to Portugal, Spain and the United States, Myrdal handed the floor over to his assistant, Vaclav Kostelecky, to report on their trip to Ireland. Kostelecky praised the arrangements of the Irish government for their visit, highlighting their meetings with ministers and government officials. Expressing the hope that Ireland would participate more actively in the work of the UNECE from now on, Kostelecky mentioned the excellent contributions of Irish experts in the matter of town planning and statistics in the past.

After the official lunch finished, Myrdal again urged O'Sullivan that Dublin should appoint a permanent delegate to Geneva or if that was not possible at least assign a member of staff in the Berne legation to look after UNECE affairs. While O'Sullivan did not comment on this remark, he ventured in his report that such a suggestion was impractical. Myrdal then proceeded to set out his views on Ireland's relatively poor economic performance since the end of the second world war. Highly critical of the apparent lack of economic leadership and its outmoded political system, Myrdal argued that Ireland would benefit by adopting best European practice to improve economic development and overcome its economic dependence on Britain. Rather taken aback by this onslaught, O'Sullivan retorted rather undiplomatically that Ireland's economic problem could not be assessed solely based on a short trip to Dublin. In particular, he took offence at Myrdal's view that the unwillingness to define the role of religion in Ireland might be holding the country back economically. This exchange perfectly illustrates the gap between the outlook of international experts working in international

---

[85] Ibid., Minutes of 219th meeting of the Inter-Departmental E.R.P. Committee, 7 June 1956.
[86] NAI DFA 2001/9/158, O'Sullivan to Murphy, 19 June 1956. (Quotation marks in the original).

organisations and that of many Irish diplomats and civil servants in the late 1950s. It is worthwhile therefore to quote O'Sullivan's account of the conversation at length.

> [Myrdal] went on to describe how Ireland would benefit from closer contact with economic methods in Europe and, feeling perhaps that he could let his hair down in the presence of someone obviously as junior a man as myself, became more frank. He said that it could perhaps be held that economic development in Ireland was retarded by the last war, but here we were ten years after the war and Ireland had made no progress whatever. No lead had been given to the Irish people, and this he ascribed to a system of government based on political difference which occurred a long time ago and no longer had any meaning. He was astonished, he said, by the apparent absence of a typical Irish way of life and the fact that everything appeared to be copied from England, on which we were as dependent as was Scotland. We should, he felt, create a political system based on facts and not on ancient quarrels, and we should, using the best methods we could find on the European continent, build an economic and social system with some independence of Britain. We should, furthermore, decide once and for all how great a part religion was going to play in the destiny of our country.
>
> I did not feel called upon to comment on this sermon, some of which is true enough and some false, beyond saying that the Irish way of life is not to be judged from a short visit to Dublin and that it was unrealistic to hold that the lack of economic development is brought about by a preoccupation with religion, although it was regrettably true enough that a preoccupation with economic development had caused some countries to abandon whatever religion they had. This was probably a tactless remark to make to a doctrinaire socialist from Sweden, but I felt that at that stage tact had gone by the board.[87]

This exchange reflects a clash of two very different worldviews: that of economism favouring technocratic government for growth promotion and that of Irish nationalism favouring the protection of Irish culture over materialism.

This clash of worldviews mirrored the policy debate domestically. In this period, T. K. Whitaker and a group of forward-thinking officials in the Department of Finance started embracing ideas similar to those expressed by Myrdal about economic development. As part of this strategy, they advocated liberalising the Irish economy and opening it to foreign competition.[88] This

---

[87] Ibid., O'Sullivan to Murphy, 19 June 1956.
[88] J. J. Lee, *Ireland, 1912–1985: Politics and Society* (Cambridge 1989), pp. 341–5.

emerging policy debate in Ireland reflected, albeit belatedly, the discussions elsewhere about the desirability of economic growth and its planability. The work of international organisations like the OEEC and UNECE played an important part in informing and shaping this debate through its reports analysing economic development in Europe. These developments left their imprint on the Irish policymaking community. The demands for extensive statistical information from American Marshall Plan administrators led to the establishment of the Irish Central Statistics Office as a separate agency.[89] At the same time, the Marshall Plan added impetus to international attempts to standardise economic statistics, including national income estimates.[90] Indeed, Irish statisticians were in the forefront of advocating the use of national income analysis for the purposes of economic policymaking and planning in Ireland.[91] In this sense, Ireland did benefit from studying developments in other small European countries through international cooperation, but the question remains whether it could have been done to a much greater extent, as Myrdal suggested.

Ireland and international cooperation in the late 1950s

The debate over Ireland's economic development was only just starting. While some groups seemed more interested in opening up the Irish economy, others continued to cling to protectionist inclinations of economic nationalism. Following his visit to Ireland, the Dublin Chamber of Commerce decided in September 1956 to invite Myrdal to speak at its annual dinner in November.[92] Because it seemed unlikely that he would accept, the Department's secretary, Seán Murphy, contacted McCann for a suitable replacement from the UNECE secretariat. At the same time, Murphy tried to prevent an unsuitable speaker being invited to address the chamber of commerce:

> Should Mr. Myrdal be unable to come I wonder if you could suggest some speaker from the Geneva Office of the U.N. who has an economic and commercial background. We should, of course, avoid Iron Curtain U.N. officials, protagonists of G.A.T.T., but it might be possible to suggest someone of some importance connected with ECOSOC which I understand does a lot of its work in Geneva.[93]

---

[89] Whelan, *Ireland*, pp. 112–6.

[90] Till Geiger, 'Strumento analitico o modello di crescita? L'influenza americana nell'elaborazione delle statistiche europee sulla crescita economica dopo la seconda guerra mondiale'. *Nuova Civiltà delle Macchine* 17, no. 3 (1999): 24–40; Till Geiger, 'Economists, national income accounting and western European reconstruction: A revolution in western liberal governmentality?' manuscript submitted for consideration, August 2005.

[91] Ronan Fanning, 'Economists and governments: Ireland, 1922–52,' in Antoin Murphy (ed.) *Economists and the Irish economy from the eighteenth century to the present day* (Dublin, 1983), pp. 151–4.

[92] NAI DFA 2001/9/158, letter O'Shields to Myrdal, 5 Sept. 1956.

[93] NAI 2001/9/158, MacWhite for Murphy to McCann, 11 Sept. 1956.

Murphy's letter sounded a definite note of caution about the potentially pernicious views held by international civil servants working for international organisations. Slightly less surprising was the desire to rule out a speaker from an eastern bloc country. Nevertheless, this statement reveals the anti-communist bias of the department in spite of Ireland's neutrality. In his reply, McCann informed Dublin that no one of equal stature to Myrdal worked in the United Nations offices in Geneva since the headquarters of the Economic and Social Council was based in New York, a view shared by Swiss officials in the Political Department in Berne.[94]

At the same time, the Irish government started to consider its response to the Soviet proposal for an All-European Agreement on Economic Co-operation. When the Soviet proposals were received in Dublin, the Department of External Affairs asked all other departments for their comments. Only the Department of the Taoiseach responded saying it had no observations to offer on the Soviet demarche. Given the general lack of response, the Department of External Affairs raised the matter at the next meeting of the Foreign Trade Committee. The representative of the Department of Industry and Commerce objected immediately to the proposed agreement as unacceptable because of the unconditional most favoured nation clause contained in Article 5 of the Agreement. Acceptance of this article would have meant that Ireland had to grant all signatories the same access to Irish markets as it only granted Britain at the time. Therefore, the Committee decided that Ireland should support moves by other western countries to reject the Soviet proposal during the forthcoming informal discussions within the OEEC. In the light of these discussions, Cosgrave agreed that Fay should not actively intervene in the debate on the Soviet proposals, but explain that Ireland did not support the Soviet proposals because the agreement undermined the OEEC by strengthening the UNECE.[95] The department adopted the same line a few months later, rejecting the Soviet proposal for an UNECE body on the peaceful use of atomic energy.[96]

Over the next few months, the Berne legation became more involved in UNECE affairs. In October 1956, Myrdal contacted the legation to draw its attention to a fellowship programme for young economists to enable them to gain experience of international economic problems for a year at the UNECE offices in Geneva.[97] After hearing that the Irish government seemed to be labouring under the misapprehension that these fellowships (funded by the United Nations Technical Assistance Administration) were open only to civil servants, Kostelecky rang the legation in Berne to stress that the competition was open to any young qualified economists a government would want to

---

[94] Ibid., McCann to Murphy, 27 Sept. 1956.
[95] NAI DFA 408/137/33, minute by Belton for Cosgrave, 14 Sep. 1956; minute by Kirwan for Warnock, 11 Oct. 1956.
[96] Ibid., Fay to Belton, 25 Feb. 1957.
[97] NAI 2001/9/158, Myrdal to McCann, 11 Oct. 1956.

nominate.[98] It is unclear whether the Irish government in the end nominated any candidates for this fellowship.

In his report on the 12th session of UNECE in April 1957, McCann noted that the Soviet Union returned to using the meeting to attack the formation of the European Economic Community (EEC) and Euratom as furthering the aggressive purposes of NATO and a revenge-seeking Germany. In contrast to the aggressive tone of the Soviet delegation, western representatives tried to keep the discussions of the Soviet proposals civil, while succeeding in watering down the Soviet proposals for increased economic co-operation between eastern and western Europe, leading to the adoption of innocuous compromise resolutions.[99] At the 12th session, Myrdal left his post as executive secretary in April 1957. O'Sullivan was relieved that his successor, the Finnish ambassador to London, Sakari Tuomioja, held much more conservative views on economic matters. Given his cautious demeanour, O'Sullivan hoped that he would avoid the controversies caused by Myrdal's forthcoming style and blunt views on ECE policy.[100]

At the 14th session, Ireland was represented by Josephine McNeill, Ireland's minister to Switzerland, and Denis Holmes, secretary of legation in Berne. Again the report showed that the session was dominated by the concerns of the UNECE secretariat about the compartmentalisation of member states into rival groupings due to the creation of regional trade agreements. The report noted that the tone of the meeting was more cordial and less confrontational than at previous sessions. The Irish representatives noted with interest that the UNECE resolved to give greater attention to less developed regions in Europe.[101] At the 15th session in April 1960, western countries were forced to defend their regional trade agreements against Soviet criticism. For example, Sweden defended the formation of EEC, EFTA and the Organisation for Economic Co-operation and Development as steps towards the multilateral integration of European economies and closer economic co-operation throughout the world.[102] Intriguingly, the Irish delegates did not intervene in the debate on the economic survey at the 15th session, even though the survey discussed the economic problems of Ireland and the agricultural economies of the Mediterranean rim (Turkey, Greece, Southern Italy, Spain and Portugal) in considerable detail. Again the Irish delegates felt it would be desirable if the delegation was briefed in advance on Ireland's economic situation in order to comment during the debate. For example, the

---

[98] Ibid., McNeill to McCann, 12 Nov. 1956. McCann returned to Dublin in October 1956 to take up the post of assistant secretary in charge of the economic division of the Department of External Affairs. He was replaced by Josephine McNeill.

[99] NAI DFA 408/137/33, 'Some political aspects of the twelfth session of the Economic Commission for Europe which opened in Geneva on 29 April 1957', minute by McCann.

[100] NAI 2001/9/158: O'Sullivan to Murphy, 27 April 1957.

[101] NAI DT S16023B, Summary of report of Irish delegate at 14th session of the UNECE, 30 Jun. 1959.

[102] Ibid., 'ECE–15th session', Holmes to Secretary, 2 May 1960.

survey was deeply sceptical about the Irish plans to expand agricultural exports to western Europe and critical of the country's high capital-output ratio, reflecting an extremely low efficiency of capital investment.[103]

After being admitted to the United Nations, the Department of External Affairs ensured that Ireland would be represented at the annual session of the UNECE, realising the political importance of the country's presence at the meetings of international organisations. However, the delegations were not properly briefed and could do little more than report on the proceedings. Charged with a watching brief, delegates were ill-equipped to participate in international economic co-operation. At the same time, the lack of interest from the economic departments was even more surprising.

Conclusion

This chapter has shown that Ireland was far less isolated due to its wartime neutrality in the immediate postwar period than historians have generally presumed. Despite some continued annoyance over Ireland's wartime neutrality, the British and American governments generally supported Ireland's involvement in postwar international cooperation. British and American officials encouraged the Irish government to apply not only for United Nations membership but also to join the newly specialised United Nations organisations such as the FAO and the various temporary bodies trying to provide relief to war-torn European countries. In marked contrast to the welcoming approach of British and American officials, Irish policy-makers remained reluctant to participate in the postwar international co-operation unless such an involvement could be shown to serve Irish interests in preserving the country's sovereignty and economic recovery. Due to this narrow outlook, Irish policymakers tended to use international fora to complain about the small allocations of fertilisers and coal Ireland was receiving. In this context, Ireland's attempts to bypass the existing international machinery for allocating coal and fertilisers annoyed American policymakers in particular.[104] While the shared economic crisis taught other governments a valuable lesson about the interdependence of European economies, Irish policymakers seemed not to appreciate the value of international cooperation in overcoming Europe's economic problems. As Ireland was better off economically than most countries in the immediate postwar period, Irish policy-makers concentrated on restoring Ireland's pre-war trading relationship with Britain rather than on expanding its economic links with other European countries through economic cooperation in the OEEC or the UNECE. Paradoxically therefore, wartime neutrality did not isolate Ireland from international cooperation in the immediate postwar period, but rather the

---

[103] Secretariat of the Economic Commission for Europe, *Economic Survey of Europe in 1959* (Geneva, 1960), chapter 7; NAI DT S16023B, 'ECE–15th session', Holmes to Secretary, 12 May 1960.
[104] Geiger, 'Why Ireland,' 200–1.

conviction that neutrality and self-reliance had served the country well and should form the basis of national policy.

After 1947 Ireland's involvement in the Marshall Plan did draw the country into the world of international cooperation with multilateral organisations. The conditionality of American aid forced Irish policymakers to strengthen its administrative capabilities by expanding the Department of External Affairs and establishing a Central Statistics Office.[105] However, this external pressure ended after the end of the ERP. As a consequence, Ireland remained on the sidelines of the moves towards further European integration. The Department of External Affairs remained involved in multilateral co-operation, but assumed the role of a clearing house, keeping other government departments informed about developments abroad. At the same time, those officials representing Ireland in organisations such as the OEEC remained convinced of the value of international cooperation. For example, Ireland's representative to the OEEC, William Fay, was dismayed by the failure of the Department of Industry and Commerce to defend Ireland's economic interests at meetings of international organisations such as the UNECE in 1956:

> This amazing statement, which apparently represents that Department's policy since they have allowed it to go on record, has already been translated into practice by the fact that the Department of Industry and Commerce have never sent a representative to the OEEC, however often they were pressed to do so in connection with meetings of Technical Committees. It would seem that they do not consider that the OEEC ever touches on 'vital interests'. One might ask when such issues do, in fact, arise, who is to determine it. On the international plane one would think that the other Departments would accept the view of the Department of External Affairs that the vital interests of the State were involved when the latter Department thought so. At least this avowal, or rather abdication by the Department of Industry and Commerce, makes it somewhat odd to think that that Department objects to the Department of External Affairs representing the country on economic matters. It would now seem that we have no alternative to do so.[106]

Such critical voices joined those in other departments. For example, T. K. Whitaker argued that the Department of Finance could not wait for the Department of Industry and Commerce to develop a strategy to overcome the country's economic malaise.[107] While the Department of Industry and

---

[105] Kennedy, 'Challenge of multilateralism', 118–22; Whelan, *Ireland*, 112–6.
[106] NAI DFA 408/137/32, Fay to Warnock, 18 Apr. 1956.
[107] Lee, *Ireland*, p. 343.

Commerce remained stuck in an isolationist mould without any inkling of how international cooperation might allow Ireland to overcome its growing economic malaise, the Department of External Affairs increasingly realised the value of international cooperation after the country's accession to the United Nations in 1955.

While accession to the United Nations led Irish foreign policymakers to belatedly discover internationalism, Irish policymakers more generally had not yet learned that international cooperation within multilateral organisations allows national governments to pursue their own national policies more effectively.[108] This lesson would be learned over the coming decade as the country became more involved in international cooperation at the United Nations and sought to join the EEC. Within this process, Irish policymakers embedded international economic cooperation as a major guiding principle into Irish foreign policy.

---

[108] Gunnar Myrdal, *Realities and illusions in regard to inter-government* organizations (London, 1955). A similar argument has been made more recently by Alan Milward, *The European rescue of the Nation State* (London, 1992).

Chapter Three

Ireland and the Middle East at the United Nations, 1955–2005

RORY MILLER

Introduction

At the time of its entry into the United Nations in 1955 Ireland, out of a total of twenty states with which the recently established republic had formal relations, only had *de facto* diplomatic relations with two Middle Eastern states: Egypt and Israel.[1] Nevertheless, the Arab world was aware of Ireland's anti-colonial credentials and its policy of neutrality, and thus welcomed its entry into the United Nations.[2] While Israel, which as early as 28 May 1948 had formally expressed its desire to 'establish a relationship of sympathy and friendship between [the] people of Eire and Jewish people in Palestine to [the] mutual advantage of both', hoped that Irish entry into the international forum would result in the development of closer bilateral ties.[3] Over the following half century Ireland's involvement in United Nations efforts to contribute to peace, stability and prosperity in this most troubled of regions proved a defining aspect of the state's United Nations policy.

Ireland's First United Nations Test: The Suez Crisis 1956

The first opportunity for, not to mention test of, Irish United Nations diplomacy towards the Middle East came at the United Nations General Assembly during the autumn of 1956, with the Suez crisis. The previous July, Egyptian president Gamal Abd al Nasser had nationalised the Suez Canal. Both the French and British governments were infuriated by this move and viewed it

---

[1] Patrick Keatinge, *A Place Among the Nations: Issues in Irish foreign policy* (Dublin, 1978), Appendix II.
[2] National Archives of Ireland (hereafter NAI), Department of Foreign Affairs (hereafter DFA), 305/311/1, memorandum on discussion between Irish and Saudi Arabian ambassadors to Spain, 10 Oct. 1956.
[3] NAI, Department of the Taoiseach (hereafter DT), S14330, telegram, Shertok to MacBride, 27 May 1948.

as a challenge to their economic security and prestige. Britain was responsible for the military defence of the canal and felt humiliated by the Egyptian action; France viewed Nasser as the major patron of the anti-French rebels in Algeria and both saw the act as a blow to their international standing as Great Powers.[4] Anglo-French discussions were followed by a French approach to Israel regarding the possibility that the Jewish state might participate in a military action to retake the canal.

In the last days of October 1956 Israeli troops crossed the Egyptian border and within a week had overwhelmed Sinai. On 5 November French and British forces landed in Egypt, ostensibly to separate the warring parties, but in reality as part of a pre-arranged plan, for which the Israeli action provided a pretext to force Nasser to denationalise the canal.

Patrick Keatinge has argued that Ireland branded Israel the aggressor in its United Nations statements on the Suez crisis.[5] This was technically correct. At the outbreak of the crisis, Frederick Boland, Ireland's Permanent Representative to the United Nations, had been instructed to support any General Assembly resolutions that had the backing of the majority of members and which called for an end to hostilities and the withdrawal of foreign forces from Egypt.[6] As such, he voted in favour of resolutions supporting an immediate ceasefire (2 November) and the creation of a United Nations force to oversee a cessation of hostilities (3 November). He also voted for a nineteen-power draft resolution (A/3309) that created the United Nations Emergency Force (UNEF) and that called on Israel to withdraw immediately behind the armistice lines of February 1949 and on France and the United Kingdom to withdraw forces from Egyptian territory.[7]

Minister for External Affairs Liam Cosgrave addressed the Suez crisis during his speech at the eleventh session of the General Assembly at the end of November 1956. Cosgrave 'deplored and condemned' the 'Anglo-French attack' on Egypt and recalled that Ireland had 'applauded' Egypt's 'struggle for freedom' from colonial rule, adding that there had always been 'friendly feelings' between the two countries. But he also expressed regret that Egypt had failed to use its independence with more 'moderation and realism', both in regard to its decision to unilaterally nationalise the Suez Canal and its

---

[4] For a detailed examination of the Suez crisis in all its complexity see Keith Kyle, *Suez* (London, 1991).

[5] Patrick Keatinge, 'Ireland', in David Allen and Alfred Pijpers (eds.), *European Foreign Policy Making and the Arab Israeli Conflict* (The Hague, Boston, Lancaster, 1984), pp. 18–30, p. 18.

[6] NAI DFA 305/173 II, External Affairs to Boland, 1 Nov. 1956, cited in Joseph Skelly, *Irish Diplomacy at the United Nations 1945–1965: National interests and international order* (Dublin, 1997), p. 53.

[7] On 2 Nov. a United States draft resolution (A/3256) was adopted as Resolution 997 (ES-I). On 4 Nov. draft resolutions A/3276 and A/3275 were adopted as resolutions 998 (ES-I) and 999 (ES-I) respectively. On 5 Nov. draft resolution (A/3290) was adopted as Resolution 1000 (ES-I). On 7 Nov. the General Assembly adopted Resolution 1002 (ES-I). See *Official Records of the General Assembly Emergency Special Session*, 1–10 Nov. 1956, pp. 126–7.

effort to 'encompass the destruction of Israel'. He continued that Israel's neighbours 'must be ready to accept as a fact the existence of Israel and must renounce their projects for the destruction of that country'.[8]

Cosgrave's criticism of Egypt's past behaviour must be viewed, at least in part, in terms of his staunch anti-communism and hence his concern lest the Arab world move closer to the Soviet Union. Indeed, in the course of his speech he pleaded, as a the foreign minister of a 'traditionally friendly and firmly anti-imperialist' country, that Egypt refrain from drawing the Soviet Union into the Middle East. But his criticism of Egypt for its anti-Israeli stance was nonetheless notable, as was his call for the Arab world to 'accept as a fact the existence of Israel'.[9]

This conciliatory and even-handed approach to the conflict taken by Ireland's foreign minister was repeated in January 1957 during a General Assembly debate on a draft resolution calling for Israeli compliance with previous draft resolutions and withdrawal behind armistice lines. At this time the Irish delegation restated its earlier condemnation of Israel's attack on Egyptian territory, but it also argued that the draft resolution introduced by twenty-four Asian and Arab states was 'a little too one-sided and a little too limited to be of real service'.[10] In particular it was argued that the draft resolution failed to tackle the matter of the underlying differences between Egypt and Israel and that 'more is needed' than simply calling for Israel to withdraw its troops. As such, though voting in favour of paragraph two of the resolution that called for the Secretary-General to continue his efforts to 'secure the complete withdrawal of Israel', Ireland abstained on the first paragraph which expressed 'regret and concern [at] the failure of Israel to comply' with earlier resolutions.[11]

Irish Peacekeeping in the Middle East: 1958–78

Frank Aiken succeeded Cosgrave as Minister for External Affairs (he also became Tánaiste), following Fianna Fáil's election victory in March 1957. He would hold this post until his retirement in 1969. Aiken is remembered as the architect of Ireland's policy of adopting an independent position at the United Nations and in entrenching Irish neutrality in international affairs.[12]

---

[8] See statement by Cosgrave, at General Assembly Plenary Meeting 603, 30 Nov. 1956, *Official Records of the General Assembly* (hereafter *ORGA*), 11th Session, vol. 1, p. 452.

[9] Ibid., p. 454.

[10] NAI 2001/43/98, memorandum on Irish involvement in the aftermath of the Suez Crisis of 1956 at the United Nations, 1 June 1967.

[11] See record of General Assembly Plenary Meeting 642, 19 Jan. 1957, *ORGA*, vol. II, p. 952. For the wording of the draft resolution that Ireland abstained on see Document A/3501/Rev.1, in *ORGA, 11th Session, Annexes, 1956–1957*, p. 44.

[12] On Aiken's contribution to the development of Irish foreign policy see 'Frank Aiken: A Tribute', *Ireland Today, Bulletin of the Department of Foreign Affairs*, 999, June 1983, p. 7 and Aoife Breathnach's chapter in this volume, below pp. 182–200.

From his earliest speeches before the General Assembly it was clear that Ireland's new foreign minister was determined to play a formative role at the international body in a number of major areas ranging from decolonisation to nuclear non-proliferation and United Nations peacekeeping: all issues that had great relevance to the Middle East.[13]

Aiken took control of Irish foreign policy at a time of significant upheaval in the Arab world. In February 1958, Syria and Egypt joined together to form the United Arab Republic (UAR) under the leadership of the Egyptian president. Nasser's claim to be the champion of Arab unity greatly worried his pro-Western neighbours, King Hussein of Jordan and Lebanon's president Camille Chamoun, both of whom faced significant challenges from pro-Nasser domestic opponents.

In June 1958, in response to Lebanese appeals over efforts by the UAR to destabilise the country and encourage rebellion, the Security Council decided to create the United Nations Observation Group in Lebanon (UNOGIL) to ensure an end to infiltration.[14] This preceded the American decision to send a marine force of 15,000 to Lebanon in July following the fall of the pro-Western regime in Iraq. It was the Irish determination to support United Nations peacekeeping that led it to make an initial contribution of five army officers to the UNOGIL force.[15] By the time that UNOGIL ceased its operations in December 1958, this contribution had grown to fifty unarmed military observers, including Colonel Justin McCarthy, the force's Deputy Chief of Staff.[16]

By all accounts this first Irish contribution to United Nations peacekeeping was a success. Secretary-General Dag Hammarskjöld praised the 'excellent service' of Ireland's UNOGIL troops, a view reiterated by the head of United Nations forces in Lebanon.[17] As the *Irish Times* noted, the Irish involvement was a

> 'source of genuine pride' and 'the emergence into the strong light of the Near East of a band of officers wearing the name of IRELAND on the sleeves on their tropical kit has demonstrated for the first time in the international field the value of Irish training and the quality of Irish officers.[18]

---

[13] See, for example, Aiken's speech at the 13th Session of the General Assembly, 19 Sept. 1958, in *ORGA 13th Session, Plenary Meetings, Verbatim Records of Meetings*, 16 Sept.–13 Dec. 1958, pp. 39–45.

[14] For an account of Irish participation in UNOGIL see Richard Heaslip's chapter, below pp. 79–116.

[15] NAI 2001/43/123, memorandum on United Nations Observation Group in the Lebanon, 29 June 1958. At the peak of its activity UNOGIL had 591 military personnel, including 469 ground observers from 21 countries.

[16] See *Irish Times*, 24 Sept. 1958 and 20 Nov. 1958.

[17] NAI 2001/43/123, Hammarskjöld to Boland, 19 Jan. 1959.

[18] *Irish Times*, 17 Oct. 1958.

[19] For an account of Irish participation in UNTSO see Richard Heaslip's chapter, below pp. 79–116.

Following the disbandment of UNOGIL several of its Irish members joined the United Nations Truce Supervision Organisation (UNTSO), which had been founded in 1948 to supervise the observance of the truces between Israel and her neighbours.[19] During the 1960s Ireland was mainly involved in providing troops for United Nations operations in the Congo (ONUC) and then between 1964 and 1973 the bulk of Irish United Nations troops were deployed in Cyprus (UNFICYP). Indeed, at the time of the June 1967 Arab-Israeli war there were only twelve Irish officers serving with UNTSO (out of a total of 178 from fourteen countries), though this small group did include a Lieutenant Colonel who headed the Israel/Syria Mixed Armistice Commission.[20] In mid-November 1967 Ireland agreed to a request by Secretary-General U Thant to increase its role in providing military observers to the Middle East.[21] This decision was especially welcome at the time because Ireland was one of only three countries (in addition to the four countries already involved: Burma, Finland, Sweden and France) acceptable to both the UAR and Israel as potential peacekeepers.[22] By 1969 Ireland was still one of only eight countries acceptable to both Israel and the UAR as a provider of additional UNTSO observers for the Suez Canal sector.[23]

By the time of the 1973 Arab-Israeli war, Irish personnel serving with UNTSO made up the fourth largest contingent.[24] In this year the majority of troops in the Irish contingent UNFICYP were transferred to Sinai to join the second United Nations Emergency Force (UNEF II), but they were withdrawn in 1974 due to domestic Irish security requirements relating to the crisis in Northern Ireland.

Ireland and the Arab-Israeli conflict at the United Nations: 1958–67

Due to its exclusion from the United Nations until 1955, Ireland did not participate in any way in the United Nations' debate over Palestine during its first decade. In particular, Ireland played no role in the deliberations of the United Nations Special Committee on Palestine (UNSCOP) which was appointed in May 1947 and whose majority report, published in September 1947, provided the basis for the General Assembly vote on partition the following November. Nor did Ireland play any role in the Security Council or General Assembly diplomatic efforts to mediate a truce and armistice during the war that followed the invasion of Israel by the combined armies of Egypt,

---

[20] *Dáil Deb.*, vol. 226, col. 1081, 9 Feb. 1967 and vol. 229, col. 1771, 14 July 1967. On the size of the various contingents to UNOGIL and the requirements for participation in the Irish contingent see NAI 98/6/401, Note concerning the selection and appointment of military observers for UNTSO, 10 July 1967 and PMUN to McCann, 3 Nov. 1967.
[21] NAI 98/6/401, letter from Thant to Cremin, 17 Nov. 1967.
[22] Ibid., telegram, PMUN to DEA, 20 Nov. 1967.
[23] Ibid., telegram, PMUN to DEA, 31 Jan. 1969.
[24] *Dáil Deb.*, vol. 268, col. 323, 23 Oct. 1973.

Iraq, Lebanon, Transjordan and Syria on 15 May 1948.[25] This conflict broke out less than twenty-four hours after the end of the British mandate and the proclamation of the state of Israel by Prime Minister David Ben-Gurion.[26]

Indeed, as noted above, it was only with the Suez crisis of 1956 that the Irish government had its first opportunity to contribute to the Middle East conflict at the United Nations. Two years later, in August 1958, Aiken spoke at length on the Arab-Israeli crisis during a speech before the General Assembly emergency session. Prior to making this statement, Aiken had been counselled by the influential Boland to delete from his speech a call for Arab recognition of Israel in its existing borders. This was on the grounds that such a move would alienate the Arab world, thus making it harder for Ireland to pursue an independent policy at the United Nations. The call might also have been viewed as an indirect Irish acceptance of Jerusalem as part of the state of Israel.[27] But Aiken did address directly the Palestinian refugee crisis which he had described as the 'greatest single obstacle' to a lasting peace in the Middle East. He called on the United Nations to 'guarantee full compensation' for the refugees covering both property lost and damages suffered as a 'result of their exile'.

Though he accepted that Israel was not exclusively responsible for the tragedy, he did call on it to state how many refugees it was prepared to accept and argued that the United Nations should 'arrange for repatriation for the maximum possible number of those who would rather return than receive full compensation'. In the words of then United Nations delegate Conor Cruise O'Brien, Aiken's 'concrete proposals'[28] on the refugee crisis were welcomed in Ireland as 'both wise and practicable'.[29] Various members of the Irish United Nations delegation, including O'Brien, Joseph Shields and Paul Keating, also made Irish concerns over the Palestinian humanitarian crisis very clear in the numerous discussions on the subject held in the Special Political and Ad Hoc Committees of the General Assembly. In subsequent years their colleagues Brendan Nolan and Noel Dorr advanced similar Irish concerns.[30]

---

[25] As part of its attempt to prevent conflict, the United Nations General Assembly appointed a United Nations mediator on 14 May 1948 (see General Assembly Resolution 186 (S.II), 14 May 1948). The United Nations Security Council also passed various resolutions aimed at finding a diplomatic solution to the conflict. See, for example, Security Council Resolution S/773, 22 May 1948; Security Council Resolution S/801, 29 May 1948; UNSSC Resolution S/875, 7 July 1948; Security Council Resolution S/1070, 4 Nov. 1948; Security Council Resolution S/1080, 16 Nov. 1948; Security Council Resolution S/1169, 29 Dec. 1948; Security Council Resolution S/1376, 11 Aug. 1949. See *United Nations Security Council Official Records* (hereafter *UNSCOR*), *3rd Year, 1948, Supplements for April–December and 4th Year, 1949, Supplement for January–December.*

[26] For the Irish reaction to the Arab invasion of the fledgling Jewish state see the *Irish Times*, 15 May 1948.

[27] For Boland's views on this matter see Skelly, *United Nations*, pp. 157–9.

[28] See meeting 159, General Assembly Special Political Committee, 26 Nov. 1959, *ORGA, 14th Session*, p. 150.

[29] *The Leader*, 28 Sept. 1957, p. 4.

[30] See meeting 105, General Assembly Special Political Committee, 13 Nov. 1958, *ORGA, 13th Session*, pp. 77–8. See also meeting 159, General Assembly Special Political Committee, 26 Nov. 1959, *ORGA, 14th Session*, pp. 150–1.

This sympathy for the plight of the Palestinian refugees at United Nations fora was the result of a sincerely held belief that while Ireland lacked political and diplomatic influence over the parties to the conflict, it did have an important, if not unique, moral position, and this belief was backed up by the first Irish financial donations to the United Nations Relief and Works Agency (UNRWA).

This United Nations body had been founded as a temporary measure by General Assembly Resolution 302 (IV) of 8 December 1949 with the mandate to carry out aid programmes to alleviate the suffering of Arab refugees who, as a result of the hostilities in Palestine in 1948, had fled to Jordan, Lebanon, Syria and the Gaza strip. However, it quickly evolved into the main provider of basic services to the refugees, regardless of whether they were registered as refugees or not, and also became a unique body in the realm of international aid by entrenching itself as a permanent organisation dedicated to the relief of one particular national group: the Palestinian Arabs.[31]

In October 1958 Paul Keating, Ireland's representative on the General Assembly Ad Hoc Committee, announced that though up to this point Ireland's 'own domestic economic problems' had prevented her from contributing to UNRWA, the Irish had been 'very conscious of the very great problem and the great source of anguish' engendered by the Palestinian refugee crisis and thus pledged a 'purely token' £1,000 (sterling) to the organisation.[32] The following year this contribution was raised to the sterling equivalent of $2,800 (US dollars) and from this time until the 1966 financial year Irish donations to the organisation totalled $126,800.[33]

This financial support for UNRWA underlined both Ireland's 'serious concern' over the Palestinian refugee problem as well as its 'appreciation' of UNRWA's role.[34] Financially, Ireland's commitment also exceeded that of most other nations during these years. With its first contribution to UNRWA in 1958 Ireland became only the thirty-first nation (plus the Vatican City) to support UNRWA financially. By 1966 it was still only one of forty-three out of the United Nations 121 members to donate funds. According to Department of External Affairs figures, Ireland ranked eleventh in Western Europe and ahead of Austria, Finland, Greece, Luxemburg and Turkey, and sixth overall in terms of its contribution as a proportion of gross national product.[35]

---

[31] The United Nations Resolution creating UNRWA envisaged the 'termination' of its relief effort 'not later' than 31 Dec. 1951. Under UNRWA's operational definition a Palestinian refugee is a person whose normal place of residence between June 1946 and May 1948 was Palestine and who lost both their homes and livelihoods as a result of the 1948 conflict. The definition also includes descendants of persons who became refugees in 1948.

[32] See meeting of the General Assembly Ad Hoc Committee, 27 Oct. 1958, *ORGA, 13th Session*, p. 9.

[33] The Irish financial contribution to UNRWA in these years can be found in *ORGA, 14th Session*, 1959 to *22nd Session* 1967.

[34] See meeting of the General Assembly Ad Hoc Committee, 20 Oct. 1960, *ORGA, 15th Session*, p. 3.

[35] NAI 2001/43/871, Nolan to O'Sullivan, 10 July 1967.

There is little doubt that this commitment to UNRWA was a direct consequence of a developing Irish foreign policy that viewed humanitarian crises with the utmost concern. But it was also directly related to Aiken's belief in the centrality of the Palestine refugee problem to the general conflict in the Middle East.

In August 1958 Aiken had referred to the deadlock between Israel and the Arabs over the refugee problem as perhaps the greatest single obstacle to the establishment of peace in the region.[36] And in his sporadic meetings with Israeli diplomats Aiken had, in the words of his own officials, 'made much of the problem of the Arab refugees'.[37] Indeed during a 1962 meeting with an Israeli diplomat, Aiken noted that as far as the Middle East was concerned, Ireland's 'main pre-occupation' was the Arab refugees. Aiken favoured compensation coupled with the repatriation of some of the refugees back to Israel.[38]

Though the early years of Aiken's period as minister marked a new beginning in Ireland's practical involvement in the humanitarian aspects of the Palestine problem, there was little parallel development in the diplomatic or political sphere during Ireland's temporary membership of the Security Council between January and December 1962. Membership of the Security Council at this time provided Ireland a rare opportunity to exert diplomatic influence at the highest forum of international diplomacy.[39] Aiken, in particular, was aware of this opportunity. In October 1962 he had personally attended a Security Council meeting to announce Ireland's joint sponsorship of a draft resolution calling for Algeria to be admitted into the United Nations.[40] The majority of Security Council business that year was dominated by events in Cuba and the ongoing tensions between India and Pakistan. However, on 20 March, in the wake of border clashes between Israel and Syria and the demand by the Syrian government that the United Nations expel Israel, Syria's United Nations representative Farid Chehlaoui brought the matter before the Security Council and asked the Council to consider the 'grave situation arising from [Israeli] acts of aggression'.[41]

This was the first time since January 1956 that the Security Council had been asked to consider a breach of the Syrian-Israeli General Armistice

---

[36] See Meeting 105, General Assembly Special Political Committee, 13 Nov. 1958, *ORGA, 13th* Session, pp. 77–8.

[37] NAI DFA PS35/1, Cremin to Boland, 17 June 1961.

[38] NAI 2001/43/119, Minutes of a meeting between Max Nurock, Israeli Foreign Ministry and Frank Aiken, the Minister for External Affairs, Dublin 24 Jan. 1962 and 31 Jan. 1962.

[39] For an account of the background to Ireland's half-term on the Security Council in 1962 see Michael Kennedy's chapter, below pp. 154–181.

[40] See draft resolution S/5172/Rev.1 proposed at meeting 1020 of the Security Council, 4 Oct. 1962, *UNSCOR, 17th* Year, p. 7.

[41] See letter from Syrian representative Farid Chehlaoui to the President of the Security Council, 20 Mar. 1962, Document S/5096, *UNSCOR, 17th Year, Supplement for January, February and March 1962*, pp. 97–8. See also *New York Herald Tribune*, 23 Mar. 1962.

Agreement on such a large scale and, just as the Suez crisis had provided an opportunity for Ireland to make its opening contribution to the Middle East conflict at the General Assembly, these clashes between Israel and her northern neighbour offered Ireland an early opportunity to involve itself in Security Council deliberations on the matter.

Boland discounted the Israeli claim that it was only acting in response to 'a series of acts of aggression and provocation' by Syria against Israeli territory.[42] He also believed that the Israeli attack on Syria was 'a major violation of the Charter'. Thus he voted in favour of the 9 April Security Council draft resolution which 'deplores [the] hostile exchange' between Syria and Israel and concluded that the Israeli attack of 16 to 17 March 'constitutes a flagrant violation of the General Armistice Agreement between the two states'.[43]

Nevertheless, Boland deliberately refrained from speaking at any of the Security Council meetings dealing with the matter in the last week of March and the first ten days of April 'as it would have been impossible for me to speak without unequivocally stigmatising Israel's action and that, I felt, would carry us into the sphere of Arab-Israeli differences to an extent which we have so far managed to avoid in the United Nations'.[44]

Boland's reluctance to become directly involved in the Middle East conflict during Ireland's half-term on the Security Council lends credence to Aiken's claim to a member of the Israeli foreign ministry in the same year that the Irish position on the Middle East was discreet and limited to private suggestions to the parties involved.[45]

Irish reluctance to use its United Nations platform to involve itself in the Middle East conflict was in part due to the preoccupation of Seán Lemass, who had succeeded de Valera as Taoiseach in June 1959, with developing the Irish economy and trade relations with Europe ahead of furthering Ireland's reputation as an outspoken and independent member of the United Nations.

Irish United Nations diplomacy and the Arab-Israeli war: June 1967

It was not until the summer of 1967, during an intense five-week period of debate on the Arab-Israeli war, that Ireland made a significant and notable contribution to Middle East diplomacy at the United Nations. On 27 June, Aiken made a speech on the crisis to the fifth emergency special session of the General Assembly that was immediately hailed as a major contribution to the United Nations debate on the conflict. For example, Arthur Lall, India's for-

---

[42] See letter from Israeli representative (Comay) to the President of the Security Council, 22 Mar. 1962, Document S/5100, *UNSCOR, 17th Year, Supplement for January, February and March 1962*, 99. The resolution was adopted by fourteen votes to zero with France abstaining. See meeting 1006 of the Security Council, 9 Apr. 1962, *UNSCOR, 17th year*, pp. 20–1.

[43] See document S/5111, *UNSCOR, 17th Year, Supplement for April, May and June 1962*, pp. 95–6, adopted by the Security Council at meeting 1006, 9 Apr. 1962.

[44] NAI 2001/43/120, Report on Syrian-Israeli border incidents, Boland to Cremin, 10 Apr. 1962.

[45] NAI 2001/43/119, Minutes of Nurock's meeting with Aiken, 31 Jan. 1962.

mer ambassador to the United Nations and the author of a 1968 scholarly analysis of the United Nations role in the Six Day War (to this day one of the most fluid and authoritative works on the subject) highlighted for special attention Aiken's 'distinctive and important statement', which he viewed as 'perhaps the most far reaching of all those made in the Assembly's debate'.[46]

On 28 June, the day after Aiken's speech to the General Assembly, Yugoslavia introduced a draft resolution (A/L.522) on behalf of eighteen non-aligned states. With regard to the issue of withdrawal, the original text called on Israel 'immediately to withdraw all its forces behind the armistice lines' and concluded with a demand that only 'after Israel withdraws its forces behind armistice lines' should the Security Council give consideration to wider questions relating to the area. On 30 June an amended version was introduced that replaced the call for Israel to withdraw its forces 'behind armistice lines' with a call for the Israelis to withdraw to 'positions they held prior to 5 June 1967', after which the Security Council should 'urgently [examine] all aspects of the situation in the Middle East'.[47]

The non-aligned draft, with its emphasis on an Israeli withdrawal independent of, and prior to, a settlement (or even an agreement), was rejected by Aiken as 'too stark',[48] and he instructed the Irish delegation to let it be known that the draft was 'unsatisfactory' precisely because 'it called for withdrawal unaccompanied by other measures'.[49]

Aiken was altogether more enthusiastic about the various discussions among those Western and Latin American representatives who hoped to find an alternative text to the Yugoslav proposal. Indeed, Aiken made a significant contribution to these deliberations among the Western European states as to whether they should introduce their own text and, if so, which country would sponsor it. At various times the Norwegian and Italian representatives suggested that if the Western countries agreed to support a Latin American draft (parallel to their own negotiations, the Western states were involved in negotiations with Latin American nations over a joint draft), then Ireland should be one of the co-sponsors representing the West.

At one point, Denmark's representative, and president of the Security Council, Hans Tabor, and Britain's ambassador, Lord Caradon, suggested that if negotiations with the Latin American states broke down, then Ireland 'should go it alone' and be the sole sponsor of a Western draft resolution. Caradon's suggestion was welcomed by both the Canadian and Dutch representatives. Although flattered by this acknowledgement of Ireland's centrality to the negotiations, Aiken favoured the idea of a Latin American draft

---

[46] Arthur Lall, *The United Nations and the Middle East crisis* (New York, 1967), pp. 151–2.

[47] For the full content of this and other draft resolutions put forward on the 4 July see meetings 1547 and 1548 of the General Assembly special session, 4 July 1967, *ORGA, 5th Emergency Special Session*, pp. 1–18.

[48] NAI 2001/43/99, Cremin to McCann, 11 July 1967.

[49] Ibid., Memorandum on 5th emergency session of the United Nations, 1967.

resolution that would be supported by the Western nations.[50]

This preference for the Latin American draft was in itself illuminating because the Latin American states were generally united in the belief that the refusal of the Arab world to recognise Israel or accept the existence of the Jewish state was the major factor responsible for ongoing instability in the region. As such, their draft resolution (A/L.523), tabled on 30 June was relatively sympathetic to Israel's predicament. This draft reaffirmed that no recognition should be given to the occupation or acquisition of territories through force and called on the Assembly to request an Israeli withdrawal. However, it also called on all the parties to end the existing state of belligerency and supported the establishment of a United Nations presence that would ensure withdrawal, an end to the state of belligerency, freedom of transit in international waterways, a full solution for the refugee problem and the establishment of demilitarised zones. It also restated earlier calls for the internationalisation of Jerusalem.

The Irish delegation found the contents of this draft resolution 'very acceptable' and Aiken himself was 'extremely satisfied'.[51] It is hardly surprising that Aiken was so enthusiastic about the Latin American draft resolution, because he had played a significant role in drafting it and had even influenced its final wording. Originally, he had argued that the first operative paragraph dealing with the issue of Israeli withdrawal should contain a reference to the 4 June ceasefire lines. However, when this proposal met with 'hesitation' from some delegations, he suggested an alternative wording calling for withdrawal from 'all the territories of Jordan, Syria and the UAR occupied as a result of the recent conflict'. This wording was ultimately adopted as the basis for operative paragraph 1(a) of the final draft (which called for Israel to withdraw its forces from 'all the territories occupied by it as a result of the recent conflict').

Aiken also suggested that operative paragraph 2, the concluding phrase dealing with a solution to the conflict, should read 'and in the negotiation of a just and durable treaty of peace and non-aggression'. He believed this wording would reassure Israel that its dual objective of recognition and acceptance in the region had international support. However, both the American and British ambassadors argued that this would lose support among the Arabs, and the final draft called simply for adherence: 'in all cases to the procedures for peaceful settlement indicated in the Charter of the United Nations'.[52]

On 4 July, the day Aiken defended his United Nations speech in the Dáil, the Irish delegation at the General Assembly voted in favour of the Latin American draft resolution and voted against the non-aligned draft, as well as against two amendments to it, an Albanian one (A/L.524) that 'strongly condemn[ed] Israel for its aggression' and a Cuban one (A/L.525) that

[50] Ibid., Cremin to McCann, 11 July 1967.
[51] NAI 98/3/86, Cremin to McCann, 12 July 1967.
[52] NAI 2001/43/99, Cremin to McCann, 11 July 1967.

condemned Israeli aggression and that of 'its principal instigator, the Imperialist government of the USA'.[53]

Ireland also voted against the Soviet draft resolution (A/L.519), which contained a preamble and four operative paragraphs that 'vigorously condemned Israel's aggressive activities and continuing occupation' and demanded the withdrawal of Israeli forces behind armistice lines. The Soviet draft also called on Israel to make good in full for all damage inflicted on the Arabs and concluded with an appeal to the Security Council to take effective measures to eliminate all consequences of Israeli aggression.[54]

None of these drafts succeeded in gaining the necessary two-thirds majority required for adoption, but even a cursory analysis of the voting shows how moderate the Irish position was. Ireland was one of fifty-seven member states to vote in favour of the Latin American draft, whereas sixty-three states either voted against (forty-three) or abstained (twenty). The non-aligned draft received fifty-three votes in favour to forty-six against, with twenty abstentions. Of the forty-six countries that opposed the non-aligned draft, forty-five voted in favour of the Latin American draft (the exception being Israel). These forty-five were joined by nine states that had abstained in the non-aligned vote (in addition, three member states voted in favour of both the Latin American and non-aligned drafts).

Ireland and the Palestine question at the United Nations: 1967–73

The special session of the General Assembly adjourned on 21 July 1967. From this point on, responsibility for the ongoing conflict once again reverted to the Security Council. In November 1967, the Security Council unanimously adopted the hugely significant Resolution 242, whose basic premise of 'land for peace', though subject to widely differing interpretations, would provide the basic framework for a negotiated settlement up to the present day. Apart from sanctioning the creation of a United Nations Middle East envoy, Security Council Resolution 242 dealt specifically with two issues central to any settlement of the Arab-Israeli conflict: the final status of territories occupied in the course of the 1967 war and the fate of the Palestinian Arab population made refugees since the birth of Israel in the late 1940s. On the question of territory, Resolution 242 called for Israeli withdrawal 'from territories occupied in the recent conflict'; while in relation to the refugee problem it simply (and vaguely) called for 'a just settlement of the refugee problem'.[55] Ireland, in line with the vast majority of United Nations member states endorsed Resolution 242 as an important contribution to a lasting

---

[53] For the voting on this and other draft resolutions put forward on the 4 July see meeting 1548 of the General Assembly Special Session, 4 July 1967, *ORGA, 5th Emergency Special Session,* pp. 13–8.
[54] Ibid.
[55] See meeting 1382 of Security Council, 22 Nov. 1967, *UNSCOR, 22nd Year,* 8.

peace and also supported the resolution's creation of a special United Nations envoy to the region.

Ireland's role at the General Assembly in the summer and autumn of 1967 was a formative one in the development of its Middle East policy. In particular, from this point on Ireland became increasingly preoccupied with the fate of the Palestinian Arab refugees. On 14 December 1967, Aiken took the floor at the UNRWA debate of the Assembly Special Political Committee, to deal specifically with the 'critically important' subject of the Palestine refugees. He praised UNRWA's 'splendid record in alleviating the lot of the refugees, in diminishing their sufferings, and in giving them that minimum sense of self-respect which is essential if the concept of the dignity of man is not to be entirely denied'. But he reminded those delegates present that the United Nations had a responsibility not simply to debate how to help UNRWA but also to 'resolve' the problem.

Thus he called on the United Nations to make 'a really extraordinary effort to break the deadlock by guaranteeing full compensation to the refugees' and to ensure that 'all refugees not repatriated should get full compensation for the property they had lost and the damage they had suffered'. He then restated his belief that the proposal that he had first put forward in 1958 'still represents the best way to tackle the problem and that [it was] best calculated to give a comprehensive and final solution'. Finally, he urged the United Nations to 'arrange for the repatriation of the maximum possible number of refugees and for full compensation, not merely resettlement, for the remainder'.[56]

He followed up this speech with instructions to External Affairs to draft a letter to the United Nations Secretary-General regarding the United Nations sponsorship of a refugee fund along the lines outlined in his proposals. By the end of 1968 the Irish position was that 'a permanent solution of the refugee problem is a *main factor* in the establishment of a durable peace in the Middle East'.[57] The following year an External Affairs memorandum on the Middle East highlighted a settlement of the refugee problem as one of three 'essential points' (together with the guaranteed freedom of communication and travel and the guarantee by the United Nations and the Great Powers against future aggression).[58]

However, Ireland attempted to avoid any support for the Palestinian refugees at the United Nations that could be interpreted as political partisanship. For example, in mid-December 1968 the Irish government rejected as 'unwise' a request by Turkey that Ireland become the only non-Muslim

---

[56] NAI 2001/43/872, statement by Mr Frank Aiken TD, Tánaiste and Minister for External Affairs of Ireland on the Question of Palestine Arab Refugees, in the Special Political Committee of the 22nd Session of the General Assembly of the United Nations, 14 Dec. 1967.

[57] NAI 2001/43/872, telegram, DEA to PMUN, 6 Dec. 1968.

[58] NAI 2001/43/102, memorandum on Irish policy in regard to the Middle East Situation, 16 May 1969.

co-sponsor of a draft resolution on the refugees.[59] Ireland also voted against Resolution 2535(XXIV) of 10 December 1969, which linked the Palestine refugee question to the 'inalienable rights of the Palestinians'. This draft resolution had been put forward during what Noel Dorr termed an 'exceptionally bitter' UNRWA debate.[60] And while Ireland did not publicly endorse the Israeli view that it was a 'one sided and harmful' development,[61] there was general agreement within the Irish United Nations delegation that Resolution 2535 was not only a conscious attempt by opponents of Israel to politicise the refugee issue, but that it was also tantamount to 'a call for the destruction of Israel'.[62]

In December 1970, Ireland chose to abstain on a similar draft resolution (A/SPC/L.198) again put forward during the Special Political Committee's UNRWA debate. Dermot Gallagher, Ireland's representative on this committee, was of the view that this draft resolution was not only 'on the lines' of Resolution 2535(XXIV) of the previous year but 'appears to be more explicit' than its predecessor. In particular, Gallagher believed that its first operative paragraph seemed to define 'inalienable rights as equal rights and self-determination' and thus it 'could be construed as being contrary to the right of Israel to exist'. This was even more the case when this first operative paragraph was combined with the second operative paragraph's call for 'full respect for inalienable rights of the Palestinian people is an indispensable element of justice and lasting peace'.[63]

As such, Gallagher recommended that Ireland refrain from supporting this 'highly political' proposal because 'support for it would be interpreted as having taken sides in the Arab-Israeli dispute ... in which we have constantly maintained a neutral stand'. He went even further and concluded with the view that an UNRWA debate was concerned with 'humanitarian' matters and as such was 'not a suitable forum for [the] introduction of political and biased resolutions'.[64]

The impact of EEC entry on Ireland's United Nations Middle East policy: 1973–78

By the time that Frank Aiken left office in 1969, Ireland's Middle East policy focused on four issues that envisaged a central role for the United Nations: settlement of the refugee problem; the withdrawal of Israeli forces to areas occupied before the 1967 war on the basis of Resolution 242; a peace treaty with firm guarantees from the United Nations, including a majority, if not

---

[59] NAI 2001/43/872, PMUN to DEA, 10 Dec. 1968 and DEA to PMUN, 11 Dec. 1968.
[60] NAI 2002/19/243, Dorr to McCann, 2 Dec. 1969.
[61] See statement to the General Assembly by Israeli Ambassador Tekoah, 10 Dec. 1969, *Israel Documents*, 1, p. 456.
[62] NAI 2002/19/243, Gallagher's memorandum on 7 Power A-A Draft A/SPC/L.198, 3 Dec. 1970.
[63] Ibid.
[64] Ibid.

all of the permanent members; and the internationalisation of the Old City of Jerusalem under direct United Nations control.[65]

Dr Patrick Hillery, Aiken's successor as minister, restated his predecessor's view that the Middle East conflict had to be tackled through United Nations channels.[66] However, Hillery was also well aware that following entry into the European Economic Community (EEC) in 1973, Ireland's Middle East policy would increasingly have to take place inside the Community as well as the United Nations. This was all the more so because after a period of false starts, these years saw an increased effort on the part of Community members to present a united foreign policy to the world. This objective had pre-occupied the Community at its Hague summit in December 1969. It had also led to the creation of the European Political Co-operation (EPC) process in 1970 in the hope of providing members with a framework through which they could consult on important foreign matters. As a former senior Irish diplomat put it 'a consequence, and corollary, of entry into the EEC' was involvement in the EPC.[67]

This was seen clearly during the October 1973 (Yom Kippur) War, which saw the invasion of Israel on its holiest day by the combined forces of Syria and Egypt, as the newly enlarged EEC attempted to coordinate its own Middle East policy and issued a declaration, which it termed its 'first contribution' to the 'search for a comprehensive solution'.[68] It was also evident in the attempt by Ireland and its EEC partners to develop a coherent Palestine policy over the following years and in Ireland's support for the establishment of the Euro-Arab Dialogue (EAD), a framework created by the 'Nine' in the aftermath of the 1973 war in the hope of improving links with the Arab world through the promotion of economic and cultural ties.[69]

The Department of Foreign Affairs, which External Affairs had been renamed in 1971, described the EAD as the 'most recent manifestation'[70] of European Political Co-operation and, at the General Assembly in September 1974, Foreign Minister Garret FitzGerald spoke very positively about the nascent EAD. The following February, at a foreign ministers' meeting in

---

[65] NAI 2001/43/102, memorandum on government policy in relation to the Middle East, 1970.

[66] Ibid., extract from speech delivered by Minister for External Affairs Dr Patrick Hillery to the General Assembly, 26 Sept. 1969. See also *Dáil Deb.*, vol. 245, col. 782, 19 Mar. 1970; NAI 2001/43/102, letter from External Affairs, on behalf of Minister for External Affairs Dr Patrick Hillery, to Joseph O'Beirne, 12 June 1970,. See also *Dáil Deb.*, vol. 246, col. 1812, 19 May 1970.

[67] See speech by Padraic MacKernan, at the 4th annual conference of the Irish National Committee for the Study of International Affairs, 20 Nov. 1981, reprinted as 'Ireland and European Political Co-operation', *Irish Studies in International Affairs*, 4 (1984), pp. 15–26, p. 16.

[68] Statement by European Community Foreign Ministers, 6 Nov. 1973, *Israel Documents*, 2, pp. 1064–5.

[69] For examples of the wide-ranging issues dealt with at these meetings, see Derek Hopwood (ed.), *Euro-Arab Dialogue: The Relations Between Two Cultures* (London, 1985).

[70] 'Irish Foreign Policy', *DFA Bulletin*, 857 (3 Dec. 1974), p. 7.

Dublin during the Irish presidency of the EEC, FitzGerald again emphasised the importance of the EAD.[71]

Despite this, Ireland still attached much importance to dealing with the Middle East conflict at the United Nations. On 14 October 1974, events took a far more serious turn when a Syrian-sponsored draft resolution calling for Palestine Liberation Organisation (PLO) participation in UNGA plenary meetings on the Palestine problem was adopted by 105 to four (with twenty abstaining). Israel dismissed this vote as 'illegal and not binding ... in any way' and the majority of EEC nations either voted against (Holland, Denmark, Belgium and Luxembourg) or abstained (the United Kingdom and Germany). However, Ireland, France and Italy voted in favour of this draft resolution. In response an Israeli foreign ministry statement expressed 'astonishment' that these three EEC member states had 'sided with the approach of the most extremist Arab states'. It also noted that the Irish vote had 'greatly dis-appointed' Israel, as it had been 'hoped' that Ireland would 'not lend ... support to an organisation of murderers, but would have preferred progress towards peace over the encouragement of Arab extremism'.[72]

The decision by Ireland, France and Italy to vote in favour of the above resolution highlighted the divergent attitudes within the Community on the subject of the PLO. Indeed, Germany and the United Kingdom had planned to vote against the resolution but decided to abstain so that the Community would not appear even more divided. But as FitzGerald noted in his autobiography, it also highlighted that in the company of France and Italy, Ireland had quickly emerged as a leading supporter of the Palestinian cause within the newly enlarged EEC.[73]

Ireland justified its vote on the Syrian draft resolution on the grounds that the Palestinian case deserved to be heard and because the PLO had the support of most of the Arab world. This latter part of the Irish defence was undoubtedly a reference to the decision of the Arab states to acknowledge the PLO as the sole legitimate representative of the Palestinian people at the Rabat Arab summit in October 1974. Nevertheless, the position that Ireland adopted at the General Assembly at this time was still quite radical. The Rabat summit had also introduced to the world the PLO's new phased strategy (first put forward in June 1974), whereby the Palestinians agreed to take whatever territory Israel offered to them as a springboard for further territorial gains until the 'complete liberation of Palestine' could be achieved.[74] However,

---

[71] 'A Just Equilibrium', text of address by the Minister for Foreign Affairs, Dr Garret FitzGerald TD, in the General Debate at the General Assembly, 25 Sept. 1974, Statements and Speeches, Department of Foreign Affairs, 1975; 'EEC Foreign Ministers in Dublin', *DFA Bulletin*, 861 (7 Mar. 1975), p. 2.

[72] Israeli Foreign Ministry statement on General Assembly Resolution 3210, 15 Oct. 1974, *Israel Documents*, 3, p. 104.

[73] Garret FitzGerald, *All in a Life* (London, 1991), p. 161.

[74] See PLO Phased Political Programme, Resolutions of the 12th Palestine National Council, 1–9 June 1974, reprinted in Aryeh Y. Yodfat and Yval Arnon-Ohanna (eds.), *PLO Strategy and Tactics* (New York, 1981), pp. 173–5.

Ireland did not endorse the PLO at every turn. For example, it refused to support any United Nations draft resolutions that would have given the PLO legal recognition on the same basis as a sovereign state and as such voted against two November 1974 draft Assembly resolutions 3236(XXIX) and 3237(XXIX). Respectively, these resolutions ratified the inalienable rights of the Palestinian people to self-determination, independence and the sovereignty of Palestine without even mentioning the existence of Israel and called for observer status at the United Nations for the PLO on the grounds that this was equivalent to granting the PLO 'legal recognition'.[75]

It is also worth noting that Ireland, in the company of all its EEC partners, voted against the 1975 General Assembly 'Zionism is a form of racism' resolution that marked the high point in international opposition to Israel's legitimacy up to that time.[76]

Irish participation in UNIFIL: 1978–2001

In 1978, after an absence of almost four years from United Nations Middle East peacekeeping, Irish troops comprising an infantry battalion, a communications section, an administrative company and staff officers based at headquarters in Naquara, departed for Lebanon as part of the newly established United Nations Interim Force in Lebanon (UNIFIL).[77] As Irish Permanent Representative to the United Nations, Paul Keating later explained in a speech to the Security Council that Ireland had agreed to participate in UNIFIL out of a sense of 'duty' to the United Nations and because it believed that the creation of UNIFIL offered an 'honourable solution to the entangled situation which had arisen'.[78]

UNIFIL was created by the Security Council in March 1978 in response to the first Israeli invasion of southern Lebanon (Operation Litani) of March of 1978, which had been initiated by Israel in an effort to neutralise the PLO threat emanating from an area of southern Lebanon that had come to be known as 'Fatahland' (after Fatah, the major constituent group in the PLO, which was headed by Yasser Arafat). The UNIFIL mandate had three essential

---

[75] Avi Beker, *The United Nations and Israel: From Recognition to Reprehension* (Lexington Mass., Toronto, 1988), p. 82.

[76] General Assembly Resolution 3379 (XXX) was passed on 10 Nov. 1975.

[77] For a more detailed study of the role of the Irish contingent see James Parker, 'UNIFIL and Peacekeeping: the defence forces' experience', *Irish Studies in International Affairs*, 2:2 (1986), pp. 63–7, p. 63.

[78] See meeting 2149 of the Security Council, 14 June 1979, *UNSCOR, 34th Year*, 7. See also Address to the 33rd General Assembly of the United Nations by Minister for Foreign Affairs Michael O'Kennedy, 28 Sept. 1978, *Statements and Speeches*, 7, 1978, DFA. The other troop contributing states were Fiji, Ghana, Netherlands, Nigeria, Norway, and Senegal. UNIFIL's total combined infantry and command staff was 5,898. Ireland contributed the second smallest infantry battalion after Senegal (577). See report of the Secretary-General on the United Nations Interim Force in Lebanon for the period 11 Dec. 1979 to 12 June 1980, document S/13994, 12 June 1980, *UNSCOR, 35th Year, Supplement April, May, June 1980*, p. 92.

elements: to confirm the withdrawal of Israeli forces from southern Lebanon; to restore international peace and security and to assist the government of Lebanon in regaining effective authority in the south.

In June 1978 Israeli forces officially withdrew from Lebanon but the raging civil war and the potential for instability on Lebanon's southern border with Israel continued to preoccupy the Security Council, which discussed the situation in south Lebanon eight times between January 1978 and June 1979. The Security Council decided not to withdraw the UNIFIL force and on 19 January 1979, and again on 14 June 1979, the Security Council extended UNIFIL's mandate for a further five months and then another six months. This marked the beginning of a process whereby the Security Council would renew the UNIFIL mandate at half yearly intervals until the summer of 2001 when the force was finally disbanded.

Almost from the start Irish participation in UNIFIL resulted in an immediate crisis in Irish-Israeli relations and tensions between the two countries on this issue were primarily played out at the United Nations. Indeed, this was seen most clearly following Ireland's election to temporary membership of the Security Council for a full two-year term beginning in January 1981.[79]

In the first weekend of June 1982 over 500 shells had landed in northern Israel and Ariel Sharon, the Israeli Minister of Defence, and Rafael Eitan, Chief of Staff of the Israeli Defence Forces, requested Cabinet approval for an operation inside Lebanon with the objective of placing Israeli population centres in Galilee beyond range of the terrorist fire. Variously termed the 'war of desperation' or the 'war of choice', Israel's invasion and subsequent entanglement in Lebanon would have a profound impact on an Israeli society divided over the war; on Lebanese society which was radicalised by the war and on the PLO, whose leadership was forced to take refuge in Tunisia and whose military infrastructure in Lebanon was destroyed.

When the Security Council convened on 5 June to deal with the crisis, Ireland voted in favour of a draft resolution that called for a practical way to force Israel to comply with demands that it withdraw from Lebanon. This draft resolution (which implied that Israel should be evicted by force) was not adopted but a less confrontational resolution calling for an immediate ceasefire, which Ireland also voted for, was adopted.[80]

Ireland also urged an immediate halt to the conflict and a ceasefire.[81] Indeed, Ireland's temporary membership of the Security Council and its status as a significant troop contributor to UNIFIL not only placed it in a unique position within Europe, but also gave it the opportunity and the

---

[79] It took its place along with Spain, Japan, Panama and Uganda which had also been elected to replace Portugal, Bangladesh, Jamaica, Norway and Zambia.

[80] Adopted as resolution 508 (1982) at Security Council meeting 2374, 5 June 1982, *UNSCOR, 37th Year*, p. 3.

[81] Ambassador Dorr, meeting 2374 of the Security Council, 5 June 1982, *UNSCOR, 37th Year*, pp. 3–4.

moral right to express its opposition to Israel's invasion in the most forthright terms.

On 1 August 1982, Israel mounted a large-scale offensive against PLO targets in Beirut. Thus, Lebanon continued to dominate the Security Council agenda during a month that saw Noel Dorr take the presidency of the Security Council for the second time (he had held this position for the first time in April 1981 when the Council was preoccupied with the situation in Namibia). During his time as Security Council president, Dorr drew attention to Israel's failure to comply with any of the seven Security Council resolutions passed on the invasion since early June.[82] He also explained that Ireland, in its role as a temporary member of the Security Council, had a 'duty' to uphold the Charter and as such, 'did not feel that the Council could simply accept that its decisions taken over a period of two months, should remain un-implemented while present fighting, destruction and serious loss of life on both sides continued'.[83] Thus, Dorr was instrumental in co-ordinating the Security Council's condemnation of Israel during August, which even saw Israel's steadfast ally the United States vote in favour of a resolution that demanded an Israeli ceasefire and called on the Jewish state to lift the blockade of Beirut and cooperate with the United Nations.[84]

Ghassan Tueni, Lebanon's ambassador to the United Nations praised Dorr's position towards the crisis during Ireland's spell on the Security Council: 'your country is a friend of my country and your valiant soldiers have been in Lebanon ever since the establishment of UNIFIL'.[85] The threat facing Ireland's UNIFIL contingent had been at the forefront of Irish foreign policy concerns at the United Nations following the 1982 Israeli invasion. Between 1981 and 1986 an Irish officer, Lieutenant General William Callaghan, commanded UNIFIL forces. By May 1985, out of 771 Irish military personnel serving overseas with the United Nations, 742 were on UNIFIL duty.[86]

Irish UNIFIL troops faced an increasingly tense and complex situation in Lebanon, especially as Israel's 1985 decision to set up a new security zone

---

[82] See, for example, his statements at meeting 2386 of the Security Council, 1 Aug. and meeting 2391 of 6 Aug. Apart from resolutions 508 (1982), of 5 June, 509 (1982) of 6 June and 512 (1982) of 19 June during these months the Security Council also passed Resolution 513 (1982) on 4 July that called for and end of the blockade of west Beirut and respect for civilian populations; resolution 515 (1982) of 29 July that demanded that Israel immediately lift the blockade; resolution 516 (1982) of 1 Aug. that called for an immediate ceasefire at a time of intense exchanges in Beirut and authorised the United Nations Secretary-General to deploy United Nations observers if requested; resolution 517 (1982), 4 Aug. that demanded an immediate ceasefire and that Israeli troops withdraw to previous positions.

[83] Statement by Ambassador Dorr, meeting 2391 of the Security Council, 6 Aug. 1982, *UNSCOR, 37th Year*, p. 9.

[84] See resolution 518 (1982) adopted at Security Council meeting 2392, 12 Aug. 1982, *UNSCOR, 37th Year*, p. 9.

[85] Ambassador Tueni at meeting 2386 of Security Council, 1 Aug. 1982, *UNSCOR, 37th Year*, p. 2

[86] *Dáil Deb.*, vol. 361, col. 1720, 12 Nov. 1985.

overlapped with part of the Irish UNIFIL sector. This resulted in increasing confrontations between Irish troops, the Israeli army and the pro-Israeli South Lebanese Army, as well as newly mobilised anti-Israeli groups such as the AMAL militia, the dominant Shi'ite group in south Lebanon, and the pro-Iranian Hizbollah (the Party of God).[87]

In May 2000, the Israeli army hastily vacated south Lebanon and re-deployed behind the international border. This withdrawal enabled Ireland to conclude its own long-time involvement in Lebanon and in mid-November 2001 the last Irish UNIFIL battalion handed over its duties to a Ghanaian contingent. Over the previous twenty-three years more than 38,100 Irish troops had served in Lebanon, forty-seven of whom had lost their lives. This contribution was celebrated in a ceremony and a 1,600 strong parade of United Nations veterans in Dublin in late November 2001, attended by President Mary McAleese and senior military and political figures.

The Irish contribution (and sacrifice) to UNIFIL had limited the spread of conflict in Lebanon and rightly earned the praise of Taoiseach Bertie Ahern, who described UNIFIL as a 'very distinguished and successful chapter in Ireland's record of United Nations service', and of Secretary-General Kofi Annan who summed up the Irish contribution to UNIFIL as 'outstanding'.[88] During its time in Lebanon the Irish force also provided significant humanitarian help to the civilian population caught up in the fighting. As President McAleese noted following her own visit to the Irish UNIFIL contingent in 1999: '[they] do more than just the job: they care about people, they care about their orphan children, they care about their social welfare, they bring a value system that speaks about the richness of the Irish people'.[89]

Gulf War I: 1990–91

On 2 August 1990 Iraq invaded Kuwait, her smaller, but far wealthier, neighbour. This action and the subsequent war between Iraq and an American-led international coalition has had profound implications for the contemporary Middle East up to the present day. For Ireland, the Iraqi invasion of Kuwait and the war that followed was of immediate concern for two primary reasons. At the time of the invasion there were an estimated fifty Irish nationals based in Kuwait as well as over three hundred in Iraq and following the invasion they, along with western nationals from twenty-one other countries, were refused permission to leave by the Iraqi authorities. Thus, the Irish government found itself facing a hostage crisis of significant magnitude. As Minister

---

[87] *Irish Times*, 8 Mar., 1 Apr. 1985, *Irish Independent*, 3 Apr. and 23 Apr. 1985.

[88] Speech by An Taoiseach, Bertie Ahern TD, at review of the last battalion to depart for service with UNIFIL, 9 Apr. 2001, Department of Taoiseach press release, Apr. 2001; Remarks by United Nations Secretary-General Annan, *UNIFIL 1978–2000: Stand Down Parade*, p. 4.

[89] Interview with An tUachtarán, Mary McAleese, *An Cosantóir*, May 1999, pp. 15–8, p. 16.

for Foreign Affairs Gerard Collins informed the Dáil, in an important and at times acrimonious debate on the Gulf crisis on 29 August 1990: 'the safety and welfare of our 350 or so citizens in Kuwait and Iraq has been, and will remain, the Government's first priority'.[90]

Indeed, while Ireland could not claim the largest number of citizens detained (that fell to the United Kingdom with 4,640 hostages), as Bobby Molloy, the Minister for Energy, told the Dáil during the same debate 'proportionately Ireland has more citizens held illegally against their will in Kuwait and Iraq than any other western nation'.[91] Nor was he exaggerating. During the month of August only six of the twenty-one western nations involved had more citizens held captive than Ireland's 350: France (530), Italy (402), Japan (508), the United Kingdom (4,640), the United States (3,580), and West Germany (740). By late September only Japan (352), France (350), the United Kingdom (1,430), the United States (1,130), and West Germany (444) had more held, while by early December only the two main members of the war coalition, the United Kingdom (1,168) and the United States (700), had more of their citizens under Iraqi control.[92]

Apart from this immediate humanitarian issue, the crisis, and in particular the economic sanctions put in place by the United Nations in the wake of the invasion, also impacted severely on Irish trade. By the late 1980s Iraq had developed into a crucial trading partner of Ireland. As a government minister explained to the Dáil in the wake of the invasion, since 1985 Iraq had been one of the 'three most important markets' in the region and in 1988 had been 'the most important market' to Ireland. Of particular importance was the Iraqi purchase of Irish beef, cattle and live animal exports. Indeed, in the second half of the 1980s Ireland sold Iraq between forty and fifty percent of its entire beef imports, accounting for IR£42.4 million of the IR£47.4 million worth of Irish goods exported to Iraq in 1989.[93] Indeed, over this time Iraq purchased up to ninety-three percent of Irish cattle and live animal exports to the Arab world.[94]

Despite the economic implications of isolating Iraq, the Irish government fully supported United Nations resolutions, including Resolution 678 of November 1990, which was designed to enable the international community to respond to the Iraqi occupation of Kuwait with armed force if necessary, without breaching Art. 2(4) of the United Nations Charter. It requested United Nations members to provide 'appropriate support' for military actions sanctioned by the Security Council. It did not oblige Ireland to take or refrain from any particular course of action, but there was an onus on all

[90] *Dáil Deb.*, vol. 401, col. 2305, 29 Aug. 1990.
[91] Ibid, col. 2379.
[92] See table of number of Westerners in Kuwait and Iraq in Lawrence Freedman and Efraim Karsh, *The Gulf Conflict: 1990–1991* (London, Boston, 1993), p. 250.
[93] *Dáil Deb.*, vol. 401, col. 2308, 29 Aug. 1990.
[94] Ibid. col. 2309.

member states of the United Nations to act in a way responsible with its membership of the international organisation.[95] The Irish government also supported the evolving programme of United Nations economic sanctions put in place against Saddam Hussein's regime over the course of the 1990s.

However, Ireland also supported the efforts of French president, François Mitterand, and his foreign minister, Roland Dumas, to use the United Nations platform to link Iraq's unconditional withdrawal from Kuwait to a resolution of the Israel-Palestine conflict. This culminated with a mid-January 1991 attempt by the French United Nations delegation to put forward a Security Council draft resolution stating that once a 'peaceful settlement' to the Kuwait crisis had been reached the Security Council would begin 'active participation' to achieve a settlement of the Palestinian problem by convening an international conference.[96]

The French failure to consult on this stance with its European partners irritated many governments within the European Union (EU). However, the Irish government welcomed these French attempts to use the United Nations to find a non-military solution. This was partly out of a desire for a peaceful conclusion to the crisis that would re-open a vital economic market; it was also due to the fact that the French call for the convening of an United Nations-sponsored international conference had long been a pillar of Ireland's Palestine policy and appealed to the Irish belief that a solution to the Palestine problem was the key to a general settlement in the region.[97]

9/11 and the 2003 invasion of Iraq

The al-Qaeda attacks on New York and Washington in September 2001 occurred at a time when Ireland was in the middle of a two-year term as a temporary member of the Security Council that had commenced in January 2001. In the wake of the attacks, Ireland voted with the other temporary and permanent members of the Security Council in favour of Resolutions 1368, which declared that the 9/11 attacks were a threat to international peace and security, and Resolution 1373 of 28 September 2001. These called on United Nations member states to introduce tough anti-terrorism measures and established a United Nations counter-terrorism committee to monitor both the implementation of resolution 1373 and the wider contribution of member states to the war on terror.

Ireland's role at the United Nations at this time was hugely significant because it took over the presidency of the Security Council for a one-month period on 1 October 2001. In a speech to the General Assembly to mark the beginning of its Security Council presidency Minister for Foreign Affairs

---

[95] See Liz Heffernan and Anthony Whelan, 'Ireland, the United Nations and the Gulf Conflict: Legal Aspects', *Irish Studies in International Affairs*, 3: 3 (1991), pp. 115–45 esp. p. 115 and pp. 126–8.

[96] Freedman and Karsh, *The Gulf Conflict*, p. 272.

[97] Also see the *Irish Times* editorial 'Politics in War', 21 Jan. 1991.

Brian Cowen argued that 'action not words' was called for in the battle to defeat the 'monster of international terrorism' and promised that, though not a member of any military alliance, Ireland 'would not be neutral in the battle ahead'.[98]

On 7 October, less than one week after the commencement of the Irish Security Council presidency, the United States began its military action in Afghanistan intended to capture or kill Osama bin Laden, neutralise Afghanistan as a base of operations for terrorists and in the words of Taoiseach Bertie Ahern, to 'eliminate this [al Qaeda] scourge'.[99]

Notably the Taoiseach used his visit to the United States in early November 2001 to lend Irish support to the Bush administration's campaign in Afghanistan. He was particularly vocal during a speech at the Forum of Public Affairs at the Kennedy School of Government at Harvard University, as well as in a meeting with President Bush at the White House.

On both occasions he set out the Irish government's view that the United States was 'quite entitled' to bomb Afghanistan under both Article 51 of the United Nations charter (that guarantees members a right to self-defence), and Security Council Resolution 1368 which, he argued, not only covered action in Afghanistan, but also action wherever the United States could provide evidence that terrorists were operating.[100]

However, Ireland also used its position on the Security Council to urge the Bush administration to build on the military victory in Afghanistan as an opportunity to reverse the view (in the words of Brian Cowen) of 'observers and commentators that the United States was heading into an era of increased unilateralism'.[101] As Richard Ryan, Ireland's Ambassador to the United Nations, put it in January 2002, 9/11 was 'not only an attack on the United States', but on the 'entire international community and the values we cherish'. As such, he continued, the United Nations should play the 'pivotal role' in the war against terror.[102]

Indeed, the end of the military phase of the Afghan campaign provided an opportunity for the Irish government to underline its support for what Cowen would later call the 'system of collective global security, founded upon the United Nations and the requirements of international law'.[103]

This was especially true regarding the Bush administration's attitude to Iraq. In late 2002, in its first statement at the Security Council on the Iraq

[98] Deaglán de Bréadún, 'Cowen decries terror attacks', *Irish Times*, 3 Oct. 2001 and 'Building Consensus', *Irish Times*, 3 Oct. 2001.

[99] Patrick Smyth, 'Harvard hears Ahern's support for Trimble', *Irish Times*, 9 Nov. 2001.

[100] Ibid.

[101] 'The Crisis of 2001–Values and Interests in the International System', Minister for Foreign Affairs, Brian Cowen, to the 2001 Conference of the Royal Irish Academy National Committee for the Study of International Affairs, 16 Nov. 2001, DFA press release, 16 Nov. 2001, http://foreignaffairs.gov.ie/Press_Releases/20011116/906.htm.

[102] Deaglán de Bréadún, 'Ireland emphasises causes of terrorism', *Irish Times*, 21 Jan. 2002.

[103] Brian Cowen, 'Only collective global security can beat terrorists', *Irish Times*, 11 Sept. 2002.

crisis, the government took a position that was widely interpreted as supporting the Franco-German approach, which opposed the use of military force without a United Nations mandate. The following month, in the wake of the United States decision to meet some French requirements in the wording of a draft resolution, Ireland in the company of all its Security Council partners (except Syria) voted in favour of Security Council Resolution 1441 that required Iraq to submit to aggressive new weapons inspections, but did not contain specific authorisation for the use of military force without a second resolution. In a speech before the National Committee on American Foreign Policy in New York Cowen continued to insist that 'it was a matter of fundamental importance that the Security Council's role be maintained in the engagement of the international community with Iraq'.[104]

This was a popular approach at home. An *Irish Times*/MRBI poll published at the beginning of October 2002 had sixty-eight percent of respondents opposed to war without a United Nations endorsement, with fifty-nine percent opposed to Ireland supporting military action that had United Nations authority. Only twenty-two percent of those polled supported military intervention.[105] Certainly, it appeared that the government was taking note of domestic opinion and moving towards the view that any war in Iraq lacking Security Council authorisation was illegal in international law. For example, during this period, *The New Republic*, an influential American weekly political magazine, placed 'neutral Ireland' in the company of 'pacifist New Zealand [and] ambivalent Canada' as one of three English-speaking countries who could not be counted on to support a war in Iraq.[106]

On 20 March 2003 Taoiseach Ahern explained that 'in the absence of an agreed further resolution by the Security Council we cannot participate in the coalition ... military action', however unlike many other European leaders at this time he refused to condemn the Anglo-American decision to invade Iraq and added '[we do however] stop short of taking unprecedented and futile gestures against friendly countries with whom we share deep bonds of democratic values and of political as well as historic ties'.[107]

Despite the refusal to support, or contribute to, a military invasion of Iraq without specific Security Council permission for such an action, from September 2001, just nine days after the Security Council passed resolution 1368 declaring the 9/11 attacks a threat to international peace and security, until the present time, the Irish government has provided over-flight, land-

---

[104] 'Peace and Security: Ireland and the United Nations', address by Minister for Foreign Affairs, Brian Cowen TD, to the National Committee on American Foreign Policy, New York, DFA press release, 25 Nov. 2002, http://foreignaffairs.gov.ie/Press_Releases/20021125/1068.htm.

[105] Patrick Smyth, 'Cabinet Faced with public hostility to war', *Irish Times*, 1 Oct. 2002.

[106] Jacob T. Levy, 'Down but Not Out', *The New Republic Online*, 26 Mar. 2002, www.tnr.com

[107] Bertie Ahern, 'Saddam, not Bush or Blair, is responsible for the crisis', *Irish Independent*, 20 Mar. 2003.

ing and refuelling rights to United States aircraft at Shannon airport. Since that time the government has continually justified the decision on the grounds that Security Council Resolution 1368 made such Irish support both 'appropriate and legal'.[108]

Conclusion

In April 2005, Cowen's successor as Minister for Foreign Affairs, Dermot Ahern, was appointed Special Envoy for United Nations Reform by Kofi Annan. It is fitting that Ahern takes up this post in the year that Ireland celebrates its fiftieth anniversary of United Nations membership. Among the many challenges that Ahern will have to face in this capacity is convincing both Israel and the Palestinians that the proposed reforms will not be detrimental to their interests. It can be argued that the Irish government's efforts not only since 9/11, but since 1955, to promote and develop the United Nations legitimacy and status as a key player in the Middle East has made the Irish foreign minister a worthy choice for this important task.

---

[108] Brian Cowen, 'It is right for Ireland to help a friend in need', *Irish Times*, 26 Sept. 2001.

Chapter Four

UNOGIL and UNTSO: 1958–60. The pre-Congo origins of Ireland's involvement in United Nations peacekeeping

RICHARD E. M. HEASLIP

Introduction

Writing in 1984 about peacekeeping operations, former Irish ambassador to the United Nations, Con Cremin, emphasised that although not formally listed in the United Nations Charter they have become a well-known feature of the United Nations system. He continued that their purpose was to defuse potentially dangerous conflict situations and he divided them into two broad categories, observer missions (unarmed) and those requiring the presence of multinational military contingents (armed) of varying size; both being based on United Nations Security Council resolutions.[1] In the foreword to Joseph Skelly's *Irish diplomacy at the United Nations*, Mary Robinson, then President of Ireland and ex officio Commander-in-Chief of the Irish Defence Forces, wrote that the book covered the genesis of Ireland's United Nations peacekeeping tradition with the contribution of several thousand troops to United Nations operations in the Congo, the Sinai, and Cyprus.[2] For both authors, Ireland's involvement with and contribution to United Nations peacekeeping is dated from the involvement of the Defence Forces in the Congo from 1960. There is little mention of involvement in two previous missions: United Nations Observation Group in Lebanon (UNOGIL) in 1958 and from late 1958 onwards United Nations Truce Supervision Organisation (UNTSO). Skelly merely explained that UNOGIL was a non-combative mission which required no change to existing Irish

---

[1] Con Cremin, 'United Nations Peacekeeping Operations: An Irish initiative 1961–1968', *Irish Studies in International Affairs*, 1:4 (1984), pp. 79–81, p. 79.

[2] Joseph M. Skelly, *Irish Diplomacy at the United Nations 1945–1965: National interests and international order* (Dublin, 1997), p. 5.

law.[3] Brigadier General P.D. Hogan, who served in UNOGIL, wrote in 1983, that even the officers in UNOGIL were not the first from the Defence Forces to perform international military observer duties on behalf of the state. He was referring to Captain Seamus McCall, who served as an observer for the League of Nations in the Spanish Civil War in the thirties.[4] However, regardless of how the Defence Forces international military observer duties started, the fact is that Ireland, in pursuance of its foreign policy, has committed itself to international peacekeeping and is particularly proud of the service of its Defence Forces personnel on United Nations missions which has continued uninterrupted from June 1958 to the present. According to P.D. Hogan, the fifty officers who served with UNOGIL in 1958 were blazing a trail which has since been followed by thousands of Irish soldiers.[5] In his view Ireland in the late 1950s was looking for a new role in the world and found this through United Nations membership. He argued that in its first steps in peacekeeping, the Defence Forces were a willing servant of the state, in tune with national feeling, and that from this starting point a strong tradition of international service was established.[6]

The professionalism, decisiveness, and foresight of senior soldiers, civil servants and diplomats of that time were instrumental in fashioning Ireland's response and commitment to United Nations peace-keeping initiatives from 1958 to 1960. These men included the often overlooked members of the Irish Permanent Mission at United Nations (PMUN) in New York, where Frederick H. Boland was ambassador, those in Dublin at the Department of External Affairs, where Con Cremin was secretary, and their Department of Defence colleagues, together with the military staffs at Defence Forces Headquarters and in particular, the Defence Forces officers who by volunteering for United

---

[3] Skelly, *United Nations*, p. 270. This observation is open to question in that there was no reference to United Nations service in Irish legislation until the hurried publication of the Defence Forces Amendment Act (No 2) 1960 which referred inter alia to the requirement for Dáil approval for the dispatch of greater than twelve unarmed members of the Defence Forces on United Nations duty. This leaves one to wonder at the legal issues associated with the deployment of the fifty Defence Forces officers to UNOGIL two years previously.

[4] P.D. Hogan, 'UNOGIL-Silver Jubilee, 1958–83 (Not so much a report, more a personal memoir)', *An Cosantóir*, (June, 1983), pp. 170–4, p. 170. Research by the author on O/5447, Captain Seamus McCall shows he had World War One service in the British Army and later saw service in the War of Independence and the Civil War (Anti-Treaty). After the Civil War he worked as a journalist with the *Garda Review* and the *Irish Press* and represented the *Irish Press* at an international media convention in Argentina in the early 1930s. Sometime after the outbreak of the Spanish Civil War in 1936 and the subsequent deployment of a League of Nations border monitoring agency, McCall was appointed as the Irish Representative on the League of Nations Land Control Scheme for Non-Intervention in Spain. In the course of this service, he functioned at the rank of Colonel and held the appointment of Chief of Staff/Chief Observing Officer, Ariege – Le Perthus Sector, Spanish Frontier, International Spanish Frontier Committee for Non-Intervention in Spain, until that mission was disbanded. Thereafter he spent time in England and returned to join the Defence Forces in Sept. 1940 when, following intervention by Frank Aiken, he served as a captain in G2 (Intelligence) Branch.

[5] A list of those who served in UNOGIL in 1958 is included as an annex to this chapter.

[6] Hogan, 'UNOGIL', p. 170.

Nations service, took that first tentative step into the unknown in June 1958.[7] This chapter outlines and assesses the pioneering work of these Irish officers in UNOGIL and UNTSO. Popular and academic opinion have both undervalued and even ignored the Irish contribution to UNOGIL (Lebanon) and to UNTSO (Israel). This dominant perspective has failed to appreciate the importance of the two missions as the origins of Ireland's involvement in United Nations peacekeeping. Through Irish involvement in these two missions there was a direct connection to the more widely remembered Irish participation in the Congo operation (ONUC), as the Irish involvement in Lebanon and Israel gave a handful of young officers experience in peacekeeping and an introduction to international military operations which would prove vital in ONUC. The challenge of working in multinational staffs in a complex international operational environment was met with confidence by each of those Irish officers. By doing so they validated the product of the officer career training and education programme conducted by the Defence Forces in the Military College. This successful endorsement of Defence Forces' officer training at all levels paved the way for the confident decision by Defence Forces Headquarters to take another step into the unknown when Ireland received the request to deploy armed infantry units for peacekeeping operations in the Congo. Ireland as a state was shedding its isolation from the international stage by its increasing engagement in United Nations issues and in the process the Defence Forces became an instrument of national foreign policy.

The most significant figure, indeed Ireland's pathfinder in this new dimension to its foreign policy, was Lieutenant Colonel Justin J.G.P.J. McCarthy. He was born in Kilburn, Middlesex, England on 15 April 1914. He started his secondary education in Ireland as a student in Clongowes Wood College, County Kildare, but after one term he returned to England and completed his education there.[8] In 1932 he joined the Defence Forces as a cadet in the 6th Cadet Class and his address on enlistment was recorded as Roughan, Kilnaboy, County Clare. Following service as a junior officer (2nd

---

[7] In June 1958 the Secretary of the Department of Defence was Hugh C. Brady who was appointed on 31 Mar. 1958 to replace Lt. Gen. (Retd.) Peadar MacMahon who held the appointment since the Department of Defence was established as a separate department in 1927. MacMahon who had previously served as Defence Forces Chief of Staff was a formative influence on the department's structure and modus operandi. National Archives of Ireland (hereafter NAI), Department of Foreign Affairs (hereafter DFA) Permanent Mission to the United Nations, New York (hereafter PMUN) 185PK/5 vol. 1 contains correspondence dated 17 Dec. 1956 from MacMahon in Defence to Murphy at Iveagh House and onward to Boland in New York showing that MacMahon had initiated inquiries 'on instructions of our Minister' suggesting Irish interest in the newly emerging concept of 'United Nations International Force such as that at present being sent to Egypt'.

[8] He was enrolled in Clongowes in 1926 and after three months he returned to Britain where he attended Wellbury, Hitchin, Hertfordshire (1926–8) and Beaumont, Windsor (1928–31). Military Archives, Cathal Brugha Barracks, Dublin (hereafter MA), Biographical Notes (extracts from personal file) 0/4530, Colonel Justin McCarthy and information from Archivist Clongowes Wood College, refer.

Lieutenant, 1st Lieutenant, and Captain), McCarthy was promoted to the rank of Commandant in 1942 and to Lieutenant Colonel in March 1945, retaining command of the 22nd Infantry Battalion for a further two years until 1947. The speed of this promotion to senior rank was due to a combination of the rapid expansion of the Defence Forces during the Emergency (1939–45) and McCarthy's personal ability. In 1947 he was posted to the Military College to the Command and Staff School where he served until 1949 when he was posted to Defence Forces Headquarters. By 1958 he was Executive Officer in the Plans and Operations Section, Chief of Staff's Branch.[9]

McCarthy left the Plans and Operations Section to lead the first contingent of Defence Forces personnel deployed outside the country on foreign service. The first element of this contingent of fifty officers was dispatched on 28 June 1958 in response to the first request to Dublin from United Nations Secretary-General Dag Hammarskjöld, for Irish involvement with the mission in Lebanon.[10] McCarthy's involvement with UNOGIL would see him appointed deputy to the chief of that mission and then to a senior staff appointment with UNTSO when UNOGIL concluded. From UNTSO, without returning home to Ireland, he deployed on a third mission to the Congo for service with ONUC. In this mission he served at UNOC Headquarters in Leopoldville, where he was killed in the course of his duties in a car accident in 1960. This remarkable record of overseas military service with three United Nations missions in two years is unique for its time and equally remarkable is the fact that McCarthy's pathfinding role and that of his Irish UNOGIL colleagues have all too often been overlooked, if not forgotten, even within the Defence Forces.[11]

Yet for those who served with McCarthy, such as Colonel Jim Croke, McCarthy was a very 'anglofied' fellow national, a consummate professional and the epitome of a distinguished senior officer holding the second most senior appointment in Lebanon.[12] During his tour of duty in UNOGIL

---

[9] The Plans and Operations section of Defence Forces Headquarters reported through the Director of Plans and Operations (Colonel) directly to the Chief of Staff. In effect this was the primary military staff section dealing with all aspects of military operations and activities being performed by or planned for the Defence Forces.

[10] MA, 'Biographical Notes Officer Casualties on Overseas Service'. See notes prepared by the Officers Records Section in respect of Colonel McCarthy.

[11] In 2001 the Defence Forces withdrew the infantry battalion from the United Nations Interim Force in Lebanon (UNIFIL) where it had served since 1978. In the special ceremony to commemorate this withdrawal from Lebanon and the casualties from all overseas missions, the Defence Forces held a special formal military parade in Dublin. In forty-three years of United Nations service, excluding the departing parade of the first battalion for UNOC and the sombre military funeral for the victims of the Niemba Ambush, this was the first and only formal military parade with full state ceremonial held in Ireland's capital city with a specific United Nations commemorative theme. To the disappointment of some UNOGIL veterans and that of the families of deceased former Irish UNOGIL UNMOs, they were not included in any aspect of this ceremony. In their opinion, this omission from such a historic military ceremonial event overlooked the contribution of the Irish UNOGIL UNMOs to the first deployment of Defence Forces to Lebanon.

[12] Croke, interview with the author, Dublin, 16 Mar. 2005.

Colonel Croke served for a time as a Duty Officer at UNOGIL Headquarters where he worked in very close contact with Colonel McCarthy. According to Croke, the efficiency and effectiveness of this multinational headquarters reflected in large measure the attention to detail and staff organisation instigated by McCarthy. Croke was particularly impressed with McCarthy's ability, *modus operandi* and professional standards as an international Chief of Staff. Additionally, Croke noted the high regard in which all at UNOGIL Headquarters held McCarthy.

The origins of UNOGIL

UNOGIL had its origins in the armed rebellion which broke out in Lebanon in May 1958 when President Camille Chamoun, a Maronite Christian, constitutionally restricted to a single six-year term, declared his intention to amend the constitution so that he could seek re-election. Disturbances by Muslims in Tripoli soon spread to Beirut and civil war threatened. The deteriorating situation in Lebanon was reported on by the Honorary Irish Consul in Beirut, Sir Desmond Cochrane, in a report to Dr Eoin MacWhite at External Affairs in Dublin. This report dated May 1958 also correctly forecast the resulting inter-communal violence.[13] Lebanon's government alleged that support for a civil war was coming from the United Arab Republic[14] (UAR) and requested support from the United Nations Security Council. Following some delay, on 11 June the Security Council adopted resolution UNSCR 128 (1958), which authorised the urgent dispatch of an 'observer group' to Lebanon in order to 'ensure that there is no illegal infiltration of personnel or supply of arms or other matériel across the Lebanese borders'. This group became known as the United Nations Observer Group in Lebanon, or UNOGIL. UNTSO, in existence since 1948 along the armistice lines between the fledgling state of Israel and its Arab neighbours to oversee the Israel/Arab problem, immediately dispatched a number of United Nations Military Observers (UNMOs) to Beirut. In this way the UNOGIL mission was established on 12 June 1958 with Major General Odd Bull of the Norwegian Air Force as its Chief of Staff.[15] In broad terms, the initial concept of operations for this mission was to establish a network of manned observation and patrol locations along Lebanon's borders with Syria to observe and report on any illegal infiltration of personnel and supply of arms across that border into Lebanon.[16]

---

[13] See NAI DFA 305/329/1.

[14] Egypt and Syria functioned as the UAR from 1958 to 1961.

[15] United Nations Website: www.un.org/Depts/dpko/co_mission/unogil.htm.

[16] NAI DFA 305/329/1 refers. On 16 June 1958 Eamon Kennedy, Chargé d'Affaires at PMUN, submitted an excellent brief and assessment to Iveagh House on the modus operandi and difficulties of those operating as UNMOs with UNOGIL. This information and that of the earlier May report from Honorary Consul Sir Desmond Cochrane was consigned to the 'Political Situation in Lebanon' file in Iveagh House and thereafter appears to have been completely overlooked when detailed information on the situation in Lebanon was subsequently required.

Irish involvement requested: the diplomatic and military response

The increasing tempo of the UNOGIL mission had little immediate impact on the routine of diplomats at the Irish Permanent Mission to the United Nations in New York. Then on 23 June 1958, a fortnight after the initial Security Council resolution on the situation in Lebanon, a flurry of cables were exchanged between the PMUN and Iveagh House over possible Irish involvement in the operation. This followed from a direct request from the Secretary-General Hammarskjöld for Irish participation in this mission. The Secretary-General's office inquired by telephone whether Ireland could provide five officers at Major (Commandant)/Captain rank. A coded cable to this effect using American Cable and Radio System was dispatched immediately to Iveagh House by PMUN at 11.59 hours on 23 June as follow:

> MOST URGENT FOR SECRETARY GENERAL'S OFFICE HAS INQUIRED TODAY ON TELEPHONE IF WE COULD URGENTLY PROVIDE FIVE OFFICERS OF QUOTE MAJOR OR CAPTAIN RANK UNQUOTE TO JOIN UN OBSERVATION TEAM IN LEBANON STOP WILL CABLE FURTHER DETAILS AFTER VISIT HEADQUARTERS THIS AFTERNOON
>
> UNEIREANN

This request was clarified later that afternoon with the urgency of the situation quite apparent in that the requirement stated the absolute necessity to deploy the officers to Beirut four days later on 27 June. The prevailing emergency and the unpredictable nature of the proposed deployment were also apparent in that although nine countries (Burma, Canada, Finland, India, Italy, Netherlands, Norway, Sweden and Peru) had committed UNMOs, there were no terms of reference for the nature of these duties or the duration of the mission. The cable urged an immediate response on the issue from Ireland, strongly recommending a favourable reply. Clarification of the terms of reference and service was eventually received and included in a third cable, providing guidance on the preferred personal skills, experience and age (25–45 years) of prospective officer observers. The cable also addressed the matter of discipline, with 'normal discipline of own national service' a matter for national authorities except for matters connected to mission duties which would be the prerogative of United Nation's Secretary-General or the senior officer designated by him. Ominously, the final condition allowed for a provision whereby 'in the event of death or total disability' the United Nations would provide $15,000 with corresponding compensation for partial disability.[17] This first rush of cables was followed by an explanatory letter to Dublin which again noted the urgency of the situation. Of particular interest is the final paragraph, which stated that

---

[17] NAI DFA PMUN, 222/13/1, cables from PMUN to External Affairs, 23 June 1958.

we, for our part, would like to express the hope that this opportunity to participate in a useful and practical task of United Nations in a vital area for world peace will not be missed. This is the first time that Ireland's participation in a joint UN team has been requested by the Organisation. It would seem fair to say that our successful participation would open the door to sharing in further efforts of this kind for which our position in the organisation is admirably suited.[18]

The correspondence on this matter was initiated by Eamon Kennedy, *Chargé d'Affaires* at PMUN. It is noteworthy that in this historic first request for military participation in a United Nations mission there was no contribution from Boland, Ireland's Ambassador to the United Nations. Kennedy, reacting to the urgency of the request and the necessity for prompt action, accurately gauged the importance of the request from the Secretary-General and realised the opportunity it presented to Ireland to take an active part in the newly evolving concept of peace-keeping.[19] The prompt positive reply requested by Kennedy's code cables was dispatched in clear cable from Iveagh House at 12.08 hours on 24 June:

PLEASE INFORM SECRETARY GENERAL GOVERNMENT AGREEABLE IN PRINCIPLE STOP DETAILS BEING SETTLED AND WILL WIRE LATER STOP REQUEST NO PUBLICITY UNTIL DETAILS SETTLED.[20]

The speed of this response suggests that, given the time differences between Dublin and New York, the government handled the matter in a most expeditious manner. The first cable from PMUN was dispatched at 11.59 local time New York Monday 23 June which means that it arrived at 18.00 hours local time in Dublin. The response was dispatched from Dublin eighteen hours later at 12.08 hours on 24 June. During this eighteen hour period,

---

[18] Ibid., PMUN to External Affairs (confidential), 23 June 1958.

[19] PMUN were very proactive on the possibility of Ireland's involvement in United Nations peace-keeping initiatives from a very early date. It is contended here that this was most probably prompted originally by correspondence from MacMahon (Defence) to Boland (PMUN) dated 20 Nov. 1956 which itself was based on the Minister for Defence's interest in the newly emerging concept of a United Nations Emergency Force (UNEF), then in the throes of initial organisation and deployment along the Gaza strip, and the legal issues associated with the possibility of Irish participation in such a force (NAI DFA PMUN 185 PK/5 vol. 1 refers). In July 1957 the opportunity to do so moved one step closer when PMUN, addressing the possibility of Indonesia's withdrawal from UNEF, speculated on the possibility of Ireland's participation as their replacement in UNEF. Guidance under strict confidential cover was sought from Dublin on this matter and Conor Cruise O'Brien, then handling this desk, sought inputs from the respective Departments of External Affairs and Defence. Defence's assessment, which included significant input by the military side, referred to a range of issues inhibiting the possibility of such participation including the necessity for amendments to the Defence Act and the poor strengths within the Defence Forces. NAI DFA 305/173/1 Pt1, United Nations Emergency International Force File with enclosure 'Memorandum for Government dated 27 Aug. 1957' refers.

[20] NAI DFA PMUN, 222/13/1, External Affairs to PMUN (clear cable), 12.08 24 June 1958.

fifteen hours of which were outside normal office hours, an entire spectrum of national decision making was activated. This included the processing of the request at first hand on receipt in External Affairs and its onward passage via established channels to the appropriate decision making authority in government, thereafter following agreement to participate, the Defence Forces Chief of Staff was instructed to provide the personnel, and finally a positive response was dispatched to PMUN.[21] The government decision must have been made overnight and most probably included input by Kevin Boland, the Minister for Defence, advised by his department and the Chief of Staff of the Defence Forces, Major General P.A. (Pat) Mulcahy. The speed at which decisions were taken links in with the sentiments expressed in the last paragraph of Kennedy's letter as part of the emerging national policy of greater involvement with the United Nations.

Selection of officers

The military authorities reacted very quickly and, guided by the terms of reference as received from New York, short listed twelve suitable officers for service in Lebanon. They then issued orders at midday on 24 June 1958 through the military chain of command for those officers to report to Defence Forces Headquarters at 10.00 hours the following day, 25 June 1958. In compliance with the strictures regarding publicity imposed by the government, and included in the clear response cable dispatched at 12.08 hours 24 June 1958 from External Affairs, the reason behind the direction to report to Defence Forces Headquarters was not communicated to the nominated officers or other military staffs. All matters regarding the short listing of personnel were conducted, according to those involved, on a very limited 'need to know' basis within the personnel branch of the Defence Forces Headquarters, i.e. Adjutant General's Branch. The Adjutant General was the head of this personnel branch which also incorporated the Officers Records Section, the repository of all officer personal files. In line with

---

[21] Government Minutes (NAI G3/24, Minutes of 8th Government, vol. 2, 11 Apr. 1958 to 16 June 1959) and Government Cabinet Minutes (NAI CAB 2/19, 8th Government, Cabinet Minutes, vol. 2, 6 June 1958 to 19 June 1959) both record a meeting for 24 June 1958, with the entire Cabinet present (except the Minister for Posts and Telegraphs), but in neither record is there any mention of a decision on involvement in UNOGIL. A search of the relevant section of the Aiken Archives at University College Dublin (Aiken Papers Section K Minister for External Affairs P104 vol. 7 (pp. 1348–1658) vol. 8 (pp. 1659–1908)) also failed to find any reference to this historic decision. However, in NAI DT CAB2/18 dated 21 Mar. 1958 Government decision S7359F is recorded regarding proposals for amendments to Defence Act 1954 facilitating service with United Nations forces which suggests that at a much earlier stage the issue of a possible positive contribution by the Defence Forces to United Nations forces was agreed in principle if not in fact. From author's research of NAI DFA 305/173/1 Pt1 and NAI DFA PMUN 185PK/5 vol. 1 it is postulated that this decision was made sometime between Nov. 1956 (See MacMahon (Defence) to Murphy (External Affairs)/Boland (PMUN) correspondence), and Sept. 1957 (Memorandum for Government) and acted on when the opportunity of UNOGIL participation was presented.

normal service practice of the time the short-listing of suitable personnel was the responsibility of this branch, acting on the instructions of the Chief of Staff. The task on this occasion was to select officers who were considered the most suitable for nomination against the United Nations criteria, bearing in mind that the request had sought experienced officers in the twenty-five to forty-five age bracket, of Major or Captain rank, with experience in unit command and as staff officers.[22]

When the list was finally approved by the Adjutant General those to be considered were notified by their respective Command Headquarters. In this manner twelve officers were notified to report to Adjutant General's Branch at Defence Forces Headquarters Dublin at 10.00 hours on 25 June. According to Colonel Patrick Lavelle, then a Cavalry Corps Captain serving in the Cavalry School Plunkett Barracks on the Curragh, he was contacted at 15.00 hours on 24 June 1958 by his Headquarters and directed to report to the Adjutant General's Office the following morning. He received no information as to the reason behind this order and noted with considerable relief the following morning at Defence Forces Headquarters that he was one of eleven officers all of whom were equally mystified as to the reason for their presence there. Within the military, being summoned to Defence Forces Headquarters in a peremptory manner without explanation and at very short notice is unusual. In fact, adding the Adjutant General's Office to this summons had all sorts of ominous connotations of a disciplinary dimension for this group of officers. For the Defence Forces of the time the general operational priority was running the Internment Camp on the Curragh and an 'Aid to Civil Power' involvement against an active IRA threat. In these circumstances, there is little wonder that those ordered to Dublin were puzzled as to why they were called.

At the appointed time the assembled group was addressed by the Chief of Staff, Major General Mulcahy, and the Adjutant General, Colonel P.J. (Pye) Hally, who informed them that the government had favourably responded to a request from Hammarskjöld to provide unarmed observers as a matter of urgency to help man the newly established UNOGIL.[23] The assembled officers were informed that in order to be considered for selection each officer must offer himself as a volunteer. Due to the urgency of the situation no time could be allowed to consult with wives or families, obliging the officers to make the decision there and then. In Lavelle's terms 'not unnaturally, it transpired that all present were volunteers' but, much to the regret of all present, [the] Chief of Staff informed them that only four would be selected.[24] Lieutenant Colonel McCarthy had already been selected by the military authorities to

---

[22] The UNOGIL terms of reference from the UN mentioned combat experience as being desirable. Fortunately from an Irish perspective given the service experience of the Defence Forces this requirement was not mandatory, otherwise it would have excluded participation by any Irish officers.

[23] Lavelle, Patrick, 'UNOGIL-Silver Jubilee, 1958–83', *An Cosantóir*, June 1983, pp. 189–93, p. 189.

[24] Ibid., p. 189.

lead the Irish observers. McCarthy's nomination to lead the group was an early decision and is apparent from the correspondence at PMUN where, despite the United Nations request for Majors and Captains, the Irish representatives were directed from the outset to request the inclusion of this Lieutenant Colonel 'with excellent French' to lead the Irish group with the acknowledgment that 'this officer is prepared to serve under an officer of equal rank'.[25] Those joining Lieutenant Colonel McCarthy (Operations Branch, Defence Forces Headquarters) were: Commandants Malachi Higgins (Air Corps, Baldonnell), Gerard Coughlan (Corps of Engineers, Eastern Command), Captains Patrick Lavelle (Cavalry Corps, Curragh) and Rory Henderson (Infantry Corps, Eastern Command).[26]

The selection of Lieutenant Colonel McCarthy to head the group being dispatched on this mission suggests that he was particularly well thought of by the military authorities. In the first instance there was a national military requirement for a ranking senior officer within the group and considering McCarthy's curriculum vitae it is apparent that his selection for this role was easily made.[27] His appointment prior to selection for UNOGIL was as Executive Officer in the Plans and Operations Branch. This last job was a very senior appointment and one with a significant ex officio input into operational considerations for any overseas deployment. Of special note too is that McCarthy had completed the Command and Staff Course at the British Army's Staff College at Camberley in England, in itself an indication of being held in high regard by the Chief of Staff and other senior figures, given that the attendance of Defence Force officers on this course has been restricted to a very select few with special potential.[28] Significantly for this mission and, most unusually for an officer of his rank at that time, McCarthy had excellent French. Colonel Jim Croke, then a young lieutenant, who later served with McCarthy as a Staff Officer in UNOGIL Headquarters in Beirut,

---

[25] See NAI DFA PMUN, 222/13/1, External Affairs to PMUN (code cable), 24 June 1958, for details. The nomination of a Lieutenant Colonel in effect gave a proper formal rank structure to the five-man group, vesting command authority in the undisputed senior ranking officer within the group. By doing so the military authorities conformed with good military practice thereby providing for a range of command, control and discipline issues likely to arise on this new mission. This procedure of having a senior ranking officer in place on each mission is standard practice in Defence Force observer and troop deployments.

[26] No explanation for the selection of these individuals is available. However, in addition to their individual personal experience this group included a range of technical military expertise covering military aviation, armour, logistics and military engineering. This in effect, whether by accident or design, ensured a comprehensive range of skills and experience within the group, suitable for a wide range of possible observer assignments in the mission area and for special staff functions within UNOGIL Headquarters.

[27] MA, Biographical Notes (extracts from personal file) 0/4530, Colonel Justin McCarthy.

[28] MA, Register of Officers Overseas Courses 1922 to 1954. McCarthy attended the 17th Staff Course in the British Army Staff College, Camberley, England, from May to Nov. 1946 with P.J. Hally who was Adjutant General in June 1958. As Adjutant General, Hally had a major input into the selection of officers for UNOGIL, and in particular the selection of the officer to lead the group.

interviewed almost fifty years later, remembered McCarthy's impeccable French.[29] To quote Croke, commenting on McCarthy's suitability for the command of the first deployment of Irish officers to a United Nations mission, 'McCarthy for many reasons was the right man, in the right place, at the right time and we could not have been better served by anyone else'.[30]

Right up to their departure there was some lingering confusion as to the exact mission in which the officers would serve. The PMUN correspondence reflects this with the matter being resolved by means of an explanatory note drawing a distinction between the proposed Lebanon mission and the other two missions in the region: namely UNTSO (in existence since 1949 as an unarmed observer organisation) and UNEF (an armed troop mission deployed since 1956).[31]

With the selection of officers completed and the relevant authorities (the government, the Department of Defence and the Department of External Affairs) in possession of basic facts regarding the mission, the media was advised of the proposed commitment of army officers to the United Nations mission in Lebanon. This was done through the Government Information Bureau which released a press statement confirming that Ireland had agreed to the United Nations Secretary-General's request to provide troops for the mission in Lebanon. The statement included the observation that 'on the assumption that suitable officers will volunteer for the service the Government propose to accede to the request'.[32] The newsworthiness of this first venture into United Nations service was also apparent from a two-column *Irish Press* featured article giving the travel details and service particulars of the officers and a photograph showing the group with the Minister for Defence, Kevin Boland, when they were received by the Taoiseach, Eamon de Valera, at Government Buildings.[33] The Weekly Bulletin of the Department of External Affairs of 7 July 1958 stated that 'the

---

[29] Croke, interview.

[30] Ibid.

[31] This confusion with the UNTSO mission was understandable given that the UNTSO mission was manning observation posts along the Lebanese/Israeli armistice line and it had dispatched some UNMOs to Beirut in an emergency deployment.

[32] *Irish Times*, 25 June 1958. The editorial in this edition of *Irish Times* also commended the government's decision to participate in the Lebanon mission.

[33] *Irish Press*, 27 June 1958. The presentation of the departing UNOGIL officers to the Taoiseach underwrote the historic nature of this first deployment on United Nations service. This was repeated in turn for all subsequent departing groups. From interviews with surviving UNOGIL veterans (Croke, Cox, Furlong, Dixon, Fagan, Ryan, O'Connell and Moran) the photo-call with de Valera was indelibly etched on their memory. According to Fagan, this meeting with, and endorsement from, a 1916 leader was particularly significant. (Fagan interview with author, Ballymore 18 Feb. 2005). In 1959 de Valera was elected President and from 1960 (ONUC) to 1971 (UNFICYP) officers of battalions departing for United Nations service were presented to de Valera in Arás an Uachtaráin. This pre-deployment visit to the President was discontinued in late 1971 in order to minimise the publicity given to troops departing on overseas service at a time of increasing domestic problems arising from the Northern Ireland troubles.

co-operation of Irish Army officers in the work of the United Nations in Lebanon has generally been welcomed as one of the ways in which the country can make an active contribution to international peace'. This sentiment was also mirrored in a statement by the leader of the opposition, Fine Gael's J.A. Costello, quoted in the *Irish Times,* who enthusiastically endorsed the action of the government in acceding to the Secretary-General's request.[34]

However, as was apparent from the manner in which the officers were approached for this duty, the exact approach to 'volunteering' was not fully resolved.[35] This eventually led to questions in the Dáil on how the officers were selected. On 9 July 1958 the issue of 'Volunteers for duty with UN' was raised when Jack McQuillan of the National Progressive Democrats, questioned Kevin Boland regarding the number of officers who had volunteered for UNOGIL. In response the minister stated that twelve eminently suitable officers were invited to volunteer and all of them did, with five being selected from this group. McQuillan referred to an *Irish Times* article that all army officers were invited to volunteer and commented to the effect that it appeared the newspaper article was misleading and that in reality the army officers were presented with a *'fait accompli'*.[36] It seems the core truth on this lies somewhere between the minister's response and the deputy's assertion when both are considered with the hindsight of Lavelle's observation. Nevertheless the 'volunteering' aspect to Defence Forces participation in United Nations service was born through participation in UNOGIL, and has remained central to each individual Defence Force member's personal commitment to the wide variety of missions that followed since then.[37]

Irish officers in Lebanon: 'explosions were a commonplace occurrence'[38]

On arrival in the mission area the Irish were assigned to their individual duty stations with Lieutenant Colonel McCarthy and Commandant Malachi Higgins sent to UNOGIL HQ and the others dispersed to countrywide outstations working with officers from twenty other countries.[39] By 1 July 1958 UNOGIL was submitting its reports to United Nations Headquarters in New York outlining the difficulties being experienced in accessing particular

---

[34] *Irish Times*, 27 June 1958.

[35] Lavelle, 'UNOGIL', p. 189.

[36] *Irish Times*, 9 July 1958.

[37] Regarding the 'volunteer' aspect, it is interesting to note the observation of Colonel Cox (deployed to UNOGIL in Sept. 1958) that it was a widely held view of the Defence Force officers of that time that they were, in the first instance, volunteers for service in the Defence Forces and, as a consequence of this, de facto volunteers for anything that was required of them as members of the Defence Forces (Cox, interview with the author, Milltown, Co. Kildare 25 Feb. 2005).

[38] Lavelle, 'UNOGIL', p. 191.

[39] Lavelle was assigned to the Saida (Sidon) Sector, Coughlan to the Tripoli Sector and Henderson to the Chtaúra Sector. See Lavelle, 'UNOGIL', p. 193. Information also from Cox and Dixon, interviews with the author, Feb. 2005.

parts of the operational area held by anti–government forces. From the out-set the operational situation faced by UNOGIL was a community divided on religious (Christian/Muslim) fault lines. The respective enclaves and dissident areas were sealed off by the Lebanese Army and Security Forces who adopted a low-profile non-interference approach. According to Lavelle, during the day the confrontation lines were relatively quiet but at night the explosions and shootings were a regular occurrence.[40] UNMOs were required to investigate these events and seek evidence of foreign involvement and interference. Eventually, by mid-July, UNOGIL became accepted by both parties and it had full freedom of movement.

As the operational situation improved for UNOGIL, political develop-ments in the region caused the Lebanese government to request United States military intervention. This arose as a consequence of increased instability in the region following a republican coup in Iraq, with serious spill-over consequences for Lebanon and Jordan. The United States informed the Security Council that it intended responding positively to the request to stabilise and protect the integrity and independence of Lebanon. Washington claimed its forces would only be deployed on a temporary mission, pending an improved United Nations capability to control the situation. UNOGIL viewed the United States intervention as an internal matter for the Lebanese government and confined its mission, in conformity with its mandate, to monitoring along the Syrian border. UNOGIL gradually achieved complete freedom of movement and sought to increase its UNMO strength to meet new contingencies.

Meanwhile, the arrival of the United States Sixth Fleet off Beirut caused the *Irish Times* to speculate as to the safety of the Irish UNMOs when the United States landed its marines on 15 July 1958. With the marines ashore in the Beirut area and the Sixth Fleet off shore, there was speculation too as to a continuing role for the UNOGIL mission and the possibility of its with-drawal. However, UNOGIL adapted to this new situation, stuck to its role and avoided any contact with United States shore elements.[41]

UNOGIL did report to New York that the intervention by United States marines impacted adversely on the inhabitants of opposition-held areas, with consequential difficulties for the UNMOs. The United Nations and UNOGIL were learning the recurring lesson of peacekeeping soldiering, namely that operational difficulties for United Nations troops arising from a superpower's presence in the United Nations peacekeeping theatre of operations were of little import if they were contrary to that superpower's strategic interests.

---

[40] Lavelle, 'UNOGIL', p. 191.
[41] *Irish Times*, 16 July 1958.

UNOGIL enlarged

After the Second World War, the delicate balance throughout the Middle East and the region's importance in the Cold War were both evident in the deployment of United States forces to Lebanon in July 1958. A similar situation developed in Jordan in July 1958 when the security situation deteriorated following an alleged UAR threat to topple King Hussein, which caused Jordan to lodge a complaint with the Security Council. Following the United States action in respect of Lebanon, Britain then decided to commit its forces in support of Jordan. Heated debates on USSR, Swedish and United States motions in the Security Council followed, but no progress was made. In this impasse, in line with his view that resolving the crisis in Lebanon was the key to restoring stability and containing the overall Middle East emergency, Hammarskjöld decided to increase the strength of UNOGIL as soon as it was possible. It was considered that this would enable it to fully carry out its mission and thus expedite the withdrawal of the United States troops.[42]

In consequence of Hammarskjöld's proposal to enlarge UNOGIL, the Irish Permanent Mission to the United Nations received a request on the morning of 28 July 1958 to provide a further five observers. Despite UNOGIL's relative freedom of movement in its mission area, the United States presence, together with the declared British intention vis-à-vis Jordan, had operational implications for UNOGIL requiring increased personnel and logistic resources. Aware of the necessity for prompt reaction to this latest request, Eamon Kennedy immediately dispatched the request to Dublin, once again strongly recommending a positive response to Hammarskjöld's request. The cable to Dublin also included extracts from the Secretary-General's correspondence to the Irish Permanent Mission to the United Nations which included inter alia the observation that the Irish in UNOGIL were performing very well: 'we have been informed by members of the Secretariat who are responsible for administering the Observer Group's operations that the five officers already assigned to Lebanon are doing a splendid job'.[43] The cable by Kennedy included an endorsement of the request which in hindsight turned out to be rather prophetic when it concluded that 'a favourable reply to this second request of the United Nations Secretary-General will help open the door wider to further participation by Ireland in the growing role of the United Nations in easing international tensions through the dispatch of forces drawn from the smaller Member States'.[44]

Once again Dublin responded promptly. On 29 July Iveagh House matched the enthusiasm of their colleagues at the Irish Permanent Mission to the United Nations. Again the ability to meet very demanding deployment

---

[42] United Nations Website: www.un.org/Depts/dpko/co_mission/unogil.htm.
[43] NAI DFA PMUN 222/13/1, United Nations Secretary-General's Office to PMUN, 27 July 1958.
[44] Ibid. Kennedy's cable to Iveagh House dated 28 July 1958 refers.

target dates was also apparent when Ireland agreed to select and deploy the next tranche of personnel to the mission area within six days, much to the appreciation of Hammarskjöld, who was then under pressure to increase UNOGIL as soon as possible. Similar requests were made to the other contributing nations through their representatives in New York. The *Irish Times* of the following day included an announcement from the Government Information Bureau that the Irish government had agreed to Hammarskjöld's request to increase Ireland's contribution to UNOGIL and that the Chief of Staff of the Defence Forces had selected five officers from those who had volunteered. These were Commandant Joe Adams (Military College) and Captains Pat White (Military College), Pat Jordan (Adjutant General's Branch, Defence Forces Headquarters), Tom Tracey (FCA Staff Eastern Command) and Chris Woods (General Training Depot, Eastern Command).[45] This party reported to Beirut on 5 August 1958. These five officers had been included in the initial short-listed twelve-man group that reported to Defence Forces Headquarters on the Adjutant General's direction on 25 June. On that occasion they were disappointed to have missed out on selection, now they were nominated to join the mission in Lebanon.[46]

The five new Irish UNMOs were processed through UNOGIL Headquarters on arrival in Beirut and were then hastily deployed to the operational sectors. White served with Lavelle in the Sidon sector and Jordan and Woods served in Tripoli. [47] Adams's and Tracey's initial operational outstation has not been located. However, interviews with Croke and Furlong suggest that Adams, Tracey and Jordan, having acquired experience of the operational situation, were subsequently withdrawn to UNOGIL Headquarters where they functioned until the mission was withdrawn in December 1958.

As the mission reconfigured in its operational profile and set about absorbing the incoming reinforcements, UNOGIL faced a problem regarding the replacement of the senior deputy (Colonel W.M. Brown of New Zealand), to its Chief of Staff Major General Odd Bull. The appointment was for an officer at the rank of Colonel but Major General Odd Bull nevertheless directed a request to Hammarskjöld for Lieutenant Colonel McCarthy to assume the appointment to replace the New Zealand Colonel. He also strongly recommended that Lieutenant Colonel McCarthy be promoted to the rank of full Colonel and included this in his letter to Hammarskjöld. On receipt of this information in the Secretary-General's office it was forwarded

---

[45] *Irish Times*, 30 July 1958.
[46] Lavelle, 'UNOGIL', p. 193; Cox, personal UNOGIL diary (in the possession of Colonel Cox); Croke and Furlong, interviews with the author (Feb. and Mar. 2005) refer.
[47] Rosalyn Higgins, *United Nations Peacekeeping 1946–1967: Documents and Commentary* (London, 1969), p. 544. Initially the emphasis was on establishing an operational presence in the field and thereafter to build the headquarters' and administrative staff sections. The organisation and operational structure for the mission provided for a headquarters command group complete with Personnel (G1), Evaluation (G2), Operations (G3) and Logistics (G4) staff sections with five operational sectors (Tripoli, Baalbeck, Chtaúra, Marjayoún, Saida) and an air squadron. This was not achieved until mid-Sept. 1958.

immediately to PMUN and then by cable to Iveagh House who replied on 2 August 1958 to the effect that McCarthy was promoted Colonel on that date. His appointment to Deputy Chief of Staff UNOGIL took place on 8 August 1958.[48] The considerations which led to his selection as the senior Irish officer, i.e. his exceptional career experience including the international dimension conferred by his staff course with the British Army, bore fruit in his selection by Major General Odd Bull to replace Colonel Brown in this appointment.[49] Commenting on the fact that an Irish colleague was now the Chief Military Observer and top man in the military hierarchy next to Major General Odd Bull, Hogan, who arrived in the mission area in late August, commented that the Irish felt very proud that one of their number had been chosen so quickly for such an important post.[50] McCarthy, only a month at UNOGIL Headquarters, and with a number of other potential candidates available to take Colonel Brown's place, had received Odd Bull's recommendation to fill a senior staff appointment at UNOGIL Headquarters. The sensitivity of this high profile appointment is best understood when viewed in the context of the demands of UNOGIL's operational priorities. At this point the operational imperative was to maintain the mission's impartiality and objectivity in a complicated operational environment, requiring it to walk a tight rope between the conflicting demands of the host government interests, those of an occupying superpower and a prevailing threat from the UAR, a belligerent adjoining state. The reality of this situation is comparable to the situation faced by Lieutenant General Seán MacEoin in ONUC a few years later, but unlike MacEoin's succession to the command of UNOC, McCarthy's appointment was not similarly publicised. In McCarthy's case, his promotion to the UNOGIL appointment was overlooked by External Affairs, the Department of Defence and the Defence Forces and was not passed to the media. It appears to have been totally overlooked and not recognised for the historic event that it was for the country, for the Defence Forces and of course for the officer concerned.[51]

By mid-August, following the election of General Chebab, former Lebanese Army Chief of Staff, to the Lebanese presidency, UNOGIL reported a noticeable reduction in tension with the ceasefire continuing to hold. Back at the United Nations in New York the veto powers, having very divergent views on the entire Middle East situation, were now close to agreement

---

[48] NAI DFA PMUN 222/13/1, PMUN to External Affairs (code cable), 1 Aug. 1958.

[49] MA, Biographical Notes on Colonel McCarthy.

[50] Hogan, 'UNOGIL', p. 172.

[51] Selection for this prestigious UNOGIL appointment was an honour for the individual and the state. This oversight by national authorities on the significance of Col. McCarthy's promotion and appointment is not easily understood except in the context of a national lack of appreciation of the achievement it represented. With the hindsight of Defence Forces experience since then, it is suggested that, being new to United Nations soldiering, Ireland had yet to understand the power-plays and intrigue of the experienced contributing nations seeking to place their representatives in influential staff appointments at the respective UN Headquarters.

on how to restore the situation. In this atmosphere negotiations began on the possibility of a United States withdrawal by mid-October 1958. UNOGIL Headquarters reported in a similar vein to Hammarskjöld and confirmed that the situation was now under the control of the Lebanese government. There was confirmation too that the United States would withdraw from Lebanon by 25 October and the British would withdraw from Jordan in the same timeframe. On the political and diplomatic scene, the Lebanese government withdrew its complaint from the Security Council, indicating that it had restored its relations with UAR.

'Can you ride a bicycle?'[52] increased Irish participation in UNOGIL

Meanwhile, adjustments of functions within UNOGIL, including the expansion of its Air Operations Group, saw a proposal for another increase in UNOGIL strength and this resulted in a further request for Ireland to provide another ten officers to the operation. Once again the national authorities responded immediately and nominated Commandants James Caseley (Southern Command Headquarters), Patrick D. Hogan (5th Battalion Eastern Command), William Carroll (Adjutant Eastern Command), Captains Thomas Furlong (Artillery Southern Command), Patrick Keogh (11th Cavalry Regiment Eastern Command), Louis Hogan (Defence Forces Headquarters), Francis O'Connor (Curragh Command), James Liddy (Air Corps Baldonnell), Gerard Gill (Engineer Corps Eastern Command) and Edward Condon (1st Battalion Western Command). According to Furlong, this group was selected from a larger number that had been called to the Adjutant General's Office in a similar fashion to Lavelle et al on 25 June. The final composition of this group followed a repeat of the volunteering and selection process experienced by Lavelle, which in Furlong's case included the appropriate answer to a question from the Chief of Staff, 'Can you ride a bicycle?'.[53] Despite the widespread Defence Forces and national interest in the Lebanon as a major news item, and the fact that Ireland had already dispatched ten officers to the mission, the proposed enlargement of Irish representation in UNOGIL was very closely guarded information within the General Staff and selected sections of Defence Forces Headquarters until the selections were announced to the media through the Government Information Bureau. Some officers, like Colonel Colm Cox, then serving as a captain in 1st Battalion in Galway and eagerly watching these unfolding events, took steps to have their interest in these matters recognised. He submitted a written request to be considered for any further Irish expansion to the mission.[54]

---

[52] Furlong, interview with the author, Bray, 15 Feb. 2005.
[53] Ibid., Furlong had been ordered to Dublin from Ballincollig, County Cork at less than twelve hours notice for this meeting with Mulcahy and Hally. He observed that some of those assembled on that occasion failed this simple test. For the remainder, having thus established their 'volunteer' status, an anxious hour's wait followed until the selection of the final ten was made.

This third group of Irish UNMO's reported to Beirut on 29 August.[55] With this deployment there were now twenty Irish officers serving with UNOGIL, but Hammarskjöld's office pressed for a further increase to this number. Reacting to these phone enquiries PMUN in collaboration with External Affairs, Defence and Defence Forces Headquarters in Dublin commenced preparations for a further increase in UNMOs. Ireland first agreed to provide ten officers, and then within five days of this request by Hammarskjöld's office, the number was raised to thirty officers.[56] The escalation in numbers was required to cater for the contingency planning in-theatre for expected changes arising from the withdrawal of the United States Marines.[57] On this occasion a medical officer from the Army Medical Service was included at the United Nations' request due in part to the rapid expansion of the mission and the necessity to provide a basic first line medical capacity for UNOGIL. Up to this point, UNOGIL was focused on developing an operational capacity and structure to cope with the evolving operational situation. As this neared achievement, it expanded the administrative and logistic structure at its headquarters, the Riviera Hotel in Beirut.[58] According to Brigadier General Pat Dixon, then the youngest and the most junior of the next group of selected nominees, the expansion of UNOGIL's administrative structures included a requirement for Military Police and Ireland undertook to provide a Military Police officer.[59] The selected officer volunteers were to be deployed to the mission area not later than 4 October and were eventually deployed in two lots, with the first group of eleven deployed on Sunday 28 September 1958.[60]

Those nominated included, in the first tranche: Commandants G. Quigley (Medical Officer) and D. Johnston (Air Corps); Captains J. Moran (Infantry, Curragh Camp), E. Russell (Infantry, Southern Command), M.F. Quinlan (Infantry, Eastern Command), J.J. Fagan (Infantry, Western Command), J.D. Mulvihill (Infantry, Western Command), B.G. Murphy (Infantry, Eastern Command) and C. Cox (Infantry, Western Command); Lieutenants P.L. Walsh (Infantry, Eastern Command) and L.P. Buckley (Infantry, Eastern Command). In the second tranche were included: Commandant E.A. Curtain (Infantry Western Command); Captains J.M. Fitzpatrick, P. Allen (Infantry Southern Command), H. Gouldsborough (Infantry Southern Command), M. O'Donnell, (Artillery Western Command) A.M. Nestor (Military Police Southern Command), T. Doyle

[54] Cox, interview.

[55] NAI DFA PMUN 222/13/1, Hammarskjöld to PMUN, 19 Aug. 1958.

[56] Ibid., memorandum by PMUN, 12 Sept. 1958.

[57] Ibid., United Nations Secretary-General's Office to PMUN, 17 Sept. 1958.

[58] Furlong, interview.

[59] Captain Ambrose Nestor was the officer nominated for this appointment. Dixon, interview with the author, Athlone, Feb. 2005.

[60] Cox, personal UNOGIL diary.

(Signals Western Command), J. Sloan (Infantry Eastern Command), W. O'Flynn (Supply and Transport Southern Command), M. Bradley (Infantry Southern Command) and T.F. Duff (Infantry Eastern Command); Lieutenants E. Sheehy (Cavalry Eastern Command), M. Carroll (Cavalry Curragh Camp), P. Croke (Artillery Western Command), F. O'Connell (Infantry Southern Command), R. McCorley (Cavalry Curragh Camp), J. Ryan (Infantry Southern Command), J. O'Brien (Cavalry Eastern Command) and P. Dixon (Supply and Transport Western Command).[61]

By this stage the Defence Forces approach to selecting, briefing, equipping and deploying personnel overseas had become better organised, if still somewhat rudimentary. In the main, medical preparation of personnel was left to United Nations resources in Beirut, but flights to the mission area were now being arranged through Cooks of Dublin, contracted agents of the United Nations, with Aer Lingus the beneficiary of this business. Equipping officers for the vagaries of the Lebanese climate saw them issued with duffle coats (courtesy of Naval Service stores), lightweight khaki 'uniform' (shirts, slacks and shorts, courtesy of purchases in Millets of Dublin) and, uniquely, blouse style 'Bulls Wool' uniform (courtesy of FCA Quartermasters).[62]

With the arrival of this final cohort of new UNMOs from Ireland and other nations the mission reached its peak strength of almost six hundred (all ranks).[63] The Irish were now very well represented at UNOGIL Headquarters, where apart from Colonel McCarthy, Commandants Higgins (Air Operations), and Adams (UNOGIL Operations) held senior staff appointments and Commandant Quigley functioned as UNOGIL's medical officer. In addition to Higgins both Commandant Johnston and Captain Liddy were Air Corps officers and qualified pilots. They were assigned to UNOGIL's Air Operations Group and were engaged in aerial observation

---

[61] NAI DFA PMUN 222/13/1, External Affairs to PMUN.

[62] Ryan, interview with author, Rathcoole, Mar. 2005 and Ryan photograph collection (in the possession of Colonel Ryan). All interviewees refer to the 'FCA Tunic' and observed that this item of military clothing, together with the Naval Service 'Duffle Coat', were a subject of envious comment by other UNMOs. Ryan's photographs clearly show the FCA tunic being worn on operational duty in Lebanon.

[63] Strength was increased from 200 on 17 July 1958, to 287 by 20 Sept. and to 591 by mid-Nov.. This included 32 non-commissioned officers in support of ground operations and 90 in the air section. By Nov. 1958, UNOGIL had 18 aircraft, 6 helicopters and 290 vehicles and it had established 49 permanently manned posts of all types. Higgins, *UN Peacekeeping*, p. 556 and United Nations Website: www.un.org/Depts/dpko/co_mission/unogil.htm refer. In addition it should be noted that the civil agency, United Nations Field Service, was also deployed to support this mission. This is an internationally recruited United Nations support echelon which provides civilian administration, technical and security personnel to deliver the appropriate support to United Nations field missions. United Nations Field Service operatives in Lebanon at this time included a number of Irish nationals. These individuals were invariably though not exclusively former members of An Garda Siochána who joined the Field Service shortly after Ireland became a member. Cox, Croke, Dixon, Furlong interviews provided the following names of these Irish Field Service personnel who served with UNOGIL in 1958, Pat McHugh, Dan McCaffrey, Pat Kennedy, Tony O'Connor, Dick O'Connor, Tom McAndrew and Dooley (Croke and Cox, interviews).

and patrols.[64] The other officers of this group were distributed to the five operational sectors (Tripoli, Baalbek, Chtura, Marjayoún, Saida) where in addition to providing officers for the operational and patrol tasks, the Irish were once again assigned to critical senior staff appointments in the Sector Headquarters in recognition of their staff skills.[65]

Meantime the United States withdrew its Marines on schedule and, with improved relations vis-à-vis Iraq and the general acceptance in Lebanon of the new Lebanese president and government by the Moslem community, the tension in the country subsided. The operational situation across the Middle East was also eased by Britain's withdrawal of its troops from Jordan on time.[66] The original problem which gave rise to UNOGIL's presence had also been resolved and in its final report to United Nations Headquarters in New York, dated 17 November 1958, UNOGIL recommended that the operation should be withdrawn. On 21 November, Hammarskjöld submitted a plan to the Security Council for the withdrawal of the operation. The plan had been drafted by UNOGIL and was acceptable to Lebanon. In accordance with that plan, the closing down of stations and substations preparatory to the withdrawal of UNOGIL began on 26 November and was completed by the end of the month. In anticipation of the administrative issues surrounding the withdrawal of the six hundred strong UNOGIL force, a number of the Irish officers were drafted into the project team at UNOGIL Headquarters to prepare and administer the final evacuation.[67] Thereafter observers were withdrawn in three phases, with the key staff, the personnel required for air service and the logistic components leaving last. The withdrawal of the main body was completed by the target date of 9 December 1958 when the mission ceased to have an operational role. The Irish officers in the Rear Party returned to Dublin in time for Christmas on 18 December and, following the precaution of overnight stay for medical processing in St Bricin's Military Hospital, they returned to their respective home stations.[68]

For some the return from the excitement of soldiering abroad was an anticlimax and, faced with the envy of their peers, they all quickly settled back into the routine of domestic soldiering. Remarkably, from the personal

---

[64] Croke, interview.

[65] Based on interviews with surviving veterans (Feb./Mar. 2005) the following was the location of the Irish UNMOs in the operational sectors. *Tripoli*: Fagan, Coughlan, Woods, Mulvhill, Jordan, Gill. *Baalbeck*: Hogan P.D., Furlong, Keogh, O'Brien, McCorley, Ryan, O'Connell, Sheehy, Duff, Moran, Carroll M. *Chtaúra*: Henderson, Curtain, Allen, Dixon. *Marjayoún*: Carroll W, Cox, Russell, Murphy, Doyle. *Saida*: Lavelle, Fitzpatrick, Walsh, Buckley, White, Sloan, Croke.

[66] The withdrawal of British troops from Jordan was monitored by a number of UNMOs provided by both UNOGIL and UNTSO. As this was a major airlift the task was entrusted to selected members of UNOGIL Air Group. Commandant Johnston of the Irish Air Corps was deployed from UNOGIL as part of this operation (Johnston photo collection and O'Connell interview with the author, Dublin, Mar. 2005 refer).

[67] Cox, Dixon and Croke, interviews.

[68] Cox, personal UNOGIL diary.

recollections of the surviving veterans, no further steps were taken to de-brief them on this historic mission, apart from a major symposium on Lebanon conducted by the Western Command UNMOs in Athlone in March 1959.[69] The Defence Forces focused attention on the prospect of the integration of the Permanent Defence Forces and FCA scheduled for September 1959. The idea of becoming involved in any further foreign service campaigns was not a realistic proposition and the challenge of integration became all-consuming. Accordingly, the UNOGIL medal parade in McKee Barracks on 11 April 1960 at which Seán Lemass, now Taoiseach, presented the medals, brought closure to this first venture into soldiering for peace.[70] Overlooked in the formality of this great occasion, the first presentation of non-national medals to serving Defence Forces personnel, was the absence of the UNMOs who remained on duty with the United Nations Truce Supervision Organisation in the Middle East.

UNTSO

The inherent instability of the Middle East region and the threat to international peace posed by the crisis in Lebanon was effectively contained by UNOGIL but its withdrawal on completion of its mission drew attention to the continuing regional fragility and the lingering threat to international peace posed by the Arab–Israeli problem. Heretofore the United Nations had deployed UNTSO to observe on the truce and adjudicate on problems arising over the armistice lines then defining the 'boundaries' of Israel. Since the 1956 Anglo-French and Israeli Suez Canal debacle, a United Nations force was deployed as a separate peacekeeping force in the Sinai. UNTSO, although an unarmed observer mission, had a wider remit over all Israel's disputed frontier and was therefore more useful as a regional peacekeeping tool. It was now decided to increase the strength of UNTSO, and selected UNOGIL personnel were headhunted for this purpose by Major General von Horn (Sweden) then the Chief of Staff of UNTSO.

UNTSO had been in existence since November 1947 when the United Nations General Assembly endorsed a plan for the partition of Palestine, providing for the creation of an Arab State and a Jewish State, with Jerusalem being assigned international status. Conflict followed the end of the British mandate for Palestine on 14 May 1948 when the state of Israel was created

---

[69] Not until 1976 did the Director of Intelligence write to surviving veterans to request them to submit their personal reports on this mission. Documents in Dixon's possession include Dixon's own copy of his report submitted in response to the request from Director of Intelligence.

[70] NAI DFA 305/329/3, Award of Medal to Irish Officers in UNOGIL refers. This file contains a copy of the Ceremonial Order 3/1960 dated 6 Apr. 1960. The file also gives insight to the protracted correspondence regarding national authorisation for wearing United Nations medals. In this first Defence Forces United Nations Medal Parade there was also a further unique historic dimension in that the Taoiseach was presenting a United Nations medal to his son-in-law Capt. Jack O'Brien (Cavalry Corps) who had served in UNOGIL.

and the Arab states went to war against Israel. This continued until both sides eventually agreed a cessation of hostilities. The United Nations, under United Nations Security Council Resolution 50/1948, deployed an international observer force of UNMOs to supervise this truce.[71] This group of military observers was designated UNTSO and it remained on to supervise the Armistice Agreements between Israel and its Arab neighbours over the following years of uneasy truce and occasional conflict.[72] Major General Odd Bull selected the UNOGIL personnel to be assigned to UNTSO and he strongly recommended Colonel McCarthy and Captain Jordan, the Irish UNMOs who were then on the UNOGIL Headquarters staff in Beirut. According to Furlong, the majority of the Irish UNMOs, having enjoyed the professionally testing operational environment of UNOGIL, were keen to transfer to UNTSO, but only McCarthy and Jordan were considered by Odd Bull.[73] Having consulted with and received the agreement of Major General von Horn, Odd Bull cabled his request to Hammarskjöld's office in New York requiring both Irish officers to be assigned to UNTSO for one year on completion of the UNOGIL mission. This request made its way via PMUN cable to External Affairs in Dublin. The communication to Dublin drew attention to this endorsement by Odd Bull of the two officers' performance of their duties and strongly recommended a positive response to their transfer to UNTSO. This was agreed very quickly by Dublin and the two officers then became the first Irish personnel to serve with UNTSO. Nationally this was a very important step and was reported as such in the national media with the Government Information Bureau emphasising the honour bestowed on the country by the selection of these officers by United Nations authorities. All of the national media published the story with very favourable comment on 17 December 1958.[74]

For both officers, once again this was a step into the unknown, a step taken in the true volunteering spirit which characterised the initial response for UNOGIL duty and a spirit that has marked Defence Forces participation in United Nations service ever since. Apart from what was gleaned from the UNTSO UNMOs in UNOGIL, there was no information available on the terms of service or other matters when McCarthy and Jordan agreed to serve with UNTSO. These administrative matters were eventually resolved and subsequent cables confirmed the transfer of both officers from Beirut to

---

[71] UN Website www.un.org/Depts/dpko/co_mission/untso refers.

[72] UNTSO also had a function as a repository of trained UNMOs available for immediate international deployment at the behest of the Security Council and this was the mission from which the core 'start-up' staff element came for UNOGIL in June 1958. In 2005 UNTSO continues to have this role.

[73] Furlong, interview.

[74] *Irish Times,* 17 Dec. 1958. This event was correctly handled by the Government Information Bureau which gave due prominence to the move to UNTSO. However, it leaves unanswered questions as to why similar action was not taken with regard to the bigger earlier story of McCarthy's promotion and appointment as Deputy Chief of Staff UNOGIL Headquarters in Aug. 1958.

Jerusalem, reporting on 18 December (Colonel McCarthy) and 19 December (Captain Jordan). Joining the new mission was soon to raise unexpected issues. At this time UNTSO had responsibility for four Mixed Armistices Commissions between Israel and each of its neighbouring states (Egypt, Jordan, Syria and Lebanon). UNTSO provided the chairman for each of these Commissions. On arrival, in recognition of his success in the UNOGIL mission, Colonel McCarthy was assigned by Major General von Horn, UNTSO Chief of Staff, as chairman of the Israel Egypt Mixed Armistice Commission (IEMAC). IEMAC functioned in the Sinai where the armed United Nations force, UNEF, was also deployed. When Dublin became aware of McCarthy's appointment as chairman of the Mixed Armistice Commission, misgivings were expressed by Dublin to PMUN regarding the possible implications for Irish neutrality. PMUN files reflect a protracted correspondence on this issue.[75] In the end the matter was resolved and an important issue relating to the deployment of Irish officers to an observer mission was established in that it was finally accepted that the duties performed by Irish personnel on a United Nations mission were those as directed by the head of the Mission, in this case Major General von Horn. There was, therefore, acceptance of the fact that such matters were operational and administrative issues within the authority and competence of the UNTSO Chief of Staff, and not a matter for consultation with governments local or national.[76] Thereafter these matters faded into the background and Colonel McCarthy's IEMAC chairmanship was commended by Major General von Horn particularly on the basis of his handling of serious incidents occurring in his (IEMAC) area of operations. There was also the professional and diplomatic manner in which he dealt with the strained command relationship between UNTSO and UNEF which had previously given rise to difficulties between the respective United Nations generals, von Horn (COS UNTSO) and Burns (Commander UNEF). Meanwhile the tensions across the Middle East, originally generated by the situation in Lebanon and exasperated by the United States and British military interventions in the region, had eased considerably. Israel and its neighbours settled into what passed for normal in their respective relations and UNTSO continued its role along the armistice lines. Jordan performed staff duty at UNTSO Headquarters in Jerusalem and McCarthy's brief in the Sinai as Chairman of EIMAC continued until they were both recommended for a further extension of their UNTSO service in December 1959.

---

[75] NAI DFA PMUN 222/13/1, External Affairs to PMUN, 6 Jan. 1959; PMUN to External Affairs, 7 Jan. 1959 and PMUN to External Affairs, 23 Jan. 1959.
[76] Ibid., PMUN to External Affairs, 7 Jan. 1959.

Ireland's first lessons from United Nations soldiering

Up to this point the preoccupation of all personnel back home in Ireland, at External Affairs, Defence and at Defence Forces Headquarters, and indeed in government, was in meeting the operational requirements and deadlines of the United Nations regarding selection and deployment of personnel to the mission area. A 'can-do' attitude had prevailed throughout, reflecting the perceived prestige accruing to the state from its first involvement in United Nations peacekeeping. Now with the completion of this first mission and the return of forty-eight Irish UNMOs from UNOGIL, the tempo of activity gave way to more mundane but still important issues. An air of relative peace and calm had returned to the Cold War realities across the Middle East and media interest in Ireland moved on to other matters. UNTSO and the Irish personnel serving there were now minor administrative matters for national civil and military administrators. Department of Defence civil servants addressing matters from their area of responsibility and expertise identified a range of problems resulting from service with the United Nations and engaged in protracted correspondence with the United Nations Secretariat in New York through External Affairs. This correspondence referred to leave, medical support, conditions of service, pensions, etc along with the matter of how this state should be reimbursed from United Nations sources for expenses arising in the course of its commitment of Irish personnel on United Nations service. The cost of the UNOGIL Mission had been calculated at £3,015–9–11 but by 8 April 1959 on the advice of PMUN this matter was not pursued.[77] Regarding costs, PMUN had quietly investigated this with the United Nations Secretariat and other contributing nations and established what costs were chargeable to the United Nations.[78] The other important personnel issues were eventually resolved to the satisfaction of all concerned. This engagement on important administrative issues arising from Ireland's first involvement with United Nations peacekeeping gave a valuable insight and experience to civil servants regarding United Nations procedures and systems and unwittingly prepared them for the Congo venture which was to follow one year later.

---

[77] Ibid., Department of Defence correspondence (9 Feb. 1959) outlined a claim for reimbursement in respect of a special clothing allowance and the additional equipment issued to each officer, plus an 'entertainment allowance' issued to Colonel McCarthy. Totalling £3,295–0–0, less the cost recovered from coats and medical kit returned to stores £279–10–1, requiring £3,015–9–11 to be paid. By 8 Apr. 1959 on the advice of PMUN this matter was not pursued by Defence. In effect, the state's first venture into United Nations soldiering cost £3,015–9–11.

[78] NAI DFA 305/329/4, contains the Iveagh House copy of PMUN letter advising as to the claim indicating that having consulted with twenty-one other UNOGIL participating countries none had claimed similar expenses. PMUN stated inter alia 'every effort should be made by Department of Defence to absorb these expenses if at all possible as it would be undesirable if not embarrassing to press these claims when such other countries as Afghanistan, Burma, Ceylon, India, Indonesia, Nepal, Peru and Thailand have not made similar claims and they would be unlikely to sympathise with our point of view'.

Another issue of more immediate importance was affecting operational matters in the mission area. This issue arose from an admonishment of Colonel McCarthy by Dublin following receipt by the Adjutant General of a memorandum from the Secretary-General to PMUN requesting the extension fo duty of McCarthy and Jordan to complete one year's service with UNTSO.[79] It appears that PMUN included a copy of all the correspondence it had on this matter in its routine dispatch bag to Dublin for onward transmission to the Department of Defence and to Defence Forces Headquarters. On receipt by the military authorities, McCarthy was written to directly by the Adjutant General, in effect severely admonishing him for going outside national military channels with his request, including a reference to the effect that the Secretary of the Department of Defence was concerned as to the 'manner in which the approach was made'. McCarthy, who had complied with United Nations procedures, felt unjustly admonished and appears to have informed his United Nations superior in UNTSO, Major General von Horn. Von Horn then wrote in defence of his subordinate, and in his letter to Hammarskjöld referred to correspondence dated 11 August from 'Adjutant General of the Irish Army' to Colonel McCarthy reprimanding him for 'gratuitously making an application to extend his service with UNTSO'. It is apparent from von Horn's correspondence that the Irish authorities, particularly Defence Forces Headquarters and the Department of Defence, were unaware of either the real nature or importance of Colonel McCarthy's UNTSO/EIMAC duties (e.g. the high profile role as Chairman of EIMAC then administering the more volatile of the Israel/Arab armistice lines). Dublin was also unaware of or overlooked the orders and administrative procedures applicable to United Nations missions in general and UNTSO in particular. All of which was compounded by the terms of the Adjutant General's reprimand to Colonel McCarthy, which also suggests a lack of appreciation of the 'independence' of United Nations missions and the attendant international status of officers deployed to those United Nations missions.

Von Horn, mindful of the proper etiquette and correct lines of communication, directed his response to Hammarskjöld's office requesting that PMUN be informed of the particular requirements of UNTSO Standing Orders, with regard to which Colonel McCarthy was fully compliant. He further commended Colonel McCarthy and his role as EIMAC Chairman in Gaza indicating that he also proposed to move him to a more senior UNTSO appointment as Chairman of ISMAC in Damascus, a much larger area of operations. The letter concluded with a velvet glove criticism of the Irish authorities when von Horn added that he would 'hate to see a fine officer penalised for a misunderstanding on the part of his superiors at the national level. I should equally hate to lose the services of this officer'.[80] This

---

[79] NAI DFA PMUN, 222/13/1, memorandum from Hammarskjöld to PMUN, 9 July 1959.
[80] Ibid., UNTSO Chief of Staff to Executive Assistant, Secretary-General (confidential), 3 Sept. 1959.

confidential letter was forwarded by Hammarskjöld's office to PMUN again under 'confidential' classification, with the request that it be passed to 'the appropriate national authorities' indicating 'this memorandum will fully clarify the misunderstanding which has apparently been occasioned by UNSG's note of 9 July 1959 requesting an extension of McCarthy's tour of duty with UNTSO'.

The entire correspondence on this matter was forwarded to Dublin for onward transmission to military authorities again under 'CONFIDENTIAL' classification on 7 October 1959 and the matter was finally resolved with the Irish authorities agreeing to both officers continuing their service with UNTSO as requested.[81] Subsequently Captain Jordan requested to be short toured and returned home in March 1960 due to his wife's pregnancy.[82]

This minor hiccup vis-à-vis national relations and communication with the Irish officers in UNTSO was an important step in awakening Defence Forces Headquarters to the sensitivities of how matters such as administrative control should be exercised over personnel deployed to a United Nations mission. After this, care was taken to ensure that communication with those in the field was done through appropriate channels. This incident also highlighted the requirement to improve direct communication with personnel deployed outside the country which up to this point appears to have depended on air mail correspondence. Later this led to the high frequency radio contact established soon after the Congo operation unfolded in 1960.

The Congo

For the early part of 1960 Colonel McCarthy's and Captain Jordan's (and later Captain O'Connor's) tour of duty was uneventful as is reflected in External Affairs and Defence files. But matters were to change for all UNTSO personnel due to the events that started to unfold in central Africa in mid-1960. The Republic of the Congo, a former Belgian colony, became independent on 30 June 1960 and within days disorder broke out. Belgium claimed the right to protect its nationals and having declared its intention to restore order, dispatched its troops to the Congo, without the agreement of the Congolese government. The Congolese government responded on 12 July 1960, by requesting that the United Nations provide military assistance to protect the national territory of the Congo against external aggression. On 14 July the Security Council approved a resolution calling for the withdrawal of the Belgian troops and authorising the deployment of military assistance to the Congolese government. In less than forty-eight hours the first contingents for what would be ONUC (United Nations Operation in the Congo) arrived in the Congo. This force also included United Nations civilian

---

[81] Ibid., External Affairs to PMUN, 7 Nov. 1959 refers.
[82] Captain Jordan was replaced in UNTSO by Captain O'Connor who had served in UNOGIL in 1958.

experts to help ensure the continued operations of essential public services. ONUC's mission was to help the Congolese government restore and maintain the political independence and territorial integrity of the Congo. In addition UNOC was required to help the government to maintain law and order throughout the country and to put into effect a wide and long-range programme of training and technical assistance. The mission was succinctly stated but the size and complexity of the task was not the immediate concern of those responsible for establishing the mission and for setting in place its command, control and operational structures. The United Nations called upon those in place across a range of missions. To lead ONUC's military component the United Nations once again drew on the expertise of those in UNTSO. Major General von Horn was directed to take control of this mission from the outset. He proceeded directly from Jerusalem to Leopoldville with a number of UNMOs.[83]

On arrival, von Horn set about establishing his headquarters and sought the assistance of Colonel McCarthy from UNTSO to function as his Chief of Staff.[84] The United Nations sought Dublin's agreement for this through PMUN and, on its receipt, McCarthy was redeployed from Jerusalem and reported to Leopoldville. Von Horn in his autobiography merely notes with some personal satisfaction that 'to my delight a plane touched down at N'Djili airport, brought in Colonel Justin McCarthy of the Irish Army, whom I had known in UNOGIL and had brought across to UNTSO'.[85] Commenting on this move Dixon observes that McCarthy's significant contribution to establishing UNOGIL in June/July 1958 had impressed Odd Bull and was also known to von Horn. That experience of orchestrating the establishment of a multinational military headquarters was unequalled amongst the available UNMOs at that time. This fact and his performance of subsequent assignments under von Horn in UNTSO made him eminently suitable for this new challenge in the Congo. In this new emerging state, the United Nations was confronted with a major challenge and UNOC struggled to establish itself while confronting a demanding, ongoing, rapidly changing, operational situation.[86] Von Horn as ONUC's military commander needed every assistance he could muster. McCarthy was a known performer and a major acquisition for this task.

At this time also Ireland was requested by Hammarskjöld to provide other officer observers for the new force and then shortly afterwards on 16 July a formal request was submitted for an infantry battalion, approximately six hundred men, later increased to two battalions, a total of twelve hundred men. Yet again, Ireland responded promptly to the call and the request was

---

[83] United Nations Website: www.un.org/Depts/dpko/co_mission/unoc.htm.

[84] Hogan, 'UNOGIL', p. 172.

[85] Major General Carl von Horn, *Soldiering for Peace* (New York, 1964), p. 184.

[86] Dixon, interview.

acceded to on 19 July with the advance elements reporting to the Congo on 22 July.

In just over twenty-five months, Ireland, having initially committed five officers to the unarmed UNOGIL mission in June 1958, had now committed in excess of twelve hundred personnel to an armed peacekeeping force many thousands of miles away from home. On this occasion the deployment of armed Defence Forces units was preceded by the speedy passage of enabling legislation.[87] McCarthy had been the senior officer in charge of those first Irish UNMOs and now on reporting for duty with Major General von Horn's staff at UNOC headquarters in Leopoldville, he became the Irish link to three United Nations missions UNOGIL, UNTSO and now UNOC. He gave himself completely to the demands of his extensive duties in UNOC Headquarters and in the performance of these duties he died in a tragic car accident in Leopoldville on 27 October 1960.[88] Subsequently, following a commendation by Major General von Horn to the Irish national military

---

[87] Skelly, *United Nations*, p. 5. See also the Defence Forces (Amendment) Act, 1960, dated 26 July 1960, and the Defence Forces (Amendment No 2) Act, 1960, dated 1 Oct. 1960, which repealed that of 26 July 1960. The Defence Forces (Amendment No 2) Act 1960 was a major revision and in doing so the necessity for Dáil Éireann approval for the dispatch of more than twelve personnel is first mentioned. This is included under Section 2, where the provision for the dispatch of Defence Forces personnel is as follows: 'for service outside the State with a particular International United Nations Force without a resolution approving of such dispatch having been passed by Dáil Éireann if, but only if – (*a*) that International United Nations Force is unarmed, or (*b*) the contingent consists of not more than twelve members of the Permanent Defence Force, and the number of members of the Permanent Defence Force serving outside the State with that International United Nations Force will not, by reason of such despatch, be increased to a number exceeding twelve, or (*c*) the contingent is intended to replace, in whole or in part, or reinforce a contingent of the Permanent Defence Force serving outside the State as part of that International United Nations Force and consisting of more than twelve members of the Permanent Defence Force.' NAI DFA 305/173/1/2, 'Proposed Irish Contingent for UNEF' also refers. In fact as a consequence of the action taken in response to the PMUN's request for national guidance vis-á-vis possible participation in UNEF (July–Sept. 1957) the government had directed that preparatory arrangements should be made by the Department of Defence to prepare an outline for a proposed amendment of Defence Act 1954. The file contains information on Government Decision S16139 dated 3 Sept. 1957 directing the Minister for Defence to prepare to amend the Defence Act 1954 with a view to making an Irish contribution to UNEF possible. This direction includes the provision that no consideration would be given to introducing a Bill to the Dáil until the need for it emerged. The Department of Defence duly prepared a 'General Scheme of a Bill' designed to give effect to the government's decision. This was submitted to the Department of External Affairs for their comment on 25 Nov. 1957 and they replied on 23 Dec. 1957. This matter continued as a live issue on the file until 25 June 1958 when a handwritten note records the observations of the Attorney General concerning the sending of Irish Officers to Lebanon and the problems of Irish Army personnel serving under an officer of the armed forces of another country. The note also records the fact that the Deputy Judge Advocate General (Senior Military Legal Officer) was consulted on this matter. The note concludes with the observation that no special legal problems were foreseen regarding the officers who had volunteered for service in Lebanon adding that it was 'understood that as far as our municipal law was concerned these officers are answerable only to the senior Irish officer accompanying them'. (Issues related to the number/size of the group and the authority of the state to deploy them outside the state appear not to have been considered at this time.)

[88] MA, Obituary Notice issued by An Rannóg Nuachta, Ceanncheathrú an Airm, 28 Nov. 1960.

authorities, he was posthumously awarded the Distinguished Service Medal, the citation for which, using Major General von Horn's phrasing states inter alia:

> For distinguished service with United Nations Forces in the Republic of the Congo, as Chief Operations Officer / deputy Chief of Staff from August to October 1960, Colonel McCarthy was instrumental in getting the first amorphous Force Staff working and his boundless devotion to duty brought it through many a crisis. He gave of his utmost beyond the call of duty. The exhausting burden of his duties contributed to his untimely death.[89]

So ended the distinguished career of Colonel Justin McCarthy. He was the first Defence Forces officer to lead an overseas deployment of Defence Forces personnel on a United Nations mission and the first to serve in three different United Nations peacekeeping operations. Tragically he was also the first Defence Forces officer to give his life in the performance of United Nations peacekeeping. To date he also remains the most senior of the eighty-five Defence Forces fatalities on United Nations operations. To commemorate this distinguished service his colleagues and cadet classmates presented the Colonel Justin McCarthy Memorial Trophy which since September 1964 is competed for annually by the senior cadets of the Military College. Apart from this there is little else to commemorate this unique record.

McCarthy's death preceded by ten days the tragedy of the Niemba Ambush, when nine Irish soldiers lost their lives, and was understandably overlooked in the scale of that tragedy. However, all these deaths so early in the UNOC mission were a harsh coming-of-age for the nation as Ireland became aware of the cost that was to be borne in the cause of peace. Participation in UNOGIL established Ireland's place 'amongst the nations of the world', UNTSO continued our tenuous engagement in peacekeeping and provided a valuable learning process as a participant of the longest United Nations observer mission. Participation in ONUC followed and at that critical juncture in Cold War world politics, Ireland established itself as a reliable member of the United Nations peacekeeping club of neutral and non-aligned states. Involvement with the United Nations and other organisations in the cause of peace has continued since then and has now become an accepted dimension of Defence Forces service and of Irish foreign policy.

---

[89] MA, *Orduithe Gnáthaimh Ginearálta Brainnse an Árd Aidiúnach* (OGG 10 1967). General Routine Order 10/1967, signed by Major General Seán Collins Powell on 30 May 1967, notifying that the Minister for Defence had awarded the Distinguished Service Medal (Second Class) posthumously to Colonel Justin McCarthy.

Conclusion

Since joining the United Nations Ireland has participated in over thirty peacekeeping missions dispersed over the five continents. Uncompromised by superpower affiliations or influence, Ireland has also established an enviable reputation as an impartial 'honest broker' over this period. In effect it has through its involvement in peacekeeping lived up to the expectations of those for whom participation in and commitment to the United Nations Organisation was the grand strategy to establish Ireland's place on the world stage. This achievement is now a matter of historical record and one to which the Defence Forces peacekeeping operations have made a significant contribution. The genesis of that Defence Forces involvement in peacekeeping operations remains UNOGIL, closely followed by UNTSO, the mission in which the Defence Forces has retained a continuing unbroken presence since December 1958.

In reflecting on the significance of these missions there is a requirement for proper recognition of the pathfinding role of Colonel McCarthy and his forty-nine Irish UNOGIL colleagues. At a personal level their 1958 experience of foreign soldiering in the cause of peace infused fifty Irish participants with a personal confidence in their professionalism and a belief in their ability to hold their own on the international stage. Through this process and the opportunity afforded by these early missions in the Middle East, those graduates of national military education and training establishments were tested in an active, demanding, international operational environment and were not found wanting. Considered from the United Nations perspective the quality, strength and flexibility of resources provided by Ireland was impressive, together with the speed with which these were deployed to the mission area. This positive performance from a first time participant in peacekeeping marked Ireland as being eminently suitable for the 'peacekeeping club' of reliable, neutral/non-aligned nations and therefore a future contender for early consideration for challenging peacekeeping missions.

From the national perspective, the role and performance of its UNMOs in this first mission was a recognition of the calibre of the respective Irish officers and validation of national military training and expertise. The early weeks of UNOGIL tested and forged Ireland's ability to react quickly and positively to an emerging international security challenge. This in turn contributed to national confidence regarding peacekeeping matters, thereby facilitating a positive response by the government in July 1960 to the Secretary-General's request for Irish troops for ONUC. In addition, participation in UNTSO, together with the instructive lessons this provided for national civil and military administrations, was instrumental in preparing all concerned for the major escalation to participation in armed troop missions which emerged with the problem in the Congo in 1960.

At a more functional level participation in the 1958 Lebanon mission also raised the public profile of the Defence Forces with the publicity and media coverage it generated, ensuring the unparalleled success of the Defence Forces 1958 recruiting campaign. Minister for Defence, Kevin Boland, moving the estimates for his department on 29 April 1959, stated that the 1958 recruiting campaign for the Defence Forces was the most effective since 1950 due to the high profile conferred on the Defence Forces from United Nations service.[90] Those recruited during this campaign became the trained soldiers of 1960 and from this trained resource the battalions and companies for ONUC were drawn, which were in turn commanded, staffed, trained and led by many of the UNOGIL veterans.

---

[90] *Dáil Deb.*, vol. 174, col. 1273, 29 Apr. 1959 and comment in *Irish Press* Dáil Report 30 Apr. 1959 refer.

UNOGIL (June/Sep. 1958) – NOMINAL ROLL

Rank[91]	No[92]	Name		Date Deployed to Lebanon[93]	UNOGIL Duty Sector,[94] Miscellaneous Military Service[95] and post-Military Service Information[96]
Lt. Col.	0/4530	McCarthy, Justin	RIP	28 June	UNOGIL Duty Sector: UNOGIL HQ Beirut. Promoted Col. during service with UNOGIL. Was transferred to UNTSO in Dec. 1959 and to UNOC in 1960. Killed in a car accident while serving with UNOC. Awarded DSM posthumously.
Comdt.	0/4624	Johnston, Desmond	RIP	28 Sep.	UNOGIL Duty Sector: UNOGIL HQ Beirut and Amman Jordan. Oversaw the 1958 withdrawal of British Forces from Amman Jordan. Retired voluntarily in the rank of Comdt. and on retirement became manager of a hotel.
Comdt.	0/4724	Higgins, Malachi	RIP	28 June	UNOGIL Duty Sector: UNOGIL HQ Beirut Air Element. Retired in the rank of Lt. Col.
Comdt.	0/4779	Caseley, James	RIP	28 Aug.	UNOGIL Duty Sector: not identified. Retired in the rank of Col.

[91] Rank shown is that held by each officer on posting to UNOGIL.
[92] Officers service numbers from NAI DFA 305/1/129/1, Ceremonial Order for Medal Parade, 6 Apr. 1960.
[93] Individual deployment dates to UNOGIL from NAI DFA PMUN, 222/13/1 and Cox Diary (date of last group's departure is estimated and is based on cable information).
[94] UNOGIL Duty Sector information from Hogan, 'UNOGIL', Cox, UNOGIL Diary, and interviews with surviving UNOGIL veterans.
[95] Details of rank on retirement (age grounds and voluntary) from MA Numbers Book.
[96] Post service information based on information from interviews with surviving UNOGIL veterans.

Rank	No	Name			Date Deployed to Lebanon	UNOGIL Duty Sector, Miscellaneous Military Service and post-Military Service Information
Comdt.	0/4944	Curtain, Eoin		RIP	11 Oct.	NOGIL Duty Sector: Chtúra. Retired voluntarily in the rank of Comdt. and on retirement became UCD Sports Facilities Manager.
Comdt.	0/4957	Hogan, Patrick D.	RIP		28 Aug.	UNOGIL Duty Sector: Baalbeck. Retired in the rank of Brig. Gen.
Comdt.	0/4976	Carroll, William		RIP	28 Aug.	UNOGIL Duty Sector: Marjayoún. Retired in the rank of Brig. Gen.
Comdt.	0/5184	Quigley, John J.		RIP	28 Sep.	UNOGIL Duty Sector: UNOGIL HQ Beirut. Functioned as UNOGIL Medical Officer. Retired voluntarily in the rank of Comdt. and on retirement became Chief Medical Officer with Aer Lingus.
Comdt.	0/5752	Adams, Joe		RIP	5 Aug.	UNOGIL Duty Sector: UNOGIL HQ Beirut. Retired in the rank of Col.
Comdt.	0/5958	Coughlan, Gerard	RIP		28 June	UNOGIL Duty Sector: Tripoli. Held the Director of Engineering appointment. Retired in the rank of Col.
Capt.	0/5135	Condon, Edward	RIP		28 Aug.	UNOGIL Duty Sector: not identified. Retired in the rank of Col.

Rank	No	Name		Date Deployed to Lebanon	UNOGIL Duty Sector, Miscellaneous Military Service and post-Military Service Information
Capt.	0/5156	Keogh, Patrick	RIP	28 Aug.	NOGIL Duty Sector: Baalbeck. Held the Director of Cavalry appointment. Retired in the rank of Col.
Capt.	0/5157	Lavelle, Patrick	RIP	28 June	UNOGIL Duty Sector: Saida. Retired in the rank of Col.
Capt.	0/5781	White, Pat	RIP	5 Aug.	UNOGIL Duty Sector: Saida. Retired in the rank of Lt. Col.
Capt.	0/5789	O'Donnell, Michael J.	RIP	4 Oct.	UNOGIL Duty Sector: not identified. Retired in the rank of Lt. Col.
Capt.	0/5956	Murphy, B.G. (Bertie)	RIP	28 Sep.	UNOGIL Duty Sector: Marjayoún. Retired voluntarily in the rank of Capt.
Capt.	0/6111	Furlong, Thomas		28 Aug.	UNOGIL Duty Sector: Baalbeck. Retired in the rank of Lt. Col.
Capt.	0/6318	Nestor, Ambrose M.	RIP	4 Oct.	UNOGIL Duty Sector: UNOGIL HQ Beirut. Functioned as UNOGIL Military Police Officer. Retired voluntarily in the rank of Comdt. and on retirement joined the Zambian Police.
Capt.	0/6356	Woods, Chris	RIP	5 Aug.	UNOGIL Duty Sector: Tripoli. Retired voluntarily in the rank of Comdt. and on retirement joined a Building Society.

Rank	No	Name		Date Deployed to Lebanon	UNOGIL Duty Sector, Miscellaneous Military Service and post-Military Service Information
Capt.	0/6375	Tracey, Tom	RIP	5 Aug.	UNOGIL Duty Sector: Saida. Retired voluntarily in the rank of Comdt. and on retirement joined Civil Defence.
Capt.	0/6377	Russell, Edward (Ted)		28 Sep.	UNOGIL Duty Sector: Marjayoún. Retired in the rank of Col.
Capt.	0/6378	Fitzpatrick, Joe M.	RIP	4 Oct.	UNOGIL Duty Sector: Saida. Awarded DSM for action in Congo. Retired in the rank of Col.
Capt.	0/6383	Hogan, Louis	RIP	28 Aug.	UNOGIL Duty Sector: Beirut. Became Defence Forces Chief of Staff. Retired in the rank of Lieut. Gen.
Capt.	0/6386	Allen, Patrick	RIP	4 Oct.	UNOGIL Duty Sector: Chtúra. Retired in the rank of Lt. Col.
Capt.	0/6393	Gouldsborough, Harry	RIP	4 Oct.	UNOGIL Duty Sector: not identified. Retired in the rank of Lt. Col.
Capt.	0/6394	Henderson, Rory		28 June	UNOGIL Duty Sector: Chtúra. Completed his service as Aide-de-camp to President de Valera. Retired in the rank of Col.
Capt.	0/6398	Quinlan, Michael F.	RIP	28 Sep.	UNOGIL Duty Sector: not identified. Retired in the rank of Lieut. Col.

Rank	No	Name		Date Deployed to Lebanon	UNOGIL Duty Sector, Miscellaneous Military Service and post-Military Service Information
Capt.	0/6658	Gill, Gerard	RIP	28 Aug.	UNOGIL Duty Sector: Tripoli. Held the Director of Observer Corps appointment. Retired in the rank of Col.
Capt.	0/6702	Jordan, Pat	RIP	5 Aug.	UNOGIL Duty Sector: UNOGIL HQ Beirut. Moved to UNTSO with Col. McCarthy. Held the senior military legal appointment of Deputy Judge Advocate General. Retired in the rank of Col.
Capt.	0/6760	Sloan, J. (Noel)		4 Oct.	UNOGIL Duty Sector: Saida. Retired voluntarily in the rank of Comdt. and on retirement joined Irish Industrial Gases.
Capt.	0/6858	Liddy, James	RIP	28 Aug.	UNOGIL Duty Sector: Beirut and UNOGIL Air Element. Killed in service flying accident.
Capt.	0/6871	O'Connor, Francis	RIP	8 Aug.	NOGIL Duty Sector: not identified. Retired in the rank of Col.
Capt.	0/6881	Doyle, Tom	RIP	4 Oct.	NOGIL Duty Sector: Marjayoún. Retired voluntarily in the rank of Capt. and on retirement worked with Alexandra College and the Law Society.

Rank	No	Name		Date Deployed to Lebanon	UNOGIL Duty Sector, Miscellaneous Military Service and post-Military Service Information
Capt.	0/6931	Moran, James		28 Sep.	UNOGIL Duty Sector: Baalbeck. Retired voluntarily in the rank of Capt. and on retirement was employed in IBEC.
Capt.	0/6967	Bradley, Michael	RIP	4 Oct.	UNOGIL Duty Sector: not identified. Retired voluntarily in the rank of Comdt. and on retirement pursued a legal career.
Capt.	0/7108	Fagan, James J.		28 Sep.	UNOGIL Duty Sector: Tripoli. Retired in the rank of Col.
Capt.	0/7113	Mulvihill, J.D. (Dermot)	RIP	28 Sep.	UNOGIL Duty Sector: Tripoli. Retired in the rank of Col.
Capt.	0/7261	MacConchoille (Cox), Colm		28 Sep.	UNOGIL Duty Sector: Marjayoún. Retired in the rank of Col.
Capt.	0/7284	O'Flynn, William		4 Oct.	UNOGIL Duty Sector: not identified. Retired voluntarily in the rank of Comdt.
Capt.	0/7366	Duff, T.F. (Des)		4 Oct.	UNOGIL Duty Sector: Marjayoún. Retired voluntarily in the rank of Capt.
Lieut.	0/7355	O'Brien, Jack	RIP	4 Oct.	NOGIL Duty Sector: Baalbeck. Aide-de-camp to Taoiseach Seán Lemass. Retired voluntarily in the rank of Comdt. and on retirement established and managed a private security company.

Rank	No	Name		Date Deployed to Lebanon	UNOGIL Duty Sector, Miscellaneous Military Service and post-Military Service Information
Lieut.	0/7356	Sheehy, Edward (Ted)		4 Oct.	UNOGIL Duty Sector: Baalbeck. Retired in the rank of Col.
Lieut.	0/7371	Carroll, Mark	RIP	4 Oct.	UNOGIL Duty Sector: Baalbeck. Died in service.
Lieut.	0/7373	Croke, P. (Jim)		4 Oct.	UNOGIL Duty Sector: UNOGIL HQ Beirut and Saida. Retired in the rank of Col.
Lieut.	0/7410	Walsh, P. L. (Leo)	RIP	28 Sep.	UNOGIL Duty Sector: Saida. Retired voluntarily in the rank of Capt. and on retirement joined the Zambian Police.
Lieut.	0/7411	Buckley, Leo P.	RIP	28 Sep.	UNOGIL Duty Sector: Saida. Retired in the rank of Col.
Lieut.	0/7416	O'Connell, Fergus		4 Oct.	UNOGIL Duty Sector: Baalbeck. Held the appointment of Defence Forces Quartermaster General. Retired in the rank of Maj. Gen.
Lieut.	0/7422	McCorley, Roger	RIP	4 Oct.	UNOGIL Duty Sector: Baalbeck. Awarded DSM for action in Congo. Retired in the rank of Col.
Lieut.	0/7423	Ryan, John		4 Oct.	UNOGIL Duty Sector: Baalbeck. Retired in the rank of Col.
Lieut.	0/7449	Dixon, Pat		4 Oct.	UNOGIL Duty Sector: Chtaúra. Retired in the rank of Brig. Gen.

Chapter Five

Ireland's contribution to the United Nations Mission in the Congo (ONUC): keeping the peace in Katanga

EDWARD BURKE

Introduction

'*We are flying into the unknown.*'
Michael O'Halloran, *Irish Press* journalist accompanying the
32nd Battalion to the Congo.[1]

United Nations Secretary-General Dag Hammarskjöld's request for troops from Ireland to serve in the Congo caught the Irish government and the Irish Army by surprise. The Chief of Staff of the army, Lieutenant General Seán MacEoin, was summoned on a Sunday morning to General Headquarters (GHQ) in Dublin, where the Minister for Defence, Kevin Boland, told him of Hammarskjöld's initiative. The extent of Ireland's previous involvement in United Nations deployment overseas had been confined to sending fifty officers abroad as part of the United Nations Observation Group in Lebanon (UNOGIL) and as part of United Nations Truce Supervision Organisation (UNTSO) from 1958.[2] MacEoin later reflected that the army had not

> given any serious thought to participation in a United Nations operation with troops, apart from a short study that was done by our plans and operations people in GHQ, which reckoned at the end of some brief deliberations that in our situation at the time the most we could afford was a reinforced company; at the very best 250–300 soldiers all ranks.[3]

---

[1] Michael O' Halloran, 'A flight into the unknown', *Irish Press*, 28 July 1960.
[2] For an account of Irish participation in these missions see Richard Heaslip's chapter in this volume, pp. 79–116.
[3] Seán MacEoin, 'The Congo (ONUC): The Military Perspective', *Irish Sword*, Summer 1995, pp. 43–7, p. 43.

In 1959, the Irish believed they were prepared to send 300 soldiers on peace-keeping duties; by August 1960 just under 1,400 Irish troops were serving in the Congo in a United Nations force of approximately 17,000 men.[4] This increase was due to a combination of political pressure and public enthusiasm to meet Hammarskjöld's request and MacEoin's desire that the Irish Army would find a renewed purpose following a period in the doldrums after the end of the second world war.[5] Ireland was still an emerging player on the international stage – it had achieved its independence less than forty years prior to the Congo crisis and secured United Nations membership only five years previously. Like many other young states, including newly independent states in Africa, Ireland yearned for an opportunity to be noticed and praised.

This chapter focuses on Ireland's participation in the United Nations Operation in the Congo (ONUC). The Congo was then, as now, a country riven by civil war. Katanga, a province in the south-east of the Congo, which declared its independence from the central government in Leopoldville (now Kinshasa) shortly after Congolese independence, and where Irish diplomat Dr Conor Cruise O' Brien served as Hammarskjöld's Personal Representative from June to November 1961, is a name synonymous with the Irish contribution to the United Nations presence in the Congo.

The initial deployment of the United Nations to the secessionist state of Katanga played a crucial role in creating the circumstances in which the United Nations would operate in subsequent months and years in trying to negotiate, and eventually force, the reunification of the Congo. The chapter concentrates on this early period in order to understand how the United Nations attempted to deal with the Katangan secession and why this caused so many problems for the Irish troops who served in Katanga. Ireland provided key leadership in Katanga even before Cruise O'Brien's appointment. Colonel Harry Byrne was the United Nations Force Commander in Katanga from August to December 1960. This period also coincided with the deployment of the 33rd Irish Battalion to the Congo. These troops served in Katanga from August 1960 to January 1961, and it is through their experiences and testimony that the chapter will evaluate the United Nations presence in Katanga.

---

[4] The Irish Army at that time contained approximately 8,500 enlisted regulars. For details of UN troop numbers in the Congo, see *The Blue Helmets. A review of United Nations Peacekeeping* (New York, 1985), pp. 344–6.

[5] It was this desire to give the army a renewed sense of purpose that prompted MacEoin to recommend Irish participation in the UN Operation in the Congo (ONUC): 'we said to hell whether they were well prepared or not, it was worth it to give 700 men an opportunity of this experience … The meeting of this challenge – the participation of a country with an unprepared army in the tropics – was magnificent, and in fact it was that very response that resulted in what a good many people, including myself, thought a bit rash. This was the sending of a second battalion of a few weeks later.' MacEoin, *The Military Perspective*, p. 44.

The Belgian Legacy

'We have always defended the law, particularly in the field of international relations, but keeping order and safeguarding lives is a duty which surpasses all others. Belgium has recognized the independence of the Congo – yes. But not any kind of independence.'[6]

Editorial of *La Libre Belgique*, 9–10 July 1960.

In trying to understand the situation in Katanga when the Irish deployed there in August 1960, it is necessary to appreciate the origins of the conflict that led to Katanga seceding from the Congo. From the moment of the Belgian departure, Congolese independence got off to an unpromising start. On 30 June 1960, King Baudoin of Belgium was in Leopoldville to partake in celebrations marking the Congo's independence. He made a speech in Leopoldville in which he praised the enlightened policies of King Leopold II and the Belgian legacy in bringing civilisation to the Congo. This outraged the incoming Congolese government and Patrice Lumumba, the newly elected prime minister, reacted with a passionate speech condemning the Belgian legacy in the Congo, a speech which seems unremarkable today but which, in the paranoid atmosphere of the Cold War, marked him as a potential troublemaker in the eyes of many Western observers, especially the Americans and the British.[7]

In 1959 the Belgian government was willing to allow a degree of Congolese independence but was determined to maintain its control over key economic concerns. The Congo was ill-prepared for independence and therefore highly reliant upon the Belgian colonial administration.[8] Even so, its transition from colony to nation state would never have been easy. It was a country divided into five different regions, each with a variant climate, topography and economy, as well as a myriad of languages and dialects – a country not easily united. On the eve of independence, the Congo had a population of fourteen million Congolese and an additional 100,000 European settlers. The province of Katanga was originally politically represented by the Conakat movement (Confédération des Associations Tribales du Katanga), a loose association of tribes. This soon fractured however, the Baluba tribe dominant in the north leaving to form the Association des Baluba du Katanga (Balubakat), led by Jason Sendwe. After this split, it

---

[6] Quoted in Catherine Hoskyns, *The Congo Since Independence* (London, 1965), p. 95.

[7] Leopold II was a particularly odious figure to most Congolese politicians; Leopold II had initiated a barbaric programme of exploitation in the Congo. See Adam Hochschild, *King Leopold's Ghost* (London 1998). These abuses were later documented by Roger Casement, for which he received a knighthood. Casement's Irish origins were often invoked by Minister for External Relations, Frank Aiken, including at the General Assembly (20 Sept.–17 Oct. 1960, *Official Records of the General Assembly* (hereafter *ORGA*), 15th Session (Part 1), Vol. 1 (New York, 1961), p. 481).

[8] Upon independence the Congo had a total of twenty-six university graduates (See Hoskyns, *Congo*, p. 42.).

became clear that the Conakat party, of which Moise Tshombe was leader, was determined to ally itself to Belgian interests. As early as 1959, its party manifesto contained the following passage lauding the paternal influence of the Belgians and denigrating the indigenous population:

> A sector of humanity has inherited no civilisation, no energy, no ideas, no interests to defend ... the black race has nothing behind it. It is a people without writing, without history, without philosophy, without any consistency ... let us maintain the trust of the good people who came to help us out of our state of stagnation.[9]

Request for United Nations intervention

When the Congolese armed forces, the Force Publique, mutinied in the first week of independence, it was essentially a reaction against their continued subordination to their Belgian officers (the white officer corps had been retained by the new government to prevent any sudden disruption of the armed forces). General Émile Janssens, the commanding officer of the Force Publique, had gathered a group of senior officers and NCOs together on 4 July and wrote on the blackboard the inflammatory order: 'before independence = after independence'. This was not what Congolese soldiers had in mind and some mutinied against their officers. When incidents of maltreatment of white civilians were reported in the immediate aftermath of the Force Publique mutiny, Belgians were outraged and demanded action. Prime Minister Patrice Lumumba, a tempermental yet charismatic leader, made matters worse by reversing his earlier decision to allow a slow period of transition within the Force Publique and dismissed all Belgian officers, which caused a further erosion of discipline in the Force Publique (later renamed the ANC – Armée National Congolaise – by Lumumba's government). Less than two weeks after independence, Belgian ministers Willem Ganshof and Auguste de Schryver were sent by their government in Brussels to deliver an ultimatum to Lumumba: he could either request Belgian military assistance or Belgium would intervene anyway.[10] Belgian paratroopers were ordered to reoccupy strategic points in the country and subsequently became involved in skirmishes with Congolese forces. For the recently decolonised states in Africa and Asia, this was a flagrant breach of sovereignty and a dangerous precedent to ignore. Leading African statesmen, such as President Kwame Nkrumah of Ghana, urged Patrice Lumumba to appeal to the United Nations for assistance.[11] On 14 June 1960, in response to a request from the

---

[9] Conakat Party literature, quoted in Ludo De Witte, *The Assassination of Lumumba* (London, 2001), p. 38.
[10] Hoskyns, *Congo*, p. 6.
[11] Conor Cruise O'Brien, 'The Congo: (ONUC): The Political Perspective', *Irish Sword*, Summer 1995, pp. 37–42, p. 39.

Congolese government, the United Nations was mandated to intervene in the Congo and the United Nations Operation in the Congo (Opération des Nations Unies au Congo – ONUC) was formed.

The United Nations deployment to the Congo

> '*The ONUC operations have demonstrated all too clearly that the super-vision and promotion of law and order in a setting of domestic strife and secessionist movements backed by outside interference, are scarcely compatible with the ideal of neutrality and impartiality.*'[12]
>
> United Nations Legal Officer, Roger Simmonds, reviewing ONUC in 1968.

The purpose of the United Nations presence in the Congo was ostensibly clear: to arrange for the repatriation of Belgian soldiers and to provide assistance to the Congolese government in developing their security forces to maintain law and order in the Congo. By mid-August 1960 hastily arranged contingents from eight African countries (Ethiopia, Ghana, Guinea, Liberia, Mali, Morocco, Sudan and Tunisia) and two European countries (Ireland and Sweden) had been dispatched to the Congo. African participation in ONUC was a matter of prestige: 'the whole operation was represented as a gesture of practical Pan-Africanism, a joint African effort to rescue the Congo from Belgian imperialism'.[13] Hammarskjöld was worried however that ONUC would lack an international character, that partisan African support of Lumumba might jeopardise the United Nations presence in Katanga and he had looked to his native Sweden and neutral Ireland to remedy this. The deployment of European troops to the Congo constituted 'a positive response to the western, inter alia, NATO states in neutralising the political balance in the Congo'.[14] Belgian opinion was also placated to some extent by the inclusion of European troops in the United Nations force. Con Cremin, Secretary of the Department of External Affairs, described an encounter with a Belgian Minister, the Comte de Laubespin, whom he thanked for praising the contribution of Ireland to ONUC 'and told him that our Ambassador in Brussels had, in fact, received similar expressions of satisfaction from the Belgian government, including the King, who had spoken most warmly of the presence of Irish troops in the Congo'.[15] The Belgian insistence on Irish and Swedish troops being deployed by the United Nations in Katanga would

---

[12] Roger Simmonds, *Legal Problems Arising From the United Nations Military Operations in the Congo* (The Hague, 1968), p. 45.

[13] Hoskyns, *Congo*, p. 131.

[14] Katsumi Ishizuka, *Ireland and International Peacekeeping Operations 1960–2000* (London, 2005), p. 35.

[15] National Archives of Ireland (herafter NAI), Department of the Taoiseach S16137C, confidential note by Cremin, 22 Aug. 1960.

later become a source of considerable Congolese grievance against the United Nations.[16] Katanga was to be the Achilles heel of ONUC.

Katanga secedes

'All of Afro-Asia was anti-Tshombe. They regarded Tshombe as the figure-head of their bad dreams ... here was a man playing into the hands of the whites and splitting off the rich part of Katanga from his country as a whole with incalcuable consequences.'[17]

Colonel E.D. Doyle.

Katanga far outstripped the other Congolese provinces in terms of mineral resources and it was widely accepted that the Congo's economic viability depended on this wealth.[18] The Union Minière, which controlled mining activities in the region, was estimated to be worth £177.5 million in 1959, making annual profits of up to £32 million, a vast amount of money at that time. The Union Minière had originally been controlled by King Leopold II, but now had a number of British, South African, American and Belgian investors who were greatly concerned at the prospect of any disruption of the colonial conditions which had been most profitable. They particularly disliked the prospect of Lumumba's government becoming stakeholders in the Union Minière as the Belgian administration had been previously. In 1959, Katanga was producing sixty percent of the world's cobalt and eight to ten percent of the world's copper, it had also been the principal uranium supplier for the atomic bomb programme of the United States. The Union Minière became highly influential supporters of the Moise Tshombe's Conakat party, both directly in terms of essential capital, but also through their effective lobbying of Western governments.[19]

As well as a coterie of Belgian political advisers, Belgian army officers played a significant role in the dissolution of the Congo in July 1960. Majors Weber, Crèvecœur and an almost completely white officer corps commanded the Katangan armed forces.[20] Belgium's influence upon the secession of

---

[16] The British Ambassador in Brussels, Sir John Nicholls believed that it was in Britain's interests 'to take any chance, however remote, of maintaining by agreement some sort of autonomy for Katanga if only to protect Belgian (and British) economic interests there'. He suggested several means of doing this: '(a) persuading Hammarskjöld to use only white troops, (b) infiltrating United Nations forces gradually, (c) as in rest of Congo not forcing Belgian troops out until United Nations forces are effectively in control' (United Kingdom National Archives (hereafter TNA) FO 371/146789 Telegram from Brussels Embassy).

[17] Author's interview with Col. E.D. Doyle, Dublin, 18 Aug. 2005.

[18] Alan James, *Britain and the Congo Crisis* (London, 1996), p. 31. Although Moise Tshombe is sometimes depicted as a retiring Methodist shopkeeper who was merely a Belgian-imposed stooge, this is highly inaccurate. Tshombe was highly reliant upon external assistance but his regime also had considerable support among the Bayeke and Balunda people who inhabited Southern Katanga. Tshombe was the son-in-law of the Chief of the Balunda and his Interior Minister Godefroid Munongo was of the royal house of the Bayeke. See Hoskyns, *Congo*, pp. 26–7.

[19] Ibid., pp. 31–2.

[20] Katangans are also sometimes referred to as Katangese.

Katanga was obvious and by the end of July the British *Daily Telegraph* (a newspaper not unsympathetic to empire and Western interests) had come to the conclusion that:

> The masquerade of Katanga 'independence' is becoming daily more pathetic. M. Tshombe, the self-styled President, is today far more under the domination of Belgian officials than when he was an obscure politician before Congo's independence. His regime depends entirely on Belgian arms, men and money. Without this, his Government would in all probability be quickly pulled down from within and without. The outline of Belgium's emergency policy for Katanga is now discernible. It is to protect the great Belgian financial stake here and to hold a political bridgehead in the hope of Congolese union amenable to Belgium and the West.[21]

Belgian influence pervaded all levels of Katanga's government. A Belgian intelligence officer, Colonel Vandewalle, observed that when the heads of the Belgian Technical Mission met in the Katangan capital, Elisabethville, 'all the grey matter ruling Katanga was gathered together'.[22] It was no wonder that Hammarskjöld so angered Lumumba and the African members of the United Nations when he declared on 8 August that the secession of Katanga 'did not have its root in the Belgian attitude'.[23]

Negotiations with Katanga

> *'And even if the Katanga army is completely massacred all the warriors of the Ba-Yeke and of Mwate Yamvo will riddle your soldiers with arrows.'*[24]
> Godefroid Munongo, Interior Minister of Katanga, in a conversation with Ralph Bunche, Special Representative of the Secretary-General to the Congo, 4 August 1960.

While the United Nations had deployed successfully in the rest of the Congo, confined the ANC to barracks and facilitated the evacuation of most Belgian troops, in Katanga the proposed entry of the United Nations force had been met with outright hostility.[25] The Interior Minister of Katanga, Godefroid

---

[21] Ibid., p. 125.

[22] de Witte, *Lumumba*, p. 42.

[23] United Nations document S/4417, Secretary-General's Report to the Security Council, 8 Aug. 1960, quoted in Hoskyns, p. 167. The extensive assistance provided by Portugal and South Africa was also vital to Katanga's survival. Jules Gérard-Libois, *Katanga Secession*, (Wisconsin, 1966) p. 282. For an account of the Portuguese and South African attitudes during this period, see Kevin O'Sullivan's chapter in this volume, pp. 201–223.

[24] Hoskyns, *Congo*, p. 163.

[25] It should be noted that General Alexander, a British officer seconded to the newly established Ghanaian Army, was perceived to be overstepping the United Nations mandate when he disarmed the mutinous Force Publique (now renamed the Armée National Congolaise – ANC) and that these weapons were later returned much to the chagrin of the United Nations Force Commander, General Carl von Horn and his Irish Staff Officer, Colonel Justin McCarthy. See Carl von Horn, *Soldiering for Peace* (New York, 1964).

Munongo, threatened to resist a United Nations presence by any means possible. Essentially, the Katangan regime called Hammarskjöld's bluff; the Secretary-General's Military Adviser, the Indian Brigadier General Indar Rikhye, recalled that

> it was neither possible nor permissible to consider fighting their way into Katanga, and therefore the cooperation of the Belgians – who had not only their troops there but also advisers who influenced Katangese leaders and led the Katanga gendarmerie – was vital if the United Nations were to succeed.[26]

Hammarskjöld sought to reassure Tshombe and his advisers that ONUC deployment to Katanga was not part of a United Nations plan to coerce the province to end its secession from the Congo. He successfully guided a resolution through the Security Council which declared that while United Nations entry into Katanga was necessary, it also reaffirmed that ONUC 'will not be a party to or in any way intervene in or be used to influence the outcome of any internal conflict, constitutional or otherwise'.[27] With chaos reigning elsewhere in the Congo in August 1960, he did not want the United Nations forces to have to fight their way into Katanga, or to have to fight to stay there.

On 12 August, Hammarskjöld flew into Elisabethville to open negotiations with Thsombe's regime for United Nations entry to Katanga. Tshombe was flanked by Belgian officials, who successfully manoeuvred Hammarskjöld into being photographed beside the secessionist Katangan flag and in another politically sensitive gesture provided Hammarskjöld with lodgings in the Union Minière guesthouse in Elisabethville. The visit was further compromised when a group of Baluba, who had arrived in Elisabethville to petition Hammarskjöld, was promptly arrested upon the orders of Major Weber. Rikhye 'gently chided Weber for the undue use of force by his police and left it at that'. He also noted that: 'On arrival I found that the northern Balubas, the Balubakat, as opponents of Tshombe's Conakat party were a constant target for harrassment and physical attack, and that we would therefore have to provide protection for them as a priority'.[28]

The Belgians would later declare that Hammarskjöld had accepted eight out of ten conditions put to him by Tshombe. Pierre Davister, a Belgian journalist sympathetic to Katanga, described the reaction in Elisabethville:

---

[26] Indar Jit Rikhye, *Military Adviser to the Secretary-General: UN Peacekeeping and the Congo Crisis* (London, 1993), p. 43.

[27] James, *Britain and the Congo*, p. xviii.

[28] While some commentators quoted in this text prefer to use 'Balubas' as a plural, I have used the more conventional plural of Baluba. Rikhye, *Military Adviser*, p. 43.

It was beyond anything one could have hoped for. The ruling team of d'Aspremont and Rothschild [two senior Belgian officials in Katanga] could not believe its eyes! Little Ambassador Rothschild especially was literally bursting with joy and one had only to see his little eyes sparkling with delight, to hear his bursts of piping laughter, to know that he had some say in drawing up the Ten Commandments of Moses (Moise)! ... certainly the whole of the 'Katanga solution' had consisted up to this moment of a terrific bluff ... it had come to this: the Secretary-General of the United Nations had accepted to enter officially into *pouparlers* with an unrecognised state.[29]

The establishment of United Nations Eastern Command in Elisabethville and the deployment of United Nations troops in Katanga occurred soon after Hammarskjöld's negotiations.[30] The directives issued by the officer in charge of Eastern Command, Colonel Byrne, gave an indication as to why those favourable to Katanga were particularly pleased at the terms of the United Nations entry to the province.

Directive No. 1 to United Nations troops issued from Eastern Command Headquarters, Elisabethville on 22 August, recognised the primacy of the Katangan gendarmerie in policing Katanga, even in areas where the regime had no popular support such as in the north of the province. Amazingly, the United Nations Directive seemed to imply that Katangan consent was required for the United Nations to act as a force for public order: 'Primary responsibility for public order belongs to the local security authorities. Upon their request for assistance made to our units, however, United Nations troops may take action *in their place*'.[31] Lieutenant Colonel Richard Bunworth, Commanding Officer of the 33rd Irish Battalion, would later report that they were issued 'a threat by Mr. Munongo to shoot United Nations troops if they interfered with the local authorities in the performance of their duties'.[32] Although the overall Force Commander of ONUC, the Swedish Major General Carl von Horn, had instructed the United Nations force to protect all civilians from atrocities, Katanga appeared to be an exception:

Police and civil authorities may not control or in any way interfere with United Nations operations, personnel, property, vehicles or aircraft; *United Nations troops may not in any way interfere with police control of all other persons and property.* They are however to report to this HQ, through appropriate confidential channels, any incidents

---

[29] Pierre Davister, *Katanga enjeu du monde,* quoted in Conor Cruise O'Brien, *To Katanga and Back: A UN case study* (London, 1962), pp. 91–2.

[30] Later Sub-Command Eastern Province (SCOMEP).

[31] Military Archives, Cathal Brugha Barracks, Dublin (hereafter MA), 33rd Infantry Battalion Unit History, Annex C – Directive No. 1 (confidential).

[32] Ibid., introductory letter from Col. Bunworth.

arising from the exercise by the local authorities of their police powers.[33]

Lieutenant Colonel Bunworth later regretted that this policy of non-interference did not prevent atrocities being committed by Katangan forces:

> To have one's military potential so restricted in the presence of the Balubakat who could see armed United Nations forces standing by when these people were engaged in the unequal military struggle and could NOT realise the helplessness of our United Nations troops.[34]

Pierre Davister concluded in the Belgian journal, *Pourqoui Pas?*, that:

> The bluff of yesterday may now become a sordid reality. If the internal organisation of Katanga can be strengthened, if the United Nations troops limit themselves to their role as a police force and if the existence of Katanga's security forces becomes more than a myth, then Lumumba can go boil himself an egg; he will have lost the game.[35]

Lumumba reacted furiously to what he felt was the United Nations de facto recognition of an illegal secessionist regime. He bitterly condemned Hammarskjöld, who had not consulted him or the Baluba opposition in Katanga. He demanded the removal of all non-African troops from Katanga, their replacement with Ghanaian and Guinean troops and an immediate commitment by the United Nations to end the secession of Katanga.[36] Lumumba was greatly disliked by many within the United Nations for his personal attacks on Hammarskjöld. They were not alone; his rash appeal to the Soviet Union for assistance in ending the secession of Katanga had appalled many in the West. A personal letter from Eamon Kennedy at the Irish Permanent Mission to the United Nations in New York to Con Cremin in Dublin (PMUN) sums up this obvious distaste for Lumumba: 'The nigger in the wood-pile is the government itself, which means Lumumba. No one here seriously doubts this.'[37]

---

[33] Ibid., Annex C – Directive No. 1 (Confidential), my italics.

[34] Ibid., introductory letter from Col. Bunworth.

[35] Pierre Davister, *Katanga enjeu du monde*, quoted in Hoskyns, *Congo*, p. 173.

[36] Hoskyns, *Congo*, p. 174. Patrice Lumumba wrote to Hammarskjöld: 'It is incomprehensible to me that you should have sent only Swedish and Irish troops to Katanga, systematically excluding troops from the African States ...' Letter dated 15 August from Patrice Lumumba, quoted in Rosalyn Higgins, *United Nations Peacekeeping 1946–1967* Vol. III (Oxford, 1980), p. 133. While Swedes and Irish were initially deployed, several African contingents were added soon after. Lumumba emphasised the threat of Swedish troops to the Congolese: 'The Swedes are only Belgians in disguise'. See Brian Urquhart, *Hammarskjöld* (London, 1982), p. 429.

[37] A Western policy of tolerating Katanga's secession until a more amenable leader had replaced Patrice Lumumba seems to have been pravalent in the UN during the early existence of ONUC. NAI DFA PMUN File 429 (M/13/6 Vol. 1), Kennedy to Cremin, 28 Aug. 1960.

United Nations tasks in Katanga

*'Above everything else we lacked experience and consequently it was very
difficult for us to visualise what a U.N. Peacekeeping Mission entailed.'*[38]
Lieutenant Colonel Richard Bunworth, Commanding Officer of
the 33rd Battalion.

The 33rd Irish Battalion prepared to deploy in Katanga in mid-August 1960,
being transported by the United States Air Force to the Congo via Wheelus
Air Force Base in Libya, following a similar route to the 32nd Battalion under
the command of Lieutenant Colonel Mortimer 'Murt' Buckley, which had
deployed to Kivu Province a month previously.[39] Colonel Harry Byrne had
been hurriedly appointed Force Commander for the Provinces of Kivu and
Katanga a few days before their arrival, with responsibility for 4,800 United
Nations troops. In Elisabethville, Colonel E.D. Doyle recalls establishing contact with the Belgian troops in Katanga in order to arrange their repatriation.
This was to be the first of the tasks assigned to Colonel Byrne's command in
Katanga. Colonel Doyle, who was then a signals officer, remembers that Byrne
and his staff were received in a hostile manner by Colonel Champion at the
Belgian Army Headquarters in Elisabethville, whom they had asked to brief
them regarding the Belgian military in Katanga: 'We had no idea we were
going to Katanga until six o' clock the night before. We were being briefed in
French about a map we had never really looked at before'.[40] Listening to the
cold, rushed presentation of Colonel Champion describing the Belgian Army's
positions in Katanga, Doyle reflected that Byrne would have a very difficult
task in gaining cooperation from this officer. Commandant Kevin O'Brien
turned to the United Nations Political Representative in Elisabethville and
asked him to compliment Colonel Champion on the logical deployment of
the Belgian Army. It was a masterstroke; Colonel Champion beamed with
approval and O'Brien received a cup of coffee and a trace of the map, which
saved an estimated three days' work for Byrne's staff. The 33rd Battalion was
to take control of Kamina air base and it was through here that Belgian troops
began to withdraw. The 33rd had been surprised by this task, they were dispatched to the Congo with such haste that little time had been available in
Ireland to gain even a rudimentary knowledge of Katanga. Colonel Donal
Crowley, then a young captain serving with 'A' Company recalled:

> Meeting Belgians was a surprise, I didn't expect to be meeting Belgian
> military officers but we did down at Kamina, at the Belgian Air Force
> School and they were very helpful to us. They were very experienced
> fellows.[41]

---

[38] MA, 33rd Infantry Battalion Unit History, introductory letter from Col. Bunworth.
[39] Kivu is the province directly to the north of Katanga.
[40] Doyle interview.
[41] Interview with Col. Donal Crowley, Dublin, 12 Aug. 2005.

Unaware of the Belgian civil, police and military presence, the Irish had a limited grasp of the political chasm that divided Katanga:

> Little was known of the delicate balance which existed between the two main political parties in Katanga – Conakats on one side led by Moise Tshombe and the Balubakats on the other side led by the exiled Jason Sendwe.[42]

Despite their sudden arrival, the Irish coped admirably in adapting to their role at Kamina. A much more onerous task for the Irish and the United Nations was the removal of those Belgian officers who had been seconded to serve with the Katangan forces.

The fate of the Belgian Technical Mission to Katanga was a subject of much discussion at the United Nations: where did technical assistance end and external aggression begin? On one point the views of the Afro-Asian group at the United Nations and those of Belgium coalesced: that the withdrawal of Belgian 'technicians' would likely prove a fatal blow to Katanga's hope of maintaining its secession, and the collapse, according to the Belgians, of an oasis of law and order in the Congo.[43] The United Nations Force Commander, General von Horn, was sympathetic to Katanga, 'having seen the chaos in the five other provinces which had followed the flight of the Belgians, it struck me as little short of madness to contemplate disrupting a well-organised state like Katanga'.[44] The British were of the opinion that the United Nations could be relied upon to act favourably towards Tshombe's regime in the short-term at least. The British Deputy Permanent Representative to the United Nations, Harold Beeley, in a report to the British Foreign Office, gave an account of a conversation with Hammarskjöld, with whom he was on excellent terms, where the Secretary-General warned 'he could no longer "protect" Tshombe if his violent outbursts became public knowledge'.[45] Hammarskjöld considered that Lumumba was 'clearly a Communist stooge' and that he himself had 'conceived the United Nations operation as a means of preventing the Soviet penetration of Africa'.[46] The French were also anxious to preserve a Western sphere of influence in the Congo through the maintenance of the Belgian presence after independence.[47] Within Katanga itself, the British Consul in

---

[42] MA, History of the 33rd Battalion, introductory letter from Col. Bunworth.

[43] *United Nations Yearbook 1960* (New York, 1960), p. 60.

[44] Von Horn, *Soldiering*, p. 218.

[45] TNA FO 371/146790, Relations with Katanga. Beeley also relates that he had to be smuggled out of the basement of the building where he met Hammarskjöld so as not to draw suspicion regarding their regular amiable meetings.

[46] TNA FO 371/146778, the Secretary-General's intentions with regard to military operations: the constitutional and administrative plan, quoted in James, pp. 67–8.

[47] Sir John Nicholls, the British Ambassador to Brussels, describes the views of the French Foreign Ministry subsequent to discussions on Katanga and the Congo: 'French government feel strongly that Western Powers should do nothing which might impede restoration of Belgian influence' (TNA FO 371/146777 Telegram from Sir John Nicholls, Brussels to Foreign Office London, 18 Aug. 1960).

Elisabethville, Anthony G. Evans, considered that the United Nations Political Representative in Elisabethville, the New Zealander Ian Berendsen, was a sound supporter of Katanga's secession, but lacked the charisma to influence others: 'Berendsen, whose sympathies are all with Katanga, is a cold and hesitant personality. He lacks the character and drive necessary to impress the acceptance of his views on his superiors'.[48] Colonel E.D. Doyle, who was at ONUC HQ in Elisabethville, disagrees with this conclusion. He did not believe that Berendsen was working in any way independently from the United Nations to advance Katangan interests, but that he was 'the epitome of a proper international civil servant ... he took Hammarskjöld's policy and he applied it'.[49] Although Hammarskjöld and the United Nations would later appreciate the degree of support that Lumumba had in the Congo, and Special Representative Rajeshwar Dayal would seek ways of including him in a potential compromise government, in August 1960 it was clear that Hammarskjöld was unsympathetic to Lumumba and Baluba demands to end Katanga's secession by force. This was to be a source of resentment for the Baluba in northern Katanga in their attitude towards the United Nations.

ONUC Command

'Unfortunately, we were not "any army", we were a United Nations Force in which logic, military principles – even common sense – took second place to political factors.'[50]

Major-General Carl von Horn, Force Commander of ONUC.

Whatever the alleged sympathies of the United Nations Secretariat to the secession of Katanga, the reluctance to reunite the Congo by more robust means is understandable, given the chaotic state of the Congolese central government from the beginning of independence. By September, central government had collapsed. President Joseph Kasavubu had dismissed the Lumumba government, and Lumumba dismissed Kasavubu in turn. Within a few weeks, the United Nations groomed Chief of Staff of the ANC, Colonel Joseph Mobutu had taken control of the capital and declared temporary military rule.[51] The United Nations acted with caution in Katanga; its presence had been initially tolerated as long as it did not threaten the viability of the Katanga secession. Colonel Byrne's task was made even

---

[48] Doyle interview, Dublin, 18 August. Col. Doyle is also of the opinion that Evans was 'an excitable little Welshman', given to drawing the wrong conclusions. Berendsen's immediate superior was Rajeshwar Dayal in Leopoldville, an Indian diplomat particularly disliked by the Katangese and the Western Powers.

[49] Ibid., Col. Doyle believed that the reunification of the Congo was inevitable given time, which the United Nations had to allow for: 'We saw the secession of Katanga as something that couldn't be sustained' (Doyle interview).

[50] Von Horn, *Soldiering*, p. 146.

[51] Brig.-Gen. Rikhye recounted in his memoirs the paternal guidance given by the Moroccan Gen. Ben Hammou Kettani to Mobutu during this period. See Rikhye, *Military Adviser*, p. 104.

more difficult given the confused nature of ONUC Command. Von Horn was regarded as a very poor Force Commander by Brigadier-General Rikhye, and as 'completely useless' by the Ghanaian Chief of Staff, Major-General Hugh Alexander (Rikhye later ascribed part of the cause of von Horn's ineptitude as being the combination of a 'good chef and a well-stocked cellar').[52] Von Horn and Rikhye often worked at cross-purposes, Rikhye issuing orders to the troops without von Horn's consent, which confused the chain of command. ONUC Command in Leopoldville appears to have been quite disorganised. Lieutenant General Seán MacEoin, when appointed Force Commander of ONUC in January 1961, was amazed to find that there were 172 staff officers, but that approximately 140 had been allocated almost no duties at all.[53] General Alexander, in a private report to President Nkrumah of Ghana, dated 28 April 1960, which was also forwarded secretly by Alexander to the British High Commissioner in Ghana and later, despite being a Ghanaian report, ironically marked 'UK Eyes Only', was of the opinion that 'the military inexperience of McKeon (sic), the present military commander, and his predecessor von Horn' was to blame for ONUC difficulties in Katanga.[54] Alexander was unfair here, both to MacEoin and von Horn, as he was either not aware or simply unsympathetic to the obvious reality that in United Nations operations military expediency will often be sacrificed for political necessity. Lieutenant Colonel Bunworth expressed this same frustration for the 33rd Irish Battalion in Katanga when he observed that:

> To be equipped and trained in the traditional use of infantry weapons, yet circumscribed in their use by the well-known and accepted United Nations policy of avoiding the use of force … was a situation difficult to accept in its finer points … often it meant that our soldiers had 'to turn the other cheek' when confronted by hostile tribesmen.[55]

This policy, according to Bunworth, was to have 'some tragic results'.[56]

The Baluba Revolt in North Katanga and the Rikhye Neutral Zones

'What exactly will be the duties of our Force? Will they be to protect the lives and property of farmers or the lives and property of the natives?'[57]
                                        Frank Sherwin TD, Dáil Éireann, 20 July 1960.

While some in ONUC regarded the Baluba as a politically unsophisticated, primitive people, there was nevertheless a distinct hostility among the Baluba

---

[52] Rikhye, *Military Adviser*, p. 128 and TNA DO 195/173, 'Statements and Reports made by General Alexander on the Situation in the Congo' (Top Secret).
[53] MacEoin, *Congo*, p. 46.
[54] TNA DO 195/173, 'Statements and Reports made by General Alexander on the situation in the Congo' (Top Secret).
[55] MA, 33rd Infantry Battalion Unit History, introductory letter from Col. Bunworth.
[56] Ibid.
[57] *Dáil Deb.*, vol. 183, cols. 1887–8, 20 July 1960.

in North Katanga towards the secessionist regime in Elisabethville. Colonel E.D. Doyle remembers that 'they knew about the "United Congo" in north Katanga ... the kids had a symbol for it'.[58] Anthony Evans, the British Consul in Katanga, was particularly concerned about the Baluba youth movement: 'The Baluba youth, especially in the towns, are politically-minded; most of them worship Sendwe and Lumumba'.[59] The Baluba uprising in late August and September was seen as a grave threat to Katanga, as it was feared that the ANC would join up with the Baluba guerrillas. The Katangan regime had been well equipped by its benefactors, however, and had even acquired a small air force. The Irish in Katanga were to bear witness to the aftermath of attacks by these Katangan aircraft. An Irish Army Medical Officer, Commandant Beckett, later reported treating 120 Baluba for horrific burns, many of them children.[60] The UN avoided taking action to restrict the Katangan regime's use of airfields, in contrast to its refusal to allow Patrice Lumumba access to the airport at Leopoldville.[61] Colonel Crowley recollects that the gendarmerie, in suppressing the Baluba revolt, would go at great speed through Baluba villages 'firing as they went'.[62] Jules Gérard-Libois, a Belgian in Katanga during this period, attempted to evaluate the extent of the violence at the end of 1960:

> The numbers of rebels killed since the beginning of 'reprisal' operations of the Katangan army was evaluated at about 7,000. We know what figures of this kind mean in Africa. Generally it is necessary to multiply by two, by three, by ten or even more if the result obtained is not to be far short of the truth ... Entire villages were razed and automatic weapons literally mowed down entire ranks of youths who – it must be agreed – marched idiotically to their death.[63]

Gangs of Baluba youth, armed with bicycle chains, bows and arrows and emboldened by drugs and witchcraft, were to prove as much an irritation to their own population as they were to the well-trained, Belgian-led mobile patrols that swept north Katanga.[64] It was in this highly volatile area that Irish peacekeepers were operating in late 1960.

---

[58] This symbol was the raising of the index finger in support of one, united Congo, Doyle interview.
[59] TNA FO 371/146663, 'The Internal Political Situation in Katanga Province 1960', letter from Evans, 28 Sept. 1960.
[60] McCaughren, Tom, *The Peacemakers of Niemba*, Browne and Nolan, 1966, p. 45. Also, Military Archives Dublin, History of the 33rd Battalion, account of patrol undertaken by Captain Pat Condron
[61] Jules Gérard-Libois, *Katanga*, p. 130.
[62] Crowley interview.
[63] Gerard-Libois, *Katanga Secession*, p. 126.
[64] The Baluba war parties committed many atrocities in North Katanga, with accounts of mutilation and burnings frequently appearing in the Western press. More were also invented, including stories of Irish soldiers being eaten alive. See George Martelli, *Experiment in World Government: An Account of the UN Operation in the Congo, 1960–1964* (London, 1966), p. 63.

As a means of ending the violence, Brigadier-General Rikhye negotiated with the Katangan regime the establishment of neutral zones, which Irish troops were to patrol, replacing the Malians in many areas with whom relations with the Katangans 'had greatly deteriorated'.[65] Rikhye was aware of the 'brutal measures the gendarmerie had adopted in repressing lawlessness', and believed the mediation of the United Nations was the only means to secure a cessation of the violence. There were two problems with this assessment: firstly, the United Nations 'had to gain the confidence not only of Tshombe but also of the Belgians' and secondly, Rikhye implied that the Baluba were guilty of 'lawlessness' but the laws they were defying were those of Katanga, a secessionist state they did not subscribe to. Restoring 'law and order', when no mutually acceptable law existed between the two belligerents would prove to be an increasingly difficult task for the Irish in Katanga.[66]

Rikhye overlooked in his memoirs a troubling aspect of the agreement over the neutral zones in the predominantly Balubakat-held north of the province, the perception that United Nations troops were merely fulfilling the same role as the white-officered Katangan gendarmerie. The United Nations agreed to protect Katangan owned mines, railways and factories. The gendarmerie were supposed to be confined to barracks in North Katanga (this was frequently not observed), while the United Nations would also conduct long-range patrols to 'restore law and order'. The British Consul in Elisabethville reported to the Foreign Office that in negotiations with Tshombe, Rikhye had 'expressed great appreciation for the Katangan point of view … and he agreed to proposals whereby United Nations forces would assume reponsibility for the rebellious areas of north-central Katanga'.[67] Rikhye should not have wondered why Tshombe would accept such an agreement. He hoped that the United Nations would act as a police force in north Katanga, suppressing Baluba 'lawlessness'. To the credit of the United Nations forces in Katanga, they did not fulfill the role envisaged for them by the Katangan and Belgian authorities. Evans complained a few weeks later that

> it was to be expected that United Nations troops would be less efficient than the Belgians in maintaining law and order but their initial passivity coupled with a refusal to allow the Gendarmerie to operate freely, together with the inevitable fraternisation with the local populace encouraged the Balubas to revolt.[68]

Colonel Byrne was clear in his orders that United Nations soldiers were not to actively take the side of the Katangan gendarmerie in repressing the Baluba revolt.

---

[65] MA, 33rd Infantry Battalion Unit History.
[66] Rikhye, *Military Adviser*, p. 121.
[67] TNA FO 371/146790, Evans to Foreign Office, 26 Oct. 1960.
[68] Ibid., Evans to Foreign Office, 19 Nov. 1960.

The 33rd Battalion in North Katanga

'Time and time again I was delighted with the humour that seemed to keep the Irish going under handicaps which would have driven the average European to despair ... transport was an especial nightmare. Byrne told me that it was impossible to mount the number of patrols which should have been going out – an unsatisfactory state of affairs which was to lead to unnecessary losses later on.'[69]

Major-General Carl von Horn, ONUC Force Commander.

Colonel Byrne had moved his headquarters in Katanga to the northeast after the Rikhye Agreement, to the town of Albertville on Lake Tanganyika. He brought the 33rd Irish Battalion with him, Colonel Juhlin of the Swedish contingent being appointed Deputy Commander in Katanga and assuming responsibility for the south. The geographical area that the Irish were asked to garrison and patrol was a daunting responsibility for 700 men. Added to this was the severe shortage of vehicles that the 33rd Battalion had to patrol with. The Transport Section history, compiled for the Battalion records on return to Ireland, made this clear:

> The total allotment of vehicles leaving Ireland was 10 Land Rovers and 5 jeeps. This was inadequate to meet the tasks the Battalion was called upon to perform, and throughout the sojourn in the Congo, the Unit was continually hampered by the lack of reliable transport.[70]

Locally acquired trucks were described as unreliable and unsuitable for military operations and the Irish did not deploy armoured cars to the Congo until January 1961.[71] A confidential report would later conclude (without irony) that, 'Irish transport is inadequate for mobile conditions'.[72] In reviewing communications, the 33rd Battalion records state that because of the unconventional distances the 33rd had to patrol, it did not possess enough radios of an adequate type. It was this same lack of radio equipment that would be called into question after a patrol under the command of Lieutenant Kevin Gleeson was attacked on 8 November 1960 near the town of Niemba in north Katanga. The Irish Minister for Defence, Kevin Boland, was either ignorant of the situation in the Congo regarding transport and other equipment, or else he deliberately misled the Dáil, when in reply to a question from Liam Cosgrave, he stated: 'I have no information which would suggest that our troops have been required to undertake the patrolling of areas which are too

---

[69] Von Horn, *Soldiering*, pp. 201–2.

[70] MA, 33rd Infantry Battalion Unit History, Annex M, Transport Section.

[71] These were Ford Mk. VI armoured cars armed with a single .303 Vickers Machine Gun. Irish troops later used British Ferret armoured cars, American M-113 APCs and Swedish APCs.

[72] University College Dublin Archives Department (hereafter, UCDA) P104/6301.

large in relation to their organisation or equipment'.[73]

Because of the rapid deployment of the 32nd and 33rd Irish battalions to the Congo and a lack of experience of overseas service, training in advance of departure from Ireland had been limited: 'Training consisted primarily of weapon firing, wireless and NO team training was ever possible'.[74] The Irish had not the modern weapons of the Belgian-armed Katangan gendarmerie, a comparision between the two was made in a report later seen by the Minister for External Relations, Frank Aiken. It demonstrates how neglected the army had been in resources in the period after the Second World War. Comparing rifles, the report states: 'The FN [semi-]automatic rifle produces considerably greater firepower than our No. 4 rifle and at a range much greater to our Gustav [sub-machine] gun'.[75] The Irish were good marksmen but their rifles were, for the most part, single shot.[76] The Irish also simply had no means of stopping the Katangan armour: 'Except for Energa launchers, which are barely effective at very close range, in the nature of a suicide squad, we have no defense against armoured cars, while our armoured cars can be stopped easily by their 75mm guns'. Yet the 33rd Battalion did not even have any armoured cars, which were available to subsequent battalions deployed to the Congo. They were also completely vulnerable to air attack and unrestricted Katangan reconnaissance flights. The report claims that the Irish did have mortars, but again this was not the case for the 33rd Battalion. If the Irish were ordered to resist by force Katangan incursions into an area, they may have had serious difficulties doing so. Operating in an area with no actual peace to keep, Irish soldiers were vulnerable to attack.[77]

---

[73] *Dáil Deb.*, vol. 184, cols. 1284–5, 17 Nov. 1960. Aside from the infamous woollen uniforms that the Irish had to wear in the early period of their deployment to the Congo, the unit history of the 33rd also records the incredulity of receiving a delivery of boots which contained a leaflet with instructions on 'how to care for your Arctic boots'. MA, 33rd Infantry Battalion Unit History.

[74] Ibid., 33rd Infantry Battalion Unit History, Annex G , Operations Section History. Declan Power makes the point that training had changed little since 'the Emergency': 'At a time when armies around the world were gradually being prepared for counter-insurgency operations or full-blown conventional operations in Europe, Irish troops' basic training was heavy on square bashing, marksmanship and the obligatory spit and polish'. Declan Power, *Siege at Jadotville, The Irish Army's forgotten battle* (Dublin, 2005), p. 59.

[75] The Lee Enfield, a bolt action rifle with a 10 round magazine, has a rate of fire of 6 rounds per minute while the next-generation FN, a semi-automatic rifle with a 20 round magazine, has an effective semi-automatic rate of fire of 60 rounds per minute. The Carl Gustav M-45 sub-machine gun fired a 9mm round with a magazine capacity of 36 rounds and is for close quarters combat.

[76] Crowley interview.

[77] UCDA P104/6301. In the aftermath of Niemba, Fine Gael TD, Gerald Sweetman, speaking in the Dáil, asked to know what equipment the army had requested that year and why had it been refused. Oscar Traynor, Minister for Justice, replied for the government: 'The Deputy is asking a question in regard to equipment requisitioned or requested by the Army Authorities and I am saying it would not be in the public interests to give that information'. Mr Sweetman: 'Did the House not get an assurance from the Minister for Defence that any equipment wanted by the troops in the Congo that could be made available would be made available? Why is that assurance being broken?' Mr Traynor: 'I am not admitting that it was broken'. Mr Sweetman: 'No, the Minister is not, but will the Minister get an answer from the Minister for Defence to that question'. *Dáil Deb.*, vol. 186, col. 931, 15 Feb. 1961.

The British authorities in neighbouring Uganda (in 1960, still a colonial territory) were also monitoring the Irish presence in the Congo. In an intelligence report to London in October 1960, the Special Branch of the Ugandan Police related information received through their contacts with the intelligence officer of the 32nd Battalion, Commandant Fleming. The report stated that

> morale is allegedly low amongst the Irish troops, this being attributed to lack of activity and their somewhat negative role. This consists of what may be best considered as Police patrol work and they have little or no authority to intervene in incidents. A further contributory factor is the shortage of supplies ... The general attitude is that most of the Irish troops would welcome an early return to Eire.[78]

Irish officers would no doubt have resented any insinuation that their troops suffered from poor morale (especially from the British authorities), yet, if this was the case, it was not uncommon to the ONUC contingents. The lack of a clear mandate for the United Nations troops in dealing with the internal conflict of the Congo affected most contingents to varying degrees. Irish troops were resented by both the Baluba and the European settlers for not wholeheartedly siding with either (the Katangans were very ungrateful to the United Nations troops who were trying to protect local European assets as well as often saving the lives of Europeans who were in danger of attack). Prominent Belgians complained to the British Police Commissioner in Uganda, who remarked in a report to London that the settlers in Kivu (where the 32nd Battalion was based) believed that 'no United Nations troops could be worse than the Irish, and the impending arrival of the Nigerians is welcomed by them'. The European settlers were outraged that the Irish did not disarm the ANC in North Katanga and Kivu.[79]

---

[78] It is interesting to note that the Irish were also seeking information from the British. According to the Ugandan police, Comdt. Fleming was concerned to know if a certain UN official, Jean David of Haiti, had any Communist leanings. Cooperation between the British authorities in Uganda and Comdt. Fleming appears to have occurred intermittently during the Irish presence on the Ugandan border. Comdt. Fleming also seems to have agreed to warn the British of any possible escalation in Kivu that might affect Uganda. TNA FO 371/146651 Special Branch Report and Intelligence Summaries on the Congo and Ruanda-Urundi: Report on Irish Troops, 30 Oct. 1960. An Irish regiment of the British Army based in Uganda was also put on notice to offer any assistance it could to the Irish UN troops. This seems to have been arranged on a very informal basis through a retired British officer in Dublin. See MA, Major H.E.D. Harris, '"Operation Sarsfield" – The Irish Army in the Congo, 1960', p. 9.

[79] TNA FO 371/146651, the Commissioner also related that the Belgians were 'extremely critical of the lack of discipline and general untidiness of the Irish troops'. These Belgian attacks on the Irish were not confined to the settlers, a sense of betrayal by their fellow Europeans was evident in the Belgian domestic press, which would escalate considerably during Conor Cruise O'Brien's UN appointment to Katanga.

Baluba suspicion

White troops in the Congo experienced a good deal of mistrust from the local population, which sometimes confused them with Belgians or mercenaries: 'The natives, until they got to know us, thought we were an extension of the Belgian occupation force who left within hours of our arrival. We were walking a very tight rope.'[80] When Lieutenant Kevin Gleeson went on patrol in the vicinity of Nyunzu (a town in north Katanga) in early October, he wrote that, upon meeting some local Baluba there, he had 'great diffficulty convincing the leader that I was not a Belgian officer but ONU'. Sergeant Hugh Gaynor wrote: 'They wanted to kill the seven of us but decided against it when they realised that if we opened fire on them they could not get near us'.[81] Lieutenant Colonel Bunworth recalled that the potential for confusion of Irish United Nations soldiers with Belgians in the Katangan gendarmerie was exacerbated by the similarity of some equipment used by both forces: 'The Katangese Gendarmes used vehicles similar to those of the 33 Inf. Bn. And their headgear was similar to the United Nations beret. This had given rise to some concern in high United Nations echelons.'[82] In some instances, due to the intense humidity, the paint on United Nations helmets had also faded 'to a colour that approximated Belgian helmets', although this was soon rectified, an alternate source of blue paint being found.[83] While it seems apparent that the Baluba found it convenient to deliberately confuse the Irish for Belgians in order to try and intimidate them into acquiescing to their demands, it also is likely that there were genuine cases of mistaken identity. This was the first United Nations mission to Africa and the good intentions of soldiers in blue helmets were not taken for granted.[84] The United Nations Commander in Katanga, Colonel Byrne, concluded: 'In an area where the white man is anathema to the Balubakat warrior, it has been difficult to depend upon the Blue Helmet and U.N. goodwill as a means of protection'.[85]

On 29 September 1960, Byrne issued Directive No. 2 from Eastern Province HQ to all contingents, including the 33rd Irish Battalion. In it he noted that 'it is evident from recent events in Katanga that troops of ONU must henceforth take a very determined stand in assisting in the maintenance of law and order'. He urged that 'every effort short of the use of arms must be made to persuade people in improper possession of arms to surrender

---

[80] MA, Col. Edward Russell, 'Memories and Thoughts of the Congo 30 Years ago'.

[81] Tom McCaughren, *The Peacemakers of Niemba* (Dublin, 1966), pp. 28–9.

[82] Lt. Col. R.W. Bunworth, 'Niemba Recalled', *An Cosantóir*, Oct. 1980, pp. 283–7.

[83] Doyle interview.

[84] The Irish were not alone in facing this danger, United States, Canadian and Austrian United Nations personnel were all viciously assaulted in the Congo during the early deployment of ONUC on being mistaken for Belgians or Belgian 'spies'. See Rikhye, *Military Adviser*, p. 83 and pp. 174–6 for accounts of these incidents.

[85] Col. Harry Byrne quoted in McCaughren, *Peacemakers*, p. 95.

equipment and to return peacefully to their homes'. In doing this he ordered that United Nations contingents 'coordinate the activities of your force with those of local security forces and so avoid unnecessary duplication of patrols, guards etc'.[86] This order was highly unusual in that the 'local security forces' must have referred to the local Katangan authorities, who had been responsible for a number of atrocities against rebellious Baluba during the course of the previous weeks. While Byrne had specified in his earlier directive that such coordination should not involve joint patrols with the gendarmerie, the Katangan patrols that were engaged in the brutal suppression of the Baluba in the north, were nevertheless hardly the type of force the United Nations should have wished to coordinate activities with.[87] Initially the United Nations had accompanied the Katangan gendarmerie on patrol to monitor their activities. A United Nations Observer unit under the command of a Swedish officer, Colonel Mollersvard, had been established for this purpose. Colonel Byrne quickly realised however that this might create a perception of collaboration between the United Nations and Katanga and the unit was dissolved. Colonel E.D. Doyle believes that 'from that short association they [the Baluba] may have thought that we were part of it ... it wasn't a good idea'.[88]

Manono

> *'Keep that, you'll want it soon.'*[89]
>
> Commandant Jacques, the Belgian Commanding Officer of the
> Katangan gendarmerie at Manono, upon surrendering his pistol to
> Commandant Pearse Barry.

In mid-September the 33rd Battalion was faced with an extremely precarious situation in the town of Manono in north Katanga. The area surrounding Manono was of great economic importance to the Katangan regime due to its tin and copper mines. The Katangan administration seemed unwilling to retreat from the area despite being virtually surrounded in the gendarmerie headquarters by hostile Baluba who had occupied much of the town. The Commander of the Irish United Nations garrison, Commandant Pearse

---

[86] MA, 33rd Infantry Battalion Unit History, Annex D.

[87] Tom McCaughren also refers to a United Nations communiqué sent on 17 Oct., which stated: 'The occupation by UN Forces will not exclude an effective collaboration with the Katanga Government'. McCaughren, *Peacemakers,* pp. 120–1.

[88] Doyle interview. Doyle also relates that although the United Nations were aware of the need to stress their impartial peacekeeping credentials, they remained on reasonable terms with the gendarmerie's Belgian officers. Their commanding officer, Col. Crevécoeur, even had an Irish connection. As a Belgian cadet evacuated from Dunkirk in 1940, he had later been stationed in Lurgan and liked to talk about his favourite pubs in Northern Ireland and Dublin.

[89] MA, 33rd Infantry Battalion Unit History, B Company, Account of the Baluba Uprising in Manono.

Barry, tactfully negotiated the evacuation of 'the more contentious members of the Tshombe administration who had placed themselves under U.N. protection and whom Commandant Barry wished out of the way'.[90] But the Baluba were furious with the Irish, however, who they saw as protecting the beleaguered Belgian officers of the Katangan gendarmerie. Barry reported:

> The Balubas could not understand why B Company did not shoot the Belgian officers and police who had killed so many of their men. Mistrust of, and hostility towards, us was mounting. For a month or so after the uprising there was a distinct possibility of a Belgian attack on our camp.[91]

The Baluba claimed to be suspicious that Barry was a Belgian: 'Pearse had one disadvantage. He had fair hair and blue eyes and at some stage with the Baluba there would be an argument ... they would say: "Who's this Flemand?" For some reason they disliked the Flemands more than the French-speakers'.[92] Barry believed that the Belgian officers of the Katangan gendarmerie wanted an attack upon the Irish so as to get them on their side and they were very bitter at the Irish success in arranging their evacuation out of Manono, the gendarmerie surrendering their arms to Barry's Company. Barry was later decorated for his calm leadership at Manono.[93]

The prelude to Niemba

'I have seen enough murder, misery and filth to do anyone.'[94]
Sergeant Hugh Gaynor, Niemba garrison, October 1960.

While the Irish would often be greeted in a friendly manner by the Baluba population of north Katanga, there was also a number of Baluba war parties to be contended with. After a train was halted in the town of Niemba, its contents looted and three Europeans abducted, a patrol under the command of Commandant Patrick Keogh was dispatched with the next train to try to assess the situation.[95] When they reached Niemba train station 'the very

---

[90] Ibid.
[91] Ibid.
[92] Doyle interview.
[93] Comdt. Barry's account of his time in Manono makes for interesting reading in that it demonstrates the degree of confusion as to interpreting the UN mandate for the Congo in the case of Katanga. Barry relates that he used his reading of the Irish newspapers' reporting of the UN attitude towards Katanga to assist him in making decisions in Manono. MA, 33rd Infantry Battalion Unit History.
[94] Sgt. Hugh Gaynor, correspondence cited in McCaughren, *Peacekeepers*, p. 47.
[95] Niemba is described by the 33rd Battalion records as a village 'due West of Albertville, about 60 miles by rail and 85 miles by road. It consists of a railway station and a group of administrative buildings, and three hundred yards away the business section of the village consisting of one street of shops and stores. Surrounding the village itself are several native villages.' By the time the Irish garrisoned Niemba in early October, most of its inhabitants had fled. MA, 33rd Infantry Battalion Unit History, Chapter 5 – Niemba.

ground seemed to erupt with armed and furious Balubas ... all appeared to be drunk or drugged or both'.[96] Despite the pleadings of the Swedish interpreter, Lieutenant von Bayer, the situation looked very bleak: 'One Baluba had an arrow in his bow and the string pulled back, with the poisoned tip only a few inches from Company Sergeant Sullivan's broad back ... it seemed that Comandant Keogh's party was doomed'. The patrol thought themselves very fortunate to be able to retreat to the train and get away from Niemba. It seems very probable, however, that the Baluba must have known that Keogh and his patrol were United Nations soldiers, Belgian officers would have been killed without hesitation. Nevertheless, they were clearly angry with the Irish Blue Helmets.

The Irish returned to Niemba with a reinforced patrol, the gendarmerie had given the United Nations a limited period in which to secure the town before they would intervene. Towards this end, the Irish maintained radio contact with a Belgian officer who was observing from a Katangan aeroplane. The Irish secured the town, which had been thoroughly ransacked. Soon afterwards a gendarmerie patrol of eight Belgians and approximately twenty Congolese arrived at the town. They had been on patrol for six weeks and had apparently seen action daily. Upon Bunworth's inspection of Niemba later that day, he ordered that the Belgian-led patrol be given a hot meal. Soon afterwards the same patrol killed one Baluba and wounded another in the town who they claimed were sneaking up on the Irish positions. Commandant James Burke treated the wounded Baluba (later an Irish soldier would also shoot another suspected Baluba scout). Bunworth then ordered the town to be garrisoned under the command of Lieutenant Kevin Gleeson of 'A' Company, who took command of the Niemba garrison on 8 October.

Lieutenant Gleeson adhered to his orders to conduct patrols and 'show the flag', but was increasingly frustrated by Baluba roadblocks. On 22 October his men removed tools left at a roadblock on the Niemba-Manono road by a Baluba work party. This coincided with a period of intense activity by Katangan forces in the Manono area, and it is likely they were constructing roadblocks to prevent the gendarmerie penetrating north to Niemba. Gleeson sensed that Baluba resentment at his presence was building and expected an attack on Niemba and later Albertville: 'Last night I was awake nearly all night as I was afraid they would fire across at my house and kill me in bed'.[97] He later informed Donal Crowley, a Captain of 'A' Company, that he was going to have his bed changed as the Baluba knew were he was sleeping.[98] A week before Lieutenant Gleeson was attacked near Niemba, Lieutenant Jerry Enright advised Gleeson on defending his garrison's perimeter: 'We had a chat about local defence of the two buildings he was occupying

---

[96] MA, 33rd Infantry Battalion Unit History, Account of Patrol to Niemba.
[97] Ibid., p. 50.
[98] Crowley interview.

and I got him to clear fields of fire, bushes and the like, thinking that the attack would be on the two houses'.[99] In a letter to his wife, Gleeson tried to sound optimistic and reassuring: 'I hope everything goes well in the next few weeks. I don't expect trouble anyway although I am in the hottest spot of the Irish battalions.'[100] But the signs were ominous. At the end of October all Gleeson's local workers at the garrison refused to continue to work for the Irish and Gleeson was also informed that many of the locals had sent their families away from the area because they were expecting the imminent arrival of a war party.

The prospect of an attack upon an Irish garrison or patrol in Katanga was steadily building throughout October. On 20 October, Lieutenant Vincent Blythe came very close to firing on a hostile group of Baluba near Monongo. An attack had also seeemed very likely at Senge-Tshimbo where a group of Baluba armed with crude weapons such as bicycle chains and clubs made to attack an Irish patrol. After the entreaties of the patrol's interpreter, they stopped only five yards from the Irish.[101]

Niemba

'I wanted so much to get out of this God-forsaken country of filth, sweat and heat, and savages. I think I prayed it might be so.'[102]

Private Joe Fitzpatrick, survivor of the Niemba attack.

On 7 November 1960 Commandant P. D. Hogan set out with a patrol of twenty men from Battalion Headquarters in Albertville to travel to Niemba. On arrival, he led a patrol with Lieutenant Gleeson and a further twenty men from the Niemba garrison towards Manono to attempt to clear the road of barriers erected by the Baluba. They were halted soon afterwards at the River Luwuyeye where the bridge had been destroyed. Hogan decided to return to Albertville, but as he was preparing to do so, he was made aware of activity in the bush and a man armed with a bow and poisoned arrows was discovered near the roadside. Hogan was assured by unarmed locals that the man was merely a hunter and subsequently instructed Gleeson to return to the bridge the next day to try and continue towards Manono. Commandant Hogan's patrol had narrowly avoided a serious engagement; the 'hunter' was actually part of a war party which had decided not to attack because of the

---

[99] Author's interview with Brigadier-General Jerry Enright, Kildare, 13 Sept. 2005. Enright, then a lieutenant in 'B' Company, later went on to be the Commanding Officer of the 50th Battalion in the Lebanon (UNIFIL).

[100] Ibid.

[101] MA, 33rd Infantry Battalion Unit History, 'Incident at Senge-Tshimbo'. Brig. Gen. Enright remembers the strain of his service with the 33rd in the Congo: 'Every patrol you went out on was a nightmare if you like, with the roads, the lack of transport, everything was against you … the heat, the lack of food. I think for two months we had biscuits and beans, day in day out, for two months.'

[102] *Irish Times*, 15 Nov. 1960.

patrol's unexpected strength (almost fifty men).[103]

The next day, 8 November, Gleeson prepared to return to the bridge at the River Luwuyeye. At approximately 10.00 am, he had travelled out with two men to inspect part of the Manono road. On his return, he decided to travel to the bridge in the early afternoon with ten men in a two-vehicle patrol (an Irish Land Rover and a locally acquired pick-up truck). The patrol consisted of Lieutenant Kevin Gleeson, Sergeant Hugh Gaynor, Corporal Liam Dougan, Corporal Peter Kelly, Trooper Anthony Browne, Private Matt Farrell, Trooper Tom Fennell, Private Joseph Fitzpatrick, Private Tom Kenny, Private Gerry Killeen and Private Michael McGuinn. They were armed with four Gustav M-45 submachine guns, and four standard rifles. Their most significant firepower was two Bren guns operated by McGuinn and Fennell – these light machine-guns could fire 120 rounds per minute in 30-round magazines and could be fired from the hip if necessary. The patrol's Medical Orderly, Private Farrell, was unarmed.[104]

Upon arrival at the destroyed bridge, Gleeson became aware of armed Baluba in the vicinity. He approached the bridge with Gaynor, Dougan and Kelly and summoned Kenny to join them as he 'was attached to the [army] engineers in Clancy Barracks'.[105] Gleeson himself had spent some time attached to the Army Engineers and he discussed with Kenny how best to get the patrol across the river. Kenny suggested 'going down the river bank a bit to try to find a shallow spot'.[106] Gleeson forded the river and walked 100 yards down the road on the other side. Fitzpatrick recalled, in a statement given to Commandant Patrick Liddy, how the patrol apprehensively observed ten minutes of Baluba movement in the bush. Meanwhile, he witnessed Gleeson 'running up to meet three Balubas who were on the road and whom I saw going into the bush'.[107] After ten minutes, a large war party emerged on to the road.[108]. At this point, Gleeson ordered Gaynor to get the vehicles turned to go back towards Niemba. It was too late:

> The Balubas began running towards us, shouting and screaming. Lieut. Gleeson told us not to fire, until he gave the order … Lieut. Gleeson called out to the Balubas 'Jambo' and some other things. The Balubas continued to come on. When they were half-way towards us Lieut. Gleeson gave the order to fire.[109]

---

[103] Ernest Lefever, Wynfred Joshua, *United Nations Peacekeeping the Congo 1960–1964*, US Arms Control and Disarmament Agency, Washington DC., 1966, Volume 3: Appendix: Establishment of UN Protected Neutral Zone in North Katanga, October 17th, 1960, pp. 6–7.

[104] MA, 33rd Infantry Battalion Unit History, Chapter 5 – Niemba.

[105] MA, 33rd Infantry Battalion Unit History, Chapter 5 – Niemba, Statement of Thomas Kenny, 'A' Company.

[106] Ibid.

[107] Ibid., Statement of Joseph Fitzpatrick, 'A' Company.

[108] Both Ptes. Kenny and Fitzpatrick estimated that the patrol had been initially attacked by a party of approximately forty Baluba.

[109] Ibid, Statement of Joseph Fitzpatrick.

Thomas Kenny recalled that Lieutenant Gleeson instructed the patrol not to fire until fired upon. While this was in accordance with United Nations instructions, the Baluba were armed with very basic weapons, deadly from a very short range, at which the advantage of the Irish weapons would be considerably reduced. The Baluba attacked the Irish patrol with clubs, bows and arrows, bicycle chains and spears, some of which were made out of fish-hooks. When the war party rushed past the first vehicle of the Irish convoy, the Irish opened fire 'except Sgt. Gaynor, McGuinn and Fennell and the medical orderly. McGuinn and Fennell were the Bren gunners. Their weapons were in the car in front of us and it was now over-run with Balubas.'[110] Kevin Gleeson was wounded twice, in the arm and leg, as he retreated to the rest of the patrol, situated behind the land rover. Kenny recalled: 'Lieut. Gleeson had an arrow in his knee. He turned to me and told me he was going to die'.[111] The patrol retreated across the river to a small rise. According to Joseph Fitzpatrick, Gleeson quickly ran out of ammunition: 'I saw Lieut. Gleeson drop his Gustav. He had no more ammunition. I heard him shout to us: "Run for your lives."'[112] The Baluba surrounded Lieutenant Gleeson, Sergeant Gaynor, Corporals Kelly and Dougan, Privates McGuinn and Farrell.[113] Fitzpatrick, in an interview published in *The Irish Times* on 15 November, described seeing Gleeson being overwhelmed by Baluba: 'A lot of them reached him at the same time and they were howling like animals. Our officer went down under a hail of blows from knives and clubs.'[114]

Private Fitzpatrick recalled in his statement to Commandant Liddy that the scrub on the side of the road where he had run for cover was very thick and it was difficult to ascertain what was going on around him. He was separated from the rest of the patrol in a group containing Privates Killeen and Fennell and Trooper Anthony Browne:

> Pte. Killeen fired a burst from his Gustav and told us to carry on. At the foot of the slope I turned and saw a Baluba almost on top of me with a hatchet raised in his hand. I shot him with my rifle ... I carried on across a narrow swampy piece of ground and Pte. Fennell ran around it on my right. There was a long kind of hedgerow and I took cover in it. I could hear many Balubas now all around me ... I realised they had found one of our lads when I heard screams. I heard

---

[110] Ibid., Statement of Tom Kenny. Various estimates were later given as to how many Baluba were killed by Irish fire during this attack. Gen. von Horn, the United Nations Force Commander cited eleven Baluba fatalities. Von Horn, *Soldiering*, p. 213. A considerable number may have been wounded; ten of these were later arrested at Manono hospital. McCaughren, *Peacemakers*, p. 101.

[111] MA, 33rd Infantry Battalion Unit History, Statement of Tom Kenny.

[112] Ibid, Statement of Joseph Fitzpatrick.

[113] It is possible that only two of this group still had loaded weapons at this point. Statement of Tom Kenny.

[114] 'Report by Peter Younghusband', *Irish Times*, 15 Nov. 1960. This interview bears the hallmark of journalistic editing, but is accurate in its general account of the attack.

Pte. Killeen's voice. He was on my left about 10 yards away. I looked up and saw Killeen bleeding from the head. He had an arrow in his shoulder. He was surrounded by Balubas. The Balubas were beating him with clubs and hatchets. He was screaming. I opened up with my rifle. Killeen came across to where I was and fell down beside me ... I tried to pull out the arrow but I knew it was a fish hook because the flesh was coming out with it. Killeen was in great pain. Killeen died beside me in about ten minutes ... There were still occasional bursts of Gustav fire.

Kenny was struck by three arrows in trying to escape the Baluba onslaught. Like Fitzpatrick, he was armed with a Lee Enfield rifle. He recalled the Baluba isolating and surrounding different soldiers. He himself was struck in the neck by an arrow, before being beaten to the ground by a group of Baluba, who pulled the arrow from his neck:

They beat me for some time on the head. At this point a Gustav opened up again. I knew it was Browne on my right. The Balubas backed away from me and then made a charge over me towards the sound of the shots ... Sometime later I heard moans on my left. I couldn't move with pain.[115]

Trooper Anthony Browne was later posthumously awarded the Bonn Mileata Calmachta, the Irish Army's most prestigious decoration for bravery, on the basis of Kenny's testimony.[116]

Ireland reacts

'And because of what happened at Niemba the name Baluba is engraved in Irish myth and legend, the name is a very byword for savagery and evil.'[117]

Cathal O' Shannon, *Irish Times* journalist in the Congo.

It was presumed initially by the Niemba garrison that Gleeson's patrol had been delayed by a Baluba roadblock. The patrol had no radio and therefore no means (if indeed they had time) to inform the garrison of an attack. Even if they had a radio, there was nothing the remaining soldiers at the Niemba post could have done in immediate response, Gleeson had set off that day in

---

[115] MA, 33rd Infantry Battalion Unit History, Statement of Tom Kenny.

[116] Thomas Kenny has recently cast doubt upon this part of his own testimony as recorded in the unit history of the 33rd. He now claims that Browne did not save his life. Interestingly, there is no official witness to Kenny's statement as there was in the case of Fitzpatrick. Thomas Kenny interview, 'Morning Ireland', RTE Radio 1, September 11, 2005 and MA, 33rd Battalion, 'Statement of Thomas Kenny'.

[117] Cathal O' Shannon, 'Irish Soldiers Die at Niemba', paper in Mr. O'Shannon's possession.

the only two vehicles available to the Irish there. At 18.30, Corporal Lynch at Niemba reported to Albertville that the patrol had not returned. Eventually after Lynch radioed HQ in Albertville several times that evening to report Gleeson's failure to return, Lieutenant Jerry Enright and twelve men were dispatched from Battalion HQ in Albertville to Niemba to locate the patrol. During the next few hours, Lieutenant Enright began to fear for the worst: 'I anticipated something serious had happened. They should have been back walking by that time. I didn't divulge what I was thinking, but I knew.'[118]

They arrived at Niemba at 03.45, and after a short break, arrived at the bridge at approximately 05.00. At 06.00, Sergeant Nolan found the first traces of blood. Shortly afterwards the bodies of Lieutenant Gleeson, Sergeant Gaynor, Corporal Dougan, and what was thought to be either Private McGuinn or Private Kenny, were found:

> We found four bodies: Gleeson, Gaynor and two others. They were about a hundred yards off the roard, stripped ... the clothes had been taken off them ... We searched around for more bodies .... I suppose people get panicky at that stage. Some of the soldiers, they were so shocked. They fell asunder in my eyes anyway. They were beginning to see people in the bushes and hear noises .... I'm sure there wasn't anybody initially, so I fell them in and marched them up and down the road just to bring them back to their senses.[119]

At 09.00 Private Fitzpatrick emerged from the bush. Fitzpatrick had spent the previous night wandering the bush trying to locate the road to Niemba. A few hours after the attack, he heard jeep engines nearby and had shot into the air to attract attention (he was fortunate not to have been located by Baluba, as the only vehicles in the area at this time are likely to have been the captured Irish Land rover and pick-up or other Baluba transport). Fitzpatrick also recalled hearing 'singing and roaring in the native village all through the night ... just before dawn, I saw that I was close to two native houses, so I moved off to try and find the river. I stumbled over four bodies on my way. They were Pte. Farrell and Tpr. Fennell and two black men.' A few hours later he returned to the site of the attack and encountered the patrol of Lieutenant Enright.[120]

After assisting Fitzpatrick, Lieutenant Enright became aware that there was some Baluba activity in the bush: 'We did fire some shots. I think we saw a limited number of Baluba, but it was a morale booster to fire weapons just in case we needed to do it .... We certainly fired the Bren guns.'[121] Shortly

---

[118] Enright Interview.

[119] Ibid. Gen. Enright recalls that the memory of Niemba was a considerable burden for some years afterwards: 'I think Niemba affected me quite a while...There was no counselling in those days'.

[120] MA, 33rd Infantry Battalion Unit History, Chapter 5 – Niemba.

[121] Enright interview.

afterwards, Enright radioed Battalion HQ in Albertville to inform them that he was returning immediately to the Niemba garrison.[122]

Commandant P.D. Hogan led a convoy of approximately seventy men from Battalion HQ in Albertville to Niemba later that day to help secure the area, recover bodies and look for survivors. An Ethiopian patrol under Lieutenants Girmatesma and Abagaz had already arrived from Nyunzu with approximately thirty-five men to assist with the search and reinforce the garrison in case of further attack. They asked that only three Irish would accompany them to the bridge, as they feared that there would be another clash between the Irish and the Baluba. Colonel Donal Crowley (then a young captain and a friend of Lieutenant Gleeson's) took a patrol of thirty-six men with him to the site of the attack regardless: 'We decided to do that ourselves, but we were looking for our own men'. The next day, almost two days after the attack, on 10 November, delirious from his wounds and dehydration, Private Tom Kenny was found by an Irish patrol. He was 'a truly pathetic sight'.[123]

In Dublin, the day after the attack (9 November 1960), Taoiseach Seán Lemass was presiding over the Fianna Fáil Ard Fheis when he was informed that a patrol of Irish soldiers had been attacked, with many feared killed. There was reportedly one badly wounded survivor, three were missing, including an officer, and seven bodies had been located. A statement to that effect was released later that day to the press. On 10 November, the *Irish Times* led with the headline: 'Ten Irishmen killed in Congo Ambush', with the information that ten bodies had been recovered and there was one Irish survivor, Private Fitzpatrick. This was incorrect: Tom Kenny was found that same day and Anthony Browne may also have still been alive.[124]

Meanwhile in Albertville, Colonel Byrne and his staff were deeply shocked and angered by what had happened: 'Tonight the men of Ireland in this horribly hot climate are cold with anger' he told journalists, who observed that he was visibly upset.[125] While the Irish were certainly on edge (two men were shot accidentally in Niemba after the attack with one fatality), orders not to retaliate or take offensive action were obeyed and a plan to capture Niemba railway station from a Baluba war party was rejected. The Irish

---

[122] Ibid.

[123] MA, 33rd Infantry Battalion Unit History, Chapter 5 – Niemba. Kenny heard the approach of the patrol of Comdt. P.D. Hogan to the site of attack: 'On the road I heard the sound of guns and the noise of cars approaching … I saw an officer come over to where I was. It was Comdt. P.D. Hogan, the Second-in-Command of the Battalion. He asked who I was. I saluted and reported to him that I was 808457 Pte. Kenny.' Statement of Tom Kenny. The firing Kenny heard was apparently Capt. Crowley shooting over the head of a Baluba who had appeared on the side of the road. The Irish hoped to capture the man to gain information. McCaughren, pp. 82–3.

[124] In a case of mistaken identity, the parents of another Kenny in the 33rd Battalion were informed that their son had been killed.

[125] Col. Byrne also did not believe that the Baluba were capable of such an attack on Irish soldiers: 'This does not look to me like the work of mere raiding tribesmen'. 'Confused Reports of Further Fighting' *Irish Times*, 11 Nov. 1960.

were ordered to withdraw from Niemba on 11 November, the day after Kenny was found: nine bodies had been recovered, two survivors had been found and only Trooper Browne remained unaccounted for. The 33rd Battalion unit history records that on 11 November: 'Col. Byrne told Col. Bunworth that he had decided to cancel the joint Irish-Ethiopian patrol which was to go to the ambush area next day to resume the search for Trooper Browne's body'. He had come to this decision because he was convinced that the search of the day before was sufficiently thorough to locate the body if it were in the area.[126] This would imply that Colonel Byrne was certain that Anthony Browne was dead. Yet the same day he gave an interview, which was published in the *Irish Times* on 12 November, in which he stated: 'We hope we will find the missing man'.[127] It is not known exactly how long Anthony Browne survived after the initial attack at the bridge – by 11 November it was presumed he was dead.[128] Information received by Irish officers who returned to the area to search for Browne's remains in 1962, suggests that he survived the attack by an unspecified number of days: 'Apparently some days after the ambush, wounded, exhausted and starving he had called some women at the outskirts of a village and asked them for food and directions to the railway line, offering them 200 Francs'.[129] Local Baluba fighters were informed and a party of them later found and killed Browne.[130]

Shortly after evacuating the garrison at Niemba, the Irish found the road blocked by Baluba. Colonel Donal Crowley recalls that the Irish were not in the mood for talking: 'A few strong men went for them … they didn't want us to pass'.[131] On 14 November, the *Irish Times* reported that Irish soldiers were withdrawn from Niemba 'because their officers feared that they may take reprisals against the Balubas'.[132] The decision to withdraw probably had more to do with the reluctance of Colonel Byrne to deploy the large garrison that would be required to maintain a United Nations presence in the area: 'To continue to garrison Niemba would have called for a much larger force than originally stationed there, as it was now a very hostile area'.[133] The men at the garrison were also becoming increasingly nervous, one soldier was hysterical and was evacuated by a Norwegian United Nations helicopter on

---

[126] The unit history of the 33rd states that after hearing testimony from Pte. Kenny, it was presumed Trooper Browne was dead: 'He said that Trooper Browne had saved his life by firing on the Balubas while he, Kenny, was being beaten by them. He said that the Balubas then turned on Browne and killed him.' MA, 33rd Infantry Battalion Unit History, Chapter 5 – Niemba.

[127] 'Military Funeral for Congo Victims', *Irish Times,* 12 Nov. 1960.

[128] Enright interview.

[129] MA, 33rd Infantry Battalion Unit History, Chapter 5 – Niemba.

[130] Gen. Enright reflected that the inability to find Browne affected some in the 33rd profoundly in the weeks after leaving Niemba: 'It was constantly being spoken about … and should something be done, could something be done?'

[131] Crowley interview.

[132] 'Search for Trooper Browne Called Off'. *Irish Times,* 14 Nov. 1960.

[133] Col. Harry Byrne, quoted in McCaughren, *Peacemakers,* p. 92.

10 November, along with Kenny, Fitzpatrick and Private Shields, who had been shot accidentally by another Irish soldier the night before. On the night of 10 November, before the Niemba garrison was evacuated, there was further firing in the camp, at shadowy figures in the bush, which the sentries thought were Baluba. Lighting cords were severed and the garrison had to rely on the headlights of a land rover for light. A young soldier, Private Davis, who had lied about his age to enlist in the army, was shot in the confusion, dying on the road to Albertville that night in the care of the medical officer, Commandant Burke.[134] Given these events and the likelihood of further fighting, including the possibility of an attack on Albertville, Byrne felt it wiser to evacuate United Nations troops from Niemba.

In the aftermath of the tragedy that occurred at Niemba, and given the acute awareness in Ireland of the grieving families of those bereaved, critical questions about the Irish casualties were avoided, even in Dáil Éireann.[135] Nevertheless there was some concern that mistakes had been made, Frank Sherwin remarked that 'there is grave disquiet among the public that a body of men alleged to have the latest firearms could have been overwhelmed by a primitive body of any number with bows and arrows'.[136] A number of questions were put regarding the state of army equipment, especially about the lack of radio equipment available to Gleeson's patrol. Minister for Defence, Kevin Boland, replied that: 'It is extremely doubtful if it would have been of any avail in the circumstances prevailing on that occasion'.[137]

The unit history of the 33rd Battalion states clearly that radios for all patrols were necessary. In the case of Anthony Browne, if it had been communicated by radio that Gleeson's patrol had encountered a war party of Baluba, then a strong patrol sent out quickly may have had a chance of finding Browne before he wandered too far from the road – it was very fortunate that Private Kenny was not discovered by hostile Baluba first. Instead a vulnerable, small patrol, of a similar type to Lieutenant Gleeson's, was sent to Niemba under the command of Lieutenant Enright. Nevertheless, given how quickly the patrol was overwhelmed, radio contact may have been impossible anyway. Enright also recalled that it was very difficult to establish radio contact from that particular site near the bridge.

Kevin Boland also observed that there was 'no reason to believe that an attack like this might happen'.[138] This does not seem logical when one looks at the experience of the 33rd Battalion in Katanga prior to what occurred at

---

[134] MA, 33rd Infantry Battalion Unit History, Chapter 5 – Niemba.

[135] On 24 Nov. 1960, during Taoiseach's Question Time, former Fine Gael Minister, Patrick Lindsay TD, asked the government 'through prior consultation with Deputies who put down questions of this kind, to ensure that the least possible publicity will attach to them and thus save the feelings of bereaved relatives …?' Brendan Corish TD interjected: 'The newspapers will take care of that', *Dáil Deb.*, vol. 185, col. 278, 24 Nov., 1960.

[136] Ibid, col. 276, 24 Nov. 1960.

[137] Ibid, col. 278, 24 Nov. 1960.

[138] Ibid, col. 277, 24 Nov. 1960.

Niemba. Unfortunately, at the bridge near Niemba the Irish were unprepared to resist an attack from the outset, the Bren guns were never taken out of the pick-up truck and Sergeant Gaynor was unarmed, having left his Carl Gustav sub-machine gun in the Land Rover. The Irish were therefore down to only seven weapons to resist a sizeable war party and they had not taken up a defensive position, despite earlier observing armed Baluba on the roadside.[139] This was a point later emphasised by Colonel Patrick Curran in a speech to the 34th Battalion departing for the Congo in January 1961 as summarised by the *Irish Press*: 'While their mission was one of peace they should never forget their Security drill. If they were sent to clear a roadblock they should never be caught off guard. If attacked they should know exactly what to do and not be caught by surprise.'[140] Lieutenant Gleeson did neglect to take defensive precautions at the bridge, but Jerry Enright believes that Gleeson demonstrated considerable courage by exposing himself in order to try and calm the Baluba war party:

> It's very fine to say that you should be defensive and you should be ready to fire … Procedure at that time was that you waited and you parleyed with them … He had no interpreter, that was a big draw-back. These people were in a frenzy and you couldn't explain to them, you didn't have the language … He went out on a limb and was isolated completely.[141]

It is too easy perhaps to be critical in hindsight; this was after all a small group of courageous Irishmen in incredibly difficult circumstances, men who were expected to wage peace in a military capacity.

Why were they attacked?

'It is a mystery to me why my men were attacked.'[142]
        Lieutenant Colonel Richard Bunworth, interviewed two days after
                        the attack on Lieutenant Gleeson's patrol.

---

[139] 'To patrol towards Manono was difficult and always dangerous', Col. Bunworth, *Niemba Recalled*, p. 284. See also statements of Pte. Tom Kenny, Pte. Joe Fitzgerald, MA 33rd Infantry Battalion History, Chapter 5: Niemba.

[140] *Irish Press*, 21 Jan. 1961. The UN Force Commander, Gen. Carl von Horn, is sympathetic to the dilemma faced by UN soldiers in ONUC as to when to open fire. However, he also believed that 'this sort of misfortune would not have happened to the battle-experienced Tunisians or Moroccans. But although the Irish had no combat experience, the basic fault lay in the grave shortage of vehicles which had precluded any chance of their being properly trained in patrol work.' Von Horn, *Soldiering*, p. 212.

[141] Enright interview.

[142] Ibid., 'Two Irish Wounded in New Congo Clash', 11 Nov. 1960, The article alleged that two Irish were wounded 'in action against a large force of Balubas. A number of the fierce tribesmen were killed or wounded.' The new clash reported was actually accidental due to accidental firing by Irish soldiers. Col. Bunworth, according to the UPI Correspondent was 'tired looking and with an audible tremor in his voice'. Ibid, 11 Nov. 1960.

In the days following the attack at Niemba, Jason Sendwe, the Balubakat leader, claimed that the Baluba had mistaken the Irish soldiers at Niemba for Belgians. This was rejected by the United Nations who insisted that the Irish were known in the area as part of the United Nations mission. Although Commandant Barry did report intercepting a Baluba war party near Manono on 9 November, who told him that there had recently been a fight in Niemba with the Belgians and that they were on their way to assist, Sendwe's explanation is unlikely.[143] A more plausible explanation is that the Baluba were suspicious of white soldiers and the United Nations in general. The Irish had a great difficulty communicating with the local population in Katanga, relying on the services of two Swedish interpreters and occasionally local Europeans for translation and information.[144] The Baluba would certainly have resented the Irish for removing their roadblocks, guarding the trains and assets of Katangan companies and the contact they had with the gendarmerie. While the Irish believed they were engaged in the 'protection of the permanent assets of the Congo' and keeping Katanga economically stable, the Baluba may have equated this with keeping the secessionist state of Katanga viable. Colonel E. D. Doyle has observed that: 'The south had a vested interest in stability, and the north had a vested interest in chaos'.[145] According to Conor Cruise O'Brien, Lieutenant Colonel Buckley had a very reasonable explanation as to why Gleeson's patrol was attacked, which he stated to the Minister for External Affairs, Frank Aiken:

> A small-scale civil war had been going on in the area for months. Tshombe's forces had been using the bridge to gain access to the refractory area and punish it by burning villages. The Baluba had accordingly destroyed the bridge. When they found the United Nations party engaged in repairing the bridge, they saw the United Nations as abetting their enemies and helping them to reinvade their home territory. So they attacked the party engaged in mending the bridge. It's very sad … but as a Kerryman, I can't see anything mysterious about it.[146]

Buckley was referring to the Irish Civil War.

Tshombe used the deaths of the Irish at Niemba as political capital. He gave a statement on a visit to the 33rd Battalion in Albertville in which he argued that:

---

[143] MA, 33rd Infantry Battalion Unit History, Chapter 5: Niemba.

[144] Crowley interview.

[145] Doyle interview.

[146] Conor Cruise O' Brien, *Memoir: My life and themes* (London, 1999), p. 205. *The Irish Times* quoted Hammarskjöld's Representative in the Congo, Rajeshwar Dayal, as saying that the attack had occurred because: 'Katangese forces, under Belgian leadership, had incited Baluba tribesmen to near desperation', *Irish Times*, 11 Nov. 1960.

the Baluba tribesmen have shown their contempt for the gentlemanly manners of the United Nations troops by killing that Irish patrol. The Balubas need help but they only appreciate that help if it is given to them by strength – the United Nations must show them who is the boss.[147]

The *Irish Press* reported that Bunworth 'assured Mr. Tshombe his troops would do all in their power to restore order to the strife-torn North'.[148] Meanwhile, the British consul at Elisabethville, Anthony Evans, informed the Foreign Office of the Irish attitude in Katanga post-Niemba: 'Colonel Harry Byrne, Chief of Staff, and himself an Irishman, is at his wits end to know what to do. He impressed upon General von Horn … that nothing less than a state of war existed.' Evans concluded that

> In fact the whole of the United Nations operation in North Katanga is a dismal failure and there appears no prospect of a successful pacification unless the same brutal methods, so roundly condemned in the Katanga gendarmerie, are adopted and enforced by military equipment. Byrne himself would like his troops to move over to the offensive, the present passivity is killing his troops' morale he says. Though after this ambush, United Nations troops are firing first and asking questions afterwards.[149]

Although Evans was a friend of Colonel Byrne, there appears to be no evidence that the Irish engaged in the aggressive behaviour Evans ascribes to United Nations troops. There were serious allegations levelled against the Nigerian, Moroccan and Ghanaian contingents during their time in the Congo. After Niemba, United Nations soldiers were keenly aware that another attack from a Baluba war party was a distinct possibility. Ernest Lefever observed that United Nations patrols in Katanga began to engage Baluba war parties before they attacked:

> Patrols in the area frequently met situations in which the personnel were surrounded by partisans armed with primitive weapons such as

---

[147] 'Irish Regroup as Katanga Grows Tense', *Irish Press*, 15 Nov. 1960.

[148] Ibid., 17 Nov. 1960. The *Irish Press*, quoting an unnamed Irish officer, went on to blame Sendwe for inciting the Balubas into targeting the United Nations on a United Nations sponsored tour of North Katanga. This is refuted by United Nations testimony that there was a great upsurge in support for the Organisation after his visit. Col. E.D. Doyle, who accompanied Jason Sendwe on his tour, concurs (Doyle interview). The Irish demonstrated a good deal of political naivety in their relations with the Katangan regime. Aside from this assurance to Moise Tshombe, the 33rd Battalion had also previously entertained Neill Maclean, a noted Conservative MP of the 'Katanga Lobby', and a delegation of the Katangan Foreign Ministry to lunch in Albertville in North Katanga.

[149] TNA FO 371/146790, letter on Irish Patrol, 19 Nov. 1960. Col. Byrne appears to have been quite shaken in the days after Niemba. When he was asked by a UPI correspondent, whether talks with the Baluba had accomplished anything, 'he replied bitterly: "I've got two men dead. What good do you think talking did?"' 'Confused Reports of Further Fighting', *Irish Times*, 12 Nov. 1960.

bows, bicycle chains, spears and clubs .... In such situations UN personnel often interpreted the self-defense restrictions as liberally as possible, shooting to kill before they were surrounded.[150]

The Moroccans, Nigerians and Ghanaians were to adhere to this policy. The situation in North Katanga certainly was tense during November and December and accusations were rife that the United Nations was going on the offensive against the Baluba. The British Consul, Anthony Evans, was unequivocal in his reports to London that the Irish took revenge on the Baluba after Niemba:

> UN troops do not hesitate to take reprisals against the Baluba. Berendsen knows this goes on all the time, but I do not think he reports it. I overheard instructions being given to an Irish officer joining the Battalion at Albertville: 'As soon as you see an African on patrol, shoot it at once. On no account talk first'.[151]

I have not found any evidence to support Evans' claims regarding the 33rd Battalion in the aftermath of Niemba. Colonel E.D. Doyle remembered a conversation with Evans in Elisabethville: 'After Niemba he said to me that the Irish were doing very well up the country: "I believe that they're showing the Baluba who's in charge, giving them a good doing up". I said: 'Mr. Evans, you are completely misinformed if you would believe that'.[152] The Irish attitude did harden after Niemba, albeit not to the extent desired by the British Consul: 'It was a turning point. After that our attitude was certainly different ... We weren't going to permit anything like that to happen again.' Jerry Enright was to return to Niemba on one more occasion before the departure of the 33rd from the Congo. The marked change in how the Irish deployed on this occasion is striking:

> We went out on a train to Niemba ... We alighted from the train and Comdt. Barry told me to do a platoon attack on a hill near the station ... When we got near the top of the hill, there was a lot of dense growth there, we opened fire before we moved up to ensure nobody was there, our attitude had changed. We were prepared to fire.[153]

The Irish succeeded in capturing a number of wounded Baluba at the hospital at Manono who were believed to have taken part in the ambush at Niemba and they were later handed over to the Katangan authorities for trial. Unfortunately, there was no other authority to hand them over to; the United

[150] Lefver, Joshua, *United Nations Peacekeeping in the Congo*, p. 349.
[151] TNA FO 371/146663, Political Relations: UK and Katanga, letter on UN activities, 8 Dec. 1960.
[152] Doyle interview.
[153] Enright interview.

Nations was in a legal vacuum, reluctant to recognise Katangan law but determined to see the Baluba prisoners brought to trial. Sentenced in September 1961, they received remarkably lenient sentences of two to three years, which is not surprising, given that another Irishman, the United Nations Representative in Katanga, Conor Cruise O'Brien, was proving to be an implacable opponent to Katanga's continued secession.

Conclusion

> *'By midnight 18 January all our men had arrived back in Dublin safely by the dispensation of a kind Providence and the skill and care of the officers and men of the United States Air Force.'* [154]
>
> The Return of the 33rd Battalion to Ireland.

Soon after Niemba, the Moroccan, Ethiopian and Nigerian contingents were engaged in serious confrontations with the Baluba, who had firmly decided that the United Nations was not acting in their interests. It is reasonable to conclude that the Irish had been placed in a highly unenviable position in Katanga. They were short of weapons, suffered from poor logistical support, and were in an impossible political situation in that they were expected to safeguard the economic interests of the Union Minière, the control of which had instigated the secession of Katanga in the first place. The Katangan regime expected the Irish to take their side in suppressing the Baluba, this was evident at Manono, but the Irish followed their United Nations orders exactly, the wisdom of which they rarely questioned. After Niemba, there was no retribution for the cruel deaths of Lieutenant Gleeson and his patrol. The Malian Battalion had also been attacked by the Baluba. Demoralised they withdrew from Katanga, their Battalion Commanding Officer cited the following reasons:

> Unceasing provocation by Katanga gendarmerie have placed the latter (the Baluba) on the defensive. United Nations is regarded by local population as accomplice of popular persecution and offering protection only to whites. Population consequently resolved to treat as an enemy force ... for the sake of my units I cannot execute any mission of this kind in present circumstances. [155]

The Moroccans also withdrew from Katanga and the Congo as a whole. In Ireland, Lemass refused to take a political viewpoint on the Congo situation and consistently restated the view of the Secretary-General. He maintained that Ireland had undertaken a role it could not relinquish and he stressed the

---

[154] MA, 33rd Infantry Battalion Unit History, Endnote.

[155] *ORGA, 15th Session, Vol. 1* (New York, 1960), p. 57. Gen. von Horn described the Malians as a 'first-rate' battalion whose departure he greatly regretted (von Horn, *Soldiering*, p. 201).

importance to mankind of the task to which we have been committed, and that we could not, in conscience or in honour, withdraw from it so long as there is, *in the judgment of the United Nations*, a continuing need for help.[156]

Ireland continued to send battalions to the Congo for more than three years, despite the risk of casualties like those which occurred at Niemba. It was a remarkable commitment to the United Nations in one of its most difficult periods.

The Congo experience galvanised the Irish Defence Forces, and the Irish people were extremely proud of its commitment to the United Nations. After witnessing the almost 400,000 people who thronged the streets of Dublin for the funeral of those who died near Niemba, the London *Observer* correspondent could not believe that: 'not one voice has been raised for recalling the Irish contingent'.[157] The Irish rallied around an ideal eloquently summed up by Colonel E. D. Doyle almost forty-five years later, when discussing his own contribution in the Congo:

> We were doing something. Soldiers for the first time in history were trying to preserve lives rather than destroy them. We hoped to solve disputes between nations and peoples and we would make force and war less necessary. And I'm proud to have done that, to have added whatever little in individual odds to that cause.[158]

---

[156] *Dail Deb.*, Vol. 185, Col. 781, 7 December 1960. My italics.
[157] *The Observer*, 13 Nov. 1960.
[158] Doyle interview.

Chapter Six

'Persuade an alternative European candidate to stand': why Ireland was elected to the United Nations Security Council in 1961[1]

MICHAEL KENNEDY

Introduction

Ireland has on three occasions served on the United Nations Security Council: from 2000 to 2002, from 1981 to 1982 and on the first occasion through 1962 for a part term. The two most recent terms have attracted some academic interest.[2] In contrast, almost no research has been undertaken into the 1962 term. It receives only passing mention in Joseph Skelly's *Irish Diplomacy at the United Nations; 1945–1965: National interests and the international order*.[3] Skelly focuses on wide policy issues and, in a book of broad brush strokes, specific episodes are often overlooked. One of the questions Skelly leaves unanswered is how and why in December 1960, after only five years of United Nations membership, Ireland found itself poised to serve on the Security Council.[4] Writing in *Irish Studies in International Affairs* in

---

[1] I would like to thank Noel Dorr, former Irish Ambassador to the United Nations and Secretary-General of the Department of Foreign Affairs for reading a draft of this paper, for his comments and most helpful criticisms.

[2] For the 2000 to 2002 term see John Doyle, 'International and domestic pressures on Irish foreign policy: an analysis of the UN Security Council term 2001–2', Centre for International Studies, Dublin City University, working paper 5 of 2005, available at www.dcu.ie/~cis/2005_5.pdf (accessed 14 August 2005) and also his 'Irish Diplomacy on the UN Security Council 2001–2', in *Irish Studies in International Affairs*, vol. 15 (2004), pp. 73–101 and for the 1981–82 term, see Ben Tonra 'The internal dissenter (II): Ireland', in Christopher Hill and Stelios Stavridis (eds.), *Domestic Sources of Foreign Policy – West European Reactions to the Falklands Conflict* (Oxford, 1996)..

[3] Joseph M. Skelly, *Irish Diplomacy at the United Nations; 1945–1965: National interests and the international order* (Dublin, 1997).

[4] On page 239, when dealing with the Cuban missile crisis, Skelly simply mentions that Ireland had 'recently been elected for a one-year term' to the Security Council.

1996, former Secretary-General of the Department of Foreign Affairs and former Ambassador to the United Nations, Noel Dorr, described the 1962 term as 'now almost forgotten'.[5] This chapter examines Irish policy towards the Security Council from 1955 to 1961 to see how and in what context the decision taken in December 1960 to embrace Security Council membership in 1962 arose.

Non-permanent membership of the Security Council 1946–1955

On the establishment of the United Nations, the membership of the Security Council was eleven, with six non-permanent members joining the five permanent members. When electing the non-permanent members due regard was to be given to 'the contribution of members of the United Nations to the maintenance of international peace and security'.[6] It was to be an unfulfilled aspiration. Candidates were instead picked according to membership of regional geographic blocs. There was no procedure laid down to ensure the equitable distribution of seats between these groups. The structural weaknesses of the Security Council became apparent in the early years of the Cold War. The distribution of non-permanent seats became a contested issue as the United Nations divided between East and West. In 1946 the first session of the General Assembly came to what became known as the 'Gentleman's Agreement' on the distribution of non-permanent seats. It was later disparagingly referred to by the Indian Delegate Vijaya Pandit as an 'arrangement privately arrived at between some of the powers'.[7] The terms of the agreement were never published, but under it the non-permanent seats were allocated to six regions: one to the Commonwealth, one to Western Europe, one to Eastern Europe, one to South America, one to the Middle East and one to Central America. There was no Asian seat, nor was there a seat for the African members of the United Nations.

The Department of External Affairs felt that the 'Gentleman's Agreement'

> whether it was or was not intended to be a long-lasting arrangement, was a reasonable one and met very well the criterion of the United Nations in general (and the Security Council in this particular context) [that it] should reflect as far as possible the realities of the world situation.[8]

---

[5] Noel Dorr, 'Ireland at the UN: 40 Years On', *Irish Studies in International Affairs* vol. 7 (1996), pp. 41–62, p. 52.

[6] United Nations Charter, Chapter V, Article 23.

[7] Quoted in National Archives of Ireland (hereafter NAI), Department of Foreign Affairs (hereafter DFA) 417/128/2 part IA, memorandum 'Gentleman's Agreement of 1946 relating to the Geographical distribution of the non-permanent seats in the Security Council' (hereafter, 'Memorandum: Gentleman's Agreement'), Oct. 1956.

[8] NAI DFA 417/230/2, MacDonagh to Ronan, 1 July 1961.

Until 1955 the 'Gentleman's Agreement' 'worked admirably'.[9] The seats for Western Europe, South America, Latin America, the Middle East and the Commonwealth were elected on the first ballot. Only in the case of the Eastern European group were there problems. By the time of Ireland's admission to the United Nations, the election for the Eastern European seat had become 'a source of controversy and deadlock'.[10] External Affairs considered that this aspect of

> the Gentleman's Agreement has not worked out too well as in every other session there were differences of opinion, usually between Communist and non-communist candidatures on the 'Eastern European seat'.[11]

The conclusion of the 10th General Assembly was delayed by several days when deadlock arose over filling the Eastern European seat. The United States promoted the Philippines and the Soviet Union, supported by Britain, promoted Yugoslavia. The British based their stand on the 'Gentleman's Agreement' while the United States argued that they were supporting the creation of an Asian seat. The deadlock was ended by an informal agreement between the Philippines and Yugoslavia to split the two-year term between them. Adopting an orthodox position, External Affairs felt this move to be 'quite against the letter and spirit of the Charter which makes no provision for resignation from the Security Council'.[12]

A more significant source of controversy than problems over the Eastern European seat was that the 'Gentleman's Agreement' could not take account of the increase in the membership of the United Nations which took place from 1955. To the new members from Africa and Asia, the geographical distribution of non-permanent seats looked far from equal. Supporting the new members, the Latin American states and Spain placed the reform and realignment of the non-permanent seats onto the agenda for the 1956 Assembly. How to ameliorate Cold War tensions, meet the concerns of the new United Nations members and still keep the Security Council functioning as efficiently as possible was the complex scenario facing the Assembly from the mid-1950s.

Irish attitudes towards Security Council reform 1955 to 1960

On Ireland's joining the United Nations, External Affairs had to respond to the complex web of demands described in the preceding section. Dublin initially

---

[9] NAI DFA 417/128/2 part IA, 'Memorandum: Gentleman's Agreement'.
[10] NAI DFA 417/230/1, 'Slate for 16th Session of the General Assembly'.
[11] NAI DFA 417/128/2 part 1A, memorandum on General Assembly item No. 62, Eoin MacWhite, 28 Aug. 1956.
[12] Ibid.

lacked any policy on reform of the Security Council. As an interim measure, the Irish Consul General in New York, John Conway, told an unofficial caucus of Western European states simply that Ireland would agree to the creation of two additional non-permanent seats. External Affairs felt that 'some increase is necessary in view of the greatly increased membership of the United Nations and the lack of representation for Asian countries'.[13]

Under these proposals there would be one new seat for Asia and one new seat for Western Europe. Eastern Europe would now have a designated seat, leaving two seats to be divided between Western Europe. When Paul Keating was pressed by a British diplomat on Ireland's position on possible Northern and Southern European non-permanent seats, the Irish diplomat replied equivocally that 'Ireland's position on the periphery of Europe did not necessarily tie her in with either of the proposed blocs … we had much in common with both'.[14] Or, he might have thought privately, with neither. Any move towards a Northern and Southern grouping was bad news for Ireland, as 'here we are in the same position as Austria of not fitting in too easily in either grouping'.[15] Ireland might be 'cold shouldered for ever' in the Northern grouping and the Southern grouping was 'more amorphous [and] more inclined to compete against each other'.[16]

In a memorandum on Security Council reform, Keating's colleague Eoin MacWhite argued that 'our attitude to the question of the increase must be affected by the answer we give to the question "Do we wish at some time to serve on the Security Council?"'.[17] He added, 'whatever misgivings we may have about the answer it is obvious that if we are continuously passed over it will be a definite blow to our international standing'. These views were no mere academic speculation. Responding to a Foreign Office telegram on possible candidates for the Western European seat, which had left out mention of Ireland, the Commonwealth Relations Office considered Ireland's eligibility should be 'borne in mind in case another opportunity should occur when we may be able to register it'.[18] Britain 'should certainly not wish to see the Irish Republic debarred from election to the Security Council because the other European countries concerned have agreed upon a new system of rotation which, deliberately or otherwise, excludes her altogether'.

MacWhite's analysis shows that there was no early pressure building up in Dublin to stand for election to the Security Council. Sure of its Western European position, but unsure if it fitted more naturally into the Northern or Southern components of the group, Ireland's United Nations policy remained firmly rooted in the Assembly with no aspirations for higher office,

---

[13] Ibid., 'Memorandum: Gentleman's Agreement'.
[14] Ibid., Keating to Murphy, 16 July 1956.
[15] Ibid., memorandum on General Assembly item No. 62, 28 Aug. 1956.
[16] Ibid.
[17] Ibid.
[18] TNA FO 371/153601, Storar to Uffen (confidential), 11 May 1960.

yet with a realisation that to be continually passed over in favour of the members of the Benelux and the Scandinavian groups for the Western European seat would be detrimental to Ireland's international position.

The Assembly discussed Security Council reform in 1956 with agreement to create two new non-permanent seats. The non-communist European countries realised that the Afro-Asian bloc would not be happy with the two new seats as

> the proposed distribution could not be argued to be altogether fair from an arithmetical point of view ... the Afro-Asians would thus have only two seats for 24 [members], whereas Europe other than Eastern Europe would have 2 for 16 and Eastern Europe would have 1 for 8.[19]

Irish Permanent Representative to the United Nations Frederick Boland reported that the Afro-Asian bloc was 'dissatisfied' with the proposals and 'wanted increase[d] representation on the enlarged Council for themselves'.[20]

The Soviets now demanded that one of the non-permanent seats on the reformed Council be reserved for Eastern Europe. This group included Finland, Turkey, Greece and Yugoslavia, but the Soviets insisted that the occupant of the seat would always be a member of the Communist bloc. They threatened to block enlargement of the Security Council until they got their way. When the Soviets added that they would veto any increase in membership until Communist China took her permanent seat on the Council, Boland concluded that 'the Soviet attitude puts an end, of course, to any question of increasing the membership of the Security Council for the present'.[21]

Boland reported in early 1957 that 'a major row' was developing over Security Council reform.[22] The Afro-Asian and Latin America groupings had been brought together as a result of 'intrigues' by India's Krishna Menon and were proposing to increase the number of non-permanent seats by four.[23] One seat would go to the European states; the other three would be divided between the Afro-Asians and the Latin Americans. This would, Boland considered, reduce European influence still further. The Soviets and the United States were likely to oppose the move and 'a major struggle is anticipated ... it is not unlikely that a deadlock will ensue with the result that the membership of the Council will not be increased at all'.[24]

Ireland was brought closer to the fray over the Western European seat in 1958 when Italy offered Dublin 'reciprocal' support if Ireland supported Italy

---

[19] NAI DFA 417/128/2 part 1A, Boland to Murphy (confidential), 14 Dec. 1956.
[20] Ibid., Boland to Murphy, 10 Jan. 1957.
[21] Ibid., Boland to Murphy, 18 Dec. 1956.
[22] Ibid., Boland to Murphy, 10 Jan. 1957.
[23] Ibid.
[24] Ibid.

in succeeding Sweden on the Security Council. In a revealing aside, the Secretary of the Department of External Affairs, Con Cremin, minuted that 'I am not sure whether we will in fact be seeking membership of that body in the next two or three years whereas we are now looking for a seat on ECOSOC'.[25] Italy, like Ireland, had joined the United Nations in December 1955, was attempting to wrest the Western European seat from the grasp of the Benelux and the Scandinavians and hoped that Ireland would join her in this task. Cremin's remarks show that Ireland, despite its strengthening record in the General Assembly and despite Boland's strong profile, did not at the time envisage running for Security Council membership. An ECOSOC seat was the limit of Ireland's United Nations aspirations.

At the 1959 General Assembly, Canada, Panama and Japan stepped down as non-permanent members of the Security Council. A crisis ensued over who would succeed to the seat vacated by Japan. The Eastern Bloc supported Poland, whereas the West sought Turkey. Deadlock ensued as the United States with others sought to prevent Poland's election. Ireland, along with the Eastern Europeans, the Scandinavian states, a small number of Afro-Asian countries, several Commonwealth states, and the Latin American states, had voted for Poland. Like Ireland, these states considered that 'failure to elect Poland would be a breach of the so-called "Gentleman's Agreement" of 1946'.[26] Fifty-one successive ballots were held, Ireland on each occasion voting for Poland, but neither candidate got the required two-thirds majority.

Ireland stuck rigidly to its preference for the Poles because Minister for External Affairs Frank Aiken 'believed that under the Gentleman's Agreement … the Soviet Bloc should have a seat on the Council in addition to that held by the Soviet Union itself'. Aiken also favoured Poland because of 'the particularly warm feelings which Ireland has for Poland and the Polish people whatever may be thought of the present Polish regime'.[27] In a wider context, support for Poland was part of a larger change in the stance of Irish United Nations policy that Aiken undertook in 1958 towards active independence and non-alignment away from his predecessor Liam Cosgrave's strongly pro-Western stance.

Non-alignment meant support for the United Nations as an institution. Ireland held that the United Nations could not be left without a legally constituted Security Council. One solution was a split term between Poland and Turkey, continuing the pattern begun by Yugoslavia and the Philippines. In contrast to its previous opposition to this arrangement, Ireland now supported a split term and would not, as some governments did, switch their vote to Turkey. In the final hours of the 14th Assembly a compromise was reached after discussions between the Soviets and the United States. Turkey

[25] NAI DFA PMUN 289, note by Cremin, 27 May 1958.
[26] Ibid, Boland to Cremin (confidential), 18 Jan. 1960.
[27] NAI DFA 417/230/2, MacDonagh to Ronan, 1 July 1961.

withdrew her candidature, and Poland, now the only candidate, was elected on the understanding that she would resign on 30 December 1960, leaving Turkey to contest the vacancy for 1961.

From the General Assembly, under both Cosgrave and Aiken, Ireland supported the limited reform of the Security Council. Ireland desired the equitable distribution of non-permanent seats and the constitution of a Security Council that reflected the realities of the world power system and the global spread of United Nations membership. At no time prior to December 1960 did Ireland envisage that it would serve on the Security Council.

Ireland supported the Latin American proposals when the General Assembly voted on the enlargement in December 1960 as well as an Afro-Asian amendment 'urging the principle [of] broader representation on existing Councils pending Charter amendment'.[28] Yet Ireland was against a further amendment put forward by the Afro-Asian bloc calling for the immediate redistribution of seats. When the entire resolution on the enlargement of the Council was put to a vote, Ireland abstained. The 1960 resolution on Security Council reform was defeated by a narrow majority. This move incensed the Afro-Asian bloc. They were now determined 'to undermine the traditional arrangements by attempting to raid seats held by other groups'.[29] This determination fed into the growing tensions between the old imperial states and newly independent states that had recently joined the United Nations. It provided the immediate context to the 1960 elections to the Security Council and created the scenario where Ireland was reluctantly forced to seek Security Council membership.

The presidency of the 15th Session of the General Assembly

Ireland's desire for advancement in the United Nations was moving in directions other than the Security Council. Following his successful chairmanship of the Fourth Committee of the Assembly in 1958, the Committee which dealt with problems of decolonisation, a strong body of opinion developed favouring Boland running for the presidency of the Assembly in 1960 when it was Europe's turn to hold the seat. Canvassing began in earnest in November 1959 when the Czechoslovaks proposed that their Deputy Foreign Minister, Jiri Nosek, 'the perennial candidate of the East European countries for this position' should run.[30] The Eastern bloc had never held this high assembly office, but the United States would not let Nosek go forward without a fight. They urged Britain to approach Boland to run against Nosek before Boland had even announced his candidature. The American Ambassador to the United Nations, Henry Cabot Lodge, met with Boland telling him that Washington would support him to the hilt.

---

[28] NAI DFA PMUN 289, telegram, UNEIREANN to ESTERO, 6 Dec. 1960.
[29] TNA DO 181/109, telegram no. 735, 14 Dec. 1960, Foreign Office to Lisbon, 14 Dec. 1960.
[30] NAI DFA 417/215/4, Keating to Cremin, 25 May 1959.

Getting Boland to run was 'destined to forestall Communist success [as] it is widely felt that [he] is the Western European candidate most likely to be universally accepted'.[31] Indeed the Foreign Office saw United States support for Boland solely as a blocking move against the Czechs similar to United States support for Turkey over Poland in the 1959 Security Council elections. London was anxious to avoid a repetition of these difficulties and the British Ambassador to the United Nations, Sir Pierson Dixon, foresaw considerable Anglo-American disagreement emerging over early American support for Boland's presidency.[32]

Aiken, in New York for the General Assembly, cabled Dublin that he 'strongly recommend[ed] Governmental approval of candidature without delay'.[33] Lemass agreed 'subject to its being absolutely assured that USA support would be announced immediately after the announcement'.[34] Aiken's reference of Boland's candidature to Lemass for government approval illustrates that the Minister for External Affairs did not always have a free hand when it came to United Nations policy. It might have 'appeared as if Ireland had, in effect, two Foreign Ministers', with Lemass dealing with Europe and Aiken 'largely given his head as Minister for the UN', but Aiken and Lemass worked together on foreign policy issues when the need arose.[35] The confidential reports from the Irish Permanent Mission to the United Nations for the period covered by this chapter show that Lemass was sent a steady stream of reports from New York and the annotations indicate that he read them.

Boland had a personal reputation for impartiality and his term as chair of the Fourth Committee in 1958 had been an apprenticeship allowing him to seek higher office. As it was the calibre of the individual, rather than the standing of his country, that was supposed to be the chief factor when choosing a president, his chairing of the Fourth Committee suggested that Boland would be a strong independent candidate. Ireland's increasingly non-aligned position in the Assembly since Aiken had become minister in 1957 gave Boland support from the Afro-Asian bloc. But with Washington also so quick to offer Boland support, those seeking to damage his candidature could call his true independence into question. Impartial as he was as a diplomat, Boland was known to be ideologically strongly pro-Western. As Conor Cruise O'Brien cynically, but honestly, put it in his autobiography, through Boland the Assembly would have a President 'who was known to be personally

[31] NAI DT S13750C, memorandum 'The Presidency of the 15th Session of the General Assembly', 7 Nov. 1959.

[32] TNA FO 371/153613, Dixon to Foreign Office, 6 Jan. 1960.

[33] NAI Department of the Taoiseach (hereafter DT) S13750C, UNEIREANN to ESTERO, 6 Nov. 1959.

[34] Ibid., minute by Moynihan, 7 Nov. 1959.

[35] Noel Dorr 'Ireland at the United Nations', in Ben Tonra and Eilis Ward (eds.), *Ireland in international affairs: interests, institutions and identities* (Dublin, 2002), pp. 104–28, p. 116.

committed to the United States, but whose delegation's credentials as "non-aligned" were acceptable in the third world'.[36] This dual position was the basis of much of Ireland's success in the United Nations in the early 1960s.

Boland's election campaign can in retrospect be seen as a proxy-canvass for Ireland's Security Council candidacy. Of course it was not seen to be so at the time. However, the manoeuvring, tabulating of possible votes, discussions and appeals gave Aiken and the Irish delegation important prior knowledge of their standing in the Assembly. It provided an excellent intelligence assessment of where Ireland stood in the opinions of the member states that not only elected the president of the Assembly, but also elected the non-permanent members of the Security Council.

External Affairs analysed Boland's position in a memorandum which was sent to Lemass as well as to Aiken. They felt that though Boland would 'have the solid support of the Western European group as well the good-will of most members', he would be opposed not on personal or national grounds, 'but because it is the feeling of the Soviet Bloc that it is its turn to have the Presidency in 1960'.[37]

Election to the presidency was by a simple majority vote and External Affairs felt that Ireland could count on Western European support, the support of the 'Old' Commonwealth, South America and a number of Asian countries. Of the African states, External Affairs felt that only Tunisia and Morocco were likely to support Boland and 'of course' the Communist Bloc would oppose him. Though Cremin thought extremely highly of this analysis, he made the point that given Ireland's work on the Fourth Committee of the General Assembly, he 'would personally be rather surprised if we did not get some African support, both on general and personal grounds'.[38] Boland recognised how important Afro-Asian support would be to his candidature and was quick to take on board the Afro-Asian hint that 'American support for our candidature is harmful to us rather than otherwise' telling Dublin that American 'over-eagerness … would be tantamount to giving us the kiss of death'.[39]

Aiken approved of Boland announcing his candidature on 22 December 1959. One of the minister's first actions was to seek British support for the Irish Permanent Representative. Boland was well known in London, having served as Irish Ambassador to Britain from 1951 to 1955. The British Ambassador to Ireland, Sir Ian Maclennan, replied in a non-committal manner that though London had taken a 'sympathetic note … it is not their practice to give early undertakings of support'.[40] It later transpired via Boland

---

[36] Conor Cruise O'Brien, *Memoir: My life and themes* (Dublin, 1998), p. 196.
[37] NAI DT S13750C, memorandum 'The Presidency of the 15th Session of the General Assembly', 7 Nov. 1959.
[38] NAI DT S13750, Cremin to Moynihan, 10 Nov. 1959.
[39] NAI DFA 417/215/1, Boland to Cremin, 2 May 1960.
[40] University College Dublin Archives Department (hereafter UCDA) P104/6271, Maclennan to Aiken, 21 Jan. 1960.

that the British mission to the United Nations had been working with Washington to promote him and had been instructed to 'discourage other Western European candidacies and do what they could to further mine'.[41] Boland was not aware that London was initially only promoting him against Italy's foreign minister[42] and sought to reserve its position on Nosek until nearer the Assembly. London was, however, playing a balancing act between Washington and Dublin. Maclennan was told secretly by London that if he considered the Irish felt that 'we have to some extent let them down', by not openly supporting Boland strongly, he was to seek immediate further instructions from London.[43] Maclennan personally told Cremin that the fact that his government

> are not prepared to commit themselves at this stage does not mean that they will not support Mr Boland's candidature. He personally hopes very much that they will and expressed the view that Mr Boland's election would be a source of considerable gratification to all those in England who, knowing him, thought highly of him.[44]

Cremin, Maclennan reported to London, 'took it quite philosophically', and so no further instructions on London's part were necessary.[45] In fact Cremin had received prior knowledge of the likely British position from a dinner party conversation,[46] and by the time of Maclennan's reply had already sent a memorandum on Britain's attitude to Irish missions abroad.[47] Once it became clear in London that Eisenhower was pushing Boland's candidature 'with considerable vigour',[48] the Foreign Office knew that Britain's attitude would have to change, noting that 'it looks as though we will have to follow the American lead before too long'.[49]

The conclusions for Anglo-American and Anglo-Irish relations of this episode are interesting. That London was prepared to endure possible Anglo-American upset over the United States initial support for Boland in early 1960 is a sign of their annoyance at Washington's blinkered cold war attitude towards the running of the Assembly, compared to their own position of preferring a more equitable distribution of offices. However, when London finally came out in support of Boland's candidature the reasons given were resonant of the improvements in Anglo-Irish relations that had taken place since Lemass had become Taoiseach in 1959. Absent was any British concern

---

[41] Ibid., Boland to Cremin, 20 Jan. 1960.
[42] Giuseppe Pella.
[43] TNA FO 371/153613, Foreign Office to Dublin, 18 Jan. 1960.
[44] UCDA P104/6271, confidential note by Cremin, 23 Jan. 1960.
[45] TNA FO 371/153613, Maclennan to Foreign Office, 22 Jan. 1960.
[46] With the Dutch Ambassador to Ireland Dr Petrus Kasteel.
[47] NAI DFA 417/215/1, confidential note by Cremin, 9 Jan. 1960.
[48] Ibid., Boland to Cremin (confidential), 13 Jan. 1960.
[49] TNA FO 371/153613, minute by O'Neill, 20 Jan. 1960.

over how Ireland might act at the United Nations, a concern that had run through British policy towards Ireland's membership of the League of Nations and the Council of Europe. Now Britain's close links with Ireland were amongst the main reasons for British support of Boland.

Boland was worried by the 'position of leadership' that the United States was adopting towards his candidacy, particularly that it might 'cause some resentment in the Western European group'.[50] The Irish Ambassador to the Netherlands[51] wondered whether between possible rival candidatures, 'it would be difficult for the Netherlands not to support the representative of another partner in the European Economic Community', in this case Pella of Italy still seemed a likely candidate.[52] In fact in January 1960 'the Six' were by no means supportive of Boland's candidature, as Ireland 'was not one of their group' and was 'unsound on certain issues'.[53] This was possibly a reference to Ireland's non-membership of NATO, or to its increasingly non-aligned stance at the United Nations.

Cabot Lodge told Boland that Eisenhower sought 'to clear up the question of a possible Italian candidature as soon as possible and to go ahead and rally maximum support for me without delay'. Eisenhower considered that 'an Irish Catholic president of the Assembly in 1960 was "an excellent idea"'. But, Boland added 'there seemed to be a hint of American internal politics in this – but, perhaps, no more than a vague hint'. He was correct. Lodge told the British that 'the election of a Communist as President of the Assembly would inject an "absolutely devastating" element into the United States presidential campaign … the Democrats would be bound to make a partisan issues of it', attacking Eisenhower's policy of seeking accommodation with the Russians and adding 'a most undesirable element into the campaign'.[54]

Cremin met Vijaya Pandit, now Indian Ambassador to Ireland, at a cocktail party in Dublin on 22 January and mentioned Boland's candidature. She did not indicate how India might vote, but appeared to 'favour Mr Boland's being elected, remarking that the Assembly would have in him an excellent President'.[55] Mme Pandit pointedly added that 'the attitude of the "new" countries could be very important', to which Cremin agreed, adding that Ireland hoped it 'would have a certain volume of support from them as, apart from other factors, it is our impression that they were happy with the way in which Mr Boland had conducted the affairs of the Fourth Committee in 1958'.[56] As it turned out, India did not support Boland or vote for him. Prime Minister Jawaharlal Nehru had indicated that India's neutralist policy

[50] TNA FO 371/153614, British Embassy, Rome, to Foreign Office, 27 Jan. 1960.
[51] Brian Gallagher.
[52] NAI DFA 417/215/1, Gallagher to Cremin, 21 Jan. 1960. He had Italy in mind.
[53] TNA FO 371/153614, British Embassy, Rome, to Foreign Office, 27 Jan. 1960
[54] TNA FO 371/153613, Beeley to Foreign Office (confidential), 19 Jan. 1960.
[55] UCDA P104/6271, confidential note by Cremin, 23 Jan. 1960.
[56] Ibid.

suggested logically that India should vote for Nosek as there was never been an Eastern European president of the Assembly.[57] India's ultimate lack of support for Ireland was more than likely due to Krishna Menon than Nehru. Menon, as Boland put it 'probably has a rod in pickle for us' on account of Ireland's Tibet policy at the General Assembly.[58]

Following weeks of speculation it was officially announced on 3 February that the United States would support Boland's nomination. At the same time, by agreement with Washington, and following consultation with the Commonwealth, Britain let it be known at the United Nations that they would expect to vote for Boland.[59] At this news, Maclennan reported, Cremin 'expressed lively satisfaction'.[60] London based its support for Boland on his making 'an excellent President', Britain's 'close links with Ireland' (this being the case made to the Soviets, by Minister of State at the Foreign Office Sir David Ormsby-Gore) and the 'dangers to our policy of détente if this issue is injected into the United States Presidential election campaign'.[61] Lodge's arguments had won Britain over, but London, not wanting 'a collision between the Six and the rest of Western Europe', had also waited until they had heard officially from Rome that foreign minister Pella would not proceed with his candidature.[62]

In the aftermath of the Anglo-American announcements and with Boland's candidacy 'well launched', External Affairs calculated that Boland had forty almost certain votes, including Ireland's own vote; Nosek only had fourteen.[63] Boland was only two votes short of the majority vote of forty-two needed for election. As of early February, Dublin could confidently assert that 'all in all, it seems at this stage that Ambassador Boland's candidature is virtually assured of success'.[64] Despite a heavy canvass by the Soviets in favour of Nosek, by the end of June Dublin had twenty-three formally pledged definite votes. Ten further were 'very likely' and nine were 'likely'. This was in contrast to the ten that were probable for Nosek and the mere handful for new entrant, Ambassador Thor Thors of Iceland. Thors' candidature was something of a sideshow at which External Affairs were 'rather puzzled'.[65] He, with little support from Reykjavík, and indeed from the other Scandinavian states, hoped to step in as a compromise candidate should there be deadlock between Boland and Nosek.[66]

[57] NAI DFA 417/215/1, Nehru to Aiken, 7 Sept. 1960.
[58] Ibid., Boland to O'Brien, 13 April 1960.
[59] The word 'expect' was explicitly chosen over 'intend'.
[60] TNA FO 371/153614, telegram no. 3, Dublin to Commonwealth Relations Office, 4 Feb. 1960.
[61] TNA FO 371/153613, Foreign Office to Dixon (priority and confidential), 23 Jan. 1960.
[62] TNA FO 371/153614, telegram no. 94, Foreign Office to UKMISUN, 29 Jan. 1960.
[63] NAI DFA 417/215/1, Cremin to Boland (confidential), 5 Feb. 1960.
[64] NAI DT S13750C, memorandum 'Ambassador Boland's candidature for Presidency of 15th Session of United Nations General Assembly', 11 Feb. 1960.
[65] NAI DFA 417/215/1, Cremin to Kiernan (confidential), 5 Feb. 1960.
[66] The Scandinavian states would later vote for Thors.

London put in a word for Boland during a meeting of Commonwealth ministers in London in May 1960; Boland was 'an excellent candidate and as a representative of Ireland free from any cold war taint'.[67] Aiken now wished Boland to pursue the campaign 'with the closest attention and not [to] neglect any step which could ensure success'.[68] Though Ireland was no longer a member of the Commonwealth, Boland was not shy in using his 'friendly and helpful' contacts with 'old Commonwealth' members Canada and Australia to further his election bid.[69] With Aiken's agreement, Boland asked the Canadian Ambassador to the United Nations[70] to rally his support with Brazil, and Australia's Permanent Representative to the United Nations,[71] to help make contacts with the representatives of the Philippines and Thailand. He also looked for information from Britain from her missions in Latin America, leading the British Mission to the United Nations to comment that 'he is of course handicapped by the fact that the Irish Republic is not represented in many of these countries. He did not ask us to lobby on his behalf, but merely to let him know where we thought the weak spots lay.'[72]

To overcome this 'handicap' in South America, Boland travelled to Argentina in June 1960, using the occasion of ceremonies to mark the 150th anniversary of the country's independence to meet a number of Latin American foreign ministers and seek their support in his election bid. The British meantime approached over thirty of their posts in Latin America, Asia and Africa to take soundings on Boland's position. By early August the tally suggested to London that Boland had twenty-five firm commitments and ten to fifteen probable votes, bringing Boland near to the required majority. Nosek, by contrast, could only manage a probable thirty votes, assuming he got Arab support. It appeared to London that Boland 'has the edge on Mr Nosek, even allowing for the disruptive influences of the candidature of Mr Thors'.[73] By August, despite uncertainty over Japan's support, Ireland was 'fairly satisfied' with Boland's candidature; the British mission to the United Nations reporting this to London, added that Boland 'should have no difficulty in getting elected'.[74] By the end of August 1960, with the Assembly only weeks away and in a climate of increasing Cold War tensions, Boland felt confident that he had forty-two votes.[75]

The canvass had allowed the members of the General Assembly to make up their minds on Boland, and, by extension, on Ireland as a United Nations

---

[67] TNA FO 371/153614, Dixon to O'Neill (confidential), 2 May 1960.

[68] NAI DFA 417/215/1, Cremin to Boland (confidential), 7 May 1960.

[69] NAI DFA 417/215/4, Boland to Cremin, 16 June 1960.

[70] Charles Ritchie.

[71] Sir James Plimsoll.

[72] TNA FO 371/153615, Moore to Tahourdin (confidential), 16 May 1960.

[73] TNA FO 371/153616, memo by Scott, 'Presidency of the 15th Session of the UN General Assembly', 2 Aug. 1960.

[74] TNA FO 371/153616, Moore to Scott (confidential), 12 Aug. 1960.

[75] Ibid., Warburton to Uffen, 30 Aug 1960.

member suitable to hold high office. Problematic positions such as the views of Britain and the EEC states had been ironed out, though the lack of Indian support would remain. Viewed in the light of future developments over the Security Council Ireland had now a solid body of support behind it in the Assembly. Though the election to the presidency and elections to the Security Council followed different procedures, the former requiring a majority of votes, the latter a two-thirds majority, and while the presidency was about the election of an individual and the Security Elections that of a country, Ireland and her diplomats, though only five years in the United Nations were both well-regarded and deemed capable of serving in the institution's senior positions.

Deadlock continues: the Security Council elections at the 15th Session of the General Assembly

For the 15th General Assembly, Dublin concentrated on winning the presidency for Boland. The Irish Minister in Lisbon[76] was warned by Dublin that there were 'no grounds for complacency ... we are only a few votes short of [a] majority and anticipate Arab states will fill deficiency'.[77] External Affairs awaited the Security Council elections with interest. The value of Ireland's voting for a Security Council candidate was calculated in terms of votes gained for Boland's presidency. For example, Ireland preferred the UAR to fill the Arab seat, but reckoned that Jordan was more likely to vote for Boland as President.

Portugal and the Netherlands fought it out to succeed to the Western European seat to be vacated by Italy. Portugal, like Ireland a United Nations member since 1955, was attempting to break what it saw as a Benelux and Scandinavian hold on the Western European seat. This attempt was unlikely to appeal to the Afro-Asian bloc because of Portugal's record on the Fourth Committee of the Assembly. The Netherlands felt that it was entitled to stand in 1960, having withdrawn from the fray in 1958 to ensure Italy's election. Lisbon promised that it would support Boland for the presidency if it got Ireland's support for its Security Council candidature. External Affairs considered that Portugal was 'not the most desirable candidate' and if it became clear that Portugal did not vote for Boland as President of the Assembly, Ireland would 'retaliate'.[78]

In a minute to O'Brien, Keating set out the pros and cons of supporting Portugal or the Netherlands. Both, he felt, were 'unpopular as colonists among the Afro-Asian group'.[79] Ireland, he argued, did share an interest with Portugal in seeing that prior member countries do not try to establish to our detriment an overriding right to succession of the seats on the various organs

---

[76] Frank Biggar.

[77] NAI DFA 417/215/2, code telegram, External Affairs to Biggar, 29 Aug. 1960.

[78] Ibid., Keating to Ronan, 8 Sept. 1960.

of the United Nations merely because they have enjoyed this privilege in the past. Hence in line with our policy of rotation of office, Portugal has a case.

Keating added, though O'Brien disagreed, that while Ireland had in the past accepted that its sympathies lay with Southern rather than Northern Europe, this did not always work to Ireland's advantage nor was reciprocated. As regards bilateral relations, a show of friendship towards Portugal, given a desire to develop air links and the expectation that Ireland and Portugal would soon clash in the General Assembly over decolonisation, were reasons to vote for Portugal; on the other hand, the Netherlands, Keating argued, had a democratic government and Ireland had stronger trade links with the country, leading him to conclude that 'a further development of friendship would appear to be more profitable than friendship with Portugal'. Keating plumped for the Netherlands, but urged that support for The Hague could be linked 'on the basis that the Benelux countries would be more reasonable about ECOSOC and would agree to a more equable rotation of the seats on all the Councils'.

Boland reported to Dublin on 9 March that 'difficulties have developed' with respect to the Western European seat at the 15th session of the General Assembly.[80] Portugal had already begun canvassing for the Italian seat, despite 'widespread feeling that the Portuguese decision to seek the seat was very injudicious'.[81] It was 'hoped and believed' that Portugal would withdraw in favour of the Netherlands. Nonetheless, Lisbon continued with what Kennedy later called 'its ill-starred candidature'.[82]

Dublin felt that Portugal was advancing 'unduly optimistic claims … there is not one Western European country which has unequivocally promised support'.[83] Iveagh House sought an 'evaluation of … [the] prospect of Portuguese success generally'.[84] Boland and his colleagues rejected the Portuguese claims. The Irish Permanent Mission to the United Nations expected Portugal to withdraw, but pending this they were prepared to promise the Netherlands support at the end of any Portuguese term. Somehow news of this Irish position got back to Lisbon and Minister to Portugal Frank Biggar cabled External Affairs on 23 April that he was 'still under [the] heavy pressure gauge' about the Security Council seat.[85] Allegations were made to him by Lisbon that Boland and his colleagues in New York were positively favouring the Dutch. This led to a 'broad hint [that the] Portuguese decision in the case of Presidency deserves reciprocating'. This Biggar suggested, put Lisbon's vote for Boland on the line. O'Brien wished to 'put Mr Biggar "out

---

[79] Ibid., unsigned memo from Keating to O'Brien, 9 Mar. 1960.
[80] NAI DFA PMUN 289, Boland to Cremin, 9 Mar. 1960.
[81] Ibid., Boland to Cremin, 9 Mar. 1960.
[82] NAI DFA 417/233/1, Kennedy to Cremin, 19 June 1962.
[83] NAI DFA 417/215/2, handwritten memo from Keating to O'Brien, 11 Apr. 1960.
[84] NAI DFA PMUN 289, ESTERO to UNEIREANN, 11 Apr. 1960.
[85] NAI DFA 417/215/2, decode of telegram from Biggar to External Affairs, 23 Apr. 1960.

of pain" as quickly as possible'.[86] He considered that Portugal lacked clout in the United Nations, and was unlikely to vote for Nosek. The Netherlands had the support of Belgium, Luxembourg and a handful of other states, but most states were undecided. It was yet too early for Ireland to make a definite decision which to support.

The Western European group was concerned about this division in their ranks and Kennedy attended a meeting of the group on 21 May 1960 that aimed to sort matters out. In the light of the 'embarrassing and potentially dangerous situation' that would arise out of this disunity in the group, 'the general consensus of the meeting was that the proposed arrangement' of the Netherlands standing aside in 1960 in favour of Portugal, on condition of an understanding that it would get the support of the Western European group in 1962 was 'a sensible solution'.[87] Kennedy did not intend to speak, owing to a lack of instructions from Dublin, but since all the other members of the group except Yugoslavia had spoken and 'the great majority seemed well-disposed to the proposed agreement' Kennedy decided to speak up, bearing in mind that Ireland was going forward as a candidate for the presidency of the General Assembly, simply stating that he did not have possession of the views of his government but 'the proposed agreement was an eminently sensible one'. To this seemingly anodyne statement he added a tribute to the 'spirit of co-operation' between the Portuguese and Netherlands delegations before stating more firmly, and paraphrasing the words of the Portuguese Ambassador that 'rival candidatures, pushed to a vote, could only weaken Western European candidatures in these difficult times'. He added, when reporting to Dublin, that 'although I did not, of course, refer to the Presidency, the point was not lost, I feel'.

It was only after the Netherlands withdrew its candidature that Aiken finally decided that Ireland would support Portugal. While this decision was based on 'general political factors' and 'despite the fact that the Netherlands has a better record in the United Nations', Aiken was conscious that Ireland had 'in the past been somewhat critical of Portugal's attitude' in relation to Mozambique and Angola and Aiken did not want 'to create the impression of a fundamental lack of goodwill to Portugal', a country which, Dublin noted, had not held any office in the United Nations.[88]

O'Brien told Cremin that though 'we are of course, committed to Portugal … their candidature is very deficient in merit'. Keating was concerned that Portugal would be a liability on the Security Council when questions such as apartheid were before the United Nations and 'other African problems are erupting'. There was even a chance that Portugal itself might be brought to account for its colonial policies before the Security Council. But

---

[86] Ibid., O'Brien to Horan, 23 Apr. 1960.
[87] NAI DFA PMUN 289, Kennedy (for Boland) to Cremin, 21 May 1960.
[88] Ibid., Cremin to Biggar (confidential), 21 May 1960.

the Portuguese pushed their 'self-nominated' candidature strongly and through 'emotional insistence' became the choice of the Western European group.[89]

The underlying political consideration for Dublin was to do nothing to upset the Portuguese given their support for Boland's candidature, though O'Brien added that 'we have no way of knowing whether they keep their promise to us or not'.[90] Ireland would therefore vote for Portugal, a conclusion which greatly pleased the Portuguese Foreign Ministry, which informed Biggar that it was 'sure that our government's decision would give particular pleasure to Dr Salazar and to the Foreign Minister, having regard to the special sympathy existing between Ireland and Portugal'.[91]

Ireland would support Portugal in 1960 and the Netherlands in 1962. The Dutch decision to step down was based, Keating felt, 'on NATO preoccupations lest a split vote lose the seat for Europe'.[92] Though NATO deliberations which had led to the initial choice of the Netherlands as a candidate annoyed Dublin, it was a question on which Ireland would have to be careful as 'our co-operation may affect our presidential chances'. However, in the longer term, Ireland agreed with the NATO position and what most concerned Keating was, like NATO, to 'save the seat for Europe'. Portugal would be

> a most unpopular candidate with the Afro-Asian powers and if they have no alternative Western candidate they may decide that the Gentleman's Agreement gives them very little and is obsolete. Consequently the proposed manoeuvre may in fact lose Western Europe the seat and thus our own chance of getting on the Council, should we wish to, in the future.[93]

This was prophetic as to the final outcome, the Ireland/Liberia agreement to split the seat, but it also shows that no-one in External Affairs had considered that it was the right time for Ireland to put itself forward as a Security Council candidate.

The picture was now complicated further when Boland reported that the Portuguese candidature was 'apparently not certain to be successful'.[94] India was working hard trying to rally support in the Afro-Asian bloc to prevent Portugal from being elected. Ireland was staying on the sidelines in this new dispute. When Cremin passed on Aiken's thoughts on 'points on which we might concentrate' on raising at the 1960 Assembly, it was Tibet, the

---

[89] TNA DO 181/109, telegram no. 426, Dean to Foreign Office, 22 Dec. 1960.

[90] NAI DFA 417/215/2, note from O'Brien to Cremin, 12 Sept. 1960.

[91] Ibid., Biggar to Cremin, 18 May 1960. Biggar felt that this point was made with 'something more than normal diplomatic courtesy'.

[92] Ibid., Keating to O'Brien, 16 May 1960.

[93] Ibid.

[94] NAI DFA PMUN 289, Boland to Cremin (confidential), 21 June 1960.

dissemination of nuclear weapons, South West Africa, the Law of the Sea and Africa that concerned Aiken, nowhere was the Security Council election mentioned.[95] Twelve items on the 'main contentious items likely to arise' at the Assembly were included in a memorandum for the information of the government; again the elections to the Security Council did not feature.[96]

Aiken departed for New York on 17 September with all indications that his main interest in the Assembly would be in the area of disarmament. The *Irish Times* attempted to highlight differences between Aiken and Lemass over foreign policy, suggesting that there might be a more pro-western tinge to policy following a speech by Lemass 'in which he defined Ireland's position in the ideological ... field to be on the side of democracy and freedom and against the Communist ideology'.[97] Aiken had also recently delivered a speech in Bonn in favour of a united Germany, but it seemed that Ireland would maintain her role as an independent country without apparent ties to the two blocs.

By the opening of the General Assembly it was uncertain whether the Indian sponsored Afro-Asian move would succeed to scupper Portuguese chances of election, but Dublin was warned that if it did, the term would be split between Portugal and an Afro-Asian state, with Portugal serving the second year. Before the elections to the Security Council took place the election of the President of the General Assembly was held.

'The Greatest Diplomatic Gathering the World has ever seen':[98] the 15th session of the General Assembly

Ireland's profile in the United Nations increased considerably when Boland was elected President of the Assembly on 20 September. Irish diplomats had underestimated his support: Boland received forty-six votes against Noesk's twenty-five and Thors's nine. Conway wrote to Cremin that 'I need hardly tell you that all of us were highly pleased with Fred Boland's election'.[99] The *Irish Press* reported that it was 'the most signal honour Ireland has yet been paid at the United Nations'.[100] It was recognition of Ireland's quickly and firmly established independent line on issues facing the United Nations. As the 'representative of a small neutral nation', Boland was capable of bringing about 'the calm atmosphere in the Assembly which we all desired'.[101] Lemass cabled Boland that he was 'very glad indeed to hear of your election[,] warmest congratulations'.[102] The Taoiseach later added that Boland's election

---

[95] NAI DFA 417/215, Cremin to Boland, 23 June 1960.
[96] Ibid., 'The General Assembly of the United Nations', 7 Sept. 1960.
[97] *Irish Times*, 6 Sept. 1960.
[98] UCDA P104/6339, 'F. Boland's speech on election as President, 1960'.
[99] NAI DFA 417/215, Conway to Cremin (confidential), 21 Sept. 1960.
[100] *Irish Press*, 6 Jan. 1961.
[101] TNA FO 371/153616, telegram no. 1649, Foreign Office to UKMUN, 2 Sept. 1960.
[102] NAI DT S13750C, telegram Lemass to Boland, 21 Sept. 1960.

was a cause of justifiable pride for the Irish people. It was an indication of Ireland's status among the nations and a tribute to the independent part that we had taken in United Nations affairs.[103]

The attendance of Khrushchev and Eisenhower gave the Assembly, which was attended by fourteen other heads of state, an atmosphere filled with nervous energy. In Boland's own words there was 'a general air of drama and excitement in the Assembly'.[104] Boland was now the primary figure in the hierarchy of the Assembly and in that context, senior even to Secretary-General Hammarskjöld. His task was to control the debates and to call to the speaker's rostrum some of the most famous and important political figures of the day: Eisenhower, Khrushchev, Macmillan, Tito, Nasser, Nkrumah and Castro. In addition, the President also had important and delicate behind the scenes roles to play, roles where Boland's three decades of diplomatic experience were essential. It was, Boland later wrote to Lemass, 'a very tough and trying assignment'.[105] It was 'an Assembly of fateful decision ... an Assembly of high opportunity'.[106]

In his acceptance address Boland said that he would endeavour, while in the chair 'to discharge the duties incumbent on me as to merit and receive the trust and confidence of the Assembly as a whole'.[107] However, as President, Boland 'encountered more problems of procedure, faced more temperamental outbursts and received more criticism than most Assembly Presidents have run into in a year'.[108] He became one of Khrushchev's targets as the Russian launched an attack on the integrity of the United Nations. In retrospect, Boland could only suppose that this had been 'for reasons of his own, of which there is no generally accepted explanation'.[109]

The climax of this 'unheard-of tension and disorder' came on 13 October with four hours of squabbles on the floor of the Assembly. During the debate on colonial freedom, Eduard Mezincescu, the Romanian Minister for Foreign Affairs, waving his fist in the air, accused Boland of being unfair to the Soviet Bloc, with the riposte 'I can only hope that the Irish people enjoy the same measure of freedom as the Romanians'.[110] This was the moment when, as president, Boland had to act. He felt that 'the very structure of the United Nations seemed to be tottering on the brink of disintegration'.[111] In attempting to silence the Romanian for references to the chair and unparliamentary behav-

---

[103] Ibid., transcript of remarks from *Irish Press*, 22 Sept. 1960.

[104] Ibid., Boland to Lemass, 3 Nov. 1960.

[105] Ibid.

[106] UCDA P104/6339, 'F. Boland's speech on election as President, 1960'.

[107] Ibid.

[108] NAI DFA 417/215, transcript of Associated Press report by Tom Hoge 'Testing time for Boland. Firm and fair hand on United Nations debates' (undated).

[109] NAI DT S13750C, Boland to Lemass, 3 Nov. 1960.

[110] NAI DFA 417/215, transcript of Reuters report 'Communist uproar cuts short United Nations session'.

[111] NAI DT S13750C, Boland to Lemass, 3 Nov. 1960.

iour during a general din in the Assembly Boland, his face flushed with right-eous indignation, broke his President's gavel as 'the obviously angry Irishman' ended the session abruptly.[112] It was, Aiken wrote to Dublin, the culmination of 'an extraordinary few weeks'.[113]

It was an unprecedented action, but in taking it Boland received a standing ovation from the great majority of those present. Boland had shown his mettle and his diplomatic skills to the states of the world and confirmed to them that he was a worthy president. He left the Assembly chamber with the Secretary-General and refused to meet the press. Interviewed in the weeks following, Aiken argued that Khrushchev's attempts to attack the United Nations, to fire Hammarskjöld and various other Soviet threats would only strengthen the United Nations, adding that new members 'might incline to take the United Nations too much for granted if a violent attempt had not been made to paralyse it'.[114] Boland felt that Khrushchev's actions had galvanised the Afro-Asian bloc in support of the United Nations as 'from being at first bewildered and dismayed by the Soviet tactics, they gradually began to resent and criticise them'.[115]

By early December 1960 Irish diplomats had a prominent position in the Assembly. Boland was automatically identified with Ireland and reflected credit on the country; he was openly being talked of as a possible successor to Hammarskjöld as Secretary-General. An *Irish Press* journalist covering the Assembly was told that 'Your president is the best Assembly president we have ever had'.[116] Aiken addressed the first committee on the non-dissemination of nuclear weapons. He then made a high profile speech on decolonisation to a plenary session of the Assembly, guaranteed to increase Ireland's image among the Afro-Asian states as a supporter of the principle of freedom for nations and of the work of the United Nations to reduce poverty, disease and illiteracy worldwide.

The 'chief compromiser': Ireland decides to put its name forward[117]

Meanwhile, the crisis over the Security Council continued. The Afro-Asian group, with India's Krishna Menon leading the calls, was making a determined move to oppose Portugal's candidature, a candidature India's Prime Minister Nehru considered to be 'provocative'.[118] Unnamed elements were suggesting that the Western European Group should nominate another candidate. This rankled the Europeans who held that they should choose their own candidate unhindered by outside interference. France and Britain

[112] NAI DFA 417/215, transcript of UPI report, no title, no date.
[113] NAI DFA 313/36/3, Aiken to Cremin, 13 Oct. 1960.
[114] *New York Journal*, 25 Oct. 1960.
[115] NAI DT S13750C, Boland to Lemass, 3 Nov. 1960.
[116] Desmond Fisher, *Irish Press*, 6 Jan. 1961.
[117] *Irish Press*, 10 Jan. 1961.
[118] TNA DO 181/109, 'Portugal and the Security Council', undated, but Oct. 1960.

considered that the Western European Group 'should be united in defence of its rights as a group to make its own nominations for elections to European vacancies on the Councils'.[119] The Western European group agreed to continue to support Portugal, this being communicated indirectly to the Afro-Asian group through a statement to the press. Privately the Foreign Office was discussing 'the danger of losing control of these elections', if neither Portugal nor the Netherlands was elected. They began to realise that 'we might in the last resort even have to look outside NATO for a quick solution on this occasion'.[120] Even so, the Foreign Office considered it preferable to 'pull a NATO rabbit out of the hat'.[121]

Representatives of the Western European Group[122] were despatched to undertake exploratory discussions with the Latin American and the Afro-Asian groupings over the redistribution of Council seats. The desire was to reconcile the differing points of view as developments had reached 'a serious stage'.[123] The Afro-Asian states, now making up just under fifty percent of the General Assembly, continued to flex their muscles against Portugal. They gained the support of the *New York Times*, which argued that 'as the one European country still possessing large-scale colonies in the old-fashioned sense, Portugal should have been the last nation to be put up by her European colleagues'.[124] O'Brien told a meeting of the Western European Group that Ireland was anxious 'to ensure that the Security Council was not crippled by a vacancy resulting from a deadlocked election'.[125] Privately, Dublin had for some time considered it 'unlikely' that Portugal would be elected.[126] London held similar feelings and was working on a strategy to rescue the situation following Portugal's probable failure. Telegrams passed between London and New York debating whether 'infinite deadlock', the loss of the seat to Western Europe or the election of a 'less desirable European country' was the preferred option.[127]

The Security Council elections went ahead on 9 December.[128] Voting for a candidate to replace Italy was suspended after seven ballots, during which votes for Portugal fell from fifty to thirty-eight and for Liberia rose from thirty-two to fifty-five. Portugal's failure led to a 'frank meeting' between members of the Western European group 'with a view to deciding our best course of action'.[129] There was every danger of losing the seat for Western

---

[119] NAI DFA PMUN 289, 'Meeting of Western European Group, 11th October 1960'. Sir Patrick Dean had replaced Sir Pierson Dixon in July 1960.

[120] TNA DO 181/109, Uffen to Warburton, 25 Oct. 1960.

[121] Ibid.

[122] The Netherlands, Spain, Italy and Greece.

[123] NAI DFA PMUN 289, 'Meeting of Western European Group, 15th November 1960'.

[124] *New York Times*, 2 Dec, 1960.

[125] NAI DFA PMUN 289, 'Meeting of Western European Group, 15th November 1960'.

[126] NAI DFA 417/215/2, Ronan to Cremin, 12 Oct. 1960.

[127] TNA DO 181/109, telegram no. 2491, Foreign Office to New York, 2 Nov. 1960.

[128] Chile and the UAR elected for two years and Turkey elected for one year.

[129] TNA DO 181/109, telegram no. 1561, Dean to Foreign Office, 9 Dec. 1960.

Europe. What had been a campaign to deny the seat to Portugal had become one to gain it for the Afro-Asian bloc. Portugal's candidature was dead, the Afro-Asians would agree only to a split term between and African state and a Western European candidate other than Portugal.

It was essential that 'an alternative European candidate be persuaded to run with the optimistic aim of being elected for two years and the compromise objective of eventually agreeing to a split term'.[130] None of the western states consulted was greatly enamoured at the prospect of serving a split term with Liberia. The Netherlands refused to run, still smarting after having been dropped in favour of Portugal, so too did the Norwegians and it was unlikely that the Greeks or the Cypriots would run as it would 'expose' them to 'the hazards of running against Liberia, who must now be regarded as an Afro-Asian candidate'.[131] The Greeks also thought it inappropriate to stand in a year in which Turkey was a Security Council member. All Britain could come up with at this stage was Iceland, and if they were 'unwilling to assume this role, we doubt any one will'. Britain and America agreed that action had to be taken very quickly before 'those Afro-Asian countries who are still not involved commit themselves to voting for Liberia in all circumstances'.[132] London was 'dismayed by these developments ... all the alternatives unattractive', but worst of all was that 'we should allow ourselves to be pushed around by the Afro-Asians on this issue'.[133] An adjournment was the best move if no western state would come forward.

By 14 December it was decision time. The British made 'urgent efforts to persuade an alternative European candidate to stand'.[134] In order of preference they proposed Denmark, Ireland or Iceland. Denmark was ahead of Ireland as it was a NATO member. Britain was desperately trying to retain the Western European seat for Western Europe as, if it were lost, London could 'say good-bye to our chances of expecting to get 7 affirmative votes on any controversial issue in the Security Council'.[135]

That day British Ambassador to the United Nations, Sir Patrick Dean 'privately put the proposition' to Boland that Ireland stand. Boland in turn passed it on to Aiken, who was still in New York and who was, it was reported, 'interested'.[136] In contrast to the accepted view of Aiken running Irish United Nations policy from New York with little contact with or interest in what Dublin thought, Aiken decided 'to telephone to his Prime Minister' to get Lemass' opinion and his and the Cabinet's agreement that Ireland might stand. The following day Aiken cabled Dublin that 'Norway has agreed to

[130] Ibid.
[131] Ibid.
[132] Ibid.
[133] Ibid., telegram no. 3072, Foreign Office to UKMUN, 10 Dec. 1960.
[134] Ibid., telegram no. 1625, UKMUN to Foreign Office, 14 Dec. 1960.
[135] Ibid., Campbell to Tahourdin, 22 December 1961.
[136] Ibid.

step into the breach. We need not bother further'.[137] It transpired that both states were willing to run for a split term and had come forward at the same time. Ireland could step back; the deadlock had been resolved. Aiken did not want Ireland to go forward for election and hoped that Norway would run.

But all changed on 16 December when Norway withdrew its candidature. It would not stand if there were another candidate in the running. Aiken telephoned Cremin just after midnight on 17 December that he was 'trying to find some other solution but that ultimately we may have no alternative but to agree' to run.[138] Cremin then informed Aiken that Lemass felt that if in Aiken's view 'it was necessary for us to accept, the Government would have no objection'.[139] There was still great reluctance on Aiken's part to allow Ireland's name to go forward. Lemass left the final decision with his foreign minister, giving him the full support of the Cabinet and leaving Aiken in no doubt what his own views were.[140] Lemass 'had requested the Minister for External Affairs ... to avoid accepting Irish membership, if at all possible'.[141] Lemass was as reluctant as Aiken to put Ireland forward, yet he realised that in certain circumstances Ireland might have no alternative. Later on 17 December Cremin cabled Aiken with some revealing news: 'British have now put it to us strongly that we should accept Security Council seat in event of Norway feeling unable to do so'.[142] This further British *démarche* is remarkable. Lemass had up to now instructed Aiken that he 'might accept if a deadlock arose which could not otherwise get resolved'.[143] Cremin, developing his previous discussion with Aiken, continued that 'in the circumstances [the] Taoiseach considers [that] we should be more [than] ready to accept if [there is] no suitable alternative. Have so informed British'.[144] Under British pressure Lemass had moved from avoiding membership 'if at all possible', to being 'ready to accept' if no alternative candidate emerged.

The discussions on 16 and 17 December reveal a scenario very different to the usual picture of Irish policy at the United Nations. Firstly, they bring Seán Lemass to the centre stage of Ireland policy at the United Nations. Lemass took his final decision following the British *démarche* on 17 December without seeking Aiken's advice. The British action shows a remarkable closeness in Anglo-Irish relations less than two years into Lemass'

---

137 NAI DFA PMUN 289, UNEIREANN to ESTERO, 15 Dec. 1960.

138 NAI DT S16137G, note by Cremin, 17 Dec. 1960.

139 Ibid.

140 That said, the Cabinet had not even been informed of these developments as the note of a Cabinet discussion on 20 December of which no formal minute was taken reveals that 20 December was the first occasion on which Lemass informed the Cabinet of the 'difficulties which had arisen in the selection of a member of the Security Council'. (NAI DT S16971A, 'pink slip' note by Moynihan of unminuted discussion, 20 Dec. 1960.)

141 NAI DT S16971A, 'pink slip' note by Moynihan of unminuted discussion, 20 Dec. 1960.

142 NAI DFA PMUN 289, ESTERO to UNEIREANN, 17 Dec. 1960.

143 NAI DT S16971A, 'pink slip' note by Moynihan of unminuted discussion, 20 Dec. 1960.

144 NAI DFA PMUN 289, ESTERO to UNEIREANN, 17 Dec. 1960.

seven years as Taoiseach and an unusual degree of sidelining of Aiken over United Nations policy. Maclennan had spoken to Cremin who went direct to Lemass, over Aiken, and obtained the Taoiseach's agreement that Ireland would stand if no other candidate came forward. Following a telegram to New York, Aiken, with Lemass' say so, allowed Ireland's name to be put forward as a candidate, in order to prevent the possibility 'that the Council would not be able to function because it did not have its full complement of members'.[145]

Portugal withdrew its candidature. It would not agree to the Western European seat being divided between two rivals. Ireland had come second when the General Assembly held an unrestricted poll in which members could vote for countries other than Liberia and Portugal. In this ballot Liberia received forty-five votes, Ireland thirty-six, Portugal seven, Cyprus three and Nigeria and Ghana one each. Two further ballots were held; first Liberia received forty-eight and Ireland thirty-eight, then Liberia forty-four and Ireland forty. Then there were three restricted ballots in which members could vote only for Ireland or Liberia. These were all inconclusive. In the last such ballot the two states tied with forty-five votes each. Boland, as President, now suggested deferring the balloting 'in the hope that through contacts between the parties concerned, we can approach this matter with a better hope of success later in the evening'.[146] A fifteen-minute adjournment was called and consultations took place between the delegations. When the Assembly resumed 'after a remarkably complex series of negotiations', Boland announced that an informal agreement had been reached whereby Liberia would be the only candidate for election and, if elected, would serve through 1961, at the end of the year withdrawing in favour of Ireland.[147]

Subsequently, on the fourteenth ballot Liberia was elected, receiving seventy-six votes out of the eighty-five cast. This gave the Western European seat 'an African association'.[148] It was a turning point in the history of the Security Council. It was a pointed victory for the Afro-Asian grouping over the Portuguese. Not all Western European group members were pleased with the outcome; Italy and Spain felt that Ireland had been 'unjustly rewarded for disloyalty to the group candidate'.[149] Writing in January 1961, Desmond Fisher of the *Irish Press* recounted how an un-named African foreign minister told him that 1960 '"was to have been Africa's year at the United Nations ... instead it has turned out to be Ireland's year." He laughed when I suggested "as a compromise" that we call it "Afro-Irish year".'[150] And so it had been. In addition to being almost certain to being elected to the Security Council in

[145] *Cork Examiner*, 21 Dec. 1960.
[146] Ibid.
[147] TNA DO 181/109, telegram no. 1711, UKMUN to Foreign Office, 20 Dec. 1960.
[148] NAI DFA 417/233/1, Kennedy to Cremin, 19 June 1962.
[149] TNA DO 181/109, telegram no. 426, Dean to Foreign Office, 22 Dec. 1960.
[150] *Irish Press*, 10 Jan. 1961.

1961, Ireland, through Boland had held the presidency of the General Assembly and in the last week of December 1960 it was announced that the Chief of Staff of the Defence Forces, Major-General Seán MacEoin, would take over command of ONUC, the United Nations peacekeeping force in the Congo. As another delegate told Fisher, 'It looks as if Ireland is turning this place into a one-nation United Nations'.

Election: October 1961

During the summer of 1961 External Affairs began considering policy for the upcoming session of the General Assembly. Despite some noises by India to the contrary, 'the general assumption' was that Ireland would be successfully elected to the Security Council in October 1961 for 1962.[151] With Boland stepping down as President of the General Assembly, Ireland was not seeking a vice-presidency and, with Security Council membership in mind, nor was Dublin seeking the chairmanship of any of the General Assembly's Committees. Prior to the Assembly session Aiken decided that Ireland would not make a major intervention in the 1961 General Debate 'as some of the topics which it might be appropriate to cover in an intervention (e.g., and in particular, Berlin) are in such a delicate stage that it is better to avoid saying too much about them at the moment'.[152]

The parameters of Irish foreign policy had changed dramatically since December 1960 as on 1 August Ireland applied for full membership of the EEC. On Boland's suggestion, the Irish United Nations delegation would intervene on suitable occasions after the conclusion of the general debate 'as the Assembly is likely to be in more or less permanent session with the various important matters coming before it'.[153] The question of election to the Security Council was not included in a wide-ranging agenda prepared for the government on 11 September 1961, but in adopting a lower profile than at previous assemblies, Dublin was taking nothing for granted in the Security Council vote. There would be no hostages given to fortune that might lose Ireland the half-term seat following Liberia's stepping down.

The 1961 general election campaign also intervened and consequently Aiken did not intend to attend the Assembly session. Lemass had informed the Dáil on 2 August that there would be a general election between the middle of September and October. Aiken was ordered to stay in Dublin, as 'the Taoiseach would be anxious that all members of the Government would be here for the campaign'.[154] Accordingly, on 17 September the Irish delegation, without Aiken, left for New York. Its members were Seán Morrissey

---

[151] NAI DFA 417/230/1, Boland to Cremin, 21 June 1961.
[152] NAI DFA 417/230/9, Cremin to Ronan, 13 Oct. 1961.
[153] Ibid.
[154] NAI DFA 417/230, Ronan to Boland, 9 Sept. 1961. Lemass was elected Taoiseach on 11 Oct. and formed a minority government.

(Legal Adviser, DEA), Seán Ronan (Counsellor, Political and United Nations section, DEA) and Noel Dorr (Third Secretary, Political and United Nations section, DEA).[155]

The first round of voting for Security Council seats took place on 30 October. The vote to replace Liberia was taken first. In opening the voting no reference was made to the trials of December 1960 or the agreement reached between Liberia and Ireland. Soon after the votes were counted, the Irish Mission to the United Nations cabled Dublin that 'Ireland [was] elected [a] member of [the] Security Council for 1962 by 83 out of 97 valid votes. Romania obtained 10 votes'.[156] Three members of the Assembly were absent and three votes were declared invalid.

Some days after Ireland's election, Boland wrote to Cremin that 'it was immediately assumed by members of the Assembly that the Soviet Bloc had decided to vote against us'.[157] However, Boland had already told Cremin by phone the day after the election that 'this does not seem to have been the case'. Boland received congratulations and assurances that they had voted for Ireland from Poland and the Soviet Union soon after the voting had taken place. Boland felt that it was 'unlikely that they would have assured us that they had voted in our favour if, in fact, they had not done so'. Someone was circulating rumours. It later transpired that the 'Brazzaville group' (excepting Dahomey) had voted for Romania 'under a misapprehension'.[158] It seemed that the group 'not being very familiar with United Nations procedure' did not realise that Romania was not a candidate for the one-year term for which Ireland was elected. But following the drama of December 1960, it was a relatively low-key affair for Ireland. Ireland took its seat on 1 January 1962. As the *Irish Times* noted on 3 January 1962, 'Ireland is entering the Security Council at the most critical juncture of the organisation's troubled history. Right at the start the circumstances have ordained that Ireland disposes of the decisive vote in the first emergency issue that is coming up – Pakistan's complaint against India about Kashmir'.[159] The circumstances surrounding the Cuban Missile Crisis of October 1962 were as yet invisible.

Conclusion

Noel Dorr has written of 1960 as 'an annus mirabilis' in Ireland's policy at the United Nations. With Boland's election as president and his heroic chair-

---

[155] They would be joined by Gerard Woods (Consul General, Boston), Frank Coffey (First Secretary, Irish Embassy, London) and Seán Ó hÉideáin (Consul General, Chicago).
[156] NAI DFA 417/230/2, UNEIREANN to ESTERO, 30 Oct. 1961.
[157] NAI DFA PMUN 289, Boland to Cremin, 4 Nov. 1961.
[158] Ibid., Boland to Cremin, 4 Nov. 1961.
[159] *Irish Times*, 3 Jan. 1962. In 1962 the Security Council would hold 38 meetings, as against 68 in 1961 and 71 in 1960. Twelve meetings were devoted to the situation in the Caribbean, eleven to the Kashmir question, eight to Palestine, four to the admission of new members to the United Nations, one to the situation in the Congo and one to the appointment of the Secretary-General and the report of the Security Council to the General Assembly. Two meetings were held in private.

ing of a most troubled assembly, Ireland's growing role in ONUC and the appointment of General Seán MacEoin as force commander of over 20,000 peacekeepers in the Congo, 1960 was a high point of Irish activism at the United Nations.[160] Viewing this catalogue of high profile activity it is easy to forget the events of 14 to 20 December 1960 when Ireland suddenly found itself poised for membership of the Security Council.

Ultimately, the December 1960 move was a surprise. The background from 1955 to 1960 shows that Ireland did not actively seek Security Council membership on any occasion up to 1960, a position in marked contrast to the 1981–82 and 2000–02 terms where detailed canvasses were carried out. However the Minister for External Affairs and his department were well aware of the problems facing the Security Council. Aiken sought a Security Council that, despite problems over the veto, operated, underlying the importance to him of a United Nations that though an imperfect organisation, at least functioned. It was certainly within the ideological parameters of Irish United Nations policy to consider Security Council membership, but the sources suggest that little consideration had in fact been given to such a move. Aiken's contact with Lemass via Cremin underlines the significance of the step he was about to commit Ireland to. The reference to Dublin at the very least suggests that Aiken was taken aback by the British suggestion, seemingly having not considered it himself.

That Ireland should desire to break the electoral deadlock in December 1960 was one consideration, that she should be judged able to fill the gap by the other members of the General Assembly was another. Ireland's pro-western outlook, her quasi-non-alignment and anti-colonial stance left her perfectly situated compared to other candidates who would not share a term with Liberia or were not acceptable to the Afro-Asian bloc. Ireland's flexible United Nations policy that looked to the west and the developing world, together with Aiken's and Boland's combined personal standing, crossed the many divisions in the 1960 General Assembly. The presidency and Ireland's emergence as a compromise candidate are inextricably linked. Boland's campaign put Irish United Nations policy before all members of the General Assembly. It was for them to judge Ireland's policies when taking a decision on Boland's suitability to hold the presidency. By extension, though it is apparent only in retrospect, when Ireland emerged as a compromise candidate for the Security Council, the canvass for the presidency and Boland's high profile as a successful president had created an environment of immediate support for Ireland which then allowed Ireland to stand for the Security Council. Ireland would not have emerged as a compromise candidate had she not followed an active United Nations policy through the late 1950s. Yet Aiken's activism notwithstanding, the canvass for Boland's presidency was, in hindsight, Ireland's canvass for Security Council membership.

---

[160] Noel Dorr 'Ireland at the United Nations', in Ben Tonra and Eilis Ward (eds.), *Ireland in international affairs: interests, institutions and identities* (Dublin, 2002), pp. 104–28, p. 114–5.

Senior members of the Irish diplomatic service with Eamon de Valera, Iveagh House, September 1945. Left to right: (front) John Dulanty, Joseph Walshe, Eamon de Valera, Robert Brennan, Thomas J. Hearne, Frank Gallagher (Government Information Bureau), Frederick H. Boland, Michael MacWhite, Seán Murphy, (back) John J. Hearne, Thomas J. Kiernan, Leopold Kerney, Michael Rynne (Courtesy of the University College Dublin Archives Department).

11th Session of the United Nations Economic Commission for Europe, Geneva, Spring 1956. The Irish delegation, Hugh McCann and J.G. Molloy are in the bottom left-hand corner (Courtesy of the United Nations Library, Geneva).

4th Group of officers in the Taoiseach's office prior to their deployment to Lebanon on 28 September 1958. Adjutant General Colonel Hally is seated with Taoiseach Eamon de Valera. Standing from the left are Capt. Fagan, Lieut. Buckley, Comdt. Quigley, Capt. Moran, Comdt. Johnson, Capt. Russell, Capt. Quinlan, Lieut. Walsh, Capt. Mulvihill, Capt. Murphy and Capt. Cox (Fagan Photo Collection) (Courtesy of Colonel James Fagan).

Dublin Airport departure of 3rd Group of Irish officers to UNOGIL – 28 August 1958. Picture taken at Dublin Airport showing Chief of Staff, Major General Mulcahy, accompanied by Adjutant General, Colonel Hally and Colonels Gray and Flynn of the General Staff on the tarmac at Dublin Airport with the third group of officers to deploy to UNOGIL. Those leaving for Lebanon are all on the aircraft steps and include (in ascending order): Comdt. Casseley, Capt. O'Connor, Comdt. Carroll, Capt. Keogh, Capt. Liddy, Capt. Condon, Comdt. P.D. Hogan, Capt. Gill, Capt. Furlong and Capt. L. Hogan (Furlong Photo Collection) (Courtesy of Lieutenant Colonel Thomas Furlong).

Baalbeck Sector officers with Col. Justin McCarthy. This thirty-three strong international group was photographed on the occasion of a visit to UNOGIL Sector Headquarters in Baalbeck by Col. McCarthy (front row in white uniform) in 1958. Baalbeck was a very active sector and the largest Irish group was deployed there. Including McCarthy, twelve of those present in this group are Irish, Comdt. P.D. Hogan (over McCarthy's right shoulder), Dan Dooley (Irish civilian serving with UN Field Service, partially obscured by McCarthy's head); grouped together next to Dooley and to the right in the second row are Lieut. O'Brien and Capt. O'Connor, and again to the right in the third row Lieut. McCorley, Capt. Moran, Lieut. Ryan, and Lieut. O'Connell (partially obscured by officer in dark uniform), with Capt. Keogh on the extreme right in the second row. Capt. Furlong is on the left in the elevated rear row (in front of the draped UN Flag) with Lieut. Sheedy second to Capt. Furlong's right (Moran Photo Collection) (Courtesy of Captain James Moran).

Con Cremin, Secretary of the Department of External Affairs (1957–63) (centre) with (left) Seán Ronan, Department of External Affairs, undated, but 1950s (Courtesy of Council of Europe Archives).

Members of the Irish delegation to the United Nations. Left to right: unknown, Conor Cruise O'Brien, Frank Aiken, Frederick Boland, Joseph Shields (Courtesy of the University College Dublin Archives Department).

Members of the Irish delegation to the 13th Assembly of the United Nations General Assembly, 1958. Left to right: Eoin MacWhite, Sean Ronan, Frank Aiken, Frederick Boland, Conor Cruise O'Brien, Eamon Kennedy (Courtesy of the United Nations Archives, New York).

Minister for External Affairs, Frank Aiken, Colonel W. Empey, General Seán Mac Eoin (Chief of Staff, Defence Forces), Minister for Defence, Kevin Boland, August 1960 (Courtesy of Military Archives, Cathal Brugha Barracks, Dublin).

An Taoiseach Seán Lemass, accompanied by Colonel Richard Bunworth, reviewing the 33rd Battalion on its departure from Baldonnell for the Congo, Summer 1960 (Courtesy of Military Archives, Cathal Brugha Barracks, Dublin).

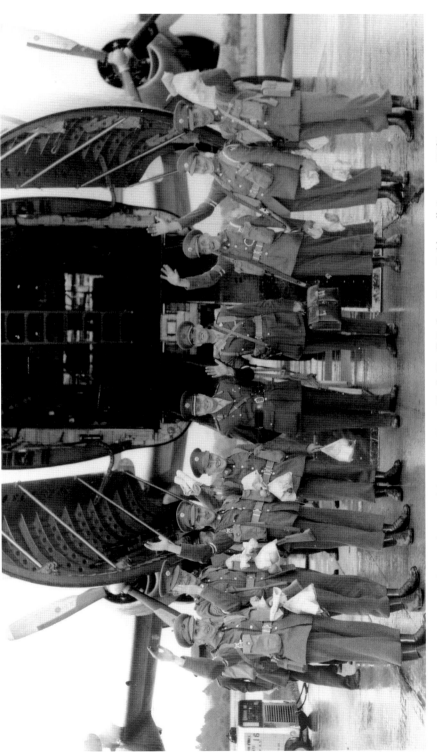

Officers and men of the 33rd Battalion with General Seán Mac Eoin, Chief of Staff, Defence Forces, Baldonnell, Summer 1960 (Courtesy of Military Archives, Cathal Brugha Barracks, Dublin).

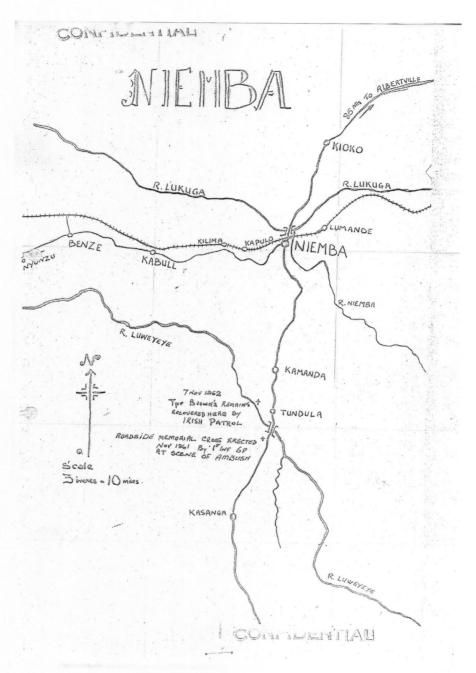

Map of the Niemba region, from the Battalion History of the 33rd Battalion (Courtesy of Military Archives, Cathal Brugha Barracks, Dublin).

Frank Aiken addressing the United Nations General Assembly (Courtesy of the University College Dublin Archives Department).

25th Irish Infantry Group, first UNEF troops to cross the Suez Canal, 14.35 hrs GMT, 9 November 1973 (Courtesy of Colonel Senan Downes, HQ Western Brigade).

First Garda contingent to serve with the United Nations overseas, March 1989 (Courtesy of An Garda Síochána).

Sgt Paul Reid (Courtesy of An Garda Síochána).

DROPS vehicles of the Irish Transport Company operating in trying conditions with KFOR, Kosovo, 2004. (Courtesy of Lieutenant Colonel Dan Murphy, Army Press Office).

It would be tempting to argue that Security Council membership was the crowning moment of Ireland's annus mirabilis, but ultimately it seems this would be incorrect. If Portugal had not persisted in its desire to contest the Netherlands for the seat vacated by Italy and if Liberia, following its own Afro-Asian agenda, had not also stood for the seat, the situation that allowed Ireland to step in as a compromise candidate would not have arisen. Given Keating's very real concern about Ireland's standing in the Western Group and the Western Group's feelings about Ireland, it is unlikely that Ireland could otherwise have been elected to the Security Council in the 1960s. Ireland would not easily have emerged as an agreed Western Group candidate given the powerful forces at play within the group and Ireland's own non-membership of NATO. Ireland's nomination could only emerge by the acclamation of the Assembly in a time of crisis. When Ireland's name was put forward, the state had nothing to lose by standing. Dublin could use the opportunity to further build its claim to be one of the states that sought to damp down crises in the United Nations before they flew out of control. Ireland's candidature emerged because of her active policy in the Assembly from 1958 to 1960, but it did not emerge as a part of that policy.

Chapter Seven

A friend of the colonial powers? Frank Aiken, Ireland's United Nations alignment and decolonisation[*]

AOIFE BHREATNACH

Frank Aiken, Ireland's Minister for External Affairs from 1951 to 1955 and 1957 to 1969, is cast by many historians as the figure representing the moral high ground of Irish United Nations policy.[1] He appears as a radical and his personal commitment to decolonisation is not in doubt. A revolutionary turned democrat, he sympathised with the new African nations emerging into independence out of colonial rule in the 1950s. In 1960, the year of Africa, Aiken addressed the seventeen new United Nations members from Africa and Asia as equals in the General Assembly, welcoming their admission to the world body as a demonstration of the principle of self-determination. Describing Ireland as one of the 'recently emerged nations who form nearly half this Assembly',[2] Aiken clearly believed that Ireland was part of a fraternity of anti-colonial nations, but the Irish attitude to the United Nations differed significantly from that held by the recently emancipated African and Asian states. Ireland's experience as a part of the United Kingdom from 1801 to 1922 may have been difficult, but it was far removed from the imperial, racist rule endured by many former African colonies. Advising new United Nations members in 1960, Aiken sought to impress upon them the importance of grave and moderate diplomacy. However, the new members, 'articulate because so long without an audience, angry because so long humiliated, demanding because so greatly in need',[3] wished to shape the United

[*] The author wishes to acknowledge the support of the Irish Research Council for the Humanities and Social Sciences in the funding of this research.
[1] This perception relates particularly to the years 1957–60, as a previous article has outlined, Aoife Bhreatnach, 'Frank Aiken: European federation and United Nations internationalism', *Irish Studies in International Affairs*, 13 (2002), pp. 237–49, p 241.
[2] Frank Aiken, *Ireland at the United Nations 1960* (Dublin, 1960), p. 12.
[3] T. B. Millar, *The Commonwealth and the United Nations* (Sydney, 1969), p. 15.

Nations in a way that often conflicted with the interests of the larger powers, their former colonial masters. From eighty members in 1956, the General Assembly expanded to 126 states by 1968.[4] Those new members changed the politics and concerns of the General Assembly, and this chapter will analyse how Aiken formulated Irish United Nations policy under these changed conditions. How Ireland positioned itself in the United Nations was always a complicated affair as bilateral concerns and internal United Nations politics had to be borne in mind. When the United Nations discussed a large power oppressing a small nation, the Irish delegation had to consider the merits of the case as well as the politics of alignment in the Assembly. Aiken's role as a policy-maker and his actions as Minister for External Affairs will be closely examined in two case studies: the first United Nations resolution on Tibet in 1959 and, second, United Nations attempts to deal with the emerging crisis over Southern Rhodesia in 1960.

Tibet 1959: 'Belling the Cat'

In the United Nations, the status of Tibet was inextricably linked to that of the representation of Communist China in the General Assembly.[5] The General Assembly vote on Tibet in 1959 illustrated how the United States could use Ireland's reputation as a non-aligned state to its advantage. In the context of a United Nations divided by Cold War politics, the phrase 'Belling the Cat' referred to the practice of smaller countries initiating a debate where the Eastern powers could be criticised.[6] Thus, under the auspices of an uncommitted nation, Tibet could be discussed in the General Assembly, thus ostensibly avoiding a Cold War debate. The United States could thereby criticise Red China's aggression without endangering the support of the Afro-Asian bloc, who resented the United States stance on Chinese representation. Ireland, ostensibly opposed to the United States position on China and as a small nation with anti-colonial credentials, was a reputable sponsor of resolutions on Tibet in the General Assembly. On 14 September 1959, the United States ambassador, James J. Wadsworth met Aiken to encourage an Irish initiative, saying that Ireland's 'association with the proposal would greatly add to its weight'.[7]

---

[4] Inis L. Claude, *Swords into Ploughshares: The problems and progress of international organization* (New York, 4th edition, 1984), p 89.

[5] For an analysis of Aiken's policy on the 'China vote' from 1957 to 1961 see Aoife Bhreatnach, 'Frank Aiken: European federation and United Nations internationalism', *Irish Studies in International Affairs* (2002), pp. 237–49.

[6] The National Archives, Kew, London (hereafter TNA), DO 35/10625, Pink to Crosthwaite, 24 July 1957.

[7] National Archives of Ireland, Dublin (hereafter NAI), Department of Foreign Affairs (hereafter DFA) 440/15, memorandum by Boland, 15 Sept. 1959. There is a disparity between the date and the United States ambassadorial appointee: Henry Cabot Lodge was Ambassador from 1953 to 1960 and Wadsworth was his successor. However, the document is clear that Aiken spoke to Wadsworth.

Aiken was surprised by the United States suggestion, but had 'a good deal to say' about Tibet in his speech on Chinese representation.[8] He did not intend to remain silent on Tibet. It was a conspicuous example of a small nation oppressed by a powerful neighbour. Following Aiken's 'China vote' speech on 21 September 1959, which expressed in equal measure his belief in the importance of discussion and a stern condemnation of Chinese aggression,[9] the Irish delegation explored the possibilities for a resolution on Tibet. Ireland's Permanent Representative to the United Nations, Ambassador Frederick Boland, was worried because sponsorship from 'middle of the road rather than [the] strongly pro-western' delegations approved by the United States was difficult to acquire; but Aiken did not share his concerns. His 'disposition [was] to pursue the idea whatever co-sponsors eventually come forward'.[10] His disregarding of the United States' preference for a 'middle of the road' co-sponsor illustrated his resolve to initiate a General Assembly discussion, and was coupled with a certain disregard for the political consequences. An eminently reputable co-sponsor was eventually secured in Malaya.

The British Permanent Representative to the United Nations, Sir Pierson Dixon, received information on Irish and Malayan efforts from the American delegation, demonstrating the extent of United States involvement in the Tibet question.[11] However, attempts to direct the Irish and Malayan delegations to fulfil United States ends were not entirely successful. The Americans considered inviting the Dalai Lama to address the General Assembly in order to publicly condemn Chinese oppression.[12] The British feared this would set a precedent in which the General Assembly would provide a platform for non-members, with worrying consequences for their interests as an imperial state. Aiken was also opposed to the idea, though for different reasons:

> Mr. Aiken has told the Americans that he is strongly opposed to any such move which would put the item in a cold war context and have an effect entirely different from what he had intended when he asked for inscription.[13]

Aiken voiced adamant objections to the American idea. As Dixon told the Secretary of State in London:

> He had said that if the Americans persisted in the design of turning his item to purposes quite different from his own, he would go to

---

[8] Ibid., memorandum by Boland, 15 Sept. 1959.
[9] Frank Aiken, *Ireland at the United Nations 1959* (Dublin, 1959), pp. 3–7.
[10] NAI DFA 313/36/2, 'Report No. 3', 25 Sept. 1959.
[11] TNA FO 371/141601, Dixon to London, 21 Sept. 1959.
[12] *Irish Times*, 10 Oct. 1959.
[13] TNA FO 371/141602, UKUN to Foreign Office, telegram no. 534, 30 Sept. 1959.

Washington and expostulate with Mr. Herter. Mr. Boland told me the Malayans held the same opinion.[14]

Though the suggestion for inscription by Ireland of the Tibetan question originated with the Americans, Aiken quite legitimately perceived the item as his own initiative. He refused to allow the Americans to manipulate the Irish resolution for their own ends.

The first draft of the resolution was shown to the United States delegation by 19 September 1959.[15] It called for respect for the fundamental rights of the Tibetan people and the restoration of their civil and religious liberties.[16] By 8 October the resolution had been 'watered down'. The call for the 'restoration of civil and political liberties' to Tibet had been replaced by a call for 'respect for the fundamental human rights of the Tibetan people and for their distinctive cultural and religious life'. This redrafting was necessary because 'any stronger version might fail to obtain the overwhelming majority which the sponsors sought'.[17] The British attempted to influence the Irish and the Malayans to modify the resolution but it was felt ill-advised 'to get too far out of step with two, in their way, robustly "free" countries in a matter with as much ideological content as this'.[18] Despite accepting some 'minor modifications' the co-sponsors did not yield to British pressure to expunge the human rights aspect of the resolution.[19] Consequently, the British felt unable to support a draft described as moderate, but 'not fully responsive to our view of the situation'.[20] They were anxious to curtail the development of the Assembly in the area of human rights, stating that they did 'not, however, wish to give any currency to the idea that the Assembly is necessarily competent to "express its opinion" about human rights in a particular case'.[21] As Aiken was eager to expand the competence of the United Nations in the interests of small nations and the rule of law, the British were alert to the dangers of such powers or judgments operating against their interests. This divergence of goals reflected a contrast between a former colonial power and a small nation rather than a specific Anglo-Irish difference.

Between 7 and 21 October, Aiken delivered five speeches on Tibet, illuminating a number of common themes. He was anxious to assure delegations that the Irish and the Malayans did not seek a Cold War debate but rather that they spoke to uphold the Charter and defend the rights of small nations. Aiken declared his opposition to the establishment of 'a kind of a cold peace

---

[14] Ibid., Dixon to London, telegram no. 540, 30 Sept. 1959.
[15] NAI DFA 313/36/2, minutes of delegation meeting, 19 Sept. 1959.
[16] *Irish Times,* 30 Sept. 1959.
[17] Ibid., 8 Oct. 1959.
[18] TNA FO 371/141603, Gore-Booth to McDermot, 9 Oct. 1959.
[19] Ibid., McDermot to Gore-Booth, 12 Oct. 1959.
[20] TNA FO 371/141604, UKUN to Foreign Office, telegram no. 648, 17 Oct. 1959.
[21] Ibid., telegram no. 1327, 20 Oct. 1959.

– a peace in which flagrant acts of oppression and injustice would be passed over in total silence as if they had never occurred'.[22] He described the United Nations as the 'political conscience' of the globe and stressed the necessity of upholding its moral authority. To avoid a Cold War debate, Aiken stressed the colonial dynamic of China's invasion of Tibet. The wider consequences both for the rule of law and the global emergence from colonialism concerned Aiken: 'actions like that of China in Tibet have more than a local effect. They set the clock back the world over.'[23] Striking in his speeches was frequent reference to Ireland's past under British rule and his expressions of sympathy with another oppressed small nation. His twin themes of the rule of law and the Charter of the United Nations were interwoven with his conscious identification of Ireland's position as a small newly independent nation.

The British, who had voted for the inscription of the debate on Tibet, attempted to prevent a vote in order to avoid the delicate position of opposition. Aiken was prepared to strongly resist a procedural motion since it would be 'impossible to explain [it] to public opinion'.[24] The United States support of the Irish stance caused the British procedural motion to falter. Britain abstained when the vote was called. The resolution was adopted by a vote of forty-five to nine, with twenty-six abstentions, on 21 October 1959. The General Assembly had registered its disapproval of the Chinese action but the resolution did not register international support for Tibetan sovereignty.[25] The human rights aspect of the resolution was a compromise issue, chosen to avoid more complex political questions. The drafting process and the desire to secure a majority vote were likely to produce a concession on an ideological issue even while Aiken sought to make a definitive statement on the oppression of small nations.

The American delegation praised the Irish handling of the item, and Ambassador Henry Cabot Lodge Jr 'congratulated the Minister, warmly expressing the view that the whole operation had been splendidly handled from first to last'.[26] The success of the vote did not unduly alarm Sir Pierson Dixon, who dryly commented that 'Mr. Aiken can now go home with a feather in his cap'.[27] The Cold War objective of registering international repugnance of Communist China had succeeded, but Aiken had also strengthened the General Assembly's remit on tackling human rights issues. The vote had asserted the 'moral obligation and legal right' for discussion of such issues claimed by the Irish and Malayans.[28] Boland reported that initial opposition within the United Nations had changed into 'a prevailing feeling

---

[22] Frank Aiken, *Ireland at the United Nations 1959* (Dublin, 1959), p. 44.

[23] Ibid., p 47.

[24] NAI DFA 313/36/2, 'Report 3' by Boland, 27 Oct. 1959.

[25] *Irish Times*, 21 Oct. 1959.

[26] NAI DFA 313/36/2, 'Report 3' by Boland, 27 Oct. 1959.

[27] TNA FO 371/141604, Dixon to Foreign Office, telegram no. 682, 21 Oct. 1959.

[28] *Irish Times*, 30 Sept. 1959.

[that] ... it was better to have had the matter raised and disposed of as it was and that the United Nations would have been in a weak position if it had simply swept the question of Tibet under the rug'.[29]

Aiken refused to allow the Cold War to restrict his criticism of imperialist aggression. He did not champion the Tibetan issue to alleviate criticism from the China vote, but Seán Lemass saw benefits to Irish action on Tibet:

> The Taoiseach has now expressed his great pleasure at the result of the vote and his satisfaction with the nature and quality of the Minister's interventions. He feels that there were considerable advantages in the Minister's taking the course he did and that our stand on this particular issue can do us nothing but good.[30]

For Lemass, the United Nations was an international political arena where Ireland's alignment was carefully judged by other members. He also felt that Irish United Nations policy was as concerned with tactics as with principle. Though the vote served a United States aim, and for Lemass a political purpose, it also served Aiken's end of strengthening the United Nations. The possibility of three different interpretations of the same vote illustrates that there was no such thing as a 'straight vote' in the General Assembly.

Southern Rhodesia: colonial mediation

While Tibet was both a colonial and a Cold War matter, communism was not a complicating factor when the issue of Southern Rhodesia came before the United Nations. Instead, colonialism, Anglo-Irish relations and wider perspectives on alignment within the United Nations were central to Irish decision-making. As part of its withdrawal from southern Africa, Britain created the Federation of Rhodesia and Nyasaland from Southern Rhodesia, Northern Rhodesia and Nyasaland (now Zimbabwe, Zambia and Malawi respectively). The territories were intended as an interim measure until the Africans achieved full independence, but the colonists were reluctant to relinquish their superiority over the natives.[31] Britain possessed final legal authority over the territories, although in practice the white minority had complete control over the government. Southern Rhodesia had long occupied an ambiguous position as a self-governing colony, but when Britain negotiated a new federation constitution in 1961 that removed the British veto over

---

[29] NAI DFA 313/36/2, 'Report 3' by Boland, 27 Oct. 1959.
[30] NAI DFA 440/115, Cremin to Boland, 24 Oct. 1959.
[31] See A.J. Hanna, *The Story of the Rhodesias and Nyasaland* (London, 1965); Leonard T. Kapungu, *Rhodesia: The struggle for freedom* (New York, 1974); Elaine Windrich, *Britain and the Politics of Rhodesian Independence* (London, 1978), Ian Phimister, *An Economic and Social History of Zimbabwe, 1890–1948* (London, 1988); Michael Charlton, *The Last Colony in Africa: Diplomacy and the Independence of Rhodesia* (Oxford, 1990); Mordechai Tamarkin, *The Making of Zimbabwe: decolonisation in regional and international politics* (London, 1990).

Southern Rhodesian affairs, the newly independent anti-colonial Afro-Asian states protested. They were angered at British abandonment of the African population in Southern Rhodesia to the tender mercies of a white minority government that had banned the African opposition party, the African National Congress, in 1959. The African population in Southern Rhodesia held an unofficial referendum in July 1961 and overwhelmingly rejected the new constitution. With the wishes of the country's majority in mind, the newly independent African states ensured that Southern Rhodesia became a major colonial dispute at the United Nations.

At its 16th Session (1961–62), the General Assembly sought to ascertain the precise legal status of Southern Rhodesia: was it self-governing or a colony? The battle on the issue was joined in the Fourth (Trusteeship) Committee, where Tadhg O'Sullivan ably represented Ireland. The Afro-Asian members called on the Fourth Committee to refer the question of the status of Southern Rhodesia to the Special Committee on Colonialism, known as the Committee of seventeen. The British argued for the special autonomous status of Rhodesia, claiming they had no right or power to demand anything from the Rhodesian government. The Afro-Asian group argued that Southern Rhodesia could not be self-governing, since 2¹/₂ million of its inhabitants were denied the vote on racial grounds. Between such polarised views, the position of moderate states, such as Ireland and Sweden, became important. In January 1962 the British embassy in Dublin 'hoped' the Irish would follow the United States, 'Old' Commonwealth nations and the Scandinavians in opposing the Afro-Asian bloc.[32]

Under Article 73 (e) of the United Nations Charter, Britain was required to inform the United Nations of its colonial territories, but the British were adamant that Southern Rhodesia was not included. Ireland did in fact support this British position, and Western and 'middle of the road' delegations – Ireland included – had attempted to co-ordinate tactics, but no course was chosen. The British attitude to the debate was uncompromising:

> The British government strongly feels that moves of this kind in the Fourth Committee represent an attempt to widen the field of activity of the United Nations so as to embrace areas in which it has hitherto no competence. It is felt that if such moves continue they could only result in the withdrawal of cooperation by the UK and other major powers, thus ultimately weakening the influence of the United Nations.[33]

Colonial disputes had alienated France and Portugal from the United Nations and Britain felt similarly pilloried over Southern Rhodesia. The

---

[32] NAI DFA PMUN 319 (J/53), DEA to PMUN, telegram no. 30, undated.
[33] Ibid., O'Sullivan to Cremin, 9 Feb. 1962.

United States believed that the Afro-Asians were sponsoring a 'mischievous move' with dangerous implications for the internal situation in Southern Rhodesia. Fearing the United Nations might offend the national interests of powerful countries and over-extend itself, O'Sullivan advocated opposing the Afro-Asian resolution.[34] Aiken offered a very different assessment of the situation. He was 'somewhat doubtful about the wisdom' of opposition:

> On the legal side the question arises whether the territory can claim to be self-governing to such an extent as to put it beyond the reach of the dominant power or, in other words, whether whatever the practice has been, the legal position is precisely as represented by the opponents of the resolution. The Minister feels that if there is a doubt on this point, the United Nations has a right to enquire into the problems.
>
> The political aspect raises a number of problems. There is no doubt that the Rhodesian government are following very strong policies. Furthermore, they cannot claim to be representative of the population when the vast bulk of the people have little or no say in government. It is likewise true that some members of the governments and in particular Sir Roy Welensky [Prime Minister of the Federation of Rhodesia and Nyasaland] have taken a strong stand against the United Nations and there is therefore a risk that a vote against the resolution could be represented as implying approval of their attitude or that our so voting might in the extreme case be represented as a vote for Welensky.[35]

Aiken felt that there was a strong case for voting against the British position, which was defined as 'power without responsibility'.[36] His argument was typical of his policy of United Nations expansion, which sought an international system based on justice and the rule of law. United Nations mediation in a colonial issue could only further the process. Clearly Aiken did not agree with the Southern Rhodesian government and its policies. Interestingly, here he was not concerned with an Irish vote being perceived as supportive of colonial powers, but being associated with opposition to the United Nations. Nonetheless, after a discussion with Boland, Aiken reversed this position. It appears that the legal argument, the foundation of the British case, was used convincingly:

> The Minister agrees that in the circumstances ... we may vote against the resolution. He accepts that there is a good legal case in favour of it. He is however, uneasy about possible misrepresentation of the vote

---

[34] Ibid.

[35] Ibid., Cremin to Boland, telegram no. 43, undated.

[36] Elaine Windrich, *Rhodesian Independence*, p 7.

... and he feels that it would be well to obviate such misrepresentation by our making a short statement which might include the following points.

One: We are voting against the resolution because we feel that if the United Nations is to retain its efficacity it must behave in a responsible fashion and not waste time and energy enquiring into matters which are perfectly obvious.

Two: The legal position in this matter seems to be quite clear.

Three: Non-inclusion under 73(e) has not hitherto been questioned during the life of the United Nations and its self-governing status has been admitted internationally by its participation in a number of instruments including GATT.

Four: In 1960, it was not suggested that Southern Rhodesia should come into this category.

Five: If United Nations set up a committee and legally based judgment it could only arrive at one conclusion, viz., that the territory cannot be classified as non-self-governing.[37]

This reversal of position was quite startling. The second point slavishly followed the British interpretation of the legal position of Southern Rhodesia. The Irish, echoing the British, would brook no argument: 'the legal position in this matter seems to be quite clear'. The third and fourth points emphasised the 'self-governing' status of Southern Rhodesia, denying the more ambiguous constitutional position. Aiken's suggestion of debating residual doubts was replaced by categorical denial of the need to discuss Southern Rhodesia. With Boland's advice he moved from holding a moderate independent position, to sharing a British interpretation of the resolution.

However, the British had resigned themselves to defeat in the Fourth Committee, hardly bothering to organise the debate or the vote. Latin American backing was vanishing and even Norway's support for Britain was beginning to waver. Under such circumstances, Boland's assessment of the Irish position changed: 'I propose to abstain in vote if a negative vote would put us in invidious company'.[38] Who constituted 'invidious company' was unclear, but the withdrawal of support by the 'middle of the road' states would have left Ireland as the sole moderate defending Britain. Ireland supported a failed British procedural move to block the vote but abstained when the resolution was put to a vote. The resolution was passed, with fifty-seven in favour, twenty-one opposed and twenty-four abstaining. Britain had suffered the first of many defeats on Southern Rhodesia.

Boland's comprehensive report is a fascinating insight into the tensions caused by the colonial issue between the Afro-Asian and Western blocs. It

---

[37] NAI DFA PMUN 319 (J/53), Cremin to Boland, telegram no. 44, 22 Feb. 1962.

also provides a clear exposition of Boland's diplomatic style, described as being in 'the distinctly unenthusiastic Talleyrand tradition'.[39] Boland disapproved of a debate in which 'the constitutional aspect of the matter played a relatively secondary role compared with the racial issue':

> The issue on which the Afro-Asians were concerned to get a decision was not the extent of Southern Rhodesia's autonomy and independence from Britain but whether a territory like Southern Rhodesia, which excluded a large majority of its population from the franchise on legal grounds could properly be said to be self-governing at all! Emotionalism played a larger part in the debate than legal argument!
>
> There is a growing feeling here at United Nations that unless the activities of the powerful Afro-Asian bloc can somehow or other be kept within the bounds of reason, serious harm to the United Nations may result. Britain is regarded here as having a relatively good record on colonial questions.[40]

Boland may have felt that the Africans were hysterical over franchise rights but the increasing support among the white minority for the extreme right threatened the prospect of racial equality. Africans believed that 'colonialism must be wiped out in Africa before any post-colonial independent state can feel secure'.[41] This was an attitude that Aiken, a staunch anti-partitionist in an Irish context, may well have understood. But African fears were not appreciated by Britain, who condemned the excesses of the Afro-Asian states. The danger of Britain feeling under siege, and adopting a 'detached, disinterested attitude' towards the United Nations was advanced by the 'Old' Commonwealth, principally Canada and Australia, and by the Nordic countries, principally Sweden. Boland acknowledged Ireland's general agreement with these countries in colonial debates, but defended Ireland's abstention on the Southern Rhodesian vote, where many Western powers had supported Britain.

Boland then outlined his vision of Ireland at the United Nations, a vision in which the delegation exerted its influence to the advantage of the United Nations and the western bloc:

> More than any of the countries of the West, we occupy a special position vis-à-vis the Afro-Asian bloc. In several respects, we are more favourably placed than they are to exert a mediatory and moderate influence on the Asian and African delegations.

---

[38] Ibid., Boland to Cremin, 23 Jan. 1962.

[39] Conor Cruise O'Brien, *To Katanga and Back: A UN Case study* (London, 1962), p 35.

[40] NAI DFA PMUN 319 (J/53), Boland to Cremin, 26 Feb. 1962.

[41] Julius K. Nyerere, 'Rhodesia in the context of Southern Africa', *Foreign Affairs* 44:3, Apr. 1966, p. 374.

> Such importance as we enjoy as a member of the United Nations derives largely from the possibility of constructive action open to us – more than to any other European country ... We cannot hope to maintain our position vis-à-vis the Afro-Asians however, unless we are prepared to give occasional proof of our freedom of action and our willingness to take an independent line. This is what we did ... when we found some of the middle-of-the-road delegations with which we normally vote taking one line (Canada, Nordic states etc.) and others (Mexico, Venezuela, Japan, Malaya etc.) taking a different one. In all circumstances, I believe the vote we cast was the correct one.

The Irish were conspicuously alone among Western European members in abstaining on the resolution. Boland reassured Cremin that though the Irish were popular with anti-colonial delegations, the former colonists were not displeased:

> The British were neither surprised by, nor resentful of, our vote. Indeed ... Sir Patrick Dean said he imagined that resolutions such as that on Rhodesia put us in somewhat of a difficulty. He realised that, for a European country, we had a special standing with the Afro-Asians; he thought it was very useful that we had that position and he readily understood that we should want to maintain it.[42]

It was likely that Sir Patrick Dean, the British Permanent Representative to the United Nations, expressed satisfaction with Ireland's 'special standing' not from expansive generosity but because the moderate Irish position could be exploited to Britain's benefit. Boland was already an ally in this cause. In 1957, he had outlined an approach to colonial issues that was very congenial to British interests:

> Boland expressed indignation at the nonsense talked by the anti-colonialists ... he recognised that it was difficult for Britain or the other colonial powers to defend themselves on this issue, but thought that something could be done by smaller countries and in particular by Ireland ... he did not see why the Irish delegation should not bring a little realism into the 'colonial' debates by drawing attention to the British record since the war.[43]

Aiken, whose speeches often referred to his country's turbulent history, may not have directly advocated defending beleaguered colonial powers.[44]

---

[42] NAI DFA PMUN 319 (J/53), Boland to Cremin, 26 Feb. 1962.
[43] TNA DO 35/10625, Pink to Crosthwaite, 24 July 1957.
[44] See for example, Aiken, *Ireland at the United Nations 1957*, p. 6, pp. 23–4; Aiken, *Ireland at the United Nations 1958*, p. 28; Aiken, *Ireland at the United Nations 1959*, p. 37; Aiken, *Ireland at the United Nations 1960*, pp. 13–5.

However, Boland realised that to maintain some moderating influence, occasional votes had to be cast with the 'wilder anti-colonialists'. Politically astute in a manner that his minister never was, Boland was instrumental in formulating Irish United Nations anti-colonial policy.

In May 1962, the special committee on colonialism reported to the Secretary-General. It found that Southern Rhodesia did not qualify as a self-governing territory within the meaning of the Charter. Furthermore, it did not agree that the constitution would guarantee African rights.[45] The report's findings undermined the legal basis of British arguments which stressed that the provisions of article 73 (e) did not apply to Rhodesia. This report changed the terms of the Irish position, which, as Aiken told Noel Browne in the Dáil, had previously opposed 'some artificial and totally beside the point enquiry'.[46] In June 1962, the Afro-Asian bloc introduced a draft resolution supporting the conclusions of the special committee. The draft urged the British government to call a constitutional conference involving all sections of the Rhodesian population, to take immediate steps to restore African rights and to ensure the release of all political prisoners.

The report of the special committee prompted Aiken to rethink Irish policy. In early June 1962, Boland was told that his minister believed that 'the British government should be exhorted to postpone the steps there contemplated until such time as a more satisfactory internal system has been incorporated in the constitution'. Aiken favoured supporting a moderate draft resolution which would urge the British government to use its 'special influence' in Southern Rhodesia to effect reform.[47] Aiken was unconvinced of British impotency in internal Rhodesian affairs, hoping for change while the government was 'still legally in a position to influence developments'.[48] Boland discussed Aiken's proposal with Sir Patrick Dean, who did not agree that Britain should postpone the implementation of the Southern Rhodesian constitution. Boland reported: 'It is quite clear that the British government strongly resents efforts to push them at this moment when they are doing their best to solve the federation problem and improve matters in Southern Rhodesia'. He advised caution until the forthcoming 17th Session.[49] The Irish did not formulate an alternative resolution on Southern Rhodesia, and abstained on the Afro-Asian resolution. Boland's speech on 29 June represented his minister's views. Firstly, Boland stated that the 1961 Constitution did not provide justice for the African population. Secondly, he expressed concern that the constitution would divest the British government of power

---

[45] NAI DFA PMUN 257 (J/37/62), 'Notes on the 17th regular session', 10 Sept. 1962.

[46] *Dáil Deb.*, vol. 193, col. 1042–3, 7 Mar. 1962.

[47] Donal Lowry discusses this point, but with regard to the position of the Labour government in 1965, in his article 'Ulster resistance and loyalist rebellion in the Empire', in Keith Jeffery (ed.), *An Irish Empire* (Manchester, 1996) pp. 203–4 and pp. 212–3.

[48] NAI DFA PMUN 319 (J/53), DEA to PMUN, undated.

[49] Ibid., Boland to Cremin, 27 June 1962.

to influence Southern Rhodesian politics and legislation. Finally, Boland urged the British government to postpone the implementation of the constitution, pending a constitutional conference.[50] Irish analysis of British influence over Southern Rhodesia altered only when the report of the special committee made the legal argument untenable. However, the legal approach to Southern Rhodesia's 'special position' remained the core of Irish policy. Aiken refused to accept the Afro-Asian thesis that Britain, as the 'administrative authority', shouldered full responsibility for Southern Rhodesia, since this 'did not correspond to the political realities of the territory'.[51]

Joe Sweeney of the American embassy in Dublin discussed Southern Rhodesia in the United Nations with Con Cremin. The State Department was worried about the possibility of a United Nations resolution framed in 'harsh and intemperate terms' being debated. In an interesting example of side-door diplomacy, Sweeney asked if Aiken would speak to the British:

> Washington thinks it might be well if the Minister were to speak once more to the British Ambassador. The State Department is of the opinion that the British still retain 'substantial political and legal authority' which gives them room for manoeuvre.[52]

It seems Aiken had already spoken to the British on behalf of the United States. The indirect method used by Washington suggests that American representations were meeting stiff British resistance. Aiken raised Southern Rhodesia with the British Ambassador in Dublin, Sir Ian Maclennan, on 30 August 1962, suggesting that the British government 'would be very wise to postpone the operation of the present constitution', and call 'a conference for purposes of drafting a new constitution which would give fuller rights to the native population'. However, Aiken's argument did not meet with any success. The British ambassador painted a gloomy picture of Britain trapped 'between the devil (represented by the United Nations) and the deep sea (represented by the white population in Southern Rhodesia)'. Aiken repeated his concerns about the coming United Nations session and addressed the argument put forward by Maclennan that the African population was not cooperating in implementing a new constitution:

> He went on to say that a change must come in Southern Rhodesia as Africa is on the march and the trend cannot be reversed. Southern Rhodesia in its present state provides an excellent excuse for all kinds of troublemakers. Furthermore, in his view, the existing electoral law does not meet the situation as it has put the financial qualification for voting away beyond the average income of the natives.

---

[50] Ibid., 'Notes on the 17th regular session', 10 Sept. 1962.
[51] *Dáil Deb.*, vol. 196, col. 1459, 4 July 1962.
[52] NAI DFA PMUN 319 (J/53), note by Cremin, 31 Aug. 1962.

The ambassador did not think any movement along the lines suggested by the minister could be possible. He suggested the United Nations ask the African population to register for elections to be held under the new constitution. Aiken pointed out that African opposition to the constitution was understandable:

> The Minister pointed out that no date has been fixed in the Southern Rhodesian Constitution for the attainment of a majority in Parliament by the Africans. This was in contrast with the position in other former British territories where, while a date was not fixed, steps were taken to bring the population forward by definite stages obviously leading to independence. To the Southern Rhodesian natives the present situation must seem likely to endure forever – as in South Africa.

The ambassador rejected this, saying 'the Africans could achieve dominance in 10 years and he did think that they were being unreasonable'. Maclennan ended the discussion stressing 'the essential impotence of the British government in relation to the territory'.[53] Aiken had failed to persuade the British to effect change in Southern Rhodesia.

Aiken was in New York when Southern Rhodesia was again discussed. At a delegation meeting he defined the Irish attitude to the Southern Rhodesian issue. His policy hoped to influence British actions in Southern Rhodesia by advocating the postponement of elections in Southern Rhodesia, the liberalisation of electoral law to give a greater African vote within a short space of time and Africanisation of the civil service.[54] The objectives of Irish policy on Southern Rhodesia were straightforward, but the methods revealed differences within the delegation. O'Sullivan believed the Irish could play a significant role; the promotion of 'a moderate solution to this problem as a whole'.[55] O'Sullivan and Aiken favoured a mediatory role, modifying extreme passages of an Afro-Asian resolution whose language echoed Chapter Seven of the Charter, which empowers United Nations intervention.[56] The United States supported the tabling of a moderate resolution and Aiken asked O'Sullivan to prepare such a draft. Boland, on the other hand, advocated a more circumspect course. He advised against exerting a moderating influence on the Afro-Asians, for fear the Irish would be labelled 'pro-colonialist'. He did not favour tabling a moderate resolution in the face of Afro-Asian opposition. Boland appeared to place a higher value on perceived Irish detachment from the western group than Aiken or O'Sullivan, who favoured an active policy.

---

[53] NAI DFA PMUN 257 (J/37/62), note by Cremin, 4 Sept. 1962.
[54] NAI DFA PMUN 273 (J/50/61), 'Minutes of the delegation meeting', 22 Sept. 1962.
[55] NAI DFA PMUN 319 (J/53), O'Sullivan to Aiken, 5 Oct. 1962.
[56] Chapter 7 of the United Nations Charter is entitled 'Action with respect to threats to the peace, breaches of the peace, and acts of aggression'.

Boland counselled caution and was anxious to reserve the Irish position.[57]

The British were also anxious for the Irish to remain silent on Southern Rhodesia. Aiken met Sir Patrick Dean on 11 October. Dean explained that it would be 'very embarrassing to the British delegation if just at that particular moment we put down or circulated privately the draft resolution about Southern Rhodesia which we had in mind'. He wondered, since the debate had 'not really begun yet', whether the Irish, who would 'lose nothing', would consider withholding the resolution, 'for the time being'. Aiken replied that since he had not yet reached a decision about specific action in the Fourth Committee, 'he was ready to fall in with the British request that we should do nothing "for the time being"'.[58] Britain feared criticism from all shades of United Nations opinion. A 'strong' Afro-Asian resolution was expected, but criticism from a moderate state was harder to stomach.

The Taoiseach was asked whether the Irish should promote a Southern Rhodesia policy which was 'strenuously opposed' by the British.[59] Lemass, after discussion with Cremin, counselled against leading a frontal attack on the British position: 'It is important at the present conjuncture to avoid giving unnecessary offence to Britain unless the reasons for doing so are entirely cogent'. Precisely why avoiding giving offence to British feelings was so important at this point was not outlined. However, Lemass reminded Aiken that Southern Rhodesia was not a 'live issue in public opinion' or in the Oireachtas. He did not regard the Southern Rhodesian problem 'as sufficient to justify our creating unnecessary resentment in London'. Lemass was also wary of United States and Canadian motives. He suspected the former of 'inducing us to shoulder a responsibility those governments are not prepared to assume'.[60] Boland and Lemass were not in favour of the Irish voicing moderate opinion on Southern Rhodesia. Lemass was alert to the bilateral implications and did not support Aiken's suggestion of a draft resolution. He was careful not to oppose the course outright, but his preference for a favourable vote for an existing resolution, as an alternative to tabling an Irish resolution, made clear his reservations. Aiken again spoke to Cremin about the Southern Rhodesian vote on 31 October:

> The Southern Rhodesian issue has become 'rather hot'. The British had been in touch with the Minister, who told them that we proposed to vote in favour of the Afro-Asian draft resolution, making an explanation of our vote which would indicate that we do not agree with all of the text. The British had wished us to abstain but the Minister had

---

[57] NAI DFA PMUN 273 (J/50/61), 'Minutes of the delegation meeting', 6 Oct. 1962.

[58] NAI DFA PMUN 319 (J/53), memorandum by Boland, 16 Oct. 1962.

[59] Ibid., O'Sullivan to Cremin, 11 Oct. 1962.

[60] NAI, Department of the Taoiseach (hereafter DT) S16057G/62, DEA to PMUN, 15 Oct. 1962.

explained that this would not be possible, as in principle he favours the resolution.[61]

The Taoiseach agreed with Aiken's course.

Despite encouragement from moderate circles in the Fourth Committee, the Irish delegation did not propose an alternative to the Afro-Asian resolution. Ireland attended two meetings of the moderate group before Aiken decided against the initiative. This change possibly occurred after Lemass' telegram. Instead, Ireland voted for a resolution which called for the suspension of the new constitution and forthcoming general election; the convening of a constitutional conference; the extension of full political rights to the whole population.[62] While declaring that 'the question was not a legal but a delicate and dangerous political one which must be faced with courage and imagination',[63] the Irish did not agree with designating Britain 'the administrative authority', believing it obscured the constitutional and political realities of the situation.[64] The Irish did not fully support either constitutional interpretation and steered a middle course between the polarised positions. Britain applauded the Irish speech, which praised the 'liberal and progressive' British constitutional tradition, for its 'moderation'.[65] Irish moderation had also prevailed upon the Afro-Asian sponsors to amend the operative paragraph, making it more acceptable to the Secretary-General.

O'Sullivan's report on the proceedings draws attention to the influence, however limited, of moderate opinion in the United Nations. Britain feared the Irish vote would encourage other moderate delegations to oppose their position. Norway had received instructions to support Ireland's vote, and Britain feared the Irish stance would receive widespread Scandinavian support. The Irish vote as a determining factor for a number of moderates increased British pressure, which included a phone call to the minister. O'Sullivan felt that moderate corridor action had influenced United States policy, which for the first time publicly favoured intervention by the British government. Britain, it was hoped, realised fully the need for negotiations to solve the Southern Rhodesian problem. Though the opportunities for mediation on colonial issues by Ireland were 'extremely limited', the Afro-Asian bloc attached 'particular value to independent policies such as the present one which, they feel, have a strong moral effect when adopted by countries which they regard as being among the friends of the colonial powers'.[66] Both East and

---

[61] Ibid., note by Cremin, 2 Nov. 1962. Although Aiken spoke to Cremin in Irish, the conversation was summarized in this memo in English.

[62] NAI DFA PMUN 265 (J/41/63), 'Memorandum for Information of the Government', 9 Sept. 1963.

[63] NAI DFA PMUN 319 (J/53), O'Sullivan to Cremin, 7 Nov. 1962.

[64] Ibid., PMUN to DEA, 1 Nov. 1962.

[65] Ibid.

[66] Ibid., O'Sullivan to Cremin, 7 Nov. 1962.

West hoped the Irish would, by principled example, moderate bloc allegiances.

Ireland's influence was valued by the diplomatic service of a fading imperial power under siege. Attempts 'to encourage in the newer [United Nations] members a consistent sense of responsibility' preoccupied London:

> In this process the Irish are playing an important and useful part. Not only do they themselves set a notable example of restraint and common sense, but they regularly use their influence with the newer members to induce in them a similar approach. Because of her high reputation and of the fact that she is a 'non-aligned' state, Ireland is particularly well placed to do this ... at the United Nations the Irish adopt a generally responsible and helpful attitude on colonial questions and appear to understand and sympathise with our difficulties.[67]

The congenial company of Frederick Boland was probably a contributing factor to this analysis. However, Aiken commented that 'by and large he felt that the United Nations recognised that Britain had done a good job in her overseas policies'.[68] Whatever Boland's influence, Aiken was not rashly anti-British. Approvingly, the British noted: 'Without compromising its independence it [Ireland] has consistently been ready to be helpful to us'. The issue of Southern Rhodesia was a 'recent occasion for gratitude', and Irish 'sympathy and understanding' was hoped for in future colonial discussions.[69]

Irish involvement in the Southern Rhodesia issue concluded after the unilateral declaration of independence by Ian Smith in November 1965. During the debates in the Fourth Committee, the Irish position was important. Though O'Sullivan acknowledged the relative powerlessness of his delegation to calm anti-colonial rhetoric, the British appreciated what little moderating influence the Irish possessed. Aiken robustly denounced imperialism, but he was not reflectively hostile towards former imperialists. In 1960, he had appealed to the expanding Afro-Asian bloc for 'moderation and prudence' in its conduct of international relations. He was fully aware of the power of the newly independent countries in colonial matters and in 1962 refused to contemplate membership of the newly constituted Committee of Twenty-Four. The United States Ambassador to Ireland, Matthew McCloskey, asked if Ireland would replace the United States on the committee, but Aiken realised 'our voice carries no weight in such groupings where Afro-Asian members pursue their way in a straight line'.[70]

---

[67] TNA DO 181/9, brief for Lord Dundee regarding Aiken and Lemass visit of 19 Mar. 1963.

[68] Ibid., record extract, Lord Dundee, Seán Lemass, Frank Aiken at Foreign Office, 19 Mar. 1963.

[69] Ibid., brief for Sir Saville Garner's June 1962 visit to Dublin, by Kimber and Smallman.

[70] NAI DFA PMUN 257 (H/1), note by Cremin, 7 Sept. 1962.

Conclusion

The extent to which Ireland adopted a principled anti-colonial stance in the United Nations needs careful analysis. Boland ensured that a moderate opinion of Britain prevailed, even as Ireland portrayed itself as fraternally part of the anti-colonial camp. A former guerrilla fighter, Aiken may have embodied successful anti-imperialism but his revolutionary days were far behind him. He counselled caution and restraint, appreciating the difficulties facing Britain as it tried to disentangle itself from Africa. The impatience of African nationalists and their fears of permanent oppression in Southern Africa were less easily comprehended. Yet, in spite of his sympathy for colonial powers, Aiken was not willing to allow them to dictate Irish policy as his resistance to British and American interference on the Tibetan resolution demonstrates. Throughout, Aiken, Boland and Lemass were aware of how votes and resolutions in the General Assembly and on Committees positioned Ireland in the context of United Nations politics. Ireland's alignment – pro-Western and independent, anti-colonial and European – was sufficiently complex to permit multiple interpretations, especially since blocs formed and reformed on the basis of individual issues and votes. On fluid issues such as Southern Rhodesia, voting policy was a means to demonstrate that alignment, as well as a statement about British responsibility for the territory. The restrained and carefully charted Irish policy demonstrated a reconciliation of two apparently disparate objectives: moderate independence on colonial issues in the United Nations and easy bilateral relations with a waning imperial power.

In addition to the internal United Nations manoeuvrings and alignments, Lemass was sensitive to the bilateral implications of the United Nations forum. Aiken had little difficulty with approaching the British on behalf of the Americans, but Lemass had no intention of annoying the British when one of the most powerful countries in the world would not openly broach the delicate issue of Southern Rhodesia with them. The minister's willingness to act for other countries was explained by Thomas J. Kiernan, Irish Ambassador to the United States:

> Anything in the nature of 'do this for me and I'll do something for you', was not wanted, but 'here's something I'd like you to do. This will help my policy' then that was something that was bound to get a positive response.[71]

Lemass however was not inclined to do favours unless tangible gains for Ireland resulted. Boland believed that the status accorded to Ireland by the Afro-Asian bloc could be used as a voice of reason in the United Nations, a belief that Aiken shared. Yet there was a difference in how that reasonable

---

[71] John F. Kennedy Library Oral History Program, Thomas J. Kiernan, recorded interview by Joe O'Connor, 5 Aug. 1966, p 15.

counsel was deployed: Aiken sought a powerful United Nations, a world body where all issues could be discussed, while Boland worked to moderate what he saw as the excitable and excessive demonstrations of the 'wilder' anti-colonials. Though the counsel of Tadhg O'Sullivan was helpful, Aiken struggled to articulate his somewhat abstract policy against the combined intellects of Boland and Lemass. Irish United Nations policy arose from the interaction of these policy-makers with each other, as well as from the complex and shifting politics of the Assembly.

Chapter Eight

'The cause of nationality is sacred, in … Africa as in Ireland': Ireland and Sub-Saharan Africa at the United Nations, 1960–75[1]

KEVIN O'SULLIVAN[2]

Introduction

On 10 September 1970 the Irish Permanent Representative to the United Nations, Cornelius (Con) Cremin, remarked on the success of Ireland's early years at the United Nations: 'We … more or less by accident, had an unusually good initial start … circumstances lent themselves well to positions which tended to give our delegation a certain prominence, e.g. the problem of Algeria, and the movement towards decolonisation in Africa which up to 1960 was in an incipient stage'.[3] Cremin's statement reflected the widely-held view that the late 1950s and early 1960s were the 'glory years' of Ireland's contribution to the United Nations. His comments also reflected a view of Ireland's relationship with the Afro-Asian states crucial to understanding the reasons for this change. Implicit in his reference was the idea that Ireland's role in United Nations circles had, by 1970, been overtaken by the arrival of newly-independent African and Asian states intent on making their voices heard. Ireland, indeed, had championed many of these states in the decolonisation debates at the General Assembly's meetings – particularly in the Fourth Committee – thus giving the delegation the 'prominence' Cremin referred to. It was not surprising, however, that Ireland had been overtaken at

[1] Irish Minister for External Affairs, Frank Aiken, paraphrasing Charles Stewart Parnell, in an address to the United Nations General Assembly (UNGA) Plenary Meeting, 6 Oct. 1960, A/PV.890.
[2] The author wishes to acknowledge the support of the Irish Research Council for the Humanities and Social Sciences in the funding of his research.
[3] National Archives of Ireland (NAI), Department of Foreign Affairs Files (DFA), 417/220, Cremin to Ronan, 10 Sept. 1970.

the forefront of Third World issues. Having been afforded the opportunity to express for themselves their aspirations and hopes for the future of their continent, many (though not all) of the African states and leaders were more than willing to make their voices heard in the completion of its liberation. Although still mindful of the need to obtain the support of those western states, like Ireland, supportive of their cause, they no longer relied on them to the same extent to force African issues to the top of the United Nations agenda.

The focus here falls on the period from 1960 (which became known as 'the year of African independence') to 1975 when the independence granted to the former Portuguese colonies of Mozambique and Angola left only South Africa, Namibia, and Rhodesia under white minority control. This chapter examines the perceptions of African issues in Ireland, looking at the organisations and groups that helped inform opinion, and the public and government identification with the goals of the African states. It also looks briefly at the role of the United Nations in Afro-Irish relations in a narrower sense by examining the importance of New York in facilitating diplomatic contacts and links. The main focus of the chapter is on three examples of foreign policy-making; the decolonisation process in Rhodesia, the decolonisation process in Portuguese Africa and the development aid policy of the Irish government. These examples facilitate the analysis of the development of policy over time and serve to highlight the central tenets of the Irish approach, the factors that influenced policy-making, and the flexibility and responsiveness of the Irish to African political developments.

Sub-Saharan Africa and the United Nations 1960–75[4]

The agenda of the United Nations during the first years of Ireland's participation was dominated by the ending of the colonial era in Africa. When the Irish delegation first took its seat in the General Assembly in 1955, there were only two delegations of 'free' (excluding South Africa) sub-Saharan African states present – Ethiopia and Liberia. The rapid expansion that followed affected the very nature of the organisation's agenda as the majority of African states interpreted their non-alignment as 'the right to make choices on the basis of each issue's merits, regardless of the interests of the Cold War alliances'.[5] The simple fact that the influx of African states gave them a

---

[4] For a more detailed introduction to African issues at the United Nations, see, for example, Gwendolen M. Carter, 'The impact of the African states in the United Nations', in Robert K.A. Gardiner, M.J. Anstee and C.L. Patterson (eds.), *Africa and the world* (Oxford, 1970), pp. 19–27; Catherine Hoskyns, 'African states and the United Nations, 1958–1964', in P.J.M. McEwan (ed.), *Twentieth-century Africa* (London, 1968), pp. 458–75; and Edmond Kwam Kouassi, 'Africa and the United Nations since 1945', in Ali A. Mazrui (ed.), *UNESCO general history of Africa VIII: Africa since 1935* (Oxford, 1993), pp. 871–904.

[5] Margaret Legum, 'Africa and nonalignment', in J.W. Burton (ed.), *Nonalignment* (London, 1966), p. 57.

numerical advantage, particularly when added to the numbers of Asian states present from the first wave of post-war decolonisation, meant that several major African concerns were continually kept to the fore. The apartheid policies of the South African government, first raised by the Indian delegation in 1946, were discussed extensively, particularly in the Special Political Committee. By extension, the future of the South West African Trust Territory (Namibia) or rather South Africa's control of it, remained an extremely contentious issue, thought of by Ireland's External Affairs Minister, Frank Aiken, as central to the resolution of conflict in southern Africa.[6] From the mid-1960s onwards, the agenda of the Fourth Committee was dominated by the decolonisation of Portuguese Africa and Southern Rhodesia, examined below, as the tensions escalated within the territories themselves. In addition, the United Nations frequently found itself confronted with disputes resulting from the decolonisation process, most notably in the Congo, but also in Somaliland, Togoland, the Cameroons and Ruanda-Urundi. In later years, as the political liberation of the continent proceeded, the African states became increasingly concerned with questions of economic equality and liberation from what they perceived as neo-colonial domination, as well as with eliciting support from the world community in response to individual events such as the famines that devastated parts of the continent in the mid-1970s.

There were, however, limitations to the powers of the African states. The very nature of the international system and the dominance of cold war politics meant that in spite of their numbers, the Africans often found it difficult to press home their advantage. The extremity of their language and proposed responses often alienated those whose support they sought to elicit, including Ireland. The limited influence of the African states was, however, perhaps best captured in the lengthy process involved in the defeat of apartheid in South Africa. In that case, the role of the African states was overshadowed by the sometimes reluctant approach of the major powers. Their unwillingness to match the actions demanded by the African states allowed South Africa to maintain a relatively comfortable existence. As Jack Spence commented in 1971, the South Africans' fear came from nationalist movements within their own country, rather than pressure from the United Nations. For them, that organisation, Spence stated, 'could only be as effective as its most powerful members were prepared to allow it to be'.[7]

---

[6] See Aiken's address to the UNGA on 3 Oct. 1966 in *Ireland at the United Nations 1966* (Dublin, n.d. [1967?]), pp. 14–21, and also his statement to Seanad Éireann in 1967, *Seanad Deb.*, vol. 63, col. 399, 7 June 1967: 'I feel that the best way to get rid of [apartheid] in South Africa and in Rhodesia is to get South Africans prized out of South West Africa'.

[7] Jack Spence, 'South Africa and the modern world', in Monica Wilson and Leonard Thompson (eds.), *The Oxford history of South Africa II: 1870–1966* (Oxford, 1971), p. 523.

Sub-Saharan Africa and the Irish imagination

In Ireland, these events seeped slowly into the public imagination; interest and knowledge remained generally low unless aroused by some major incident or by Irish involvement in an issue. Africa was viewed mainly in simplistic terms, from the missionaries' 'penny for a black baby' campaigns to *The Economist*'s exaggerated remarks about an 'Afro-Irish Assembly' at the United Nations.[8] For many Irish people perceptions of Africa were bound up in images of Irish missionaries working in African rural communities, images reinforced in the Lenten campaigns initiated by Trócaire (the Catholic aid organisation) from the early 1970s. The magazines of missionary orders also provided the Irish public with a window on Africa, important in informing them of the poverty of conditions that existed in many areas, and the difficulties facing Irish missionaries in those environs.

In the majority of cases however, these images were divorced from the high politics of the countries concerned. As Garreth Byrne wrote in 1974, the 'Black Baby image … kept countless Irish people in ignorance of African culture'.[9] Instead the missionaries concentrated on the provision of basic needs such as medical, educational and church-related services. It was only on occasions such as the huge public outcry surrounding the Nigerian civil war in the late 1960s, fuelled by missionary reports of famine and the plight of the secessionist Biafran region, that the missionaries' ability to mobilise support was visibly manifested.[10] Even then the emphasis was less on the political than on the humanitarian element. Others, such as Bishop Donal Lamont and the Irish missionaries who became involved in the war of independence in Rhodesia, became embroiled in the politics of the countries of their missions, but never had the same impact on public opinion in Ireland. Nor did they overtly seek it, in this case concentrating instead on the politics within Rhodesia itself.[11] They were, however, known and remembered by those in the Department of External Affairs. Recollecting his experience of international sanctions against Rhodesia, one prominent missionary praised the Irish government for allowing his order to operate as unhindered as possible.[12]

---

[8] *The Economist*, 19 Dec. 1959. This piece is discussed, with proper reference to its exaggeration, in T.D. Williams, 'Irish foreign policy, 1949–69', in J.J. Lee (ed.), *Ireland 1945–70* (Dublin, 1979), p. 139; and Noel Dorr, 'Ireland at the United Nations', in Ben Tonra and Eilís Ward (eds.), *Ireland in international affairs: interests, institutions and identities; essays in honour of Professor N. P. Keatinge FTCD, MRIA* (Dublin, 2002), p. 115.

[9] Garreth Byrne, *The Afro-Irish connection* (n.p., 1974), p. 3.

[10] See Enda Staunton, 'The case of Biafra: Ireland and the Nigerian civil war', *Irish Historical Studies*, 31: 124 (Nov. 1999), pp. 513–35.

[11] See Donal Lamont, *Speech from the dock* (London, 1977); Terence Ranger, 'Holy men and rural communities in Zimbabwe, 1970–1980', in W. J. Shiels (ed.), *The Church and war; papers read at the twenty-first summer and the twenty-second winter meeting of the Ecclesiastical History Society* (n.p., 1983), pp. 443–461; and Terence Ranger and Mark Ncube, 'Religion in the guerrilla war: the case of Southern Matabeleland', in Ngwabi Bhebe and Terence Ranger (eds.), *Society in Zimbabwe's liberation war* (Oxford, 1996), pp. 35–57.

[12] Interview with Fr Seán Coughlan, O.Carm., Dublin, 5 March 2004.

For the most part, however, missionaries were deemed capable of looking after their own interests and did not request assistance from the Irish government. External Affairs often raised the safety of Irish missionaries as a factor for consideration in policy-making, yet rarely, apart from the obvious Nigerian example, were they forced into concrete action.

In Ireland itself, the very proliferation of missionary orders resulted in a lack of co-ordination, and hindered any ability they might have had to impart their knowledge of African politics to the Irish public. The goals of the Irish Missionary Union, established in 1969, to 'integrate the Irish missionary movement into the Irish Church more fully, to promote co-operation ... and to gather information'[13] referred more to the expansion of the faith and the ability to surmount practical difficulties faced on the ground. Their fears, such as the loss to the Church of 'the working-man' in the 'new industrial revolution' in the newly-independent states, had little impact on the comprehension of African politics amongst those at home.[14] The majority of the Irish public retained stereotypical images of Africa formed by and reinforced by missionary magazines, occasional visits by missionaries to parishes and schools, and by tales of soldiers who had served their time as peacekeepers with the United Nations force in the Congo.

By the early to mid-1970s the situation was beginning to change slowly, as the work of aid organisations and the increasing numbers of teachers, engineers, nurses and others working in Africa brought to Ireland stories of their experiences in different African nations. The public outcry surrounding the Nigerian civil war – crucial in making the Irish public aware of the importance of development aid – also highlighted the importance of single major events to arouse public opinion. Foreign policy issues, the Irish Anti-Apartheid Movement (IAAM) bemoaned, were 'rarely publicly debated'.[15] The IAAM's mobilisation of opinion against events such as the South African rugby tours of 1965 and 1969-70, therefore, was crucially important in providing a concrete, visible example of the impact of apartheid policies to the watching Irish public. Given the reluctance of the Department of External Affairs to engage in discussion on policy issues, the role of groups like the IAAM, the United Nations Association, university societies, and discussion groups such as Tuairim, was to maintain and encourage an undercurrent of debate. From an African standpoint, the IAAM played a central role in educating the public. From its inception in 1964, the group continually implored the government to take the strongest possible stance on apartheid and, subsequently, on the Rhodesian and Portuguese African issues.[16] It also reinforced the relationship

---

[13] Richard Quinn, *The missionary factor in Irish aid overseas* (Dublin, 1980), p. 29.

[14] Joseph McGlade, *The missions: Africa and the Orient* (Dublin, 1967), p. 20.

[15] Irish Anti-Apartheid Movement (IAAM), *Annual report 1971–72* (Dublin, 1972).

[16] For a brief introduction to the history of the IAAM, see David M. Scher, '"How is it that such a small group of people can pressure governments ...?" A history of the Irish Anti-Apartheid Movement', in Donal P. McCracken (ed.), *Ireland and South Africa in modern times (Southern African-Irish Studies*, Vol. 3, 1996) (Durban, 1996), pp. 136–70.

between Ireland and the decolonisation struggle by forging strong links with the United Nations Special Committee on Apartheid, which visited Dublin on several occasions, and by using its excellent contacts in media and other circles to bring its case prominently before the Irish public.

The relationship between Ireland and the decolonisation struggle was reinforced in other ways by the government itself which asserted Ireland's solidarity with the cause of Africa's newly emerging and emergent states. In their addresses to the General Assembly, Irish ministers were keen to stress the state's position as 'the only Western European country which has had experience ... of a long historic epoch of foreign rule and of resistance to that rule'.[17] In debates on African issues, the Irish delegation continually reiterated its special affinity with events on that continent brought on by the state's own experience with colonialism. Both Aiken and the then Taoiseach Seán Lemass invoked Parnell's pledge to the 'sacred' principle of nationality 'in Asia and Africa as well as in Ireland' and reasserted the importance of that thinking to the Irish government.[18] This idea was reiterated in the press, both in Ireland and abroad. In the British journal *The Spectator* in 1960, Erskine B. Childers reminded readers of Ireland's role 'both to champion, *and* to help interpret to other countries, the demands and sensitivities of Afro-Arab-Asians,'[19] while Bernard Share wrote in the *Irish Times* in 1966 of 'Ireland's unique position as a European nation with strong anti-colonialist views'.[20]

Noel Dorr's recollections of his early days in the Department of External Affairs reflected the influence of both media, as he left for the Permanent Mission in New York in 1961 'imbued with a highly romantic view ... [which] I had absorbed from the press in Ireland and from service in a junior capacity in the United Nations Section of the Department'.[21] Though the view was 'highly romantic', it also had practical implications for Ireland. Aiken was viewed by many African politicians with a respect that came not only from his role at the United Nations, but also from his revolutionary past. As Hurwitz has suggested, Ireland's experience of colonial domination gave it 'a different attitude towards decolonisation and self-determination' from its western partners.[22] This attitude in the eyes of the African states was one of the factors that gave Ireland the prominence accorded to it by Cremin in the statement quoted at the outset of this chapter. Indeed, Ireland retained a large degree of the respect that had been cultivated during its early years at the United Nations through to and beyond the 1970s, particularly in its

---

[17] Frank Aiken's address to the UNGA, 6 Oct. 1960, A/PV.890.

[18] Ibid., and Seán Lemass's address to the UNGA, 17 Oct. 1963, A/PV.1245.

[19] Erskine B. Childers, 'Unbeholden Diplomacy', *The Spectator*, 29 Apr. 1960.

[20] Bernard Share, 'Two men on a Continent', *Irish Times*, 16 Aug. 1966.

[21] Noel Dorr, 'Ireland at the United Nations: 40 years on', *Irish Studies in International Affairs*, 7 (1996), p. 48.

[22] Leon Hurwitz, 'The EEC and decolonisation: the voting behaviour of the Nine in the UN General Assembly', *Political Studies*, 24: 4 (1976), p. 442.

negotiations as a member of the EEC. It was under Ireland's first presidency that the Lomé Agreement between the EEC and the Afro-Caribbean states was signed in 1975, and the state built on its reputation to come to prominence as a negotiator at the United Nations Conference on Trade and Development (UNCTAD) in Nairobi in 1976.

Afro-Irish diplomacy at the United Nations

Ireland's role in the latter negotiations coincided with a period of great expansion in the Department of Foreign Affairs to cope with the demands of EEC membership. In addition to the changes in Iveagh House, a new Irish embassy was opened in Kenya in 1979, becoming the second, after Nigeria (opened in 1960), in sub-Saharan Africa. The limitations in the period prior to this of having only one Irish embassy were obvious. The small staff made it extremely difficult to cover the activities across an entire sub-continent, and meant that political reporting was often extremely lacking on issues outside the immediate vicinity of Nigeria and its surrounding states. The poverty of direct diplomatic exchange thus gave special importance to Patrick Keatinge's statement that for Ireland 'the United Nations was the principal window on the diplomatic world'.[23] Indeed, Aiken, so reticent to expend funds on expansion, was adamant that Ireland could do 'any work that we have to do, with the permanent representatives of the countries in which we are not represented by diplomatic missions'.[24] The relatively frequent concentration of foreign ministers and prominent officials from across the globe in the corridors of the United Nations buildings in New York allowed Irish ministers to meet officials from states with whom they might have little or no other contact.

Friendships were struck between officials at the Irish Permanent Mission and those from other countries, such as that between Con Cremin and the Somali Ambassador Abdulrahim Abby Farah. These allowed for discreet conversations and exchanges of information to be made without recourse to official channels. Friendships such as these could be useful in obtaining details of upcoming proposals, or friendly warnings of opposition to future positions. They were also, as indeed was the United Nations experience as a whole, particularly prior to the expansion of the Department of Foreign Affairs, important in broadening the understanding of Irish representatives of African issues. Irish representation on the committees of the General Assembly, when manpower could afford it, particularly the Fourth Committee, the Special Political Committee, and the Committee on South-West Africa, allowed them to come into contact with issues on which they had little or no previous knowledge. It also forced them to take positions and

---

[23] Patrick Keatinge, *A place among the nations: Issues of Irish foreign policy* (Dublin, 1978), p. 215.

[24] NAI 2000/14/259, 'Transcript from the tape recording of the Tánaiste's speech at United Nations Association', 23 Feb. 1968.

to listen and question the representatives of the independence movements that came before the Assembly.

Examples of Irish policy

As time progressed, however, the use of the United Nations as a focus for Ireland's international diplomacy was displaced by newer avenues of exchange, not least those operating through Brussels and the medium of the EEC. Policy itself was adapted to changing circumstances accordingly. The remainder of this chapter will focus on this process of adaptation by using three examples of policy-making to examine the influences that affected the Irish position. The emphasis in choosing these examples has been on encompassing as broad a time period and range of issues as possible, in order to highlight both continuity and change. The Rhodesia question raised issues of decolonisation, bilateral relations, and Ireland's relationship with the structures of inter-national organisation. The future of Portuguese Africa posed similar questions, but in addition exhibited elements of European influence. Both were bound up to some extent in issues of aid at the United Nations, particularly through the various funds established to support victims of political repression in southern Africa. In an Irish context, the heightened awareness brought on by the response to the Nigerian civil war helped foster the creation of this different environment in policy-making. Its more humanitarian emphasis, in combination with the analyses of the first two examples, provides an interesting introduction to Irish United Nations policy in the first half of the 1970s.

Rhodesia[25]

On 29 October 1962, Tadhg O'Sullivan, Ireland's representative on the Fourth Committee, told its general debate on Southern Rhodesia that 'the hard core of the problem in Africa had now been reached – the presence of strong white minorities with vested interests in Central and Southern Africa'.[26] O'Sullivan's comments reflected the increasingly intransigent stance taken by the Southern Rhodesian government, led by the Rhodesian Front (RF) Party, whose approach preyed on the apprehensions of the territory's white minority. They feared that Britain's decision to break up the Central African Federation, which they had dominated, and the process towards independence for its other constituent parts, Nyasaland (Malawi) and Northern Rhodesia (Zambia), would mean enforced African majority rule. Failed attempts by the British to negotiate a settlement led the RF, led by Ian

---

[25] For an introduction to the history of the Rhodesia question, see Robert Blake, *A history of Rhodesia* (London, 1977); Martin Meredith, *The past is another country: Rhodesia 1890–1979* (London, 1979); W.H. Morris-Jones (ed.), *From Rhodesia to Zimbabwe: behind and beyond Lancaster House* (London, 1980); and Peter Godwin and Ian Hancock, *'Rhodesians never die': the impact of war and political change on white Rhodesia, c. 1970–1980* (Oxford, 1993).

[26] Tadhg O'Sullivan, UNGA Fourth Committee, 29 Oct. 1962, A/C.4/SR.1364.

Smith, to announce its Unilateral Declaration of Independence (UDI) from Britain on 11 November 1965, in the process effecting the entrenchment of their minority rule. The response of the international community was to introduce economic sanctions and to isolate the illegal Rhodesian regime. Although made mandatory by the United Nations Security Council in 1966, the sanctions served only to galvanise the Rhodesians in their effort to retain their hold on power. They were aided in these efforts not least by the South Africans and Portuguese, but also by divisions within the African nationalist movement, and by the failure of the British to secure settlement in successive negotiations aboard *HMS Fearless* and *HMS Tiger* in the Mediterranean in 1966 and 1968 respectively. The turning point came, arguably, in 1972, when the Pearce Commission, set up by the British to assess the African reaction to the RF-written 1971 constitution, reported a resounding rejection of the document. It represented also an end to the primacy of the constitutional approach as a frustrated African population increasingly rejected the use of non-violent methods. The ensuing escalation of the guerrilla war forced the Rhodesian government into further concessions, and their cause was not helped by South Africa's withdrawal of support in the mid-1970s. The loss of their two closest allies (after the 1974 revolution had brought democracy to Portugal) eroded their ability to resist international sanctions and by 1979 they were forced to agree to majority rule and the creation of the modern state of Zimbabwe.

Central to the Irish government's stated policy was a commitment to 'the aspirations of the people of Southern Rhodesia for independence based on majority rule'.[27] In practical terms, this support translated into occasional Irish attempts to mediate in the process of its achievement. In 1962, the Irish representative at the Fourth Committee called on the British government to intervene as a 'third party' following the African population's rejection of Southern Rhodesia's 1961 constitution.[28] This method of direct representation to the British was repeated again, albeit in a more private forum, by Aiken in the years following UDI. In 1966 he overcame his reservations regarding sanctions to urge the British to 'make them obligatory' in order to increase the pressure on the Rhodesian regime.[29] Seven years later, Garret FitzGerald, in his capacity as Minister for Foreign Affairs, reiterated this commitment in the Fine Gael-Labour stance on southern Africa, reflecting on Ireland's dedication to a policy 'in line with our historic position as a nation which has suffered from colonialism and various forms of discrimination' and to 'human rights and the dignity of the individual'.[30] That government would also put its words into practice by its involvement in attempts at a settlement to the situation in the 1970s, and its central approach was marked by continuity from preceding governments.

---

[27] Kirwan, UNGA Fourth Committee, 3 Nov. 1969, A/C.4/SR.1841.
[28] Tadhg O'Sullivan, UNGA Fourth Committee, 29 Oct. 1962, A/C.4/SR.1364.
[29] NAI 2000/14/50, Note by O'Sullivan, 31 March 1966.
[30] *Dáil Deb.*, vol. 265, col. 750, 9 May 1973.

If Irish support for the 'ultimate objective' of the African states was unquestionable, however, the means of achieving this objective often went beyond what they felt they could agree to.[31] The Irish approach, as articulated by Aiken when speaking on the South West African issue, was to find a solution that combined 'practicability and effectiveness' with high moral principles.[32] O'Sullivan's intervention in a Fourth Committee debate on 18 October 1963 was indicative of this tempered approach. His delegation 'wished very much to support the general stand taken by the African countries, and had received instructions to that effect', he had told the meeting.[33] In this case, however, the inclusion by the Afro-Asians of a statement in their draft resolution which termed the Rhodesian situation 'a threat to international peace and security' went beyond what the Irish delegate felt he could support. Such resolutions led the Irish on numerous occasions to abstain, vote against, or at least strongly outline their reservations. Time and again, Irish delegates cited extreme elements of draft resolutions, such as 'the call for the use of force against Britain' (1969),[34] or the condemnation of Britain for refusing 'to take effective measures' (1972),[35] as reasons holding them back from full support of Afro-Asian resolutions.

Taking this line did not mean that the Irish were not open to accommodating the African states' views. In late October 1965 the Irish delegation indicated its inability to support part of an Afro-Asian sponsored resolution in the Fourth Committee on grounds that made African delegates question the sincerity of the Irish commitment to majority rule. O'Sullivan had told them in his explanation of Ireland's opposition to paragraph 3 of the draft resolution (A/C.4/L.795) that

> it was said [in the paragraph] that the United Nations would oppose any declaration of independence which was not based on universal adult suffrage. He wondered how the Committee could claim to know, at a distance, that the African leaders ... would not accept an arrangement which would bring majority rule in a few years.[36]

Following objections by both the Cameroon and Liberian delegations, and a private comment to O'Sullivan from the Kenyan delegate,[37] the decision was made to revise the Irish position on the paragraph. O'Sullivan clarified that

---

[31] NAI 2000/14/48, de Paor, for Cremin, to McCann, 30 Oct. 1967.

[32] Frank Aiken, address to the UNGA Plenary Meeting on 11 Dec. 1967 in Ireland, DEA, *Ireland at the United Nations 1967* (Dublin, n.d. [1968?]), p. 21.

[33] Tadhg O'Sullivan, UNGA Fourth Committee, 18 Oct. 1963, A/C.4/SR.1451.

[34] NAI 2002/19/31, 'Southern Rhodesia: Explanation of vote after vote on draft resolution A/C.4/L.936', 3 Nov. 1969.

[35] Carmel Heaney, UNGA Fourth Committee, 30 Nov. 1972, A/C.4/SR.2009.

[36] Tadhg O'Sullivan, UNGA Fourth Committee, 27 Oct. 1965, A/C.4/SR.1540.

[37] NAI 2000/14/46, 'Extract from Irish delegate's report on the 4th Committee (20th Session)', n.d. [1966?].

Ireland had not meant 'opposition to the introduction of universal suffrage' but rather that 'it might be advisable not to insist upon the inclusion of such a categorical statement in an official text'.[38]

Where the Irish felt themselves unable to compromise was on the question of violent decolonisation. Aiken maintained that 'the rule of law, rather than the rule of force' should 'finally determine the emergence of all the peoples of Africa to national and democratic freedom'.[39] To him, it followed that Ireland 'could not support a call which might indirectly encourage people in Southern Rhodesia to take up arms against impossible odds'.[40] The parallels between the nationalist movements and Ireland's own struggle for independence were obvious, and were recognised by officials in External Affairs. On the margins to a 1967 letter quoted above, one unidentified official had handwritten: 'we sought such support in 1919!'[41] The Ireland of the 1960s, however, and particularly the problems in Northern Ireland, left no room to support any organisation involved in armed struggle. Nor could a state so committed to the use of United Nations institutions and the proper implementation of international law for the resolution of conflict be seen to support violent decolonisation.

The Irish were also very careful to delineate between what could be decided by the General Assembly, and what issues should have recourse to a Security Council decision. On the Rhodesia question, they took a similar line to that taken on the South African issue. There, the Irish position was clear: 'resolutions of the General Assembly are not legally binding but have the force of recommendations. Ireland considers herself, therefore, to be under no obligation to comply with Assembly resolutions to which she has expressly objected before their adoption.'[42] When the need arose to bolster its stated support for United Nations mechanisms with action the Irish government was more than willing to comply. This was particularly evident in relation to the Irish approach to economic sanctions, a policy, as stated above, to which they had been previously opposed. Just ten days before the recommendation by the Security Council on 22 November 1965 that all member states make provision to end trade with Rhodesia (sanctions would be made mandatory just over a year later, in December 1966), Aiken's department had vetoed the inclusion of a passage beginning 'While in the light of our own past experience, we have little faith in economic sanctions ...' from a proposed press release to be made by Lemass.[43] Again, the reference to Ireland's own historical circumstances, notably the economic war of the 1930s, was obvious, but

---

[38] Tadhg O'Sullivan, UNGA Fourth Committee, 1 Nov. 1965, A/C.4/SR.1544.

[39] *Dáil Deb.*, vol. 201, col. 942, 3 Apr. 1963.

[40] NAI 2000/14/48, de Paor to McCann, 30 Oct. 1967.

[41] Ibid.

[42] NAI DFA 305/94 VI, 'Extract from Memo for Government on XVIII Session of UNGA', 9 Sept. 1963.

[43] NAI 97/6/229, Draft Statement for issue on behalf of the Government, 12 Nov. 1965.

dedication to the supremacy of the Security Council led them to support the move to the last detail. An economic break with Rhodesia was an easy decision for many states, including Ireland, to make. Ireland had no diplomatic ties with Rhodesia, nor did her trade amount to much; Irish imports were only £219,696 and exports only £8,901 in the first eight months of 1965.[44] This small amount of trade was easily restricted by the government through the implementation of a licensing system agreed between the Department of External Affairs and the Department of Industry and Commerce on a case by case basis. It was rather the minute detail in their monthly reports to the United Nations, and the repeated concern of Aiken that goods were being imported to Britain via Ireland, that illustrated Ireland's strong commitment. In the returns of trade to the United Nations for February 1968, for example, the only exports to Rhodesia were 'other animals not for food (dogs)'.[45]

This commitment allowed the Irish government to exhibit simultaneous support for Britain, which was wholeheartedly behind the implementation of sanctions. Although Noel Browne's 1963 comments that the government was 'placating the British', 'selling out',[46] and 'on the side of the white colonists'[47] might be taken with a pinch of salt, they illustrate the way in which Irish policy was sometimes construed as overly supportive of the British approach. Even in the suggestions they offered for a solution to the problem, the Irish exhibited a clear awareness of the discomfort of the coloniser. They rejected resolutions at the General Assembly that called for Britain to go beyond the bounds of negotiation (i.e. to use force), and reiterated their support for the British involvement in the process of negotiated settlement. After UDI, and with the implementation of the Anglo-Irish Free Trade Agreement in the same year, the Irish came under additional pressures as a result of their commitment. Seen by the British as a possible back door for entry of Rhodesian goods, as Aiken feared, they were susceptible to repeated and often irritating representation from British officials. Made particularly through the British embassy in Dublin, the frequency and nature of these calls were such that in 1966 Aiken instructed one of his officials to tell the British that the Irish government could not agree to its actions 'being policed'.[48]

It was simply another influence to be borne in mind in the construction of policy. While mindful of the British concerns, the Irish asserted their independence and made judgement on the issue according to their position as a small state in the international system. They were influenced by various

---

[44] *Dáil Deb.*, vol. 219, col. 12, 23 Nov. 1965.
[45] NAI 2000/14/58. Imports of tobacco remained Aiken's major concern, and as late as June 1968, tobacco of Rhodesian origin was being imported into Ireland; NAI 2001/43/160, O'Sullivan to Wardlaw, 24 June 1968.
[46] *Dáil Deb.*, vol. 193, col. 1043, 7 Mar. 1962.
[47] *Dáil Deb.*, vol. 196, col. 1460, 4 July 1962.
[48] NAI 2000/14/50, note by O'Sullivan, 31 Mar. 1966. See also NAI 2002/19/32 for examples of British representations.

different core principles, not least of which were their commitment to decolonisation and adherence to international law. As Aiken noted in a proposed reply to a question tabled in the Dáil, 'Southern Rhodesia is a territory for whose external relations Britain is responsible', making it difficult and undesirable for the Irish to become involved.[49] The Rhodesian question was, like the question of South West Africa, one on which a principled stance might be maintained, but, like policy on Vietnam, one in which direct involvement was not significant, apart from the aforementioned links with missionaries. By the mid-1970s, the effects of economic sanctions on Rhodesia were beginning to be felt, the result not only of South Africa's decision but also of the individual efforts of many small actors like Ireland to enforce the restrictions. It was thus in the detail that the Irish approach had maximum effect.

Portuguese Africa[50]

The Portuguese African issue shared centre stage with the Rhodesian and South African issues in the decolonisation debates of the 1960s and early 1970s. Confident of their importance to the Cold War effort (they were members of NATO and governors of an important base in the Azores), efforts to force the Portuguese to decolonise were met with intransigence. In 1961 the brutal suppression of an armed uprising in Angola drew the attention of the world to the situation in Portugal's African colonies. It also signalled to the world the intentions towards armed struggle of the independence groups. Better organised than their Rhodesian counterparts, the liberation movements operated loosely in a collective known as the Conference of Nationalist Organisations of the Portuguese Colonies (CONCP), which allowed them to direct collective pressure on the international stage. The Portuguese response was true to its role as a member of what O'Sullivan had termed the 'hard core' of white resistance. In 1960, Dr Franco Nogueira of the Portuguese Foreign Office told the Irish Minister to Lisbon, Frank Biggar, not 'to place too great hopes on the United Nations. Its original character had been greatly modified by the admission of the Afro-Asian states'.[51] Nogueira reiterated the point to Biggar's successor J.W. Lennon in 1962, and observed that 'Portugal was not greatly concerned with the United Nations voting, as her mind was made up on the course she had to follow'.[52] Their attitude towards

---

[49] NAI 2000/14/45, O'Sullivan to Brennan, 15 Nov. 1965.

[50] For an introduction to the history of decolonisation in Portuguese Africa, see Gervase Clarence-Smith, *The third Portuguese empire 1825–1975: a study in economic imperialism* (Manchester, 1985); Basil Davidson, 'Portuguese-speaking Africa', in Michael Crowder (ed.), *The Cambridge history of Africa: volume 8 from c. 1940 to c. 1975* (Cambridge, 1984), pp. 755–810; Norrie MacQueen, *The decolonisation of Portuguese Africa: metropolitan revolution and the dissolution of empire* (London, 1997); and Malyn Newitt, *Portugal in Africa: the last hundred years* (London, 1981).

[51] NAI DFA 313/11G, Biggar to Cremin, 14 Sep. 1960.

[52] NAI DFA 313/11H, Lennon to Cremin, 10 May 1961.

the United Nations was matched only by the continued pressure of the Afro-Asians whose actions helped to force the adoption of sanctions prohibiting the sale of arms by the Security Council in November 1965. While remaining relatively unmoved by United Nations pressures, the war of attrition being waged in its colonies wore down the Portuguese resistance, not least by the large proportion of state expenditure needed for its continuation. In April 1974, Marcelo Caetano, the successor to the long-serving Salazar as leader of Portugal, was overthrown in a coup. The moves towards democracy in Portugal that followed helped accelerate the process of decolonisation in its colonies and in 1974 the Cape Verde Islands and Guinea-Bissau celebrated independence, to be followed in 1975 by Mozambique and Angola.

Although Ireland had little direct link with the colonies themselves, – only ten missionaries (all based in Angola) in 1968[53] – links with the metropolitan centre meant that a legation was maintained throughout this period in Lisbon. Indeed, this representation was upgraded to embassy status in the late 1960s, although the position of ambassador was not filled until after the revolution of 1974, due, according to Garret FitzGerald, to 'concern at the failure of Portugal to take action with regard to its colonial territories'.[54] Diplomatic representation at this level kept Irish minds open to the possibility of influencing the Portuguese while simultaneously reinforcing the 'historical ties of friendship' between the two states. Indeed, it was these very ties of friendship, the Irish argued, that 'compelled' them 'to urge Portugal to revise its policy'.[55] External Affairs' internal response to the violence in Angola in 1961 underlined this fact. Portugal's position, they stated, was 'very weak ... barbarous action from a supposedly civilised country'.[56] Although they retained the links of friendship, to support the Portuguese would, they argued, 'be contrary to [the] Irish tradition of support for the theory of self-determination and the liberty of foreign-dominated countries'.[57]

As in the case of Rhodesia, this support manifested itself in both vocal and voting support for the independence process. Successive External Affairs memoranda on the subject repeated this commitment. In 1964, one such memorandum read 'Ireland will continue to support the principle for self-determination and independence for the territories under Portuguese administration'.[58] A further reiteration of this commitment in 1967 stated that 'Ireland's policy for urging self-determination and independence for these territories will be maintained',[59] and a 1969 memorandum described how Ireland would 'continue its policy of urging self-determination and

---

[53] 'Irish Missionary Personnel in Developing Countries: Statistical Analysis March 1968', supplement to *Catholic Missions: Annals of the Propagation of the Faith*, April 1968.

[54] *Dáil Deb.*, vol. 275, col. 922, 5 Nov. 1974.

[55] Tadhg O'Sullivan, UNGA Fourth Committee, 5 Dec. 1966, A/C.4/SR.1654.

[56] NAI DFA 305/218/13 Pt I, unsigned note, 'Angola', 30 Aug. 1961.

[57] Ibid.

[58] NAI 2002/19/10, 'Extract from Memorandum To Government', 13 Nov. 1964.

[59] NAI 2002/19/11, 'Extract from Memorandum for Information of Government', (1967).

independence for the Portuguese territories'.[60] The method of support remained constant also, and echoed Ireland's position on the Rhodesia question. When voting in favour of resolutions put forward by the Afro-Asian states, Ireland often felt it necessary to qualify its position, with reference to the language and content (generally the recourse to economic sanctions, to which we shall return) of the resolution. The words 'our vote in favour of the resolution is not to be taken as approval of all of its contents' were frequently uttered by the Irish delegation and were in accordance with their sentiment that General Assembly resolutions were of limited power and could be followed, if at all, with reservation.[61]

In holding this position of qualified support, Ireland not only illustrated its dislike for extreme pronouncements, but also its commitment to bringing about the most constructive solution. It was no surprise to find Ireland, in December 1962, in the company of 'all Western delegations and practically all Latins' in stressing the need to tone down a draft resolution on the sale of arms to Portugal put before the Fourth Committee by the Afro-Asians.[62] In the complex debate that followed, Ireland became involved with Sweden in suggesting a compromise text, which, although rejected by the NATO states, eventually led to the adoption of an Italian amendment. Although the outcome of the debate, which was centred on the sale of arms to Portugal, would not have impacted on Ireland directly, it is interesting to note the nature of the delegation's involvement, moving from their original position in order to achieve a compromise and way forward. As a telex to Iveagh House noted, 'we supported [the Italian] amendment and made it clear in speaking on the draft resolution that this formula was closer to our own position than was the Swedish-Irish suggestion which had been put forward as a compromise'.[63]

The evidence was clear also that from an early stage the stance taken by the Afro-Asian states was beyond what the Irish were prepared to support, and had resulted in the reservations outlined above. In a handwritten note to Seán Ronan of External Affairs in January 1962, Paul Keating commented that a General Assembly resolution on Angola appeared 'much too strong for us to support. The problem arises whether now that it is tabled the African countries can accept anything weaker than this pre-emptive phrasing.'[64] The Afro-Asian states' efforts to have Portugal expelled from the United Nations and consistent recourse to sanctions in General Assembly resolutions continued to frustrate the Irish. They were, however, only two elements to the extreme nature of the Afro-Asian approach. On 30 November 1973, Ireland abstained on Resolution 3070 of the General Assembly which called

---

[60] Ibid., 'Extract from Memorandum for Information of Government', 6 Sep. 1969.
[61] Ibid., 'Text of Explanation of Vote on the Draft Resolution A/C.4/L.842 on Question of Territories under Portuguese Administration, Fourth Committee, 5th December 1966'.
[62] NAI DFA 305/218/13 Pt I, telex, UNEIREANN to ESTERO, Dublin, 6 Dec. 1962.
[63] Ibid., telex, UNEIREANN to ESTERO Dublin, 13 Dec. 1962.
[64] Ibid., handwritten note, Keating to Ronan, 22 Jan. 1962.

on the body to re-affirm the legitimacy of armed struggles in states under colonial domination. In explanation Garret FitzGerald told the Dáil that the government was 'not prepared to support guerrilla activities'.[65] It read like a reiteration of the Frank Aiken ministry's distaste for violent decolonisation, and as Thomas Mulkeen wrote in 1973, captured the essential nature of the Irish approach: while 'South Africa's and Portugal's racial policies are unjustifiable on any grounds, [Ireland] also believes that physical force is not the business of the United Nations'.[66] Nor could it be seen to support the use of force, given, as stated earlier, the difficult circumstances facing the government in Northern Ireland at the same time. Ireland's position echoed also that of Sweden, which gave direct humanitarian support to the liberation groups, not only in Portuguese Africa, but in South Africa, Rhodesia, and South West Africa, but was simultaneously careful to stress that 'the search for non-violent solutions' was 'a basic principle' in its foreign policy.[67]

The Irish government was also involved in a process (if not continual, then periodic) of re-evaluating its position in order to align itself to the most constructive approach. A handwritten note by Hugh McCann to the then Minister for External Affairs, Patrick Hillery, commented on a General Assembly vote in December 1970, observing that 'were it not for [the] Secco [United Nations Security Council] mission's report implicating Portuguese armed forces in [the] invasion of Guinea I would have been inclined to recommend abstention so as to encourage Portugal to go further on de-colonisation'.[68] The note was a reflection of Ireland's commitment to this constructive approach, and of the importance of the open channels of communication between the two governments.[69] It was also clear that Ireland's opposition was, as stated, to 'the colonial policy of the government of Portugal',[70] rather than to the Portuguese state itself, a fact that manifested itself again in Ireland's opposition to the expulsion of Portugal from the United Nations.

With this opposition, the Irish also re-emphasised their support for the institutions of the United Nations, participation in which forced Portugal and South Africa's exposure to the influences of the world polity. This support for the institutions extended once again to the question of sanctions. With a commitment similar to that expended on Rhodesian sanctions, the

---

[65] *Dáil Deb.*, vol. 270, col. 1113, 20 Feb. 1974.

[66] Thomas Mulkeen, 'Ireland at the United Nations', *Eire-Ireland*, 8:1 (Spring 1973), p. 5.

[67] Tor Sellström, *Sweden and national liberation in southern Africa: Volume I – formation of a popular opinion (1950–1970)* (Uppsala, 1999), p. 343.

[68] NAI 2002/19/12, handwritten note by McCann to Hillery, 8 Dec. 1970, appended to 'urgent' note from Ronan to McCann, 7 Dec. 1970. In this incident, Portuguese troops had been implicated in an invasion from Guinea-Bissau of neighbouring independent Guinea, which they had, of course, denied.

[69] Ibid., see particularly the note by Ronan on two meetings with the Portuguese Ambassador to Dublin, 21 Oct. 1970.

[70] Tadhg O'Sullivan, UNGA Fourth Committee, 5 Dec. 1966, A/C.4/SR.1654.

Irish implemented Security Council Resolution 218 of 23 November 1965 which requested states to refrain from supplying arms to Portugal which might be used for the maintenance of the Portuguese territories in Africa. The use of *economic* sanctions against Portugal, although never subject to a Security Council resolution, was rejected by the DEA in a 1964 memorandum which commented that '(a) it would be well-nigh impossible to establish an effective system of economic sanctions and (b) such sanctions would strengthen the Portuguese Government in its intransigence, thereby (c) making even worse the plight of the victims of Portuguese colonial rule'.[71] Echoes could again be seen of the memories of the economic war of the 1930s, and the Irish, from Aiken through to FitzGerald, illustrated a genuine belief in sanctions as a last resort solution.

A measurement of Fine Gael/Labour policy on sanctions must be gauged more from their opposition to their implementation against South Africa, since events in the Portuguese case ran ahead of their ability to have any significant effect on policy. Rather, their involvement coincided with the introduction of a new element into the Irish approach. Illustrating a sensitivity not only to Portuguese politics, but also to the role of the EEC in promoting democracy in Europe, the coalition government had made the decision in July 1974, on FitzGerald's recommendation, 'that Ireland should also recognise Guinea-Bissau when Portugal has done so'.[72] In his memorandum to the government on the question, FitzGerald exhibited a sensitivity to the positions of the other eight EEC countries, but also reiterated that it was 'important that Ireland should be among the first of the West European countries to recognise the new Republic [since] Ireland has, over the years, consistently affirmed the right of colonial countries and peoples to self-determination and independence'.[73]

His comments illustrated the changing interaction between core Irish values and developing circumstances which influenced Irish decision-making. His delay in according recognition to Guinea-Bissau, after, as a frustrated IAAM remarked, 'more than 80 states had already done so',[74] marked the importance of the new EEC forum for the expression of policy. That policy retained a large measure of the consistency seen in the approach to Rhodesia. The commitment to the freedom of the African territories remained primary but was once again tempered by Ireland's commitment to various other core values. The importance of United Nations institutions, the overly extreme language and support for violence from the African states, and the influence of bilateral friendships and exchanges interacted in a manner similar to that seen on Rhodesia to form a constructive approach to decolonisation that was

---

[71] NAI 2002/19/10, 'Extract from Memo to Government dated 13/11/64, 19th Session of United Nations General Assembly'.
[72] NAI 2005/7/500, Department of Foreign Affairs memorandum for Government, 31 July 1974.
[73] Ibid.
[74] IAAM, *Annual Report 1973–74* (Dublin, 1974).

responsive again to pressures from coloniser and colonised, and exhibited an awareness of Ireland's position as a member of the western group of states.

Development aid

By the fall of the Caetano regime in 1974, much of the focus for the African states at the United Nations was on closing the wide economic gap between them and the developed world. The 1960s had been designated by the General Assembly as the First Development Decade, and had aimed at a contribution to overseas development aid from states of 1.0% of GNP. By the 1970s, this figure having not been reached in almost all cases, the target for the Second Development Decade was reduced to 0.7% of GNP. In Ireland prior to the 1970s, aid policy had been implemented on an ad hoc, intermittent basis. There was very little in the Fianna Fáil approach pre-1973 that allowed it to be seen as 'cohesive', and nothing that approached the drive that would lead FitzGerald to request a Minister of State to deal with the workload relating to development aid in 1975.[75] External Affairs was more than aware of these limitations, describing its approach in 1965 as 'rather haphazard'.[76] In terms of contribution to United Nations funds, Ireland's stance could best be termed as conservative. Apart from its contributions to the World Food Programme, its financial support was minimal. The United Nations Fund for victims of apartheid, for example, established by the General Assembly on 16 December 1963, was deemed in March 1966 to be inappropriate for an Irish contribution as it was not 'under the control of the Secretary-General'.[77] Although some officials in External Affairs worried about 'the extremely low level of Ireland's contributions to the United Nations Voluntary Agencies as compared with those of other countries in Western Europe', contributions to the main southern African funds remained minimal.[78] In 1967 Ireland's contribution to the United Nations Trust Fund for South Africa (UNTSA) stood at only US $1,000, while the decision to contribute to the United Nations Special Educational and Training Programme for Southern Africa (UNSETPSA) was not made until later that year, over three years after its creation by the Security Council.[79]

Although Ireland still remained one of a relatively small proportion of states subscribed to these funds, its reluctant support undermined somewhat its commitment to the cause of the African states. Towards the late 1960s and early 1970s, the question of development aid began to take on a further dimension, particularly after the appointment of Hillery as minister, with the

---

[75] Garret FitzGerald, *All in a life: an autobiography* (London, 1991), p. 191.
[76] NAI 2002/19/299, Draft memorandum for the government, 'The size and nature of Ireland's contribution to development aid', Aug. 1965.
[77] NAI 98/3/58, Brennan, commenting on Aiken's decisions with regard to United Nations funds relating to southern Africa, to Cremin, 9 Mar. 1966.
[78] Ibid., O'Sullivan to Whitaker, 5 Sept. 1967.
[79] Ibid.

growth of a strong awareness of a broader European approach. Referring to the decision in the Third Programme for Economic Expansion to increase official aid to developing countries to more than £1m, Donal O'Sullivan at External Affairs wrote to the Department of Finance in 1969 to request an increase in Ireland's contributions. He noted that Hillery was 'concerned lest our extremely modest performance in certain important aspects of the aid field should subtract from the country's general international standing and prestige', but, most tellingly, worried that such a performance 'could indeed come under unfavourable notice in the context of our application for membership of the European Economic Communities'.[80]

This theme was continued in an October 1970 External Affairs memorandum. While the document noted Ireland's role as one of 'the developed nations that have adopted a forward policy in opposing apartheid and racial discrimination in southern Africa', its comparative figures with similar states at the United Nations reflected extremely unfavourably on Ireland. This was particularly the case in comparison with fellow EEC aspirant Denmark, whose contributions of US $60,012 to the UNTSA, and US $92,335 to the UNSETPSA were vastly larger than Ireland's contributions of US $1,500 and US $5,000 respectively.[81] The memorandum, which also compared Ireland's contributions (unfavourably in all cases) with Austria, Belgium, Finland, and Norway, illustrated not only the continued awareness of the policies of other European states, but also of the importance of outward expressions of support to the viewing world, including the Irish public. This was evident also in the submission to the Department of Finance in October 1971, when a recommendation to increase the contributions to both of the above funds was accompanied by a comment by Hillery that 'a sizeable increase in our contributions generally would be welcomed by public opinion' in Ireland.[82]

Hillery's latter comments were indicative of the new public interest in issues relating to Third World aid, particularly prominent following the creation of the aid organisation Africa Concern (later shortened to Concern) and the huge amount of public support that surrounded the Nigerian civil war. It was not until FitzGerald's decision to introduce a comprehensive programme of official development aid that structure and direction were given to the government policy. The EEC, of course, had an impact, particularly through its decision in 1974 to meet the target of 0.7% GNP contribution to development aid set by the United Nations. Contributions through the EEC's multilateral projects also absorbed some of the increase in Irish funds, although the absolute contributions to United Nations funds increased significantly in the following years. In 1974, the Irish government's total aid contribution amounted to £2.5m, and rose to £3m in 1975 and £4.6m in

---

[80] Ibid., O'Sullivan to Murray, 7 Aug. 1969.
[81] Ibid., Department of External Affairs memorandum for the government, 'Proposed contributions to international aid agencies', 5 Oct. 1970.
[82] Ibid., McDonagh to Murray, 15 Oct. 1971.

1976.[83] The contributions to the UNTSA and UNSETPSA had also increased significantly by 1974 to US $6,000 and US $12,000 respectively, although they remained nowhere near those of Denmark earlier in the decade.

Questions of economic equity, however, and complex theories of neo-colonial domination were in many ways even less accessible to the ordinary Irish person than political questions such as the Congo had been in the 1960s. Paul Keating, Ireland's Permanent Representative to the United Nations, told an interviewer in 1980 (shortly before his death) that Ireland then was 'much more active in a United Nations context ... than we were required to be in the 1950s', but realised that it didn't 'sound so dramatic' in 1980.[84] As Holmes, Rees and Whelan's investigation of Irish voting at the United Nations in the 1980s revealed, the complexities of the situation had increased greatly as Ireland itself had become more developed and more industrialised, leading it to be less supportive of the Third World on economic issues.[85]

Ireland's support for development aid represented a new chapter in its support for the African states. Although it might justifiably be accused of having been behind its companion western 'moderates' in the 1960s and early-1970s, the Hillery ministry's very awareness of the importance of development aid as an expression of support illustrated the changing circumstances at the United Nations. Limited by different factors to those involved in the Rhodesian and Portuguese cases, the policy of successive ministers represented a response to the prevailing influences and circumstances. Aiken's reticence towards funds not established by the Security Council reiterated his support for the Charter. Hillery's tentative moves towards increasing Irish contributions revealed awareness to increased domestic pressure, the EEC accession process, and the changed financial circumstances in the state. These changed circumstances were, before the oil crisis of 1973 held them back to a small degree, exploited in turn by FitzGerald, whose support for the African states manifested itself most visibly in his commitment to development aid.

Conclusion

What bound the approach of all three ministers (this analysis has excluded Brian Lenihan, whose spell as minister in early 1973 was too short to have any significant effect) was Ireland's commitment to the advancement of the African states. In the earlier examples of the Rhodesia and Portuguese African issues, the most concrete expression of support involved their struggle for political independence. Having achieved this political advancement to

---

[83] Figures from Keatinge, *A place among the nations*, p. 183.

[84] '"A line which might have been helpful": interview with Paul Keating, Ireland's Permanent Representative at the United Nations', *Cara: the inflight magazine of Aer Lingus*, 13:5 (September/October 1980), p. 19.

[85] Michael Holmes, Nicholas Rees, Bernadette Whelan, *The poor relation: Irish foreign policy and the Third World* (Dublin, 1993), p. 164.

a large extent by the mid-1970s, the independent African states shifted their focus towards freedom from economic domination, poverty, and hunger. The famines of the early 1970s thus required a different response to the deaths in Angola in 1961, even if, centrally, the goals and identifications were the same.

As Hillery told the Dáil in 1972, for a small country like Ireland, 'the role of Government is not to try to impose a grand "foreign policy design". It is rather to steer and develop our many existing contacts in accordance with some general ideas of what we stand for and what we want to achieve.'[86] In the case of Africa, those general ideas were centred on Ireland's commitment to the decolonisation process, and to international institutions, and were, as Hillery's statement suggested, subject to adaptation according to circumstance. In the cases examined in this chapter, the Irish attempt to 'steer' its contacts was most evident in the case of Portuguese Africa, but also to some extent in Anglo-Irish relations on the Rhodesian issue. It transferred itself later to Irish involvement in the process of European Political Co-operation (EPC) and the subsequent influence this brought to Irish policy. What accession to the EEC did not result in, however, as studies by Lindemann, Foot, and Hurwitz have shown, was a dampening of the core commitment of Ireland towards the Third World.[87] It provided, rather, an alternative method of articulation for Irish policy, and afforded it access to new forms of multilateral co-operation. The commitment to multilateral aid via the EEC provided an excellent example of this, as increases at that and at bilateral level were matched by an overall increase in funds that benefited Ireland's contribution to aid via the United Nations.

The reaction to the new EEC environment illustrated the need for Irish policy to be flexible and maintain the ability to adapt to changing circumstances. Although many of the Irish statements retained an almost banal consistency, the continual process of re-evaluation of policy to the most constructive approach (see McCann's comments on Portugal in 1970) exhibited the influence of conflicting factors in policy-making. Noel Dorr's assertion that Ireland 'sometimes found ways to rationalise a vote for resolutions couched in terms that went well beyond anything which it could possibly have lived with in an earlier era'[88] illustrated the difficulties faced in striking a balance between these varying commitments at times. At times it could seem, as the IAAM put it, that positive votes were merely support 'hedged around with reservations and qualifications'.[89]

---

[86] *Dáil Deb.*, vol. 260, col. 385, 18 Apr. 1972.

[87] Rosemary Foot, 'The European Community's voting behaviour at the United Nations General Assembly', *Journal of Common Market Studies*, 17: 4 (June 1979), pp. 350–360; Hurwitz, 'The EEC and decolonisation'; and Beate Lindemann, 'Europe and the Third World: the Nine at the United Nations', *The World Today*, 32: 7 (July 1976), pp. 260–269.

[88] Dorr, 'Ireland at the United Nations', p. 118.

[89] IAAM, *Annual report 1973–74*.

Apart from the obvious limitations regarding support for violent decolonisation, Ireland's belief in the United Nations system, and particularly the primacy of the Security Council, brought it into conflict with the African states. Most obvious in the repeated abstentions on resolutions relating to Rhodesia and Portuguese Africa, the effects of this policy were evident also in the Fianna Fáil approach to development aid. Support was given only to funds that were set up directly by the Security Council or other bodies, such as the Food and Agriculture Organisation, that were deemed competent. In the case of development aid, however, the refusal to support in this manner was not matched by any great commitment to those funds that were within the Irish sphere of competence, at least until the 1970s, and this therefore left Ireland behind many of its European contemporaries.

Ireland's physical presence in New York, allowing for the development of diplomatic contact with African states, the 'development' element to Hillery's comments, was, while important, matched by the influence of bilateral links of other kinds, such as those exhibited between Ireland and Britain and Portugal. The limitations placed on Irish actions in this way were, however, balanced to some extent by the outlet they allowed for direct representation. Bilateral relations with the individual states involved allowed the Irish to impress on them their own particular view of the situation. They also illustrated the interaction of forces commanding Ireland's attention.

It was the attempt to reconcile each of these factors to a coherent policy that caused Ireland to be open to criticism on occasion, such as that laid at its door by both the IAAM and TDs such as Noel Browne.[90] Although Ireland may not have had the affluence of states such as Sweden or Norway to pursue extensive programmes of humanitarian support, what was perhaps more important was that it had not a sizeable vocal popular opinion pressing for a change in policy, as was the case in the former two states.[91] The Irish state, as the *Daily Express* put it in 1960, may have 'come of age' as a result of its involvement in peacekeeping in the Congo,[92] but popular opinion had to wait until the early 1970s to elicit enough support to create an environment ready for change. By then Irish affluence had increased and the numbers of organisations and writers calling for the instigation of a better development aid policy created a new focus for Irish people in their outlook on Africa.[93]

---

[90] Browne was, indeed, also a member of the IAAM and frequently made his opinion heard at meetings of the group.

[91] For a description of the African policies of Norway and Sweden, see the publications relating to them in the excellent 'Nordic countries and southern Africa' series published by the Nordic African Institute, Uppsala: Tore Linné Eriksen (ed.), *Norway and national liberation in southern Africa* (Uppsala, 2000); and the two volumes by Sellström, *Sweden and national liberation in southern Africa: Volume I*, and *Sweden and national liberation in southern Africa: Volume II – solidarity and assistance (1970–1994)* (Uppsala, 2002).

[92] *Daily Express,* 11 Nov. 1960.

[93] See, for example, the criticisms levelled at the government in Jerome Connolly, *The third world war* (Dublin, 1970); Declan O'Brien, *Ireland and the Third World: a study of government aid* (Dublin, 1980); Mary Sutton, *Irish government aid to the Third World – review and assessment* (Dublin, 1977); and also in the newsletter published jointly by Trócaire and the Irish Commission for Justice and Peace, *One World.*

In accordance with this new focus, by 1980 Ireland's role at the United Nations had, in Keating's words, lost the 'glamorous position that it had … [and] become somewhat routine'.[94] Involvement in the EEC, the focus on bilateral aid, the increased number of non-governmental organisations, and the changed international environment shifted the focus of Ireland's African policy. The IAAM, of course, continued to keep its voice raised, most famously seen during the Dunnes Stores strikes of the 1980s. It operated, however, in an environment different to that of the 1960s and early 1970s, and Irish foreign policy had to adapt accordingly, emphasising Hillery's concern with flexibility and adaptability. As has been evident throughout this chapter, in the policy-making of a state like Ireland, the ability to assimilate different approaches into a cohesive policy was central. As T. Desmond Williams stated, in the international system 'What states are really free to do is always subject to some restrictions and constraint'.[95]

---

[94] *Cara,* 'Interview with Mr Paul Keating', p. 19.
[95] Williams, 'Irish foreign policy', p. 137.

Chapter Nine

Ireland at the United Nations, 1965–69: evolving policy and changing presence

GREG SPELMAN[1]

By 1965 the locus of Irish foreign policy was shifting from New York and the United Nations to Brussels and the European Economic Community. Nevertheless, Ireland's policy at the United Nations, particularly while Frank Aiken remained Minister for External Affairs (and Tánaiste), remained conspicuous on various issues in the General Assembly. These included the non-proliferation of nuclear weapons, the financing of peacekeeping, Soviet repression of the 'Prague Spring' in Czechoslovakia in 1968, the Vietnam War, where Ireland was conspicuous by its silence on the issue in the General Assembly, the representation of China at the United Nations, and various decolonisation problems in Southern Africa. Dublin's policy on these issues was typical of Ireland's neutral stance at the United Nations. It manifested a heterogeneous and often paradoxical mix of aspects characteristic of Western policy and also certain elements common to non-alignment.

But Irish policy at the United Nations during the mid to late 1960s was forced to undergo an evolution. This was as a result of shifting priorities in Dublin, but evolution was also necessary to accommodate the changing balance within the General Assembly that had emerged in the early 1960s. During the high point of Ireland's activism at the United Nations, from 1957 to 1961, Ireland was counted among a small number of neutral and 'middle power' states that held the balance of power and could exert considerable influence over various issues. In the early 1960s, however, there was an influx of non-aligned and newly independent African and Asian countries into the General Assembly, which altered that balance and challenged Ireland's ability to maintain an active United Nations policy.[2] Nevertheless, in the

---

[1] Dr Spelman is writing in a personal capacity; the views he expresses in this chapter are his own.

[2] For further details see Kevin O'Sullivan's chapter 201–223.

mid-1960s Ireland regained a semblance of its previous activism. Aiken was especially concerned by the failure of the United Nations members to fully support peacekeeping missions, by opposition to plans for a treaty on the non-proliferation of nuclear weapons and by the worsening situation in southern Africa. Aiken attempted to create a more active Irish role at the General Assembly in the late 1960s. He sought a greater Irish influence over the United Nations response to these issues.

Ireland's policy with respect to Cold War issues – episodes where there were clear divisions of East and West and that were of significance to Washington's political and strategic interests – was often in accordance with United States policy at the United Nations. However, Ireland continued to be a strong advocate of decolonisation. Similarly, it maintained a strong and independent line on disarmament and peacekeeping, which provided the strongest manifestation of its activism. Ireland was thus able to reassert some influence at the General Assembly, particularly in the debates pertaining to matters on decolonisation, disarmament and peacekeeping.

On matters such as the financing of peacekeeping and disarmament, the members of the United Nations were often divided between the permanent members of the Security Council and the small states that comprised the bulk of the General Assembly. On these issues, Ireland was a strong advocate of multilateral diplomacy and of initiatives aimed at curbing the privileges of the more powerful states. Thus, Irish policy was part of a common commitment by small states, especially neutrals and others outside the alliance system, to multilateral diplomacy and the United Nations system to promote order and stability in the international environment.[3] In many respects, the Irish delegation felt a particular exigency to promote multilateral diplomacy and disarmament because heavy defence spending did not underpin Ireland's neutrality. This made Ireland unique among the European neutrals. Irish policy on disarmament and peacekeeping at the United Nations was the fundamental component of its efforts to pursue 'milieu goals'.[4]

The financing of peacekeeping operations

From 1965 Ireland sought to achieve agreement on the financing of peace-keeping missions. It was a strong supporter of peacekeeping operations and, therefore, had a particular interest in ensuring their reliable financing. In 1965 Aiken submitted proposals to reform the system of peacekeeping,

---

[3] Whereas Ireland's policy on disarmament and peacekeeping prioritised international order over international justice, other aspects of Ireland's United Nations policy reversed this hierarchy, especially in the case of decolonisation.

[4] Arnold Wolfers, *Discord and Collaboration: Essays on international politics* (Baltimore, 1962), p. 74. For discussion of Irish pursuit of milieu objectives refer to Catherine E. Manathunga, 'The Evolution of Irish United Nations Policy 1957–61: "Maverick" Diplomacy and the Interaction of "Possession" and International "Milieu" Goals', unpublished PhD thesis, University of Queensland, 1995.

focusing on the restoration of mandatory assessments of United Nations member states.

The Irish initiatives were formulated in response to the crisis of the 19th General Assembly session of 1964, which left the United Nations substantially in debt to contributors to peacekeeping missions, including the Irish government. The crisis was caused by the refusal of France and the Soviet Union to pay their contributions for the peacekeeping operations in the Congo and the Middle East. This meant that they were both in arrears of their financial obligations for the preceding two consecutive years and, therefore, in violation of Article 19 of the United Nations Charter. Under this article both countries should have been punished by the forfeiture of their votes at the General Assembly. However, in June 1965 the General Assembly waived Article 19 and sought voluntary contributions to clear the debts of the defaulters.[5]

Aiken formulated proposals to establish the financing of peacekeeping on a sound basis.[6] Following the termination of the Congo operation in 1964 for financial reasons, Aiken was concerned that the United Nations role in maintaining international peace and security was being undermined and was being reduced to a forum for international debate.[7] He sought the inscription of the financing of peacekeeping on the agenda of the General Assembly at every session[8] from 1965 to 1968.[9] The Irish delegation also took the lead in the discussions on the issue and in the campaign to restore reliable funding arrangements. Aiken's proposals for the re-institution of mandatory assessments were translated into draft resolutions in 1965, 1966, and 1967. At the 20th General Assembly session in 1965 the proposals broadly addressed the issues of authorisation and financing of peacekeeping operations, but by the following session they had been revised to deal only with the issue of financing. The Irish proposals, as a resolution, had been adopted by a narrow margin by the Special Political Committee in 1966 at the 21st General Assembly session, though they were not pressed to a vote in the plenary session.[10]

All the permanent members of the Security Council resisted the Irish proposals, and France and the Soviet Union led the opposition. The perpetuation of voluntary subscriptions would give them an effective financial veto over the United Nations, in addition to their formal veto as permanent members of the Security Council. It would provide an avenue for

---

[5] National Archives of Ireland (hereafter NAI), 2000/14/300, Memorandum for the Information of the Government on the General Assembly of the United Nations – 22nd Session, 30 Aug. 1967.

[6] Patrick Keatinge, *A Singular Stance: Irish Neutrality in the 1980s* (Dublin, 1984), p. 50.

[7] *Cork Examiner*, 9 Feb. 1967.

[8] Except for the 5th Emergency Special Session of 1965.

[9] The issue was inscribed thus: 'Comprehensive review of the whole question of peace-keeping operations in all their aspects: report of the Special Committee on Peace-keeping Operations'.

[10] NAI 2000/14/300, Memorandum for the Information of the Government on the General Assembly of the United Nations – 22nd Session, 30 Aug. 1967.

scuttling operations that avoided the public fallout ensuing from a formal veto, or the penalties accrued by breaching Article 19 of the Charter. France's public justification for its position was that peacekeeping was an enforcement action and, therefore, under the exclusive authority of the Security Council. Most Western countries supported France's opposition to the Irish proposals and, as the apportionment of expenses by the United Nations was based on national wealth, these states also bore much of the financial burden of peacekeeping.[11]

Although frustrated by intransigence of the Soviet Union and France, and supportive of the General Assembly being responsible for apportionment, neither Britain nor the United States would support the Irish proposals.[12] But in March 1967 Ireland's Permanent Representative to the United Nations in New York, Con Cremin, neutralised the United States in the debate by extracting an assurance from the delegate in charge of peacekeeping affairs, Ambassador Max Finger, that he would not veto a scale of mandatory assessments or the Irish proposals as a whole.[13]

On numerous occasions and at various sessions in New York, Soviet diplomats and adherents of the French-Soviet position met with members of the Irish delegation in an attempt to dissuade Ireland from raising Aiken's proposals and, especially, from producing them in draft resolution form. The high point of this pressure occurred in early 1967 during the lead up to the convening of the 5th Special Session, which had been called specifically to address the issue of the financing of peacekeeping and the deteriorating situation in Namibia.[14] The Soviet Union accused the Irish delegation of seeking to 'undermine the Charter', in an attempt to facilitate 'the establishment of colonial and neo-colonial systems in various areas of the world'.[15] Further, the Soviet delegation warned that, if they continued to pursue the proposals, Moscow would 'review her position in relation to the United Nations'.[16] This rhetoric was typical of Soviet diplomacy at the United Nations during this period, as Moscow frequently framed its arguments in anti-colonial language in a bid to appeal to the non-aligned states that formed the pivotal voting bloc in the General Assembly.

France pursued a more subtle strategy to avoid accusations of bullying a small member state, though French newspapers remained openly critical of the Irish position.[17] France successfully undermined Ireland's support base,

---

[11] NAI 2000/14/322, Cremin to McCann, 8 Feb. 1967.

[12] The United States supported the concept of mandatory assessments, but could not support the particular method prescribed by Ireland because it could require the United States to bear a greater proportional financial burden than permitted by Congress.

[13] NAI, Department of Foreign Affairs (hereafter DFA) 417/249/1, Cremin to McCann, 27 Apr. 1967.

[14] The crisis in Namibia and the Irish response is referred to later in this chapter.

[15] *Irish Times*, 15 Apr. 1967.

[16] NAI 98/3/286, Cremin to McCann, 31 Mar. 1967.

[17] NAI 98/3/287, Memorandum on Peacekeeping, 4 Oct. 1967.

which was comprised primarily of the large bloc of small, developing, disempowered and non-aligned states. These countries supported the concept of mandatory assessments, but were reluctant to force a confrontation with the permanent members of the Security Council. They were also aware of the lack of an explicit endorsement of peacekeeping in the United Nations Charter[18] and were concerned that a peacekeeping system not supported by the Soviet Union and France could plunge the organisation into an even deeper crisis.[19] In 1967, the permanent representatives at the United Nations from key non-aligned states, including Egypt, India and Yugoslavia,[20] as well as the Chairman of the Committee of Thirty-Three,[21] Mexico's Permanent Representative, Ambassador Francisco Cuevas Cancino, attempted to persuade the Irish delegation to drop its proposals, specifically because of the objections of France and the Soviet Union.[22]

This undermining of the support base allowed France to stall the Irish proposals. France was able to provide an illusion of progress by supporting the establishment of a committee devoted to peacekeeping, but ensured that its influence on that body would perpetuate stagnation.[23] France and the Soviet Union would only support deliberation in the Committee of Thirty-Three, not the General Assembly. The discussions in the Committee of Thirty-Three had previously demonstrated regression, rather than progression in achieving a consensus.[24] Further, while the proposals were before the committee, the United Nations membership gradually came to tacitly accept the limitation of that body's role – to examine only observer missions – rather than its mandate of conducting a comprehensive review of all aspects of peacekeeping.[25] A barrage of criticism from the Irish delegation, particularly during the General Assembly session in 1968, failed to achieve any progress.

Whereas the Irish proposals had enjoyed widespread support at the 20th and 21st General Assembly sessions in 1965 and 1966, from the Fifth Special Session in 1967 support began to rapidly decline. The Irish delegation decided not to introduce its proposals at the Fifth Special Session in 1967, following the lack of progress and increasing suggestions of open opposition from the United States delegation. After the Fifth Special Session, the debates

---

[18] Responsibility for the administration of peacekeeping was not clearly delegated to a particular United Nations body. Many commentators have suggested it was articulated in 'chapter six and a half'. Chapter six refers to the 'Pacific Settlement of Disputes' and chapter seven to 'Action with respect to Threats to the Peace, Breaches of the Peace and Acts of Aggression'.

[19] NAI 98/3/292, Cremin to McCann, 23 Feb. 1967.

[20] NAI 98/3/286, Cremin to McCann, 31 Mar. 1967.

[21] This was the Special Political Committee on Peacekeeping that had been established in 1965 to discuss in depth the problems of peacekeeping and formulate proposals to review all aspects of the question.

[22] NAI 2000/14/370, memorandum, 'Background on Peacekeeping', undated.

[23] NAI DFA 417/249/1, memorandum 'Report on the Fifth Special Session – Peacekeeping'.

[24] NAI 98/3/286, Cremin to McCann, 25 Apr. 1967.

[25] NAI 2000/14/378, memorandum 'Report on Peacekeeping at the 23rd General Assembly Session'.

on peacekeeping became increasingly superficial and brief and advocates of progress resigned themselves to stagnation. The 22nd General Assembly Session in 1967 consolidated this position, as the issue was pushed back on the agenda and had increasingly fewer meetings allocated for its discussion.

Non-Proliferation of nuclear weapons

The issue of non-proliferation of nuclear weapons had been a central aspect of Irish policy since the early years of its membership of the United Nations. The Irish delegation had provided crucial leadership in the General Assembly on the matter. Aiken had been instrumental in first raising the issue at the 13th General Assembly session in 1958 and in driving momentum behind non-proliferation following that session. In 1958 the Irish proposals for non-proliferation initially attracted little support, but over the next three sessions momentum grew. The joint statement of agreed principles for disarmament negotiations of September 1961 between the United States and the Soviet Union was instrumental in giving an impetus to the Irish non-proliferation agenda. That agreement was followed by the General Assembly unanimously adopting Resolution 1665(XVI), of which Ireland was the sole sponsor, calling for the formulation of a non-proliferation treaty (NPT).[26]

From 1961 to 1967 political relations between the Soviet Union and the United Nations had been strained by the Vietnam War and other Cold War issues. This delayed action being taken on the Irish non-proliferation resolution of 1961. But by early 1968 the two powers had agreed on the text for an NPT, which they presented to the resumed 22nd General Assembly session for its endorsement.[27] Whereas the superpowers were both committed to the conclusion of an NPT, support for the instrument among the rest of the United Nations membership was 'anything but overwhelming'.[28]

Crucially for the potential success of the NPT, there was limited support among the other permanent members of the Security Council and threshold nuclear weapon states. France was resolutely opposed to the NPT, as were other members of the European Economic Community (EEC), most notably Italy. The French President, Charles de Gaulle, objected to the NPT due to the fact that it was negotiated bilaterally by the Soviet Union and the United States, and because it did not sufficiently address vertical proliferation, particularly in his view the widening gap between the superpowers and the other possessors.[29] De Gaulle also deemed the sections of the NPT concerning security guarantees (termed negative security assurances), which were essential for the support of the small powers, as contrary to French interests

---

[26] Joseph M. Skelly, *Irish Diplomacy at the United Nations, 1945–1965: National interests and the international order* (Dublin, 1997), p. 264.

[27] NAI 2000/14/370, Report on the 22nd General Assembly Session.

[28] *Foreign Relations of the United States, vol. XI: Arms Control and Disarmament*, Document 231: Bohlen to Rusk, 5 Apr. 1968.

[29] *FRUS*, vol. XI, Document 231: Bohlen to Rusk, 5 Apr. 1968.

and national security as they opened up France to attack by other nuclear weapon states. France's nuclear deterrence strategy was predicated on its willingness and capacity to act unilaterally, pre-emptively and with nuclear weapons if it was directly threatened, due to doubts that the interests of the United States would necessarily prompt the defence of Western Europe.[30] This policy of unilateral security was one of a number of disagreements Paris had with its NATO partners that had led to the rift in 1966, and in the subsequent French withdrawal from NATO command.[31]

France had critical support from the People's Republic of China,[32] and the threshold nuclear states, which shared France's concerns about sections of the NPT. The threshold states comprised a large and diverse group whose members pursued this agenda to different extents, but it principally included Argentina, Brazil, Egypt, India, Israel,[33] Japan, Pakistan, Romania, South Africa, Sweden, West Germany and Italy. They were concerned about their exclusion from an established hierarchy of power that was based on the possession of nuclear weapons, the potential for nuclear blackmail, as well as the inequalities of obligations between the nuclear and non-nuclear states articulated by the NPT.[34] There were also specific, regional concerns as India was anxious about nuclear blackmail from the People's Republic of China, Pakistan about its relations with India, and Egypt about the acquisition of nuclear weapons by Israel.[35] The EEC states (especially France, Italy and West Germany) were also concerned about the sections of the NPT which could endanger regional cooperation in the peaceful development of nuclear energy through the European Atomic Energy Agency.[36] A large group of African states also were opposed to the NPT, including both francophone states and countries intent on using endorsement of the NPT as a lever for the two superpowers to intervene in Namibia and Southern Rhodesia.[37]

The Irish delegation took an active role in the efforts to marshal support for the NPT, particularly at the 22nd General Assembly session in 1967. Acknowledging that it was a collateral measure, Aiken argued that complete disarmament was not a realistic immediate goal and would take many years to achieve.[38] By contrast, the conclusion of an NPT was an achievable,

---

[30] Walter Laqueur, *Europe In Our Time* (New York, 1992), pp. 324–5.

[31] R. C. Macridis, 'French Foreign Policy: The Quest for Rank', in R. C. Macridis (ed.), *Foreign Policy in World Politics: States and Regions* (7th edn) (London, 1989), p. 52.

[32] The People's Republic of China opposed the NPT, but it was not directly represented at the United Nations and, thus, its influence in the debate was limited.

[33] Although termed a threshold state at this time, Israel almost certainly possessed nuclear weapons by the time the NPT was formulated in 1968.

[34] Keesing's Research Report, *Disarmament: Negotiations and Treaties, 1946–1971* (New York, 1972), p. 273.

[35] NAI 98/3/86, Cremin to McCann, 20 Apr. 1967.

[36] United Nations Department for Disarmament Affairs, *The United Nations and Disarmament*, p. 76.

[37] NAI 98/3/87, Cremin to McCann, 11 Apr. 1968.

[38] University College Dublin Archives Department (hereafter UCDA), P104/6930, extracts from Aiken's Statements at the United Nations on NPT.

immediate objective of the United Nations and, therefore, the 'single most important and urgent disarmament measure facing the United Nations'.[39] Aiken argued for the necessity of the inclusion of negative security guarantees to enhance international peace and security and increase the appeal of the NPT.[40] To further this objective, he proposed the establishment of a two-tiered United Nations Guarantor Force to accompany the NPT. This force was envisaged as including contingents drawn from non-nuclear states and backed by the nuclear powers.[41]

Due to its influence in debates on the issue, Ireland was active in campaigning on the merits of the NPT. Its campaign focused on Dahomey, the leader of the francophone countries opposing the treaty.[42] Cremin met with his counterpart from Dahomey, Ambassador Zollner, on 28 May 1967. At that meeting, Cremin was successful in persuading Zollner to revise his country's position.[43] Zollner's public justification for the change in position was the introduction of some minor amendments in the General Assembly on 31 May. The Irish campaign had various degrees of success with different countries and it managed to help reverse the voting positions of the francophone African countries: Dahomey, Togo, the Democratic Republic of the Congo and Chad. Ireland also successfully prevailed on the Netherlands to persuade other members of the EEC to support the NPT and drop their insistence on regional, rather than international, inspection measures.[44]

The campaign of the supporters of the treaty culminated in the United Nations overwhelmingly supporting a resolution that annexed the text of the NPT, endorsed its provisions and called for widespread adherence at a resumed 22nd General Assembly session in 1968.[45] Ireland's role in the achievement of the NPT was recognised by the international community when Aiken was invited to Moscow in July 1968 to be the first signatory of the NPT, and when Ireland became the first country to ratify the Treaty.

The Conference of Non-Nuclear-Weapon States

After the NPT was finalised in 1968, the main disarmament issue at subsequent General Assembly sessions was consideration of the work of the Conference of Non-Nuclear-Weapon States. The purpose of the conference was to facilitate the cooperation of the non-nuclear weapon states in ratifying the NPT.[46]

---

[39] NAI 2000/14/300, Memorandum for the Information of the Government on the 22nd General Assembly Session of the United Nations, 30 Aug. 1967.

[40] NAI 2000/14/370, Report on Non-Proliferation of Nuclear Weapons at the 22nd General Assembly Session.

[41] Ibid.

[42] Dahomey, from 1975 known as the Republic of Benin.

[43] NAI 98/3/87, Cremin to McCann, 24 June 1968.

[44] *FRUS,* vol. xi, Document 211: Foster to Johnson, 2 Oct. 1967.

[45] A/ PV.1672, 12 June 1968, pp. 6–7.

[46] *Official Records of the General Assembly* (hereafter *ORGA*) – 23rd General Assembly Session, Document A/7445, Report of the First Committee, p. 14.

Ireland had always opposed the holding of the conference for fear that it would be hijacked by the threshold nuclear states and used as a forum to undermine international support for the NPT.[47] These fears were realised when the threshold group used the conference to propose possible alternatives to the treaty.

At the 23rd General Assembly session in 1968, the threshold states' opposition manifested itself in an effort to convene the United Nations Disarmament Commission to deliberate on the peaceful uses of nuclear technology. By referring to this body, rather than to the International Atomic Energy Agency (IAEA), the objective was to maintain the issue of non-proliferation on the agenda of the United Nations and refocus debates on nuclear matters towards nuclear disarmament and not nuclear energy. Ultimately this tactic sought to delay the NPT coming into force until such time as greater concessions were obtained from the superpowers.[48] These alternatives never translated into international agreements because there was little support from countries outside this group.[49]

Ireland supported the efforts of the 'Finnish group', a group of non-threshold, non-nuclear states led by Finland. They responded to the Latin American initiative with a draft resolution that sought to have the peaceful uses of nuclear technology discussed by the IAEA. Driven by its experiences of bureaucratic stagnation in the peacekeeping debates of the mid-1960s, the Irish delegation unsuccessfully sought a more overt endorsement of the NPT and dismissal of the report from the Conference of Non-Nuclear Weapon States.[50] The Irish initiatives generally failed to solicit sufficient support within the Finnish group, as they were regarded as too antagonistic towards the threshold group. Ireland also co-sponsored a number of successful resolutions including overt endorsement of the role of the IAEA, rather than the United Nations Disarmament Commission, in order to avert the derailing of the NPT.[51]

Irish United Nations policy and the Cold War: Vietnam versus Czechoslovakia

Ireland's United Nations policy on Cold War issues during the mid to late 1960s was typically formulated within a United States orientated pro-Western context. This was due to the large Irish-American community in the

---

[47] NAI 2000/14/378, Report on General and ENDC Disarmament Questions at the 23rd General Assembly Session.

[48] *ORGA* – 23rd General Assembly Session, Document A/7445, Report of the First Committee, pp. 14–9.

[49] NAI 2000/14/378, Report on General and ENDC Disarmament Questions at the 23rd General Assembly Session.

[50] Ibid.

[51] *ORGA* – 23rd General Assembly Session, Document A/7445, Report of the First Committee, pp. 14–9.

United States, increasing United States investment in Ireland and pervasive anti-communist sentiment in the Irish political culture.[52] This was most clearly evident in Ireland's disparate responses to the United States involvement in Vietnam and the Soviet invasion of Czechoslovakia in 1968.

Vietnam was not a debated agenda item at the General Assembly, though it was customary for many delegations to refer to the issue, especially during the general debate. For example, at the 22nd General Assembly in 1967, seventy-six of the 122 delegations to the United Nations referred to the conflict in Vietnam during the general debate, with many Western countries calling on the United States to cease its bombing of North Vietnam.[53] Although the official position of the Irish government involved supporting calls for a peaceful solution, the Irish delegation was among the minority of delegations that customarily did not address the Vietnam conflict. This was despite the fact that the Irish public and media remained gripped by events in Vietnam. The Irish government came under repeated attack in the Dáil for its silence on Vietnam, with claims that it had betrayed its republican roots and its independence in order to serve American interests.[54]

Aiken's customary justification for silence at the United Nations on Vietnam was that the Irish government could not exercise any influence on the matter until such a time as the permanent members of the Security Council came to an agreement that would remove the division in the General Assembly.[55] It was argued that debate in the United Nations would not contribute to any positive outcome, as it would merely descend into exchanges of polemical rhetoric. Whenever Aiken, or any member of the Irish delegation, did make reference to the conflict, it was in the general context of South-East Asia and the necessity for the establishment of an 'Area of Law'.[56] The statements of the Irish government were limited to expressions that it saw little hope of an end to the war in Vietnam and no hope for a permanent peace until such an eventuality.[57]

Whilst the Irish government was silent on United States involvement in Vietnam, Dublin's response to the Soviet invasion of Czechoslovakia involved a condemnation of Moscow that was framed in ideological terms. In a statement to the press on 21 August 1968, Aiken criticised the Soviet Union for violating the United Nations Charter, the principles of territorial integrity and political independence. He called for a Security Council resolution demanding the immediate withdrawal of Soviet troops and the cessation of

---

[52] Patrick Keatinge, *The Formulation of Irish Foreign Policy* (Dublin, 1973), pp. 164–5.

[53] NAI 98/3/73, note on attitude of the Holy See to Vietnam.

[54] *Dáil Deb.*, vol. 226, col. 891, 8 Feb. 1967; *Dáil Deb.*, vol. 255, cols. 2702–4, 28 July 1971.

[55] *Dáil Deb.*, vol. 216, col. 481, 9 June 1965.

[56] These were formal proposals by Aiken designed to lessen Cold War tension by formally establishing neutralised regions that were otherwise of strategic rivalry. For further discussion, refer to Skelly, *United Nations*, pp. 161–5.

[57] *Dáil Deb.*, vol. 230, col. 1917, 7 Nov. 1967; UCDA, P104/6906, Memorandum for the Information of the Government on the Situation in Vietnam, 1 Feb. 1968.

their interference in Czechoslovakian internal affairs.[58] Taoiseach Jack Lynch took the opportunity to reiterate that Ireland was Western, 'far from ideologically neutral', though it still maintained 'an independent role in international affairs'.[59]

The Irish delegation raised the issue of Czechoslovakia in the First Committee during the debates on disarmament, accusing the Soviet Union of violating the United Nations Charter and various United Nations resolutions regarding use of force and violations of sovereignty.[60] Cremin also raised the issue directly with the Soviet delegation. He reiterated the criticisms made during press statements and United Nations speeches and justified this by citing Ireland's history, its United Nations policy and its attitude towards the United Nations Charter.[61] The language and arguments resembled points voiced at the United Nations by other countries with respect to United States involvement in the Vietnam conflict.

Although Ireland supported omitting the issue of Vietnam from the agenda of both the Security Council and the General Assembly, it supported inscription of the Czechoslovakian issue. The Security Council met to discuss Czechoslovakia, but the Soviet veto ensured that it produced no resolution on the crisis.[62] Despite an acknowledgement that, like the Vietnam issue, a debate on Czechoslovakia could be counterproductive, Ireland supported inscription on the agenda of the General Assembly.[63] Cremin argued that the General Assembly should express world opinion, which would encourage the Czechoslovakians to continue their liberalisation.[64]

The Irish delegation was often reticent when articulating its policy on Cold War issues because it was concerned about being seen as overtly partisan. This did not hold true when communist states were guilty of transgressions and in situations where pro-Western Irish denunciation could be justified as not being ideologically driven. Such a distinction between Irish diplomacy concerning perceptions of United States and Soviet imperialism was evident on Irish policy and stances on the invasion of Czechoslovakia, as opposed to the Vietnam situation during the late 1960s. It was also apparent in other precedents, such as with respect to Chinese action in Tibet, compared to that on the insertion of United States and British troops in Lebanon and Jordan, respectively, a decade earlier.

---

[58] UCDA P104/6898, Press Release on the situation in Czechoslovakia, 21 Aug. 1968.

[59] *Irish Independent*, 22 Aug. 1968, p. 8.

[60] NAI 98/3/87, Cremin to McCann, 26 Nov. 1968.

[61] Ibid., Cremin to McCann, 5 Sept. 1968.

[62] NAI 98/3/63, Cremin to McCann, 23 Aug. 1968.

[63] Ibid.

[64] Ibid., Cremin to Ronan, 30 Aug. 1968.

The Middle East [65]

The Middle East crisis was a complex policy concern, as it encompassed various issues including colonisation, race relations, regional border disputes, violations of international law and defiance of United Nations resolutions. It was also a political Cold War battleground, where there was a clear exercise of patronage by the superpowers and a distinct East-West division that characterised voting patterns on the various draft resolutions and declaratory speeches at the United Nations. More importantly, it can be deemed a Cold War issue for Ireland because the Irish voting pattern and the position taken by various Irish speakers were more consistent with its policy on Cold War issues, rather than, for example, on decolonisation. Although Ireland did not formally recognise the state of Israel until 1963,[66] the Irish delegation invariably supported the resolutions proposed or supported by the West, and not those of the Arab states or the Soviet Union.

At the 5th Emergency Special Session in 1967, Ireland opposed, along with most of the West, pro-Arab Yugoslavian, Soviet, and Albanian draft resolutions on the subject.[67] These draft resolutions, which ultimately were defeated, called for the immediate and unconditional withdrawal of Israel from the occupied territories, condemned the West (specifically the United States, Britain and West Germany) as aggressors and as active participants in the conflict, denounced Israel as an aggressor and Western colony, and urged enforcement action against Israel.[68] Only three Western states (France, Greece and Spain) supported or abstained on these draft resolutions.[69] Ireland also supported the defeated Latin American draft resolution, which called for an end to a state of belligerency, as well as an Israeli withdrawal from occupied territories. The Latin American draft resolution articulated the general Western position and, as a consequence, was opposed by both the Arab states and the Soviet bloc.[70]

Aiken's intervention in the debate on 27 June emulated the sentiments of the speeches of the Western bloc. Although Israel had launched a pre-emptive attack, Aiken refused to identify Israel as the aggressor or the instigator of the conflict and defended its right of self-defence. He also called for the establishment of a stable and long-term peace in the Middle East, through

---

[65] See also Rory Miller's chapter, above pp. 54–78.

[66] Paula Wylie, 'The Virtual Minimum: Ireland's Decision for De Facto Recognition of Israel, 1947–9', in Michael Kennedy and J. M. Skelly (eds), *Irish Foreign Policy, 1919–1966, from independence to internationalism* (Dublin, 2000), p. 154.

[67] During this period at the United Nations, Albania was the mouthpiece of the communist People's Republic of China, which had not yet acquired membership of the United Nations.

[68] *ORGA* – Fifth Emergency Special Session Annexes, Document A/L.519, Soviet draft resolution; *ORGA* – Fifth Emergency Special Session Annexes, Document A/L.522/Rev.3, Yugoslav draft resolution.

[69] A/PV.1548, 4 July 1967, p. 15.

[70] Ibid., p. 17.

respect for mutual recognition of various principles. He articulated various necessary conditions, including the withdrawal of Israel's forces from territories it had occupied, but also the recognition of Israel's right to exist.[71] When Cremin spoke in explanation of Ireland's votes on the substantive draft resolutions before the General Assembly, he explicitly indicated that he viewed the pro-Arab draft resolutions produced by Yugoslavia, Albania and the Soviet Union as partisan. He stated that their refusal to address the underlying tension in the region would only serve to exacerbate existing tensions and dismissed the Albanian and Soviet texts as unnecessarily rhetorical and condemnatory.[72]

At subsequent United Nations sessions Ireland's voting positions continued to accord with its Western partners, just as its explanations of votes continued to echo the statements of Western delegations.[73] Even when addressing the humanitarian aspects of the crisis, Irish representatives urged that the refugee situation could only be properly addressed through resolution of the broader political issues and a lasting peace.[74] Although Aiken came under heavy criticism in the Dáil from Fine Gael for being too receptive to the Arab position by calling for a withdrawal of Israeli troops, the linking of this call to recognition of the right of existence was a clear acknowledgement of Israel's diplomatic position.[75]

At this time, the call for recognition of Israel's right to existence was opposed by the Arab states and was the defining feature of the Western and Israeli position on the issue. But it was also the recurrent theme of Ireland's policy on various resolutions brought before the General Assembly regarding the Middle East. The Arab diplomatic position was fundamentally based on the view that the state of Israel was an illegal and illegitimate construction.[76] Therefore, the Arab states and their supporters considered that United Nations action should be confined to merely ordering or compelling Israel's withdrawal from the occupied territories. This position was seriously challenged by the resounding defeat of the Arab states during the Six-Day War, which would later result in a grudging acceptance of the recognition of Israel's right to existence and the birth of Resolution 242 of 22 November 1967. This resolution called for both the withdrawal of Israeli forces 'from territories occupied' in the conflict, as well as an end to the state of belligerency and the recognition of all the states in the region.[77]

Aiken's speeches on the Middle East crisis also included concrete peace

---

[71] A/PV.1538, 27 June 1967, p. 5.

[72] A/PV.1546, 3 July 1967, p. 4.

[73] NAI 2000/14/370, Report on the Palestinian Refugees.

[74] NAI 2000/14/378, Report on Palestinian-Arab Refugees at the 23rd General Assembly Session.

[75] *Dáil Deb.*, vol. 229, cols. 1132–5, 4 July 1967.

[76] A/PV.1573, 28 Sept. 1967, p. 9.

[77] *Official Records of the United Nations Security Council*, Security Council Resolution 242 (1967) of 22 Nov. 1967.

proposals aimed at lessening tension in the region. He called for the formulation of a peace treaty guaranteed by the United Nations and all the permanent members of the Security Council. Aiken insisted that this was necessary to avoid repeated outbreaks of violence every few years, avert the escalation of violence into a nuclear arms race and create an environment conducive to a lasting peace. Aiken also called on the permanent members of the Security Council to refrain from further discord in the Middle East and formally guarantee his proposed treaty of peace and non-aggression by the Middle East states.[78] In his speech, the Irish Minister for External Affairs also advocated a settlement of the refugee problem, by resurrecting proposals that he initially raised in 1958, calling for the restoration of property or the payment of reparations by the United Nations to those displaced.[79]

The Arab states viewed the proposals with mixed interest. The more extreme members of the Arab bloc advocated denouncing the Irish proposals as they implied an acceptance of Israeli occupation of Palestinian territories, but others considered the proposals as 'sincere and disinterested [and] the first real sign of fresh thinking on an apparently intractable problem'.[80]

The representation of China at the United Nations

The representation of China had been one of the major Cold War issues debated by the United Nations since it was first considered in 1950. The Soviet Union and the United States mustered support for their respective positions, with the Soviets seeking the replacement of Taiwan with the People's Republic of China, and the United States seeking to maintain the status quo with Taiwan holding the Chinese seat and Communist China being excluded from the United Nations. Since the communists assumed power in mainland China in 1949, the regime had demanded the expulsion of the nationalists from the United Nations and their replacement with communist delegates. This was prevented until 1971 by United States opposition to the admission of the communist regime to the United Nations.

Between 1957 and 1971, when the United States capitulated to pressure in the General Assembly and ceased its opposition, Ireland supported the inscription of the discussion of the representation of China on the agenda of the General Assembly. This was evident both in its declaratory speeches and in its voting, despite provoking swift and substantial direct and indirect pressure from the United States. Ireland's support for the discussion of the issue was a courageous defiance of United States policy, as Ireland and the Scandinavian countries (except Iceland) were the only Western supporters of this view.[81] The stance of the Irish delegation shocked the United States

[78] A/PV.1538, 27 June 1967, p. 4–6.
[79] Ibid., p. 5.
[80] NAI 2000/14/370, Report on the Palestinian Refugees.
[81] NAI 98/3/273, Report on the Representation of China.

government, Irish Americans, the Irish media and the opposition in the Dáil. Consequently, Washington attempted to involve the Vatican and even managed to solicit the cooperation of Cardinal Spellman of New York in attempting to persuade the Irish delegation to reconsider its position. On 28 November 1957, the Irish vote on the issue of the representation of China prompted a motion of 'Disapproval of the Government's Foreign Policy' in the Dáil.[82]

Despite the criticism of the Irish position and the United States perception of its Cold War implications, until 1961 Ireland took a position on the procedural aspect of the question, not the substantive issue. As the procedural question was the focus of debate, both the Taoiseach and the Minister for External Affairs went to great lengths to emphasise that the question before the General Assembly was not one of whether the People's Republic of China should be admitted, but whether the question of Chinese representation should be discussed. They indicated that Ireland had not yet made a decision on the substantive issue of the representation of China.[83] Despite his criticism that Irish policy from the mid-1960s was a reversal of policy from the position taken in 1957,[84] former Irish diplomat Conor Cruise O'Brien unequivocally stated in 1962 that Ireland did not have a policy on the substantive issue in 1957.[85]

In 1965, the People's Republic of China was not a member of the United Nations and the Chinese seats were occupied by the Republic of China (Taiwan). The General Assembly was essentially divided into two camps on the China issue. The first involved those members who advocated the immediate and unconditional replacement of the representatives of Taiwan with those of Communist China. The proponents of this view included the representatives of Cambodia and Albania, who were Beijing's primary spokespeople while it remained unrepresented, as well as the Soviet bloc, various Asian and African countries and a small number of Western states. These Western states included the Scandinavian countries (except Iceland), Britain and France.

The United States was the principal opponent of this view and had pressed support for its Two-China Policy, which maintained that both Communist China and Taiwan had the right to independent membership of the General Assembly, with Beijing taking control of the seat on the Security Council.[86] Irish policy on the representation of China was premised on this position from 1964 to 1970.[87] Washington succeeded in perennially

[82] Keatinge, *Formulation*, p. 206.

[83] NAI 98/3/273, Report on the Representation of China.

[84] *Dáil Deb.*, vol. 241, col. 1877, 28 Oct. 1969.

[85] Paul Sharp, *Irish Foreign Policy and the European Community: A study of the impact of Interdependence on the foreign policy of a small state* (Aldershot, 1990), p. 182.

[86] NAI 98/3/273, Report on the Representation of China.

[87] NAI 2000/6/281, Memorandum for the Information of the Government on the 24th General Assembly Session.

undermining its opponents by achieving recognition that the question was an 'important question' and, thereby, required a two-thirds majority, rather than a simple majority. It was a procedural ploy that was instrumental in continually denying Beijing admission.[88]

Ireland's support for the United States position continued until 1970, when Minister for External Affairs Patrick Hillery instigated a change in policy. Between 1965 and 1969, Ireland avoided making declaratory speeches or explanations of its vote because Aiken and the Irish delegation considered that the debate was polemical, that the Irish position had not changed from previous sessions and that it had been adequately explained on those previous occasions.[89]

In 1966, Ireland's allegiance to the Two-China Policy led it to support an Italian draft resolution, which sought to have the United Nations establish a committee to study the situation and make recommendations for 'an equitable and practical solution to the question'.[90] Two years later at the 23rd General Assembly, Ireland joined the list of co-sponsors, which also included Belgium, Luxembourg and Chile. The proposal was promoted as a means of making progress towards the objective of universality, but it was generally viewed by member-states to have been inspired by the United States. The supporters of the People's Republic of China categorically rejected the Italian proposal as an initiative aimed at postponing its admission.[91] This view was given credence by a letter from the Belgian Permanent Representative, who was one of the co-sponsors, to the President of the General Assembly in 1968.[92] It outlined Belgium's views on the study to be undertaken by the committee in the event of the draft resolution being adopted and, specifically, its pre-judging of the outcome in favour of a Two-China solution.

Ireland refused to co-sponsor the text when it was first produced in 1966 out of a concern that it did not push a Two-China solution. The Irish delegation elected to co-sponsor the proposal in 1968 specifically because it envisaged such a solution.[93] It was also significant that the United States supported the Italian draft resolution and, in fact, at the session during which Ireland joined the list of co-sponsors, the text was replicated from those used at previous sessions precisely because it had United States endorsement. The proposal was considered as embodying specifically United States orientated Western interests and it failed to gain necessary support in 1966, 1967 and 1968. With these failures and diminishing support each year, it was dropped in 1969.[94]

---

[88] A/PV.1602, pp. 2–4, 21 Nov. 1967.

[89] NAI 2000/14/370, Report on the 22nd General Assembly Session.

[90] NAI 2000/14/378, Report on the Representation of China at the 23rd General Assembly Session.

[91] Ibid.

[92] NAI 98/3/273, Cremin to McCann, 18 Nov. 1969.

[93] Ibid.

[94] NAI 2000/14/378, Report on the Representation of China at the 23rd General Assembly Session.

In 1969, the Irish delegation under Patrick Hillery, who had succeeded Aiken following the June 1969 election, continued to adhere to Aiken's policy on the representation of China. This policy was perpetuated through the direction of Cremin. It caused problems at ministerial level, because Hillery did not agree with Aiken's policy or its continuation by the Irish United Nations delegation. On his appointment as minister, Hillery acknowledged his inexperience and the lack of time available to him to properly examine the issues on the agenda of the General Assembly. He accordingly granted Cremin and the Irish delegation significant latitude in their decision making.

It was not until after the vote in debates at the 24th General Assembly session in 1969 that Hillery made clear his displeasure with the Irish position.[95] His dissatisfaction was channelled through Seán Ronan, Assistant-Secretary at the Department of External Affairs, who passed on his minister's views to Cremin along with a request for greater background information on the major debates at the United Nations. Hillery's change of policy was previewed in the Dáil a month before this, when he made a very vague and brief reference to the representation of China in a speech that crucially made no reference to, or defence of, the Two-China Policy. This was contrasted with the custom of his predecessor who had invariably explicitly defended the Two-China policy.[96]

Hillery believed that Ireland needed to change its position, particularly after the Italian proposal ceased to be forwarded. He was also increasingly swayed by the expanding support of Western countries for the replacement of Taiwan with the People's Republic of China; especially that of Belgium, Italy and Canada who were in the process of considering formal recognition of Beijing. Hillery was conscious that Sweden, Norway, Denmark, the Netherlands, Britain and France had already recognised the communist regime and supported its admission, even if it was at the expense of Taiwan.[97] It was clear that the United States and its supporters, including Ireland, were becoming increasingly isolated and fighting a losing battle to promote the Two-China Policy. As a result, Hillery was concerned that Ireland's support for this policy could be interpreted as opposition to the admission of the People's Republic of China and preferred abstaining on the issue.[98] Therefore, in 1970, and in response to the direction of his minister, Cremin announced that Ireland's position had altered due to a 'desire for some progress' on the issue. Ireland continued to support the argument that any alteration in the representation of China that could result in the expulsion of Taiwan from the United Nations should be deemed an important question. At the same time,

---

[95] NAI 98/3/273, Cremin to McCann, 18 Nov. 1969.
[96] *Dáil Deb.*, vol. 241, col. 1877, 28 Oct. 1969.
[97] NAI 98/3/273, Cremin to McCann, 18 Nov. 1969.
[98] Ibid., McCann to Cremin, 20 Nov. 1969.

Ireland abstained on, rather than opposed, the perennial substantive draft resolution to replace the representatives of Taiwan with those of the People's Republic of China.[99]

In 1971, Ireland supported the draft resolution seeking the replacement of Taiwan with the People's Republic of China. It decided to support the replacement of Taiwan at the same session that the United States ceased its opposition to the measure and the General Assembly approved the proposal. Nevertheless, Hillery rejected the suggestion that Ireland's policy was influenced by the reversal of policy by the United States.[100] He insisted that his change in Ireland's policy was simply because he 'saw no logic in the seat for the largest nation in the world being held by Taiwan'.[101] The People's Republic of China was the largest nation in the world, with one quarter of the world's population, and was a nuclear power, having tested its first fission nuclear weapon in 1964 and thermonuclear weapon three years later.

Hillery was sincere about the lack of United States influence over Irish policy on that particular issue, because the United States was increasingly impotent to halt the desertion by Ireland and other Western states from the Two-China Policy. Since he had been appointed minister in 1969, Hillery had consistently sought to reverse Ireland's stance on the issue and berated the Irish delegation in 1969 when it perpetuated its support for the Two-China Policy. This was two years prior to any indication that the United States would reverse its policy. Washington had unilaterally removed some minor restrictions on travel in and trade with Communist China in 1969 and held discreet talks at a diplomatic level.[102] But the first hint of a public reversal of policy at a diplomatic level had come in early 1971 when President Richard Nixon used the official name, 'People's Republic of China', instead of the usual United States terminology – Red China or Communist China – to describe the regime in Beijing. The thaw in relations was confirmed in July of that year, when Nixon also announced that he had received an invitation to visit Beijing, which he intended to accept.[103]

Ireland and decolonisation at the United Nations[104]

Ireland's policy on decolonisation issues at the United Nations had always shown a significant departure from conventional Western policy. Ireland had gained its independence from Britain in 1922. Consequently, its first generation of political leaders, which included Frank Aiken, remained focused on national liberation and political independence. Further, its history

[99] A/PV.1913, 20 Nov. 1970, p. 11.
[100] *Dáil Deb.*, vol. 255, col. 2919, 29 July 1971.
[101] Interview on-line with Dr Patrick Hillery, 30 Mar. 2002.
[102] Henry Kissinger, *Diplomacy* (New York, 1994 edition), p. 723.
[103] Frank Freidel, *America in the Twentieth Century* (4th ed.) (New York, 1970), p. 393.
[104] See also Aoife Bhreatnach's and Kevin O'Sullivan's chapters above pp. 182–200 and pp 201–223.

of affiliation with the Third World in the form of missionary activity, provision of education, and administration of schools and hospitals, fuelled its anti-colonial sentiment.[105] Ireland's reputation for supporting decolonisation was established during the early period of Irish neutrality at the United Nations between 1957 and 1961. But this was a period when the balance of the General Assembly gave disproportionate weight to 'middle powers' and in the period 1965–1969, Ireland's policy was forced to evolve.

Ireland's policy on decolonisation was conspicuously divergent from Western norms, as Western European countries were the primary colonial powers. While the West did not actively advocate the perpetuation of colonialism, many western states were reluctant to surrender the economic benefits arising from the inertia of their earlier period of colonial exploitation. The minority regimes of Southern Africa provided access to valuable mineral resources (including gold, diamonds and uranium) and an export market for steel, agriculture, industrial equipment and armaments.[106] South Africa also housed a large proportion of the United States' space and missile tracking installations. Its seas provided an alternate route between the Indian and Atlantic Oceans to bypass the unstable Suez Canal zone. South African air and naval facilities were significant for United States forces and South Africa provided a crucial pro-Western presence in Africa.[107] These ongoing economic relationships, as well as cultural, political and strategic links, deterred the former colonial powers from supporting any General Assembly resolutions advocating forceful means to eliminate control by minority colonial regimes.[108]

Ireland's anti-colonial United Nations policy manifested itself on various issues, but was most prominent in the mid to late 1960s on the issues plaguing Southern Africa. These included apartheid in South Africa, the illegal minority white regime in Southern Rhodesia, the perpetuation of Portuguese colonial control over Guinea, Angola and Mozambique, as well as South Africa's continued occupation of Namibia.

Ireland had historically adopted a more assertive position than most other Western countries on Southern African issues and it had been associated with Afro-Asian countries as a supporter and co-sponsor of resolutions and efforts to achieve the inscription of items. The Irish delegation had often been instrumental in bringing issues such as apartheid to the attention of the General Assembly. Ireland's diplomacy on Southern Africa was also distinct from other Western states because it involved support for the referral of such issues to the Security Council. In this respect, Ireland supported the implementation of sanctions against Portugal and the minority white regime in

---

[105] UCDA P104/7258, transcript of an interview by Aiken with John O'Shea of radio station WJRZ, Newark, New Jersey, 5 Sept. 1966.

[106] James Joll, *Europe Since 1870: An International History* (London, 1990), p. 475.

[107] *FRUS* vol. XXIV, Document 403, Goldberg to Rusk, 29 Oct. 1965; Document 600: National Policy Paper – South Africa, Washington, 18 Jan. 1965.

[108] Trevor Salmon, *Unneutral Ireland: An ambivalent and unique security policy* (Oxford, 1989), p. 34.

Southern Rhodesia, as well as the use of force against South Africa. In contrast, most Western states opposed such actions as extreme and unrealistic,[109] as well as a violation of Article 2.7 of the United Nations Charter, which protected against United Nations interference in matters of 'domestic jurisdiction'.

Namibia

The deteriorating situation in Namibia was considered by the Irish delegation to be the most pressing decolonisation issue in the region. Namibia had been a German colony that was occupied by South Africa during the Great War, with authority from the League of Nations following the end of the war. In 1945, Pretoria refused to transfer its mandate to United Nations trusteeship and from 1948 made efforts to integrate the territory into South Africa. In 1966, and in response to the extension of apartheid to the territory, the United Nations terminated South Africa's mandate over Namibia with the passage of Resolution 2145(XXI).[110] Pretoria rejected the resolution as contrary to the United Nations Charter[111] and the rulings of the International Court of Justice,[112] and refused to terminate its control.[113] Neither France nor Britain supported Resolution 2145(XXI) and, therefore, the right of the United Nations to even discuss the matter. Furthermore, France openly defied the United Nations embargo on the sale of arms to South Africa.

Aiken considered South Africa's refusal to terminate its administration as representing 'a clear case of aggression by a would-be colonial Power against a weak neighbouring people'[114] and an effort at 'territorial expansion'.[115] He also viewed Namibia as a 'test case' for the United Nations, as the failure to implement Resolution 2145(XXI) 'would be a crippling if not a fatal blow' to the United Nations capacity to take collective action to suppress international aggression.[116]

Under Aiken, the Irish delegation advocated pragmatic and effective action on the issue to terminate South Africa's control. Aiken did not consider either the Afro-Asian or Western proposals to end Pretoria's grip on the territory as meeting those criteria. The Afro-Asian bloc argued for the establishment of a United Nations Council for Namibia to assume administration of the territory and oversee the withdrawal of South African security

---

[109] *FRUS*, vol. XXIV, Document 600: National Policy Paper – South Africa, Washington, 18 Jan. 1965.

[110] NAI 2000/14/267, Report on Fifth Special Session – Namibia.

[111] South Africa regarded the resolution to be in violation of Article 10 and associated articles of the United Nations Charter, which limited the powers of the General Assembly to discussion and recommendations.

[112] In 1966 the International Court of Justice had ruled that the termination of a mandate by the League of Nations required bilateral agreement between the United Nations and the administering power, which in the latter case had not been given.

[113] NAI 2000/14/266, South African Memorandum on Namibia, Apr. 1967.

[114] NAI 2000/14/267, Report on Fifth Special Session – Namibia.

[115] Ibid.

[116] Ibid.

forces, but failed to address the issue of Pretoria's recalcitrance in relinquishing control. The Western bloc proposed the appointment of a Special Representative for Namibia, to be nominated by the Secretary-General, who would study the situation and report back to the General Assembly. Whatever the findings of the study, Western delegates categorically rejected the use of coercive action.[117]

Aiken recognised that Resolution 2145(XXI) did not have mandatory force and relied on either South African capitulation or the hope that the Security Council would share the General Assembly's view and institute enforcement measures. As Pretoria rejected the legality of Resolution 2145(XXI) and refused to terminate its control of Namibia, it was clear that progress would only be achieved in the event of Security Council action. It was inevitable that the South African government would reject any overture from the General Assembly, especially as it would likely be pressed by the smaller states. Consequently, Aiken met with Marian Anderson of the United States delegation and urged her to amend a Western draft resolution on Namibia to substitute references to the General Assembly with references to the Security Council. Furthermore, he indicated that unless she did so, Ireland would not support the Western text.[118] Aiken was unsuccessful with Anderson and met with the United States Permanent Representative to the United Nations, Ambassador Arthur J. Goldberg, four days later and attempted to convince him of the necessity for the amendments. Aiken did not believe that South Africa would fight to keep Namibia, particularly because the majority of the white population in Namibia was German (rather than South African) and the capital investment was primarily foreign. Despite his efforts, Aiken could not persuade the United States to support his amendments.[119]

On 16 May 1967 and following these rebuffs, Aiken met with a contact group[120] for a proposed compromise draft resolution and again urged the inclusion of a clause referring the matter to the Security Council. On behalf of the co-sponsors, Chief Simeon Ola Adebo of Nigeria indicated that he agreed with Aiken's rationale, but could not include such a clause because of the opposition it would engender from the West.[121] For this reason the *Irish Press* described Aiken's policy as 'taking a stronger line than the Africans themselves'.[122]

The Irish efforts to strengthen the resolution before the General Assembly failed when a compromise draft resolution was produced on Namibia. The resolution established a Council for Namibia to administer the territory until

---

[117] Ibid.
[118] NAI 2000/14/266, Cremin to McCann, 25 May 1967.
[119] Ibid.
[120] The contact group comprised Ethiopia, Nigeria, the Philippines, Chile and Mexico. Denmark, Finland, Iceland, Norway and Sweden were also in attendance at the meeting.
[121] NAI 2000/14/266, Cremin to McCann, 18 May 1967.
[122] *Irish Press*, 12 Dec. 1967.

it achieved independence and to report on its work, with no contingency for South African intransigence and no reference to the Security Council.[123] Due to this omission, Ireland refused to support the text, stating that no resolution passed by the General Assembly could induce a change in the situation of Namibia. The rest of the West also abstained but, unlike the Irish, these states opposed any action being taken other than dialogue.[124]

By the opening of the 22nd General Assembly later in 1967, Aiken's views had gradually gained support among African and Asian representatives following continued intransigence in Pretoria.[125] The African Group introduced a text that was overwhelmingly supported on 16 December 1967 as Resolution 2325(XXII). The text of this resolution corresponded closely with the text of the resolution adopted on the subject at the previous session, except for the addition of a paragraph, requesting the Security Council to take steps to enable the United Nations to fulfil its responsibilities of administration.[126] Most Western states strenuously objected to the inclusion of the paragraph and its reference to Chapter Seven of the United Nations Charter. The inclusion of the paragraph prompted Ireland to support the resolution and Cremin referred to previous speeches by the Tánaiste and reiterated that reference to the Security Council was essential for 'effectiveness and practicability'.[127]

Most Western states abstained in the vote, unwilling to be seen to be endorsing South Africa's action or the extension of apartheid. But position speeches made clear their objections to the referral to the Security Council.[128] Their concern over the possibility of this eventuality had resulted in efforts during 1966, 1967 and 1968 by various members of the Western European and Others (WEO) Group[129] to persuade its members to present a unified front on the issue of Namibia. Their objective was to prevent the General Assembly from recommending the action advocated by Ireland. Concerns about infringements of sovereignty led to the politicisation proposal being dropped during 1967,[130] though it was resurrected in 1968 during the discussions on Namibia in an effort to avoid Security Council referral.[131] While

---

[123] NAI 2000/14/267, Report on Fifth Special Session – Namibia.

[124] NAI 2000/14/370, Report on the 22nd General Assembly Session of the United Nations.

[125] Ibid.

[126] *ORGA* – 22nd General Assembly Session, Documents A/L.540 and Add.1 and 2*, Somalian draft resolution, pp. 25–6.

[127] A/PV.1742, 16 Dec. 1968, p. 5.

[128] A/PV.1693, p. 9, 14 Oct. 1968; NAI 2000/14/378, Report on Namibia at the 23rd General Assembly Session.

[129] The WEO Group was a group that comprised Western Europe (including the EEC) and new world Western states of similar political, historical and cultural characteristics, such as the United States, Australia, New Zealand, Canada and South Africa. Its only formal function involved elections to United Nations offices and organs, to ensure shared or proportional regional representation. But because of the correspondence of political, cultural, economic and strategic interests, the WEO Group usually voted along similar lines.

[130] NAI 98/3/86, Cremin to McCann, 20 Jan. 1967.

[131] NAI 98/3/87, Cremin to McCann, 22 Jan. 1968.

there was no agreed framework for political cooperation, many countries agreed to oppose initiatives pertaining to Namibia, such as the Irish proposal to refer the matter to the Security Council.

Apartheid in South Africa[132]

Ireland's anti-apartheid movement provided an influential voice in Irish politics with its substantial Catholic missionary influences and mass demonstrations in Dublin, which were influential in Irish United Nations policy.[133] Although almost every member of the United Nations, except South Africa and Portugal, claimed to be opposed to the principle and practice of apartheid, most Western countries opposed or abstained on resolutions critical of South African racial policies.[134] Interventions were rare as some, like France, minimised involvement due to a refusal to accept the validity of the United Nations debates,[135] and others were only roused by the need to defend themselves against accusations that they were not committed to ending apartheid.[136]

In 1966, for the first time, Ireland supported the General Assembly resolution labelling apartheid 'a crime against humanity' and calling for the implementation of universal mandatory economic sanctions against South Africa. Ireland supported the resolution as a whole despite having reservations about various clauses and, due to these concerns, abstained on various paragraphs when put to separate votes, including those that deemed apartheid to constitute a threat to international peace and security and were critical of South Africa's trading partners.[137] Nevertheless, the Irish delegation signalled that it believed sanctions were necessary to ensure Pretoria's compliance in ending apartheid.[138]

During the General Assembly session of 1966, Ireland joined opposition to a United States amendment to Resolution 2396(XXIII) on apartheid in South Africa. The United States was seeking to delete operative paragraph four, recommending the implementation of mandatory comprehensive sanctions. Most Western countries supported the amendment; nevertheless, Ireland and the majority of General Assembly member-states ensured it was defeated.[139]

In the resolutions passed on Southern Africa, Ireland's support for decolonisation was characterised not only by the resort to action under

---

132 See also Kevin O'Sullivan's chapter pp. 201–223.

133 Keatinge, *Formulation*, pp. 283–4.

134 NAI 2000/14/370, Report on apartheid at the 22nd General Assembly Session.

135 *ORGA* – 22nd General Assembly Session, Document A/6914, Report of the Special Political Committee, pp. 53–5.

136 A/SPC/SR.564, p. 75, 10 Nov. 1967.

137 NAI 2000/14/300, Memorandum for the Information of the Government on the 22nd General Assembly Session of the United Nations, 30 Aug. 1967.

138 Ibid.

139 *ORGA* – 23rd General Assembly Session, Document A/7348, Report of the Special Political Committee, pp. 7–11.

Chapter Seven, but also resolutions that included clauses condemning the trading partners of the minority regimes for encouraging the perpetuation of apartheid. Although these trading partners were left unnamed, it was widely recognised that they were primarily wealthy Western states,[140] including the United States and the former colonial powers of Western Europe, such as France and Britain.[141]

From 1967, the Irish delegation shifted its policy further when it supported all the paragraphs of the resolution on apartheid when put to separate votes, including that condemning South Africa's major trading partners, in addition to the resolution as a whole.[142] Ireland was concerned that the situation in Southern Africa was becoming 'more explosive' and was on the brink of racial war, with the increasing unity of South Africa, Portugal and Southern Rhodesia to suppress their opponents.[143] Ireland also supported the paragraph condemning South Africa's trading partners specifically because it believed that various member states and financial interests had encouraged South Africa to perpetuate its policies. Certain member states, most notably France, had sold arms to South Africa during 1967, despite the existence of a Security Council arms embargo. Further, South Africa's purchases of military equipment had been increasing as the race relations in the country deteriorated.[144] Nevertheless, Ireland would not support United Nations enforcement action against South Africa for its use of apartheid, until after the Security Council sanctioned such involvement on the issue of Namibia. Aiken considered Pretoria's actions in the latter instance to constitute a stronger case, under the United Nations Charter, for such intervention.[145]

Ireland took a more cautious approach towards the efforts of the Afro-Asian bloc to expel South Africa from the United Nations Conference on Trade and Development (UNCTAD). At the second UNCTAD meeting in New Delhi in March 1968, the membership, led by its Afro-Asian delegates, voted to expel South Africa from the body until such time as South Africa abolished apartheid. While African countries were leading an initiative in the General Assembly to legitimise this decision, Western states opposed the effort with the United States, Britain and Canada indicating that they would

---

[140] Ireland also had to defend the accusation from the International Monetary Fund (IMF) that it was one of South Africa's major trading partners. Ireland had expanded its trade significantly with South Africa in the mid-1960s and the Irish government was concerned about the effect this had on Ireland's international image. Nevertheless, the Irish government rejected the validity of the IMF's trade statistics, as they included commodities that arrived at Shannon Airport and were dispatched to other countries. See NAI 96/3/95, Dorr to Holmes, 4 Dec. 1969; and NAI 96/3/95, Notes for the Permanent Representative of Ireland to the United Nations for 22nd General Assembly Session).

[141] *ORGA* – 24th General Assembly Session, Document A/7348, Report of the Fourth Committee, pp. 7–11.

[142] NAI 2000/14/370, Report on apartheid at the 22nd General Assembly Session.

[143] Ibid.

[144] *ORGA* – 22nd General Assembly Session, Document A/6914, Report of the Special Political Committee, pp. 53–5.

[145] NAI 2000/14/266, Background Note on Namibia.

revise their support and participation in UNCTAD.[146] Although Western opposition was not sufficient to prevent the Second (Economic and Financial) Committee passing the resolution to expel South Africa from UNCTAD, the resolution did not attract the necessary two-thirds support to pass in the plenary session. Ireland along with the other Western states present and most of the Latin American states opposed the resolution.[147]

The Irish government believed that Pretoria's presence in these forums would better allow the effective use of public opinion and moral condemnation against the South African government.[148] As one of the West's most vocal critics of apartheid in South Africa, Ireland wanted the opportunity to make its position clear. But more importantly, Dublin was concerned about the legal validity of the expulsion effort and the increasing propensity on the part of the Afro-Asian bloc to use their numerical influence to pass unrealistic or unconstitutional resolutions. This view was supported by the legal counsel of the United Nations, Constantine Stavroupoulos, who claimed the move was contrary to Articles Five and Six of the United Nations Charter, which specified that such an action could only be contemplated after a recommendation of the Security Council, because membership of UNCTAD was a right involved in membership of the United Nations.[149] The Soviet bloc, which usually rallied behind the Afro-Asian anti-colonial cause, also refused to support the attempted expulsion of South Africa.[150]

The Portuguese Territories in Africa

Ireland supported the General Assembly resolutions critical of Portugal's control of its African territories for similar reasons to those on Pretoria's use of apartheid and control of Namibia. These included resolutions that contained operative paragraphs which deplored those foreign financial interests that obstructed the independence of the indigenous populations, provided that this was only interpreted as pertaining to those financial interests that impeded progress towards independence, not all foreign investment. Ireland also supported the inclusion of the operative paragraph 'deploring' the aid that Portugal received from NATO.[151] As in the case with South Africa, Portugal's acquisition of war materials and arms accelerated as its repression of the indigenous population intensified.

As it supported punitive action against South Africa, from 1966 Ireland had supported recommendations that the Security Council implement

[146] NAI DFA 305/94/5, Dorr to Cremin, 2 Dec. 1968.

[147] A/PV.1741, 13 Dec. 1968, p. 13.

[148] NAI 2000/14/300, Memorandum for the Information of the Government on the 22nd General Assembly Session of the United Nations, 30 Aug. 1967.

[149] NAI DFA 305/94/5, Dorr to Cremin, 2 Dec. 1968.

[150] A/PV.1741, 13 Dec. 1968, p. 13.

[151] *ORGA* – 24th General Assembly Session, Document A/7352**, Report of the Fourth Committee, pp. 1–4.

mandatory sanctions against Portugal.[152] Lisbon defied all pressure on it to relinquish its colonies in Mozambique, Guinea and Tanzania, which it considered to comprise part of 'Metropolitan Portugal'. At the 21st General Assembly in 1966, Ireland had been the lone Western nation supporting the resolution passed on the issue of the Portuguese territories in Africa, which labelled the situation a threat to international security and called for the Security Council to impose mandatory sanctions. At the same time, the Irish government did not intend to sever diplomatic relations with Portugal until obliged to do so by Security Council resolutions. The overt justification for this was that the communication of disapproval about colonial practices was impossible without open diplomatic channels.[153]

Aside from Ireland and the Scandinavian countries, economic sanctions against Portugal and South Africa were vociferously opposed by most Western states. These countries minimised their participation in the debates on decolonisation, but interjected when it came to protecting their trading interests, arguing that the maintenance of relations was essential to exert influence over the policies of the minority regimes of Southern Africa.

Southern Rhodesia[154]

Ireland's position on Southern Rhodesia was more nuanced, considering the complex nature of that regime's relationship with Britain following its unilateral declaration of independence. The Irish delegation did not support the calls for the use of force to end the illegal regime in Southern Rhodesia and abstained on resolutions on the issue, specifically because they contained operative paragraphs which called for this course of action.[155] But Ireland's opposition to the use of force against Southern Rhodesia was qualified and it expected a solution through negotiations, an avenue which had not yet been sufficiently exhausted.

Aiken was conscious that Southern Rhodesia was a British colony and technically, if not practically, remained under the control of London. Therefore, he was reluctant to advocate a course of action unless endorsed by Britain. He supported the British and widely acknowledged that the application of Article 2.7 of the United Nations Charter, preventing United Nations involvement in the internal politics of a member-state, as it incorporated a unilateral secession from administration by Britain and had no foreign involvement. This had been recognised by the General Assembly as

---

[152] *Dáil Deb.*, vol. 226, col. 373, 14 Dec. 1966.

[153] *Dáil Deb.*, vol. 241, col. 1866, 28 Oct. 1969.

[154] See also Kevin O'Sullivan's and Aoife Bhreatnach's chapters above pp. 201–223 and pp. 182–200.

[155] Southern Rhodesia (Zimbabwe) had been a British colony, which gained self-government in 1923. In 1962 the white supremacist party, the Rhodesian Front, won power from the United Federal Party, which had been attempting to expand the rights of the African population, and began negotiations with Britain for independence. Those negotiations collapsed in 1965 and the leader of the Rhodesian Front, Ian Smith, responded with a unilateral declaration of independence (UDI).

the initial resolution passed on the situation in 1966 called on London to take the necessary measures to end the illegal regime.[156] The General Assembly only sought direct intervention by the Security Council when it decided that Britain was not acting with sufficient alacrity. London was reluctant to resort to the use of force, because of the opposition of the British electorate and the political instability in Britain that military intervention in Southern Rhodesia might have engendered.[157] Ireland had implemented sanctions against Southern Rhodesia when they were voluntary (specifically because they were urged by London) and also when they became mandatory.[158]

Aiken was sceptical about the efficacy of voluntary sanctions, but made an exception in the case of Southern Rhodesia at the urging of London.[159] He was reluctant to implement any sanctions unless they were endorsed by major trading partners and the Security Council. Aiken believed that without such involvement, economic sanctions would be ineffective, would only impact negatively on the victims of apartheid, and would diminish the authority and prestige of the United Nations.[160] Further, the Irish government was concerned that supporting voluntary sanctions would result in Irish exporters and workers losing jobs to countries not participating in sanctions, who would use the opportunity to expand their trade, and would have a disparate effect on participating countries.[161]

But the Irish government supported the imposition of mandatory universal sanctions by the Security Council against both Portugal and South Africa.[162] It was because of its mandatory and comprehensive nature that Ireland had supported the arms embargo against South Africa embodied in Security Council Resolutions 181 and 182 of 1963 and Resolution 191 of 1964.[163] Ireland also complied with Security Council Resolution 253 (1968) imposing comprehensive mandatory sanctions against Southern Rhodesia.[164]

---

[156] NAI 2000/14/300, Memorandum for the Information of the Government on the 22nd General Assembly Session, 30 Aug. 1967.

[157] Joll, *Europe Since 1870*, p. 474.

[158] The decision of the Irish government to apply sanctions against Southern Rhodesia was a rare case where considerations for the EEC application encroached into the area of United Nations policy. The Economic Division of the Department of External affairs favoured the imposition of selective sanctions, rather than a comprehensive embargo. All six members of the EEC adopted the former, and the latter was adopted by Britain. The Economic Division was concerned that the imposition of comprehensive sanctions would be interpreted in Common Market capitals as evidence that Ireland remained adherent to British policy (NAI 2000/14/52, Economic Division to Ronan, 16 Aug. 1967).

[159] *Dáil Deb.*, vol. 233, col. 1638, 3 Apr. 1968.

[160] NAI 2000/14/300, Memorandum for the Information of the Government on the 22nd General Assembly Session of the United Nations, 30 Aug. 1967.

[161] *Dáil Deb.*, vol. 241, cols. 1750–1, 23 Oct. 1969; *Dáil Deb.*, vol. 226, col. 980, 9 Feb. 1967.

[162] *Dáil Deb.*, vol. 241, col. 1751, 23 Oct. 1969.

[163] *Dáil Deb.*, vol. 232, col. 1769, 27 Feb. 1968.

[164] NAI 2000/6/609, Memorandum for the Government on the implementation of United Nations Security Council Resolution 253 (1968), 18 Feb. 1969.

Conclusion

Ireland's impact at the United Nations had been out of proportion for a state of its size in the period from 1957 to 1961. Frank Aiken brought to the United Nations a unique and often conflicting mix of policy imperatives inherent in Ireland's political culture, including anti-colonialism, neutrality as well as cultural and political ties to the West. Aiken remained chairman of the Irish delegation and exerted a strong presence in New York until 1968. He retired the following year. However, Ireland's capacity to maintain its role as a broker and proponent of compromise initiatives as a 'middle power' had diminished by the mid-1960s due to the shift in the composition of the General Assembly.

After a brief period of apathy in the early 1960s that gave an illusion of success for activism and the role of the 'middle powers', the permanent members of the Security Council reasserted their presence in the United Nations from the mid-1960s by paralyzing its security procedures. Many of the newly admitted small states also confined their objectives to preserving their sovereignty in order to protect their recently won autonomy and limited budgets from the demands of international public servants. Others increasingly used their numerical advantage to redirect the scope and nature of debates to focus on Third World rights, issues and objectives, which were not often conducive to a compromise role. Therefore, countries such as Ireland and other 'middle powers' were marginalised, given little opportunity for the activism that had characterised their earlier United Nations policies and were forced to evolve their approaches in the mid to late 1960s.[165]

Ireland's policy on the financing of peacekeeping operations was, in many respects, the final effort at serious activism of the Irish delegation in the arena of the United Nations during the 1960s. The Irish delegation was gradually forced to accept the reality and dominance of great power politics and the Third World majority in the General Assembly. By 1969, the Irish proposals were effectively emasculated by bureaucracy and committees. Ireland maintained a key role on disarmament, especially the diplomacy surrounding the General Assembly deliberations on the NPT. Although the treaty was negotiated by the superpowers on a bilateral basis, Ireland played a central role in marshalling support among United Nations member states.

On a range of Cold War issues – the admission of the People's Republic of China, Vietnam, and the Middle East – Ireland's voting was invariably and conventionally Western and it adopted United States positions as its locus. In these situations, Ireland clearly voted along with the rest of the United States-led West and minimised its speeches to avoid drawing attention to itself. On only one significant Cold War issue had there been a shift in Irish policy at the General Assembly during this period – the representation of China – and

---

[165] Sharp, *Irish Foreign Policy and the European Community*, p. 25.

that came at the instigation of Patrick Hillery in 1969 and 1970. Hillery's appointment and the shift in policy on the representation of China were signs of Ireland increasing identification with Europe and with its impending admission to the EEC.

In the early 1960s, during Ireland's first application for membership of the EEC, France had criticised Ireland for exhibiting a United Nations policy that was more associated with non-alignment than with conventional Western diplomacy. The criticism was particularly aimed at Ireland's policy on decolonisation because Irish diplomacy on such issues invariably brought it into conflict with the member-states of the EEC, the United States, Britain and other key Western countries. These countries were either former colonial powers, or those who had trading interests that brought them into conflict with the advocates of decolonisation. Nevertheless, in the mid-late 1960s Irish diplomacy on decolonisation evolved under changing circumstances, but continued to be the most unyielding aspect of Irish United Nations policy, due to its link with Ireland's national identity and historical experience. This was most apparent from 1966 and on issues such as Gibraltar, where there were clear parallels with the situation in Northern Ireland, as well as with the numerous issues of Southern Africa. Ireland was a vocal presence in the General Assembly on decolonisation and, in the case of Southern Africa, a key proponent of the intervention of the Security Council and the use of force against South Africa. Ireland's policy in this respect was in contrast to the majority of Western countries, who were reluctant to participate in debate and only did so to articulate very general condemnation of racially based policies, without addressing the specifics of the issues before the United Nations.

Therefore, Ireland maintained a strong approach to various issues at the United Nations in the mid to late 1960s, most notably peacekeeping, disarmament and decolonisation. That approach was forced to evolve as the General Assembly membership transformed; disarmament was increasingly removed from the province of the United Nations and tensions on some issues escalated. Nineteen-sixty-nine was an especially pivotal year as it signified the retirement of Aiken who had been a driving force in Irish United Nations policy from 1957. The year also saw a virtual end to two key policies at the United Nations, with a substantial diminution of Ireland's promotion of its peacekeeping proposals, and the realisation of a decade-long objective with the formulation and endorsement of the NPT. The formulation of the NPT also symbolised the increasing relegation of disarmament matters to a bilateral basis between the superpowers. This year was also significant for contributing to a change of emphasis in Irish foreign policy with a redirection of energy towards Europe following the retirement of de Gaulle and the removal of France's veto over expansion of the EEC. The Hague summit of that year brought eventual Irish admission to the EEC within reach.

Chapter Ten

1969: A United Nations peacekeeping force for Northern Ireland?

NOEL DORR

I

Introduction

'[A] model from which students of diplomatic technique can learn much': this is how Andrew Boyd of *The Economist*, writing two years later, described the events of August 1969 when Ireland, for the first and only time, tried to put the Northern Ireland issue formally on the agenda of the United Nations.[1]

Today, there is a cordial partnership – perhaps even a degree of personal friendship – between the Taoiseach, Bertie Ahern, and the British Prime Minister, Tony Blair, as they work closely together to bring the long and winding peace process in Northern Ireland to a successful conclusion. In contrast, in the late 1960s at the start of the troubles in Northern Ireland, the relationship between the two governments was a good deal more distant – and sometimes strained. Even then, however, the approach taken at the United Nations was quite unlike that followed by other countries whose disputes come before the Security Council. Ireland's request to the Council for a United Nations peacekeeping force did indeed cast the two countries into opposing roles. But despite this, the episode was conducted with courtesy and with a degree of that adversarial restraint which has often characterised Anglo-Irish relations, even at moments of high tension. Now that times have changed greatly it is of interest to look back at this largely forgotten episode: how did it come about and was Boyd too kind in his assessment of how it was handled?

The Irish Permanent Representative at the United Nations at the time was Con Cremin. Eleven years later he wrote an interesting, but cautious

---

[1] Andrew Boyd, *Fifteen Men on a Powder Keg: A History of the UN Security Council* (New York, 1971), p. 329.

account of the handling of this episode in New York.[2] More recently, Ronan Fanning, working from the archives and from interviews, has given a broader and more comprehensive account of the response of the British and Irish governments to the Northern Ireland crisis over the whole of the two-year period 1968–69.[3] The present, more personal memoir, elaborates on Cremin's account of the events of August-September 1969 at the United Nations and seeks to situate those events against the general background of Ireland's approach to the Northern Ireland issue at the United Nations over the first decade and a half of Ireland's United Nations membership.

II
Background: 1956–1969

Ireland was admitted to the United Nations at the end of 1955 and by 1969 it had fourteen years experience as a member state. Irish delegations had played an active role each year at the annual session of the General Assembly and the speeches and initiatives of the Minister for External Affairs, Frank Aiken, especially in the late 1950s and early 1960s, had had a considerable resonance at home. Freddie Boland's presidency of the General Assembly in 1960 had received wide coverage and had won great respect.[4] Ireland had also established a good record in United Nations peacekeeping in the Congo and in Cyprus; Irish soldiers had died abroad on United Nations service;[5] and Conor Cruise O'Brien's book on his experiences in Katanga had attracted wide attention.[6] All of this contributed greatly to rooting deeply in domestic opinion the conviction that, if Ireland did not exactly 'bestride the United Nations like a colossus' as *The Economist* unwisely put it in 1960, it had certainly played an honourable role in the work of the organisation. So it was understandable that, when trouble erupted in Northern Ireland in the late 1960s, many Irish people were ready to see the United Nations as a world moral authority, with a capacity for peacekeeping, which might have a helpful role to play.

Over the years, Frank Aiken had made references to the partition issue from time to time in speeches to the General Assembly; and other members of the Irish delegation had touched on it sometimes in debates in committees on other issues.[7] But Ireland had not raised the issue of Northern Ireland

---

[2] Con Cremin, 'Northern Ireland at the United Nations August/September 1969', *Irish Studies in International Affairs* 1:2 (1980), pp. 67–73.

[3] Ronan Fanning, 'Playing It Cool: the Response of the British and Irish Governments to the Crisis in Northern Ireland, 1968–9', *Irish Studies in International Affairs* 12 (2001), pp. 57–85.

[4] See Michael Kennedy's chapter above pp. 154–181.

[5] See the chapters above by Richard Heaslip (pp. 79–116) and Edward Burke (pp. 117–153).

[6] Conor Cruise O' Brien, *To Katanga and Back: A UN case study* (London, 1962).

[7] Conor Cruise O'Brien, for example, gave a lengthy analysis of 'this general question of partition' in a debate on Korea and Vietnam in the Special Political Committee on 14 Oct. 1957. He spoke at some length about 'self-determination' in a First Committee debate on Cyprus on 11 Dec. 1957. He

formally at the United Nations despite the fact that, as minister, Aiken received letters from time to time in the mid-1960s from certain Irish-American groups pressing him to do so. As a member of the delegation in those years, I remember helping to draft replies for his signature. Those were the years of Lemass and Lynch meetings with Terence O'Neill, the Prime Minister of Northern Ireland, a time of 'hands across the border', and the replies we drafted focused on this approach. In Irish government circles, there was also a memory of the unsuccessful and unfortunate 'sore thumb' policy followed at the Council of Europe where the partition issue had been raised constantly in the early 1950s. The policy had achieved little but the boredom and irritation of other delegations. Aiken preferred to focus on establishing a respectable record for Ireland as 'a good United Nations member'.

Did he have in mind that, once this had been established, Ireland might then raise the issue in some way in the United Nations? I may be imputing later thinking to him but I am inclined to doubt it. His instinct, I think, as a Northerner himself, would have been that the Northern Ireland question was essentially a matter for the peoples of Ireland, and of Britain and Ireland, to resolve between themselves: taking it to an international forum would have been a confession of failure which would achieve nothing.

If the issue of the partition of Ireland as such had been raised formally in the General Assembly in those years, it would in any event have been difficult to get support for Ireland's case. One problem would be the Agreement of 1925: after the collapse of the Boundary Commission, the then government of the Irish Free State had in effect accepted partition in return for a financial settlement. That Agreement was signed before the Fianna Fáil party entered the Dáil; and Eamon de Valera's government in the 1930s, like all later Fianna Fáil governments, refused to accept its validity. However, if the partition issue became a matter of legal argument internationally, or if it were ever submitted to the International Court of Justice in The Hague, then the issue would be judged on legal, and not on political grounds. In that case the existence of that Agreement would be a serious obstacle from the viewpoint of the Irish government.

It might seem, of course, that playing it as a 'colonial issue' at the United Nations would prove a trump card. But, equally, that argument, if not carefully handled, could go wrong: many newly independent countries,

---

[7] *contd.* told the Committee on that occasion 'Self-determination, as applied by the United Kingdom, in our experience is an elastic doctrine. It can cover the whole of the British Isles and cause them to be so called, or it can cover the North-Eastern corner of one of the islands. What it does not cover is what one would naturally and normally expect it to cover – self-determination for the people of the island of Ireland.' The partition of Ireland was also touched on by the Permanent Representative, Freddie Boland on 21 Feb. 1957 in a First Committee debate on Cyprus and on 26 Nov. 1957 in a debate on West Irian. Other members of the delegation also referred to it on occasion in other Committees. In more recent times, the practice has been for the Minister for Foreign Affairs in his General Debate speech at the start of each annual session to report, generally in positive terms to the General Assembly on progress in the peace process.

which had themselves learned to live with the division of whole peoples separated by the illogically drawn borders of the colonial era, would be wary of the idea of changing borders now, especially after an interval of fifty years. In any case, most member states would see it as essentially a dispute about the territory of Northern Ireland: should it remain part of the United Kingdom or become part of a new united Ireland? In such cases, there is a strong tendency to look to the wishes of a majority of the population in the territory in question – an approach which, in the case of Northern Ireland would serve to confirm and consolidate the Unionist position.

Another possibility might have been to raise the question solely as an issue relating to the human rights – or more specifically the civil and political rights – of the minority in Northern Ireland. This would certainly have drawn attention to the problem. But in Ireland we have tended too easily, in the past at least, to believe that if wrongs can only be brought to world attention, they will be righted. Sadly, this is not always the case. It certainly was not so in the late 1950s and early 1960s. It seems to me questionable whether 'internationalising' the issue in this kind of adversarial way – and probably having to return to it regularly at each annual session – would have achieved much more in practice than the futile 'anti-partition' campaign of the early 1950s at the Council of Europe. It would also have meant relying on general provisions in various Articles of the Charter. In those years, negotiation of what is today quite a dense network of United Nations Conventions on human rights issues, with provisions for 'peer review' by other member states, was only just beginning. And some important Western countries took the rule in the Charter against intervention by the United Nations in a state's internal affairs so seriously that they had even been dubious about voting for resolutions calling for action against apartheid in South Africa.

Exchange of memoranda 1958

I recall that, nevertheless, in early 1958, Conor Cruise O'Brien, writing from the department in Dublin, and the permanent representative, Freddie Boland responding from New York, had exchanged memoranda about the possibility of asking to have the issue of Irish unity placed on the agenda of the General Assembly. Interestingly enough in view of his later position, it was O'Brien who promoted the idea while Boland opposed it strongly. O'Brien even went so far as to draft a possible resolution. This would have the Assembly, in the preamble, '[recognise] that the principle of self-determination is applicable to the people of Ireland'; '[note] that the island of Ireland is a historical as well as a geographical unit' and '[note] also that the present division of the island is contrary to the wishes of the great majority of the inhabitants'. The resolution in a single operative paragraph would then '[call] on all those concerned, including the Governments of Great

Britain, of Ireland, and of Northern Ireland, to discuss the problem, with a view to making progress towards a peaceful, just and democratic solution'.

The practice in the General Assembly is to assign various items on its agenda, according to subject matter, for debate in one or other of seven specialised committees. All member states are represented in each of these committees. When a resolution, after detailed debate, has been adopted by a committee, it is referred onward to a plenary meeting of the General Assembly for final approval. O'Brien's view was that, if we placed the issue on the Assembly agenda, it would be referred for debate to the Special Political Committee; and he believed that it would be possible to get that committee to adopt the kind of resolution he envisaged. It would not be possible however to get it through a plenary session of the Assembly. So he proposed a somewhat convoluted procedural approach. Once the committee had adopted the resolution, Ireland would approach Canada and India informally and ask them to propose a compromise resolution. This would delete the pre-ambular paragraphs about self-determination from the Irish draft resolution and leave only the operative paragraph calling on the three governments to enter into discussions about 'a peaceful, just and democratic solution'. The General Assembly would then approve this text.

This, he felt, would bring 'the problem of Partition' to the forefront of world attention; possibly bring movement; and, in any case, give new heart to the minority in Northern Ireland. But it would be necessary also, he thought, to tell the United Nations that there was no question of coercing the Northern Ireland majority. To meet this point, the resolution would need to avoid calling for an all-Ireland plebiscite; it would have to be clear that no solution would be imposed on a recalcitrant local majority; and there would be a new emphasis on economic cooperation between North and South. In this way, so he argued, it would be possible to combine a 'co-operative' with a 'United Nations' approach to the Northern Ireland issue.

Boland, responding a month later, took a diametrically opposite view: he argued that it would simply not be possible to combine the two approaches; and in any case, a positive case for raising the issue, as proposed, had not been made. There was no certainty that a resolution would even get through the Special Political Committee. Even if Ireland did get a resolution advocating talks through the Assembly, it would have to report back to the United Nations a year later that the talks had got nowhere. It would then be fated to continue pursuing the issue, vainly, year after year. In any case, the Unionist majority in Northern Ireland would see the initiative as a new form of coercion by the South; and in any debate, the British delegation would rest their case on the 1925 Agreement and offer, if necessary, to submit the issue to the International Court of Justice in The Hague where it would be decided on legal and not political grounds. This was something the Irish government could not accept.

This exchange of memoranda across the Atlantic between two heavy-weights in the Irish Foreign Service, was, to my knowledge, the only serious consideration given to raising the issue of Northern Ireland formally at the United Nations over the fourteen year period between our admission to United Nations membership and 1969. I have sometimes wondered if it is just possible that Conor made the proposal simply in order to have Boland shoot it down – what a billiards player might call a cannon, off Boland, aimed at Aiken. On balance I doubt this. In any case, his proposal to raise the issue formally was never pursued.

III

Derry: August 1969

By the summer of 1969, however, the whole situation had changed. Leaders of the Nationalist minority in Northern Ireland were agitating vigorously for civil rights; reforms initially envisaged by the Northern Prime Minister, Terence O'Neill, were slow in coming and opposed by many Unionists; and there had been sporadic violence against civil rights marchers and others of the minority. In August 1969 the situation became extremely serious. The Apprentice Boys parade in Derry on 12 August led to violent disturbances; the trouble spread; and Nationalist areas in Derry and Belfast came under attack. Policing by the RUC was inadequate at best; at worst, it appeared that some of the police in Derry and in Belfast had themselves been among the attackers. The British government decided to deploy troops on the streets in both cities to protect Nationalists; and refugees from Belfast were crossing the Border to seek safety in the South. Emotions were high in the South as well as in the North; and in Dublin, as we now know, the Taoiseach Jack Lynch faced serious divisions within his own government about what was to be done.[8]

Already, before the parade, the Irish government had been apprehensive about what might happen. Dr Hillery, who had been appointed Minister for External Affairs only two months before, travelled to London on 1 August.[9] There he had a meeting at the Foreign Office, kept private at the time, with the Foreign Secretary in the Labour government, Michael Stewart. Hillery warned the Foreign Secretary that the Apprentice Boys' parade of 12 August

---

[8] Ronan Fanning, who interviewed Hillery on 20 June 2001, gives a graphic account of the atmosphere in the Irish Cabinet in his paper 'Playing It Cool', pp. 73–74: 'When Hillery got back to Dublin Lynch warned him that his Cabinet colleagues were "very excited": Lynch "was particularly surprised at Lenihan." Hillery likened one of the subsequent emergency Cabinet meetings to "a ballad session ... They were all talking patriotic ... I remember being sure our army was not as well armed as the B Specials, not to talk of the British army."'

[9] At this point his title in English was still 'Minister for External Affairs', which had been the usage in countries of the Commonwealth. Dr Hillery himself was later responsible for the change in the title of the post to 'Minister for Foreign Affairs' – although interestingly enough the title in Irish 'Aire Gnóthaí Eachtracha' has remained unchanged.

had been 'deliberately stepped up': there would be some seventy bands as against about seventeen in previous years. Derry, he said, had become 'a powder keg' and something could be started there which it might be very difficult to contain.[10] He would prefer to see the parade banned. But if this was not possible, the sponsors should at least be required to limit it to the normal size and keep it to a particular area; the B Specials should not be allowed a role in policing it; and the British government should arrange for impartial observers.

The Foreign Secretary, to say the least, was not very receptive. It was better to control the parade than to ban it, he said – this was an approach which had proved correct recently in Bermuda. Although the British government was kept in close touch with the situation, primary responsibility for the area lay with the Northern Ireland government. There were now some hopeful signs that that government was taking steps towards reform. In any case he had to say that 'there is a limit to the extent to which we can discuss with outsiders – even our nearest neighbours – this internal matter'.

Although Dr Hillery was clearly dissatisfied with this response he had to conclude that there was no possibility of taking the matter further with the British side at that point. He concluded the discussion with a warning of the danger of a 'spill over' into violence: if this happened he would come under increasing pressure to act. His predecessor (Frank Aiken), he said, had gone to the United Nations during a previous outbreak of trouble in Derry although he did not raise the problem formally before any United Nations body. However, if violence should occur in Derry it might well spill over into the South and then he, as minister, would have to deal with the situation and 'it might have to be raised'.

Aiken's New York meeting: April 1969

In speaking of Aiken having gone previously 'to the United Nations', Dr Hillery was referring to an episode in late April 1969. At that point, the Irish government was already concerned about growing trouble in Derry, following the Burntollet and other civil rights marches, and it had sent Aiken, as Minister for External Affairs, to brief the Secretary-General, U Thant on the situation.

In view of what happened later, it is interesting to look back at the press conference which Aiken gave in New York on 23 April 1969 after his meeting with the Secretary-General. He first laid out for journalists, at some length, what was then the standard Irish account of partition with quotations from Asquith and Churchill about its impermanence. He recalled that 'not even one Irish member [of Parliament] voted for the Partition of Ireland – for the 1920 Act'. He expressed his hope for 'the restoration of Irish unity' by peaceful means and for a continuation of 'the evolution that has gone on

---

[10] NAI DFA 2000/6/557, 'Notes of a discussion at the Foreign Office, Friday 1 August 1969'.

amongst the Unionists in the North ... [so that] ... we can have a settlement in the mutual interests of all the people of all parts of Ireland'. Having laid out this standard background however, he made it clear that his focus was not on ending Partition but on civil rights and on the need for reform in Northern Ireland. When asked whether he might bring the issue at some stage to one of the United Nations bodies which dealt with the remnants of colonialism, he responded that 'the best way ... is to settle this between ourselves'; and when pressed about bringing it to one of the United Nations human rights bodies, he stressed that the only purpose of his visit was to keep the Secretary-General, 'the principal officer of the international organisation for peace' informed.

Perhaps his most interesting response, in the light of later events, was his answer to a journalist who asked whether he had discussed with the Secretary-General '... the possible use at any time of a United Nations Peace-keeping Force to maintain the peace in Northern Ireland?' Aiken replied 'I didn't. The Government have taken no decision to ask for a Peacekeeping Force and I think there is sufficient wisdom if it can only be energised in our section of the world, in these islands off the North West of Europe, to settle this problem.'[11]

August 1969 – the Apprentice Boys parade

By August 1969, however, Aiken who, by then, had led successive Irish delegations to the United Nations General Assembly for twelve years, had gone from office; and in a deteriorating situation the view of the Irish government on this point had changed, as Dr Hillery had warned Michael Stewart obliquely on 1 August that it might.

On Wednesday 13 August 1969, the day after the Apprentice Boys parade, there was an emergency meeting of the Irish government. That afternoon, while the government was still meeting, it sent word to the Secretary of the Department of External Affairs[12] to issue an instruction to the Irish Ambassador in London[13]: he was 'to convey immediately to the British government the request that they arrange for the immediate cessation of the police attacks on the people of Derry'.[14] The ambassador was on leave so, in his absence, the chargé d'affaires, Kevin Rush, acting on the instruction, sought an appointment with the Foreign Secretary. He too was on leave, so Rush met late that afternoon with Lord Chalfont, Minister of State, who was handling business at the Foreign Office during the holiday month of August.

---

[11] Quotations are taken from a verbatim transcript of Aiken's press conference in New York on 23 April 1969, published by the Department of External Affairs (of Ireland) as 1/69 in the series 'Statements and Speeches'.

[12] Hugh McCann.

[13] Jack Molloy.

[14] NAI 2000/9/2, G.C. 13/11, 13 Aug. 1969.

It is interesting to note the speed with which this meeting was arranged which may indicate that the British government, in a change from the Foreign Secretary's complacency of 1 August, was by now seriously concerned. Rush received the instruction from Dublin at 3.30 pm: an hour and a half later he was received by Chalfont in his room at the Foreign Office.

Rush brought with him an aide-memoire setting out the text of the message he had been asked to convey. However, while he was in an ante-room at the Foreign Office waiting to be taken in to Chalfont, he received another telephone call from the department in Dublin. This presumably was the result of a further decision of the Cabinet. He was now also to request the British government to apply immediately to the United Nations for the urgent dispatch of a peacekeeping force to the Six Counties of Northern Ireland and (to say that) the government has instructed the Irish Permanent Representative to the United Nations to inform the Secretary-General of the foregoing.[15]

Immediately thereafter Rush was taken in to see Chalfont. He handed over the aide-memoire which he had prepared on the basis of the earlier instruction and supplemented it orally by reading out the text of the later message which he had just received by telephone in the waiting room. The Foreign Office official acting as note-taker, duly noted this text.

Chalfont was courteous enough in his response but he maintained the standard position of the British government at the time: he would note all that had been said and convey it to the Home Office which was the responsible department; personally, he could not for a single moment accept that the police were attacking the people of Derry; and as to the United Nations, the issue was 'an internal affair of the United Kingdom, it was not a matter which it would be appropriate to raise at the United Nations'. When showing Rush out, the Foreign Office note-taker confirmed with him his own impression of what Rush had said: the Irish government was requesting the British government to take up the matter of a peacekeeping force with the United Nations – the Irish government was not proposing to do this itself. Two days later, in an aide-mémoire to the Embassy, the Foreign and Commonwealth Office confirmed the position taken by Chalfont: the British government did not regard a United Nations peacekeeping force as either appropriate or necessary and therefore did not propose to accede to the request of the Irish government.

Also on 13 August 1969, the day after the Apprentice Boys parade, the Taoiseach, Jack Lynch, in a television statement expressed his 'deep sadness' at the tragic events in Derry and elsewhere. He noted that the Irish government had 'acted with great restraint' for several months: they had made their views known to the British government on a number of occasions but they had been 'careful to do nothing that would exacerbate the situation'. It was clear now 'that the present situation cannot be allowed to continue … [and]

---

[15] Ibid.

'clear, also, that the Irish Government can no longer stand by and see inno-
cent people injured and perhaps worse'.[16] Lynch went on

> It is obvious that the RUC is no longer accepted as an impartial police
> force. Neither would the employment of British troops be acceptable
> nor would they be likely to restore peaceful conditions – certainly not
> in the long term. The Irish Government have, therefore, requested the
> British Government to apply immediately to the United Nations for
> the urgent dispatch of a Peace-keeping Force to the Six Counties of
> Northern Ireland and have instructed the Irish Permanent
> Representative to the United Nations to inform the Secretary-General
> of this request.

Lynch announced that the government was sending army field hospitals to
the border to cater for those of the injured who did not wish to be treated in
Six County hospitals; and he went on to raise the possibility of talks about
re-unification:

> Recognising, however, that the re-unification of the national territory
> can provide the only permanent solution for the problem, it is our
> intention to request the British Government to enter into early nego-
> tiations with the Irish Government to review the present constitu-
> tional position of the Six Counties of Northern Ireland.

On 15 August, Dr Hillery, who had been recalled urgently from a holiday in
the West of Ireland,[17] travelled to London to meet his British equivalent.
After some delay he was received eventually at the Foreign Office by Lord
Chalfont, Minister of State at the Foreign Office, and Lord Stoneham, his
counterpart at the Home Office. This was the holiday period and the Foreign
Secretary, Michael Stewart, was still away. Chalfont was reluctant and far
from gracious about the meeting. He began by saying that he considered it
'useful' to have discussions on these matters.[18] But he qualified this with what
seemed like a slight reproof: 'I am personally sorry that it was not possible to
have a prior agreement regarding your visit'. He maintained the official position that 'anything happening there [i.e. in Northern Ireland] is an internal
matter to be dealt with by the Home Department' [i.e. the Home Office].

---

[16] NAI 2000/5/12, 'Statement by the Taoiseach Mr J. Lynch', 13 Aug. 1969. The popular memory
has it that Lynch said that the Irish government can no longer stand *idly* by (emphasis added) but
the word 'idly' does not appear in the text which I have which was issued at the time or in the collected volume of Lynch's statements and speeches at this time (*Speeches and Statements on Irish Unity,
Northern Ireland, Anglo-Irish Relations August 1969–October 1971*, Government Information Bureau,
Dublin 1971 p. 2). Ronan Fanning notes that a draft prepared by the Department of Foreign Affairs
for possible use by the Taoiseach did include the word ('Playing it cool', p. 73).
[17] Fanning in 'Playing It Cool' mentions that the minister was on a painting holiday in Achill (p. 72).
[18] NAI 2000/6/558, confidential report of discussion at Foreign Office, London, 15 Aug. 1969.

Dr Hillery recalled that he had told the Foreign Secretary on 1 August that the Irish government was seriously perturbed about what might happen if the Apprentice Boys parade went ahead in Derry on 12 August. 'On that occasion I accepted the point that the control of the situation was at present in your hands but not that it is solely your internal affair'. Now, he went on, 'There is trouble for all of us – serious, grave trouble'. He told Chalfont and Stoneham that

> this situation is not one that can be handled by a partisan peace-keeping force. So perhaps your troops and ours could be combined together to form a peace-keeping force acceptable to both sides or alternatively, there could be a United Nations force.

Chalfont accepted that there was concern on the part of the Irish government and he understood why they were anxious to discuss the matter. But the maintenance of law and order in the United Kingdom was

> primarily our [i.e. Britain's] concern. This responsibility is exercised in concert with the Government of Northern Ireland ... As regards the need for a United Nations or international intervention, we consider it is simply not necessary. It is well within our capacity to deal with the situation not only for juridical reasons, but because we are confident we can deal with it in an impartial way. The presence of any international or joint force in the area would be totally irrelevant and here I might add that our view is shared by the Secretary-General of the United Nations.

Later Chalfont, apparently responding to what the Taoiseach had said on television on the evening of 13 August, said

> I find it irrational although perhaps psychologically predictable, to say that the presence of troops is intolerable to anybody. How can the presence of troops in towns of the United Kingdom be intolerable to anyone except the people in those towns? It isn't anyone else's business.

Hillery asked to talk to the Prime Minister, Harold Wilson, but he was on holidays in the Scilly Isles. Chalfont said he would report to him, and to the Home Secretary, what Hillery had said but he could not hold out any hope of talks with the Prime Minister.

It is interesting that Chalfont could say to Hillery that the United Nations Secretary-General, U Thant, shared the view of the British government on the question of an international force. So far as I know, there is no evidence that the Irish side were aware that U Thant had been consulted on such a proposal at this stage. However, the United Kingdom, like the other four Permanent Members of the Security Council, enjoys something of a special status at the United Nations: one might surmise that Chalfont had received a report from the British representative who may perhaps have sounded out U Thant privately after Lynch's statement of 13 August.

Did the Irish government at this point really expect that the British government would agree either to set up a joint peacekeeping operation with the Irish side, or to request the United Nations to send a peacekeeping force? In retrospect it seems unlikely. But in any event, the proposal had now been put and rejected. The Irish government was under severe pressure at home and, as we now know, it was internally divided between 'hardliners' and those who favoured a more 'level-headed' approach to the Northern crisis. So on his return to Dublin, the government decided that the Minister for Foreign Affairs, Dr Hillery should go at once to New York to ask the Security Council for such a force. He left for New York on the afternoon of Saturday, 16 August 1969.

The government had met earlier that same day – a Saturday meeting was a most unusual event – and it had considered a 'Memorandum for the Information of the Government' prepared by the Department of External Affairs under the heading 'Bringing the Situation in the North of Ireland before the UN'.[19] This document considered various options both for the approach which might be taken and the United Nations body in which it could be raised.

As to how to approach the question, it said that there were three possibilities: it could be raised as a threat to the peace; as an issue of self-determination; or as a human rights question. As where to raise it, the memorandum, in what seems like an excessive attempt to be exhaustive, suggested that that could be done in any one of five main organs of the United Nations – not only in the Security Council or the Assembly but also in the Economic and Social Council, or with the Secretary-General or at the International Court of Justice. Of these, it suggested, the most relevant seemed to be the Security Council, which would make it necessary to imply in some way that there was a 'threat to the peace'; or, alternatively, the General Assembly, where the main emphasis would probably have to be on 'human rights'. The memorandum then gave an estimate – presumably on the basis of a report from Cremin in New York – of what the reaction in the Security Council would be if an effort were made to raise the issue there: the 'maximum affirmative vote' in the Council in favour of placing the issue on the agenda would be eight, whereas nine positive votes would be needed. In view of later events it is interesting that it advised the government that

---

19 NAI 2000/6/558.

Ireland would have no right to participate in the discussion about the placing of such an item on the Security Council Agenda and only if it were to be admitted to debate would we be invited to participate, without vote, in the subsequent discussion.

For this reason, the memorandum concluded, raising the issue in the General Assembly 'seems to be the most profitable course'. However this did not preclude raising it eventually in the Security Council 'although such action has practically no prospect of success, if for no other reason than because of the British attitude and the fact that Britain has a veto'.

It is clear from this that there was some awareness in Dublin of the difficulties, at least among External Affairs officials with a good knowledge of the United Nations. The government, nevertheless, went ahead; and within hours, Dr Hillery, who had taken over from Frank Aiken only two months earlier, was on his way to New York to raise – or seek to raise – the issue with the United Nations Security Council.

On the face of it, it should have been obvious that his mission to seek a peacekeeping force was a difficult one which was unlikely to be successful without the support, or at least the acquiescence, of the government of the United Kingdom. The United Kingdom was, after all, a Permanent Member of the Council with the right of veto. It is true that the request for a peace-keeping force would be submitted under Chapter 6 of the Charter which deals with 'Pacific Settlement of Disputes' rather than under Chapter 7 which deals with 'Threats to the Peace'. The distinction is important: when the Council takes a decision under Chapter 6, 'a party to a dispute shall abstain from voting'; in a vote under Chapter 7 on the other hand, the veto right applies, so the United Kingdom would be able to block a decision.

The first question, however, was whether the Council would even agree to consider the question. The United Kingdom would certainly argue strongly that Northern Ireland was a purely internal matter; and it would point to Article 2.7 of the Charter which states clearly that the United Nations is not authorised 'to intervene in matters which are essentially within the domestic jurisdiction of any state'. Indeed in arguing that it was an internal matter, the United Kingdom might conceivably call the United Nations Charter itself in evidence: the Charter explicitly names 'The United Kingdom of Great Britain *and Northern Ireland*' (emphasis added) as one of the five Permanent Members of the Security Council. At that stage, United Kingdom governments took a rigid legal approach to the constitutional position of Northern Ireland within the United Kingdom: they had not yet come to accept, as they did from 1973 onwards, that, whatever the formal legal position, the Irish government must have a substantial role to play in any settlement of the Northern Ireland troubles.

Even if the Council did debate the issue, a further question would follow from the argument that Northern Ireland was an internal matter for the

United Kingdom. The principle that a United Nations peacekeeping force could operate only with consent was clear: in 1967, U Thant had felt obliged to withdraw UNEF I, the United Nations force in Sinai, when Egypt withdrew the consent it had initially given for its presence. How then could the Council agree to send a peacekeeping force to Northern Ireland over British objections?

Even if those considerable difficulties could be overcome, further questions would arise. Would the United Nations be willing to involve itself in an internal policing role of indefinite duration in a developed country of Western Europe? United Nations peacekeeping at the time was still, in some ways, on an uncertain footing, especially as regards financing. When the Security Council agreed five years previously, to send a United Nations peacekeeping force to Cyprus, France and the Soviet Union had both abstained on the key paragraph of the resolution setting up the force – even though the force would have the consent of Cyprus itself, as well as Greece, Turkey and the United Kingdom.[20] The United Nations force in the Sinai, interposed between the organised forces of Israel and Egypt, with their consent, had been successful enough before its withdrawal in 1967. The Congo experience of the early 1960s, on the other hand, had shown how difficult – and even dangerous – it was for the United Nations to be drawn into dealing with a chaotic situation within a state. There were other questions too: who would take part in such a force; how would it be received in a divided society where the majority community would probably oppose its very presence; how long would it remain; and, even if welcomed initially, would it soon become part of the problem itself, subject to attack from both sides, as indeed happened later with the British army?

Looking back now, more than a generation later, we might ask a further question about this episode: was its basic aim to obtain, or merely to be seen to ask for, a United Nations peacekeeping force? No doubt the Irish government at the time believed in a broad and general way that a United Nations peacekeeping force could help. But to those who knew the United Nations, the odds were against getting such a force: the memorandum for the government from External Affairs of 16 August, basing itself no doubt on reporting by Cremin in New York, had concluded, bluntly enough, that 'such action has practically no prospect of success'. Undoubtedly, the 'hardliners' in government, with little knowledge of the United Nations, would have discounted this assessment by what they would think of as the faint-hearted officials of External Affairs. But, we can see now that yielding to the hardliners to the extent of being seen to 'take the issue to the United Nations', served a useful purpose in itself in helping Jack Lynch to ride the turbulence in the

---

[20] See *Yearbook of the United Nations. Special Edition: UN Fiftieth Anniversary 1945–95* (The Hague, 1995) p. 76. The resolution as a whole was adopted unanimously by the Council but the USSR, France and Czechoslovakia abstained on operative paragraph 4.

Cabinet and, more generally, to defuse tension in the South. It also, to a degree, added to the pressure on London to bring needed reform to Northern Ireland. A cynic might perhaps also think that it was intended to provide a basis from which the Irish government could say 'I told you so' later, if it felt a need to criticise the role or the actions of the British army in Northern Ireland.

In retirement, eleven years on, the late Con Cremin, who had succeeded Freddie Boland as Ireland's Permanent Representative (that is, Ambassador) to the United Nations in New York, published an account of this whole episode.[21] It is accurate and correct, as anyone who knew Con Cremin would expect. But it is also carefully written and circumspect: those of us who knew him would expect no less. It does not quite convey the enormity of the task which faced Dr Hillery, and the degree of improvisation which necessarily followed the sudden decision to send him to New York to appear before the Security Council; and it is cautious too, about referring to some of what the delegation learned at the time of the likely attitude of countries represented on the Council.

IV
New York – The Security Council

In his published paper, Cremin recounts how he, as Irish Permanent Representative, wrote on Sunday 17 August 1969 to the Spanish Ambassador who was President of the Council for that month to ask for an urgent meeting. This was Jaime de Pinies: a strong and colourful character who was reputed to have served on both sides in the Spanish Civil War. He spent most of his career as Spain's United Nations representative and at one point was elected to serve for a year as President of the General Assembly. At this time, he represented Franco's Spain. I came to know him well later, as a colleague on the Security Council, to which Spain was again elected, along with Ireland, in 1981–82. At that stage, he spoke, with equal conviction, for a new democratic Spanish government. He boasted to me many times that he personally had played a large part in securing a hearing for Dr Hillery. No doubt he felt that there is an affinity between Spain and Ireland. In any case, Spain had its own long-standing dispute with Britain about Gibraltar.

The presidency of the Security Council rotates alphabetically, on a monthly basis, among the fifteen member states on the Council. While the representative holding the presidency cannot impose his or her views on other member states, a good president will consult widely with colleagues and seek to promote agreement. De Pinies, in his capacity as president at this time, took an active approach to his role.

Cremin's memoir, published eleven years later, mentions that Dr Hillery had conversations with each member of the Security Council and that he

---

[21] See pp. 253–254 above.

kept in very close touch with the President (de Pinies) and the Secretary-General but he does not go into detail on any of these exchanges. In fact, Dr Hillery and he met informally, with de Pinies at his residence, that Sunday morning before he sent his formal letter requesting a meeting of the Council. De Pinies was helpful to his Irish visitors.[22] He advised them on the terms of the letter which Cremin was later to send to him in his capacity as President of the Council for that month: it should stress the urgency of the situation and also the possibility that events in Northern Ireland would lead to 'international friction'. This echo of a phrase in Chapter 6 (Article 34) of the Charter which deals with the 'Pacific Settlement of International Disputes', would bring the question more clearly within the remit of the Council.

Cremin's letter, carefully drafted to take account of these suggestions, was duly sent to de Pinies early that Sunday evening. De Pinies lost no time in consulting, as he was required to do, with other member states about the Irish request to hold a meeting of the Council. He was able to tell Cremin shortly after ten that Sunday evening that he had spoken to all but one of the fifteen representatives.[23] There seemed to be general agreement that a meeting should be called but this of course was only a first step – it did not mean that the Council would necessarily agree to discuss the issue. De Pinies' own thinking at this stage, which he may have discussed with his French colleague, seems to have been that the issue would be placed on the agenda of the Council and, after both sides had been heard, he would propose that the members of the Council would wish to reflect on what had been said. He, speaking as President, would then express the Council's concern about the situation and its hope that all concerned would refrain from anything which might aggravate it. He would then adjourn the meeting and leave the date of any future meeting to be determined in consultations.

I think we may conclude from this that de Pinies probably realised already from his consultations that Sunday evening that it was very doubtful if the Council would ever agree to send a peacekeeping force to Northern Ireland. The procedure he had in mind would, however, seize the Council of the issue, formally at least, and allow it to express concern in a very general way, while saving face and honour all around.

On that same Sunday evening, 17 August, Lord Caradon, the British Permanent Representative, who had been away, telephoned Cremin at his residence and remonstrated with him, gently enough, for not telling him, Caradon, in advance that Ireland was going to raise the Northern Ireland issue in the Security Council. Cremin replied that he had assumed that, after Hillery's meeting with Chalfont on 15 August, he, Caradon, would have been fully briefed by London. Caradon then suggested that he meet Dr

---

[22] The account which follows of contacts with Security Council members draws on a memorandum by Ambassador Cremin of 16 October 1969. Copy in the possession of the author.

[23] He could not reach the Ambassador of Paraguay but seems to have spoken to his deputy.

Hillery. He did so at noon on the following day, Monday, in an area between two of the delegates' lounges in the United Nations building.

Caradon, a large, agreeably benevolent man, was at the time a major figure at the United Nations where he had represented the United Kingdom since 1964. If I recall correctly he actually had an apartment lower down in the same building as Cremin, his Irish colleague. He had the rank of Minister of State in Harold Wilson's Labour government. As Sir Hugh Foot, he had been the last British Governor of Cyprus. He was a brother of Michael Foot, later leader of the Labour Party and one of three Foot brothers, known affectionately, if my memory is correct, as 'the three left Feet'. He had a disarming way of responding to criticism of Britain's colonial record by boasting that it had given 600 million people their independence in his lifetime. As I heard him repeat this many times in United Nations debates, I sometimes wondered if he ever thought of the corollary – if it was Britain which granted them independence, then it must have been Britain which deprived them of that independence in the first place. He was popular at the United Nations however, and I do not recall that anyone ever picked him up on the point.

The atmosphere at the meeting, as noted later by Cremin, was 'rather cold'. Caradon did most of the talking. He spoke of the danger of initiating action without knowing precisely where it might end up. He held firmly to the British position that the issue could not appropriately be discussed by the Security Council: Article 2.7 of the Charter precluded United Nations intervention in internal affairs; and Northern Ireland was an integral part of the United Kingdom. So much for what was clearly his formal position. But, he then said, the Irish letter had been sent and the question now was how to resolve the matter with least detriment. The letter would of course have received world-wide publicity and this, he thought, would meet one of the Irish side's possible objectives: it could remain on file and be followed later by other explanatory documents. What he was implying was that, once it had gained some publicity for its initiative in raising the issue, Ireland would decide not to pursue its request to the Council actively at the present time. He must have known that that would not be sufficient.

He then went on to float a second idea which evoked no immediate reaction from the Irish side but which, in retrospect, we can see now as highly significant in that it foreshadowed the way in which the issue was actually dealt with later in the Council. An alternative, Caradon said, could be that, since the minister had come to New York, and since it was impossible to have the item placed on the agenda of the Council, the minister might still be given an opportunity of making a statement. This might meet many of the considerations which lay behind the Irish request to the Council. Dr Hillery listened quietly but did not respond on this point.

On that Monday evening, 18 August, in the course of a reception, there was another significant exchange. Ambassador Max Jakobson, the representative of Finland, which had a seat at the time on the Council, phoned Cremin during the reception and told him that he had been thinking about a possible procedural approach which the Council might take and had found wide acceptance for it. Jakobson was another distinguished United Nations figure who was a candidate for the post of Secretary-General later, in 1971. He might well have been elected but it was said that the Soviet Union believed that his Jewish background would make him unsuitable to deal with the problems of the Middle East. During his phone call, Jakobson outlined to Cremin an approach which, in fact, he went on to propose in the Council two days later: that, in a departure from normal procedure, Dr Hillery should be allowed to address the Council at the stage when it was considering whether or not to accept the issue on its agenda.

A short time later, de Pinies, who was also at the reception, met quietly in a corner with Hillery and Cremin and told them that as a result of his consultations with other Council members, he had concluded that it was now improbable that Ireland would gain the nine votes necessary to place the issue on the agenda of the Security Council. In these circumstances, the best formula to follow would be that outlined already by Jakobson on the phone to Cremin. Significantly enough, de Pinies thought that the idea for such an approach had originated with the United Kingdom. If true, this would mean, in effect, that it had been suggested to Finland by Caradon.

On the following day, Tuesday, 19 August, Jakobson phoned Cremin again and said that he doubted if the Irish request would receive enough votes to be place formally on the agenda. He again outlined to Cremin the procedural approach which he had in mind. He said that he had now polled all members of the Council and had found that it would have general support – although Britain did not like it and wanted to have the Irish request rejected. He asked Cremin to let him know during that afternoon whether or not Ireland would find it acceptable. Cremin later noted that he and the minister, Dr Hillery 'were quite satisfied by then that we did not have the requisite number of votes'. So he phoned Jakobson about 3 pm to say that the Irish side would not object.

At lunch-time that day, de Pinies had confirmed to the Irish side his earlier estimate of the position: his private head-count showed only seven votes in favour of the Irish request to place the issue on the agenda, two short of the necessary nine. Pakistan, Spain, China, Paraguay and Colombia would probably vote in favour; the Soviet Union and Hungary were reticent but he thought that they would do so; he was doubtful about the Africans (Algeria, Nigeria, Senegal and Zambia) – indeed he understood from Algeria that it would probably not vote in favour. Jakobson later suggested to Cremin that the position of the African members on this kind of issue would be influenced by their concern about the effort at secession by Biafra, which had led to the civil war then raging in Nigeria.[24]

---

[24] That is to say that they might be wary of any talk of Irish unity since, in their eyes, it would seem to involve 'secession' by Northern Ireland from the United Kingdom.

Cremin also learned from Ambassador Yost of the US that he had instructions to abstain – because the issue was one of domestic jurisdiction, it was not a threat to international peace, and Britain was taking measures to improve the situation. His French colleague, Berard, was helpful enough in private, advising that the key thing for Ireland was not to suffer a defeat. But, at a meeting with the Irish side on Monday 18 August, he also drew attention to the strong position which France had traditionally taken in regard to the bar in Article 2.7 of the Charter on intervention by the United Nations 'in matters which are essentially within the domestic jurisdiction of any state'. In retrospect, one can surmise that it is most unlikely that France would have gone so far as to vote in favour of the Irish request to put the issue on the agenda. Finland too, if it came to it, would abstain: Jakobson in his phone call had told Cremin this. The United Kingdom of course would oppose. As to the fifteenth member of the Council, Nepal, Cremin had kept in touch with its representative, General Khatri, but de Pinies' view was that he was very erratic.

Later in the afternoon of Tuesday 19 August, de Pinies confirmed that the meeting of the Council had now been fixed for the following day. He also said that there was by then agreement among the members of the Council to follow the procedure suggested by Finland. The United Nations Legal Counsel was perturbed, he said, because he feared that it could open the door to abuse of Council procedures. However, de Pinies said that they could take it that the meeting would follow the Finnish approach: he thought this would be the most satisfactory result from an Irish viewpoint. Dr Hillery confirmed that the Irish side had already told Jakobson that Ireland would not object. Still later, about 8.45 pm, de Pinies phoned Cremin again to urge that in what was by then expected to be Dr Hillery's speech to the Council the next day, there should be an emphasis on the tension and friction along the border in Ireland: this was necessary because several Council members had told him privately that they were not satisfied that Cremin's original letter requesting a Council meeting had shown sufficient evidence of a threat to *international* peace (my emphasis). Cremin noted this but said that they would have to be careful not to overstate the case as this 'might serve to nourish tension'.

Following all of these exchanges, de Pinies called a Council meeting for Wednesday morning to consider the Irish request to put the item on the agenda. (Initially the meeting was to take place on Tuesday 19 August but the Council was still preoccupied at that point with a complaint by Lebanon against Israel.) The Council eventually convened to consider the issue about lunchtime on Wednesday 20 August.

Meetings with the Secretary-General

Over the days before the meeting, Dr Hillery had also been in contact with the Secretary-General, U Thant. U Thant himself tells us of these meetings in his autobiography:

> I met with the Irish ambassador and Foreign Minister several times in 1969 and offered to mediate the dispute. Specifically I proposed that, if both Dublin and London agreed, the question could be looked into by a third party, with or without my involvement. I had in mind the names of two statesmen who were universally recognised to be impartial: Lester Pearson, former Prime Minister of Canada, and Earl Warren, former Chief Justice of the United States. While Dublin appeared receptive to the idea, however, London remained silent. And later, while not referring directly to my proposal, London many times reiterated its position that 'the matter does not lend itself to intervention from outside.[25]

When the Security Council met eventually at lunch-time on Wednesday, Cremin's letter of the previous Sunday was the only item on its provisional agenda. The agenda at this stage, however, could only be provisional: the first business for the Council would be to agree to its adoption. For this, a positive vote from at least nine of the fifteen members would be necessary. This meant that an abstention by any Council member would have the same effect as a vote against.

At the start of the meeting, Lord Caradon, the British representative, objected to the formal approval of the agenda. He said he would not discuss the substantial issues raised in the Irish letter to the President of the Council – he would keep to the principle: the United Nations could not intervene in matters of domestic jurisdiction. Northern Ireland was an issue within the domestic jurisdiction of the United Kingdom; and, in consequence, the United Nations was precluded from dealing with it under Article 2.7 of the Charter which overrides any other Charter provision. The United Kingdom delegation had always believed that the Council should consider all issues properly raised before it but this issue could not properly be raised.

Immediately after Caradon had finished, Jakobson, the Finnish representative, intervened to make the proposal which he had outlined to Cremin on the previous day. He had doubts about the right of the United Nations under the Charter to intervene in this matter. However, he noted that Dr Hillery as Irish Foreign Minister, had come to New York to explain the situation and

---

[25] U Thant, *View from the UN* (London, 1977) p. 55. Con Cremin, in referring to U Thant's memoirs in his essay in *Irish Studies in International Affairs* says on p. 68 that U Thant also mentioned Dr Ralph Bunche, Under-Secretary-General and winner of the Nobel Peace Prize.

present his case in detail; and he suggested that before deciding on the agenda, the Council should hear him as a courtesy, in case the agenda might eventually not be adopted.

Caradon responded that this was a most unusual procedure, for which there were few, if any, precedents. Nevertheless, he said,

> for the reasons and on the basis which has been proposed by the Ambassador of Finland, and as a matter of courtesy to the visiting Foreign Minister who is with us, I would certainly raise no objection to this proposal and I look forward to hearing what the Foreign Minister has to say to us.[26]

The scenario, first mentioned in passing by Caradon to Hillery two days previously, and picked up later by Jakobson of Finland who may perhaps have been encouraged privately by Caradon, was now beginning to play itself out in public in the Council. As a result, Dr Hillery was centre stage; and he now had a full chance to explain the position of the Irish government in relation to Northern Ireland.

Surprisingly enough in retrospect, if my recollection is correct, he had travelled alone to New York with no officials to help in the preparation of the address to the Council in which he was to challenge the position of the United Kingdom, a Permanent Member. The speech had to be prepared in the Irish Permanent Mission to the United Nations once he arrived in New York.[27]

Notwithstanding the short time available, the speech would have to be carefully drafted – and it was. For an Irish domestic audience it had to maintain consistency with the theology of Irish nationalism at the time by situating the whole problem of Northern Ireland against the background of the partition of Ireland in 1920–21. But it also had to avoid treating partition as such as the issue to be brought before the Council. Instead it had to focus on discrimination and the slow pace of reform in Northern Ireland. It had somehow to show that Article 2.7 which bars the United Nations from intervening in 'matters which are essentially within the domestic jurisdiction of any state', was not a barrier to consideration by the Council: it did this by citing the cases of Cyprus and apartheid in South Africa. It also had to explain the point of the initiative of the Irish government: its conviction that,

---

[26] Provisional Verbatim Record of the 1503rd meeting of the Security Council S/PV 1503 20 August 1969.

[27] My memory is that this was done largely by the Permanent Representative Ambassador Con Cremin and Paddy MacKernan, a junior colleague drawn in for the occasion from the Irish Consulate General in New York – though no doubt other officials in the Irish Mission helped. Paddy MacKernan, who was then Deputy Consul-General, was subsequently Irish Ambassador in Washington and in Paris, Permanent Representative to the EU and, like Cremin well before him, Secretary (General) of the Department of Foreign Affairs.

for historic reasons, the British army, then deploying on the streets of Belfast and Derry, would not be acceptable there in the longer term and that a United Nations peacekeeping force was needed instead.

When Dr Hillery had set out all this at length, Zakharov, the Soviet Union representative supported his request that the issue be accepted formally on to the agenda of the Council. Zakharov spoke briefly, and somewhat inaccurately, of discrimination in Northern Ireland as shown, he said, 'by the fact that the right to form a government ... belongs only to one religious community, the Protestants'. In addition to taking measures 'to put an end to the persecution' of those fighting discrimination, the British government, he said, must 'see to it that the necessary conditions are created for the solution of problems in conformity with the wishes of the people of Northern Ireland'. It was an intervention – the only such intervention – in favour of putting the item on the agenda. Dr Hillery no doubt welcomed support from any source, but could be forgiven if he swallowed hard at the terms in which it was expressed.

Caradon then responded, following as we might now speculate, the choreography required by the Jakobson procedure. Dr Hillery's speech, he said, was 'careful and restrained' but of course he could not possibly agree with a lot of what had been said. He did not want to be drawn into a debate on the substance. Nevertheless, he went on to deal with the issues raised.

As to the constitutional position, he said, this was not an international matter: the Irish Republic had, over the years, recognised the fact of partition and had accepted its consequences. There had, for example been meetings between the Prime Minister of the Republic and the Head of Government in Northern Ireland to discuss such matters as cooperation on tourism and electricity supply. He acknowledged that the Foreign Minister shared 'the purposes of reconciliation and the reduction of intense feeling and the restoration of order'. But he should be aware of the dangers of intervention. Now that British troops had been deployed on the streets in Northern Ireland, there was a peacekeeping force already there – and there could be no better or more impartial force. 'Talk about a peacekeeping force being introduced against the wishes of the country concerned [was] a contradiction in terms'. He agreed with Dr Hillery about the importance of human rights; and he cited in full the statement issued by Downing Street about this which had been issued after a meeting on the previous day between Prime Minister Wilson and the Northern Ireland Prime Minister, Chichester Clark. He noted too that 'the Civil Rights Movement in the North is directed not to the transfer of Northern Ireland from the United Kingdom but to internal reform'. The programme of reform was under way.

At the close of his speech he stressed again to members of the Council that to breach the principle of domestic jurisdiction would have the most serious consequences.

We have gone out of our way and departed from established practices in order to pay respect and courtesy to the visiting Foreign Minister and enable him to speak to us today.

He had, he said, heard a suggestion, in consultations, that having heard the minister, the Council might wish to adjourn the meeting. He would have expected it to vote in the normal way on the adoption of the provisional agenda. However, he went on

I would say to you, Sir, that we would not complain if the Council decided to adjourn. But I should make it very plain that we should accept such a decision on the clear understanding that the wish of the Council is not to accept and proceed with the item proposed.

This was a very clear hint to the other Members of the Council that the United Kingdom was ready to accept the scenario canvassed privately by Jakobson, the Finnish representative, which indeed, it may have had a hand in suggesting to him in the first place.

The next step in the careful choreography was taken by Ambassador Muuka, the Zambian representative. He intervened to say that '[i]t is our feeling, a feeling which is shared by other members of the Security Council, that in the light of the statements made this morning it might be wise of the Council to adjourn a decision [on whether or not to adopt the agenda]'. Accordingly, he proposed formally that the meeting be adjourned.

Cremin in a later report said that he had been told afterwards by de Pinies that this approach had been discussed in advance in private 'consultations' that morning between members of the Security Council.[28] It was understood among the members, at this point, even before the formal meeting started, that the Zambian representative would make this proposal and he (Muuka) had been 'very annoyed' that Caradon had mentioned it first at the formal session. This raises a question: had the Zambian been encouraged privately in advance to make this proposal? If so, by whom – by de Pinies, by Jakobson, perhaps even by Caradon? At this stage we cannot know. But if he had indeed been encouraged by Caradon, then his subsequent annoyance at Caradon's 'jumping the gun' in public would be understandable.

Jaime de Pinies, as President, recalled for the Council the rule which required him to put such a proposal to the vote immediately, without debate.

---

[28] It was, and is, the practice for the representatives of the member states of the Security Council to hold private 'consultations' before meetings of the Council in an effort to reach agreement. These consultations are held in a small room behind the Council chamber. They are informal; they take place in English, without interpretation; and there are no TV cameras, records or notetakers present. Some believe that they can be helpful at times in working out an agreed scenario and avoiding polemics in the Council chamber; others deplore them as allowing major states to avoid taking responsibility publicly for the positions they take in drafting resolutions etc.

Noting quickly that there had been no objection to the Zambian proposal, he said he would declare it unanimously adopted. He then adjourned the meeting. The music stopped; the dance – if indeed that is what it was – was over. The Council did not take up the issue again – then or since.

Dr Hillery, before leaving New York for home, did not have another opportunity to meet with Lord Caradon but, at Hillery's request, Cremin later told Caradon that while Hillery did not agree with the substance of the British position, he was grateful for the way Caradon had handled the issue. Caradon thanked him warmly for this. Later still, Cremin was told by a contact in the British Mission that Caradon had been very impressed by the minister. There was honour, it seems, on both sides, between opponents – or should they be described as, in some degree at least, partners, constrained by the situation to join eventually in what became a carefully arranged dance?

I followed these events from the Irish Embassy in Washington where I was based at the time. One month later, I went to New York to join the Irish delegation to the annual session of the General Assembly, as I had done for each of the previous three years. Dr Hillery as minister came out again from Dublin to lead the delegation in the opening weeks of the session. By then what we can now see as the underlying objective of the government's initiative of mid-August had been achieved: the issue had been seen to have been 'taken to the United Nations'; and Dr Hillery had had a hearing for his case. In any event, the immediate crisis had eased somewhat. The issue now at the United Nations – though this would not have been admitted, or perhaps even recognised by the Irish side at the time – was how to withdraw gracefully to a less exposed position.

This was achieved under cover of what appeared to be, and may even have been intended by some to be, another advance – a formal request that the issue which Dr Hillery had sought to raise with the Council should now be placed on the agenda of the General Assembly.

Here again, as in the Council, the first item was consideration of a 'provisional agenda' leading to a decision about which items should be accepted formally for debate by the Assembly. This is done by a twenty-five person General Committee comprising the Assembly President and Vice-Presidents and the Chairmen of the main Committees. Dr Hillery appeared before this Committee to make his case on 17 September 1969. He focused mainly on the procedural question of the competence of the Assembly to deal with such an issue. In a reprise of events in the Security Council four weeks previously, Lord Caradon replied. He pointed to the urgency with which the British government was pressing ahead with reform and argued that, while human rights issues could be discussed in the Assembly, the Irish request went well beyond that: it should be withdrawn. The Soviet Union again supported the proposal to put the item on the Assembly's agenda. The US found itself in an 'unhappy dilemma' and waited to hear Dr Hillery's response to Caradon's statement.

I recall sitting in the meeting hall listening to these exchanges with other colleagues (who, like me, had helped to prepare the material) and feeling a degree of surprise at the time at hearing Dr Hillery's measured response. The core of it was not a renewal of the argument for debate in the General Assembly but an acceptance of Caradon's personal good faith in saying that reforms in Northern Ireland would be put into effect urgently. Dr Hillery said he would reflect on this. In such a meeting, a willingness 'to reflect' is an important signal for those alert to hear. Nigeria now intervened: it proposed that further consideration of the request to put the issue on the agenda should be suspended for a period to be decided by the Chairman. This proposal was accepted by the Committee and the Irish request remained formally on the table. It was not raised again. Whether or not this was the intention – and no doubt some of those involved would deny that it was – a graceful withdrawal had been achieved: Ireland had retreated in relatively good order from its exposed position of mid-August.

V

Conclusion: Was it a defeat?

In the quotation from his book on the Security Council with which I began, Andrew Boyd saw it on the contrary as a well-judged and well-executed example of how the United Nations should be used as a point of reference and a help in defusing tensions which might otherwise lead to conflict.[29] It is possible of course that Boyd exaggerated the extent to which the participants at the time had consciously choreographed, rather than extemporised, the dance in which they engaged in the Council chamber.[30]

Con Cremin would have been in a good position to judge. In his 1980 paper he commended Boyd's account as 'interesting' and 'well done'. But he added a qualification: 'one statement could be interpreted to have an implication which would not be valid'. This was a reference to Boyd's comment that Caradon and Hillery in a 'quiet talk … evidently found that … they could trust each other to play their parts in the Council with dignity and what may be termed "style"'. Cremin acknowledged that Caradon and Hillery did indeed have a talk but he rejected 'any inference that they, as it were, worked out a scenario for the Council session'. This is no doubt, strictly speaking, true: they did not explicitly work out a scenario. But experienced politicians and diplomats do not always need to be literal or heavy-handed in their approach. It is significant that Cremin's own account of their meeting,

---

[29] Boyd, *Fifteen Men*, pp. 318–329.

[30] I think Boyd was friendly in earlier years with some members of the Irish delegation such as Conor Cruise O'Brien and that he had a very sympathetic attitude towards Ireland. It may even have been he who was responsible for the leading article which appeared in *The Economist* in 1960 under the rather extravagant heading 'The Afro-Irish Assembly': it began, if my memory serves, by saying that 'Ireland bestrides the UN like a colossus'. *The Skibbereen Eagle* could hardly have done better.

to which I referred earlier, mentions that on that Sunday evening, 17 August, Caradon floated to Dr Hillery, an idea for how the issue might be handled which was virtually identical to that proposed later by Finland's Jakobson. Cremin's report records that 'The Minister listened quietly' but it appears that he did not offer any reaction. However, that was indeed the approach which the Council eventually followed three days later.

It would be of interest to see what light further research in the British archives might throw on the position of the Foreign Office at the time. Was Caradon instructed from London to take the position he did? Or was it rather that he, a political figure of some substance, felt free to interpret his instructions with greater latitude than a career diplomat might have done?

In summarising the whole episode, I think I should quote again from Boyd:

> in this case the 'defusing' potential of an airing in the Council was exploited with unusual deftness. The Irish government at home faced a general demand that it should do something, and a specific demand that it should take the matter to the United Nations. Its action enabled it to claim that it had responded to both these demands; that it had pushed its case as far as the Council would allow it to go; and that it had thereby added to the pressure on the British government to put the right kind of pressure on the Ulster Unionists. Yet it could not be accused by any level-headed person of having further inflamed an explosive situation. The brief and measured exchanges in the Council (and the marked silence of no less than eleven of its fifteen members) had the opposite effect.[31]

The eventual outcome of all that had happened was that no decision was ever taken by the Security Council on the request by Ireland for a peacekeeping force because the issue was never formally inscribed on the agenda of the Security Council. If it had been, there was no chance in practice that the Council would have agreed to send a United Nations peacekeeping force to Northern Ireland over British objections. But, with the acquiescence of the British representative, Lord Caradon, the Irish Foreign Minister, Dr Hillery had been allowed to present his case in full to the Council when the preliminary procedural issue of whether or not to put the item on the agenda was being debated. This was the important thing for the Irish public at home at the time who were not well versed in the niceties of United Nations procedure.

Now, thirty-six years later, with the heightened passions of the time largely spent, we can also see it as one of a series of steps through which successive Irish governments were able gradually to establish that they had a

---

[31] Boyd, *Fifteen Men*, p. 328.

substantial role to play in relation to Northern Ireland – contrary to the initial British view that 'the Irish Question' had been settled definitively in 1921–22 and that, in consequence, the Republic was now a 'foreign country'.

The first formal acceptance that this did not reflect the reality of Northern Ireland came three years later: a Green Paper published by the British government in the year before the Sunningdale Conference of 1973, acknowledged that 'the Irish Dimension' was an intrinsic part of the problem which would have to be given expression in any settlement. The phrase was vague enough but it became the basis for the effort to set up a Council of Ireland as part of the Sunningdale settlement. Seven years on from the collapse of Sunningdale, the two Haughey-Thatcher meetings of 1980 introduced a new theme: Northern Ireland should be set within a wider context – 'the totality of relations' between the two islands. Five years further on, in the Anglo-Irish Agreement of 1985, the British government agreed to set up an Anglo-Irish Intergovernmental Conference, served by a standing joint Secretariat in Belfast. This, for the first time gave the Irish government a formal, legally institutionalised, role – less than executive but more than con-sultative – in relation to the affairs of Northern Ireland. Later still, in the 1990s, consultation and cooperation through the Conference became even closer – though still with occasional ups and downs and moments of temporary turbulence.

In the late 1980s and early 1990s various exchanges behind the scenes prepared the way for what subsequently became a 'cessation of military activ-ities' by para-military groups. The Downing Street Declaration agreed in 1993 between the two governments was important in charting a new way ahead. Finally, following the paramilitary ceasefires, negotiations between representatives of the two governments and of all of the main parties (includ-ing some with links to paramilitaries) resulted in the Good Friday Agreement of 1998 (which many Unionists prefer to call the Belfast Agreement). This Agreement, approved in simultaneous referenda North and South, as well as by the two sovereign parliaments, opened the door to a wholly new era. As part of that Agreement, all concerned, including Unionists in Northern Ireland, now fully accept that Dublin and London, the two sovereign gov-ernments, must continue to act together in partnership to deal with the dif-ficult legacy of history to the peoples of both islands.

This is not to say of course that any of this could have been, or was, fore-seen in 1969. 'Taking the issue to the United Nations' was largely one of the responses by a divided government to the need to be seen to 'do something' in a time of crisis which it could do little to resolve directly. But as one of several steps which helped at least to channel, though not wholly to defuse, emotions in the South, the decision to send Dr Hillery to New York, and his handling of the issue there, must be seen now as having been a reasonable success. He did not get what he had been sent to ask for – a United Nations force. He did not even succeed in getting the question put formally on the agenda of the Security Council. But he did get something which seemed important at the time – a chance to present the government's case on the Northern Ireland issue before the world forum.

Conor Cruise O'Brien wrote long ago about the useful role which the United Nations can serve in ritualising conflict as a way of avoiding real bloodshed. This may have been a good example. In any event, the episode is now history; times have changed; and relations within the island of Ireland, and between Britain and Ireland, seem to be set on a much happier course.

Chapter Eleven

Ireland and Collective Security[1]

BEN TONRA

The aim of this chapter is to reconsider Irish foreign, security and defence policy in the light of the state's fifty-year long commitment to the United Nations system of collective security. It will contrast that commitment with Ireland's ambivalence towards collective defence and will argue that the 'neutrality' debate in Ireland is premised upon a misunderstanding of collective security that has the potential to pose major policy challenges. The chapter opens with a brief outline of the distinction between collective security and collective defence. It will proceed to review the execution of Irish foreign policy through both the League of Nations and the United Nations and will attempt to outline the relationship between an Irish commitment to collective security with the tradition of Irish military neutrality. Finally, the chapter will conclude with an analysis of the potential policy challenges to be faced by Ireland should a more robust and effective system of collective security be agreed in a United Nations context.

Security and defence

Collective security embodies the idea that states within the international system join together on the basis of an agreed set of norms and then commit themselves to the defence of an international order so established through a multilateral institution. That multilateral institution is, in turn, vested with the legal and political legitimacy to determine the existence of any threat to that agreed order and has the consequent obligation and (it is assumed) the capacity to address such threats, up to and including the use of military force.

    Collective security and collective defence are associated but distinct concepts. The concept of collective security was arguably first promoted by Immanuel Kant and posited as a means by which an international peace

[1] This chapter is adapted from a longer study of Irish foreign policy to be published as *European Republic and Gobal Citizen: Irish Foreign Policy in Transition* in Autumn 2006 by Manchester University Press.

might be secured. It was later applied in practice through the establishment of the League of Nations in the aftermath of the First World War. Collective defence, by contrast, is understood to be a bilateral or regional agreement among a sub-set of states that agree that a military attack against any member of the alliance is deemed to be an attack against all. They further agree to meet any such attack with a collective military response.

Thus the distinctions between collective security and collective defence may be summarised as follows.

- Collective security is operationalised through a multilateral institution in which member states agree to be bound by decisions of that institution. A collective defence – although founded by treaty – does not bind states in precisely the same way.
- The nature of 'threat' in a collective security system is usually broader and is often seen in a more long-term context. In a collective defence system 'threats' are usually understood to be military and near immediate in nature.
- In a collective security system the 'threats' are usually seen to originate within that system of states. In a collective defence system the threat is assumed to be external to that specific group of states.
- Effective collective security is usually viewed as being a more elusive goal than that of collective defence since the former must be constructed on a near universal base from among a heterogeneous group of self-interested states, while the latter is usually composed of a smaller, politically committed sub-group of self-selected states.
- It is also argued that the cost of enforcing collective security can be perceived to be quite high while the immediate benefits of such enforcement are less obvious.

Collective security is usually understood to be a more effective long-term approach to security than that pursued by individual states defending themselves in isolation. Weaker states find themselves incapable of providing for their own defence while those states with adequate resources for defence may find themselves embroiled in a local or regional arms race that serves to detract from, rather than enhance, their long-term security. Moreover, while collective security institutions are predicated upon strengthening international cooperation, the more traditional balance of power system – where each state fends for itself – is seen to lead to competition and a greater potential for conflict.

Some critics, however, see the concept of collective security as being illusory, if not misguided. While states may be formally obligated to sustain a system of collective security – they may well choose – in any individual case – to refuse to abide by decisions made through multilateral channels or explicitly to oppose or subvert them for reasons of national self-interest. Such interests, moreover, are more often framed in a short-term immediate context rather than a longer strategic one. A collective security system has also the potential to turn a comparatively minor dispute into a much larger systemic one – particularly if the dispute becomes embroiled in the calculations of the larger powers within the collective security system. Thus, the interests of protagonists within smaller conflicts may be traded among the larger powers in a complex system of logrolling and strategic balancing.

Irish security and defence policy

The start of a debate on Irish security and defence policy in this context is a contest over the roots and nature of Irish neutrality. In the traditional academic literature Irish neutrality is characterised as being exceptional and differentiated from that of other European neutrals.[2] At the same time, it is argued that neutrality is deeply rooted in Irish history, first identified with Wolfe Tone's publication in 1790 of a pamphlet dedicated to Irish neutrality in the Anglo-Spanish War. This tradition of neutrality is then traced through the anti-conscription campaign of the First World War, state neutrality in the Second World War and Ireland's rejection of NATO membership and subsequent military neutrality during the Cold War. Neutrality can also be traced through the major figures of the nationalist and republican movements; from Wolfe Tone 'the father of Irish Republicanism' through the nineteenth century's Young Irelanders, the Irish Republican Brotherhood, Arthur Griffith – founder of Sinn Féin and co-founder of the Irish Neutrality Association – James Connolly, the Irish Citizen Army's declaration that it served 'neither King nor Kaiser but Ireland', and Roger Casement. Thus, neutrality is painted as a long-standing principle of Irish engagement in the world – both before and following statehood – and is often linked strongly with an anti-imperialist view.

Others see neutrality in a far more contingent context – and one largely shaped by pragmatic necessity and/or an atavistic need to define the state's identity in opposition to Britain. This tradition would highlight the very partial nature of Irish neutrality in the Second World War, with the roots of that neutrality resting upon concerns with domestic security and the very explicit linkage of neutrality with partition both during the war and subsequently in the 1949 rejection of NATO membership.[3] Furthermore, it is argued, Ireland declared itself to be a firm, ideologically-committed part of the 'West' during the Cold War and never practised neutrality as defined and/or required in international law. In particular, attention is usually drawn

---

[2] See Patrick Keatinge, *A Singular Stance: Irish Neutrality in the 1980s* (Dublin, 1984); Trevor Salmon, *Unneutral Ireland: An Ambivalent and Unique Security Policy* (Oxford, 1989).

[3] See Eunan O' Halpin, *Defending Ireland: the Irish State and Its Enemies since 1922* (Oxford, 1999); Eunan O' Halpin, 'Irish Neutrality in the Second World War', in Wylie, N. (ed.) *European Neutrals and Non-Belligerents during the Second World War* (Cambridge, 2001).

to the fifth and thirteenth Hague Conventions of 1907 that demand that neutral states deny assistance to all belligerents in time of conflict. This is then contrasted with the reality of Irish foreign and security policy practice.

This debate is effectively summarised in the 1996 White Paper on Irish foreign policy where it is argued that neutrality 'has taken on a significance for Irish people over and above the essentially practical considerations on which it was originally based'.[4] The White Paper further argues that 'Many have come to regard neutrality as a touchstone of our entire approach to international relations' even though the practice of Irish foreign policy is not 'dependent on our non-membership of a military alliance'. This assessment is echoed by former Senator John A. Murphy, who argued that while 'There is a respectable body of evidence to suggest that (neutrality) is firmly rooted in the history of the State', it was also a pragmatic policy and '... not all that principled. Much of it was simply an anti-English tactic, and anti-English strategy.'[5] Similarly, for former Taoiseach Garret FitzGerald, Irish neutrality has 'developed its own ethos in many peoples' minds and despite its dubious origins actually came to be widely seen as virtuous. He goes on to note, somewhat ruefully perhaps, that '(the) afterglow of moral rectitude associated with our military neutrality during the Cold War remains quite potent'.[6]

In outlining this debate, however, neutrality needs also to be linked to what is seen as a very strong commitment to international law, multilateral institutions and collective security. Here a number of diplomatic historians have identified this as a much stronger and more consistent foreign policy line even than that of neutrality.[7] Reviewing Irish government policy and diplomatic practice in the Commonwealth, the League of Nations and subsequently in the United Nations and even the Council of Europe, they have identified a powerful and ongoing policy commitment to the rule of law, collective security structures and their associated multilateral institutions. This is reflected in the comment of Taoiseach Bertie Ahern that 'Our policy of military neutrality has always gone hand in hand with support for collective security based on international law'.[8]

Arguably, however, not only has neutrality to be contextualised by a commitment to collective security, it may in fact be superseded by it. Thus, in the League of Nations, for example, de Valera – the architect of Irish wartime

---

[4] See http://foreignaffairs.gov.ie/information/publications/whitepaper/chp2.asp. Section 2.26.
[5] *Seanad Deb.*, vol. 96, col. 1105, 2 Dec. 1981.
[6] *Irish Times*, 19 Apr. 1995.
[7] Michael Kennedy, *Ireland and the League of Nations, 1919–1946: International Relations, Diplomacy and Politics* (Dublin, 1996); Joseph Morrison Skelly, *Irish Diplomacy at the United Nations, 1945–1965: National Interests and International Order* (Dublin, 1997); M. Kennedy and J.M. Skelly (eds.), *Irish Foreign Policy 1919–1966: From independence to internationalism* (Dublin, 2000); M. Kennedy and E. O' Halpin, *Ireland and the Council of Europe: from Isolation Towards Integration* (Strasbourg, 2002).
[8] *Irish Times*, 20 May 1999.

neutrality – is seen to have faced down significant, sustained and unprecedented domestic political opposition in order to support League sanctions against both Fascist Italy and Franco's Spain.[9] It was the League's ultimate inability to censure Italy for its Abyssinian invasion and the subsequent and obvious contempt for the League held by the major powers, which is argued to have finally determined Ireland's path to neutrality.[10] As Fianna Fáil Deputy Conor Lenihan argued in parliament, de Valera's commitment to neutrality only arose 'as a result of the failure of one of the great internationalist projects, namely, the League of Nations, under the jackboot of fascism in the 1930s. It was only for that reason that he opted progressively for a position of neutrality.'[11]

In the immediate post-war world, de Valera assessed the potential of United Nations membership for the Irish State and its Chapter VII provisions for collective security. He subsequently noted in the Dáil that the obligations of membership included that of 'going to war at the bidding of the Security Council'.[12] Such an obligation clearly made neutrality untenable, but he argued that this was – particularly for a smaller state – a necessary outcome since 'It would be fatal for the small nations, including ourselves, who have any hope of collective security, to think that they can in the end dodge their obligations'.[13]

Thus, while military neutrality – or 'non-membership of military alliances' – may be said to define Irish defence policy, it does not encapsulate Irish foreign and security policy. Since Irish policy makers are willing to devote considerable effort to the pursuit of collective security, it may be more appropriate to describe Irish security policy as being one of military non-alignment within the context of an overriding commitment to collective security and the consequent pre-eminent position of the United Nations.[14] As a militarily non-aligned security actor, the issue for Irish policy makers is then understood to be the identification of the most appropriate and effective structures through which an Irish contribution may be made to regional and international collective security. For the Labour Party's Eamon Gilmore, for example, Ireland has to 'rethink its traditional policy of neutrality' and so shift to 'a concept which concentrates on the multilateral building of peace'.[15]

The foundations of Irish security policy are defined by the 1996 White Paper on foreign policy as being:

---

[9] Michael Kennedy, 'The Irish Free State and the League of Nations, 1922–32', *Irish Studies in International Affairs*, 3:4 (1992), pp. 9–23.

[10] Patrick Keatinge, *The Formulation of Irish Foreign Policy* (Dublin, 1973), p. 157.

[11] *Dáil Deb.*, vol. 535, col. 617, 2 May 2001.

[12] *Dáil Deb.*, vol. 102, col. 1319, 24 July 1946.

[13] *Dáil Deb.*, vol. 102, col. 1466, 25 July 1946.

[14] Daniel Keohane, *Realigning neutrality? Irish defence policy and the EU, Occasional Paper 24* (Paris, 2001). Available at http://www.iss-eu.org/occasion/occ24.html.

[15] *Dáil Deb.*, vol. 446, col. 332, 20 Oct. 1994.

- a policy of military neutrality, embodied by non-participation in military alliances
- the promotion of the rule of international law and the peaceful settlement of disputes
- the promotion of greater equity and justice in international affairs through efforts to eliminate the causes of conflict and to protect human rights
- a commitment to collective security through the development of international organisations, especially the United Nations
- a willingness to participate in peace-keeping and humanitarian operations throughout the world
- participation in the construction of the European Union as a way of overcoming age-old rivalries in Europe
- the promotion of an active policy of disarmament and arms control
- a commitment to regional co-operation, especially in Europe, through the promotion of, and participation in, regional organisations such as the Organisation for Security and Co-operation in Europe, and the Council of Europe.

In support of that policy, the 2000 White Paper on Defence provided for a three-brigade structure of just over 10,500 troops to meet the full range of tasks arising from its own threat assessment. The Defence Forces, comprising the Permanent Defence Force – the Army, the Air Corps, the Naval Service – as well as the Reserve Defence Force, are specifically tasked with participation in overseas missions in the cause of international peace, as well as meeting the requirements of domestic security which are defined as providing 'military personnel in an operational role in an aid to the civil power (ATCP) capacity'.[16] According to the White Paper: 'The external security environment does not contain any specific threats to the overall security of the State' with Ireland therefore facing 'a generally benign security environment'. Since the 2001 attacks on the United States that assessment has been revised to conclude that, according to the Minister for Defence in 2003, while there is 'no credible threat to this country'[17] immediately arising from international terrorism the fight against it is one in which, according to Taoiseach Bertie Ahern, Ireland 'will continue to play its part to the fullest in tackling'.[18]

Internationally, the Defence Forces have a nearly fifty-year record of peacekeeping and peace support operations overseas, ranging across Europe, Africa, Asia and the Middle East. In 2005 more than 850 troops were dedicated – through several multilateral mechanisms (United Nations, NATO and EU) – for assignment to overseas mission. Significantly, the participation

---

[16] Department of Defence, *White Paper on Defence (2000–2010)*, available at http://www.defence.ie/website.nsf/home .

[17] *Dáil Deb.*, vol. 561, col. 1312, 19 Feb. 2003.

[18] *Dáil Deb.*, vol. 541, col. 94, 3 Oct. 2001.

of Irish troops in such operations is highly valued at both official and public levels – lending substance to Ireland's commitment to collective security and contributing to achievements such as Ireland's heading the poll in the 2000 election of members to the United Nations Security Council. Peacekeeping has also been described by the government as being 'a matter of justified public pride' and 'an integral element of how we see ourselves in the world'.[19] These missions are also popular with the Defence Forces themselves – with some estimates calculating that more than 65 percent of Irish troops have served overseas in one or another capacity.[20]

Since the end of the Cold War and in the context of the post-2001 attacks on the United States, however, Irish security policy has come under renewed scrutiny. The state is understood to be seeking to adapt itself to a new security environment that, it is argued, is based even less on national defence and much more upon mechanisms designed to deliver collective security. In this changing environment, the international security architecture is also seen to be evolving with the United Nations, NATO and European Union all facing new challenges. While the United Nations remains the central multilateral focus for an Irish contribution to international collective security, there are claims that regional actors such as NATO, OSCE and the EU have their own roles to play and that Ireland must ensure that it is centrally placed in this new security architecture if it is to maximise its influence and participation therein.

For some, any such analysis must entail a critical, root and branch review of Irish security policy and that this will result in a full commitment to regional security structures, even at the expense of neutrality. For advocates of this position: 'We must accept the fact that neutrality, as we have known it, is no longer a necessary mark of Irish independence' and 'what was appropriate for the emerging Republic of Ireland in the middle of the last century may not be the best way forward for our modern, confident state'.[21] In even stronger terms a former Minister of State for European Affairs argues that the 'farcical eulogising of "neutrality"' must end and the 'pretence of Ireland's neutrality' should give way to a debate on the form and content of a European common defence that includes Ireland'.[22]

Others, however, insist that neutrality as currently conceived and expressed (as non-membership of military alliances and therefore of NATO and any common EU defence) is entirely consistent with a full and whole-hearted engagement in international and regional collective security structures.

---

[19] Department of Foreign Affairs, *Ireland and the Partnership for Peace: An Explanatory Guide* (Dublin, 1999).

[20] Lt.-Col. Oliver A.K. Macdonald, 'Peacekeeping Lessons Learned: An Irish Perspective', *International Peacekeeping*, 4:3 (1997).

[21] *Seanad Deb.*, vol. 173, col. 1285, 25 June 2003.

[22] Gay Mitchell, *Time to end chaos within the Government on Irish defence policy and to abandon the farce of Irish neutrality, Statement, 15 March 2005* (Dublin: Fine Gael Press Office, 2005).

According to Minister of State for European Affairs, Dick Roche TD, 'Ireland's policy of military neutrality remains viable in the context of the new security challenges ... (and) fully relevant in circumstances where the emerging challenges have moved from traditional defence towards crisis management'.[23]

Finally, for a third constituency, Irish neutrality has already been hollowed out to such an extent that it has lost all substantive meaning. Over the course of Irish EU membership, through a series of treaty and extra-treaty developments and as a result of other government decisions 'Our neutrality has been taken away, not as a result of any one decision or following public debate, but bit by bit until we reached the stage where we were told by politicians and so-called intellectuals that our neutrality no longer makes sense'. For this group it is urgently necessary for 'Ireland to act like a neutral country' in both the spirit and letter of that concept.[24]

Policy challenges

In facing what is argued to be a new security environment and an evolving security architecture, a number of challenges have arisen to confront Irish policy makers, commentators and the broader public.

The first such challenge is making an appropriate response to changes in the ways in which the United Nations pursues multilateral security – and, in particular, the use of military forces in peace support missions. As noted above, for nearly fifty years, Ireland has been centrally engaged in United Nations peacekeeping operations. This has entailed an Irish commitment to more than forty United Nations-commanded missions, involving 39,836 tours of duty – four times the total size of the Irish Defence Forces – and resulting in the deaths of 82 Defence Forces personnel.

However, the United Nations has been presented with what are argued to be its own new realities arising from its post Cold War experience. In 1992 the United Nations' 'Agenda for Peace' foresaw a more robust and interventionist role, and no longer assumed that United Nations forces would have to operate with the consent of parties to a dispute.[25] The deaths of more than forty United Nations peacekeepers in Somalia in 1993 put paid to that ambition. The United Nations' subsequent failures in the former Yugoslavia 1992–5 – and in particular the July 1995 massacre of approximately 8,000 men and boys at Srebrenica – further underscored the limitations of traditional United Nations commanded operations. In 2000, the United Nations published a critical analysis of its own peacekeeping operations conducted by a 12-member expert panel under the chairmanship of former Algerian

---

23 *Seanad Deb.*, vol. 173, col. 1310, 25 June 2003.
24 *Dáil Deb.*, vol. 561, col. 1000, 18 Feb. 2003.
25 Boutros Boutros Ghali, *An Agenda for Peace* (New York, 1992).

Foreign Minister, Lakhdar Brahimi.[26] This report argued, inter alia, that the traditional United Nations peacekeeping model was inadequate to address the tasks being presented. A major evolution in United Nations peacekeeping practice subsequently resulted, with a shift in focus to regional security organisations as being the agents to carry out United Nations mandated missions. Moreover, those missions were more complex and now relied upon a more robust force structure – giving them the capacity to intervene forcibly in support of mission goals.

The Irish state responded by opting into these newly emerging structures. Some fifty Irish military police, for example, were contributed to the Stabilisation Force in Bosnia and Herzegovina (SFOR) in July 1997. This was a United Nations-mandated operation in support of the 1995 Dayton peace agreement but it was commanded and operated through NATO. This raised a number of queries not least of which was how could an Irish government 'countenance the sending of Irish troops to serve under NATO command in Bosnia and still claim that Ireland has not abandoned its renowned policy of active neutrality'.[27] The response from the Minister for Foreign Affairs underlined the emerging dilemmas for traditional United Nations contributors in that the SFOR operation was 'an important expression of the new mutually reinforcing and co-operative security architecture that is developing in Europe' and that as a long-standing 'advocate of co-operative approaches to security,' Irish participation would 'be a concrete example of our commitment to inclusive co-operative security in Europe' and would 'enable Ireland to experience directly the new approach to European peacekeeping'.[28]

Critics insisted, however, that by buying into this 'new' model of peacekeeping 'the United Nations' role has been usurped by NATO', and that effective international peacekeeping could only be properly assured by strengthening the United Nations rather than participating in ad hoc mechanisms which had the effect of marginalising the United Nations system.[29] Instead, it was argued, the Irish priority should be given to the United Nations' own Standby Arrangements System (UNSAS) to which the Irish government had committed a potential maximum of 850 troops and also to SHIRBRIG – the Danish-sponsored United Nations Standing High-Readiness Brigade, to which Ireland was an observer.

As the United Nations moved towards using regional security and defence organisations as the subcontractors for some of its peacekeeping and peace 'making' operations, a second challenge for Irish foreign policy quickly arose. This was how Ireland could and should relate to the core transatlantic and European security and collective defence organisation, NATO.

---

[26] Lakhdar Brahimi, *Report of the Panel on United Nations Peace Operations* http://www.un.org/peace/reports/peace_operations/report.htm.
[27] *Dáil Deb.*, vol. 476, col. 1089, 19 Mar. 1997.
[28] *Dáil, Deb.*, vol. 476, col. 1090, 19 Mar. 1997.
[29] *Dáil Deb.*, vol. 507, col. 865, 1 July 1999.

By 1961 and 'irrespective of the question of partition, important as that is' the Minister for Foreign Affairs Frank Aiken viewed non-membership of NATO as a 'contribution which Ireland can make in international affairs' by playing its part, free from alliances, in 'reducing tensions between States, and in forwarding constructive solutions for the sources of such tensions'.[30] This also facilitated the sending of Irish troops on United Nations peacekeeping missions to locations where 'combat troops of nations belonging to NATO and other military blocs are not acceptable'.[31] Throughout the 1960s and 1970s, questions on the prospects for NATO membership were dismissed on the basis that a decision had been reached in 1949 and the government had no intention to revisit the issue. By 1988, the government no longer relied upon partition as any part of its explanation. Instead, the Minister for Foreign Affairs now noted that 'Ireland's policy of military neutrality necessarily implies non-membership of military alliances such as NATO.[32]

In its own evolution following the end of the Cold War, the North Atlantic Alliance first revised its strategic concept in 1991 and then in 1992 offered itself as a means for multilateral peacekeeping missions first under the auspices of the OSCE and later for the United Nations. At the same time, NATO's relationship with former Warsaw Pact adversaries was changing, as membership demands from states in central and eastern Europe multiplied. NATO began now to straddle the line between being a structure for the collective defence of its members and taking on many of the attributes of a regional collective security actor. In 1994, with the launch of its 'Partnership for Peace' initiative, the Alliance sought to square that particular circle in what was characterised by a former United States Ambassador to NATO as a 'two-for-one' deal; offering both an antechamber to full membership for those that sought it as well as a structure designed to facilitate confidence-building measures and collective security among NATO members and non-members in Europe.

For Irish policy makers, this evolution posed something of a dilemma. Non-membership of military alliances – and specifically of NATO – had become, over time, part of the very definition of Irish neutrality. Now, NATO was taking on tasks and characteristics of a collective security organisation, working with both the OSCE and the United Nations in a new European security environment.

Initially, NATO's Partnership for Peace initiative was characterised by the Irish government simply as a 'new form of co-operation' in the evolution of Europe's security architecture.[33] On the publication of the 1996 foreign policy White Paper, however, the government sought consideration of whether or not Ireland should participate in 'this co-operative initiative

---

[30] *Dáil Deb.*, vol. 189, col. 461, 17 May 1961.

[31] *Dáil Deb.*, vol. 189, col. 462, 17 May 1961.

[32] *Dáil Deb.*, vol. 382, col. 1028, 21 June 1998.

[33] *Dáil Deb.*, vol. 437, col. 2094, 27 Jan. 1994.

which the vast majority of OSCE member states have already joined' and which had already 'assumed an important role in European security co-operation, particularly in such areas as training for peacekeeping and humanitarian operations'.[34] Opposition to the 'NATO-sponsored' and 'ill-named' organisation centred upon the view that it represented a kind of 'second hand membership of NATO'.[35] In opposition, the Fianna Fáil leader, Bertie Ahern, went so far as to argue that such was the gravity of any proposed link to NATO that Irish participation in the Partnership for Peace could only be legitimately secured by a consultative referendum. Anything else he insisted would be 'a serious breach of faith and fundamentally undemocratic'.[36]

While Irish troops served under NATO command in the SFOR operation – which was itself denounced by MEP Patricia McKenna as 'an attempt to get us into Partnership for Peace by the back door'[37]– the government was nonetheless unable to secure agreement from within its own governing coalition to pursue participation. The Minister for Foreign Affairs underscored his own support for the Partnership and insisted in early 1997 that the issue was being kept under constant review.[38] With the General Election of 1997 and subsequent change of government to a Fianna Fáil-Progressive Democrat coalition, the new Minister for Foreign Affairs (Fianna Fáil's Ray Burke TD) assessed Partnership for Peace as he had when in opposition, as representing a second-class membership of NATO that would fundamentally compromise Ireland's military neutrality.[39]

This analysis changed within weeks with the appointment of a new Fianna Fáil Minister for Foreign Affairs (David Andrews TD). His position soon shifted from one in which Irish participation was 'not a tenable proposition'[40] to one where he looked forward 'to an open and well informed debate on Partnership for Peace in the House in due course'.[41] This provoked vigorous political exchanges not only on the principle of joining the NATO-sponsored security framework but also the means by which such a decision was to be made, i.e. with or without a consultative referendum. Following a preliminary Dáil debate in January 1999, publication by the government of an explanatory guide and the June 1999 European Parliamentary elections, the Government decided in favour of membership. By resolution of the Dáil on 9 November 1999 Irish participation in the Partnership for Peace and the associated Euro-Atlantic Partnership Council (EAPC) was agreed.

---

[34] Ibid.
[35] *Dáil Deb.*, vol. 436, cols. 1294–6, 1 Dec. 1993.
[36] *Dáil Deb.*, vol. 436, col. 1322, 2 Dec. 1993.
[37] *Irish Times*, 23 Jan. 1997.
[38] *Dáil Deb.*, vol. 474, col. 961, 6 Feb. 1997.
[39] *Dáil Deb.*, vol. 480, col. 899, 30 Sept. 1997.
[40] *Dáil Deb.*, vol. 480, col. 1504, 2 Oct. 1997.
[41] *Dáil Deb.*, vol. 487, col. 974, 19 Feb. 1998.

While Irish participation in NATO-specific operations – whether under a United Nations or OSCE framework – has been problematic, similar challenges have emerged in the 2000s as NATO and the European Union have developed bilateral agreements, procedures and even institutional links so as to coordinate between them on the use of military forces. Such links have been justified officially on the basis that the EU '... is likely to remain dependent on NATO infrastructure and transport capacity, as the United Nations-mandated operations such as SFOR and KFOR have shown'.[42] These links have, in the eyes of at least some critics, created a situation in which the Union has become a subset of NATO and the Union's own foreign and security policy agenda is indistinguishable from that of the Atlantic Alliance. This has the obvious implication for Irish security and defence policy that participation in EU structures and operations is seen to draw Ireland closer towards the NATO alliance and is thus argued to further erode Irish neutrality.

This then is the third policy challenge – the construction and development of a European Security and Defence Policy within the European Union and its relationship with the United Nations and international collective security.

While the original European Community treaties contained no reference to defence – or indeed to foreign policy – it has been noted that considerable effort was made in the early 1960s by the Irish government and the Taoiseach, Seán Lemass, to underline Ireland's political commitment to the European project while at the same time making it clear that membership of the Communities had no immediate impact upon neutrality. According to the Minister for External Affairs, Patrick Hillery, speaking in 1970 'there is no question of making any military commitments at any place. We have not been requested to do so. There is no question of our doing so.' but nonetheless, he went one, from the point at which a common European defence might emerge in the future 'we would defend Europe if the defence of Europe became necessary'.[43]

That formulation gave rise to considerable and ongoing scepticism, particularly since, by the time EC membership negotiations actually opened, the member states of the then European Communities had established a process of foreign policy cooperation which came to be titled European Political Cooperation (EPC). According to Senator Mary Robinson in 1972, these informal political commitments were 'evolving an external policy for the Community so that Europe will speak with one voice'.[44] Such an eventuality, according to the Minister for External Affairs, was 'an ideal to which the Government fully subscribe and for which I believe – in fact, we

---

[42] *Dáil Deb.*, vol. 533, col. 998, 2 Mar. 2001.
[43] *Dáil Deb.*, vol. 246, col. 1373, 13 May 1970.
[44] *Seanad Deb.*, vol. 72, col. 570, 1 Mar. 1972.

are certain – there is a ready response in the Irish nation as a whole'.[45] Others were not so sure.

For Senator John A. Murphy, 'membership (of a military alliance) is inevitable and implicit in our continued participation in the European Political Cooperation talks and in the harmonisation of foreign policy which is an increasing tendency in the Community'. Such concerns were also evident in a 1981 parliamentary debate during which a newly installed Fine Gael-Labour coalition government took issue with its immediate Fianna Fáil predecessor as to how much ground had been lost in defending neutrality within EPC. For the incoming Taoiseach, Garret FitzGerald, the former Foreign Minister, Brian Lenihan, had 'put this country's position (on neutrality) at risk ... which has required considerable efforts by this Government to retrieve'.[46]

The proposed formalisation of EPC as Title III of the Single European Act in 1986 gave rise to further political debate, as it was alleged that the treaty potentially represented 'a serious erosion of Irish neutrality'[47] and one which could 'certainly be interpreted as posing a challenge to our neutrality'.[48] For the Fine Gael Minister for Foreign Affairs, Peter Barry, however, the treaty's provisions posed 'no threat to this country's sovereignty, neutrality or ability to take independent decisions on foreign policy matters'.[49] Despite its parliamentary passage as an international treaty, a court challenge was launched and, following defeat at the High Court, the plaintiff won on appeal before the Supreme Court. There it was held that Title III purported to 'qualify, curtail or inhibit the existing sovereign power to formulate and to pursue such foreign policies' and that it was 'not within the power of the government itself to do so'.[50] The government was thus forced to present the Single Act before the electorate as an amendment to the constitution.

Subsequent European treaty changes were equally contentious in the area of security and defence policy. The 1993 Maastricht Treaty established the Common Foreign and Security Policy (CFSP) and gave a treaty base to its associated decision making structures. For its part, the 1999 Amsterdam Treaty provided for the progressive framing of a common security and defence policy that, it was argued, could deliver humanitarian and rescue tasks, peacekeeping tasks and tasks of combat forces in crisis management, including peacemaking – the so-called Petersberg Tasks. The 2003 Nice Treaty added nothing of substance but it did provide a treaty base to the new Political and Security Committee (COPS) whose role was to offer policy recommendations and to manage CFSP/ESDP on a day-to-day basis on

---

[45] *Dáil Deb.*, vol. 247, col. 2068, 25 June 1970.
[46] *Dáil Deb.*, vol. 330, col. 310, 21 Oct. 1981.
[47] *Dáil Deb.*, vol. 365, col. 2173, 30 Apr. 1986.
[48] *Dáil Deb.*, vol. 370, col. 1922, 9 Dec. 1986.
[49] Ibid.
[50] Supreme Court 1986 No. 12036P.

behalf of EU ministers in the General Affairs and External Relations Council.

For some, these treaties – individually and collectively – threatened the bases and substance of Irish neutrality. They represented the culmination of 'a sustained effort to transfer decisions on foreign and security policy to Europe'[51] as 'Irish neutrality has been progressively and systematically eroded by successive EU treaties'.[52] Indeed, the referendum on the Amsterdam Treaty alone was deemed to be 'our last chance to avoid the complete abandonment of Irish neutrality' according to Patricia McKenna MEP.[53] For others, however, these treaties were a pragmatic response to Europe's new security challenges and were fully consistent with the tradition and practice of Irish neutrality to date. Additional safeguards – such as the 2002 constitutional amendment precluding Irish participation in a European common defence and the various Declarations sought from EU partners and/or appended unilaterally to instruments of Irish treaty ratification – were all designed to underline that fact.

Of particular interest over time has been the evolution of a relationship between ESDP and NATO. The involvement of NATO in ESDP is understood to be rooted in the fact that in fulfilment of its own security agenda the Union is likely to have to rely upon the transportation, intelligence and communications infrastructure of the North Atlantic Alliance – unless it is either to act without such infrastructure or is to attempt to obtain its own. Detailed arrangements, under the so-called 'Berlin Plus' framework, have been put into place so as to allow for the use of NATO assets by the EU. These arrangements include a coordinating role for the Deputy Supreme Allied Commander of NATO, on the allocation of NATO resources for a specific EU-commanded operation and the creation of links between NATO and EU military planning units. For critics 'the Irish Government is steadily being sucked into the NATOfying of the EU under the guise of peacekeeping and humanitarian missions … Ireland's neutrality is on a crash course with Fortress Europe'.[54] For the government, these arrangements are seen as 'a necessary dimension of ESDP' but they are also governed by the principles of 'non-discrimination between member states and (the) autonomy of decision-making by both organisations'.[55]

The European Union's Rapid Reaction Force (EURRF) is the military framework that gives substance to the ambitions behind the ESDP. Initiated at the 1999 EU Helsinki Summit, it was declared to be partially operational in October 2004. The initial aim was to have available a full force complement

---

[51] See http://www.workers-party.org/ .
[52] *Dáil Deb.*, vol. 553, col. 1014, 25 June 2002.
[53] *Irish Times*, 8 July 1997.
[54] Fox, Carol, 'European Defence Debate, Peace and Neutrality Alliance (PANA) briefing paper no.2', (Dublin, 1996).
[55] *Dáil Deb.*, vol. 533, col. 998, 28 Mar. 2001.

of up to 60,000 soldiers which could be deployed to theatre within 60 days and sustained there for up to one year. That target was subsequently adjusted to the creation of up to 13 Battlegroups, each of which would comprise about 1,500 troops, and which would include combat and service supports. These Battlegroups are said to be designed to be deployed within 15 days and sustained in the field for at least 30 days. In the period 2004–2005 EU-commanded military forces were engaged in three major military operations. These were in Macedonia (Operation Concordia), the Democratic Republic of Congo (Operation Artemis) and in Bosnia Herzegovina (Operation Althea). The last of these represented a transfer of command from NATO's SFOR operation to the EU (Althea-EUFOR) of the 7,000 multilateral troops deployed in support of the Dayton Peace Process. Irish Defence Forces personnel participated in two of these operations – but were precluded from participation in Operation Concordia because this operation did not have formal United Nations Security Council authorisation.

This necessity for United Nations authorisation arises from the 'triple lock' on Irish peacekeeping. This requires a government decision, Dáil authorisation and a United Nations mandate for the participation of more than twelve armed members of the Defence Forces in international peace support operations. The Defence (Amendment) (No. 2) Act 1960, which provides for the deployment of Irish troops overseas, was drafted at a time when United Nations peacekeeping missions were of a specifically 'police' nature and when it was assumed that the United Nations would raise such forces on its own behalf. The Act was amended in 1993 deleting a reference to 'the performance of duties of a police character' so as to enable Irish forces to participate in the United Nations' military mission to Somalia (UNOSOM II). The 1960 Defence Acts still require, however, that such missions are 'authorised or established by' the United Nations. As a result of a 1999 Chinese veto in the United Nations Security Council, such authorisation was not forthcoming for a proposed peacekeeping mission in Macedonia and the United Nations was able only to indicate its 'strong support' for such a mission. This, however, was judged to be insufficient by the Attorney General in providing for Irish participation.

In 2005, the Irish government indicated that while it supported the EU Battlegroup concept in principle and would seek to participate, it faced legal difficulties. These related to the training of both Irish troops overseas as well as that of foreign-commanded troops in Ireland. Moreover, the nature of the Battlegroup concept – and its assumption of rapid deployability – was seen as militating against the participation of Irish troops, relying as they must on prior United Nations authorisation of such a mission. For one military analyst, 'Ireland's unique experience in peacekeeping, peace enforcement and anti-terrorist operations along with her world-class ordnance disposal and Special Forces personnel' would be an invaluable contribution to the EU

Battlegroups and thereby to the Union's security and defence policy.[56] For others, however, Irish participation would only serve the purposes of 'Europe's military and economic elites', which would further sideline the United Nations.[57]

For its part, in December 2004, the United Nations released its report from the High-Level Panel on Threats, Challenges and Change, entitled *A more secure world: our shared responsibility*. Having been commissioned by the Secretary-General to review the United Nations system so that it might more effectively address contemporary security challenges, the report made a series of substantial recommendations. Among these, it looked specifically at the use of force to address a broadened range of security challenges.

The report contended that Article 51 of the United Nations Charter remains an appropriate mechanism to address threats of a serious – but not imminent nature. Through this procedure, it is up to the Security Council to assess the evidence of a threat to collective security and then to determine what action is to be authorised. The potential use of military action – as part of a spectrum of response to threats – is understood to be the very corner-stone of an effective collective security policy. That policy, however, must also recognise that while not all states share the same perception of threats, we must acknowledge that the threats themselves are frequently inter-connected. As Foreign Minister Dermot Ahern has remarked

> The threats posed by terrorism and weapons of mass destruction are distinctly peripheral to the concerns of some, whose own concerns relate more to their next meal, or to where their children can get an education, or to the threat of violation and massacre through the fail-ure or perversion of the institutions of their state.[58]

Nonetheless, it is also acknowledged that the United Nations' security guar-antee is meaningless if it is not backed up by the capacity and willingness – in extremis and under carefully controlled conditions – to employ military force.

For the Irish state this can be a problematic issue in a public discourse where 'neutrality' has been partially conflated with issues of anti-militarism and indeed pacifism. While the United Nations may be extolled as the only valid legitimator of the use of force in collective security there then frequently arises the question as to the legitimacy of the United Nations' own decision making. In the run-up to the United Nations debate on Iraq and a decision on the use of force, for example, there were frequent arguments in the Irish

---

[56] *Irish Times*, 10 Jan. 2005.

[57] *Irish Times*, 11 Jan. 2005.

[58] Address by Minister for Foreign Affairs, Dermot Ahern, at Harvard University, 14 Mar. 2005. Available at http://www.irelandemb.org/press/03152005.html.

debate that if the United Nations were to authorise the US-led multilateral force then Irish neutrality would have to be invoked to forestall any Irish involvement in what would still be argued by some to be an illegitimate conflict.

Conclusions

It is here that the crux of the Irish policy dilemma on neutrality and collective security rests. Is neutrality – as it has been applied in the past – simply the default policy position in the absence of an effective collective security system, or does neutrality in a sense 'trump' the collective security goal in circumstances to be judged by the Irish body politic – or a substantial section thereof?

The emerging links between NATO and, in particular, the European Union and the United Nations are problematic on the other side of the debate. If the European Union – either of its own volition or in concert with other agencies such as NATO and/or the OSCE – is increasingly to take on the mantle of a collective defence agent and a tool of collective security, how can Irish foreign and security policy be situated within such a matrix? Are EU actions in support of peacekeeping and peacemaking only legitimate when formally authorised by the United Nations, or is there scope for the Union to exercise a collective security role in Europe with, perhaps, only the tacit support of a majority of the Security Council – when, for example, a veto wielding member rejects the possibility of collective action? Indeed, to what extent does the collective defence of the European Union and its member states not depend upon the success of collective security in Europe?

Several issues arise from these reflections. The first is the extent to which there is a broad consensus that Ireland can and should make a substantial contribution to missions defined in terms of international peace and security. There is also a broad consensus that Ireland's contribution thus far in United Nations peacekeeping and peacemaking has been honourable and worthy. The second issue, however, is the bitter division that immediately becomes evident when choices must be made about the appropriate institutional framework through which it is legitimate for Ireland to make that contribution.

Thus, while there is a generally shared commitment to the primacy of the United Nations, it is often to an idealised version of the United Nations, a 'transformed' United Nations that is sought. The 'actually existing' United Nations is seen as being frequently compromised by the politics to be found within the chamber of the Security Council and the dominance of the veto-wielding global powers therein. This then is the starting point for a subsidiary debate as to the potential for other actors, such as the EU, to act in support of collective security. Can or should the EU seek to legitimate its own military actions? In the absence of formal United Nations authorisation, can such actions be deemed to be consistent with the United Nations charter, inter-national law and broader political considerations of ethics and justice? Were such a debate to open at the fiftieth anniversary of Ireland's membership of the United Nations it would be an opportunity to both celebrate and hon-our the contribution that has already been made as well as establish Ireland's commitment to a more effective United Nations collective security policy.

Chapter Twelve

Ireland's participation in United Nations peacekeeping: a military perspective

JOHN TERENCE O'NEILL

Introduction

Ireland's long and honourable tradition of service in United Nations peace-keeping operations has been frequently acknowledged in studies of Ireland's role in international affairs. 'The heart of Ireland's foreign policy' has, according to Taoiseach Bertie Ahern, 'always been support for international collective security and engagement in peacekeeping and humanitarian operations'.[1] But while such a statement might suggest consistent and enthusiastic Irish support for United Nations endeavours in the field of conflict containment or resolution, in reality Ireland's support for the organisation and its activities has been far from unreserved. Participation in peacekeeping operations has in many instances been marked by an extremely cautious approach and heavily influenced by a variety of factors. These include concern about domestic security, a desire to be perceived as neutral, and a long-standing aversion to spending more than is absolutely necessary on defence.[2] And while the performance of Irish troops abroad might justifiably be a source of national pride, it is unlikely that more than a small fraction of the population could, the Congo and Lebanon apart, name the location of any of the missions on which Irish security personnel have served. Moreover, while there might be general acceptance that overseas experiences have developed the skills of the troops, the impact which the diversion of resources to a high-profile overseas role has had on the internal security role of the army, has gone largely unrecognised.

---

[1] *Address at European Movement National Conference on Partnership for Peace, Dublin,* 29 Mar. 1999, p. 3.
[2] For the background see Theo Farrell, '"The Suicidal Army": Civil Military Relations and Strategy in Independent Ireland', in Tom Garvin, Maurice Manning and Richard Sinnott (eds.), *Dissecting Irish Politics: essays in honour of Brian Farrell* (Dublin, 2004), pp. 48–65.

A question of commitment

Ireland's position on United Nations membership was initially extremely uncertain. Eamon de Valera, in May 1945, indicated Ireland's willingness to become a loyal member of any league that might be formed for collective security,[3] a sentiment endorsed in 1946 by the Secretary of the Department of External Affairs, Frederick Boland.[4] However, concern as to the potential financial consequences of United Nations membership caused de Valera's successor as Minister for External Affairs, Seán MacBride, to declare in 1948: 'these organisations are of great value but with our limited resources, I must be careful not to overload my administration'.[5] Dublin was alarmed by the approval of the United Nations for collective military action following the outbreak of war in Korea in June 1950. Ireland, Boland noted, was unprepared to participate in such military action and he was concerned that entry into the United Nations could have implications for Irish neutrality. In the light of its military response to the war in Korea, Boland even considered halting Irish plans for United Nations membership due to what he described as the 'most unwelcome and inopportune honour' of possible Irish entry into the United Nations at a time when it was involved in a war.[6] However, Timothy O'Driscoll, Assistant Secretary at the Department of External Affairs, observed that Sweden, a determined neutral, had not found the United Nations response to the Korean War in conflict with its own neutral status and United Nations membership.[7]

These remarks implied a clear difference in the observance of neutrality in both states. The question that consequently arises is: how did Irish and Swedish neutrality compare? Permanently neutral states – which Sweden, neutral since 1814 presumably was, and which Ireland, from the statements of its politicians and diplomats wished to be regarded as – must, under international law, prepare for their armed defence in accordance at least with the prevailing international standard, i.e. the military efforts of comparable states, especially those in their vicinity.[8] In World War II, Sweden had mobilised 592,000 well-equipped troops and was considerably better prepared for any attack than neutral neighbours Norway and Denmark.[9] Neutral Ireland had only managed to muster 42,500 troops and 'one of the most serious problems which had to be contended with during the present

---

[3] Joseph M. Skelly, 'Ireland, the Department of External Affairs and the United Nations, 1946–55: a new look', *Irish Studies in International Affairs* 7 (1996), pp. 63–80, p. 69.
[4] Ibid., p. 71.
[5] Ibid., p. 74.
[6] Ibid.
[7] Ibid., p. 78.
[8] Hanspeter Neuhold, 'Permanent Neutrality in Contemporary International Relations', *Irish Studies in International Affairs* 1:3 (1982), pp. 13–26, p. 19.
[9] Klaus Richard Böhme, 'The Principle Features of Swedish Defence', *Revue Internationale D'Histoire Militaire* 57 (1984), pp. 119–35, p. 127.

emergency', the Chief of Staff, Lieutenant General Dan McKenna, wrote in 1944 'was the almost complete lack of modern equipment. Not only did this problem haunt us throughout the emergency and retard progress at every step, but, in addition, it had a crippling effect on organisation, training and combat efficiency'.[10]

Overcoming reservations and, still distinctly less than a 'determined' neutral, Ireland joined the United Nations in December 1955. An undoubted factor in arrival at this decision was Boland's argument that small nations should welcome membership of an organisation intended to provide an international collective security system.[11] Ireland's implied reliance on the United Nations' collective security provisions invited the question: what did, or could, Ireland bring to any collective effort to oppose or repel aggression against another member state? The answer was 'nothing': it had neither the men nor military resources to engage in any such action.

The critical issue of resources inevitably surfaced in 1957 with the possibilities of a request that Ireland provide a contingent for United Nations Emergency Force I (UNEF I). External Affairs minister Frank Aiken took the view that refusing such a request would be inconsistent with Ireland's position regarding preservation of peace through collective action.[12] However, the Minister for Defence, Kevin Boland, expressed the opinion that having regard, not only to ordinary day-to-day requirements such as training, guard duties, etc, but also to the actual and potential internal security commitments, it would not be possible to undertake the additional commitment of providing a contingent for service with the United Nations.[13] This was hardly surprising: the army stood at a mere 8,846 and was woefully ill-equipped. It had four obsolete tanks, for which spare parts were not available, seventy-nine obsolete 'armoured cars', whose armour was virtually negligible, and only twenty-four artillery pieces. Meanwhile, the recrudescence of IRA activity in 1956 highlighted the need for greater concern about internal security, while the opening of the interment camp in the Curragh (for 120 IRA detainees) stretched manpower resources to the limit.[14] In these circumstances, training was and could only be geared towards engagement in conventional warfare. The question of training for possible employment in foreign theatres did not arise. Ireland was neutral and the army would – if ever – be employed in what

---

[10] Military Archives, Memorandum on Defence Forces, 11 Oct. 1944, p. 25. In December 1939 as war loomed, Taoiseach de Valera asked the Defence Forces for details of likely military requirements. The relatively modest list of personnel and military resources provided by the army was summarily dismissed by the Department of Finance. The threat from Britain, the Department claimed, could be dismissed and even if it materialised, consideration had to be given to avoidance of unnecessary suffering and excessive destruction. Ibid., pp. 62–3.

[11] Skelly 'A new look', p. 69.

[12] National Archives of Ireland (hereafter NAI), Department of Foreign Affairs (hereafter DFA), 305/1/173/1, 29 Aug. 1957.

[13] NAI DFA 305/173/1, 20 Aug. 1957.

[14] John Duggan, *A history of the Irish Army* (Dublin, 1990), pp. 235–8.

would effectively be a token gesture of resistance to attack by a foreign power. Since a request for an overseas contingent did not materialise in 1957, potentially painful decisions were put off for another day.[15]

The request for troops for the Congo operation (ONUC) raised again the issues of neutrality and resources. Ireland, like Sweden and Yugoslavia, was chosen because it did not belong to any bloc, while Taoiseach Seán Lemass declared that the United Nations request was due to 'the special position occupied by Ireland in relation to world affairs'.[16] There was, however, uncertainty as to the precise purpose of the operation, and the role of the troops. Adrift on a tide of uncertainty, Ireland chose to take a lead from Sweden,[17] whose action in the international field was viewed by members of the Department of External Affairs as 'independent, disinterested and honourable'.[18]

However, remaining totally independent would, for Ireland, be considerably more difficult than Sweden. The latter had not changed its non-aligned policy in order to escape a heavy burden of military expenditure.[19] Sweden spent 85% more per capita on defence than NATO neighbours Norway and Denmark: 13% of its national budget going on defence.[20] Its air force was the third strongest in Europe and most of its weapons were home produced. Swedish men between the ages of nineteen and forty-five were conscripted for five months and the armed forces, when mobilised, would be just above 500,000.[21] Most importantly, Sweden had rich natural resources and a thriving economy. Ireland's military resources remained essentially unchanged since 1957, when participation in UNEF I was mooted. By the late 1950s Ireland was seeking admission to the European Economic Community, a move which, if accomplished, would link it directly to a clearly Western community and it was in United Nations debates a consistent supporter of the United States. The same could not be said of Sweden.[22]

Within ONUC there was a significant difference between the quality of weapons and equipment available to the Swedish and Irish contingents. The consequences of Irish troops' unpreparedness for the challenging and always potentially dangerous role of peacekeeping was soon apparent. In November 1960, Baluba tribesmen using bows and arrows and machetes killed nine

---

[15] See also Richard Heaslip's chapter in this volume, pp. 79–116.

[16] *Dáil Deb.*, vol. 183, cols. 1875–81, 20 July 1960. Swedish parliamentarians also saw their country as occupying a 'special' position. See Kjell Goldmann, 'The United Nations Forces Use of Force in the Middle East, Congo and Cyprus' (Translated by the author), Stockholm University, Nov. 1965, pp. 1–11.

[17] Lemass stated: 'if any circumstances should arise which would prompt Sweden to withdraw its contingent, it is a fair assumption that the same circumstances would cause us to take a similar decision'. *Dáil Deb.*, vol. 183, cols. 1887–8, 20 July 1960.

[18] Conor Cruise O'Brien, *To Katanga and Back: A UN case history* (London, 1962), p. 14.

[19] Krister Wahlbeck, *The Roots of Swedish Neutrality* (Stockholm, 1986), p. 80.

[20] Irene Scobbie, *Sweden: Nation of the Modern World* (London, 1972), p. 149.

[21] Nicklas Granholm, (Swedish Military Historian), email to author, 12 July 2005.

[22] Denis Driscoll, 'Is Ireland Really Neutral?', *Irish States in International Affairs* 1:3 (1982), pp. 55–61, p. 56.

Irish soldiers of an eleven-strong patrol at Niemba. Four of the patrol were equipped with single-shot rifles, totally inappropriate for use in bush country.[23] The Swedes, in contrast, had come well-provided with Carl Gustaf sub-machine guns, of which the Irish had only a very limited number.[24] Equally critical to the role of the troops was the transport provided. The United Nations Force Commander in the Congo noted in relation to the Niemba incident that while a certain cause of the tragedy was the Irish personnel's lack of combat experience, the basic fault lay in the grave shortage of vehicles, which precluded any chance of their being trained in patrol work.[25] The Irish battalion had been provided with a mere fifteen Land Rovers and jeeps, and had to be furnished by the United Nations with some like-sized vehicles acquired locally. All deteriorated rapidly in the trying conditions.[26] Swedish troops had an abundance of sturdy troop carriers and formidable armoured cars drawn from their second-grade home stocks of approximately 500.[27] Irish equipment inadequacies were again highlighted in September 1961 when an Irish company (150 soldiers) was ordered to Jadotville. Having just one truck and two jeeps, the Irish were forced to turn to the Swedes to transport the bulk of men and stores, and even then were forced to leave behind their most potent weapon, the 81mm mortar.[28] Under sustained attack from overwhelming forces and lacking the transport to break out, the Irish were forced into a humiliating surrender, a development which compromised the United Nations effort to end the attempted secession of Katanga.[29]

Developments in the Congo also tested Ireland's claim to 'neutrality'. The decision to row in behind the Swedish Secretary-General Dag Hammarskjöld, who supported the 'pro-Western' Conglese President Joseph Kasavubu in his power struggle with his Soviet and African-backed Premier Patrice Lumumba, placed it at odds with the many new African states with whom it believed it had a long-standing special relationship.[30] Equally, at a time when Ireland was seeking EEC membership, supporting United Nations-approved strong measures against Belgian- and French-backed Katanga, the mineral rich south-eastern province of Congo which attempted secession following Congolese independence in 1960, involved alienating

[23] See also Edward Burke's chapter below pp. 117–153.
[24] Granholm, ibid.; Military Archives, Cathal Brugha Barracks, Dublin (hereafter MA), 'History of the 33rd Battalion'.
[25] General Carl Von Horn (Sweden) in the *Irish Times*, 8 Nov. 1985.
[26] Personal recollection of the author.
[27] Granholm, Ibid.
[28] John Terence O'Neill, 'The Irish Company at Jadotville Congo 1961: Soldiers or Symbols?', *International Peacekeeping* 9: 4 (Winter 2002), pp. 127–44, p. 132.
[29] For further details see Declan Power, *Siege at Jadotville. The Irish Army's forgotten battle* (Dunshaughlin, 2005).
[30] Norman McQueen, 'National Politics and the Peacekeeping Role: Ireland and the United Nations Operations in the Congo', *War and Society* 6:1 (May 1988), p. 102.

two established founder members of the community. The engagement of Irish troops in armed conflict in Katanga, albeit under a Security Council resolution, could be viewed as intervention in the internal affairs of another member state, while the controversial role in Katanga of former External Affairs official, Dr Conor Cruise O'Brien,[31] the loss of many lives including those of Irish soldiers[32] and the surrender at Jadotville, did not accord with the 'neutral' image which politicians and people wished to project.

There were, however, certain grounds for satisfaction. The deaths at Niemba had propelled 'little' obscure Ireland into world headlines and continued engagement (in ONUC) – many states had withdrawn for assorted reasons – helped foster the image of Ireland as a committed supporter of United Nations' efforts to contain the conflict. The performance of the troops had been widely acclaimed and for many Irish people, the army was at last being seen to be doing something, and something useful at that. There were other reasons to be pleased. The United Nations had paid generously for the use of the troops, the replacement of obsolete equipment and assorted expenses.[33] Peacekeeping was, therefore, a role which Ireland could play in world affairs without apparently forfeiting its claim to neutrality. And by playing up the value of this role, it was possible to divert attention from the ongoing failure to equip the army for its primary tasks of defending the state against external and internal threats.

For the army, the experience of peacekeeping represented an opportunity to engage in a new and totally unexpected role. It allowed Irish troops to measure their training and skills against personnel from other armies, introduced them to a world they would likely never otherwise have encountered, earn extra money and enjoy six months in the sun. For some, there had been the opportunity to apply their military training in combat and they emerged with a confidence in their ability to function as 'real' soldiers. Overall, acquaintance with contingents from other countries, both European and African, plus some bitter experiences brought home to Irish peacekeeping troops the limitations of the equipment with which they were provided. For Irish military analysts, a particularly important lesson was the ease with which, on a so-called Chapter VI operation, 'mission-creep' could transform what had begun as a 'policing' operation, into armed confrontation.

The Congo experience highlighted the risks and responsibilities associated with placing military forces at the disposal of an international body such as the United Nations, particularly where the objective was unclear, the nature

---

[31] Alan James, 'The Congo Controversies', *International Peacekeeping* 1:1 (Spring 1994), pp. 44–58.
[32] Sixteen Irish soldiers were killed in the Congo. See Eunan O'Halpin, *The Irish State and its Enemies since 1922* (Oxford, 1999), p. 272.
[33] These included allowances to officers and men, extra food issued prior to departure, transport of troops, telegrams, telephone calls, postage, employment of temporary chaplains, overtime, freight charges. Total £1,706,145. Details of money recovered from the United Nations, Management Accounts Branch, Dept. of Defence, 30 Oct. 2002 (pages not numbered).

and scale of the action uncertain, and the attitude and capabilities of other participating states still to be established. Faced in December 1961 with a situation where the troops had become engaged in armed conflict for which they were unprepared, Dublin had the option of doing nothing and risking heavy casualties, withdrawing from the operation and 'losing face', or reinforcing. It had chosen the latter, but this choice was possible only because of a benign domestic security situation. Demonstrating independence and responsibility, it had been shown, required providing contingents with the numbers and equipment necessary to ensure adequate self-protection.

The request to provide a contingent for UNFICYP in Cyprus, while seemingly an endorsement of the Irish role in the Congo, did not meet with an immediate positive response. With President Makarios of Cyprus unwilling to accept Third World contingents as peace keepers, attention was directed to European 'neutrals', Ireland, Sweden, and Finland. Ireland, however, was not 'neutral' over the issue of potential solutions to the conflict in Cyprus. It opposed the Turkish solution of the partition of the island, Frederick Boland suggesting that union of the island with Greece (which both Greece and the Greek Cypriots had long sought) was not only the best solution, but also an important factor in the defence of the West.[34] Sweden meanwhile was unwilling to join without another neutral: it became, as Alan James described it, a situation of 'after you Claude, no, after you Cecil'.[35] Concern about possible intervention by Great Britain, Greece, or Turkey – although these states were entitled, indeed required under international treaty,[36] to do so in certain circumstances – was overcome largely through a desire to maintain the image of a strong United Nations supporter. Ultimately, it was the decision of Finland and Sweden to participate which led to Ireland's involvement.

A further cause for Irish hesitation was the issue of finance. The government regarded the voluntary funding arrangement for the Cyprus operation as a grave and unwise departure from the principle of collective responsibility. To demonstrate its stand on the issue, it undertook to pay overseas allowances to the troops as well as equipping the contingent prior to departure.[37] This equipment did not, however, include the jeep-type vehicles that would obviously be required. Since the bulk of Ireland's original stocks of such vehicles had been sent to the Congo and abandoned there, none was now available. External Affairs Minister Frank Aiken expected that transport, supplies and ammunition would be provided by Britain, but Seán Lemass, anxious to avoid any misunderstanding regarding relations between British and Irish

---

[34] Norman McQueen, 'Irish Neutrality: The United Nations and Peacekeeping Experiences 1945–1965', unpublished PhD Thesis, New University of Ulster, 1981, p. 274.

[35] Alan James, '"After you Claude, No After you Cecil". The Problems of Assembling the United Nations Cyprus Force March 1964', Paper to the Pearson Peacekeeping Centre, July 1998, p. 8.

[36] For details see Katsumi Ishizuga, *Ireland and International Peacekeeping Operations 1960–2000* (London, 2004), p. 92.

[37] Ibid., p. 95.

contingents, insisted that any charges for provision of these items be sent direct to the United Nations – they were.[38]

Opposition contributions to the debate on the proposed Irish involvement focused on the need for the provision of armoured vehicles and the numbers to be provided. Since inadequate armaments in the Congo had brought about Irish casualties[39] and the factions on Cyprus were known to be heavily-armed, there was a clear need for greater protection and 'muscle'. Aiken argued that the Irish contingent should be as fully and heavily equipped as the Swedish and Canadian battalions and arrangements were made for the purchase of eight Panhard armoured fighting vehicles. There was meanwhile some concern also about the depletion in the numbers of soldiers left at home; one Dáil deputy asking, 'Were the Irish slowly proving that they did not need an army'?[40] Ultimately, 639 soldiers were sent to Cyprus on 19 and 20 April 1964.

The issues of numbers and associated costs became more acute with the request for two extra companies (approximately 400 officers and men) to bring Ireland in line with the roughly 1,000-strong forces provided by Canada, Denmark, Finland, Sweden and Great Britain.[41] While the Minister for Finance Charles Haughey argued that the sending of the extra troops and eight more armoured fighting vehicles would be too heavy a burden to bear, Aiken maintained that only by showing its total commitment could Ireland argue effectively for a fairer system of United Nations financing of peacekeeping operations. Aiken's view prevailed and the extra troops were sent to Cyprus in August 1964. The initiative had its hoped for roll-on effect: Haughey later wrote to Aiken: 'I am very pleased to see that your long campaign to recover money due to us from the United Nations in respect of the Irish contingents in Cyprus has been a success'.[42]

The operation revealed an aspect of peacekeeping operations not normally commented upon, namely the differing perceptions between governments and their troops on the question of the 'good' and 'bad' parties in the dispute. The Irish government and Irish diplomats had at the outset taken a distinctly pro-Greek line, although, by supporting the United Nations in its maintenance of the 1974 cease-fire line – effectively partition – that position would now seem to have been reversed. Meanwhile, the Irish troops, having witnessed the plight of Turkish Cypriots following the violence of 1963, having been denied freedom of movement by Greek Cypriot authorities, and having observed Makarios smuggling in large numbers of Greek troops and heavy equipment, were at odds with their political leaders.[43]

---

[38] Ibid., p. 76.
[39] Ibid., p. 78.
[40] *Dáil Deb.*, vol. 208, col. 1112, 7 Apr. 1964.
[41] United Nations Document 5/5679, 2 May 1964, p. 1.
[42] NAI 2000/43/96, Haughey to Aiken, 16 Aug. 1967.
[43] Assorted Irish Officers, interview with author, Mar.-May 2005.

In the performance of their duties, Irish troops had the distinct advantage of having in their ranks large numbers of personnel with considerable experience in the Congo. Some of the Swedish troops might also have served in the Congo, but the bulk of personnel were, like those from Finland and Denmark, conscripts. And while such personnel might be well-trained, equipped, and motivated, they were on a one-off tour. British troops, while well-trained and equipped, regarded peacekeeping as not 'proper' soldiering. Canadian personnel, seeking to keep an edge on their soldiering skills, tended to be unnecessarily confrontational.[44] Since Ireland had such limited numbers to call upon, many returned to the mission at regular intervals. In this way, they acquired detailed knowledge of the people, terrain and the dangers. The skills in crowd control, mediation, and establishing of good relations developed in the Congo were employed to good effect in the new theatre. Officers familiar with Western operational procedures slotted well into staff appointments, many coming to occupy senior positions.[45] Critical to the effective functioning of all ranks was that Irish peacekeepers spoke English, this enabling them to communicate effectively with all parties, including local leaders.

Whereas many of the problems encountered in ONUC had arisen from lack of reliable transport, no such problems attended the operation in Cyprus. The contingent had an abundance of vehicles (forty-eight jeeps per battalion), provided and maintained by the British Army.[46] This facilitated routine patrolling, the immediate dispatch of reserves to trouble spots, and a generally effective conduct of operations.

The clash of interests

Dismissing the suggestion of a possible Permanent Defence Force (PDF) intervention in Northern Ireland in the early 1970s, Taoiseach Jack Lynch said: 'a military intervention is just not possible'.[47] That such a statement was required reflected the prevailing ignorance of the army's capabilities at this time amongst the political elite and general population alike.

The movement of troops to the Border to help establish refugee camps following riots in Belfast and Derry in August 1969 bordered on the shambolic. Trucks carrying personnel and stores broke down within minutes of leaving barracks and a move that should have been accomplished in a matter of hours, became spread over days.[48] Troops subsequently located in Border posts suffered from an acute shortage of vehicles in which to patrol; there was

---

[44] General M.J. Murphy, interview with author, 12 Oct. 1997.

[45] For example, Force Commander Major Gen. James Quinn (1976–81), Major Gen. Michael Minehane (1992–4).

[46] MA, 'History of 40th Bn.'.

[47] NAI DFA 305/14/396/1, 20 Aug. 1971.

[48] Personal recollections of the author.

as yet no effective replacement for the transport sent to the Congo almost ten years earlier. What few Land Rovers remained were purchases made in the mid-1950s, in such poor condition that all patrols were advised to bring along tow ropes, assuming such were available. Once again, with attention focused on the overseas role of the Irish troops and the bulk of requirements there having been met by the United Nations, little or no thought had been given to the resources required for their fulfilment of the internal security role.

Performance of this domestic role in the 1970s would, however, reveal the benefits of overseas experience. Many of the still small army (9,200 men) were by now skilled in patrolling, and remaining calm in potentially explosive situations. Junior officers and NCOs had honed their leadership skills and all ranks were quite familiar with the assorted weapons and explosives employed by subversive elements. Acquaintance with some British army units with whom troops had co-operated in Cyprus, facilitated effective liaison and reduced the risk of misunderstanding and confrontation. Increasingly, developments at home exposed again the limitations of resources and impacted on overseas commitment.

Following the outbreak of war between Israel and Egypt in 1973, Ireland was asked to provide troops for UNEF II. Inability to provide the standard battalion-sized contingent resulted in the single company now remaining in Cyprus being directed to the Sinai where they were reinforced by another company from Ireland. As they were being dispatched, the Minister for Defence, Paddy Donegan, emphasised the need to recruit more men due to the security situation, and the Minister for Foreign Affairs, Garret FitzGerald, said it was 'not without careful thought' that the provision had been agreed.[49] The group thus established had few resources beyond their weapons and uniforms, and were entirely dependent upon other UNEF II contingents for such essentials as transport and tentage. Trucks – provided by the Egyptians – were in such a dilapidated state that Israeli liaison officers were unwilling to travel in them,[50] while Minister Donegan noted: 'it has been pointed out that at some stage the men could experience difficulty obtaining food'.[51] Their lot was made even more parlous by political complications. Ireland had not at this time established diplomatic relations with Israel and, deployed on the Israeli side of the ceasefire line, the peacekeepers became effectively hostages in the hands of the Israelis.[52]

The government decision to withdraw from UNEF II in 1974 following the Dublin and Monaghan bombings in May of that year did little to boost numbers at home and was, according to John Duggan, looked on from

---

[49] *Dáil Deb.*, vol. 273, cols. 1715–6, 27 July 1974.

[50] Col. S. Downes in an interview with the author, 14 May 2005.

[51] *Dáil Deb.*, vol. 268, col. 817, 30 Oct. 1973. The men subsisted on pack rations.

[52] Bertil Stjernfelt, *The Sinai Peace Front* (London, 1992), p. 67.

abroad as a cosmetic charade which ignored serious United Nations problems on the ground.[53] Both superpowers during the crisis had put their forces on red alert and United Nations officials, Irish diplomat Noel Dorr observed, would have been a bit disappointed in Ireland, which they had always thought of as so reliable, withdrawing its troops for domestic reasons in such a climate.[54] In an effort to undo the damage the government later offered a full contingent for UNFICYP, but the United Nations did not take up the offer.[55]

Recruiting campaigns in the early 1970s helped boost army strength to approximately 12,000, but in 1976 and 1977 there were losses of 1,200 and 1,100 respectively.[56] Minister for Defence Donegan attributed, with some justification, such significant wastage to difficult working conditions.[57] Such conditions might arguably have been tolerated had the troops the prospect of a break overseas from the dreary routine, but that prospect seemed now remote. Increasingly troops were conscious of the much more favourable conditions enjoyed by the gardaí alongside whom they were working and the unavailability of overseas allowances was all the more acutely felt.

Dáil debates on defence matters in the early 1970s reveal a general failure to consider what would be required if the Defence Forces were to fulfil their designated tasks. Major Vivion de Valera observed that the peace-time strength of the army had been worked out in the context of post-war needs: 'That strength was eroded in order to save money … we now find ourselves with an army insufficient for our current needs … it is geared towards a security job and that is wrong',[58] and went on: 'we may go to the extreme of regarding the army as an auxiliary police force and nothing else'. Meanwhile, criticism was heaped on Dr Conor Cruise O'Brien for daring to suggest that in a Doomsday situation, the army could at best hold a town the size of Newry,[59] although this was a view with which army personnel would have wholeheartedly agreed. Former minister Neil Blaney, when considering the internal security problem declared: 'We should try to get the United Nations interested in our problem here: we seem to be very fine members of the United Nations when something is required of us, but when we have required something of that body, the goods do not seem to be delivered'.[60] And while Minister for Defence Donegan announced 'whether we like it nor not, there will be a need in the years to come for an Irish army of considerable proportions and great equipment',[61] what he had in mind was not made clear.

---

[53] John Duggan, *A history of the Irish Army* (Dublin, 1990), p. 263.
[54] Ishizuga, p. 101.
[55] Ibid, p. 100.
[56] *Dáil Deb.*, vol. 311, col. 951, 13 Feb. 1979.
[57] *Dáil Deb.*, vol. 312, cols. 949–55, 9 Mar. 1979.
[58] *Dáil Deb.*, vol. 285, col. 966, 3 Nov. 1975.
[59] *Dáil Deb.*, vol. 275, cols. 332–5, 29 Oct. 1974.
[60] *Dáil Deb.*, vol. 268, col. 811, 30 Oct. 1973.
[61] *Dáil Deb.*, vol. 285, col. 1003, 3 Nov 1975.

The general naiveté surrounding the state of the army and its equipment was particularly evident in the debate on the proposed purchase of armoured personnel carriers (APCs). Rejecting criticism of such vehicles, Donegan was forced to argue that an APC was 'not a pugnacious sort of weapon, but a vehicle in which one can move personnel'.[62] Former Taoiseach, Jack Lynch, expressed support for the purchase of an Irish-assembled Timoney APC on the basis that Belgium had purchased some and that 'what was good enough for the Belgians was surely good enough for us'.[63] The Timoney was, however, intended primarily for use in the Low Countries and the South African veldt, and would have proved useless in an overseas operational theatre such as Lebanon, or even along the Irish border with Northern Ireland. Even the Panhards eventually purchased, while highly useful in Ireland, proved underpowered for the upcoming UNIFIL operation in South Lebanon.

Involvement in UNIFIL provided a welcome opportunity to restore Ireland's tarnished image in United Nations peacekeeping.[64] Not only was a full battalion provided, but also its abundant equipment, which included refrigerated ration trucks, made the Irish the envy of other contingents. Such 'support' would not, however, be sustained. By 1982, ninety percent of those vehicles were in a highly dangerous state: Dublin passed responsibility for replacement to the United Nations, whose replacement procedures took nine to twelve months.[65] There was, however, no shortage of volunteers, most of whom had previous peacekeeping experience and were by now confident that United Nations operations were their true metier.

Confidence and experience were required in what was to be at all times a dangerous environment. Small groups deployed in isolated posts were highly vulnerable to attack by any or all local parties. It was, therefore, vital that they were seen to be impartial. The position of the Irish troops was not, however, improved by Foreign Minister Brian Lenihan's expression of support in February 1980 for the role of the Palestine Liberation Organisation in representing the Palestinian people.[66] Equally, the government response to developments in Lebanon, while indicative of concern for the troops welfare, was in some respects, less than helpful. The death of one Irish soldier in a confrontation with Israeli-backed militia at At-Tiri in April 1980 and the murder two days later of a further two Irish troops by the same militia in the presence of an Israeli agent presented the government with a difficult choice. It could fail to respond and risk further deaths, or attempt to bring pressure to bear on Israel, knowing that such a move could be counter-productive. By way of responding, Ireland hosted a conference in Dublin in May 1980

---

62 *Dáil Deb.*, vol. 750, col. 1334, 16 Dec. 1970.

63 *Dáil Deb.*, vol. 298: col. 433, 29 Mar 1977.

64 See also Rory Miller's chapter, pp. 54–78.

65 Recollections of the author.

66 Robert Fisk, 'At-Tiri, or Bosnia Avoided: The Irish in UNIFIL 1978–95', *The Irish Sword* 20 (Summer, 1996), no. 79, pp. 59–70, p. 63.

which was attended by eleven troop-contributing states. But while the conference indicated the strength of feeling on developments, the states had no effective tools to influence the Israelis. With all contingents convinced that Israel could, and did from time to time, raise the tension, relations between the Irish and the Israeli troops and Israeli-backed militia were at all times difficult, the Irish being perceived to be more firm in dealing with Israeli-supported militia than other contingents.[67] And though frustration with the operation's lack of progress caused Nigeria, Senegal and even the pro-Israeli Netherlands to withdraw, Ireland remained engaged. These withdrawals created greater opportunities for Irish officers to assume staff appointments and, totally familiar with United Nations procedures, such personnel were highly suitable for and increasingly employed on the many operations launched in the 1990s.

Apart from the issue of casualties, the most frequently advanced reason for questioning continued participation in UNIFIL was that of cost, with Dáil statements presenting the United Nations as in arrears with payment. However, much misunderstanding arose through presentation as 'a loss' delayed payments of the notional figure agreed between the United Nations and governments for provision of the troops. In reality Ireland had a steady income from the United Nations. Information from the Department of Defence stated that in 1991 'receipts in respect of arrears of UNIFIL troops (£10,162,647) were higher than anticipated', while in 2001 estimated receipts from United Nations (£7,261,678) 'were greater than expected due mainly to the payment of arrears of contributions by member countries'.[68] This information received no media coverage.

More 'robust' engagement

In contrast to UNIFIL, the request to provide a contingent for the operation in Somalia, UNOSOM II in 1993, in this case a transport company, resulted in considerable deliberation. Secretary-General Boutros Ghali's reference to 'peace enforcement', invocation of Chapter VII, and the presence in the United Nations force of a significant-sized and heavily-armed United States element, suggested an attempt to impose a solution by military means. Minister of State for Defence, Seamus Brennan, sought to present Ireland's approach as non-threatening. The United Nations, he declared, was not going to Somalia with aggressive intent: 'The mandate is designed in such a way that the United Nations Force will be in a position to respond if subjected to aggression by local gangs'.[69] But since authority to engage vigorously in self-defence was always a feature of Chapter VI (peacekeeping) operations,

---

[67] Ibid., p. 63.

[68] Memorandum 'Details of money received from the United Nations, Management Accounts Branch, Department of Defence, 13 Oct. 2002. Memorandum in the author's possession.

[69] *Dáil Deb.*, vol. 432, col. 2155, 24 June 1993.

including ONUC, the move from police action to 'something else' aroused concern.[70] Because of the nature of the Irish role, it was possible for supporters of participation to present the Irish as acting under Chapter VI within a Chapter VII mission. But while the Irish would in the course of their work be escorted by well-armed other contingent elements, they actually possessed considerable weaponry.[71] Had they become engaged in combat – which they did not – the question of whether they were engaged in a Chapter VI or a Chapter VII action would have been purely academic.

Ireland emerged unscathed from the shambolic operation in Somalia. It had not been embroiled in the fighting, nor had its troops been contaminated by accusations of brutality levelled against several other contingents. Dáil debates presented Ireland's involvement not as an indication of its commitment to United Nations endeavours, but as an altruistic gesture and a manifestation of its neutrality. Minister David Andrews saw the sending of a unit as 'reflecting the will of the Irish people arising from their generosity to the people of Somalia',[72] declaring: 'we are born missionaries whether in army uniform or clerical garb'.[73] He further stated: 'we have a moral role to play within the United Nations as a small island on the periphery of Europe'.[74] Deputy Haughey supported this view: 'Ireland is a neutral country, we promote peace and justice and basic human rights through diplomacy and negotiation, and we are well respected for the role we play ... we can rely on our missionary work ... and our peacekeeping by the United Nations troops'.[75]

The transport company had done an excellent job with vehicles (MAN diesel trucks), the bulk of which were over ten years old, but refitted and repainted to appear as new. The state had leased the transport to the United Nations and on completion of the mission, it was returned for service on domestic duties. Ireland had discovered a niche role which would allow continuing participation in United Nations operations, engagement of small numbers, minimal extra expenditure and welcome monetary compensation.

Into the unknown

After the Cold War, expectations that conflicts could in a less polarised world be resolved rather than contained had received a setback in Somalia. But if 'peace-enforcement' had been discredited, even in the eyes of the United Nations Secretary-General, there remained the perceived option of 'robust peacekeeping'. The prescription for such action is captured in Michael Ignatieff's call for combat capable warriors under robust rules of engagement

---

[70] *Dáil Deb.*, vol. 432, col. 2157, 24 June 1993.

[71] A senior officer engaged in the operation in an interview with the author, 18 May 2005.

[72] *Dáil Deb.*, vol. 429, col. 417, 6 Apr. 1993.

[73] *Dáil Deb.*, vol. 438, col. 1553, 10 Feb. 1994.

[74] *Dáil Deb.*, vol. 443, col. 2084, 16 June 1994.

[75] *Dáil Deb.*, vol. 442, col. 1176, 11 May 1994.

with armour, ammunition, intelligence capability, and a single line of command to a national government or regional organisation.[76] This option presented problems for Ireland since as John Sanderson observes: 'in the military, we used to call these activities war not peace operations'.[77] And Ireland not merely lacked the resources referred to, but was unhappy about association with any regional alliance.

The European Union (EU) preventive deployment venture in Macedonia appeared tailor-made for a country with traditional peacekeeping experience. The task was undemanding, resources required un-taxing, and prospects of confrontation seemingly remote. However, Ireland refused to commit forces because the operation lacked a United Nations mandate. Reluctance to engage in operations other than strictly 'United Nations approved' would be a feature of debate for several years. International demand for humanitarian intervention faced Ireland with a dilemma. Given its missionary zeal and declared support for collective action, it could hardly abstain from involvement. However, UNOSOM II had demonstrated the need for resources and command structure best provided by NATO, the body from which Ireland had so long sought to distance itself.

In 1995, Fianna Fáil leader Bertie Ahern, noted that neutral Sweden, Austria and Finland had all joined the NATO-led Partnership for Peace (PfP) which he described as 'a half-way house offering a form of associated membership', but declared: 'our geographic and strategic location was not the same as theirs'.[78] Subsequently, Ray Burke, later to be Minister for Foreign Affairs, declared: 'Fianna Fáil is fundamentally opposed to Irish participation in NATO-led organisations such as Partnership for Peace', which he saw as having serious implications for our military neutrality.[79] However, with every Western European state involved except Ireland and Switzerland (which was showing an interest),[80] opposition to participation in Partnership for Peace could not be sustained; especially since Ireland's peacekeeping record was a particular asset in collective crisis management,[81] but particularly since NATO heavyweights, the United States and Britain, were involved in trying to resolve the island's internal security problem. After years of pursuing a singular stance, Ireland in 2000 accepted the reality that no one state or institution can deal by itself with the multifaceted challenges to security of the post-Cold War world.[82]

---

[76] Michael Ignatieff, 'A Bungling United Nations Undermines Itself', *New York Times*, 15 May 2000, p. 19.

[77] John Sanderson, 'The Changing Face of Peace Operations: A View from the Field', *Journal of International Affairs* 55:2 (Spring 2002), pp. 277–88, p. 277.

[78] *Irish Times*, 2 June 1995.

[79] *Dáil Deb.*, vol. 479, col. 524, 14 May 1997.

[80] Patrick Keatinge, *Towards a Safer Europe: Small States Security Policies and the European Union: Implications for Ireland* (Dublin, 1995) p. 47.

[81] Ibid., p. 115.

[82] Defence White Paper, p. 17.

In many countries, including the former Cold War adversaries, neutral states were now seen as involved in a web of mutually reinforcing security co-operation. This security interdependence involving the United Nations, OSCE, EU, NATO, and WEU was, in the 2000 White Paper on Defence, seen as having played a role in reducing the risk of war between states within Europe, as well as facilitating co-operation for the management of regional conflicts such as in the Balkans. Even the PfP, which Ireland joined in December 1999, was now accepted as contributing to this process and facilitating planning and co-operation for the Petersberg tasks.[83]

The operational tasks identified in the Petersberg Declaration of June 1992, namely humanitarian rescue and peacekeeping, and employing combat forces in crisis management including peacemaking, were all largely in line with earlier efforts by the United Nations to maintain international peace and security. The major difference was in the resources available to PfP members as distinct from any other United Nations member states, including Ireland. Since the other members of PfP were members of NATO, had been members of the Warsaw Pact or neutrals who saw the need to maintain substantial well-armed forces, Ireland's resources made it the exception. But whereas the potential roles in the new scenario would be challenging and require substantial numbers and modern arms and equipment, large investment in these was never likely.

Even during the heightened international tensions of the 1980s when defence against external aggression was officially the primary task of the Defence Forces, the resources required were manifestly inadequate. With the Cold War past and the internal security threat apparently reduced by the Good Friday Agreement, expenditure on defence would be even less a priority. In December 1999, arrangements were made for the purchase, over a five-year period, of forty MOWAG APCs.[84] But while this was a welcome development, funding would come not through additional investment but through a reduction in the strength of the forces and the sale of six military barracks.[85] The prospect of ever-reducing numbers had to be considered against the undertaking given by Ireland in October 1998 to commit 850 troops to peacekeeping under the United Nations Stand-By Arrangement System (UNSAS). And while 850 might be in line with contributions to earlier United Nations operations, the figure would now be expected to cover for PfP as well as 'conventional' United Nations requests.

The Senate debate on PfP membership revealed, even among learned members, an ongoing inability or unwillingness to address the issue of army resources. On the matter of equipment, Senator David Norris declared: 'we should not be swayed by their (the army's) requirement for toys'.[86] Senator

---

[83] Ahern, Address at European Movement Conference, p. 3.

[84] *Dáil Deb.*, vol. 500, col. 156, 9 Feb. 1995.

[85] *Dáil Deb.*, vol. 512, col. 1008, 3 Feb. 1999.

[86] *Seanad Deb.*, vol. 161, col. 42, 16 Nov. 1999.

Dr Mary Henry, while criticising United Nations and PfP, lamenting the loss of 7,000 to 8,000 lives in former Yugoslavia observed: 'one realises what can happen when there are no forces to keep warring factions apart'.[87] Neither offered any suggestion as to how to address such problems without resort to the 'toys' and numbers that PfP could provide. The commitments involved in membership of PfP were soon apparent.

In 1999, Ireland provided the United Nations-mandated Kosovo Force (KFOR) with a one hundred strong Transport Company tasked with providing equipment and material to military units and humanitarian organisations. Pressed into service were many of the by now twenty-plus year old MAN trucks earlier used in Somalia. While these vehicles were mechanically sound, the combination of vehicle and trailer proved unsuitable for movement of goods from Thessaloniki to the mission's area. Moreover, the other contingents were all accustomed to movement of forces by Demountable Rack Offloading and Pickup System (DROPS) vehicles with container lifts. This was a totally new 'league': it was no longer a matter, as in earlier operations, of just providing bodies and hoping to get by. For would-be participants, the question was: what assets are you bringing? In the event DROPS vehicles were purchased and returned with the Company to Ireland in 2003, providing the army with a morale-boosting asset. The Transport Company would be replaced by a 200-strong well-armed infantry unit.

Returning to Ireland's preferred option, 213 troops were provided for the United Nations mission in Ethiopia and Eritrea (UNMEE), the first contingent arriving in December 2001.[88] The group engaged in extensive humanitarian work raising funds through its own resources and being provided by the Irish government with €200,000. The work of the force was hugely advantaged by the presence in the initial six months of the United Nations Stand-By Force High Readiness Brigade (SHIRBRIG).[89] This body, which addressed the need for swift and effective United Nations deployment capabilities, included neutrals Sweden, Finland, and Austria. However, Ireland, once again being the exception, had only observer status.[90] The contingent was withdrawn in July 2003 and thus resources became available for dispatch of a contingent to Liberia in December of that year.

The successful setting up of UNMIL (United Nations Mission in Liberia) was also facilitated by the work of SHIRBRIG and the speedy arrival of the 427-strong Irish contingent. This body, which provided the Force Commander's Rapid Reaction Force and a short-term (six months) Special Force Unit, was very well-equipped, having twenty-one MOWAG APCs,

---

[87] *Seanad Deb.*, vol. 161, col. 26, 16 Nov. 1999.

[88] In contrast to ONUC, this small force was equipped with twenty three-quarter-ton vehicles, eight heavy MAN trucks and six MOWAG APCs (Irish Army sources).

[89] Col. R. King, in an interview the author, 10 July 2005.

[90] One senior observer at SHIRBRIG Headquarters speaks of the embarrassment at his inability to explain to Scandinavian officers Ireland's non-participation, interview with author, 18 Aug. 2005.

four armoured fighting vehicles, twenty-six jeeps, eleven trucks and other assorted vehicles, had an excellent logistic back-up,[91] and could therefore undertake its task with confidence.

In the early weeks, the battalion (the contingent was quickly supplemented with a Swedish company) helped stabilise the situation in the capital and opened the way to the interior for other contingents. The robust approach which met with a favourable reaction from the war-weary population, was the consequence of availability of high-quality equipment and robust rules of engagement. However, for Ireland, forming the cutting edge of a Chapter VII mission represented an extraordinary change in political attitude. Having for decades failed to equip the army for defence of the state, it was now prepared to have its troops, if necessary, wage 'war' under Chapter VII in a country thousands of miles away from Ireland.

Conclusion

Ireland's approach to United Nations operations was, from the start, marked by a desire to be regarded as a 'good' United Nations member, tempered by concerns as to the consequences of involvement. Reaction to the Congo operation revealed contrasting views on the role of the troops: while some lauded the efforts to bring peace through patience and negotiation, many took satisfaction from the performance of the 'fighting Irish' in armed conflict. With only a fraction of the population acquainted with military affairs, the serious problems that the operation exposed went largely unobserved, and analysis of the activity in which the troops had been involved was not undertaken. Deaths in the Lebanon, while lamented, were in general presented as inevitable or in a noble cause.

The image of professional forces playing a useful role abroad had steadily reduced the motivation for serious examination of the role(s) and capability of the army. The army had ventured into United Nations operations with extremely limited and largely obsolete equipment, and uncertain as to the nature of the activity and its ability to perform. Experience gained on a variety of operations and on internal security had produced a well-trained and experienced force. Exposure to the demands of overseas roles had also resulted in acquisition of some state-of-the-art equipment, which arguably would not otherwise have been seen as required.[92] The army could, therefore, 'deliver' on future operations if just provided with numbers and more equipment. However, once again, there arises the issue of political commitment.

The declaration of support for international collective security and peacekeeping by successive governments would suggest that the Defence Forces constituted a key element in foreign policy. However, the army's efforts

---

[91] Information gained from Defence Forces sources.

[92] Such as Javelin Anti-Armour Systems, MOWAG APCs and CBRN (Chemical Biological Radiological Nuclear) early warning equipment.

abroad as well as at home have consistently been handicapped by government failure to provide necessary resources.[93] This failure follows in large measure from the perception and presentation of Ireland as an impoverished, small state 'on the periphery of Europe', but also from an interpretation of neutrality characterised by what Ronan Fanning calls 'a sense of emotional self-satisfaction'.[94]

Still resistant to membership of NATO and dragging its feet on involvement in proposed EU defence arrangements, Ireland's policy, particularly given its so-called 'moral role' should logically be one of wholehearted commitment to United Nations peacekeeping activities, whether these be conducted by the Organisation or a regional body acting under Chapter VIII of the United Nations Charter. However, the ability to meet potential demands is being eroded by a steady reduction in defence expenditure and an associated paring down of numbers.[95] This trend is seen as ill-advised.

At a time when the Irish economy is booming, enlargement of the Defence Forces by 3,000 to 4,000 would eliminate the risk of another debacle such as that in 1969 and the problems of the 1970s. Equally importantly, a significant increase in numbers would allow Ireland to make available 1,500 to 2,000 personnel at any time for overseas operations. Meaningful contributions rather than the mere nominal presences currently provided would be in keeping with the 'special position' of which Seán Lemass spoke in 1960 and with the missionary spirit so often spoken of in relation to Ireland's role in peacekeeping.

---

[93] The number of MOWAGs provided for KFOR (6), is less than half that available to other contingents (author in discussion with officers recently returned from service in KFOR (June, 2005)).

[94] Ronan Fanning, 'Irish Neutrality – An Historical Review', *Irish Studies on International Affairs* 1: 3 (1982), p. 33.

[95] Financial allocation to defence expenditure has dropped each year from 1995 (1.3% of GNP) to 2004 (0.7% of GNP). Defence Forces Annual Report, 2004, p. 50.

Chapter Thirteen

The legal framework governing Irish participation in peace operations

RAY MURPHY

Introduction

This chapter explores the municipal legal bases for Irish and Canadian participation in United Nations operations. It aims to examine, inter alia, the laws governing the decision to participate in such operations, and further issues concerning the status under municipal law of members of the respective armed forces of both countries. Canada and Ireland share a long tradition of involvement in peacekeeping operations. Although Canada is a larger and more influential country than Ireland, both states share a 'middle power' political image on the world stage. Since 1971, participation in peacekeeping has been identified as an integral and important part of Canada's defence policy. In Ireland such an identification began in the early 1960s. The legal system of each country is significantly different, and the municipal legal basis for participation in peacekeeping and related operations reflects this. Despite this, on analysis, the aim and effect of different provisions contained in the two respective legislative frameworks can be said to be the same. In Ireland, the Defence Acts 1954 to 1998 govern the operation and organisation of the Defence Forces. The operation of the Canadian armed forces is governed by a legislative enactment called the National Defence Act, which came into force in 1950 and is revised periodically.

In Ireland, the Constitution of 1937 is the primary source of law and all Acts or Statutes enacted must be consistent with its provisions. Unlike Ireland, which is a unitary state, Canada is a country organised on a federal basis with areas of responsibility assigned to the federal or provincial governments in its constitution.[1] Section 91 of Canada's Constitution Act gives the federal government exclusive authority over 'militia, military and naval service, and defence'.[2]

[1] Lt. Col. K. Carter, 'The Legal Basis of Canada's participation in United Nations operations', *International Peacekeeping* 1 (4) (1994), pp. 116–8.
[2] Section 91, The Constitution Act, 1867 (The British North America Act, 1867), 30 & 31 Victoria, c. 3.

At first glance, the most striking similarity between the legislative frame-work governing the respective armed forces of Canada and Ireland is that in both jurisdictions there is no mention of the aims of defence or security policy, or the actual mission of the armed forces themselves. This has more to do with history than any other reason. Canada, like Ireland, had a series of Militia Acts to govern the establishment and maintenance of the armed forces. Neither country has any real independent military tradition and both states are relatively new members of the international club of recognised states. This is a politically expedient way to conduct defence matters, as each government can determine the priorities and mission of the state's armed forces. The problem with this, despite the fact that Canada and Ireland have well established and strong democratic institutions, is that it allows the ruling party of the day more discretion than is necessary in a parliamentary democracy. It also reduces the parliamentary control exercised over the armed forces. While it is true to state there is no serious threat to democratic insti-tutions in either state, the maximum parliamentary control over all elements of defence and security issues is the hallmark of a healthy democracy. One of the many controversial issues surrounding the formation of a European Rapid Deployment Force and Irish participation is that of democratic con-trol. Just who or what will command or control the force is not yet clear.[3] There does not appear to be any definition of the term defence in any of the relevant legislation in either jurisdiction, and one must look to Irish and Canadian government policy statements to determine what is included in the term. For Canada, these are usually found in federal government 'white papers', which are published from time to time, and in Canadian parliamen-tary debates. Up to recently, Ireland had a much less clear defence policy than that of Canada. This has now changed with the publication of a government white paper on defence and other reports.[4] Prior to this, reference had to be made to Dáil Éireann debates and ministerial statements to determine, as best one could, what the policy was.

Despite the different juridical basis for participation in United Nations operations, the decision whether or not to participate in either the traditional peacekeeping operation or the more pro-active enforcement action missions of recent years, is an executive decision in both countries. Given the similar parliamentary democracy system prevailing in Canada and Ireland, the most important practical consideration is whether the party or parties in govern-ment have a sufficient majority in parliament or Dáil to ensure support for the proposal. Approval for matters of this nature is usually a foregone con-clusion, though it would be necessary for the relevant minister to acquaint

---

[3] Jonathan Eyal, 'Democratic accountability key to success of European defence force', *Irish Times*, 21 Nov. 2000.
[4] See Department of Defence, *White Paper on Defence* (Dublin, 2000), and Department of Defence, *Defence Forces Annual Report* (Dublin, 1999, yearly to the present).

himself or herself with the background information to avoid appearing uninformed during the debate. Under the Defence (Amendment) (No. 2) Act 1960 the Dáil must approve the sending of troops abroad when the numbers exceed twelve.[5] In practice this means that approval is required in almost all situations. On the other hand, in Canada, there appears to be no constitutional requirement to have the decision reviewed by the legislature, but the unwritten rules embodied in certain 'constitutional practices' require that the parliament be consulted on the matter.[6] The actual decision to participate is made by the Governor in Council, which is the executive arm of the government. The Governor in Council is formed by the governor general, the queen's representative in Canada, whose role in such decisions is procedural rather than substantive.

When Ireland was first admitted as a member of the United Nations in 1955, the government of the day led by John A. Costello did not consider that any enabling legislation was required to allow the country to participate in all United Nations activities and meet the obligations which membership entailed.[7] In the United Kingdom, on the other hand, the United Nations Act 1946 had been passed in order to give effect to certain provisions of the United Nations Charter. This Act, however, referred specifically to Article 41 of the Charter relating to measures not involving the use of armed force and to decisions taken by the Security Council only.[8] Since the Supreme Court decision in *Crotty v An Taoiseach*,[9] serious doubt has been cast on the constitutionality of Ireland's commitments under the Charter.[10] Other constitutional issues arise regarding the command and arrest of Irish troops

---

[5] Section 2, Defence (Amendment) (No. 2) Act, 1960.

[6] Carter, op. cit. (n. 1).

[7] When Costello was questioned by de Valera on the need to pass legislation due to the acceptance of Ireland's application for membership, he replied that so far as he knew 'ratification is not necessary nor is any legislation required'. The obligations, he said, were now less onerous than had been anticipated in 1946 and any military commitments under the Charter were 'entirely within our own control'. *Dáil Deb.*, vol. 153, cols. 1601–8, 15 Dec. 1955. This was a reference to Article 43 of the United Nations Charter which relates to the use of armed force, see Goodrich, Hambro and Simons, *Charter of the United Nations* (3rd. ed.) (New York, 1969), pp. 317–26, and B. Simma (ed.), *The Charter of the United Nations – A Commentary* (Oxford, 1995), pp. 636–9. For a comprehensive discussion of the obligations of Irish membership of the United Nations see L. Heffernan and A. Whelan, 'Ireland, The United Nations and the Gulf Conflict: Legal Aspects', *Irish Studies in International Affairs* (1991), pp. 115–45.

[8] Section 1 (1) of the United Nations Act, 1946 states: 'If, under *Article forty-one* of the Charter ... (being the Article which related to measures not involving the use of armed force) the Security Council of the United Nations call upon His Majesty's Government ... to apply any measures to give effect to any decision of that Council, His Majesty may by Order in Council make such provision as appears to Him necessary or expedient for enabling those measures to be effectively applied ...'
For a discussion on the legal status of British armed forces and related issues, see P. Rowe, *Defence – The Legal Implications* (London, 1987).

[9] [1987] Irish Reports 713. See J. Casey, *Constitutional Law and Ireland* (3rd. ed., Dublin, 2000), pp. 214–8.

[10] See Heffernan and Whelan, op. cit., (n.7), pp. 128–137 and Ray Murphy, 'Kosovo: Reflections on the legal aspects', *Irish Studies in International Affairs* 11 (2000), pp. 7–31, esp. pp. 18–9.

abroad by members of an international United Nations force who are not Irish citizens. These issues could also arise in the context of Irish participation in European Union security arrangements or peacekeeping operations in the future.

There are also problems in relation to the arrest and taking into custody of members of the Defence Forces and the Canadian forces when carried out by international military police that are not part of either the Irish nor the Canadian contingent respectively and these are outlined below. None of these issues was addressed in the Defence (Amendment) Act 1993 or the more recent 1998 Act. The 1993 Act was passed to allow the Defence Forces to participate in an international United Nations Force that is not simply of a police or peacekeeping nature, and effectively permits the participation of Defence Forces personnel in any kind of United Nations military operation. However, it is inadequate for the needs of the Defence Forces today, and amending legislation is required to put participation in international missions on a satisfactory statutory basis.

Municipal legal basis for Canadian and Irish participation in peace-keeping

Canada

The possibility of Canadian involvement in a major war during the 1930s was uppermost in the minds of politicians when the then prime minister, Mackenzie King, was responding to a question put regarding Canada's future role in the event of a war in Europe. The policy of the government, he declared, is that parliament will decide what is to be done.[11] However, this declared policy was not reflected in the provisions of the National Defence Act, which came into force in Canada in 1950. The Act does not require that parliament give its formal approval or consent to the despatch of Canadian forces on service abroad, whether in a United Nations or other capacity. Under Section 31 of the Act, the Governor in Council has power to place the Canadian forces on active service, a status that is usually conferred on troops involved in armed conflict. Despite the fact that there is no specific legal requirement, there is a parliamentary tradition in existence since 1950 for the government to reaffirm that Canadian forces are on 'active service' for specific United Nations, NATO and other operations involving substantial numbers of troops when such missions are considered potentially hazardous.[12] The concept of 'active service' and its legal implications under Canadian military law is confusing. The contemporary legal purpose and effect of this status is unclear, and in this regard the National Defence Act is in need of clarification.

---

[11] *House of Commons (Canada), Debates*, vol.111(1938), col. 3183.

[12] Carter, op. cit. (n. 1).

The tradition of informing parliament arose from a decision by Prime Minister Louis St Laurent during 1950 while debating the National Defence Act in the course of the Korean crisis. An undertaking was given that, henceforth, whenever significant numbers of members of the Canadian forces were to be deployed outside Canada, the decision would be announced in the House of Commons and an enabling order in Council would be tabled. However, under the National Defence Act, a Governor in Council (Cabinet) decision is all that is lawfully required to place the Canadian forces on 'active service'. Furthermore, an examination of the relevant legislation indicates that Canadian forces are not actually required to be placed on 'active service' to participate in an operation. If Canadian forces are placed on 'active service' while parliament is not sitting, parliament must meet within ten days to consider the Governor in Council decision. It is not surprising then that there is a significant amount of confusion in Canada in relation to deployment outside Canada and the concept of 'active service'. This was most recently evident during preparations for participation in the so-called first Gulf War, when the requirement to recall parliament became a matter of some controversy. In spite of the absence of a strict legal or constitutional requirement, parliament was recalled as a result of what could best be described as political necessity owing to public disquiet at how the matter was being handled.[13]

Ireland

Before the enactment of the Defence Act 1954 the statutory basis of the Irish Defence Forces was the Defence Forces (Temporary Provisions) Act 1923. Amendments to this act were passed annually, until repealed and replaced by the 1954 Act. In 1956, the question of amending the 1954 Act to allow for an Irish contribution to the United Nations Emergency Force was mentioned by the Taoiseach of the day, John A. Costello. In a reply to a question in the Seanad about the possibility of Ireland contributing troops to the Force, Costello stated, inter alia, that:

> the situation is new. We were not asked or requested to contribute, nor was it suggested that we should ... It is perhaps something that should be considered, although if we felt morally obliged to make an offer of volunteers, it would be necessary to have an amendment to the law. That is not a very serious matter ... I think it would be necessary to amend the Defence Forces Act [sic] before we could send any troops.[14]

---

[13] Personal interview, senior Canadian diplomat in the Department of Foreign Affairs and International Trade, Ottawa, 27 June 1998; and D.L Bland, *Chiefs of Defence-Government and the Unified Control of the Armed Forces* (Toronto, 1995), p. 203.

[14] *Seanad Deb.*, vol. 46, cols. 1045 and 1154, 21 Nov. 1956. It is interesting to compare Costello's statement that 'there is, in fact, no obligation on any member (of the UN) to contribute to this police force (the UNEF), but there may be perhaps considerations of humanity and a desire to

However, as Ireland was not asked to contribute troops to the Force, the question lost its urgency until 1960.

When Ireland was requested to contribute a contingent to serve as part of an international United Nations force in the Congo on 14 July 1960, the question of the legality of sending such a 'force' abroad for duty of this nature was considered and new legislation was introduced into the Dáil on 19 July, 1960. According to the long title of the Defence (Amendment) Act 1960 it was passed to authorise the despatch of contingents of the army for service outside the state with international United Nations forces for the perform-ance of duties of a police character and other related matters. In more specific terms, it was passed as a temporary measure in order to enable the government to accede to Secretary-General Hammarskjöld's request to make a contingent of Irish soldiers available to go to the Congo.[15] This statute was later repealed by Section 7 of the Defence (Amendment)(No. 2) Act 1960 which was intended as the permanent legislation to authorise, subject to the previous approval of Dáil Éireann in certain circumstances, the despatch of contingents of the Permanent Defence Forces for service outside the state with international forces established by the Security Council or the General Assembly, for the performance of duties of a police character.[16] There is no definition in the Act of what constitutes such duties; presumably it was intended to distinguish between what are now often termed traditional peacekeeping duties, and enforcement action missions pursuant to Article 42 of the United Nations Charter.[17] In any event, the Minister for Defence declined to elaborate upon its meaning when given the opportunity in the course of the debate in the Dáil. This was, and remains, an unsatisfactory position, as there are no definitive legal criteria within the municipal legis-lative framework to determine such matters. The more recently formulated policy guidelines or criteria for deciding whether or not to participate in peacekeeping or related activities are useful.[18] They do not, however, constitute legal criteria that might be used to challenge a decision of the government to

---

[14] *contd.* contribute to the maintenance of peace …' with that of the Minister for Foreign Affairs, Dr Garret FitzGerald, and Minister for Defence Paddy Donegan, seventeen years later. FitzGerald stated that Ireland's decision to contribute troops to the second UNEF in 1973 was fulfilling 'an obligation and one that we recognize to be such'. Donegan stated that 'after consideration of the request (for Ireland to contribute troops to UNEF) it was decided that, in order that our international obligations be met and our high reputation preserved, the request should be complied with'. *Dáil Deb.,* vol. 268, cols. 816–24, 30 Oct. 1973.

[15] *Dáil Deb.,* vol.185, cols. 774–81, 7 Dec. 1960.

[16] The Act extended the service of certain members of the Defence Forces and for those purposes amended the Defence Act 1954 in certain respects. It also provided for the registration of certain births and deaths occurring outside the state and the application of Section 11 of the Wills Act 1837 and Wills (Soldiers and Sailors) Act, 1918.

[17] See H. McCoubrey and N. White, *The Blue Helmets: Legal Regulation of United Nations Military Operations* (Aldershot, 1996), pp. 11–37, and Goodrich, Hambro and Simons, op. cit. pp. 314–7.

[18] Ray Murphy, 'Ireland, the United Nations and Peacekeeping Operations', *International Peacekeeping* 5 (1) (1998), pp. 22–45, esp. pp. 38–40 and *White Paper on Defence,* op. cit., pp. 59–70.

participate in a particular operation. While no such legal challenge has ever been mounted, there is significant public disquiet about security and defence issues in the context of European integration, and the possibility of such a challenge cannot be ruled out in the future.

When the Taoiseach, Seán Lemass, was moving the second reading of the Defence (Amendment)(No. 2) Bill 1960 (in December of that year) he first placed the measure against the wider background of Ireland's attitude and obligations as a member of the United Nations.[19] Although he pointed out that there was no agreement among the so called 'big powers' on the implementation of the provisions of Chapter VII of the Charter, he neglected to distinguish between enforcement action pursuant to this Chapter and what was initially intended as a preventive diplomacy mission in the Congo. However, he was careful not to claim that Ireland was being called upon to fulfil a legally binding obligation under Article 43, but that other more general provisions referred to indicated that participation in the United Nations Force in the Congo, and by implication any similar peacekeeping force, was required by the spirit of the Charter. This reflected the view that participation in United Nations forces was one of the few methods by which small nations like Ireland could come together to influence world events, and Lemass invoked Article 29 of the Irish Constitution which solemnly affirms Ireland's 'devotion to the ideal of peace and friendly co-operation amongst nations, founded on international justice and morality'.[20] The question of the validity of such a laudable contention may well be posed, but the record of Irish initiatives at the United Nations, and the participation in peacekeeping and other United Nations activities since admission, have been significant. They were certainly out of proportion to the relative size and importance of the country on the world stage.[21] In any event, much of the discussion that took place in the Dáil concerned the political situation in the Congo and the function of the Irish and other United Nations troops there.[22] At times it appeared to be forgotten by some that the Bill was intended as permanent legislation to enable the Dáil to agree to Irish participation in any similar United Nations peacekeeping mission around the world.

Parliamentary control of Canadian and Irish participation in United Nations forces

According to the 1997 *Report of the Somalia Commission of Inquiry* (the Commission), Canada has begun a new relationship with its armed forces

---

[19] *Dáil Deb.*, vol. 185, cols. 774–81, 7 Dec. 1960.
[20] *Dáil Deb.*, vol.185, col. 777, 7 Dec. 1960.
[21] See Murphy, op.cit. (n.18).
[22] For example, Deputies Browne and McQuillan in particular drew attention to the political situation in the Congo and to the dangers of the UN imposing a partition on the Congo similar to that in Ireland.

that arguably requires greater involvement by members of parliament and Canadians generally in the direction, control and supervision of Canadian forces.[23] It also identified a need to strengthen the role of parliament in the development and scrutiny of defence policy. One of the prerequisites for the control of the military and defence policy in any democracy is a vigilant parliament. During the course of the cold war, defence policy in Canada was largely determined by the perceived threat and alliance commitments of the era. There was little systematic monitoring of defence policy and military matters by parliament in general.[24] Since 1989, Canada has increasingly been called upon to engage in a wide range of United Nations sponsored operations in complex situations involving uncertain alliances with unclear mandates and inadequate resources. The Senate and House of Commons Special Joint Committee also highlighted the issue of strengthening the role of parliament in the whole process in 1994 when it reported that:

> whatever our individual views on particular issues of defence policies or operations, there was one matter on which we agreed almost from the beginning – that there is a need to strengthen the role of Parliament in the scrutiny and development of defence policy.[25]

In Canada, the different government departments involved in peacekeeping operations use a set of guidelines when determining whether Canada should participate in a particular operation.[26] In 1996, an Irish government white paper on foreign policy, and a later white paper on defence, identified a number of factors that are taken into account when considering requests for Irish participation in peacekeeping or similar operations.[27] When compared, the political criteria adopted by both countries are remarkably similar. Furthermore, in both countries experience shows that these guidelines or criteria are not applied in any strict sense. The respective governments of Canada and Ireland retain discretion to decide if the armed forces should participate in a United Nations or similar operation. The guidelines do provide a benchmark by which to examine each proposal and they also facilitate parliamentary control, albeit limited, over the decision by government whether or not to participate.

---

[23] *Report of the Somalia Commission of Inquiry*, vol. 5, 'The Need for a Vigilant Parliament', p. 1.
[24] Ibid.
[25] Parliament of Canada, Senate and House of Commons, Special Joint Committee, *Security in a Changing World*, Report of the Special Joint Committee on Canada's Defence Policy (25 Oct. 1994), p. 57.
[26] E. Reumiller, 'Security in a New World Order: A Canadian Perspective' and 'Canadian Perspectives and Experiences with Peacekeeping: General Policy Considerations' in P. O Gormaile and R. Murphy (eds.), *Conflict Resolution and Peacemaking/Peacekeeping: the Irish and Canadian Experience* (1997), pp. 15–22 and pp. 23–36, and *White Paper on Defence*, op. cit., pp. 59–70.
[27] Oliver MacDonald, 'The Irish Peacekeeping Experience and its Influence on Doctrine', O Gormaile and Murphy, op. cit. 44–57.

In Ireland, the power of the Dáil to monitor and scrutinise defence policy, in particular participation in United Nations forces, is quite limited. Under the provisions of Section 2 of the Defence (Amendment)(No. 2) Act 1960 ('the 1960 Act'), the Dáil must first approve by means of a resolution the despatch of a contingent of armed members of the Permanent Defence Forces exceeding twelve in number for service outside the state as part of an international United Nations force. Section 2 states:

> 2 (1) Subject to subsection (2) of this section, a contingent ... may be despatched for service outside the State as part of a particular International United Nations Force if, but only if, a resolution has been passed by Dáil Éireann approving of the despatch .....
> (2) A contingent ... may be despatched for service outside the State ... without a resolution approving of such despatch having been passed by Dáil Éireann, if, but only if
> (a) that International United Nations Force is unarmed, or
> (b) the contingent consists of not more than twelve members of the Permanent Defence Force, ...
> (c) the contingent is intended to replace, in whole or in part, or reinforce a ... contingent of the Permanent Defence Force serving outside the State as part of that International United Nations Force and consisting of more than twelve members of the Permanent Defence Force.

This allows the Dáil to discuss in detail the implications of Irish participation in any United Nations force prior to giving its approval. This section was discussed at length during the Dáil debate on the Bill and reservations were expressed regarding its exact implications. In response, the Minister for Defence, Kevin Boland, pointed out that it would not be possible to reinforce an unarmed force, which did not require Dáil approval, by a contingent such as would be sent to an armed force under Subsection(2)(1). [28] However, once the Dáil had passed a resolution approving the despatch of an armed contingent of over twelve personnel, then it must be left to the government to determine the size of the contingent and the duration of its mission. Similarly, the government could replace the original contingent as necessary for the duration of the United Nations mission. In this way, the government could continue sending contingents to the Congo without ever coming back to the Dáil for any authority or discussion.

It was not surprising then that in the circumstances certain deputies opposed some of the provisions contained in Section 2.[29] They considered that the Dáil was entitled to have a discussion on the merits or otherwise of

---

[28] *Dáil Deb.*, vol. 185, cols. 1133–4, 14 Dec. 1960.
[29] Ibid., col. 1139.

sending and maintaining troops abroad on a regular basis. The political situation in the Congo during the 1960s alone, and more recently in Somalia, shows that events can develop in such a way that the original mandate of a United Nations force would have to be modified or changed as a result of subsequent developments. This could bring about a situation in which the contingent going to replace the troops originally sent out with Dáil approval could find itself in totally different circumstances than originally envisaged and planned for. It could also find that the original mandate was so modified to meet these changed circumstances that it amounted to a new mandate altogether. In this way, Section 2 of the 1960 Act gave the government more discretion than was probably required. This situation has since been changed somewhat and under Section 4 of The Defence (Amendment) Act, 1993 the minister is required to make an annual report to the Dáil on the operation of Section 2 of the 1960 Act, and the Dáil may by resolution approve of the report. This provision was prompted by an opposition amendment to the original Bill after a number of deputies had expressed misgivings about the lack of parliamentary control over Irish involvement in United Nations forces.[30] In reality it amounts to a minimalist parliamentary control mechanism with which to monitor the activities of government and the defence forces in this area, but it does at least provide for some debate and it requires that the minister apprise the Dáil of all relevant matters at least once a year.

An essential element of a parliamentary democracy is that the government of the day should have to obtain the approval of parliament before taking certain action. It is difficult to sustain Deputy Lionel Booth's claim that debates on such issues should be avoided as 'ill informed debate might prove a considerable embarrassment to our troops'.[31] In any event, public statements by politicians outside the Dáil have, on occasion, caused embarrassment and even danger for Irish troops serving with United Nations peacekeeping forces.[32] The situation in Ireland contrasts with that in the Netherlands, where parliament exercises greater control and supervision over its armed forces serving with the United Nations.[33] The continued participation in UNIFIL of troops from the Netherlands was reassessed regularly. This may be one reason why, unlike the Irish government, the government of the Netherlands withdrew its contingent due to the lack of support UNIFIL received from parties to the conflict. The Netherlands armed forces are not

[30] *Dáil Deb.*, vol. 433, col. 310, 29 June 1993, and cols. 689, 718 and 722, 30 June 1993.

[31] *Dáil Deb.*, vol.185, cols. 1149–1152, 14 Dec. 1960.

[32] See Ray Murphy, 'Background to the 1980 At-Tiri Incident – A Personal Assessment', *An Cosantóir* (1988), p. 38.

[33] J.O. de Lange, 'Peacekeeping Operations of the United Nations and Public International Law – Some Legal Aspects in the Netherlands', *Netherlands International Law Review* 28 (1981), pp. 182–7. See also the Netherlands Supreme Court judgment on the despatch of troops to UNIFIL, *The State of the Netherlands V. A.1. Toonan*, Supreme Court, 8 Feb. 1980, reported in the *Netherlands Yearbook of International Law* (1981), pp. 353–6.

made available to the United Nations without constant re-examination of their role and their indefinite involvement in a peacekeeping operation may not be taken for granted.[34]

The scope of the 1960 Act was confined to matters concerning the contribution of an Irish contingent to a United Nations force established by the Security Council, or the General Assembly, for the performance of duties of a police character only. There is no elaboration in the Act on what these police duties involve. The most likely purpose of the use of the phrase was to distinguish between 'peacekeeping' and 'enforcement action'. The phrase could be construed as somewhat misleading when some of the events in which the United Nations force in the Congo was involved, particularly in Katanga Province, are taken into account.[35] The phrase also reflects the ambiguous and compromised role in which United Nations forces can find themselves, and was epitomised by the United Nations peacekeeping forces in Lebanon during the 1982 Israeli invasion.

The 1960 Act does not provide any definition of 'contingent' either.[36] It was probably considered more expedient at the time to omit such a definition. In military terms it can denote anything from the usually less than twelve Irish personnel that form the Irish Contingent with the United Nations Force in Cyprus, to the six hundred or more forming the Irish Contingent with UNIFIL.

The Defence (Amendment) Act 1993 has amended and extended the 1960 Act in significant respects. The principal amendment is contained in Section 1 which by defining an 'International United Nations Force' as an international force or body established by the Security Council or General Assembly of the United Nations, goes beyond the previous definition contained in the 1960 Act which had limited Defence Forces participation to United Nations peacekeeping operations. This brought about a radical change in Irish defence and foreign policy that was not reflected in the level of public or parliamentary debate at the time. Although the Dáil debate indicated that at least some did appreciate the wider ramifications of the change in Irish municipal law, it seemed that the Dáil as a whole did not.[37] It is unlikely that the new legislation would have had such an uncontroversial passage but for the humanitarian considerations in sending an Irish Army transport unit to Somalia and the presence of Irish aid workers in that country.

---

[34] Ibid.

[35] R. Higgins, *The United Nations Operation in the Congo (ONUC) 1960–1964* (London, 1980) and E.W. Lefever, *Crisis in the Congo – A United Nations Force in Action* (Washington DC, 1965), pp. 72–121.

[36] Defence Force Regulations CS7 governing 'A Contingent of the Permanent Defence Force serving with an International United Nations Force' states in Para 1 that 'the word "contingent" means a contingent of the Permanent Defence Force dispatched pursuant to the provisions of the Defence (Amendment)(No. 2) Act 1960 for service outside the State with a Force'.

[37] *Dáil Deb.*, vol. 433, cols. 309, 363 and 376, 29 June 1993.

There is no equivalent provision in the Canadian National Defence Act, although Section 33 provides that all regular forces are at all times liable to perform any lawful duty. This is a very broad provision that, inter alia, permits deployment in accordance with government policy to any country outside Canada. It reflects Canadian history of involvement in major conflicts outside of Canada, as well as the present commitment to the Atlantic Alliance. Looked at in isolation it might appear that there is little or no control by parliament over the deployment of Canadian forces at home and abroad. When one examines the provisions of the National Defence Act as a whole, in particular those relating to the issue of command and control, it is evident that this is not the case. In this way the issue of command and control of the Canadian and Irish forces is also intrinsically linked to the matter of parliamentary control.

A significant means of achieving greater parliamentary control in both Canada and Ireland would be the setting up of a special permanent parliamentary committee made up exclusively of elected members of the Dáil and the Canadian parliament respectively. Since its establishment in Ireland, the Joint Oireachtas Committee on Foreign Affairs has functioned well, despite the limitations of its mandate. The Standing Committees on National Defence and Veterinary Affairs in Canada have also performed a worthwhile function, but the establishment of a permanent committee could significantly improve the current situation.

The power and influence of the parliament could also be significantly enhanced by adopting one of the proposals of the Commission, namely, enacting legislation requiring that parliament receive notice of Canadian forces deployments, which in any important context would be expected to provoke a debate in parliament.[38] This would include situations when it is proposed to place Canadian forces on 'active service', or even whenever the government contemplates deploying any sizeable unit or other element of the Canadian forces outside Canada. In such circumstances, the chief of defence staff could be required to make a report to parliament on the effectiveness and readiness of the Canadian forces not simply to deploy overseas, but to undertake the proposed mission in all respects.[39] This would avoid what the Commission identified as one of the major deficiencies in the pre-deployment phase of the Somalia mission. No one seemed prepared to say that the Canadian forces were not ready to undertake such a mission.[40] Parliamentary supervision of this nature would ensure greater accountability and transparency at all levels of decision making in defence and security matters. This would avoid ill-considered decisions being taken without proper debate and consideration of the full implications of a particular course of action.

---

[38] *Report of the Somalia Commission of Inquiry*, op. cit., (n.30), 'The Need for a Vigilant Parliament', vol. 5, p. 4.

[39] Ibid.

[40] Ibid. 'The Failure of Senior Leaders', in the Executive Summary of the *Commission Report.*

The policy of sending volunteers on United Nations operations and the implications of 'active service' status[41]

From the Irish Defence Forces' point of view, Section 3 of the 1960 Act is the most significant. Under this Section, all officers and men who are appointed or enlisted on or after the date of the passing of the Act shall be liable to serve outside the state with a contingent of the Permanent Defence Forces. There is a similar provision contained in Section 2 of the Defence (Amendment) Act 1993. Wherever practicable, the Defence Forces have adhered to a policy of sending volunteers on United Nations service. In certain circumstances, however, this is not always possible. It may happen, for example, that there is a limited number of army personnel suitably qualified to fill specific appointments in a contingent.[42] At the time of the debate on this Section, Deputy Frank Sherwin, the Independent TD, and others did not consider that anyone should be compelled to serve overseas.[43] His primary fear that army recruiting might be seriously affected did not materialise. Nor did the more far-fetched scenario painted by Sherwin, of soldiers with left wing political leanings deserting to the other side in an 'ideological clash between Russia and the West', come to pass.[44] In the event, this Section of the 1960 Act did not receive very much attention in the debate and it merely brought Irish military law on overseas service into line with that of most other countries, including Canada. Nevertheless, it is an emotive subject in Ireland. Recent debates on Irish participation in some form of European defence commitment have often raised the spectre of Irish soldiers being conscripted to serve in or alongside foreign armies.[45] In the course of the debate on the Defence (Amendment) Act 1993 the question of sending volunteers on United Nations service was considered once again. [46] David Andrews, the Minister for Defence, pointed out, however, that in practice overseas missions are heavily oversubscribed and the question of compulsory United Nations service did not arise.[47] This, of course, was true at the time, but it did not change

---

[41] For an overview of the legal and disciplinary implications of participation in United Nations operations, see P. Rowe, 'Maintaining Discipline in United Nations Peace Support Operations: The Legal Quagmire for Military Contingents', *Journal of Conflict and Security Law* 5(1) (2000), pp. 45–62.

[42] In late 2000 there were a number of Irish engineers and specialist staff with UNIFIL on a non-voluntary basis owing to short-term requirements arising from the Israeli pull out and UNIFIL redeployment. In Oct. 1984, an army medical doctor instituted proceedings in the High Court to restrain the Minister for Defence from sending him to the Lebanon as part of the Irish contingent with UNIFIL. He claimed his health would be damaged by such service. His action was unsuccessful and Mr. Justice McMahon was satisfied he should not grant an injunction. *Irish Times*, 26 Oct. 1984.

[43] *Dáil Deb.*, vol. 185, cols. 892–6, 7 Dec. 1960.

[44] Ibid.

[45] Personal interviews with serving Defence Forces personnel, Dublin and Galway, 1998. See also Edward Horgan, 'Committing our troops to EU force clear breach of neutrality', *Irish Times*, 1 Nov. 2000, p. 16.

[46] *Dáil Deb., vol.* 433, cols. 309 and 363, 29 June 1993.

[47] Ibid., col. 373. Towards the end of Irish participation in UNIFIL, it was often difficult to find sufficient volunteers from the ranks of the Defence Forces due to shortage in numbers, and a degree of exhaustion and boredom with the mission.

the fact that personnel joining the Defence Forces after July 1993 are liable for service with a United Nations force of an unspecified nature.

The reality today is that it cannot be assumed that the volunteer list for missions abroad will be heavily oversubscribed, though a fresh intake of recruits or the instigation of regular recruiting to the Defence Forces could change this situation relatively quickly. At one stage in 1998 it was reported that it might prove necessary to recruit civilian staff, in particular paramedics, for service with the Irish battalion in Lebanon (UNIFIL). This was due to a shortage of personnel with specialised skills.[48] The Minister for Defence conjured up an even more drastic scenario when he said that Ireland would withdraw from participation in UNIFIL if the shortage of volunteers became chronic.[49] This statement, without any indication by the minister of his intention to address and resolve the problem, was unacceptable for a minister with responsibility for the Defence Forces and defence policy. It showed no appreciation of the causes of this problem, and a total unwillingness to accept any responsibility for the situation brought about by years of neglect.

The Canadian forces and the Irish Defence Forces consist of volunteers. Both forces are organised and divided into a regular full-time professional force and a reserve force of part-time volunteers. Under Section 33 of the National Defence Act, regular force members are liable to be deployed at any time and anywhere. Members of regular forces have also been placed on 'active service', which in the context of Canadian military law means they can be immediately deployed. This is in contrast to Irish forces, who are deemed to be on 'active service' when deployed on United Nations duties abroad, and for whom the term has radically different legal consequences, and political connotations. Section 4 of the 1960 Act lays down that members of the Defence Forces serving with armed United Nations forces shall be deemed to be on active service. This is a status usually deemed appropriate for troops participating in some kind of offensive military operation or involved in actual armed conflict. One of the effects of this section under Irish military law is that it confers unlimited jurisdiction on a court-martial, convened for the trial of an offence alleged to have been committed by a person subject to military law, while serving outside Ireland with an armed International United Nations Force.[50] Section 126 of the Defence Act 1954 is also important in this regard.

---

[48] *Irish Times*, 11 May 1998.

[49] Statement by the Minister for Defence at the annual PDFORRA (soldiers representative association) conference, reported in *Irish Times*, 5 Nov. 1998.

[50] Section 3 of the Defence (Amendment) Act 1993 applies the provisions of Section 4 of the 1960 Act to Defence Force units participating on peace enforcement missions. See the comments by Finlay, C.J., *Ryan v. Ireland, The Attorney General and the Minister for Defence* [1989] Irish Reports, 177 at 182 and M.N. Gill, 'Development of the Military Jurisdiction of the Irish Defence Forces', *Revue de Droit Penal Militaire et De Droit De La Guerre* (1980), pp. 427–433. For example a soldier cannot be tried by court martial for the offences of treason, murder, manslaughter, treason felony, rape or buggery, unless he was on active service at the time of allegedly committing the offence (Section 192, Defence Act 1954).

It lists a number of offences more severely punishable on 'active service' than at other times. This means that Irish soldiers with United Nations forces are subject to a stricter military code of discipline due to the severe punishments for certain breaches of military law while on active service.[51]

The Canadian position is different in significant respects because under Section 31 of the National Defence Act, the Governor in Council, in effect the Cabinet in Canada, has power to place Canadian forces on 'active service'. The question of placing forces on 'active service' in this way is considered important. This is reflected in the requirement that if placed on 'active service' when parliament is not sitting, parliament must meet within ten days to consider the Governor in Council decision.[52] Under Section 31, Canadian forces may be placed on 'active service' 'when advisable' by reason of an emergency, for the defence of Canada; or for action taken under the United Nations Charter, or NATO. However, unlike the situation prevailing in Ireland, the National Defence Act is permissive rather than mandatory, and Canadian forces do not have to be placed on 'active service' to participate in a United Nations sponsored operation. In fact, there appear to be no circumstances where it is a requirement or prerequisite for a particular course of action.

In practice, a somewhat unusual situation prevails with regard to Canadian regular forces in that they have been placed on 'active service' on what amounts to a permanent basis.[53] This renders the concept of 'active service' for Canadian forces somewhat meaningless, both legally and politically. This issue can cause confusion, and this was evident during the 'Gulf War' when at the beginning of the crisis many observers thought parliament would have to be recalled to allow the Canadian forces to go on 'active service'.[54] No one in the public service or in the Department of National Defence seemed to understand how Canada should actually participate in an offensive military operation or parliament's role in the decision. The then Prime Minister, Mulroney, wanted to avoid recalling parliament for domestic

---

[51] One other aspect of military law affecting persons subject to it while on overseas service that is worth mentioning is that relating to military detention. Soldiers may be awarded short periods of detention (usually 7 or 14 days) by either their commanding officers or courts-martial if found guilty of an offence under military law (see Section 178 and Sections 209 to 212 of the Defence Act 1954). This is quite common both at home and on overseas service. When a soldier is awarded this punishment he forfeits his pay for the period of his detention. However, when a soldier is on United Nations overseas service he not only forfeits his pay for the period of detention but also his overseas allowances for the same period. This anomaly has never been challenged. It is surely unjust to withhold payment of overseas allowances while a soldier serves a period of detention while overseas, as he continues to be overseas during the period in question. This almost amounts to a double punishment for the one offence.

[52] Section 32 of the National Defence Act states in part: 'Whenever the Governor in Council places the Canadian forces or any component or any unit thereof on active service, if parliament is then separated by an adjournment or prorogation that will not expire within ten days, a proclamation shall be issued for a meeting of parliament within ten days ...'.

[53] Personal interview, JAG officer, Canadian forces, Ottawa, 21 June 1998. Reserve forces are not placed on active service, and a formal Order in Council is required for any such forces to be placed on active service.

[54] Bland, op. cit., p. 203.

political reasons.[55] The Clerk of the Privy Council tried to maintain that parliament's role was only customary and not required. The Chief of Defence Staff, De Chastelain, said that the Prime Minister was not required to refer the matter to parliament.[56] This statement, though legally correct, was probably not a politically astute observation at the time. In the event, parliament was recalled.

The episode shows the confusion surrounding the law, and the status and implications of 'active service' for Canadian forces. Canadian military personnel might well argue that current commitments to the United Nations and NATO entail large numbers of Canadian forces being deployed outside Canada at any given time, and the permanent state of 'active service' reflects this. However, what is the point of 'active service' if it is a permanent status and a mere administrative convenience? This situation is unsatisfactory. The matter could be clarified by amending the National Defence Act and making it a statutory requirement to place Canadian forces on 'active service' for any operation under the United Nations Charter, NATO, the Organisation for Security and Co-operation in Europe, or any similar organisation. A further amendment could also make it a statutory requirement to refer the matter to parliament before any such decision is made. This would clear up the semantic and legal confusion surrounding the matter, and enhance parliamentary control over the Canadian forces, and in particular over their deployment outside Canada.

The policy in Ireland reflected in the statutory requirement to place troops involved in United Nations operations on an 'active service' footing does have merit. While involvement in peacekeeping and similar operations should not be equated with armed conflict, the unpredictable and volatile environment in which such operations often take place may require resort to the use of force in certain circumstances, albeit in a restrained and defensive manner. The need to maintain discipline is of the utmost importance in such sensitive situations. The situation under Irish law of enshrining this in the legislative framework governing participation has been vindicated by the nature of such operations since 1960. In this way, the legal position of Irish troops is clearer than that of Canadian forces, whose status depends on practice rather than a precise legal provision.

The practical significance for Irish troops of Section 4 of the 1960 Act became evident in 1983 when a court-martial tried a soldier for the murder of three comrades in Lebanon.[57] Under the 1954 Defence Act, a court-

---

[55] Ibid.

[56] Ibid.

[57] Private McAleavy was found guilty of all three murders on 27 Sept. 1983. He was sentenced to penal servitude for life and was discharged from the Permanent Defence Forces with ignominy (*Irish Times*, 28 Sept. 1983). The decision was appealed to the Courts-Martial Appeals Court that confirmed the finding and sentence of the court-martial. The court consisted of the Chief Justice, Mr O'Higgins, Mr Justice Barrington and Mr Justice Lynch. The judgment was unreported. See the Order of the Courts-Martial Appeals Court dated 29 Mar. 1984, and *Irish Times*, 30 Mar. 1984.

martial does not have jurisdiction in such cases unless the offence was committed while on 'active service'. In this way, Section 4 of the Act conferred jurisdiction on the court-martial to try Private McAleavy for the murders in question. Under the National Defence Act, 'active service' has no such legal significance. Nevertheless, a similar situation prevails with regard to Canadian forces who commit an offence under military law while outside Canada. Under Section 130 of the National Defence Act all federal Acts are incorporated into military law, and unlimited jurisdiction is granted to courts martial in respect of offences committed outside of Canada. Furthermore, there is a different scale of punishment for offences committed outside Canada.

Although the means by which the Canadian and the Irish legislation achieve this result is different, the net effect of the respective sections is much the same. There is one potentially important distinction. In theory, a Canadian forces member may find himself or herself liable to a stricter military code for offences committed outside Canada in a private capacity. There is no requirement that the offence relate to or be associated with official duty or service outside of Canada. This is in contrast with the code of discipline governing Defence Forces members, who must be deemed to be on 'active service' before Section 126 of the Defence Act can be invoked. There is no similarity between 'active service' under military law and what is often termed 'emergency legislation' provisions under civil law. Some might argue that 'active service' and combat situations require strict discipline and a somewhat harsher code of military law. This has not been the experience of the United States military in Vietnam or elsewhere, nor has it been the experience of Canadian forces.[58] Such situations do not justify the suspension of any of the rights or duties of an accused under military law, and neither Canadian nor Irish military law provide for any derogation.

Legality of the arrest of Irish personnel forming part of international forces

The question of placing of Irish personnel serving with United Nations forces under arrest also raises serious constitutional questions. Although the problems can arise in respect of any international United Nations force, it is convenient to focus on UNIFIL as an example.[59] The regulations applied to a number of forces have expressly provided for powers of arrest to be exercised by United Nations military police personnel.[60] At one stage, UNIFIL's standing operating procedures governing duties and responsibilities of military police purported to grant powers of arrest over any member of the peacekeeping force.[61] This appeared to grant a power of arrest over and above

---

[58] Personal interview, JAG officer, Ottawa, 21 June 1998.

[59] Although Canadian forces do not participate in this force at present.

[60] See Article 15 of the UNFICYP Regulations and UNEF Regulation 14.

[61] Personal interview, Comdt P. Murphy, Deputy Provost Marshal UNIFIL MP Company 1989/1990, Galway, June 1997.

that conferred by the military law of a participating state upon a member of its forces over another.[62] Sections 171 and 172 of the Defence Act 1954 govern the powers of arrest of members of the Defence Forces. These provisions specify those authorised to place under arrest persons subject to military law and those listed do not include military police serving with United Nations forces that are not themselves members of the Defence Forces.[63] Furthermore, they do not authorise arrests by Defence Forces personnel of persons not subject to Irish military law, i.e. members of other contingents with UNIFIL.

According to the Constitution, no citizen shall be deprived of his or her personal liberty, save in accordance with law.[64] It would appear that there is no statutory or common law basis for authorising the United Nations military police to arrest members of the Defence Forces. In fact, the matter was covered by the Chief of Staff's directive to the Irish contingent and unit commanders with UNIFIL.[65] This directive purported to authorise such powers of arrest by UNIFIL military police as may be defined by, or on behalf of, the force commander.[66] These were outlined in the UNIFIL standing operating procedures dealing with the duties and responsibilities of the military police. The issue is whether the purported granting of authority to military police personnel belonging to other contingents with UNIFIL is in accordance with Irish municipal law.[67] It would appear that the Chief of Staff's directive in relation to powers of arrest had no basis in law. Furthermore, the Minister for Defence has no authority to direct the Chief of Staff to issue such a directive for reasons already outlined. This arrangement had potential to bring about a conflict between United Nations military arrangements and the national military law of contributing states. This is not a situation unique to Irish or Canadian military forces.[68]

Sections 171 and 172 of the Defence Act 1954 are quite specific in relation to the arrest and placing in custody of persons subject to military law. These sections have not been amended to take account of the situation created by Defence Forces participation in United Nations forces. In the case of *The People (Attorney General) v O'Callaghan,* the Irish Supreme Court reinforced an earlier suggestion that Acts of the Oireachtas delimiting personal liberty would be scrutinised on general constitutional principles rather than

---

[62] Draper, op. cit. 71.

[63] Section 171 provides, inter alia, that a provost marshal, an officer or non-commissioned officer or any person subject to military law who is so authorised by any commanding officer may arrest a person subject to military law.

[64] Article 40.4.1° of the Constitution provides 'No citizen shall be deprived of his personal liberty save in accordance with law'.

[65] Personal interview, former Irish Contingent Commander UNIFIL, Nov. 1989.

[66] Ibid.

[67] This should not be confused with the question of whether members of the Defence Forces in a foreign jurisdiction may be lawfully deprived of liberty in accordance with the law of that jurisdiction, which is a separate circumstance not in issue in this case.

[68] See McCoubrey and White, op. cit., pp. 179–81.

accepted as automatically validating their contents as being in 'accordance with law'.[69] For this reason, certain arrests of members of the Irish contingent with international forces may be rendered unlawful and unconstitutional, as it appears there is no constitutional or statutory authority for extending the powers of arrest already lawfully in existence. While the common law machinery for challenging the legality of a detention by way of Habeas Corpus embodied in Article 40.4.2°-5° of the Constitution may be of limited bene-fit to a soldier unlawfully detained in a remote area of south Lebanon, according to the Supreme Court in *The People (Director of Public Prosecutions) v Conroy*,[70] the burden of proof in establishing the legality of arrest and detention is on the military authorities. Furthermore, evidence obtained from the accused during an unlawful detention will normally be inadmissible at the trial.[71]

Need to amend current legislation to reflect changing nature of peace operations

In August 2005 it was reported that the Minister for Defence was to bring proposals for participation of Irish troops in EU rapid-reaction forces before the government which would probably require a series of legislative changes.[72] In view of the number, size and complexity of contemporary peace support operations, it was deemed necessary to develop a selective response to future requests from the United Nations based on certain factors.[73] Although broad and imprecise, they are potentially useful guidelines in assessing the nature and extent of what Ireland's support should be for any United Nations peace support operation.

Taking into account the experience of Irish involvement with the United Nations mission in Somalia, the Irish government's approach to participation in enforcement operations is guided by certain criteria.[74] The criteria are as

---

[69] [1966] Irish Reports, p. 501.

[70] Supreme Court, unreported, 31 July 1986.

[71] *The People (DPP) v Shaw* [1982], Irish Reports. 1. *The People (DPP) v O'Loughlin* [1979], Irish Reports 85. *The People (DPP) v O'Higgins* (Supreme Court, Nov. 22, 1985). See generally Casey, op. cit., at pp. 381–3 and 414–22.

[72] Liam Reid, 'Battlegroup plans due before Cabinet', *Irish Times*, 16 Aug. 2005.

[73] The factors that will inform consideration of such requests will include: an assessment of whether a peacekeeping operation is the most appropriate response to the situation; consideration of how the mission relates to the priorities of Irish foreign policy; the degree of risk involved; the extent to which the particular skills or characteristics required relate to Irish capabilities; the existence of realistic objectives and a clear mandate which has the potential to contribute to a political solution; whether the operation is adequately resourced; and the level of existing commitment to peacekeeping operations and security requirements at home; see Department of Defence, *White Paper on Defence*, Dublin, Feb. 2000, p. 63 and Department of Foreign Affairs, *Challenges and Opportunities Abroad, White Paper on Foreign Policy* (Dublin, 1996), pp. 194–5. The *White Paper on Defence* outlined additional factors for consideration, including ongoing developments in United Nations peace support operations, the evolution of European security structures, and the resource implications for the defence budget.

[74] *White Paper on Foreign Policy*, op. cit., pp. 199–200.

follows: that the operation derives its legitimacy from decisions of the Security Council; that the objectives are clear and unambiguous and of sufficiency and urgency and importance to justify the use of force; that all other reasonable means of achieving the objectives have been tried and failed; that the duration of the operation should be the minimum necessary to achieve the stated objectives; that diplomatic efforts to resolve the underlying disputes should be resumed at the earliest possible moment; that the command and control arrangements for the operation are in conformity with the relevant decisions of the Security Council and that the Security Council is kept fully informed of the implementation of its decision.

The difficulties presented by the changed nature of peace operations were evident when Defence Forces personnel found themselves unable to participate in the EU-led preventive deployment mission in Macedonia. In March 1995, the United Nations established the United Nations Preventive Deployment Force (UNPREDEP), to replace an earlier United Nations mission in Macedonia.[75] This was regarded as a very successful mission. Unfortunately, the functions of the Force came to an end in February 1999, when the Security Council failed to renew the mandate due to the veto of China.[76] Speaking after the vote, the Chinese delegate said his government had always maintained that United Nations peacekeeping operations, including preventive deployment missions should not be open ended. China considered the situ-ation there to have stabilised. This view was not shared by other members of the Security Council, who especially feared a spillover of violence from Kosovo across the border. In reality it had more to do with the issue of Macedonia's policy regarding Taiwan than any issue related to peacekeeping.[77]

As a result of the inability of the United Nations to act in this case, the Secretary-General stated that a new approach would have to be adopted by the government of Macedonia and its neighbours, in consultation with regional organisations. In January 2003 EU foreign ministers approved the first ever EU peacekeeping mission, and agreed to replace the NATO peacekeeping operation that took over when the United Nations mission was vetoed by China.[78] At about 350 soldiers from a wide range of countries, the EU mission was described as small but significant.[79] The Irish Attorney General advised the government that Ireland could not contribute troops to this mission, because it did not satisfy commitments made by Ireland as part of the Seville declaration prior to the Nice Treaty referendum. This was a

---

[75] Security Council Resolution 983 (1995), United Nations Doc. S/RES/995, 31 Mar. 1995.

[76] Press Release SC/6648, 25 Feb. 1999.

[77] See 'China – Macedonia Set to Cut Ties with Taiwan', *People's Daily*, 1 June 2001.

[78] See Agence France Presse (AFP), 27 Jan. 2003 and 13 Dec. 2002.

[79] Statement attributed to German Vice-Admiral Rainer Feist, who was selected to lead the mission, see E. Saskova, 'Macedonia: Debut for Euro Troops', *Institute for War and Peace Reporting*, 25 Feb. 2003.

source of embarrassment to Irish diplomats at the Department of Foreign Affairs and the Defence Forces.[80]

The origins of Ireland's dilemma regarding participation in the peace-keeping mission in Macedonia are clear in the criteria outlined above, especially the need for the operation to derive its legitimacy from a decision of the Security Council. Under the so-called triple lock mechanism, before Ireland can participate in a peacekeeping mission it must be United Nations authorised, and approved by the Dáil and government.[81] At the Seville European Council in June 2002, the Irish government made a National Declaration. This stated, inter alia, that the Treaty of Nice does not affect Ireland's policy of military neutrality, and that a referendum will be held in Ireland on joining any future common defence. However, it is paragraph 6 of the declaration that is most relevant to the current debate. It provides that Ireland reiterates that the participation of contingents of the Irish Defence Forces in overseas operations, including those carried out under European security and defence policy, requires (a) the authorisation of the operation by the Security Council or the General Assembly of the United Nations, (b) the agreement of the Irish government and (c) the approval of Dáil Éireann, in accordance with Irish law.

No one can take issue with the necessity for parliament and government approval, but what is to happen when a permanent member of the Security Council prevents United Nations authorisation. One of the many interesting aspects of the declaration is that when the Minister for Foreign Affairs first mentioned this 'triple lock' mechanism, he referred to 'United Nations endorsement'.[82] Sometime later this became United Nations authorisation, a very significant change that was especially relevant to the situation in Macedonia.[83] The United Nations Security Council had adopted a resolution that 'welcomes' and 'endorses' the involvement and support of the European Union for the Framework Agreement to consolidate a multi-ethnic society within Macedonia.[84] However, from a legal perspective, this falls short of authorising the EU mission to Macedonia, especially when the veto by the Chinese in the Security Council is taken into account.

The Declaration has added another legal dimension to Irish participation in peace support operations. The legal basis for Irish participation in such

---

[80] Personal interview, Department of Foreign Affairs official, Dublin, Mar. 2003.

[81] See Department of Foreign Affairs Press Release, Wednesday, June 19, 2002. www.gov.ie/iveagh.

[82] Statement by the Minister for Foreign Affairs, Brian Cowan, Adjournment Debate on Seville Declaration on Neutrality, 19 June 2002, available from www.gov.ie/iveagh .

[83] Second Stage Speech by the Minister for Foreign Affairs, Brian Cowan, 26th Amendment to the Constitution Bill, 4 Sept. 2002, available from www.gov.ie/iveagh .

[84] Security Council Resolution 1371 (2001), United Nations DOC S/RES/1371, 26 Sept. 2001, paras. 4 and 5. See also Framework Agreement sighed at Skopje on 13 Aug. 2001 by the President of the Former Yugoslav Republic of Macedonia and the leaders of four political parties.

operations was the Defence (Amendment)(No. 2) Act 1960 as amended by the Defence (Amendment) Act 1993.[85]

Irish participation in peace support operations is now governed by both the Defence Acts and the Seville Declaration. However, in the case of the EU mission to Macedonia, the Seville Declaration was the decisive issue. There has been much debate in Ireland in recent years about European security and defence issues. The decision to join the NATO sponsored Partnership for Peace (PfP) was controversial, especially as the government of the day reneged on a commitment to hold a referendum on the issue. It is likely the perceived militarisation of Europe and a fear that the Nice Treaty would lead to Irish involvement in European defence issues contributed to the decision of the Irish electorate to reject the Nice Treaty in the first referendum on the issue in early 2001.[86] In order to reassure the Irish electorate on the issue of Irish military neutrality and participation in EU military operations during the second referendum campaign, the government made the Seville Declaration, which was accepted by all the EU member states. The problem that will confront Ireland in future years is participation in United Nations approved, but not formally mandated, operations.

Conclusion

The Defence (Amendment)(No. 2) Act 1960 made statutory provision for service outside the state as part of an international United Nations police force. Under the terms of this Act, the Dáil must approve the initial dispatch of members of the Defence Forces for United Nations peacekeeping; thereafter, however, considerable discretion is left to the government in determining the extent of Irish involvement. The Act also provides that members of the Defence Forces shall be liable to serve outside the state with the United Nations peacekeeping forces, and while so serving they are deemed to be on active service. In certain circumstances this confers unlimited jurisdiction on a court martial and renders the accused liable to a more severe punishment.

The 1960 Act was intended as a permanent piece of legislation to provide for potential future participation by Ireland in United Nations peacekeeping forces. For over forty years it served as the statutory basis for Irish involvement in peacekeeping missions, but it is now in need of reform and updating to reflect the changed nature of peace support operations.

The Defence (Amendment) Act 1993 made provision for Irish involvement in United Nations forces not of a peacekeeping nature. This is the most

---

[85] See Ray Murphy, 'Ireland: Legal issues arising from participation in United Nations operations', *International Peacekeeping* 1 (2) (Kluwer, 1994), pp. 61-4; and Ray Murphy, 'Legal Framework of United Nations Forces and Issues of Command and Control of Canadian and Irish Forces', *Journal of Armed Conflict Law* 4, pp. 41-73.

[86] A second referendum was held in 2002, and on this occasion a clear majority voted in favour of Irish ratification of the Nice Treaty thus clearing the way for enlargement of the EU.

significant development in the municipal legal basis for Irish involvement in United Nations forces to date. It permits participation in any kind of United Nations operation and makes all Defence Forces personnel joining after 1 July 1993 liable to service on United Nations enforcement missions. Yet in planning for future roles of this nature, it is not possible to take everything into account or to provide a definitive legal criterion of what this role must be on each occasion. The enabling legislation merely provides the general legal framework for Irish involvement. While the term police character may cause some confusion about the precise role of peacekeeping forces, it has not in any way hindered Irish participation in such forces to date. However, despite this legislation, there are still matters pertaining to such participation that require urgent attention. In particular, the question of command of members of the Defence Forces and the powers of arrest of those who are not subject to Irish military law is in need of review.[87]

There is no equivalent Act in Canada because the Canadian National Defence Act is the source document and statutory legal basis for all Canadian forces activities. Unlike the Irish practice of enacting new laws and statutory amendments to existing legislation in the form of Amendment Acts, the Canadian practice is to revise and amend the National Defence Act as deemed appropriate, without a whole new Act being enacted. The current National Defence Act is a consolidating legislative enactment incorporating all amendments since 1950.[88] In this way, a single basic Act is a comprehensive and effective way to keep legislation up to date, and preferable to the piecemeal and confusing methodology prevailing in Ireland.

Under Canadian law, the National Defence Act does not require formal parliamentary approval or consent to the despatch of Canadian forces for service abroad. There does not appear to be any constitutional requirement to have the decision reviewed by the legislature either, although rules embodied in certain 'constitutional practices' require that the parliament be consulted. Unlike the situation under Irish military law, the distinction between enforcement action and traditional police type peacekeeping duties is of little legal relevance in respect of Canadian participation in United Nations operations. Military service in Canada entails service with NATO and the United Nations as part of normal military activities. Once declared lawful and part of Canadian policy, all Canadian forces are liable under the National Defence Act to service outside of Canada. Though the deployment of Canadian forces abroad without the approval of parliament is legally permissible, the reality is that parliament must be informed if the government wants to avoid a political storm. Nevertheless, the 1997 *Report of*

---

[87] Murphy, 'Legal Framework'.
[88] Revised Statutes of Canada, 1985, c. N–5. Although the current Act is being reviewed and amendments proposed as a result of adopting certain of the Dixon Committee report recommendations, which itself was a result of the *Report of the Somalia Commission of Inquiry.*

the Somalia Commission of Inquiry highlighted the need to strengthen the control exercised by parliament over the activities of Canadian forces, and reform of the law to provide for the mandatory approval of parliament for deployment of Canadian forces abroad would be preferable to the current situation.

As all regular Canadian forces are on a semi-permanent 'active service' footing, the status has little real significance. Under Section 31 of the Act, the Governor in Council has power to place the Canadian forces on 'active service' and despite the fact that there is no specific legal requirement, there is a parliamentary tradition in existence since 1950 for the government to reaffirm that Canadian forces are on active service when specific operations involving substantial numbers of troops are considered potentially hazardous. Unlike the situation of Irish Defence Forces, Canadian forces are neither deemed nor required to be placed on active service to participate in an operation. Under the National Defence Act, a Governor in Council decision is all that is lawfully required to place the Canadian forces on active service. There is a need to clarify the status and implications of 'active service' under Canadian military law. This should be undertaken in a way that would clear up the semantic and legal confusion over the issue and enhance rather than diminish parliamentary control over Canadian forces. The most significant differences between the situation of Canadian forces and the Defence Forces is in the area of command and control. The legislative framework governing Canadian forces works well domestically and in the context of international United Nations and similar forces.

The legislative framework governing Irish participation in peacekeeping operations is now out of date. It is apparent that Canada has conducted a more thorough consideration of all of the issues, and Ireland could learn from the Canadian experience. During the summer of 2002, the United States threatened to veto the renewal of crucial mandates for United Nations peace operations unless a mechanism was agreed to prevent US personnel on United Nations related missions coming under the jurisdiction of the International Criminal Court. A solution was found, but the threat to United Nations operations was real.[89] The power of the permanent members to veto Security Council mandates at their instigation or renewal remains a real threat to United Nations authorised peace support operations. At the time Irish troops as part of United Nations operations had to prepare to return home if the necessary mandate was not renewed. Such events are quite likely in the future for a variety of reasons. The legal and political loops

---

[89] The solution was the adoption of Security Council Resolution 1422 of 12 July 2002. This effectively exempted officials and personnel, part of United Nations authorised or established operations and from a State not a party to the ICC Statute, from the jurisdiction of ICC for twelve months. It was renewed in 2002, but due to changed political circumstances it was not put forward for renewal in 2004.

Ireland chose to apply to participation in the EU mission to Macedonia were a source of some bewilderment to our EU partners, and are characteristic of Ireland's inept posturing on issues of European foreign policy and security co-operation.

The Defence (Amendment) Act 1993 is the most recent relevant piece of enabling legislation passed in Ireland providing for participation in international forces, and it is similar to the 1960 Act insofar as its terms are permissive rather than mandatory. The 1993 Act does not outline nor define the nature and kinds of operations envisaged under the Act. There is only the definition of 'International United Nations Force' as 'a international force or body established by the Security Council or General Assembly of the United Nations'. There is no mention of duties of a police character, enforcement action or 'peace enforcement'. It is a very short piece of legislation that in effect permits involvement in any kind of international United Nations force and leaves many issues undetermined. Nonetheless, its significance should not be underestimated. It provided the legal basis for participation in the United Nations sponsored, but NATO-led, operations in the former Yugoslavia and the current Chapter VII mandated mission to Liberia. One of the key questions for Ireland remains the so-called triple lock requirement, especially the need for formal United Nations authorisation of an operation. There is also the matter of participation in non-United Nations authorised humanitarian tasks such as the aftermath of hurricane Katrina in the United States, and other EU monitoring missions or operations under the auspices of the OSCE.

Chapter Fourteen

The history of Garda participation in United Nations missions

AN GARDA SÍOCHÁNA

Introduction

This chapter describes the participation of An Garda Síochána in the United Nations and specifically in those United Nations missions which involved a civilian police element. The involvement of An Garda Síochána with the United Nations began in the 1950s. Initially it was necessary for individual gardaí to resign from the force in order to serve with the United Nations. In the intervening years hundreds of its members have contributed to United Nations missions. Some have been honoured for valiant and honourable service, some have served on several missions, while others now work full-time with the United Nations. One serving member, Sergeant Paul Reid, died in the line of duty while serving with the United Nations, and this chapter is dedicated to his memory.

The contribution of An Garda Síochána to the United Nations may be divided into two categories – missions that took place before 1989, and those that took place after 1989 (owing to a requirement on members to resign from the force in order to serve with the United Nations prior to 1989). Accordingly, a specific section is included for each period.

A section which details special United Nations missions involving An Garda Síochána personnel is also included. These were often brief fact-finding missions which took place in advance of the design of a mandate for a full mission. That members of the force were selected for this pivotal work is regarded as an honour for the force and for Ireland by extension. The chapter concludes by considering the future role for An Garda Síochána in United Nations Civilian Police peacekeeping operations.

Civilian police in the United Nations

Global developments, particularly the ending of the Cold War and changes in Eastern Europe, have altered the nature of United Nations peacekeeping missions. These missions are no longer solely military but rather multi-functional operations, often with a strong police element. The United Nations Civilian Police (UNCP or CIVPOL) was deployed for the first time in the 1960s in peacekeeping operations in the Congo. Shortly afterwards it was again deployed in Cyprus and for more than thirty years it has been part of the United Nations force there. Since the United Nations mission to Namibia in 1989, the UNCP has become an increasingly important element of peacekeeping operations and has helped to restore conditions of social, economic and political stability to war-stricken societies.

UNCP currently participates in thirteen different missions around the globe. Each day more than 7,000 police officers from eighty countries go on patrol, provide training, advise local police services, help ensure compliance with human rights standards and assist in a wide range of other fields. This contributes to a safer environment where communities will be better protected and criminal activities will be prevented, disrupted and deterred. The diverse national experiences of UNCP officers and their commitment to peace and security are their best tools to promote the rule of law.

When engaged on United Nations duties, civilian police officers adhere to a specific mandate which varies from mission to mission. In some missions the mandate has been limited to monitoring the actions and activities of the local police services. In more complex missions the mandate extends to advising, training, assisting with the establishment of local police services and enhancing their work; while in others law enforcement forms part of the mandate. The civilian police officers serving with the United Nations Interim Administration in Kosovo (UNMIK) were the first to be tasked with full executive law enforcement authority.

Invariably, UNCP strives to train and develop the skills and abilities of local police services with a view to the gradual hand-over of responsibilities to the local authorities. The United Nations established two police academies, in Bosnia and Herzegovina, and in the region of 1,200 police cadets have been trained there. By 2002 approximately 4,500 locals graduated as police officers in Kosovo and are now actively engaged in policing alongside the UNMIK police. Similarly in East Timor more than 2,000 local police officers have been certified and work there with UNCP personnel from more than forty countries.

In 1993 the United Nations established a specific Civilian Police Unit to coordinate, plan and support the activities of the various missions involving a civilian police element. This unit became the Civilian Police Division in October 2000 and remains part of the Department of Peacekeeping Operations. Its goals are to:

1 support civilian police components of United Nations missions
2 enhance planning capacity for police components of United Nations operations

3   assist as appropriate with strengthening the performance, effectiveness and efficiency of local criminal justice systems, including police and corrections
4   enhance the ability to deploy rapidly a functional police component
5   improve quality representation in the field.

Garda participation on United Nations missions has had a number of beneficial effects. As well as achieving the primary aims of introducing stability and improving the policing and human rights situation in the regions concerned, such participation has also reinforced the international reputation of An Garda Síochána and has provided members of the force with a variety of experiences that can only serve to enhance the standard of policing in Ireland.

The decision on Irish involvement in a particular mission is generally determined following the receipt of a formal request from the United Nations (usually routed through the Department of Foreign Affairs to the Department of Justice, Equality and Law Reform). The latter then enters into informal consultations with An Garda Síochána and the Department of Foreign Affairs and, if necessary, seeks clarification as to the mandate and arrangements for the mission.

Factors taken into account include the nature and likely duration of the mission, level of risk, relevancy to Irish interests and the number of gardaí already serving abroad. If Irish participation appears feasible and desirable, the Minister for Justice, Equality and Law Reform formally consults the Garda Commissioner, the Minister for Foreign Affairs and the Minister for Finance who brings the matter before government for approval. If approved, volunteers from An Garda Síochána are selected and practical arrangements for their training, briefing, equipment and transport to the operational area are made. To date, this approach has not given rise to any difficulties and has the advantage of being relatively flexible.

An Garda Síochána involvement in United Nations operations pre-1989

United Nations posts were first offered to members of An Garda Síochána, with the agreement of the Irish government, in 1956. Prior to 1989 and the passing of An Garda Síochána Act, gardaí served with the United Nations on an individual basis. These members served in peacekeeping missions in Cyprus, the Lebanon and other countries, but their service was conditional upon their first resigning from An Garda Síochána and becoming United Nations employees for the period of their service. They retained the option to rejoin the force upon completion of United Nations service. The legal impediment preventing serving gardaí working with the United Nations was abolished with the passing of the Garda Síochána Act (1989) – an Act introduced to facilitate the Namibian mission and such other missions as might arise.

The main provisions of the Act were the following:

1   to empower the government to send a contingent of gardaí for service outside the state
2   to enable the government to determine the number and rank of those members to be included in such a contingent
3   to ensure that all members of such a contingent would be volunteers
4   to provide for the registration, in this state, of the death outside the state of a member of An Garda Síochána, his/her spouse or another relative while such a member is on service overseas with the United Nations
5   to provide for the registration of the birth outside the state of the child of such a member.

One member who chose to resign from An Garda Síochána to serve with the United Nations in those early years was Garda Francis (Frank) Eivers, 10236 (RIP). Eivers, a native of Roscommon, joined the force on 19 November 1952 and resigned on 28 November 1956 to join the United Nations. He was killed on 18 September 1961 while working with the United Nations in the Congo in the plane crash along with all other passengers and crew and in which Secretary-General Dag Hammarskjöld was also killed.

Frank Eivers is one of the two members of An Garda Síochána to receive the Dag Hammarskjöld Medal posthumously. The medal, which honours, recognises and commemorates all of those who have lost their lives as a result of service in peacekeeping operations under the operational control and authority of the United Nations, was presented on 21 November 2002 and was accepted by Mrs Marie-Therese De Mora on behalf of her late husband.

An Garda Síochána involvement in United Nations operations post-1989

Arising from a request from the United Nations, serving members of An Garda Síochána were first deployed on United Nations service on 14 April 1989 to participate in the mission in Namibia. To facilitate this deployment it was necessary for the government to put in place legislation allowing gardaí to serve overseas and to this end the Garda Síochána Act (1989) was enacted by the Oireachtas. Participation in this first mission to Namibia was unique and paved the way for garda contingents to serve with the United Nations on later missions in Angola, Cambodia, Mozambique, Somalia,

Western Sahara, the Former Yugoslavia, Bosnia and Herzegovina, Eastern Slavonia, and Cyprus.

Namibia (UNTAG – United Nations Transition Assistance Group)

Fifty-one members of An Garda Síochána served with the United Nations in Namibia from March 1989 to March 1990.

The contingent consisted of one chief superintendent, one superintendent, two inspectors, eleven sergeants and thirty-six gardaí.

The task of these members was primarily one of monitoring and supervision of the work of local police forces, to ensure that law and order was maintained effectively and impartially, and that human rights and fundamental freedoms were observed and fully protected. Gardaí on this mission also supervised prison and detention centres and helped to assure free and fair democratic elections and assisted in the process of returning persons displaced by hostilities.

Stephen Fanning, who had participated in a United Nations reconnaissance mission in Namibia some years earlier while serving as an Assistant Commissioner in An Garda Síochána (although then retired), was selected as the United Nations Police Commissioner for the subsequent mission.

Chief Superintendent Noel Anderson (now retired), who led the garda contingent, held the position of District Commander in the Namibian capital, Windhoek. Superintendent Peter Fitzgerald (now Deputy Commissioner) was assigned as District Commander to the troubled northern region of the country, and was based in Oshakati where armed conflict took place between the ruling South African forces and the South West African People's Organisation (SWAPO) insurgents in the early stages following deployment of civilian police to the region. Notwithstanding those initial difficulties, the Namibian mission is widely recognised within the United Nations as one of the great success stories in its history, the mandate having been fully achieved within the set timeframe.

Angola (UNAVEM II – United Nations Angola Verification Mission II)

Angola had been a Portuguese colony up to 1975. Following independence, a civil war ensued and the country became another battleground for the United States and the Soviet Union. UNITA, under the leadership of Jonas Savimbi, was supported by the Americans while the MPLA governing forces received the support of the Soviets. In the late 1980s a settlement was reached and a ceasefire agreed. As a result of the ceasefire, the United Nations established a mission in Angola to certify the demobilisation of military personnel, the creation of a national army and the establishment of a national police force. This mission was to be known as UNAVEM. Civilian police were to become involved in the process of verifying police neutrality by accompanying members of the National Police Authority on investigations. The National Police Authority consisted of nominees from both sides of the political divide (UNITA and MPLA).

Fourteen gardaí served in Angola from September 1991 to November 1992. They were deployed separately and dispatched to stations across Angola where they served with civilian police officers of other nationalities.

This contingent consisted of two inspectors, one sergeant and eleven gardaí.

The functions of monitors in Angola included the supervision and monitoring of the work of local police forces, the verification of the arrangements agreed by the Angolan parties for monitoring the ceasefire as set out in the ceasefire agreement, verification of the arrangements agreed by the Angolan parties for the monitoring of the Angolan police during the ceasefire period ensuring that law and order was maintained effectively and impartially, and that human rights and fundamental freedoms were observed and fully protected. Prison and detention centres were also supervised and there was a focus on assuring free and fair democratic elections. Similar to the Namibian mission, members of An Garda Síochána also assisted in the process of returning persons displaced by hostilities.

Cambodia (UNTAC – United Nations Transitional Authority in Cambodia)

Seventy-five gardaí served with the United Nations in Cambodia from April 1992 to July 1993. Chief Superintendent (now Deputy Commissioner) Peter Fitzgerald served as CIVPOL Chief of Operations and Superintendent Joe Dowling held the position of District Commander in Siem Riep Province in the north of the country where the Khmer Rouge carried out sporadic attacks on government forces and the local population throughout the course of the mission. The garda contingent consisted of one chief superintendent, one superintendent, seven inspectors, fifteen sergeants and fifty-one gardaí.

On 23 October 1991 the Agreements on a Comprehensive Political Settlement of the Cambodia Conflict (The United Nations Peace Plan) were signed in Paris by the four warring Cambodian factions, including the Khmer Rouge. These agreements marked the end of more than a decade of negotiations in which the United Nations Secretary-General had been closely involved. The agreements were designed to bring peace to Cambodia through the holding of free and fair elections under United Nations supervision with a view to establishing a democratic government.

In addition to the supervision and monitoring role previously carried out by gardaí while on international duty, the Cambodian mandate added the executive powers of stop, search, interrogate and arrest. This development required An Garda Síochána to take a lead role in the investigation of crimes committed by the Khmer Rouge, demobbed Cambodian military, local police and ordinary criminals. Members of the force subsequently investigated several mass murders of Vietnamese workers by Khmer Rouge forces, individual murders associated with ordinary crime, and crimes associated with the political environment.

Although the Cambodian mission claimed many international lives, Cambodia being at that time the most heavily mined country in the world, gardaí serving with UNTAC escaped unscathed apart from minor injury and illnesses including malaria. The mission was not without incident however – some members were held at gunpoint by Khmer Rouge military and others were fired upon during military operations by the Cambodian forces.

Gardaí held the prestigious roles of Mission Chief of Operations, District Commander and Chief of the Special Investigation Unit. This ensured that An Garda Síochána was at the core of the transitional authority in Cambodia. Members of the force were among the first United Nations personnel to enter Cambodia and reports show that they entered Phnom Penh even before it was reinhabited by many Cambodians after the end of Pol Pot's (Khmer Rouge) despotic regime. An Garda Síochána remained in Cambodia until the mission ended and had the opportunity to take part in the rebirth of that country after decades of destruction.

Yugoslavia (UNPROFOR – United Nations Protection Force)

Hostilities broke out in Yugoslavia following free elections in Slovenia and Croatia in 1990. These hostilities engulfed the whole of the Balkans, resulting in the deaths of at least 250,000 people. By December 1991 an estimated half a million more people fled as refugees and displaced persons. By August 1992 the number of persons directly affected by the crisis and in need of emergency humanitarian assistance was estimated to be in the region of 2.7 million.

Eighty-two members of An Garda Síochána served with UNPROFOR in the former Yugoslavia from March 1992 to January 1996. The contingent comprised four superintendents, eighteen sergeants and sixty gardaí.

The functions of the mission centred on ensuring that local police carried out their duties without discrimination against any person or any nationality, on ensuring that local police respected the human rights of all residents in the mission area. Monitors also provided assistance to UNHCR (United Nations High Commissioner for Refugees), ICRC (International Committee of the Red Cross) and other UNPROFOR recognised humanitarian agencies in support of their work to facilitate the return, in conditions of safety and security, of civilians who had been displaced by the conflict.

Sergeant Paul Reid, 20655E (RIP), was a member of the garda contingent deployed with the United Nations to the former Yugoslavia on 28 April

1995. He had served only twenty-one days in the mission area when he was killed on 18 May 1995 while on duty in the area of Sarajevo, then referred to as 'Sniper's Alley'. Sergeant Reid was the first and only serving member of An Garda Síochána to be killed while serving with the United Nations.

The Dag Hammarskjöld Medal was awarded to Sergeant Reid posthumously on 21 November 2002. The medal was accepted by Mrs Rosemarie Reid on behalf of her late husband.

Bosnia and Herzegovina (UNIPTF)

The United Nations Civilian Police (UNCP) mission in Bosnia and Herzegovina operated in a very difficult situation. Its members had to co-operate with a multi-national military force which was outside direct United Nations control and which was viewed with some hostility by elements of the local population. The representatives of An Garda Síochána made key contributions to the initial success of the mission, maintaining excellent relations with the local authorities and the NATO-led military force and establishing a new local policing structure for Bosnia and Herzegovina. Ireland's international reputation was considerably enhanced by its contribution to this mission at a key stage.

Assistant Commissioner Peter Fitzgerald (now Deputy Commissioner) was the first CIVPOL Commissioner for the International Police Task Force (IPTF) in Bosnia and Herzegovina from January 1996 to January 1997. He was in charge of the largest police force ever deployed by the United Nations up to that time. A total of 246 members of An Garda Síochána served on the mission, which ended on 31 December 2002. It was succeeded by the European Union Police Mission (EUPM) on 1 January 2003.

The Bosnia and Herzegovina deployment was widely accepted by those members who had served on previous missions as being more difficult and more stressful than any that had gone before. The political and military tensions were palpable and the plight of civilians as a result of displacement (including the transition of Sarajevo – the moving of the inter-entity boundary lines as a result of the Dayton Agreement) led to overwhelming community security problems, property rights issues and an ethnic imbalance of historical norms. One member reported spending St Patrick's Day 1996 in an old cemetery on the outskirts of Sarajevo providing security for one ethnic group that was removing the remains of its buried relatives and family members so that they could be re-interred where the new inter-entity boundary lines provided guarantees that they would not be desecrated. Others reported similar situations, including the discovery of mass graves and other atrocities.

Bosnia-Herzegovina proved to be a testing situation for the international community, the United Nations and the International Police Task Force

(IPTF). The circumstances required the application of the most acutely honed policing skills. This proved to be very fruitful for An Garda Síochána, with members securing management positions far beyond their rank; some receiving international recognition for their innovative approaches to solving the problems of the Bosnian communities, and some members were also credited with saving lives and preventing serious violence while serving there.

Eastern Slavonia (UNTAES – United Nations Transitional Administration for Eastern Slavonia)

Ten gardaí served in Eastern Slavonia from May 1997 to January 1998 (when the mission was replaced by the UNPSG mission). This contingent of gardaí was made up of one inspector, two sergeants and seven gardaí.

Inspector Declan Brogan served as Deputy Police Commissioner to the mission from September 1996 to July 1997. Prior to 1997, fifteen members served with UNTAES (from May 1996 to May 1997).

In Eastern Slavonia monitors provided assistance to UNHCR, ICRC and other recognised humanitarian agencies in support of their work to facilitate the return, in conditions of safety and security, of civilians who had been displaced by the Balkan conflict. The local police force was also overseen to ensure that they carried out their duties without discrimination against any person or any nationality, and to ensure that local police respected the human rights of all residents in the mission area. Gardaí on this mission were also involved in training law enforcement personnel and advising governmental authorities in the region on the organisation of effective law enforcement agencies. They also helped to ensure that proper conditions prevailed in terms of the holding of free and fair elections.

This mission changed over to UNPSG (United Nations Police Support Group) from 15 January 1998 to 15 October 1998. Ten members of An Garda Síochána served with UNPSG from January to May 1998 and a further ten served from May 1998 until the termination of the mission in October 1998 when it was replaced by the OSCE (Organisation for Security and Co-operation in Europe) Policing Mission to the Danube Region of Croatia. The function of the UNPSG mission was to provide guidance and support to the local police while monitoring their performance as necessary to ensure public safety, guarantee universal human rights and gain the confidence of the local population.

Cyprus (UNFICYP – United Nations Forces in Cyprus)

The UNFICYP mission to Cyprus was created by the Security Council in 1964 as a response to hostilities between the Greek and Turkish communities on the island. In 1974, the coup d'etat by Greek and Cypriot elements was followed by Turkish military intervention. The resultant hostilities were halted on 16 August with both sides agreeing to support a Security Council resolution which called for the cessation of hostilities. As a result of these events, UNFICYP readjusted its deployment so that a force would be positioned between the opposing military forces in what is known as the Buffer Zone, extending about 180 km from west to east across the island.

The police component of this mission was until the late 1990s part of the military force and reported through the military commander. Unlike most CIVPOL missions, police of different nationalities were not integrated initially, but operated as two separate police units. This position was reviewed by the United Nations and the police detachments now report directly to the Head of Mission in line with all other United Nations missions with a CIVPOL component.

To date 165 members of An Garda Síochána have been deployed with UNFICYP in Cyprus. Eighteen members are currently serving with the United Nations in Cyprus, consisting of one superintendent, two inspectors, four sergeants and eleven gardaí. They are serving in the following locations: Nicosia, Pyla, Ledra, Famagusta, Dherynia, Athienou, Dhenia and Linou.

The functions of police monitors in Cyprus include the prevention of renewed fighting by maintaining a peaceful atmosphere within which a just and lasting solution to the island's problems can be found. CIVPOL is responsible primarily in the Buffer Zone for the following activities not involving United Nations personnel or United Nations property: investigation of criminal offences committed or suspected of being committed by non-United Nations personnel; preservation of civil order in the Buffer Zone; resolution of disputes between civilians from the north and south; access control of civilians in the Buffer Zone; supporting UNFICYP in the control of civilians during demonstrations, disturbances, etc; assistance and monitoring of Cypriot police investigations in the Buffer Zone; escorts of civilian officials into the Buffer Zone, and investigations. Members of An Garda Síochána on United Nations duties in Cyprus also provide appropriate assistance to humanitarian agencies.

Mozambique (ONUMOZ – United Nations Operations in Mozambique)

A general peace agreement was signed on 4 October 1992 in Rome between the Mozambique government and the National Resistance of Mozambique (RENAMO). This agreement provided for a ceasefire and the movement of troops into designated assembly areas where weapons could be handed over to United Nations personnel. In the light of these developments, the United Nations proposed the deployment of a sizeable police observer force to Mozambique to assist in the provision of a stable and secure environment in the run up to the elections in October 1994.

Twenty members of An Garda Síochána served with the United Nations in Mozambique from April 1994 to November 1994. The contingent consisted of one superintendent, four sergeants and fifteen gardaí. These members were engaged in the supervision and monitoring of the work of the local police force, to ensure that law and order was maintained effectively and impartially, and that human rights and fundamental freedoms were observed and fully protected. Gardaí also supervised prisons and detention centres and helped to ensure free and fair democratic elections. The process of returning persons displaced by hostilities was also assisted. Gardaí investigated crimes and complaints of discrimination and/or other human rights abuses.

From 27 to 29 October 1994, Mozambique held its first free and fair multi-party elections. These elections followed a protracted civil war which claimed the lives of hundreds of thousands of people, displaced millions more and destroyed the entire economic and social infrastructure of the country. The elections represented a major success story, not only in the operation for the first time of the democratic process but also in terms of United Nations peacekeeping, peacemaking and humanitarian and electoral assistance. In Mozambique members of An Garda Síochána were, once again, central to the CIVPOL mission.

Somalia (UNOSOM II – United Nations Operations in Somalia II)

The Somalia Justice Programme was drawn up in accordance with United Nations Security Council Resolutions 814 (26 March 1993) and 897 (4 February 1994). This programme was created in anticipation of the withdrawal of United States and most Western troops by the end of March 1994 and the changing of the role of the United Nations from a peace-enforcing to a peacekeeping one. The belief of the United Nations was that the best way to bring peace to Somalia was through the re-establishment of its own police force and criminal justice system.

Four members of An Garda Síochána served with UNOSOM II from April 1994 to August 1994: one chief superintendent, one inspector and two sergeants.

Chief Superintendent Michael Murphy was appointed Head of Training for this mission in April 1994. The main function of garda personnel on United Nations duty in Somalia was the training and re-establishment of a police force in Somalia. While significant progress was achieved by the civilian police element of the mission, including the recruitment and training of 1,200 Somali police officers, due to the deteriorating security situation the mission was terminated and United Nations personnel, including the civilian police, were evacuated.

Western Sahara (MINURSO – United Nations Mission for the Referendum in Western Sahara))

Fifteen members of An Garda Síochána served with the United Nations MINURSO mission to Western Sahara from May 1995 to March 1996. A contingent had originally been requested by the United Nations in 1991 but due to political difficulties and a resurgence of fighting in the region, the United Nations did not seek the deployment of the contingent at that time.

In 1988 Morocco and the Polisario Front agreed in principle to the United Nations Secretary-General's proposal for a ceasefire in Western Sahara. On 29 April 1991 the United Nations Security Council established the MINURSO mission with responsibility for organising a referendum in which the people of the region would choose between integration with Morocco and independence. The ceasefire commenced on 6 September 1991. A transitional period commenced in June 1995 as a run up to a referendum, intended for October 1995. The role of United Nations personnel was to oversee the identification and registration of votes and to monitor the repatriation programme during this transitional period. The United Nations was unable to complete this task due to political upheaval in the region, resulting in the temporary winding down of the mission in March 1996.

The Irish garda contingent with the United Nations MINURSO mission to Western Sahara from May 1995 to March 1996 comprised one inspector, four sergeants and ten gardaí. Work responsibilities of Irish police monitors included the supervision and monitoring of the work of the local police forces, the investigation of crimes and complaints of discrimination or other human rights abuses, and the responsibility for the maintenance of law and order effectively and impartially in order to ensure that human rights and fundamental freedoms were observed and fully protected. Prison and detention centres were also supervised as was the democratic election process. Members also assisted in the repatriation of persons displaced by hostilities.

With regard to the democratic election process, the main role for members of An Garda Síochána was in assisting, identifying and registering potential voters in the referendum. For this purpose garda personnel assisted in fingerprinting and photographing all potential voters, and in maintaining the security of registration centres throughout Western Sahara, Tindouf, Algeria and Nouadhibou, Mauritania. The referendum was to enable the people of Western Sahara (approximately 280,000) to choose between independence or integration with Morocco. However, the registration of voters ceased shortly after garda personnel were deployed because agreement failed to be reached between Frente Popular Para to Liberacion de Saguia el Hamra y de Rio de Oro (Frente POLISARIO) which was seeking independence and the Moroccans who had reintegrated the territory after Shamish withdrawal in 1976.

East Timor (UNAMET – United Nations Assistance Mission in East Timor)

Nine members of An Garda Síochána served with UNAMET from June 1999 to September 1999.

Indonesia and Portugal signed agreements on East Timor on 5 May 1999, witnessed by the Secretary-General of the United Nations, requesting that he immediately establish a United Nations mission to East Timor for the purpose of conducting popular consultations through a ballot on 8 August 1999. The purpose of these consultations was to ascertain whether the East Timorese people would accept or reject the proposed constitutional framework providing for a special autonomy for East Timor within the unitary Republic of Indonesia.

Security Council Resolution 1236 (1999) requested that the Secretary-General monitor the situation in East Timor and report to it by 24 May 1999. In this report, the Secretary-General proposed the establishment of a United Nations Mission in East Timor (UNAMET) to organise and conduct the popular consultations referred to above.

The UNAMET mission included 274 civilian police. The initial duration of the mission was for three months commencing June 1999; however, it was extended until November 1999 due to the postponement of the popular consultation until 30 August 1999. The Irish contingent was due to be repatriated in late September 1999. However, due to an outbreak of hostilities in the region most of the UNAMET personnel, including the Irish contingent, were evacuated from the mission area on 8 September 1999.

The main tasks of the police monitors included acting as advisors to the Indonesian police in the discharge of their duties during the period of the plebiscite, and supervision of the escort of ballot papers and boxes to and from the polling sites.

Special missions involving An Garda Síochána

El Salvador

Deputy Commissioner T.P. Fitzgerald was appointed as the police expert on the preliminary mission to El Salvador from 9 March 1991 to 1 April 1991. He subsequently reported to Under Secretary-General Marrack Goulding on the policing requirements for the proposed mission to that country. At a later date Commissioner Fitzgerald met with Goulding in New York, where he briefed him prior to the Under-Secretary-General's meeting with the El Salvador authorities to negotiate the terms of reference for the establishment of the mission. The mission to El Salvador was then established and subsequently reached a successful conclusion.

Tajikistan

Chief Superintendent Noel Anderson served with the United Nations Mission to Tajikistan from October 1995 to February 1996 as a legal/judicial consultant to the Tajikistan authorities. He worked closely with UNHCR during this mission.

Mission to Kosovo

Prior to the outbreak of the hostilities in the region in the late 1990s, the OSCE was in the process of establishing a Kosovo Verification Mission pursuant to negotiations between United States Envoy Richard Holbrooke and the President of the Federal Republic of Yugoslavia. An agreement had been signed with OSCE and had been endorsed by United Nations Security Council Resolution 1203 of 24 October 1998. The OSCE envisaged a police component to monitor the FYR police and possibly to assist in the establishment of a new ethnically balanced local police. The government had approved, in principle, the participation of An Garda Síochána in this mission. The situation changed dramatically, however, after the United Nations took responsibility for policing Kosovo and for establishing and training a local ethnically representative police force. Approximately 3,000 armed police officers were deployed as part of the United Nations mission and because these United Nations police were armed Ireland could not participate in the mission.

Although An Garda Síochána played no contingent role in Kosovo a great honour was bestowed upon the force when Deputy Commissioner Peter Fitzgerald was appointed Auditor General of that mission, a function never before awarded to a police officer by the United Nations. Commissioner Fitzgerald was charged with carrying out a full audit of how the mission had progressed and where it now stood – the budget, manning levels, the capability of the local police to provide a service without a United Nations presence, support structures in place for the policing element – and subsequently to make recommendations on his findings. His report was submitted and accepted, resulting in the police advisors office in New York being tasked with implementing his recommendations.

2002 fact-finding mission to Israel (Jenin Refugee Camp)

In April 2002 an Israeli military operation in the Jenin Refugee Camp led to international concern that atrocities had taken place there. A United Nations Security Council resolution prompted the setting up of a small fact-finding team under the stewardship of the former President of Finland, Marti Ahtisaari. The fact-finding team consisted of a civilian, military and police component, with the entire police component consisting of members of An Garda Síochána (Deputy Commissioner Peter Fitzgerald, Assistant

Commissioner Dermot Jennings and Superintendent Pat Leahy). The team was forced to carry out its enquiries from Geneva because of circumstances beyond its control and the mission was finally abandoned without the team ever setting foot in Israel or the Jenin Refugee Camp.

2003 Iraq investigation

Following the bombing of United Nations Headquarters in Baghdad on 19 August 2003, a United Nations investigation team was established under the direction of the former President of Finland, Marti Ahtisaari. The mission consisted of military, police and civilian components with the police component again entirely made up of members of An Garda Síochána, (Deputy Commissioner Peter Fitzgerald and Assistant Commissioner Kevin Carty). The investigation required the members to carry out enquiries in Baghdad, Amman, Jordan, Geneva and New York. A report was submitted to the Secretary-General of the United Nations which led to a complete overhaul of the security apparatus within the United Nations and subsequent fundamental changes within the organisation.

2005 fact-finding team to Beirut, Lebanon

On 14 February 2005, former Prime Minister Rafiq Hariri was assassinated in a massive explosion in Beirut. This assassination prompted the Security Council of the United Nations to mandate for a fact-finding mission to Lebanon to enquire into the 'Causes, Circumstances and Consequences' of the assassination. Deputy Commissioner Peter Fitzgerald, Chief Superintendent Martin Donnellan and Superintendent Pat Leahy (all members of An Garda Síochána) were charged with carrying out these enquiries supported only by a political advisor and a legal advisor.

This again was a departure for the United Nations in as much as it was prepared to allow a single, national police service (An Garda Síochána) to be the sole providers of this internationally sensitive service. The resulting report (The Fitzgerald Report) was subsequently referred to as follows: 'If the assassination of former Prime Minister Hariri had an earthquake-like impact on Lebanon, then the Fitzgerald Report has all the makings of the Tsunami that follows the earthquake'. The Fitzgerald Report led to the subsequent international investigation which is currently underway in Lebanon regarding the assassination of the former prime minister.

United States Institute for Peace

As a result of their involvement with the United Nations, members of An Garda Síochána were invited to develop and subsequently took part in developing the 'Model Codes for Post-Conflict Justice' with the United States Institute for Peace in partnership with the Irish Centre for Human Rights.

These model codes are expected to provide a flexible workable framework for each element of the justice system in future post-conflict situations.

The future role and changing environment for An Garda Síochána in international peacekeeping

For more than sixteen years An Garda Síochána, along with other police services in the international community, has grappled with an eruption of internal state crises throughout the post cold-war world, bringing with them state collapse, civil war, breakdown of law and order, and the need for humanitarian assistance. Widespread media coverage has borne witness to the slaughter, genocide, famine, disease and vast internal and external refugee flows, leaving in their wake epic problems of disease, destruction and poverty. Scenes of carnage and devastation, mass graves, outpourings of refugees and pictures of wounded, tattered and hungry survivors have unfortunately become part of the working environment in which An Garda Síochána has earned tremendous respect from the most junior administrator to the United Nations Secretary-General.

The responses of the international community to these situations have run the gamut from doing nothing, to providing standard humanitarian goods and services, deploying military and civilian police and supporting major training, development and reconstruction efforts once hostilities have been quelled. There have been more United Nations interventions since the gardaí first went abroad as an organisation in 1989 than in all the years between World War Two and 1989. The new conflicts have taken forms that have been hard to mesh with the basic conception of the United Nations or its previous experience. The United Nations was established to deal with conflicts between states. By contrast, post cold-war conflicts have typically arisen within states – often disintegrating states. Historic grievances, ethnic tensions, and religious differences, which were suppressed during the cold-war or dominated by East-West considerations, have re-emerged in acute form.

For the states that make up the United Nations however, the presumption of sovereignty remains strong. Traditional constraints against intervention in the internal affairs of a state operate not only within the United Nations but affect the decisions and actions of other international organisations and states as well. To address the internal conflicts with which An Garda Síochána and other agencies are now confronted has required not only hard political decisions, but a slow and difficult process of rethinking fundamental international norms and legal justifications.

Beyond the volume and novelty of the new challenges, An Garda Síochána has had to contend with international problems in the area of developing coherent and effective strategies for responding to internal conflict, whether by preventive action, by efforts to end ongoing violence or by reconstruction and rehabilitation in the aftermath of conflict. Some of these conditions, conditions which set the context within which future garda deployments may take place, present problems for An Garda Síochána when considering these future deployments.

In its most fundamental aspect, the problem of policy coherence is a problem of the sheer multiplicity of actors at many levels, performing the wide variety of tasks associated with conflict intervention. Participants typically include the United Nations; specialised intergovernmental agencies, such as the World Health Organisation (WHO), the Food and Agriculture Organisation (FAO), and, of particular importance, the international financial organisations, like the World Bank; regional organisations, such as the Organisation for Security and Cooperation in Europe (OSCE) or the Organisation of African Unity (OAU); nation states, both as political actors and as donors in bilateral aid programmes; and a host of NGOs, both international and local. All have their own mandates (often embodied in their charters), agendas, constituencies and needs, not fully appreciated by others and rarely harmonised.

In this list of players there is no official or organisation with the legal authority, let alone the practical power or political and economic resources, to impose order on the actions of so many different organisations pursuing so many different objectives in so many different ways. Prime examples are the Security Council resolutions establishing the 'mandate' – the goals, objectives and broad strategy – for United Nations operations. These resolutions are necessarily the product of a political process. The language must take account of the divergent political interests of the Council members – particularly those of the permanent members – which supply most of the human, financial and political resources. This situation has begun to generate doubt as to the viability of deployment of An Garda Síochána to missions where the arming of civilian police contingents is becoming the norm.

Increasing numbers of requests for intervention and the move towards arming international civilian police has generated an interesting debate, which has not yet been resolved. How An Garda Síochána will fare in the future in terms of continued international deployments has not yet been determined. Evidence suggests that the future of civilian police deployments will include increased armed missions, an outcome which is at variance with the fundamental concepts of policing within the force. Having earned such respect on the international stage, is An Garda Síochána destined to remain at home in the future and fade into international obscurity because of conflicting national and international policy decisions regarding the carriage and use of firearms while on United Nations duty?

The developing role of the European Union in peacekeeping operations is also having, and will continue to have, implications in respect of the future role of An Garda Síochána within the United Nations. As part of its pre-accession strategy, the European Union has been actively involved in assisting the development of modern police forces in the countries of Eastern Europe and the Baltic States with particular regard to the observation of human rights. As part of its Common Foreign and Security Policy, the EU has a close interest in promoting international peace and security and there have been EU missions involving election monitoring. The primary role of the United Nations and the Organisation for Security and Cooperation in Europe (OSCE) in the area of police peacekeeping missions is recognised and the EU is looking at how it can best contribute to developments in the area.

In terms of future garda involvement in international peacekeeping operations, the probability is that An Garda Síochána will become more involved in EU missions and less involved in United Nations missions. There are several reasons for this:

1   Along with its EU partners Ireland has an interest in minimising conflicts near the borders of the EU. Conflicts such as those which broke out in the former Yugoslavia can have serious economic and social implications for member states of the EU. In addition to the danger of conflicts spreading to the border of the EU, such conflicts generate serious problems with refugees.

2   United Nations missions are increasingly becoming armed missions, and current policy is that Irish contingents will not be armed. The level of risk to personnel is one of the factors taken into account when a decision is being made to send a garda contingent abroad.

3   The primary concern has to be policing in Ireland. There are costs involved in sending garda contingents abroad and, while travel and subsistence costs are generally met by the international organisation concerned, the salaries of members serving on peacekeeping missions continue to be paid by the state. The real cost is that the gardaí deployed abroad are not available for deployment in Ireland.

4   Increasing demands are being placed on the garda Vote for domestic policing issues.

On the other hand, Ireland has a long tradition of involvement in peacekeeping missions and in the provision of assistance to developing countries. This commitment to peacekeeping is part of Ireland's foreign policy and the involvement of the gardaí in this task is a natural development of that policy. Furthermore, as members of international organisations such as the United Nations and the Organisation for Security and Cooperation in Europe, Ireland has obligations and commitments to honour. Ongoing provision of resources is required if conflicts are to be resolved and suffering alleviated.

In addition, the nature of United Nations missions is such that gardaí find themselves working alongside police from all over the world. They gain considerable experience and often are placed in positions of responsibility well beyond what they would experience at their rank in Ireland. Such missions enhance the level of expertise within the garda service overall and have confirmed that the training and overall standard within An Garda Síochána meets the highest international standards.

The Garda Síochána Act (1989) was introduced to facilitate the dispatch of contingents of An Garda Síochána for service with the United Nations in Namibia. Not surprisingly, the Act was geared specifically for service in an international United Nations peacekeeping force. There have been a number of significant developments since 1989. In particular, missions with international organisations other than the United Nations have become more common. It may now be timely to revise the existing legislation to provide, for instance, for members of An Garda Síochána who are required to exercise police powers on a mission. It would also be appropriate for the legislation to cover service with other bodies as well as the United Nations.

Chapter Fifteen

The place of the United Nations in contemporary Irish foreign policy

EILEEN CONNOLLY AND JOHN DOYLE

During the past decade, even with an increased emphasis on EU integration, the United Nations has retained a central place in Irish foreign policy. Both political discourse and public opinion polls indicate widespread support for the organisation as a source of international legitimacy and as the appropriate forum to make major decisions regarding peace and security, international human rights, and development. This support draws from both the idea that the United Nations provides the most suitable forum and safeguards for a small state in the international system and also from the identification of the ethical basis of Irish foreign policy with the founding principles of the United Nations. For the public at large the aspect of Ireland's engagement with the United Nations which has the highest profile is that of service by the Irish Army on United Nations peacekeeping missions. Acknowledging this An Taoiseach Bertie Ahern's speech to the 2005 United Nations summit began with the statement that 'We have always placed the United Nations at the very centre of our foreign policy. Many Irish soldiers have served under the blue flag, and some have sacrificed their lives in that noble service'.[1] In addition, a significant number of Irish people have direct personal experience of working with the United Nations system through involvement with United Nations humanitarian agencies and with non-governmental organisations working with, or funded by, United Nations agencies. The high level of legitimacy enjoyed by the United Nations in Irish society is indicated by its high profile use by campaigners for a no vote in referenda on alterations to EU treaties in 2001 and 2002. Here campaigners contrasted their perspective of the future of European security arrangements with 'traditional' United Nations operations – most graphically captured by the poster during the

---

[1] Speech by the Taoiseach, Bertie Ahern TD at the United Nations General Assembly on Wednesday, 14 Sept. 2005. http://www.taoiseach.gov.ie/index.asp?locID=200&docID=2157.

referendum on the Nice Treaty that starkly said 'Hello NATO, good-bye UN'.[2]

Looking beyond the rhetoric this chapter examines the position of the United Nations in contemporary Irish foreign policy. It starts with a brief examination of the first white paper on foreign policy in the history of the state, published in 1996. This paper indicates tensions between different policy objectives and also clearly establishes the priority areas of foreign policy. These four areas – peacekeeping, disarmament, human rights, and development are then examined in turn[3]. To analysis in more detail how Irish foreign policy works out in practise the chapter will then examine Ireland's record on the Security Council during its term of 2001 to 2002.

Tensions in Irish foreign policy

In the 1996 government white paper on foreign policy, which remains the state's primary foreign policy document, the United Nations is described as 'a cornerstone of Irish foreign policy since we joined the Organisation on 14 December 1955'.[4] In stating this it expressed support for the United Nations in the context of the values that underlie Ireland's foreign policy. The white paper clearly reflects the wider public perception of the ethics underlying Ireland's foreign policy. It argues:

> Ireland's foreign policy is about much more than self-interest. For many of us it is a statement of the kind of people we are. Irish people are committed to the principles set out in the Constitution for the conduct of international relations —
> * the ideal of peace and friendly co-operation amongst nations founded on international justice and morality;
> * the principle of the pacific settlement of international disputes by international arbitration or judicial determination; and
> * the principles of international law as our rule of conduct in our relations with other states.[5]

---

[2] The first (defeated) referendum was held on 9 June 2001; the second referendum, which was passed, was held on 19 Oct. 2002.

[3] *The White Paper on Foreign Policy: Challenges And Opportunities Abroad,* http://www.dfa.ie/information/publications/whitepaper/default.asp, *para 5.8.*
The continued relevance of these four areas is indicated by the fact they are the only sub-headings used for policy on the website of the Irish Mission to the United Nations; also see, for example, the speech by the Taoiseach, 14 Sept. 2005. http://www.taoiseach.gov.ie/index.asp?locID=200&docID= 2157
or address by the Minister for Foreign Affairs of Ireland, Brian Cowen, to the 59th Session of the United Nations General Assembly, 23 Sept. 2004, New York,
http://www.dfa.ie/information/display.asp?ID=1587

[4] White Paper, para. 5.7.

[5] White Paper, para. 2.40.

In making this statement the white paper is clearly aligning Ireland with the fundamental principles of the United Nations. It also discusses the way in which the government believes that these higher aspirations are essential to the self-interest of small states, in that they form the basis of an international system in which small states can best function as economic and political units. This is reflected in the assertion that

> It is precisely because Ireland is small and hugely dependent on exter-
> nal trade for its well-being that we need an active foreign policy.
> Ireland does not have the luxury of deciding whether or not to pursue
> a policy of external engagement. We do not have a sufficiently large
> domestic market or adequate natural resources to enable our economy
> to thrive in isolation. We depend for our survival on a regulated inter-
> national environment in which the rights and interests of even the
> smallest are guaranteed and protected.[6]

The argument that there is a conflict between the ethical basis of Irish foreign policy as expressed by its support for the United Nations and Irish economic interests has been dismissed strongly by the government in recent years. For example former Minister for Foreign Affairs Brian Cowen has argued against an analysis of foreign policy on the basis of values versus interests. He said it was not an either/or situation, because small states could not compete in a power-seeking international system run according to realist principles. Ireland, he argued, 'like most small nations has always known that a multilateral rules-based international order *is* in our national interest. We would like to think, and I believe with much justification that we have demonstrated this, that our commitment to liberal internationalism is also based on principle.'[7] In this he reflects the view of Robert Keohane who concludes that small-state support for multilateralism is rational, because whatever the failures of multilateral action, small- and even medium-sized states have no hope whatsoever of making an international impact if they act alone. Small states acting within international fora can play a 'systemic role' in seeking to shape codes and rules of behaviour.[8]

Although the overarching relationship between self-interest and ideals in foreign policy may not be in conflict, the relationship is not always one of coincidence: it also involves tensions when the pursuit of the economic self-interest of the state comes into conflict with its ethical foreign policy stance. Minister Cowen's argument could be seen as an attempt to deflect criticism which surrounded foreign policy decisions which appeared to be based on

---

[6] White Paper, para. 2.37.

[7] Brian Cowen, 'Challenges to liberal internationalism', *Irish Studies in International Affairs* 12 (2001), pp. 1–5, p. 2.

[8] Robert Keohane, '"Lilliputians" dilemmas: small states in international politics', *International Organization* 23(2) (1969), pp. 291–310, p. 297.

narrow economic self-interest. Two recent examples of this tension have been seen in the stance of the Irish government on the invasion of Iraq and also the position it has taken on agricultural subsidies to Irish farmers. The policy on Iraq which was critical of United States plans to invade the country was muted by consideration of the importance of United States investment for the Irish economy.[9] And the relatively good international reputation Ireland enjoys on development policy has been undermined by its strong protectionist stand on the question of EU subsidies for trade in agricultural products.

The white paper also discusses reform of the United Nations system and the role it should play into the twenty-first century. It expressed support for an enlargement and reform of the Security Council and support for General Assembly reforms to enable it to play a more important role in building international consensus on key issues.[10] On peace and security it supported the maintenance of 'the United Nations' capacity to deter aggression, 'including if necessary through enforcement action under Chapter VII of the Charter' but sought a greater focus on 'developing the United Nations' capability in relation to conflict prevention, peacekeeping and peace-making'.[11] This position was continued in the build up to the 2005 United Nations Summit.[12] Ireland's credibility on these issues was confirmed by the appointment of Foreign Minister Dermot Ahern as one of just four special envoys of Secretary-General Annan to promote United Nations reform in advance of the summit.

The white paper's four priority areas of interest for Irish foreign policy – peacekeeping, disarmament, human rights and development – are now examined in the light of the tensions that exist between the desire of the Irish state for a 'multilateral rules based international order' and the pressures of realpolitik that they face.

Peacekeeping and the challenge of EU security

Ireland has been a very significant contributor to United Nations peace support operations – in particular peacekeeping. Indeed given the comparatively small size of the Irish army that contribution has been remarkable. In August 2005 for example, only Poland within the EU (or indeed OECD) had more troops deployed on peacekeeping missions worldwide than Ireland.[13] Ireland's deployments have not followed the pattern of other developed states. In Africa – where many of the current large peacekeeping operations are deployed, the

---

[9] See, for example, *Sunday Times* (London), 23 Feb. 2003; *Business and Finance*, 13 Feb. 2003.

[10] White Paper, para. 5.47.

[11] White Paper, para. 5.28.

[12] See for example press release from Minister Ahern, 21 Mar. 2005, http://www.dfa.ie/information/display.asp?ID=1719.

[13] http://www.un.org/Depts/dpko/dpko/contributors/. More generally there have been over 50,000 tours of duty, primarily by the Irish military, but in recent years also including members of an Garda Síochána.

United Nations has had great difficulty getting commitments from developed states to provide troops. There are now almost no European or North American troops on the African continent in the major missions under United Nations command. Only in Liberia where Ireland provides 426 troops and Sweden provides just over 200 are there any significant numbers of troops from developed states.[14] Although this reflects the regionalisation of peacekeeping to some extent, that policy is also a reflection of the failure of developed states to commit resources to peacekeeping operations.

In December 2004, 771 Irish troops were deployed internationally. This included 428 in Liberia, 45 on other United Nations duties, 208 under KFOR command but with a United Nations mandate in Kosovo and 53 with EUFOR in Bosnia, again with a United Nations mandate. None of these missions was in arenas where Ireland could be said to have narrow economic or trade interests, but engagement of this type does boost Ireland's inter-national standing. There are two key questions that need to be addressed on the future development of Ireland's peacekeeping role – firstly, could Ireland do more and secondly, how will the current developments in EU security and defence policy impact on Ireland's commitments in this area?

On the first issue, it is unlikely that Ireland could significantly increase the numbers of troops on United Nations duty unless there was an increase in the overall size of the defence forces.[15] Keeping 800 troops abroad in effect means having another 800 in training getting ready to replace them and typically means 800 have just returned home – an effective commitment of 2,400. With only 8,500 soldiers in the Irish army, that is a relatively high proportion by current international standards, given other commitments for security, training etc. There is an ongoing debate about the nature of modern military training and deployment and widespread agreement that European armies are relatively inflexible and immobile. In particular, in Ireland there is a political reluctance to consolidate the army into a much smaller number of barracks; this greatly reduces the capacity for large-scale training and is a drain on resources with no military rationale. One effect of the maintenance of the current number of barracks is a reduction in the number of troops available for international duty. If the government wishes to increase Ireland's commitment to peacekeeping that will in reality require an increase in the size of the defence forces or a decision to close small barracks.

The question of the development of EU security and defence policy is a more complex one. The current commitment of a maximum of 850 troops to international duty covers both the emerging EU capabilities and the United Nations. The Irish Army could not sustain two separate deployments

---

[14] Other large United Nations missions which Ireland has been involved in since the mid-1990s have included: the United Nations Transitional Administration in East Timor (UNTAET) (Feb. 2000 to May 2002), Irish commitment over that time: 181; United Nations Mission Ethiopia/Eritrea (UNMEE) (Nov. 2001 to June 2003), total Irish commitment: 630.

[15] See also John Terence O'Neill's chapters, above pp. 299–317.

at that level if they were requested simultaneously. On one level there is a fear among some commentators that the pressure from EU partners to build an effective EU military capacity will lead inevitably to a reduced availability of Irish soldiers for United Nations duty.[16] Given the reluctance of most EU states to serve under United Nations command or to serve in Africa this might lead to a significant change in Irish practice. If the EU decides to engage in a United Nations mandated military mission there would be considerable pressure on Ireland to participate to demonstrate our support for an important EU development and inevitably this means fewer troops are available for other United Nations commanded operations.

On the other hand it is possible that if the EU were to develop a military capacity of its own to carry out significant peace support operations then this would offer the United Nations a resource which it does not currently have. States not currently participating at significant levels in United Nations peacekeeping might then feel more pressure to participate (and pay for) an EU-led operation.

For the Irish public (and internationally) it is unlikely that the EU can have the legitimacy which the United Nations possesses as a near universal organisation of states. Given the previous colonial relationships of many European states with the Global South and the growing gap of wealth between the Global North and South it will be very difficult for the EU to build the level of acceptability that the United Nations possesses. EU-led missions will inevitably take place in a context of unequal power relationships and with suspicions that the EU is seeking to develop military muscle to match its economic power.

At present there is a very limited range of operations carried out under European Security and Defence Policy (ESDP) and a judgement on the pressures they create for Ireland's traditional foreign policy priorities can only be tentative. The range of early activity has been in keeping with Irish foreign policy goals. Ireland was particularly keen to see the civilian aspects of ESDP given a central role, given domestic concerns around issues of neutrality and the high levels of public opposition to the United States invasion of Iraq. In this regard, ESDP has had a range of activity other than purely military. In fact at present there is just one significant military operation (of 7,000 troops in Bosnia and Herzegovina), three policing missions (FYR Macedonia, Bosnia and Herzegovina and DRC), one on security sector reform (DRC), one on judicial system reform (Iraq) and a post-peace agreement civilian monitoring mission in Aceh, just beginning at time of writing.

So far there has been no tension between EU and United Nations responsibilities or authority. While Ireland was unable to take part in the first ESDP

---

[16] e.g. Andy Storey, *The Treaty of Nice, NATO and a European Army: Implications for Ireland,* Afri Position Paper No. 3, 2001. This was also the view expressed by the Green Party (http://www.green-party.ie/) and by Sinn Féin (http://www.sinnfein.ie).

military mission in Macedonia because it did not have the United Nations mandate required by Irish law, this was a largely technical issue due to a threatened veto by China because of Macedonia's diplomatic recognition of Taiwan. There was certainly nothing in the character of the mission which would have raised fears of an adverse public reaction in Ireland.

The second ESDP military operation, 'Artemis' in the Democratic Republic of the Congo (DRC), was essentially a French-led affair but it had a United Nations mandate and involved much greater EU-United Nations cooperation. While there was clearly contact between the United Nations Secretariat and the French before a formal request for assistance was made, even allowing for that, an EU decision was made within a week of the United Nations request and enabling troops were on the ground within days – leading to the rapid deployment of about 1,800 troops. The Irish Army Ranger wing was offered to the French Force commander in the Congo but the offer was not taken up. There was structured cooperation with the wider United Nations Mission in the Congo and the Force, having stabilised a potentially dangerous situation in one locality, handed over to a United Nations operation. This was clearly a limited operation even in the context of the ongoing crisis in the DRC. Nonetheless it played a crucial role at a potentially difficult time and was a practical example of how well-trained and well-resourced EU troops can play a role within a wider United Nations context. It led to a memorandum of understanding between the EU and United Nations on future cooperation in crisis management.[17] This idea was developed during the Irish Presidency of the EU in 2004 when the Irish military authorities hosted a seminar on EU-United Nations cooperation in peacekeeping, with speakers including Jean-Marie Guéhenno, United Nations Under-Secretary-General, Department of Peacekeeping, and Major-General B. Neveux, Former EU Operations Commander in Operation Artemis.[18]

The positive relationship between the EU and the United Nations in the early ESDP operations took place in relatively benign environments and they were limited in scale. There are some suggestions that ESDP decisions in the counter-terrorism arena since the publication of the EU Security Strategy in 2003[19] have taken a rather narrower view and have stressed the criminal justice, border security, intelligence and military aspects over long-term commitments to dealing with the underlying causes of insecurity identified in that strategy document, such as poverty and underdevelopment.[20] If a narrow

---

[17] http://ue.eu.int/showPage.asp?id=606&lang=en.

[18] *Synergy between the United Nations and EU Military Crisis Management*, Irish Defence Forces Publication, 2004.

[19] *A Secure Europe in a Better World, the European Union Security Strategy*, agreed by the European Council on 12 Dec. 2003.

[20] John Doyle, *Analysing the causes of 'international terrorism': situating European Security and Defence Policy 2004–2005*. Working paper in International Studies, Centre for International Studies, Dublin City University, 2005.

view of security based on border controls, military force and economic power dominates ESDP in practice Ireland could find real tension emerging between ESDP activity and traditional commitments to a broader view of security.

At present Ireland remains clear in its broad commitment to the United Nations as the legitimate organisation responsible for international peace and security. It seeks not only to defend but expand the United Nations' role in that area. As part of the deliberation for the 2005 United Nations Summit in New York Ireland strongly supported the strengthening of the United Nations' right and responsibility to intervene and welcomed the agreement to establish a Peacebuilding Commission. Given the strength of Irish public opinion on this issue it is likely that government support for ESDP missions will remain within the framework of United Nations mandates.

Disarmament

Since joining the United Nations Ireland has had a public commitment to disarmament and in particular nuclear disarmament.[21] However this is clearly an area where international progress has been very limited and where a small non-nuclear state has little leverage.

Apart from discussion on nuclear weapons, the control and eventual banning of landmines has been the object of a strong international campaign. In 1997 the Convention on the Prohibition of the Use, Stockpiling, Production and Transfer of Anti-Personnel Mines and on their Destruction (1997 Mine Ban Treaty) came into force and Ireland signed and ratified the convention on the first day.[22] As Ireland only possessed 130 mines in 1997 – for purely training purposes – this was a symbolic decision designed to maximise political pressure.

Ireland was admitted to the Conference on Disarmament (Geneva) in 1999, most likely in response to the particular initiative taken the previous year when Ireland supported the Joint Declaration by the Ministers for Foreign Affairs of Brazil, Egypt, Ireland, Mexico, New Zealand, Slovenia, South Africa and Sweden, 'Towards A Nuclear-Weapons-Free World: The Need For A New Agenda'.[23] That declaration called for new initiatives on disarmament – including a commitment in principle by nuclear capable states to disarm, support for a comprehensive test ban treaty, a ban on fissile material, short-term de-escalation measures such as de-alerting and deactivating weapons, and the removal of non-strategic weapons. Based on this, Ireland was one of the sponsors of a resolution at the Conference on Disarmament (Geneva) which was passed with ninety positive votes, thirteen against and thirty-seven abstentions (which included most NATO members).

---

[21] See also Greg Spelman's chapter above pp. 224–252.

[22] http://www.icbl.org/tools/databases/country/ireland .

[23] see statement of 9 June 1998 http://www.dfa.ie/policy/nuclearfreeworld.asp.

The resolution was brought to the United Nations General Assembly First Committee (disarmament) in November 1998 and again passed with most NATO members abstaining. However without NATO support the progress as a result of the resolution was very limited.

During Ireland's two-year period on the Security Council there were no initiatives on disarmament – because the permanent five were under no particular pressure to take any action and would have blocked any initiative. There was an Irish contribution to an open meeting of the Security Council on small arms following the July 2001 United Nations conference on the illicit trade in small arms; however there were no decisions requiring action taken at the meeting and no evidence of any follow up.[24]

This general lack of progress on disarmament was reflected in the immediate reaction to the United Nations summit of September 2005 when Minister for Foreign Affairs Dermot Ahern in his only negative comment said 'I share in particular the Secretary-General's disappointment that it contains nothing on disarmament and non-proliferation, nor on the need to strengthen the Nuclear Non-Proliferation Treaty'.[25] Therefore while the public commitment to disarmament has been maintained over recent years, there has been limited room for practical action, and limited results.

Development and the role of the United Nations in generating consensus

In a world with a growing emphasis on security the United Nations plays a key role in building an international consensus on development and utilises its position to secure stronger commitments from the developed world on aid, trade and debt relief. Both in terms of the level of its aid spending and the wider context of its overall policy on aid, Ireland has been closely tied to the United Nations system. The bulk of Irish development aid goes to its priority programme countries, primarily in sub-Saharan Africa, and to supporting the work of Irish development NGOs.[26] As the development co-operation budget has grown in recent years the size of the contributions to the United Nations agencies has grown both in absolute and in percentage terms and is now larger than the contribution to the EU development programme. In 2004 approximately €66 million was contributed to United Nations agencies, representing 13.5 percent of the overall aid budget and a 50 percent increase since 2002. Following a 'peer review' of Ireland's development cooperation programme by the OECD Development Assistance Committee (DAC) in 1999[27] and the subsequent Ireland Aid Review,[28]

---

[24] Security Council meeting 2 Aug. 2001; for report see http://www.un.org/Depts/dhl/resguide/scact2001.htm.
[25] Press Release 14 Sept. 2005, Dermot Ahern (New York); text on http://www.dfa.ie/Press_Releases/20050914/1839.htm.
[26] See also Kevin O'Sullivan's chapters above pp. 201–223.
[27] OECD *Development Cooperation Review Series: Ireland, no. 35* (Paris, 1999).
[28] Report of the Ireland Aid Review committee, Department of Foreign Affairs (Dublin, 2002).

Ireland decided to target contributions to the United Nations to a much smaller number of agencies. It had funded thirty-nine separate United Nations agencies in 1999 but decided to focus its contributions on a more limited number thereafter. The criteria for selection included fit with Development Co-operation Ireland's (DCI) own programmes and a focus on poverty alleviation. While some small contributions continue, spending is now more focused. Among the larger contributions in 2004, United Nations Development Programme (UNDP) received €12.9m, UNICEF €8.5m, UNHCR €7m, WFP €2.9m, United Nations Population Fund (UNFPA) €2.5m, WHO €2.9m, United Nations High Commissioner on Human Rights (UNHCHR) €2.5m and the Joint United Nations Programme on HIV/AIDS (UNAIDS) €2.3m.[29] These eight agencies therefore receive a total of €41.5m – nearly two thirds of the overall contribution to the United Nations.

In addition to increasing its development aid budget Ireland has been a strong supporter of the United Nations' single most important initiative in the development arena – the Millennium Development Goals (MDGs) of 2000. The actual goals originated in a 1996 OECD report,[30] but came to public prominence when the 'Millennium Summit', held in New York in September 2000, adopted a Declaration committing the member states to their achievement by 2015.[31] While they have been criticised for their limited vision the success of the MDGs has been their capacity to re-engage the governments of the Global North on issues of development and to offer a simple message to the public to mobilise support, thereby ensuring government action.[32] In this regard the strength of the United Nations is clear, because even though there was nothing new in the MDGs they could be presented as a legitimate, universal set of principles around which pressure for reform could be built. So, although opinion polls show a low level of awareness on the actual 'goals' themselves,[33] there is very strong support for the policy principles contained within them. McDonnell and Solignac Lecomte suggest that because the campaigning has focused on the broad issues and not the 'goals' per se the impact of the profile given to the MDGs by the United Nations is most visible in the high levels of support for increased aid, fair trade and debt cancellation within the EU and Canada.[34]

---

[29] For further details and a comprehensive annual commentary on Ireland's ODA see Helen O'Neill, 'Ireland's Foreign Aid in 2004', *Irish Studies in International affairs*, vol. 16 (2005) (and see previous volumes for each year back to 1979).

[30] OECD DAC, *Shaping the Twenty-First Century: The Contribution of Development Cooperation*, (Paris, 1996).

[31] http://www.un.org/millennium/declaration/ares552e.htm.

[32] For a supportive but critical review see Lorna Gold, *More than a Numbers Game? Ensuring that the Millennium Development Goals address Structural Injustice* (Dublin, 2005).

[33] Ida Mc Donnell and Henri-Bernard Solignac Lecomte, *Policy Insights No.13: MDGs, Taxpayers and Aid Effectiveness* (Paris, 2005).

[34] Ibid., poll figures taken from Special Eurobarometer Wave 62.2 TNS Opinion & Social, 2005, Attitudes towards Development Aid, Brussels; and Focus Canada, Environics Research Group (2004), Canadian Attitudes toward Development Assistance, Ottawa.

Ireland has given the MDGs, and in particular Goal 8, which focuses on the responsibilities of developed states, a central place in its development policy. The development cooperation agency of the Department of Foreign Affairs, DCI, states:

> The overarching objective of Development Cooperation Ireland (DCI) is the reduction of poverty, inequality and exclusion in developing countries ... the eight Millennium Development Goals, agreed by the United Nations at a series of international summit meetings, identify some of the main causes of extreme poverty in today's world and underpin the poverty reduction policies and activities of Development Cooperation Ireland ... the Millennium Development Goals, and the specific targets set to enable their achievement to be measured, provide the context in which DCI priority sectors are decided.[35]

The MDGs in Goal 8 specify a number of areas for action by developed states – chief among them action on debt cancellation, increases in official aid and progress on reform of the world trade system to make it fairer for poor and developing states. Ireland has supported calls for debt cancellation for many years. Irish aid however is given as untied grants, therefore the government did not have any debts to cancel which made it easy for it to be on the side of the angels on this issue and reduced its leverage on those countries who needed to act. On trade issues the main policy contradiction for Ireland is around the question of export subsidies for agriculture – strongly supported by Irish agricultural interests but seen as unfair dumping in developing states. There is a growing acceptance that further cuts in subsidies will inevitably take place, but Ireland has strongly resisted any attempt to reopen the current agreed set of agricultural reforms due to be implemented in stages up to 2013.[36] One change that is marked in the Irish context is that the policy of agricultural supports which was considered a domestic/EU issue is now also discussed in terms of its impact on the developing world. However given the indirect manner in which Ireland participates in world trade talks (as the Commission takes the lead for the entire EU), and the absence of any debts due by developing countries, it is the level of development aid that has been the key focus of domestic debate on the MDGs.

The focus on aid was signalled by both the Taoiseach and by Foreign Minister Brian Cowen, speaking at the United Nations Summit and General Assembly in 2000. The Taoiseach made Ireland's first public commitment to reach 0.7 per cent of GNP by 2007 and asserted that 'the specificity of the language and the timescales [in the goals] mean that we can and will be held accountable for delivery. If we urge policy coherence and precise targets on

---

[35] http://www.dci.gov.ie/challenges.asp.
[36] *Irish Times*, 3 Sept. 2005

the United Nations, we must be individually prepared to adopt the same disciplines'.[37] Minister Cowen in turn stated that 'our aid budget is both a test and a reflection of our commitment to the values and principles set out in the Millennium Summit Declaration'.[38] That supportive attitude to the Goals and the focus on the aid target was confirmed by the Taoiseach again in 2003 when he addressed the General Assembly; 'At the Millennium Summit, I committed Ireland to reaching the United Nations target for Official Development Assistance of 0.7 per cent of GNP by 2007. Since then, Ireland has increased its ODA to 0.41 per cent, and remains committed to reaching the target by 2007.'[39] When the government later announced that it would not after all meet the United Nations target by the deadline of 2007,[40] it generated a very high level of criticism.[41] After a period of internal debate by the government, it used the opportunity of the 2005 United Nations Summit to announce a new commitment to reaching the target by 2012 – three years ahead of the deadline adopted by the EU collectively in a decision earlier in 2005. The Taoiseach's speech also announced an interim target of 0.5 per cent of GNP by 2007. The opposition parties responded with a promise to put the new schedule in legislation – something which Irish NGO's had called for to make a future weakening of this goal more difficult.[42]

Ireland's current official development aid expenditure is 0.4 per cent of GNP. This compares to an EU average of 0.35 per cent and an OECD average of 0.25 per cent. At present aid as a percentage of GNP ranges from a low of 0.16 per cent from the USA to 0.85 per cent from Luxembourg and Denmark. Apart from the two top donors only Sweden, the Netherlands and Norway meet the United Nations target of 0.7 per cent. Sweden, Luxembourg and Norway have subsequently committed spending 1 per cent of GNP on aid with target dates ranging from 2006 to 2009. Even though aid, expressed in absolute cash terms is at its highest ever level this year – it is well below the percentage figure of 0.5 per cent of GNP which is found in the early statistics collected by the OECD. The OECD has however expressed worries that some of the expected increases over the next year may not reflect real aid, for example it is estimated that a debt writeoff for Iraq could involve $15 billion which could be claimed as 'aid'.[43] This use of aid to meet foreign policy goals in the security arena is not one which has faced

---

[37] Address by the Taoiseach, Bertie Ahern, to the United Nations Millennium Summit, New York, 6 Sept. 2000.

[38] Statement by Brian Cowen, Minister for Foreign Affairs, During the General Debate at the Fifty-fifth Session of the General Assembly of the United Nations, 14 Sept. 2000.

[39] Statement by the Taoiseach, Bertie Ahern, to the General Debate at the 58th General Assembly of the United Nations, New York, 25 Sept. 2003.

[40] Interview with Conor Lenihan, *Irish Times*, 8 Oct. 2004.

[41] e.g. *Irish Times*, 17 June 2005; 20 Oct. 2004; 1 July 2005.

[42] *Irish Times*, 16 Sept 2005.

[43] OECD DAC Chair Richard Manning DAC news, http://www.oecd.org/document/25/0,2340, en_2649_33721_35317145_1_1_1_1,00.html.

Ireland to date. However there is likely to be a future debate on whether the costs of peacekeeping operations in the least developed countries could be included within the figures used to calculate aid and whether Ireland has reached the 0.7 per cent target. This would require a collective decision by the OECD Development Assistance Committee who determine what can be counted and is not a unilateral decision Ireland could make. Indeed even in the event of an OECD decision Ireland would obviously still be free to decide to reach 0.7 per cent without counting any allowed military expenditures.

Ireland has been supportive of the United Nations as an institution which can build international pressure for higher levels of aid and a more coherent development strategy. In keeping with the tension between idealism and self-interest that runs through foreign policy, its support for the United Nations reflects its belief that development and a reduction in international inequality is essential for peace and security as well as being ethical. Domestically it has also been able to use the United Nations agreed baseline standards as proof it is living up to its international commitments and to answer critics who argue that it should do more.

Human rights and the weakness of the United Nations system

Irish foreign policy regularly asserts a commitment to human rights as one of its key priorities for working within the United Nations system. However, there are well-documented weaknesses in the United Nations Commission for Human Rights and one of Kofi Annan's harshest criticisms of any United Nations body was reserved for the Commission when he said in his 2005 report *In Larger Freedom: Towards Development, Security and Human Rights for All*:

> the Commission's capacity to perform its tasks has been increasingly undermined by its declining credibility and professionalism ... a credibility deficit has developed, which casts a shadow on the reputation of the United Nations system as a whole.[44]

In this regard Ireland welcomed the creation of a separate Human Rights Council to replace the Commission at the 2005 Summit, although at time of writing it is not clear if this will be more than a change of name.

Whatever the limitations of the United Nations system in this area, Ireland's commitment to international engagement on human rights is demonstrated by the setting up of the Human Rights Unit, to coordinate activity in this area within the Department of Foreign Affairs immediately following the publication of the 1996 white paper. The following year, former President of Ireland Mary Robinson became United Nations High

---

[44] Annan, 2005, para 182.

Commissioner for Human Rights. There was considerable lobbying for the post and it was a measure not only of Mary Robinson's own standing but of Ireland's strong position at the United Nations that she received the support of Secretary-General Kofi Annan and the endorsement of the General Assembly. Ireland was also elected to the United Nations Commission on Human Rights for the period 1997–1999 and in 1999 Ireland was elected to chair the Commission session in Geneva. Minister David Andrews announced the election in Seanad Éireann saying

> It is with some pride that I tell the House Ireland has been elected to chair the session, one of the most important events in the human rights calendar. Our permanent representative in Geneva, Ambassador Ann Anderson, will conduct the proceedings and her election is a recognition of the consistent and progressive policies on human rights adopted by successive Irish Governments and a measure of her standing at the United Nations in Geneva.[45]

Ireland was again elected to serve on the Commission from 2003 to 2005 after a break of just one term. Also in 2003 Judge Maureen Harding Clark was elected as a judge of the International Criminal Court (ICC), following her nomination by the Irish government. She secured 65 out of 83 votes and jointly topped the poll.[46]

Ireland also used its term on the Security Council in 2001–2002 to promote human rights, when diplomats made a number of interventions. After the fall of the Taliban regime in Afghanistan, Ireland argued against the prevailing view on the council that political stability in Afghanistan would be threatened if the new Transitional Authority was held too tightly accountable on human rights issues.[47] In this regard Ireland organised and chaired two informal meetings in October 2002 between Council members and two Human Rights Rapporteurs who had recently undertaken official missions in Afghanistan – the Special Rapporteur on Human Rights in Afghanistan, Kamal Hossain of Bangladesh, and the Special Rapporteur on Extrajudicial, Summary and Arbitrary Executions Asma Jahangir of Pakistan. It is difficult to judge the outcomes of such briefing but they did reinforce Ireland's commitment to the issue.

After the establishment of the Counter Terrorism Committee by the Security Council under resolution 1373, the committee appointed a number of experts to assist it, primarily in the spheres of financial law and practice and legislative drafting. It decided, however, not to recruit an expert on human rights and counter-terrorism. The proposal to recruit such an expert

---

[45] *Seanad Deb.,* vol. 158, col. 356, 17 Feb. 1999.
[46] The election was among those 83 states who had signed the ICC Treaty.
[47] Details of Ireland's position on this matter are available at http://www.un.int/ireland/scstatements/sc77.htm.

was directly opposed by China and Russia and it was not actively supported by the other permanent Council members – the United States, Britain and France. Ireland, as a Council member with support from Norway, Mauritius and Mexico, pressed the need for a human rights focus in the committee's work and was commended by human rights NGOs for this stance.[48]

In another initiative, in June 2002 following the deaths of nearly 200 people in Kisangani in the DRC, the United Nations High Commissioner for Human Rights, Mary Robinson, addressed the Council in private – in 'informal consultation of the whole'.[49] This briefing was held following pressure from Ireland, and was the first time such a briefing ever happened on a specific country situation. Again the outcomes of such meetings are difficult to judge but they do add some pressure on the Council to act.

While the current international climate with its focus on countering international terrorism has narrowed the focus for human rights work Ireland has remained an active supporter of international human rights. Even with the severe limitations and lack of effectiveness of United Nations human rights structures Ireland continues to see the United Nations as the primary forum for promoting human rights and has continued to support structural reform to enhance United Nations effectiveness.

Ireland's record on the United Nations Security Council

In the last decade the period of Ireland's membership of the Security Council is clearly the high point of engagement with the United Nations system. The Security Council is both the most powerful and most prestigious body within the United Nations system, bringing together the five permanent members with ten others elected for two-year terms. It has the unique capacity to initiate a range of instruments, including mediation and diplomatic pressure, compulsory economic sanctions, and military action. Once the Council decides on a course of action it is likely that the action will gain widespread international legitimacy. The Council's key weakness is that any one of the permanent five members can veto a resolution; however this does not mean that elected members are powerless. Using the veto portrays a state as isolated on an issue. The United States, for example, has gone to great lengths to have resolutions withdrawn or opposed by other members to avoid having to use its veto. As a resolution must receive nine positive votes in order for it to pass, the combined weight of the permanent five in favour of a resolution cannot guarantee its success unless they can also persuade some of the elected ten to support it.

---

[48] Info from private source.

[49] This is a United Nations procedure, whereby an informal 'gathering' of the full Council is held, in private, without constituting a formal meeting and thereby invoking Council procedures including a written record. Further information is available at http://www.globalpolicy.org/security/informal/summary.htm.

Security Council membership placed Ireland in a high profile environment where it was required to have a public position on a range of international issues. While Ireland had been on the Council before, this term took place in a much more insecure international environment and with a greatly increased Council workload. There were 430 public sessions of the Council over the two-year period and permanent ongoing private consultations.

Ireland's election to the Council was itself a strong vindication of the country's profile within the General Assembly – because states are elected by the entire United Nations membership. It was not initially regarded as a strong candidate, lacking the diplomatic and economic strengths of its electoral rivals – Norway and Italy. The relative ease of the victory – 130 votes on the first round – was a result of a strong campaign certainly, but also Ireland's positive image within the Assembly, based in part on its voting record.

A recent statistical analysis of voting from 1990 to 2002, published in *Irish Studies in International Affairs* by Young and Rees, paints an interesting picture of Irish voting patterns that perhaps goes some way towards explaining the strong vote for Ireland in 2000.[50] Young and Rees identify what they call a progressive voting bloc of Austria, Greece, Ireland, Spain and Sweden. Of particular note was Ireland's voting record on the key issues raised by the Global South. Given the make-up of the General Assembly the concerns of developing states feature much more strongly than in the Security Council. Over the period 1990–2002 resolutions on Palestine, the Middle East more generally, apartheid (up to 1994) and colonialism represented 38 per cent of all resolutions, while human rights and disarmament represented another 31 per cent of all the resolutions. While Ireland's support for such resolutions in the 1990s was marginally lower than shown by an earlier study looking at the 1980s[51] Ireland was still the EU state most likely to support such resolutions – marginally ahead of Sweden and Austria.

The Security Council term provides an opportunity to analyse Ireland's foreign policy across a range of issues, and allows a comparison between the rhetoric and practice in a situation where Ireland has influence. In particular the Council term allows an examination of those areas where Ireland's stated policy would bring it into conflict with the USA. Specifically, decisions on Iraq, Palestine, the International Criminal Court and Western Sahara, presented Ireland with difficult diplomatic decisions.[52]

---

[50] Helen Young and Nicholas Rees, 'EU Voting Behaviour in the United Nations General Assembly, 1990–2002: the EU's Europeanising Tendencies', *Irish Studies in International Affairs*, 16 (2005).

[51] Michael Holmes, Nicholas Rees and Bernadette Whelan, 'Irish foreign policy and the Third World: voting in the United Nations General Assembly in the 1980s', *Trocaire Development Review* (1992), pp. 67–84; Jan Wouters, 'The European Union as an actor within the United Nations General Assembly', Institute of International Law, K.U. Leuven Group Working Paper (January, 2001).

[52] For a full account of the Security Council term see John Doyle, 'Irish Diplomacy on the United Nations Security Council 2001–2: Foreign Policy-making in the light of Day', *Irish Studies in International Affairs* 15 (2004), pp. 73–102.

Iraq

The issue of Iraq dominated the council during Ireland's term. Up to mid-2002 the focus was on the impact of the sanctions regime, which had been in place since the 1991 Gulf War, with many countries, including Ireland, seeking reform of the system to ensure a better flow of civilian goods into Iraq while at the same time maintaining military sanctions. After President George W. Bush's 11 September anniversary speech to the United Nations General Assembly,[53] however, and under United States pressure, the Council debates focused almost entirely on Iraq's alleged programme of weapons of mass destruction. On sanctions Ireland unsuccessfully argued that Iraq should be allowed to operate in the economic field as normally as possible, consistent with preventing it from rearming, and pending fulfilment of its obligations as set out in previous United Nations resolutions since the end of the first Gulf War.[54] At this time Ireland also argued that future sanctions regimes should have a specified time limit – to avoid a situation whereby sanctions could be kept in place by the veto power of one permanent member of the Security Council. It was clear that there would not have been a majority to impose sanctions of that kind on Iraq in 2001 if a new resolution had been required. While this approach to sanctions was applied in practice from 2001 onwards, it was not adopted as formal, standard Council policy because of United States opposition

Following the identification of Iraq by the United States as an international threat, the unanimous adoption of resolution 1441 on 8 November 2002 gave Iraq a 'final opportunity' to comply with previous resolutions on disclosure of its weapons programmes. The Irish government faced some domestic criticism for supporting the motion. In its explanation for having voted in favour of the resolution, the government explicitly stated that it was for the Security Council to decide if Iraq committed a 'material breach' of its obligations, in accordance with the use of that term in international law, and that only the Council and not individual members could then decide what action should ensue.[55] During Ireland term all of the government's decisions and speeches that are publicly re-viewable, including numerous debates, were in keeping with Ireland's public position of opposition to the continued use of such wide-ranging sanctions against Iraq, continued support for the weapons inspectors and opposition to a unilateral attack on Iraq.

After leaving the Security Council the Irish government, unlike France and Germany, took a muted and more neutral stance on the war. This was the real shift: from the position the Irish government took during 2002 while

---

[53] 12 Sept. 2002.
[54] See debate on UNSC resolution 1409, adopted on 14 May 2002, available at http://www.un.org/Docs/sc/.
[55] The Irish government's statement in relation to this resolution is available at http://www.un.int/ireland/scstatements/sc97.htm.

on the Security Council to the view it held in 2003, when war became inevitable. On this issue there was a clear tension between Ireland's economic interests, given the country's dependence on United States investment, and the more principled foreign policy position set out in the government's earlier statements on the issue. Once the Council term was over and there was a less immediate requirement to adopt and defend explicit positions, the Irish government sought to avoid taking a definitive position on developments following from resolution 1441. In particular it appeared unwilling to publicly criticise United States foreign policy, while at the same time continuing to emphasise the importance of Irish-United States economic links. However in spite of allowing United States planes to land in Shannon airport Ireland did not actively support the war and the government continued to express its preference for a United Nations mandated solution.

Palestine-Israel

Irish foreign policy has expressed sympathy with the plight of the Palestinian people and has supported political moves towards a settlement that recognises a Palestinian state. In December 2000 just before Ireland joined the Council a Palestinian-promoted draft Security Council resolution calling for a United Nations Observer Force in the Occupied Territories could only get eight votes. The United States therefore did not have to use its veto. Even though the United States lobbies heavily against resolutions critical of Israel it prefers not to use its veto because of the resulting negative publicity which affects its relations with the Arab world in particular.

In Council debates Ireland articulated its position on the conflict in the Middle East around five key themes:[57]

- the right of the Security Council to concern itself with the Middle East
- Israel's right to security within recognised borders
- the legitimate rights of the Palestinian people
- condemnation of terrorism, the counter-productive nature of Palestinian violence, Israel's excessive reaction to such violence and illegal Israeli settlements
- Israel's right to defend itself along with its obligation to do so in accordance with international humanitarian law.

Ireland abstained on a draft resolution in March 2001 which proposed United Nations observers, arguing that no observers would in practice ever be deployed and that the collapsed peace process ought to be the focus of

---

[56] See also Rory Miller's chapter above pp.54–78.
[57] For details see, for example, statements and vetoed resolution on 15 and 27 Mar. 2001, available at http://www.un.org/Docs/sc/.

activity. Whatever Ireland's motivation it was open to the charge that it had been influenced by United States pressure on this first key vote on the Palestinian question. Although the resolution got nine positive votes it was vetoed by the USA.

The Council debates on Israel-Palestine were dominated by United States attempts to avoid resolutions critical of Israel, while at the same time because of the emerging 'war on terror' the United States felt constrained in its ability to use the veto, given its need for improved relations with the Arab world. In December 2001 Ireland supported a draft resolution promoted by the Arab states and encouraged three other non-permanent Council members to vote in favour.[58] The resolution simply reiterated Council support for previous resolutions and initiatives and supported the principle of land for peace. The United States however vetoed the resolution. This veto, the negative reaction to it, and a recognition that there was now a majority on the Council in favour of moderate motions critical of Israel were important factors in pres- surising the United States towards supporting the principle of Palestinian statehood. In March 2002, faced with a moderate Arab resolution that it would again have had to veto to defeat, the United States introduced its own draft, which endorsed the principle of Palestinian statehood and welcomed the involvement of the Quartet as a mediating group in the Israeli- Palestinian conflict.[59] The United States also introduced and supported other resolutions critical of Israel. However it by no means abandoned its traditional support for Israel. In late 2002, for example, following the killing of United Nations employees by Israeli forces, the United States vetoed a draft resolution condemning the killing. The resolution was supported by Ireland.[60]

The International Criminal Court

The establishment of the ICC generated a real crisis on the Council. While United States concerns about the Court were known during the Clinton presidency, it became clear in the early days of the Bush administration that there would be active United States opposition to the ICC. By June it was known that the United States was planning to veto the annual renewals of United Nations peacekeeping operations in order to pressurise the Council to agree to an exemption for United States citizens from the ICC's mandate.

The United Nations Mission in Bosnia and Herzegovina was the first to be affected by the United States position of opposition to renewals, and only three short technical extensions of the mandate kept the mission in place

---

[58] See Security Council report for 14 Dec. 2001, available at http://www.un.org/Docs/sc/.

[59] Resolution 1397, based on the United States draft, was ultimately adopted on 12 Mar. 2002. The Quartet was the shorthand used to describe the principle that mediation in the conflict would involve the United States, the United Nations, the EU and Russia.

[60] See Security Council reports for 20 Dec. 2002, available at http://www.un.org/Docs/sc/.

until the crisis over the ICC was resolved.[61] This happened when resolution 1422, agreed on 12 July 2002, effectively gave the United States an exemption from the ICC's mandate. At the open meeting of the Council on 10 July, Ireland had said that the United States position was 'not well founded',[62] that Ireland could not agree to the mechanism that the United States sought and that Ireland believed the Rome Statute contained sufficient safeguards to prevent 'politically inspired' prosecutions.[63] Ireland and Mexico were the last two countries to agree to support the resolution, which was adopted on 12 July. While the United Nations resolution was condemned by human rights groups the controversy had the effect of raising the profile of the International Criminal Court.[64]

Western Sahara[65]

Though not generating the same publicity as either Iraq, Palestine and the ICC Ireland played quite an important role on the issue of Western Sahara and it is an interesting example of active diplomacy on a relatively low profile issue where Irish activity made a real difference and where Irish motivations were not narrowly based on any economic interest.

There was widespread acceptance that the 1991 United Nations plan for a referendum in Western Sahara on its constitutional future was unimplementable, due to differences between the occupying power, Morocco, which claimed sovereignty over Western Sahara, and the nationalist movement, Polisario. In the light of this, former United States Secretary of State James Baker, acting as the personal envoy of United Nations Secretary-General Annan, had produced a 'Draft Framework Agreement' that involved the appointment of a five-year, interim government to be followed by a referendum in which every person resident in the territory for at least one year prior to the referendum could vote. The Moroccan government had 'encouraged' Moroccan migration into Western Sahara for many years and the inclusion of these migrants on the voters' list would have almost certainly led to the integration of Western Sahara with Morocco. The United States and France strongly supported Baker's proposal. Polisario opposed this plan and instead promoted the 1991 United Nations plan for self-determination for Western Sahara.

Ireland took a principled position on this issue and was an important actor in the group that prevented the Baker plan from getting a majority on

---

[61] These extensions were agreed in resolutions 1418, 1420 and 1421.

[62] Details of Ireland's contribution to the meeting are available at http://www.un.int/ireland/scstatements/sc82.htm.

[63] See http://ods-dds-ny.un.org/doc/UNDOC/PRO/N02/469/11/PDF/N0246911.pdf?Open Element.

[64] For details of this criticism see, for example, http://web.amnesty.org/pages/icc-index-eng and http://www.amnesty.nl/persberichten/NK-PB0088.shtml, and see http://web.amnesty.org/library/Index/ENGIOR510062004 for objections to 2003 renewal.

[65] See also the chapter on garda involvement in United Nations missions, above pp. 343–361.

the Council. Ireland supported the right of the Sahroaui people to self-determination – as enshrined in the United Nations' proposed Settlement Plan – and the right to exercise self-determination in a free and fair way. Ireland's activity ensured that Baker's Draft Framework never had more than six or seven supporters. The Council ultimately adopted resolution 1429, on 30 July 2002, effectively putting off a decision on the Western Sahara issue for six months and this ultimately killed off the Baker plan. Ireland's role in preventing the Council from adopting Baker's Framework Agreement was widely recognised in the United Nations and was welcomed by Polisario.

Conclusion

The Security Council term offered a real test of whether stated priorities in foreign policy of peacekeeping, disarmament, human rights, and development would be pursued in practice against the inevitable pressures faced at that level. In coming to a judgement as to whether the traditions of Irish foreign policy were overly constrained by realpolitik during Ireland's term on the Security Council it is clear that Irish diplomats displayed a consistent support for multilateralism, for the United Nations system and for a humanitarian and human rights based approach to international relations. However, Ireland's term ended just before the United States decision to invade Iraq became irreversible. If Ireland had been on the Council at the time of the invasion, it would have found itself under much more pressure to conform to the United States position on that decision than on any other issue with which the Council had dealt over the previous two years.

Ireland, in common with the wider international community, was strongly supportive of the United States in the post-11 September 2001 period. This can be seen most clearly in activity on the UNSC in late 2001, during debates on Afghanistan and in the discussions on the Counter Terrorism Committee (CTC). Even on those issues, however, there were some minor issues of conflict between Ireland and the United States. For example, Ireland was part of the group that pressurised the United States and Britain to brief the Council immediately after they began their attack on Afghanistan.[66] The United States had simply wanted to write to the Council saying it was invoking its right of self-defence. Ireland also sought (unsuccessfully) to institutionalise a human rights perspective within the work of the CTC.

Ireland, on many occasions, opposed United States policy on issues of importance. It did so repeatedly on Palestine, on sanctions against Iraq, and on whether a second resolution was required to attack Iraq. On other less high-profile but nonetheless important issues, Ireland publicly and regularly opposed United States policy. Such issues included: seeking to re-engage the United Nations in Somalia; the United States attempt to alter United

---

[66] Council meeting, 8 Oct 2001.

Nations policy on Western Sahara; the effort in January 2001 to end the arms embargo on Ethiopia and Eritrea; and the wider debate on sanctions regimes in general, in which Ireland argued for specific time limits to be imposed for sanctions. In addition, Ireland sought to apply a United Nations mandate to the NATO operation in FYROM, against United States and British arguments. Although that initiative had little impact, Ireland did succeed in ensuring a larger United Nations operation in Timor Leste against the wishes of the permanent Council members who were seeking to curtail costs there.[67] While Ireland ultimately voted to give the United States an exemption from the operation of the International Criminal Court the United States use of a veto to block renewals of peacekeeping missions put the other members of the Council in an impossible position – either to weaken the ICC or to stall peacekeeping missions indefinitely.

In analysing Irish action other than on the Security Council, there are a number of important areas where Irish support for the United Nations has been very clear, including involvement in United Nations peacekeeping and in particular in the commitment to African mission, support for Millennium Development Goals, increases in official development aid, financial support for United Nations agencies, and a focus in other areas of the development cooperation programme on the poorest countries. In the areas where there has been less tangible results – notably disarmament and human rights – Ireland has been a supporter of attempts to strengthen the United Nations role. There are other pressures on Irish foreign policy, a reliance on United States foreign investment has clearly constrained an active policy on Iraq since 2003. Within the EU there will be future conflicts on the extent to which emerging EU security and defence policy should reflect an attempt to deal with underlying causes of conflict and insecurity rather than simply a narrow focus on criminal law, border security and military responses. However in this fifth decade of Ireland's United Nations membership there remains ample evidence of a genuine attempt to strengthen United Nations multilateralism as a key contribution to a more equal and secure world.

---

[67] See Doyle, 'Irish Diplomacy', for reports of Council meetings on United Nations website, for further details on these issues.

Notes on contributors

DR AOIFE BHREATNACH is a graduate of University College Cork and De Montfort University. She was Irish Government Senior Scholar at Hertford College, Oxford, in 2004–05 and currently holds an Irish Research Council for the Humanities and Social Sciences Post-Doctoral Fellowship in NUI Maynooth. Her first book, *Becoming Conspicuous: Irish Travellers, Society and the State, 1922–70*, will be published by UCD Press.

EDWARD BURKE is a graduate of Trinity College Dublin (BA Hons, Modern History) and has recently completed an MA in War Studies at King's College London, including a thesis on Irish diplomatic relations with the United States from 11 September 2001 to the outbreak of the war in Iraq. He has also studied at the United Nations University in Tokyo under its programme covering armed conflict prevention, management and resolution.

DR EILEEN CONNOLLY is a lecturer in Politics in the School of Law and Government at Dublin City University and is a member of the Board of the Centre for International Studies. Her research interests include the politics of development and gender on which she has published in the *European Journal of Women's Studies* and *Irish Studies in International Affairs*. She is at present leading a major research project in DCU for the Advisory Board of Development Cooperation Ireland on the role of civil society in development and the implications for Ireland's development cooperation programme.

NOEL DORR is a former Secretary (General) of the Department of Foreign Affairs (1987–95). Prior to that he served as Irish Ambassador in London (1983–87) and Permanent Representative of Ireland to the United Nations in New York (1980–83). He represented Ireland on the United Nations Security Council 1981–82. He was a member of the Irish Delegation to the United Nations General Assembly in 1961 and in 1966, 1967, 1968 and 1969.

DR JOHN DOYLE is co-director of the Centre for International Studies in the School of Law and Government at Dublin City University, where he is also director of the three MA programmes in international relations, globalisation and security and conflict studies. His research interests are in security and conflict resolution. He is editor of *Irish Studies in International Affairs*, where he published (in 2004) a review of Ireland's performance on the Security Council in 2001–02.

DR TILL GEIGER is a lecturer in International History in the School of Arts, Histories and Cultures at the University of Manchester. He has published widely on American foreign policy towards Europe, including several studies on Ireland and the Marshall Plan. His most recent publications include *Britain, and the economic problem of the cold war: the political economy and the economic impact of the British defence effort, 1945–1955* (Aldershot, 2004) and an edited volume with Michael Kennedy, *Ireland, Europe and the Marshall Plan* (Dublin, 2004).

RICHARD E.M. HEASLIP is a former Colonel in the Defence Forces. His service in the Defence Forces included extensive peacekeeping experience with United Nations troop and observer missions in Cyprus (UNFICYP), the Middle East (UNTSO, UNIFIL) and Kosovo (UNMIK). He also served in the EU Monitoring Mission in the former Federal Republic of Yugoslavia and with OSCE in the Kosovo Verification Mission. Prior to retirement he held the appointment of Senior Mission Officer for Ireland to Supreme Headquarters Allied Powers Europe in Mons, Belgium, addressing matters related to Irish participation in the 'Partnership for Peace' programme and Defence Forces deployments on UN mandated NATO-led peacekeeping operations in the Balkans and Afghanistan. He holds an MA in International Relations from Dublin City University.

DR MICHAEL KENNEDY is Executive Editor of the Royal Irish Academy's Documents on Irish Foreign Policy Series, volume IV of which was published in 2004. He has published widely on twentieth-century Irish foreign policy, including *Ireland and the League of Nations* (Dublin, 1996), *Ireland and the Council of Europe* (Strasbourg, 2000) and *Division and Consensus: the politics of cross-border relations in Ireland* (Dublin, 2000) as well as a number of edited volumes of essays, most recently (with Till Geiger) *Ireland, Europe and the Marshall Plan* (Dublin, 2004) and many journal articles. He is a Research Associate of the Centre for Contemporary Irish History, Trinity College Dublin, and is currently the Secretary of the Royal Irish Academy's Committee for the Study of International Affairs.

DR DEIRDRE McMAHON was educated at University College Dublin and Churchill College Cambridge. She is a lecturer in History at Mary Immaculate College Limerick and her most recent book was *The Moynihan Brothers in Peace and War, 1908–1918*, published by Irish Academic Press in 2004.

DR RORY MILLER is a senior lecturer in Mediterranean Studies, King's College, University of London, where he teaches courses on Middle Eastern politics and United States and European involvement in the Middle East and wider Mediterranean. He is associate editor of the Routledge academic journal *Israel Affairs* and author of *Ireland and the Palestine Question, 1948–2004* (Dublin, 2005).

DR RAY MURPHY is a senior lecturer at the Irish Centre for Human Rights, Faculty of Law, National University of Ireland, Galway. A former practising barrister and Captain in the Irish Defence Forces he served with UNIFIL in 1981–82 and 1989. He has worked for the OSCE, the European Union, Amnesty International and the Irish government in human rights and election monitoring in Africa and Europe. His main research interests include international peace operations and international humanitarian law and he has published widely in these fields. Dr Murphy is on the faculty of the Pearson Peacekeeping Center in Clementsport, Nova Scotia, Canada, and is also a member of the teaching faculty of the International Institute for Criminal Investigations and the International Institute of Humanitarian Law at San Remo, Italy.

DR JOHN TERENCE O'NEILL is a former Colonel in the Irish Defence Forces. He has served on United Nations missions in the Congo (1961), Lebanon (1982–83) and Angola (1993) and holds a PhD from Trinity College, Dublin. Terry O'Neill has published articles in *Irish Studies in International Affairs* and *International Peacekeeping*. His *United Nations Peacekeeping in the Post-Cold War Era* (co-authored with Nicholas Rees) was published in 2005. He is currently working (with Nicholas Rees, University of Limerick) on a study of the role of the United Nations in Liberia. He is a Research Associate of the Centre for Contemporary Irish History, Trinity College Dublin, and a Fellow of the Irish Centre for Human Rights, Faculty of Law, National University of Ireland, Galway.

KEVIN O'SULLIVAN is a graduate of Trinity College Dublin and holds a postgraduate research scholarship from the Irish Council for the Humanities and Social Sciences. He is currently engaged in research for an MLitt through the Department of History at Trinity College Dublin, focusing on the formulation of Irish foreign policy on Sub-Saharan Africa in the 1960s and 1970s.

DR GREG SPELMAN is an analyst at the Australian Department of Defence but retains a personal interest in Irish diplomatic history. In 2003 he was awarded his PhD from the Queensland University of Technology for his dissertation 'Reconciling a policy of neutrality with the prospect of integration: Ireland, the European Economic Community and Ireland's United Nations policy,

1965–1972'. He has published a number of articles on aspects of the history of Irish foreign policy and has presented papers on this subject at national and international conferences.

DR BEN TONRA is Jean Monnet Professor of European Foreign, Security and Defence Policy at University College Dublin where he is also Director of the Graduate School of the College of Human Sciences. He is Director of the Dublin European Institute (DEI) at the UCD School of Politics and International Relations. Outside the university he is the Project Director for EU Foreign and Security Policy at the Institute of European Affairs. His published work includes *Rethinking EU Foreign Policy: Beyond the Common Foreign and Security Policy* (with Thomas Christiansen, eds) (Manchester, 2005), *Ireland in International Affairs: Interests, Institutions and Identities* (with Eílis Ward eds) (Dublin, 2002) and *The Europeanisation of National Foreign Policies: Ireland, Denmark and the Netherlands in the European Union* (Ashgate, 2001) as well as more than two dozen journal articles and book chapters covering aspects of Irish and EU foreign and security policy.

Index

Note: 'n' following a page number indicates a footnote.